INTRODUCTION TO PSYCHOLOGY
Exploration and Application

INTRODUCTION TO PSYCHOLOGY
Exploration and Application

Dennis Coon
Department of Psychology
Santa Barbara City College, California

Introduction by W. Royce Adams

West Publishing Company
St. Paul □ New York □ Los Angeles □ San Francisco

Printed in the United States of America

Library of Congress Cataloging in Publication Data

Coon, Dennis L
Introduction to psychology.

Bibliography: p.
Includes index.
I. Psychology.
II. Title.
BF121.C625 150 77–901
ISBN 0–8299–0134–5

5th Reprint 1978

Acknowledgements

The author is indebted to the following for permission to reproduce copyrighted materials.

p. 33 From *In the Shadow of Man* by J. van Lawick-Goodall. Copyright © 1971 Houghton Mifflin Company. World rights: William Collins Sons & Co., Ltd., London. Reprinted by permission.
p. 44 Reprinted with permission of author and publisher from: Ulrich, R. E., Stachnik, T. J., and Stainton, N. R., Student acceptance of generalized personality interpretations. PSYCHOLOGICAL REPORTS, 1963, 13, 831-834.
pp. 75-76 From *The Psychology of Consciousness* by R. E. Ornstein. Copyright © 1972 by W. H. Freeman & Company. Reprinted by permission.
p. 96 From *Fields of Applied Psychology* by Ann Anastasi. Copyright © 1964 McGraw-Hill Book Company. Reprinted by permission.
p. 125 From *An Experiment in Mindfulness* by E. H. Shattock. Copyright © 1958 Hutchinson Publishing Group, Ltd. Reprinted by permission.
p. 126 From *The Psychology of Consciousness* by R. E. Ornstein. Copyright © 1972 W. H. Freeman & Company. Reprinted by permission.
p. 126 From *The Three Pillars of Zen* by Philip Kapleau. Copyright © 1966 Harper & Row, Publishers. Reprinted by permission.
p. 142 Snyder, S. G., "The True Speed Trip: Schizophrenia." Copyright © 1971 Ziff-Davis Publishing Company. Reprinted by permission of *Psychology Today Magazine.*
p. 149 Rahula, W., *What the Buddha Taught.* Reprinted by permission of Grove Press, Inc. Copyright © 1959 by W. Rahula. Second and enlarged edition copyright © 1974 by W. Rahula. All rights reserved.
p. 161 From "A Study of Dreams" by F. A. van Eeden. In *Proceedings of the Society for Psychical Research*, 1913, 26, 431-461.
p. 165 From *Gestalt Therapy Verbatim* by F. Perls. Copyright © 1969 Real People Press. Reprinted by permission.
p. 191 Gray, F., P. S. Graubard, and H. Rosenberg, "Little Brother Is Changing You." Copyright © 1974 Ziff-Davis Publishing Company. Reprinted by permission of *Psychology Today Magazine.*
p. 217 From *The Excitable Cortex in Conscious Man* by W. Penfield. Copyright © 1958 Charles C Thomas. Reprinted by permission.

p. 287 Horner, M. S., "Fail: Bright Women." Reprinted by permission of *Psychology Today Magazine.* Copyright © 1969 Ziff-Davis Publishing Company.
p. 316 From "Ten Danger Signals of Depression." Published by the National Association of Mental Health.
p. 330 From *Type A* by M. Friedman and R. Rosenman. Copyright © 1974 Alfred A. Knopf, Inc. Reprinted by permission.
p. 350 From "Healthy Personality and Self-Disclosure." In *Mental Hygiene*, 32, 1959. Reprinted by permission.
pp. 337-338 From "Sweet 16." Newsfeature, *Associated Press.* Reprinted by permission.
pp. 358-359 Huxley, A., "Human Potentialities." In R. E. Farson (ed.), *Science and Human Affairs.* Palo Alto, California: Science and Behavior Books, 1965.
p. 365 From *Human Development* by J. Lugo and G. Hershey. Copyright © 1974 Macmillan. Reprinted by permission.
p. 379 Hayakawa, S. I., "The Use and Misuse of Language." In R. E. Farson (ed.), *Science and Human Affairs.* Palo Alto, California: Science and Behavior Books, 1965.
pp. 383, 384, 385, 386, 387, 388 From *Psychology and Effective Behavior* by James C. Coleman. Copyright © 1969 by Scott, Foresman and Company. Reprinted by permission.
p.383 Ehrenburg, I., "A Last Memoir." In Cousins, N. (ed.), *What I Have Learned*, Saturday Review, 1968.
p. 401 From "On Growing Up, Learning and Loving" by E. Zigler. In *Human Behavior Magazine*, March 1973. Reprinted by permission.
pp. 402, 403 Ginott, H., *Between Parent and Child*, 1965. Reprinted by permission of Dr. Alice Ginott.
p. 405 *The Prophet* by Kahlil Gibran. Reprinted with permission of the publisher, Alfred A. Knopf, Inc. Copyright © 1923 by Kahlil Gibran; renewal copyright © 1951 by Administrators C.T.A. of Kahlil Gibran Estate, and Mary G. Gibran.
p. 427 Sheilds and Monroe, "A Ban on I.Q. Tests?" Copyright © 1976 by Newsweek, Inc. All rights reserved. Reprinted by permission.
p. 443 MMPI test reproduced by permission. Copyright © 1943, renewed 1970 by the University of Minnesota. Published by The Psychological Corporation, New York, New York. All rights reserved.
p. 451 Art Buchwald quotation courtesy of the *Los Angeles Times.*
p. 452 *The Organization Man.* Copyright © 1956 by William H. Whyte, Jr. Reprinted by permission of Simon & Schuster, Inc.
pp. 487-488 From *Catch 22* by Joseph Heller. Copyright © 1955, 1961 by Joseph Heller. Reprinted by permission of Simon & Schuster, Inc.
pp. 495, 496, 509, 514 Suinn, Richard M., *Fundamentals of Behavior Pathology*, 1st edition Copyright © 1970 by Richard Suinn. Reprinted by permission of John Wiley & Sons, Inc. Suinn, Richard M., *Fundamentals of Behavior Pathology*, 2nd edition Copyright © 1975 by Richard Suinn. Reprinted by permission of John Wiley & Sons, Inc.
pp. 509-510 From *I Never Promised You a Rose Garden* by Hannah Green (Joanne Greenberg). Copyright © 1964 by Hannah Green. Reprinted by permission of Holt, Rinehart and Winston, Publishers.
p. 514 From *Abnormal Behavior, Psychology's View* by F. B. McMahon. Copyright © 1976. Reprinted by permission of Prentice-Hall, Inc., Englewood Cliffs, New Jersey.
p. 519 From "Toward a Theory of Schizophrenia" by G. D. Bateson, D. Jackson, J. Haley, and J. Weakland. In *Behavioral Science*, 1956, 1, 251-264. Reprinted by permission.
p. 529 From *The Politics of Experience* by R. D. Laing. Copyright © 1967 by R. D. Laing. Reprinted by permission of Penguin Books, Ltd.
p. 549 From *Awareness: Exploring, Experimenting, Experiencing* by John O. Stevens. Copyright © 1971 Real People Press. Reprinted by permission.
p. 558 Lazarus, Arnold, "The Treatment of Chronic Frigidity by Systematic Desensitization." In *Experiments in Behavior Therapy*, H. J. Eysenck (ed.). Reprinted by permission of the author. Copyright © 1964 Pergamon Press, Ltd.
p. 590 From *Sexuality: A Search for Perspective* by Grummer and Barclay. Copyright © 1971 by Litton Educational Publishing, Inc. Reprinted by permission of D. Van Nostrand Company.

p. 594 From *Personal Adjustment* (2nd ed.) by S. M. Jourard. Copyright © 1963 Macmillan Publishing Co., Inc. Reprinted by permission.
pp. 595-596 From "Where Should You Touch?" by H. E. F. Donohue. Copyright © 1968 Hearst Corporation. Reprinted by permission.
p. 597 From "A Contest of Ladies" by William Sansom. In *The Stories of William Sansom*. Copyright © 1963 Hogarth Press, London. Reprinted by permission.
p. 631 From *The Authoritarian Personality* by Theodore Adorno, E. Frenkel-Brunswik, D. J. Levinson, and R. N. Sanford. Copyright © 1950 Harper & Row Publishers. Reprinted by permission.

Illustrations and Tables

Fig. 1-3 Photo courtesy of Dr. B. T. Gardner, University of Nevada, Reno.
Table 6-1 "Stanford Hypnotic Susceptibility Scale" adapted from Weitzenhoffer and Hilgard. Stanford University Press, 1959.
Fig. 6-3 "Spectrum and Continuum of Drugs." Dr. Robert W. Earle, Department of Medical Pharmacology and Therapeutics, University of California, Irvine.
Table 6-2 "Facts about Drugs" from *The Resource Book for Drug Absue Education.* Copyright © 1969 National Education Association. Reprinted by permission.
Fig. 6-4 Courtesy Dr. Lester Grinspoon, Harvard Medical School.
Fig. 6-5 From *Eyewitness Series in Psychology*, Jozef Cohen. Copyright © Rand McNally and Company. Reprinted by permission.
Fig. 9-5 From *The Behavior of Organisms* by B. F. Skinner. Copyright © 1938 D. Appleton-Century Co., Inc. Reprinted by permission of Prentice-Hall, Inc., Englewood Clifs, New Jersey.
Fig. 11-2 Premack, A. and Premack, D., "Teaching Language to an Ape." Copyright © 1972 by Scientific American, Inc. All rights reserved.
Fig. 11-3 Osgood, C. E., "The Nature and Measurement of Meaning," Psychological Bulletin 49. Copyright 1952 by the American Psychological Association. Reprinted by permission.
Fig. 12-5 From "Curiosity and Exploration" by D. E. Berlyne. In *Science*, Vol. 153, pp. 25-33, Figure 4, July 1, 1966. Copyright © 1966 by the American Association for the Advancement of Science. Reprinted by permission.
Fig. 13-4 From "Emotional Development in Early Infancy" by K. M. B. Bridges. In *Child Development*, 3, 324-341, Figure 1. Copyright © 1932 by the Society for Research in Child Development, Inc.
Fig. 14-5 Courtesy of Joseph V. Brady, The Johns Hopkins University School of Medicine.
Table 14-1 Holmes, T. H. and P. H. Rahe, "Social Readjustment Rating Scale." Reprinted with permission from Pergamon Press, Ltd. Copyright 1957.
Fig. 16-1 Fantz, R., "Origin of Form Perception." Copyright © 1961 by Scientific American, Inc. All rights reserved.
Fig. 17-2 Tanner, J. M., "Growing Up." Copyright © 1973 by Scientific American, Inc. All rights reserved.
Fig. 17-3 Dooley's World © King Features Syndicate, 1974.
Table 18-1 Terman, L. and M. Merrill, *Stanford-Binet Intelligence Scale.* Copyright 1937, (revised edition, copyright 1960) Houghton Mifflin Company.
Table 18-2 "Wechsler Scale." Copyright © 1958 The Psychological Corporation.
Fig. 18-4 From "Are I.Q. Tests Intelligent?" by R. B. Cattell. Reprinted by permission of Dr. R. B. Cattell.
Fig. 19-3 Cattell, R. B., "Personality Pinned Down." Copyright © 1973 Ziff-Davis Publishing Company. Reprinted by permission of *Psychology Today Magazine.*
Fig. 20-1 Courtesy of Illusions, Park Ridge, Illinois.
Fig. 24-2 Photograph courtesy of Albert Bandura and the American Psychological Association. Copyright © 1969 by the American Psychological Association. Reprinted by permission. From the *Journal of Personality and Social Psychology*, 1969, 13, 173-199.

Fig. 24-3 Lovaas, O. I. and J. Q. Simmons, "Manipulation of Self-Destruction in Three Retarded Children." In the *Journal of Applied Behavior Analysis*, 1969, 2, 143-157. Reprinted by permission.

Fig. 25-3 From *An Introduction to Physiological Psychology* by Allen M. Schneider and Barry Tarshis. Copyright © 1975 by Random House, Inc. Reprinted by permission of Random House, Inc.

Fig. 25-4 Reproduced by permission from Frank A. Beach (ed.), *Sex and Behavior*, New York, John Wiley & Sons, Inc. 1965.

Fig. 25-5 Reproduced by permission from Frank A. Beach (ed.), *Sex and Behavior*, New York, John Wiley & Sons, Inc. 1965.

Box 26-1 From *Liking and Loving: An Invitation to Social Psychology* by Zick Rubin. Copyright © 1973 by Holt, Rinehart and Winston, Inc. Reprinted by permission of Holt, Rinehart and Winston, Inc.

Contents in Brief

Contents

Preface

As an instructor I have learned that selection of a textbook is half the battle in teaching a course. A good text does much of the work of conveying information to students. This leaves class time free for discussion, and it leaves students asking for more. When a book overwhelms students or cools their interest, teaching becomes an uphill battle. For this reason, I have worked hard to make this a readable, comprehensible, and interesting text. Since this is a highly student-oriented book, it is appropriate to let student comments show the response to what I have tried to accomplish. The following comments were made by students who used this book in manuscript form at the University of Arizona:

> I found the book to be very humorous and interesting to read.
>
> Most of all, the text was readable. By that, I mean that it held my interest. I found myself actually reading ahead of scheduled assignments. I have even caught my brother reading this text, without encouragement from me!
>
> I found myself not only reading the assigned chapters, but also reading ahead.
>
> This is one of the most interesting textbooks I have ever read.

So, this is a book students can read and will read. Will they learn from it? Ironically, few psychology texts have made use of learning principles to teach psychology. With the help of W. Royce Adams, a reading and study skills specialist, the chapters of this book have been designed to maximize reader participation and comprehension. Basically, each chapter is built around the well-known SQ3R study-reading formula. The success of this approach is indicated by student reactions:

> The SQ3R set up, with questions and learning checks within the chapters, was a great help. Up until I took this course, SQ3R was something I had been told about but had never seen applied.

> What a pleasant introduction to college, after not having attended school for 24 years, to have a text that was interesting. I found the format much easier to learn from than previous texts as remembered. The learning checks seem to be well placed to help you remember the important facts of a section and to find out if the material covered has been comprehended.

Another unique aspect of this book is the series of "applications" sections found at the end of each chapter. In these sections an attempt was made to bridge the gap between psychological theory and practical application. I believe students have every right to ask: "Does this mean anything to me? Can I use it? Why should I learn it if I can't?" No matter how interesting or intellectually stimulating, a text that fails to show the practical consequences of adopting new ideas is irrelevant in a very basic sense. The applications sections in this book spell out how a student can make use of the principles of psychology. Again, student comments indicate a positive response to this addition:

> The applications sections are very interesting. They seem to tie in some of the basic concepts of the chapter and really apply them, which makes it easier to grasp the concepts. I especially enjoyed the ones about meditation and how to pick a psychologist.
>
> The applications sections were also something I haven't seen in other texts. This extra care taken to point out immediate uses for me, as a student, was encouraging. There are several chapters and sections of chapters I plan to save for later reference.

Readability, a format to facilitate learning, and practical applications are core features of this text, but they are not the whole story. This is a complete but non-encyclopedic introduction to psychology. Students are given a clear grasp of major concepts rather than buried in details of interest only to the professional. The presentation is balanced: I have tried to show the value of many theoretical perspectives to foster an appreciation for the unique contributions of each. Because the presentation is eclectic, I think students will find this book full of intellectual challenge; and teachers will find traditional topics covered to their satisfaction. At the same time, I have made a special effort to relate psychology to common experiences and to practical problems of daily life.

In the pages which follow, I think the reader will find an attractive blend of the theoretical and the practical, the esoteric and the commonplace. In addition, there are discussions of many of the most interesting current topics in psychology, including: biofeedback, altered states of consciousness, hypnosis, meditation, death and dying, assertive training, bimodal consciousness, sensory awareness, and dream research. A particularly important addition, I believe, is the chapter on human sexuality.

To give students maximum access to this information, use of technical jargon is minimal and the reading level of each chapter has been carefully measured and adjusted. This is a text students will be able to read with pleasure and full comprehension. For flexibility, the text is broken into 27 short chapters, each approximately half the length of a traditional chapter.

Each stands as a unit and can be read in a single session. This approach allows great freedom in ordering topics and assignments. It also gives the student a sense of completion or closure at the end of each assignment.

Each chapter is divided into five parts: Preview, Resources, Resources Summary, Applications, and Questions for Discussion. The preview is to arouse reader interest and to focus attention. The resources section presents the basic concepts of the chapter. The summary reviews major ideas, and the applications section shows how they can be applied. The final section provides additional material and questions to spur thought and discussion.

The extensive use of study aids in this text is based on the belief that students can be guided into more effective study and reading habits. After having spent countless hours teaching students the SQ3R method and other study skills, Royce Adams and I felt that a text could be designed to enhance learning and to develop study skills subtly over the course of a semester (or quarter). What we have done should be totally unobtrusive for accomplished students; for the student who does not yet know how to extract information from a text, the approach will be a welcome change.

Throughout each chapter, guide questions are used to maintain reader attention and to make reading an active learning experience. The format is not just questions and answers; it is more like a dialogue in which student questions and reactions are anticipated. The questions cue students to look for important points in the paragraphs which follow. Also interspersed throughout the text are Learning Checks. These are short, noncomprehensive quizzes that allow the reader to gauge recall and comprehension of preceding material. When learning check questions cannot be answered, the student is directed to review the previous section before reading more. Completing the Learning Checks also serves as a form of recitation to enhance learning. An excellent student workbook, prepared by Faren Akins, is available as another major study aid.

I sincerely hope teachers will find the format of this book a refreshing change from traditional texts. Student response to it has been extremely positive. If others find the approach of this text useful, I will be pleased. For me the feature which most clearly distinguishes it from others is its practicality. The applications sections are truly the heart of the text. They serve to bring psychology out of the "ivory tower" and breathe life into its concepts. Some of the topics covered in these sections are: techniques for controlling pain, how to break bad habits, how to improve memory and study skills (including a discussion of mnemonics), behavioral dieting, self-disclosure, effective parenting, conditioning pets, suicide prevention, how to find professional help, self-modification of behavior, and steps toward self-actualization. These are the things students need and want to know about psychology. This is particularly true of students who will never take another psychology class, but it applies to psychology majors as well.

The enterprise of psychology is a cooperative effort requiring the talents and energies of an entire community of scholars, teachers, researchers, and thinkers. For this reason, I am deeply appreciative of the criticisms, suggestions, and encouragement offered by the outstanding psychologists who read and reviewed portions of the manuscript for this book. The unique perspectives and talents of the following people have added immensely to the text:

Faren R. Akins, University of Arizona
William N. Colson, Norfolk State College (Virginia)
Thomas Eckle, Modesto Junior College (California)
Raymond Elish, Cuyahoga Community College (Ohio)
John P. Keating, University of Washington
Al Mayer, Portland Community College (Oregon)
Mark McKinley, Lorain County Community College (Ohio)
Don Nelson, Indiana State University
Darlene Pacheco, Moorpark College (California)
Leon Peek, North Texas State University
Harvey Taub, Staten Island Community College (New York)
Bruce Trotter, Santa Barbara City College (California)

My personal thanks to each of you.

I would particularly like to thank Clyde H. Perlee, Jr. of West's College Department for professional support above and beyond the call of duty and for his interest and friendship. It is hard to imagine a more helpful combination of professionalism and humanity than that represented by his guidance. Although a simple thank you seems woefully inadequate, I would also like to thank Janet Hansen and her associates at Hansen Graphics. Their special efforts and fine work have been a key element in the completion of this project. Judy Chaffin had the sizable task of editing the final manuscript. I am very grateful for her contribution. Readers will be, too!

Finally, I would like to thank the two unsung heroes of this project. To Janet Bollow goes credit for the design of the pages which follow. Were it not for her talent, patient good humor, and personal involvement, this book would still be a disordered stack of typed pages. Special thanks also go to Daniel Downey, whose preliminary research on Chapters 3, 12, 13, and 19 made possible the completion of each. The reader will find a more direct example of his work in the appendix. For my part, I cannot look at these chapters without seeing his efforts everywhere and feeling gratitude for his help and friendship.

DENNIS L. COON

The Psychology of Studying Psychology*

How to Communicate with Your Textbook

In the chapters which follow you will learn about memory, perception, abnormal behavior, psychotherapy, and a host of other interesting and useful topics. Since this book is your link to this information, a few words follow about how to make best use of it.

SQ3R Basically, each of the following chapters is designed around a well-known study-reading formula called the *SQ3R* method. This is a valuable five-step method for effective studying introduced over thirty years ago by Dr. Francis P. Robinson. It is designed to help a person (1) select what he is expected to know, (2) understand these ideas quickly, (3) remember what's important, and (4) review effectively for tests (Robinson, 1941). The symbols SQ3R are abbreviations for the necessary steps in effective study reading:

Step One: *Survey* = Look over the title and main headings in each chapter before reading in detail. Read captions under any pictures or illustrations. Read any summary statement or review if the chapter has one. This step should be a quick survey, taking no more than two minutes. It gives you an overall picture of what is in the chapter.

Step Two: *Question* = In order to concentrate on the content of a chapter, turn each topic heading into a question. This will increase your interest in what you read, and it forces you to focus on the content. The result is an increase in your concentration and comprehension.

*This introduction was contributed by W. Royce Adams.

Step Three: *Read* = The first *R*, in SQ3R, refers to *read.* You should read from one *topic heading* to the next, then stop. Don't go on to another heading.

Step Four: *Recite* = The second *R* stands for *recite.* After you have turned a heading into a question and read only to the next heading, you should then stop and recite; that is, try to answer the questions you asked yourself at the start of the section. Say the answer to yourself or write it down in notes. If you can't say or write the answer in your own words, scan back over the section and find the answer. Jotting down your questions and answers in a brief set of notes is often the best procedure. Once you thoroughly understand what you have read, turn the next topic or heading into a question and then read to the following heading. Again you should look for the answer as you read. Repeat this process until the entire chapter is read.

Step Five: *Review* = When the chapter has been read completely, look over your notes and check your memory by reciting the answers to questions again. Or better yet, get someone to ask you questions about each topic to see if you can answer in your own words.

Question: Does this method really work?

Many experiments have shown that using the SQ3R method improves reading comprehension and efficiency. Students who haven't learned a reading strategy tend to read straight through an entire chapter and try to remember everything. This approach is only slightly better than not reading at all! It is not wise to read a textbook as you would a novel. You must actively "dig out" information and give yourself a chance to pause and digest the information you are learning. A *survey* prepares you to read effectively. *Questioning* maintains your concentration on the subject, and it allows you to *read* in short "bites." *Recitation* of what you've read allows you to actively participate in and check up on your learning. Finally, *review* of the whole chapter ties together what you have learned and increases your understanding.

One of the most distressing experiences students have when they read is to discover after a while that they have passed their eyes over several pages but don't really remember anything. More than anything else the SQ3R method helps avoid this. That's why it's important that you *not* keep reading an assignment, but that you stop periodically, recite by taking brief notes in your own words, and review immediately after the entire chapter has been read.

Question: You said earlier that the chapters of this book are set up according to the SQ3R study formula. Can you explain that?

The SQ3R method can be used with any text. However, if you glance through this book you will notice that it is designed to help you use it. The opening of each chapter is a survey or preview of the chapter. Chapters are broken up by questions which are answered by the material which follows. Periodically, there are "learning checks" so that you can make certain that you understand the most important points. Toward the end of each chapter you will find a short review.

Effective Note-taking

Question: The SQ3R may be good for study-reading, but what about taking notes in class when it's difficult to know what the instructor's talking about?

Class note-taking is not always easy. But, generally speaking, there are two types of student listeners. One listens *passively*; the other listens *actively*. A passive listener just sits and listens and seldom hears everything because he allows his thoughts to wander away from the topic at hand. A certain idea or even a word can often trigger a passive listener into thoughts that have nothing to do with the lecture. It's the same type of loss of concentration that occurs when you are reading a chapter without controlling your thought processes through surveying, questioning, and reciting.

An *active* listener has a plan he follows. He knows he'll "drift away" on other thoughts if he doesn't help control his attention. Here's a listening-note-taking plan that works for many students. The important steps are summarized by the letters in the word LISAN.[1]

L = Lead. Don't follow. Try to anticipate what the instructor may be going to say. Try to be a jump ahead of him. When you guess wrong, it's all right because you will want to hear what he does say. As in SQ3R, try to set up questions as guides. Questions can come from the instructor's study guides or the reading assignments.

I = Ideas. Every lecture will be based around a core of important ideas. Usually an idea is introduced and examples or explanations are given. Ask questions such as: What is the main idea of this lecture? What important ideas will help support this? What part of what the instructor is saying supports the main idea? What is his purpose?

S = Signal words. Listen for words that tell you the direction the instructor is taking. For instance, here are some groups of signal words:

[1]Robert Carman and W. Royce Adams, *Study Skills: A Student's Guide for Survival*, Wiley, 1972.

There are three reasons why . . .	Here come ideas
First . . . second . . . third . . .	Order of ideas
Most important is . . .	Main ideas
On the other hand . . .	Change in idea
On the contrary . . .	Opposite idea
As an example . . .	Support for main idea
Therefore . . .	Conclusion
In conclusion . . .	Conclusion
In summary . . .	Summary coming

A = Actively listen. Sit where you can hear or where you can be seen if you need to ask questions of the instructor. Be on time. Look at the instructor while he or she talks. Bring questions from the last lecture or from your reading you want answered. Raise your hand at the beginning of the class or approach your instructor before the lecture begins. Do anything that helps you to be active.

N = Note-taking. As you listen, write down only key points or answers to questions you may already have. Organize your listening and note-taking around what you already know. Listen to everything, but be selective and don't try to write down everything you hear. Pay attention to signal words. If the lecture is not organized, you can organize your notes later. In fact, it's a good idea to review your notes and clarify any points by checking them with your textbook. Use the index of your textbook to locate key names or terms used in the lecture and follow through by reading those sections.

Taking Tests

Question: If I have read effectively and listened effectively in lecture, is there anything else I can do to improve my study skills?

One area that often gives students difficulty is test taking. Learning the material in a course is not enough. You must be able to show what you have learned on a test. If you have honestly followed the study suggestions given so far, you probably will have little to worry about when it comes time for tests. But there are some guidelines for test taking you might consider.

Objective Tests Objective tests (multiple-choice and true-false items) are often reading tests. They check on your ability to recognize a correct answer among wrong answers or a correct statement against a false one. They require little evaluation or thinking and demand more memory training than thoughtful analysis. If you are taking an objective test, try this:

1. Read the directions carefully. Don't assume that because the question has a T or F to circle or four or five items to select from that you know what to do. The directions may give you good advice or clues for the test. If the directions are not clear, ask the instructor to clarify them.
2. Read each statement or question carefully. If you have several choices for each item, read them *all* before deciding the correct answer. You may mark one you think is correct only to find the last choice says "both a and e," yet you only marked "a" as the answer.
3. Skip items you are not certain about. Go through the test answering the ones you do know. If there is time left, go back to the ones you skipped.
4. Eliminate certain alternatives. With a four choice per question multiple-choice test, the odds are 1 in 4 that you could guess the right answer. If you can eliminate one of the alternatives, your odds are 1 in 3. If you can eliminate two alternative choices, your guessing odds are 1 in 2, or fifty-fifty. Those are better odds than pure guessing.
5. There is a bit of folk wisdom that says "Don't change your answers on a multiple-choice test. Your first choice is usually right." This is generally good advice unless you feel *very* uncertain of your answer. A recent study showed that when you have strong doubts, your second answer is more likely to be correct (Johnson, 1975).

Essay Tests Essay questions are often a student's weak spot simply because of poor organization, poor or no support of main ideas, or not writing directly to the question. When you take essay exams, try the following:

1. Read the question carefully. Make sure that you note the key words, such as *compare*, *contrast*, *discuss*, *evaluate*, *analyze*, *define*, or *describe*. These words all demand a certain emphasis that should be placed on your answer.
2. Think about your answer before putting words on paper. It's a good idea to make a brief list of the points you want to make in your answer. Just list them as they pop into your head. Then rearrange your points so that you have them organized in the order you want to write them.
3. Don't beat around the bush or pad your answer. Be direct. Make a point and support it. Get your list of ideas into words.
4. Look over your essay for spelling errors, sentence errors, and grammatical errors. Save this for last. Your ideas are more important than misspelled words or poor sentence structure. You can work on those problems later if they interfere with your grade.

These tips on studying and test taking are just to get you off to a good start. In later chapters we will discuss additional techniques for improving your memory and learning skills.

Motivation

Question: All these study techniques are fine, but what if I'm just not interested in some of the courses I have to take?

Many students view school as an artificial "game" that has little connection to the "real world." But school and study are a part of every student's real world. Problems in relating to psychology as a subject—or to any course, for that matter—arise when the student can see nothing practical, useful, or even understandable in the course. Our concern in this chapter has been that you learn certain study *tools* that you can use to solve the problem of how to study effectively and meaningfully.

Even though you may not be interested or motivated to get involved in a course that does not particularly "turn you on," if you want to pass the course you have to talk yourself into mastering the fundamentals. The best thing to do in such a case is just to start studying, applying the skills we've suggested. You may not be motivated or interested to begin with, but forcing yourself to get started may be all you need. That's right. Sometimes you just have to tell yourself that interest and motivation are not going to come via a lightning bolt, but from you. In other words, it makes more sense to simply *begin.* Work hard, and real interest and motivation just might begin to creep into the picture.

A college has been called a community of learners. If you have not come to college knowing that you must adapt yourself to this community, then you may be spending your time in the wrong place. Unfortunately, most learning is a lonely process. No one can do your reading, thinking, or note-taking for you. You must ultimately decide whether or not you want to be a member of the community of learners. If you don't, leave school and come back when you are ready. If you are ready, or think you are ready, then you will have to learn to discipline yourself.

True discipline is the ability to give yourself self-direction, to face problems without fear or the need to look to others for help. This does not mean you cannot seek instructor, tutor, or friendly help when you need something explained. It means you know when you need to seek help rather than floundering around or hoping someone else will do your work for you.

Of course, just saying "I'm going to work hard at this course" is not enough. You can help find motivation and interest by controlling your reading assignments, by attending the lectures, and by pouring yourself into your studies.

There is a distinction that is made in Zen between "live words" and "dead words." Live words come from personal experience; dead words are "about" a subject. This book can only be a collection of dead words without your personal involvement. It is designed to help you learn psychology, but it cannot do it for you. You will find many helpful, useful, and exciting ideas in the pages which follow. To make them yours, you must set out to learn *actively* as much as you can. We think it will be worth the work. Good luck!

Suggestions for Further Reading

Brown, Charles, and W. Royce Adams. *How to Read the Social Sciences.* Scott, Foresman, 1968.

Carman, Robert A., and W. Royce Adams. *Study Skills: A Student's Guide for Survival.* Wiley, 1973.

Millman, Jason, and Walter Pauk. *How to Take Tests.* McGraw-Hill, 1969.

Contents

Introduction to Psychology **Unit One**

An Introduction to Psychology and Psychologists

1

Chapter Preview

Why Study Psychology?

You are a universe, a collection of worlds within worlds. Your brain is possibly the most complicated and amazing device in existence. Through the action of its 14 billion cells you are capable of art, music, science, philosophy, and war. Your capacities for compassion, affection, and dedication coexist with your capacities for aggression, hatred, and . . . murder? You are the most frustrating riddle ever written, a mystery at times even to yourself. You are at one and the same time a unique event in human history and like everyone who has ever lived. Your thoughts, emotions, and actions, your behavior *and* conscious experience, *are the subject of this book.*

Perhaps the simplest reason for studying psychology is that we are in the midst of a psychological revolution. Aldous Huxley has said:

> We have had religious revolutions, we have had political, industrial, economic, and nationalistic revolutions. All of them, as our descendents will discover, were but ripples in an ocean of conservatism—trivial by comparison with the psychological revolution toward which we are rapidly moving (Huxley, 1971).

Look around you. Newspapers, magazines, radio, and television abound with psychological information. Psychology is discussed in homes, schools, businesses, and bars. Psychology is an explosive, exciting, and ever-changing panorama of people and ideas. You can hardly consider yourself "educated" without knowing something about it.

There is another reason for studying psychology. Socrates said "Know thyself," and although we must envy those who have set foot on the moon, looked into an atom, or experienced firsthand the dreamlike landscapes of the ocean's depths, the ultimate frontier still lies close to home. Psychologist D. O. Hebb puts it this way: "What is psychology all about? . . . Psychology is about the mind: the central issue, the great mystery, the toughest problem of all" (Hebb, 1974).

Psychology is a journey into inner space. This book is a travel guide. Psychologists can't claim to have "the answers" to all of your questions, but they can show you the contours of the landscape already explored. More importantly, you may find skills in psychology that will aid you in your own search for answers. Ultimately the answers must be your own, but the study of psychology is a rich starting point. In this chapter you will find a definition of psychology, a description of various kinds of psychologists and what they do, and a brief history of ideas in psychology.

Resources

"The elephant," said the blind man as he felt the elephant's leg, "is very much like a tree."
"Why, how foolish!" said a second blind man (who had hold of the elephant's tail). "The elephant is like a rope."
The third blind man, having encountered the beast's trunk said, "You're both wrong, the elephant is like a snake."

Psychology: Psyche = Mind; Logos = Knowledge, or Study

Question: What is psychology?

A brief description of psychology will doubtless leave you in a position similar to that of the blind men. Psychology has become such an enormous beast that no short description can do it justice. By the time you have read this entire book you will begin to have an overall picture of what psychology is and what psychologists do. For now, let us just say that psychology is the *scientific study of the behavior of organisms*. Its goals are to *understand*, *predict*, and *control* behavior.

The scientific part of this definition means that psychologists have a special respect for *empirical evidence*. Empirical evidence consists of facts or information gained through direct observation and measurement rather than through opinion, argument, or appeals to authority. Psychologists settle differences by seeking empirical evidence whenever possible. Would you say it's true that "you can't teach an old dog new tricks"? Why argue about it? A psychologist would get ten "new" dogs, ten "used" dogs, and ten "old" dogs and then try to teach them all new tricks to find out!

Question: What is "behavior"?

Behavior is anything you do. Eating, sleeping, talking, thinking, and sneezing are "behaviors." So are dreaming, gambling, taking drugs, watching TV, learning Spanish, basket weaving, and reading this book. Psychologists prefer to focus on behavior because it can be observed and measured. Psychology floundered early in its development because psychologists differed in their answers to questions like: "When you look at a 'green' lawn, do you experience the same color sensation that I do?" This question can't be answered. It is too *subjective*. You may experience the sensation I call red, but if we both consistently label it green (because it happens every time we look at the lawn) we will never discover that we have had different experiences. All we can observe scientifically, or empirically, is that when we look at the same stimulus (the lawn) we respond alike: We call it green.

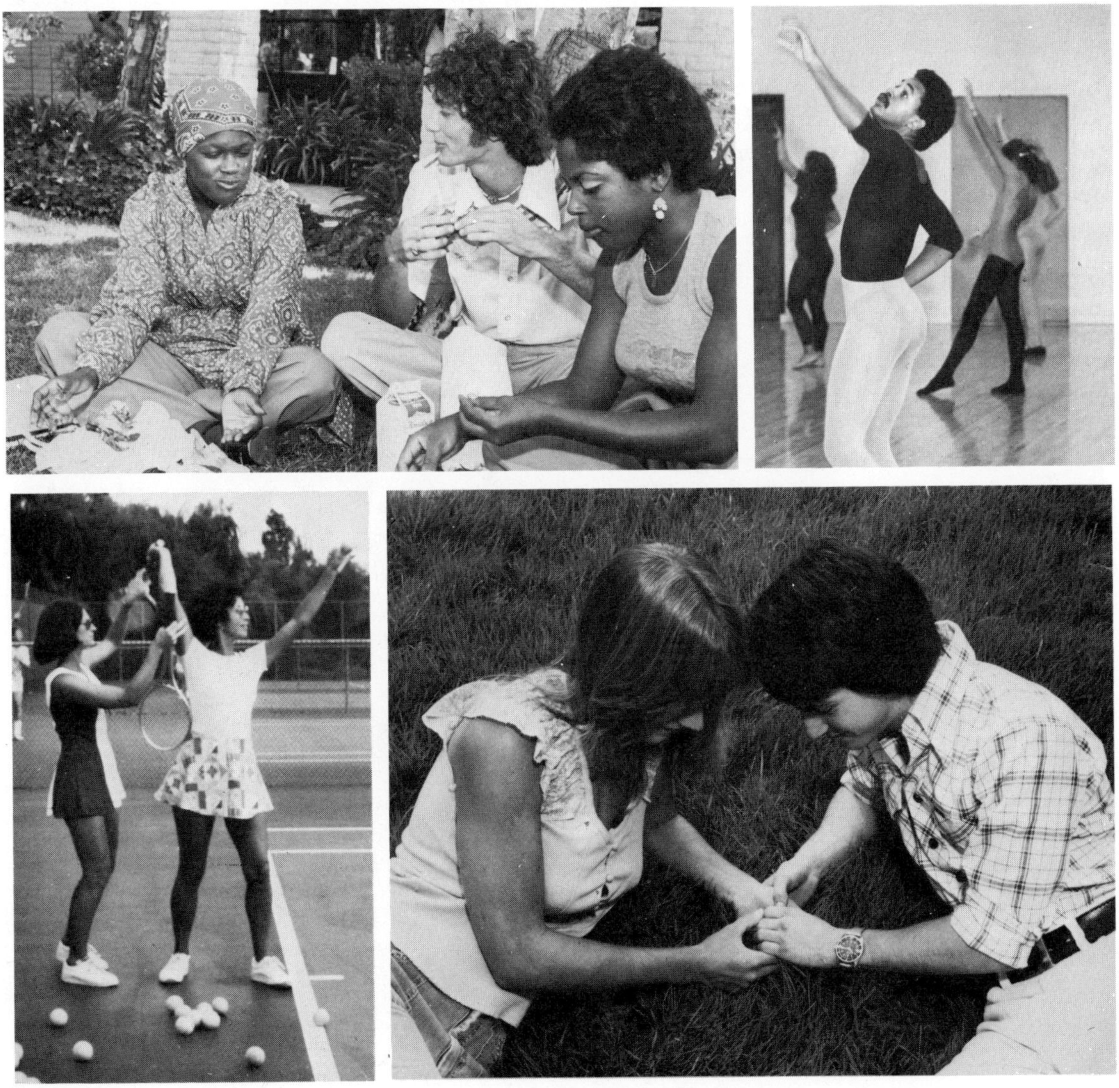

Fig. 1-1 The variety and complexity of human behavior makes psychological investigation challenging. (Photo by Marge Agin.)

Question: I've heard that psychology isn't scientific. Your definition says it is. Is it?

Psychology has been described as the "almost science" because scientific study of humans is not yet possible in all areas of research. Sometimes questions go unanswered because of moral or practical limitations. What would happen if a child were placed in a soundproof, lightproof box for the first five years of life? This question will probably never be directly answered. (However, many times an indirect answer can be obtained by studying animals.) Sometimes research must await a receptive social climate. Very little was known about human sexual response until William Masters, a gynecologist, and Virginia Masters, a psychologist, pioneered direct recording of physiological responses to sexual intercourse. Such research would have been impossible to carry out and publish twenty years ago.

More frequently, psychological questions remain unanswered because a suitable *method* does not yet exist. For years the subjective reports of people who said they never dream had to be considered accurate. Then the EEG (electroencephalograph or brain-wave machine) was developed, and it became possible to tell objectively when a person is dreaming. People who "never dream," it turns out, dream frequently and remember their dreams when awakened during one. Through use of the EEG, the study of dreaming is becoming quite scientific.

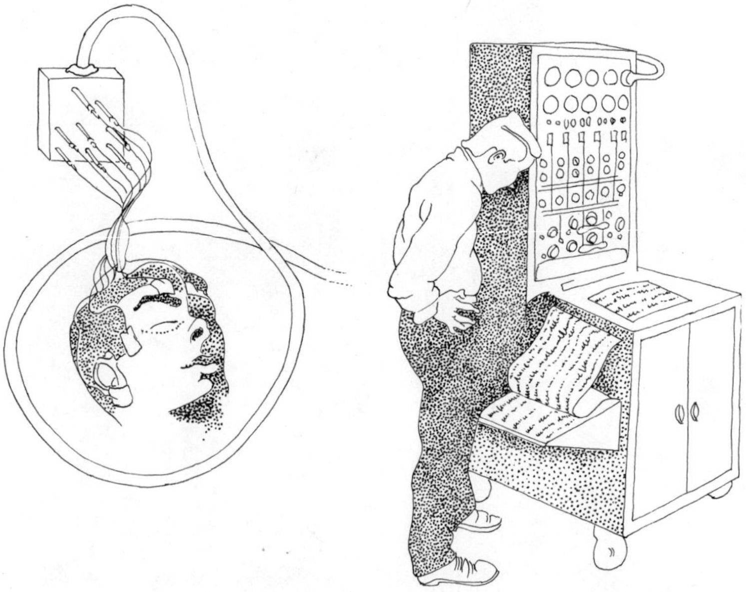

Fig. 1-2 The scientific study of dreaming has been made possible by use of the EEG, a device that records the tiny electrical potentials generated by the brain of a sleeping subject. It converts these electrical potentials to a written record of brain activity.

Question: You mentioned studying animals. What is a "rat psychologist"?

Notice that our definition says "the study of the behavior of *organisms.*" Psychologists are interested in the natural laws governing the behavior of *any* living creature—from flatworms to people. Many *comparative* psychologists (who *compare* the behavior of different species) spend their entire careers studying rats, cats, dogs, turtles, or chimpanzees. Some observers are critical of psychologists' willingness to base conclusions on the study of rats. Biologists have long been wary of the *anthropomorphic fallacy*, the temptation to attribute human thoughts, feelings, and motives to animals. Arthur Koestler has accused psychologists of reversing the error by treating humans like rats: "For the anthropomorphic view of the rat, American psychology has traded in a rattomorphic view of man" (Koestler, 1964). Elsewhere Koestler charges: "The 'cynical onlooker' might now ask . . . what is there left for the psychologist to study? The short answer is: rats" (Koestler, 1968).

But don't be too hasty in rejecting the efforts of "rat psychologists." In the same way that physicians test a new drug on animals before trying it on humans, psychologists often discover principles in simplified animal experiments that eventually prove useful in solving human problems. Sometimes principles established with animals can never be tested directly with humans. In this case animal research is especially important. Animals, serving as *models*, may provide the only information available on a

Fig. 1-3 Some of the most interesting research with animals has focused on attempts to teach chimpanzees to communicate with sign language. Here the chimp Washoe converses with a psychologist. (Photo courtesy of B. T. Gardner.)

particular topic. For example, the majority of what is known about the human brain and nervous system is based on research with animals. You just can't go around destroying parts of human brains to find out how they work. (The author, at any rate, has had a hard time finding volunteers.)

Learning Check

To improve your memory of this chapter, see if you can answer these questions. If you miss any, skim over the preceding material before continuing in order to make certain you understand what you just read.

1. Psychology is the ____________ study of the ________________ of organisms.

2. Information gained through direct observation and measurement is called ____________ evidence.

3. The *anthropomorphic fallacy* involves attributing human feelings and motives to ____________.

Answers: **1.** scientific, behavior **2.** empirical **3.** animals

A Brief History of Psychology's Brief History

Psychology as a science is less than 100 years old. Psychology, it is said, has a long past, but a short history. Those who dislike history may be tempted to add, "But not short enough!" They may be right! However, the *ideas* in psychology's past are intimately tied to its present. To understand where psychology is now, let's take a brief look at its long past and short history.

Question: *What do you mean when you say that psychology has a long past?*

Countless thinkers have pondered the question, "What is the nature of human nature?" From their efforts a body of thought known as *philosophy* emerged. This background of philosophical inquiry is psychology's "long past." Actually, all of the sciences grew out of philosophy, but psychology's connection to philosophy is very direct. The great philosophers (Plato, Aristotle, Descartes, Locke, Kant, and others) discussed psychological questions and elaborated their views of human nature. For example, Plato concluded that humans are both rational and irrational and that their behavior is the result of an interaction between desire (mainly sexual), emotion (which depends on the "heat of the blood"), and knowledge. Aristotle saw it differently. Humans, he said, function at three levels—the vegetative, sensory, and rational—and they generally seek pleasure and avoid pain. According to Descartes, the mind has three functions: intellectual cognition, volition, and sensation. The mind interacts with the body through the pineal gland. Kant felt that . . .

Question: Wait! Who is right?

That's a good question! You have noted the overlapping, conflicting, and confusing nature of these statements. For all its unquestionable value in other areas, a philosophical approach to psychological questions often became a game of words and complicated logic.

Eventually psychologists realized that the way to increase knowledge and to settle differences is to *investigate directly by observation*. As self-evident as this may seem in fields like biology or physics, we are still often tempted in psychology to accept what seems plausible or sensible rather than what *is*.

For example, see how many of these questions you can answer correctly on the basis of personal experience, reasoning, or common sense, and then we will compare your answers to those established empirically.

1. Owls can see in complete darkness. T or F?

2. The higher a person's intelligence, the greater the chance of mental illness. (Genius is next to insanity.) T or F?

3. The image of the moon is magnified by the atmosphere near the horizon. T or F?

4. Those who threaten suicide rarely actually commit suicide. T or F?

5. Through the use of hypnosis, people can be made to perform unusual feats of strength. T or F?

6. Intelligence is completely inherited from one's parents. T or F?

7. If your car breaks down, you are more likely to get help from a passerby on a busy highway than on a lightly traveled country road. T or F?

8. Punishment is the most effective way to reinforce the learning of new habits. T or F?

9. Drug addiction is one of the major causes of murder and other violent crimes. T or F?

10. A one-eyed man could not land an airplane. T or F?

Scoring this quiz is easy since all of the statements are F, false. If you missed some, don't despair, because the point is simply this: Psychology ceased to be philosophy when psychologists began to perform experiments, make observations, and seek evidence, and you will become a more critical and sophisticated observer of human behavior to the extent that you do the same.

Fig. 1-4 Wilhelm Wundt, 1832—1920. (Brown Brothers.)

Question: What about psychology's "short history"?

Structuralism Psychology's history began in the year 1879 at Leipzig, Germany. There, the "father of psychology," Wilhelm Wundt, established the first psychological laboratory. Wundt wanted to explore the mind more directly than philosophers had done from their "armchairs." He also wanted to duplicate the progress being made in other sciences. In chemistry, complex compounds were being reduced to their elements; in physics, the concept of the atom had emerged; and the cell doctrine had brought a new clarity to biology. In psychology, Wundt hoped to discover the *structure* of conscious sensory experience by *analyzing* it into its elements.

Question: How could he do that? You can't analyze experience like you can a chemical compound.

Wundt developed a method called *introspection*. Introspection is self-observation, or "looking inward," combined with analysis (separation into elements). In Wundt's laboratory, a trained introspectionist might heft an apple and then decide that he had experienced the elements "redness," "roundness," and "weight." Another example of the kind of question that might have interested Wundt is this: What are the basic irreducible tastes that are mixed together to form complex tastes as different as liver, lime, bacon, or burnt-almond fudge?

Functionalism William James, an American psychologist, felt that Wundt and the structuralists were missing the boat in their attempts to discover the structure of conscious experience. James was interested in how consciousness *functions* to adapt us to changing demands. James considered consciousness an ongoing *process*, not a collection of building blocks.

Question: What did he mean by that?

The functionalists were particularly influenced by Charles Darwin. Darwin showed that organisms *evolve* in directions that favor their survival. In practice, this means that a physical feature which functions to adapt an animal to its environment is retained through *natural selection*, or "survival of the fittest." The functionalists sought to learn the ways in which thought, perception, habits, and emotions serve as psychological tools for human adaptation.

Fig. 1-5 William James, 1842—1910. (Brown Brothers.)

Question: What effect did functionalism have on modern psychology?

The functionalists (particularly John Dewey) were especially interested in the process of education because education can be used to develop practical skills and to improve overall functioning. *Educational psychology* is a direct outgrowth of functionalism. The educational psychologist studies learning to make it more effective or to find ways of overcoming problems such as learning disabilities or reading impairment. Functionalism also spurred the development of *industrial psychology*.

Fig. 1-6 John B. Watson, 1878—1958. (Brown Brothers.)

Behaviorism: Stimulus-Response Psychology Structuralists and functionalists often disagreed among themselves because they relied heavily on subjective introspection. Behaviorist John B. Watson was troubled by this and by the fact that their methods excluded the insane, children, and animals from scientific study. Watson found that he could study animals quite effectively even though he couldn't ask them questions. He simply observed the relationship between *stimuli* and an animal's *responses* to them. With this in mind, he proclaimed in 1913: "The time has come when psychology must discard all reference to consciousness. . . . Its sole task is the prediction and control of behavior; and introspection can form no part of its method." According to Watson, the proper definition of psychology is the "science of behavior."

Watson adopted the *conditioned response*, a concept introduced by the Russian physiologist Pavlov, as a means of explaining most behavior. Pavlov had showed that a reflex response can become associated with a particular stimulus so that the stimulus will produce the reflex. Watson began to think of everything in terms of stimulus-response connections. He treated emotions and feelings as learned "gut" reflexes, and he considered thinking to be "sub-vocal speech habits" (unvoiced talking to oneself). Watson's enthusiasm for conditioning theory had obviously reached extremes when he proclaimed:

> Give me a dozen healthy infants, well-formed, and my own special world to bring them up in and I'll guarantee to take any one at random and train him to become any type of specialist I might select—doctor, lawyer, artist, merchant-chief, and yes, beggarman and thief (Watson, 1913).

Question: Would most psychologists agree with this?

Behaviorism has had a profound effect on modern psychological thought. One of the best-known and most influencial modern behaviorists, B. F. Skinner, has said,

> The environment is the key causal matrix. . . . In order to understand human behavior we must take into account what the environment does to an organism before and after it responds. Behavior is shaped and maintained by its consequences (Skinner, 1971).

Many psychologists consider Skinner's brand of behaviorism extreme. But the majority would agree that most human behavior is based on various forms of learning.

Fig. 1-7 Max Wertheimer, 1880—1941. (United Press International.)

Gestalt Psychology The German word *gestalt* means form, pattern, or whole. The *gestalt* school of thought, founded by the German psychologist Max Wertheimer, held that it is a mistake to try to analyze psychological phenomena. The gestaltists sought to study experiences as *wholes*. Their slogan was, "The whole is equal to more than the sum of its parts."

Question: What did they mean by that?

Consider the example of a melody. If the notes from a familiar tune such as "Yankee Doodle" are played in quick succession, the result is a melody recognizable on any instrument. Next we could use a new set of notes much higher or lower than the original set. Even if none of the original notes are used, the melody will still be recognizable if the *relationship* between notes is the same. Now what if the original notes were played in the proper order, but at a rate of one each hour? What would we have? Nothing. The individual notes would no longer be a melody.

The melody is somehow more than the sum of its parts. This may be why "a picture is worth a thousand words" or why a thousand words are still not enough to capture a symphony or a sunset. Some psychological experiences resist analysis. The gestalt point of view is particularly influencial in the areas of perception and personality for this reason.

Psychoanalytic Psychology As the mainstream of psychology was becoming more rigorously objective, scientific, and experimental, another important school of psychological thought was developing on a foundation of clinical insight. By working with troubled patients, an Austrian physician, Sigmund Freud, developed a theory of personality and an approach to psychotherapy that stood in sharp contrast to laboratory-based theories.

Freud's point of departure was his recognition that human mental experience is like an iceberg. Only part is exposed to view. According to

Fig. 1-8 Sigmund Freud, 1856—1939. (Historical Picture Service, Chicago.)

Fig. 1-9 Abraham Maslow, 1908—1970. (© Ted Polumbaum.)

Freud, there are vast areas of *unconscious* thoughts, conflicts, and desires which cannot be experienced directly but which continue to influence our behavior. Because these unconscious thoughts are usually of a sexual or an aggressive nature they are threatening and are therefore *repressed* (actively held out of consciousness by forces within the personality). Sometimes they are revealed in dreams, impulses, and slips of the tongue. Freud's revelations about the unconscious added an entirely new dimension not only to psychology but to art, literature, and history as well.

Freud's other contributions were his insistence that all thoughts, emotions, and actions are *determined* (nothing is an accident); his emphasis on the importance of childhood in later personality development ("the child is father to the man"); and his development of a method of psychotherapy called *psychoanalysis.*

Humanistic Psychology A fairly recent development in psychology is a point of view known as *humanism*. Humanism is sometimes called the "third force" in psychology. (Psychoanalytic psychology and behaviorism count as the other two.)

Question: How is the humanistic approach different?

Psychologists Carl Rogers, Abraham Maslow, and others developed the humanistic viewpoint to counter the negativity they saw in behaviorism and psychoanalysis. Humanists reject the Freudian idea that the personality is ruled by unconscious forces and the behavioristic idea that we are controlled by the environment. Although they admit that one's past affects personality, they emphasize the importance of *free will*, the human ability to make choices.

The humanists have also made psychologists aware of the importance of psychological needs like the needs for love, self-esteem, belonging, self-expression, and creativity. According to the humanists, such needs are as important as biological needs for food and water. For example, a newborn infant who is deprived of human love and warmth may die just as surely as he would if deprived of food.

Question: Do the humanists use a scientific approach?

Humanists collect data and seek evidence to support their ideas, but for the most part the humanists tend to be less interested in attempts to treat psychology as a science. Since they are basically interested in solving human problems, humanists show little interest in research with animals or laboratory studies of behavior. Instead, they emphasize the importance of such *subjective* factors as one's *self-image*, *self-evaluation*, and *frame of reference*.

One of the most distinctive contributions of the humanistic approach is Maslow's identification of the human need for *self-actualization*. Self-actualization is the need to develop one's potential fully, to lead a rich and meaningful life, and to become the best person one can become. According to the humanists, everyone has this potential. The humanists seek ways to allow it to emerge.

Learning Check

See if you can correctly match the following before reading further.

___ **1.** Philosophy	**A.**	Against analysis; studied whole experiences
___ **2.** Structuralism	**B.**	Analyzed experience into elements
___ **3.** Functionalism	**C.**	Emphasizes self-actualization and personal growth
___ **4.** Behaviorism	**D.**	interested in unconscious causes of behavior
___ **5.** Gestalt	**E.**	Gave rise to educational psychology
___ **6.** Psychoanalytic	**F.**	Studies stimuli and responses, conditioning
___ **7.** Humanistic	**G.**	Asked "What is human nature?"

Answers: **1.** G **2.** B **3.** E **4.** F **5.** A **6.** D **7.** C

Psychologists—Guaranteed Not to Shrink

Question: What is the difference between a psychologist and a psychiatrist?
Answer: About $20 an hour.

Confusion often exists about the difference between *psychologists*, *psychiatrists*, and a third group, *psychoanalysts*. Although many people lump all three together as "shrinks," there are distinct differences in training and emphasis among them.

A psychologist usually has a master's degree or a Ph.D. in psychology; that is, from three to eight years of specialized postgraduate training in psychological theory and research methods. Depending on their interests, psychologists may teach, do research, administer psychological tests, or serve as consultants to business, industry, government, or the military. Psychologists interested in human emotional problems and their treatment specialize in *clinical psychology*. Most psychologists now entering professional positions find it necessary to have the doctorate (Ph.D. or Ed.D.) in order to be licensed or to qualify or compete for positions. Most clinical psychologists have a Ph.D. from a school accredited by the American Psychological Association (APA).

Like clinical psychologists, psychiatrists are also interested in treating human problems, but they are trained differently. A psychiatrist is a physician. After training in general medicine, a psychiatrist specializes in personality, abnormal behavior, and psychotherapy. Psychiatrists often become "talking doctors," meaning that they make little direct use of their medical training. Instead, they spend much of their time doing psychotherapy or counseling. In practice, then, the major difference between a psychologist who is doing psychotherapy and a psychiatrist is this: As an M.D., a psychiatrist is trained to recognize and treat physical causes of psychological difficulties, and he or she can prescribe drugs and refer patients for surgery.

To become a psychoanalyst you must have a moustache and goatee, spectacles, a German accent, and a well-padded couch, or so the TV and movie stereotype goes. Actually, a psychoanalyst is simply a clinical psychologist or a psychiatrist extensively trained in the theories of Sigmund Freud and his followers. Analysts also undergo analysis themselves before applying the method to others.

Question: Are Freud's theories still used?

In practice most psychotherapists find that a flexible and *eclectic* (drawing from many sources) approach is most effective. This, plus the fact that traditional psychoanalysis is an expensive and time-consuming process, is gradually making the pure psychoanalyst something of a rare breed, but a true psychoanalyst adheres to the core of Freud's theory.

Question: What is a gestalt therapist?

There are dozens of approaches to psychotherapy. Discussion of gestalt therapy and a number of other techniques must be deferred to a later chapter (Chapter 23), but this question does raise an interesting issue. Before the American Psychological Association began a push for licensing and certification of psychologists, it was possible in many states for virtually anyone to purchase an inexpensive license and then "hang out a shingle" as a "psychologist." To be legally called a psychologist, a person must now meet a rigorous set of educational requirements. To work as a clinical psychologist, he or she must have a license issued by a state examining board. However, the law does not prohibit you from calling yourself anything else you choose—gestalt therapist, primal feeling facilitator, cosmic aura therapist, or Rolfer—or from selling your "services" to anyone willing to pay. Beware of people advertising under such self-proclaimed titles. Even if their intentions are honorable, the training of such individuals is often limited or nonexistent. A fully trained certified psychologist who chooses to use a particular type of therapy is not the same as someone "trained" only in that therapy. Unfortunately, psychology, like medicine, has attracted a fringe of opportunists, quacks, and charlatans who seek to profit by taking advantage of human needs, fears, and suffering. When the escapades of these "not-really psychologists" make the news or when a friend or relative has a bad experience with one, psychologists often pay the price in negative public attitudes toward psychology in general. This is indeed unfortunate since psychologists adhere to a professional code established by the APA which stresses: (1) accurate representation of one's professional qualifications; (2) confidentiality in handling of personal information in teaching, practice, or research; and above all, (3) protection of the client's welfare. Psychologists are also expected to make their services available to anyone who seeks them, regardless of social considerations or ability to pay.

How to Be a Psychologist—Let Us Count the Ways

Question: Do all psychologists do therapy and treat abnormal behavior?

Although it is the largest subarea, only 30 percent of psychologists are clinicians. The rest divide themselves among a range of specialties, listed in Table 1-1. Over 50 percent of psychologists are employed full-time by educational institutions. In this setting they mix teaching with research, consultation, and practice. Those who do research may do "*pure*" research, seeking knowledge for the sake of knowledge; or "*applied*" research, in which immediate uses are planned for the information gained.

Question: What kinds of things would a typical psychologist at a university do research on?

Here is a sampling of representative research topics:

Developmental "I am interested in development. I am trying to learn how people grow and change over time. My interests stretch from prenatal

Table 1-1 Kinds of Psychologists and What They Do

	Teaching	*Pure research*	*Applied research*	*Practioner*
Clinical	Sometimes	Sometimes	Often	Usually
Counseling	Sometimes	Rarely	Sometimes	Usually
Educational	Often	Sometimes	Often	Sometimes
School	Rarely	Rarely	Rarely	Usually
Personality	Often	Often	Sometimes	Rarely
Social	Often	Often	Sometimes	Rarely
Developmental	Sometimes	Sometimes	Sometimes	Often
Industrial	Rarely	Rarely	Usually	Usually
Experimental*	Often	Usually	Sometimes	Rarely

*Frequent specialties in experimental psychology are: learning, sensation/perception, motivation/emotion, comparative, and physiological.

life to death, but I am especially interested in early childhood. My colleagues and I seek the principles whereby a child develops the ability to think, speak, perceive, and learn. Broadly speaking, I am interested in how adult personality and skills emerge from childhood, but my current research is more limited. I am studying the effects of stimulating childhood environments on the development of intelligence."

Learning "I'm also interested in how people get to be the way they are, but in a much more abstract sense. I feel that most human behavior is learned. By studying various kinds of learning, conditioning, and memory in humans and animals, I am helping to construct theories about how learning occurs and what factors affect it. My dissertation was on avoidance learning. I had rats learn to press a bar in order to avoid receiving an electric shock which followed the onset of a signal light. Right now I'm studying the effects of patterns of reward on learning in pigeons."

Personality "In many ways my area is both the most rewarding and the most frustrating. Personality theorists draw on the findings of all other research areas as well as their own in an effort to create as total a picture and understanding of human personality as possible. I concern myself with the structure and dynamics of personality, motivation, and individual differences. I am studying the personality profiles of college students who score high on tests of creativity."

Sensation and Perception "How do we come to know the world? How does information 'get into' our nervous system? How is it processed and given pattern and meaning? These are my concerns. I am using an information-processing theory called signal detection to study the visual perception of random shapes."

Physiological Psychology "The brain and nervous system are my meat . . . so to speak. It is my belief that ultimately all other areas in psychology—learning, perception, even personality—will be explained by reference to the action of nerve cells or parts of the brain. I have been doing some exciting research on the role of the hypothalamus in hunger. I find that if I destroy part of the hypothalamus in the brain of a rat, he will eat and gain weight until he looks like a furry water balloon. If I destroy an area just a few centimeters away, he will starve to death while sitting on a pile of food."

Social Psychology "I study people in a group setting, or under any circumstance in which social factors play a part. Social psychologists in general are interested in attitudes, social influence, riots, mobs, conformity, leadership, racism, and a growing list of other topics. My personal interest is interpersonal attraction. I place two strangers together in a room for a short time and investigate factors which affect their ratings of attraction toward each other."

This small sample should give you some idea of the diversity of psychological research. It also gives you a hint of some of the kinds of information covered in later chapters of this book.

Learning Check

See if you can answer these questions before continuing.

1. Which of the following can prescribe drugs? Psychologist, psychiatrist, or psychoanalyst?

2. A psychologist who specializes in treating human emotional difficulties is called a ______________________ psychologist.

3. Seeking knowledge for the sake of knowledge is called ____________ research.

Match the following research areas with the topic they cover.

___ **4.** Developmental	**A.**	Attitudes, groups, leadership
___ **5.** Learning	**B.**	Conditioning, memory
___ **6.** Personality	**C.**	Brain and nervous system
___ **7.** Sensation and perception	**D.**	Child psychology
___ **8.** Physiological psychology	**E.**	Individual differences, motivation
___ **9.** Social psychology	**F.**	Animal behavior
___ **10.** Comparative	**G.**	Information processing

Answers:
1. Psychiatrist **2.** clinical **3.** pure **4.** D **5.** B **6.** E **7.** G **8.** C **9.** A **10.** F

Resources Summary

Psychology is the scientific study of the behavior of organisms. Its stated goals are to understand, predict, and in some cases control behavior. Whenever possible psychologists seek *empirical*, or objective, evidence. Psychologists study animals as well as people. One danger in studying animals is the *anthropomorphic fallacy*.

The history of psychology begins with *philosophy*. The first school of thought in psychology was *structuralism* started by Wundt. Structuralism was followed by *functionalism* and *gestalt* psychology. Three major streams of thought in modern psychology are *behaviorism*, *humanism*, and the *psychoanalytic* approach. Behaviorism emphasizes scientific study of observable stimuli and responses. Humanists study subjective experience, human motives, and the positive side of human nature as expressed through self-actualization. The psychoanalytic approach, based on Freud's theories, emphasizes the unconscious determinants of behavior.

Psychologists, psychiatrists, and psychoanalysts all work in the field of mental health, although their training differs considerably. *Clinical* psychologists who do psychotherapy represent only one of several specialties in psychology. Many psychologists do research and teach. Some of the other areas of specialization in psychology include: *educational* psychology, *school* psychology, *social* psychology, *developmental* psychology, *industrial* psychology, *experimental* psychology, and *personality*.

Applications

An Introduction to "Applications"

Question: What can I learn from psychology that will benefit me personally?

Psychology has always been one of the most relevant courses on campus. When the topic is human behavior, it is hard not to be interested. But the time has come in psychology when interest is not enough. As George Miller has said:

> the secrets of our trade need not be reserved for highly trained specialists. Psychological facts should be passed out freely to all who need and can use them. . . . There simply are not enough psychologists, even including nonprofessionals, to meet every need for psychological services. The people at large will have to be their own psychologists, and make their own applications of established principles (Miller, 1969).

To help you make the most of your learning in psychology, each of the chapters which follow includes an "applications" section. Here, information and ideas of immediate usefulness to you will be discussed. In this first applications section, Maslow's concept of *self-actualization* will be expanded upon.

Self-actualization—Let Your Reach Exceed Your Grasp

Psychologists have had a tendency to study human problems more than human strengths. A notable exception to this can be found in Abraham Maslow's studies of people living unusually effective lives. Maslow became interested in people who seemed to be using almost all of their talents and potentials. How were they different from the average person? To find an answer, Maslow began by studying the biographies of great men and women: Albert Einstein, William James, Jane Adams, Eleanor Roosevelt, Abraham Lincoln, John Muir, Walt Whitman, and others. From these he moved on to direct studies of artists, writers, poets, and other creative individuals.

Along the way Maslow's thinking changed radically. At first he studied only people of obvious creativity or high achievement. Eventually, however, it became clear that a housewife, carpenter, clerk, or student could live creatively and make full use of his or her potentials. Maslow referred to this tendency as *self-actualization* (Maslow, 1954).

As he continued his studies, Maslow found that *self-actualizers* shared a great number of similarities. It made little difference if they were famous or unknown, academically distinguished or uneducated, rich or poor, self-actualizers fit this profile:

Some Characteristics of Self-actualizers

1. *Efficient perceptions of reality.* Subjects were able to judge situations correctly and honestly

and were very sensitive to the fake and dishonest.

2. *Comfortable acceptance of self, others, nature.* Subjects were able to accept their own human nature with all its shortcomings. The shortcomings of others and the contradictions of the human condition were also accepted with humor and tolerance.
3. *Spontaneity.* Maslow's subjects extended their creativity into everyday activities. They tended to be unusually alive, engaged, and spontaneous.
4. *Problem-centering.* Most subjects had a mission to fulfill in life or some task or problem outside of themselves to pursue. Albert Schweitzer is a good example of this quality.
5. *Autonomy.* Subjects were free from dependence on external authority or other people. They tended to be resourceful and independent.
6. *Continued freshness of appreciation.* The self-actualizer seems to constantly renew appreciation of life's basic goods. A sunset or a flower will be experienced as intensely the one-thousandth time as it was the first.
7. *Fellowship with mankind.* Maslow's subjects felt a deep identification with mankind and the human situation in general.
8. *Profound interpersonal relationships.* The interpersonal relationships of self-actualizers were marked by deep, loving bonds.
9. *Unhostile sense of humor.* This refers to the wonderful capacity to laugh at oneself. It also refers to the kind of humor a man like Abraham Lincoln had. Lincoln probably never made a joke that hurt anybody. His wry comments were a gentle prodding at human shortcomings.
10. *Peak experiences.* All of Maslow's subjects reported the frequent occurrence of "peak" experiences. These were marked by feelings of ecstasy, harmony, and deep meaning. Subjects reported feeling at one with the universe, stronger and calmer than ever before, filled with light, beautiful and good, etc.

In short, self-actualizers feel safe and unanxious, accepted, loved, loving, and alive.

Question: That's a difficult list to live up to. How many people are self-actualizers?

Very few people fit Maslow's conception of a self-actualizer. It is an ideal that stands as a challenge for personal growth to us all. But self-actualization is not just an end point, it is a process. In this first applications section we would like to issue a challenge to you to make your excursion into psychology a contribution to your own personal growth. By combining the information and insights you will obtain from this book, your instructor, and your fellow students, your own progress toward full use of your unique potential can be advanced.

Questions for Discussion

1. In what ways is your behavior controlled by the environment? Do you feel that you have free will? Is there any way to tell if a "free choice" is really determined by your past?

2. How did you picture a psychologist before reading this chapter? Has your image of psychologists changed? How accurate are television and movie portrayals of psychologists?

3. Have you ever had a "peak experience"? What was it like? How did it affect you?

4. Maslow has referred to self-actualizing individuals as the "growing-tip of humanity." How does self-actualization compare to your conception of a fully functioning person? Does self-actualization place too much emphasis on impulsiveness and subjectivity?

5. Should psychologists study animals? Why or why not?

6. The goals of psychology are to understand, predict, and control behavior. Which of these goals do you find acceptable or unacceptable?

7. Is the distinction between "objective" and "subjective" information realistic? When might the "objectivity" of psychological conclusions be disputed?

8. Discuss the limitations of the following widely used "psychological" terms and insights (dubbed "psychobabble" by one critic): I "flashed on" what he meant and really felt like we were "getting into each other's heads." She's really "together," you know, really "laid back." "I hear you." He gives me "good vibes," he's really "high energy," and you can always tell where he's "coming from." You gotta "go with your feelings" and "let it happen" if you don't want to be "uptight."

Suggestions for Further Reading

A Career in Psychology. American Psychological Association, 1200 17th Street, N.W., Washington, D.C. 20036. (You can write for this one.)

Marks, R. W. (ed.) *Great Ideas in Psychology.* Bantam, 1966.

Pronko, N. H. *Panorama of Psychology.* Brooks/Cole, 1969.

Psychology Today. CRM. Available monthly.

Roback, A. A. *History of American Psychology.* Collier, 1964.

Wertheimer, M. *A Brief History of Psychology.* Holt, 1972.

Research Methods in Psychology

2

Chapter Preview

From Common Sense to Controlled Observation

Comment overheard on campus: "I don't know why he bothers taking psychology classes. Psychology is just common sense." Is psychology common sense? Is common sense a good source of information?

Consider some "commonsense" statements: Let's say that your grandfather has gone back to college. What do people say? "Ahh . . . never too old to learn." And what do they say when he loses interest and quits? "Well, you can't teach an old dog new tricks." Let's examine another commonsense statement. It is frequently said that "absence makes the heart grow fonder." Those of us separated from friends and lovers can take comfort in this knowledge—until we remember that it's also "Out of sight, out of mind!" Much of what passes for common sense is equally vague and inconsistent. Notice also that these B.S. statements work best after the fact.*

Common sense can be a set of blinders which prevent us from seeking better information or seeing the truth. Einstein reportedly said, "Common sense is the layer of prejudice laid down in our minds before we are eighteen." In the early stages of the scientific revolution *people laughed at the idea that the world is round. Anyone with eyes could see that it wasn't. They laughed at Pasteur when he proposed that microorganisms cause disease. How could creatures too small to be seen kill a healthy human? Certainly ideas like these contradicted the common sense of their time. Now*

*B.S., of course, stands for *Before Science*.

few people argue with the findings of established sciences like chemistry, physics, or medicine, but many still write off psychology as "just common sense."

Jab a hat pin into your finger. The nerve impulse carrying the sensation of pain to your brain seems instantaneous. We can go no further using casual observation. *Common sense tells us that nervous transmission is instantaneous. However, if we make* controlled observations *we arrive at a different conclusion. Before the turn of the century, German physiologist Herman Helmholtz observed that a pin poked in the ankle will produce a longer average* reaction time *than a pin applied to the hip. This simple experiment shows that nervous transmission is not instantaneous since the pain message takes some time to travel the distance between the ankle and the hip on its way to the brain.*

By using an electrical stimulus and electronic recorders to measure nerve impulses directly, psychologists have found their top speed to be 120 meters per second, almost the speed of sound. This is fast, but certainly not instantaneous. We have come a long way from our original casual observation.

Research psychologists use a number of approaches to improve upon and extend observation and to avoid the pitfalls of "common sense."

Fig. 2-1 This woman is monitoring a reaction-time experiment. A subject in a separate, darkened room has been presented with a visual stimulus. This device records the subject's brain waves and eye movements in response to the stimulus. (Photo © Van Bucher, Photo Researchers, Inc.)

Resources

Naturalistic Observation—Into the Field!

Instead of waiting to encounter haphazardly whatever they are interested in, psychologists may set out to *actively observe* subjects in their *natural setting*. A good example of this style of research is the work of Jane van Lawick-Goodall. She and her staff have been observing chimpanzees in Tanzania since 1960. A quote from her book *In the Shadow of Man* captures the excitement of a scientific discovery:

> Quickly focusing my binoculars, I saw that it was a single chimpanzee, and just then he turned my direction. . . . Cautiously I moved around so that I could see what he was doing. He was squatting beside the red earth mound of a termite nest, and as I watched I saw him carefully push a long grass stem into a hole in the mound. After a moment he withdrew it and picked something from the end with his mouth. I was too far away to make out what he was eating, but it was obvious that he was actually using a grass stem as a tool (1971).

This discovery forced many scientists to change their definition of humans because previously humans had been regarded as the only toolmaking animals.

Question: Chimpanzees in zoos use objects as tools. Doesn't that prove the same thing?

Fig. 2-2 A special moment in Jane van Lawick Goodall's naturalistic study of chimpanzees. (Photo by Baron Hugo van Lawick. © National Geographic Society.)

One of the advantages of naturalistic observation is that the behavior being studied has not been tampered with by outside influences. Only by observing chimps in their natural environment can we tell if they use tools without human interference.

Question: But doesn't the presence of human observers in an animal colony affect their behavior?

Yes. However, two advantages of naturalistic observation are that it provides a wealth of information and that *careful record keeping* avoids biased observations. In any scientific investigation it is an excellent starting point, but it does have limitations. A major problem is the effect of the observer on the observed.

Effects of the Observer The presence of an observer may change the behavior of the observed. Naturalists studying animal colonies must be very careful to keep their distance and to avoid the temptation to "make friends" with the animals. Likewise, if you are interested in student-teacher interactions in an elementary school classroom, it would hardly do for you to simply walk in and begin taking notes. A stranger in the room would undoubtedly affect both the students and the teacher. When possible, this problem is minimized by concealing the observer. For example, Arnold Gesell and his associates (1940) were able to determine at what age children develop the ability to sit up, walk, talk, and so forth, by observing preschoolers through one-way vision screens.

Correlation versus Causation A second limitation of naturalistic observation is summarized by the statement, "Correlation does not prove causation." In other words, naturalistic observation does not allow a clear determination of *causes*. Just because one thing appears to cause another does not prove that it does. This can be seen clearly in the case of some obviously noncausal relationships. For example, there is a correlation, or relationship, between the number of storks nesting in English villages and the number of births in those same towns. Does this mean that storks bring babies? Or could it mean that babies attract storks? Obviously neither. Here's another: There is a relationship between the number of churches in United States cities and the number of bars: The more churches, the more bars. Does this mean that drinking makes you religious? Does it mean that religion makes you thirsty? No one, of course, would leap to the conclusion that any one of these events *caused* the other, but in more realistic situations it is a temptation.

Doctors and nurses in New York hospitals noticed a sharp rise in the birthrate exactly nine months after the 1966 power failure in New York State. In news reports of this event it was assumed that when the lights and TVs went off, people had nothing better to do, and the result was a "baby boom" nine months later. A closer look at the birthrate would show that it fluctuates up and down all year and that the "baby boom" was but one of dozens of small peaks and therefore not necessarily linked to the power failure at all.

Learning Check

Before reading on, answer the following questions about what you have just read:

1. Psychology can rightfully be called "common sense." T or F?

2. Casual observation can reliably be used for scientific investigation. T or F?

3. Controlled observation is not as reliable as casual observation. T or F?

4. Correlation does not prove causation. T or F?

Answers: 1. F 2. F 3. F 4. T

The Controlled Experiment—Can a Horse Add?

One of the most powerful research tools available to psychologists is the *controlled experiment*. Conditions are carefully arranged in an experiment so that very reliable information is gained.

Question: What is controlled *in an experiment?*

Here is an example of what is meant by control. Psychologist Robert Rosenthal (1965) has reported the story of Clever Hans, the wonder horse. Clever Hans was a horse owned by a mathematics instructor. Hans seemed to be able to solve difficult math problems which he answered by tapping his foot. If you asked Hans "What is 12 times 2, minus 18," Hans would tap his foot six times. Hans was so astonishing that he eventually attracted the attention of an inquiring scientist who discovered how Hans was able to perform. Assume that you are the scientist and that you are just itching to find out how Hans *really* does his trick. You might make the horse's owner leave the room and then have someone else ask him questions. In other words, your *hypothesis* (a hypothesis is an educated guess) is that the owner is giving a signal. Your proposed test would either confirm or deny this possibility and thereby support or eliminate the hypothesis. By changing the conditions under which you observe Hans, you have *controlled* the situation to gain more information from it.

Incidentally, Hans could still answer when his owner was out of the room. But a brilliant series of controlled observations revealed Hans' secret. If Hans couldn't see the questioner, he couldn't answer. It seems that

Fig. 2-3 Clever Hans.

questioners always *lowered their head* (to look at Hans' foot) after asking a question. This was Hans' cue to start tapping. When Hans had tapped the correct number, a questioner would always *look up* to see if Hans was going to stop. This was Hans' cue to stop tapping!

The Classic Experiment—Untangling Cause and Effect

The simplest psychological experiment is based on creation of two groups of *subjects* (animals or people). One group is called the *experimental group*. The other is called the *control group*. The control group and the experimental group are treated exactly alike except for one condition called the *independent variable.*

Question: What is a variable?

A variable is anything which can change (vary) and which might affect the behavior of the subjects. Suppose that you have noticed that you seem to study better with music on in the background. This suggests the hypothesis that music improves learning. We could test this hypothesis by forming two groups of people. One group could study with music on and another without music. Then we could compare their scores on a test. The group exposed to music is the experimental group because the independent variable (music) is present. The group not exposed to music is the control group.

Question: Is a control group really needed? Can't people just study with music on to see if they do better?

Without a control group it would be impossible to tell if music had any effect on learning. The control group provides a *point of reference* to which scores of the experimental group can be compared. If the average test score of the experimental group is higher than that of the control group, it can be concluded that music improves learning efficiency. If the average is lower than the control group, we will know that music hampers learning. If there is no difference, we know that the independent variable had no effect on learning. In this experiment the "amount learned" (indicated by scores on the test) is the *dependent variable*. In an experiment we are asking the question, "Does the independent variable *affect* or influence the dependent variable?" (Does music affect or influence learning?) Another way to think of this is that the dependent variable in an experiment *depends on* the independent variable. (The amount learned depends on whether or not music accompanied study.)

Notice that our experiment is based upon the average learning scores for two *groups*. If we were to compare only two individuals, one exposed to music and the other not, we would not know if music made the difference in learning scores or if one person was just brighter than the other. Since intelligence is an *extraneous*, or outside, *variable* (a condition we are not interested in studying as an independent variable), it must be eliminated from the experiment. Other extraneous, or outside, variables—like the amount of study time, sex of the subject, the temperature of the room, the time of day, the amount of light, and so forth—can be prevented from affecting the outcome of an experiment by making all conditions except the independent variable *exactly the same* for both the experimental group and the control group. If every possible condition is exactly the same for subjects in the experimental group and the control group except the presence or absence of music during study, and if there is a difference between the two groups in the amount learned, then that difference *must* be caused by the music.

Question: That makes sense, but how can a variable like intelligence be removed from the experiment?

Differences in the personal characteristics of subjects that are extraneous to the experiment can be eliminated by *randomly* assigning subjects to the two groups. Random assignment means that a subject has an equal chance of being a member of either the experimental group or the control group. Even in fairly small groups this results in few differences in the number of people in each group who are geniuses or dunces, hungry, hungover, Democrat, Republican, tall, music lovers, or whatever.

To summarize, a psychological experiment usually involves at least two groups of subjects who are treated differently with regard to the independent variable. The effect of the independent variable on some behavior (called the dependent variable) is then measured while extraneous variables are held constant. In a carefully controlled experiment the independent variable can be the only possible *cause* for a change in the dependent variable.

Learning Check

1. To understand cause and effect, a simple psychological experiment is based on creation of two groups: the ______________ group and the __________ group.

2. Anything which can change (vary) and which might affect the behavior of subjects is called a __________.

3. There are three types of variables to consider:

an ______________________________ variable;

a ______________________________ variable;

and an ______________________________ variable.

Answers:

1. experimental and control **2.** variable **3.** independent, dependent, and extraneous

Placebo Effects—Sugar Pills and Salt Water

If the independent variable in the above experiment were changed from music to a drug, a problem arises. Assume that we want to perform an experiment to see if Dexedrine (a powerful central nervous system stimulant) affects learning. An accurate test of the drug would *not* occur if, before studying, members of the experimental group were given a Dexedrine pill and the control group got nothing.

Question: Why not? The experimental group gets the drug and the control group doesn't. If there is a difference in learning scores, it must be due to the action of the drug. Right?

No, because an error has been made: The experimental group and the control group have been treated differently with respect to more than just the presence or absence of the drug. Members of the experimental group swallowed a pill, and control subjects did not. Without using a *placebo*, it is impossible to tell if the drug has affected learning or if just swallowing a pill did.

Question: What is a placebo?

A placebo is a fake pill or injection. Sugar pills and saline (salt water) injections are common placebos. Neither has any *chemical* effect, but swallowing a pill or receiving an injection can have a tremendous *psychological* effect. As an example of how powerful the *placebo effect* can be, one study showed that an injection of saline solution had 70 percent of the effectiveness of morphine in reducing pain for hospital patients (Beecher, 1959). The placebo effect is well known to physicians who may prescribe placebos to relieve complaints that have no physical basis.

To control for placebo effects, a psychologist doing drug research usually employs a *double-blind* arrangement. This means that *all* subjects get a pill or injection. The experimental group gets the real drug, and the control group gets a placebo. Thus, subjects are *blind* as to whether or not they received the drug. The experimenter must also be *blind* as to whether he is administering the drug or a placebo to any particular subject. This prevents him from unconsciously influencing the subject or being influenced himself.

The Clinical Method—Information by the Case

Many psychological experiments that might prove informative or revealing are impractical, immoral, or impossible to perform. In instances such as these, information may be gained from *case studies*. A case study is an in-depth focus on all aspects of a single subject. Case studies are used heavily by clinical psychologists.

Case studies may sometimes be thought of as *natural experiments*. Gunshot wounds, brain tumors, accidental poisonings, and similar disasters have provided much information on the functioning of the human brain. One remarkable case from the history of psychology is reported by Dr. J. M. Harlow (1868). Phineas Gage, a young foreman on a work crew, had a thirteen pound steel rod blown through the front of his brain by the premature explosion of an excavating charge. Amazingly, he survived the accident, but not without undergoing a profound personality change. Dr. Harlow carefully recorded all the details of what was perhaps the first well-done case study of an accidental *frontal lobotomy* [the destruction of front brain matter].

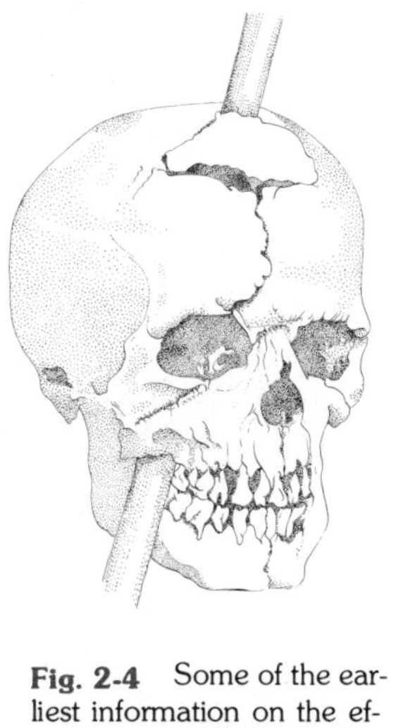

Fig. 2-4 Some of the earliest information on the effects of damage to frontal areas in the brain came from a case study of the accidental injury of Phineas Gage.

Since the psychological effects of a lobotomy might be successfully studied using lab animals as subjects, the clinical approach is not necessarily the only one available. But when a purely psychological problem is under study, the clinical method may be the *only* source of information.

A classic psychological case study is *The Three Faces of Eve* (Thigpen & Cleckley, 1957). Eve White was a mild, restrained, suburban housewife who in the course of psychiatric treatment revealed the existence of a second separate personality. This second personality, Eve Black, was the antithesis of Eve White. Eve Black was childish, mischievous, and erotically flirtatious. Eve Black knew about Eve White and openly talked about the times she had disobeyed her parents or gotten drunk and then "went in" to Eve White. After Eve Black's escapades, Eve White faced her punishment or bore her hangover with bewilderment because she did not know of Eve Black's existence. Eventually this duality was resolved when a third personality—who called herself Jane—emerged. Jane ultimately separated from Eve White's husband and began a relatively stable new life marked by the slow development of a progression of other personalities. The careful recording of all pertinent facts in a case like this is essential to psychology. *Multiple personality* is a rare event, and there is no experimental means of studying it.

Survey Method—Sampling Information

Sometimes psychologists would like to ask everyone in the world a few well-chosen questions: "Have you ever smoked marijuana?" "Have you engaged in premarital sexual intercourse?" "What is your marital status now, and were your parents ever separated or divorced?" "Do you favor abortion?" The answers to questions such as these can reveal much about significant psychological events in the lives of large groups of people. But since it is impractical to question everyone, psychologists use the *survey method*. In a survey a *representative sample** of people are asked a carefully worded series of *questions*. A careful survey can provide an accurate picture of how large segments of the general population feel about current issues, even though only a small percentage of people are polled.†

Question: How accurate is the survey method?

Modern surveys like the Gallup and Harris polls are quite accurate. The Gallup poll has erred in its election predictions by only 1.5 percent since 1954 (*Time*, 1968). This level of accuracy has not always been the case. During the 1936 presidential election, a well-known magazine, the *Literary Digest*, predicted that Alfred Landon would defeat Franklin Roosevelt by a landslide. Roosevelt defeated Landon by about 11 million votes!

Question: How could the poll have been so wrong?

*A representative sample includes the same proportion of men, women, white-collar workers, Republicans, Democrats, blacks, and so on, as found in the population as a whole.

†Some psychologists have questioned—tongue in cheek—psychology's claim that its conclusions apply to people in general. The distinguished psychologist Edward Tolman once noted how much of American psychology is based on two sets of subjects: rats and college sophomores. Tolman urged his colleagues to remember that rats certainly are not people and that college sophomores *may not be*!

The answer lies in the way that the sample was taken. Most people in the poll were contacted *by telephone*. In 1936, during the Depression, people who had phones were much more wealthy than average, and the wealthy favored Landon. The sample was biased rather than representative. Even when questions are carefully stated and the sample is representative, a survey may be limited by another problem. If a psychologist asked you detailed questions about your sexual history and current sexual activities, how accurate would your replies be? Would you be embarrassed and not completely frank? Or might you have a tendency to exaggerate your sexual experience? Replies to survey questions are not always *accurate* or *truthful*. In spite of this, much useful information is usually gained. Alfred Kinsey's (1953) famous surveys of human sexual behavior radically changed ideas about what is "normal." Prior to Kinsey's research, activities like premarital sex, masturbation, and oral sex were considered abnormal or at least unusual by many. Kinsey found that each of these activities is engaged in by sizable percentages of the population and that publically expressed attitudes contradicted actual behavior. The availability of information like that produced by Kinsey's research may eventually help remove much unnecessary worry and guilt from human sexuality.

"How would you like me to answer that question? As a member of my ethnic group, educational class, income group, or religious category?"

Fig. 2-5

Learning Check

1. If you wanted to do a controlled experiment on the effects of a certain drug, you would need to use *placebos* if two or more groups of people were used. T or F?
2. Case studies are often thought of as *natural experiments* and are used frequently by clinical psychologists. T or F?
3. Survey methods, if used correctly, are often valid means of research. T or F?

Answers: 1. T 2. T 3. T

Resources Summary

Psychology attempts to improve upon common sense and casual observation by making *controlled observations* and applying the scientific method. A starting point in many investigations is *naturalistic observation*—the careful recording of behavior in a natural setting. Two prominent difficulties in naturalistic observation are *effects of the observer* on the observed and inability to conclusively identify *causes*.

Cause and effect relations are identified by *controlled experiments*. In a controlled experiment two groups of subjects are formed. These groups differ only with regard to the *independent variable* or condition of interest as a *cause* in the experiment. Differences in the *dependent variable* (the effect) are then measured while all other conditions (*extraneous variables*) are held constant. In experiments testing drugs, a *placebo* (a fake pill or injection) must be used to control psychological expectations associated with taking a drug. Drug research also frequently employs a *double-blind* procedure so that neither subjects nor experimenters know who is receiving a drug.

The *clinical method* employs *case studies* which are in-depth studies of a single subject. Case studies provide important information on topics that could not be studied any other way.

In the *survey method* a *representative sample* of people are asked a carefully worded series of questions. Responses to these questions provide information on the attitudes and psychological functioning of large groups of people.

Applications

Prescientific Psychology: Surefire Personality Analysis

Astrology Astrology is probably the most popular of several *pseudo-psychologies* (*pseudo* means false). It is based on the assumption that the position of the stars and planets determines personality characteristics and affects behavior. Like the other pseudo-psychologies, astrology has a highly developed system that gives it the appearance of science, but it has been repeatedly disproved by scientific study.

Question: Then why does it seem to work?

Let's return to that question after considering some of the less convincing pseudo-psychologies.

Palmistry Palmistry claims that lines in the hand are indicators of personality and a person's future. Lines that are longer or shorter, more or less bent, clear or indistinct, supposedly predict destiny, fortune, length of life, occupation, and health. The fact that palmistry assumes that the hands tell the story of the whole body is hard enough to swallow, but ignoring the effects of dishwater, manual labor, or hand lotion is inexcusable.

Phrenology During the nineteenth century, a German anatomy teacher, Franz Gall, popularized the theory that personality is revealed by the skull. Phrenologists assumed that parts of the brain responsible for various "mental faculties" cause bumps on the head. By feeling these bumps the phrenologist claimed to read a person's abilities. Phrenology faded rapidly when greater understanding of the brain showed that this is impossible. For instance, the area of the brain which controls

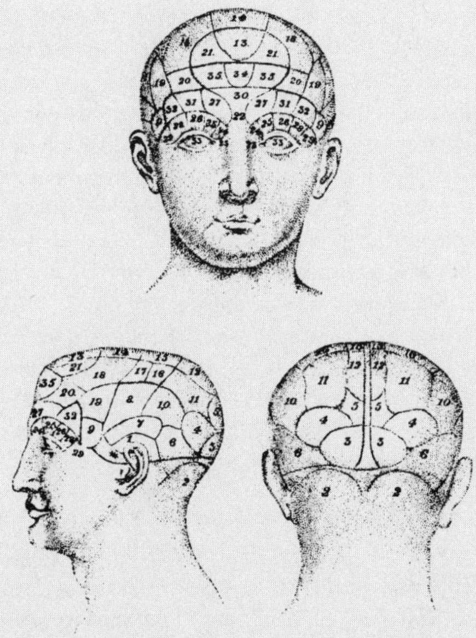

Fig. 2-6 Phrenology was an attempt to assess characteristics of various areas of the skull. Phrenologists used charts such as the one shown here as guides.

hearing was listed on phrenologist's charts as the center for "combativeness" and "destructiveness"!

Graphology Graphologists believe that personality is revealed by handwriting. Graphology is only moderately popular in the United States, but in Germany it is widely used for job placement and advancement. This is somewhat distressing to American psychologists because studies show that graphologists score close to 0 on careful tests of accuracy in rating personality (Guilford, 1959).

If the pseudo-psychologies have no scientific basis, how do they survive and why are they popular? To get an idea, read the following personality description.

> You have a strong need for other people to like you and for them to admire you. You have a tendency to be critical of yourself. You have a great deal of unused energy which you have not turned to your advantage. While you have some personality weaknesses, you are generally able to compensate for them. Your sexual adjustment has presented some problems for you. Disciplined and controlled on the outside, you tend to be worrisome and insecure inside. At times you have serious doubts as to whether you have made the right decision or done the right thing. You prefer a certain amount of change and variety and become dissatisfied when hemmed-in by restrictions and limitations. You pride yourself as being an independent thinker and do not accept other opinions without satisfactory proof. You have found it unwise to be too frank in revealing yourself to others. At times you are extroverted, affable, sociable, while at other times you are introverted, wary, and reserved. Some of your aspirations tend to be pretty unrealistic.[1]

Does this describe your personality? A psychologist read this summary individually to college students who had taken a personality test. Twenty-nine said it was an "excellent" description of their personality; thirty said it was "good"; fifteen said it was "average"; and five said it was "poor." Thus, only five students out of seventy-nine felt that the description failed to adequately capture their personality. Reread the summary, and you will see that it is stated in such general terms that it would apply to almost anyone. It also contains both sides of several personality dimensions ("At times you are extroverted . . . while at other times you are introverted"). The summary can hardly miss. Similarly, the vague generality of the descriptions and predictions of the prescientific psychologies practically ensures their acceptance. Astrology is a good example. You can always find "Leo characteristics" in a Leo. If you looked, however, you could also find "Gemini characteristics," "Scorpio characteristics," or whatever. This is an example of the *fallacy of positive instances* in which a person remembers or notices things that confirm his expectations and forgets the rest.

Casual or unscientific observation is very susceptible to the fallacy of positive instances. Awareness of this, along with your understanding of psychological research methods, should do much to make you a more critical observer of human behavior. Here are some additional pointers to sharpen your skills.

Notes on Reading the Popular Press

Suggestion 1 *Be skeptical.* Psychological reports in the popular press tend to be made uncritically and with a definite bias toward the reporting of "sensational" findings.

Example: A few years ago stories appeared in the press reporting research in Russia and the United States on "dermo-optical perception." According to these stories, people had been found who could identify colors and read print (even under glass) while blindfolded. These feats were supposedly performed using the fingertips and were given as an indication of the existence of a "sixth sense," or "x-ray eyes." Martin Gardner, a

[1]Reprinted with permission of author and publisher from: Ulrich, R. E., Stachnik, T. J., and Stainton, N. R. Student acceptance of generalized personality interpretations. PSYCHOLOGICAL REPORTS, 1963, 13, 831-834.

scientist whose hobby is magic, suggests that such "abilities" are based on what professional performers call a "nose peek." Gardner says that it is impossible to prepare a blindfold (without doing damage to the eyes) that does not leave a tiny space on each side of the nose through which a person can peek. In accordance with Gardner's criticism, the phenomenal ability of individuals who performed in the first dermo-optical perception experiments disappeared each time the opportunity to peek was more controlled (Gardner, 1966).

Here is another indication of the need to be critical or skeptical. Psychologist Philip Zimbardo tells with amusement about his mentioning to an inquiring reporter that in the back wards of two mental hospitals in which he had worked women patients seemed to use a greater number of obscenities than male patients. Zimbardo emphasizes that this was nothing more than a casual statement and that it was not based on data of any kind, but when it was reported in *The New York Times* it became an "observation" that he had "noted" over a long period of time. When *Newsweek* reported the *Times* article to its readers, the relationship that was "noted" became one that had been "found." Ultimately, *Playboy*'s version stated that "a number of psychologists, *The New York Times* reports, have found that women of every social level have become increasingly uninhibited in their use of obscene language" (*Playboy*, 1969). Zimbardo notes that the only authority mentioned to confirm this "fact" was himself (Ruch & Zimbardo, 1971)!

Suggestion 2 *Consider the source of information.* It should come as no surprise that information given by an individual or a company intent on selling a product often reflects the profit motive more than it does objective truth. Here is a typical advertising claim: "Government tests have proven that no pain reliever is stronger or more effective than Brand X aspirin." A statement like this usually means that there was *no difference* between the product and others tested in speed or effectiveness of pain relief. No other pain reliever was stronger or more effective, but none was weaker either. Keep the source in mind when reading the claims of makers of home biofeedback machines, sleep learning devices, and the like. Remember also that psychological services may be merchandised as well. Expensive courses that promise instant mental health and happiness, increased efficiency, memory, ESP or psychic ability, control of the unconscious mind, an end to the smoking habit, and so on, are usually supported by a few testimonials and many unproved claims.

An area of psychological interest that must be viewed with special caution is that of "psychic" phenomena. Stage mentalists make their living by deceiving the public and understandably promote belief in their nonexistent powers. Psychic phenomena when (and if) they do occur are quite fragile and unpredictable. It would be impossible for a mentalist to do three shows a night, six nights a week without consistently using deception.

Question: I've seen some amazing things on TV. Could you give an example of how I may have been fooled?

Here is a typical stage mentalist's routine. The mentalist picks a member of the audience "at random" and begins telling him personal things that "he could not possibly know." How does he do it? Easy! One of his many assistants stood in line outside the theatre and eavesdropped on the person's conversations before the show. The assistant then made careful note of where the person was seated and passed on the location and information to the mentalist. The mentalist then announces, "You have an aunt . . . Aunt Bessy . . . she has been very ill . . . you were thinking about her earlier this evening . . . you had a flat tire on the way here this evening."

Suggestion 3 *Ask yourself, "Was there a control group?"* The essential importance of a control group in any experiment is frequently overlooked by the psychologically unsophisticated—an error to which you are no longer susceptible! The popular press is full of reports of "experiments" performed without control groups: "Talking to

Plants Speeds Growth"; "Special Diet Controls Hyperactivity in Children"; "Food Shows Less Spoilage in Pyramid Chamber"; "Theatre Reports Increased Beverage Sales during Showing of *Lawrence of Arabia.*"

Consider the last example for a moment. Almost every year it seems a theatre somewhere will claim that a movie has had an unusual effect on viewers. If the showing of *Lawrence of Arabia* were accompanied by increased beverage sales, would this indicate that viewers had been influenced by the desert scenery? Actually, they may have been influenced, but since there is no control group (people who watch another movie under identical conditions), it is impossible to tell if the temperature in the theatre, the time of year, the kind of crowd attracted, or the movie itself affected beverage consumption.

Suggestion 4 *Look for errors in distinguishing between correlation and causation.* An earlier discussion should make it clear that it is dangerous to presume that one thing has *caused* another on the basis of correlation. In spite of this, you will encounter numerous claims based on questionable correlations. Law enforcement agencies like to point out that most heroin addicts have used marijuana. This is an interesting observation, but it does not justify the conclusion that marijuana use "causes" addiction to hard drugs. Most heroin addicts have also used milk. Lack of proof for a casual link to hard drugs is also not an endorsement of marijuana use, but it does point out how muddled thinking on important issues can become.

Here's another example of mistaking correlation for causation. Jeanne Dixon, a popular astrologer, once answered a group of prominent scientists who had declared that there is no scientific foundation for believing in astrology by saying: "They would do well to check the records at their local police stations, where they will learn that the rate of violent crime rises and falls with lunar cycles" (Dixon, 1975). Dixon, of course, is implying that the moon affects human behavior.

Question: If it is true that violent crime is more frequent at certain times of the month, doesn't it prove her point?

Far from it; increased crime could be due to darker nights, the fact that bills fall due at the first of the month, or any number of similar factors.

Suggestion 5 *Be sure to distinguish between observation and inference.* If you see a person *crying*, is it correct to assume that he is *sad*? Although it seems reasonable to make this assumption, it is actually quite risky. We can *observe* objectively that the person is crying, but the *inference* that he is sad may be in error. It could be that he has just peeled 5 pounds of onions or that he has just won the Irish sweepstakes, or that he is trying on contact lenses for the first time. Psychologists, politicians, physicians, scientists, and other experts often go far beyond the available facts in their claims. This does not mean that their inferences, opinions, and interpretations have no value; the opinion of an expert on the causes of mental illness, criminal behavior, learning problems, or whatever can be very revealing. But be careful to distinguish between fact and opinion. Here is an example that illustrates why this is important:

> A fifty-four-year-old schizophrenic patient was rewarded for holding a broom that was given to her by a ward attendant. If she held the broom after it was handed to her, she was given a cigarette by another attendant. The purpose of this experiment was to determine if rewards should be used to alter the patient's rather listless behavior (she had been hospitalized for twenty-three years and refused to do anything on the ward). Soon the patient spent much of her time holding the broom. At this point two psychiatrists were invited to observe the patient through a one-way mirror. One psychiatrist's interpretation of the "broom-holding behavior" was that it was a symbolic expression of deep-seated unfulfilled desires. According to him the broom could be a symbol for:
>
> 1. "a child that gives her love and she gives him in return her devotion.
> 2. a phallic symbol.

3. the sceptre of an omnipotent queen" (Ayllon *et al.*, 1965).

The psychiatrist *observed* that the patient spent much of her time holding a broom. He *inferred* that this had deep psychological meaning, when in fact she held the broom for one reason: She received cigarettes for doing so!

Alvin Toffler and others have suggested that we are in the midst of an "information explosion." Indeed, we are all being bombarded daily with such a mass of new information that it is difficult to adequately process it. The available knowledge, even in a limited area like psychology, biology, medicine, or contemporary rock music, is so vast that no single person can completely know and comprehend it. With this in mind, it becomes ever more important that you become a critical, selective, and informed consumer of information.

For Discussion

The Experimenter Effect

Psychological researchers face an interesting problem not shared by physicists and chemists. Human subjects are very sensitive to hints from an experimenter about what is expected from them. The *experimenter effect*, as it is called, can cause a powerful influence on a subject's behavior (Rosenthal, 1966). This is true even when animals are used as subjects.

> Twelve experimenters [psychology graduate students] were each given five rats to run through a maze. Half of the experimenters were told that they were receiving "maze-bright" rats and half believed that their rats were "maze-dull."

Question: What is a maze-bright rat?

Maze-bright and maze-dull rats have been specially bred to be either brilliant at learning mazes or very slow at it.

> At the end of the experiment it was found that the "maze-bright" rats showed superior learning compared to the "maze-dull" rats in spite of the fact that the rats were actually all of the same variety (Rosenthal & Fode, 1963a).

There was no difference between the rats! But they performed as if they really were bright or slow. The source of the difference was the expectations of the experimenters. Those who thought they had maze-bright rats, named them, handled them frequently, and fed them choice tidbits between learning trials. Experimenters who thought they had stupid rats carried them by the tail and handled them as little as possible. These handling differences affected the way the rats performed in the maze.

Psychologist Robert Rosenthal tested every student in an elementary school in the South San Francisco Unified School District. The children were given a standard intelligence test, but Rosenthal told their teachers that the test was a measure of "intellectual blooming." About 20 percent of the children in each classroom were *chosen at random*. Teachers were given the names of these students and were told that a test had predicted that they would make large intellectual gains during the coming year. At the end of the school year all the children were given the same IQ test they had taken earlier. Children who had been designated "bloomers" showed a total IQ increase that averaged 4 points more than the other students, and a reasoning IQ improvement of 7 points more. This is quite astounding. IQ scores are not supposed to change (Rosenthal & Jacobson, 1968).

Question: Then why did they improve?

Since the "bloomers" were randomly selected, the only difference between the "bloomers" and other students was *in the minds of their teachers*. When the teachers were interviewed later, it was determined that they saw the "bloomers" as more interesting, curious, adjusted, appealing, and affectionate than other students. Their expectations had created a "self-fulfilling prophecy."

The implication of this interesting spin-off from psychological research is clear. Anyone who deals frequently with people (that's just about everyone), and especially teachers, employers, supervisors, counselors, leaders, and parents, would be well advised to remember that people tend to live *up* to or *down* to one's *expectations*.

Questions for Discussion

1. How have the expectations of teachers, parents, or friends affected your self-image or your own expectations for yourself?
2. Did you attend a school that had slow, normal, and accelerated classes? What are the advantages and disadvantages of such a system?
3. What would you expect to happen to a Mexican-American child erroneously placed in a special education class because he or she has scored poorly on an aptitude test based on *English skills*? (It happens.)
4. Can you think of other situations where something similar to the "experimenter effect" has occurred?

Suggestions for Further Reading

Anderson, B. D. *The Psychology Experiment*, 2nd ed. Brooks/Cole, 1971.

Hyman, R. *The Nature of Psychological Inquiry.* Prentice-Hall, 1964.

McCain, G., and E. M. Segal. *The Game of Science.* Brooks/Cole, 1969.

Monte, C. F. *Psychology's Scientific Endeavor.* Praeger, 1975.

Van Lawick-Goodall, J. *In the Shadow of Man.* Dell, 1971.

Contents

Foundations of Human Consciousness **Unit Two**

The Biology of Behavior and Conscious Experience

3

Chapter Preview

Worlds within Worlds within Worlds

Darkness. Infinite void. Light. Energy. Photons. Electrons. Protons. Atoms. Molecules. Elements. Compounds. Air. Fire. Water. Earth. Planets. Stars. Galaxies. The universe. It is always a mind-bending experience to consider the way complex phenomena are built out of ever more intricate combinations of elements. To understand the complexities of human behavior psychologists are increasingly turning to direct studies of the brain and nervous system. Once we crack open the fragile shell of the skull we find in the truest sense "worlds within worlds within worlds."

The human brain is a mass of spongy tissue about the size of a large grapefruit. It is also the most amazing computer in existence. Weighing a little over 3 pounds, it consists of from 10 to 14 billion individual nerve cells called neurons. *All human behavior can ultimately be traced to the activity of these tiny cells. Each neuron is interconnected to many others—sometimes as many as 1,000. This arrangement provides an exceptionally large capacity for combining and storing information. It has been estimated that the number of possible interconnections between neurons in a single human brain exceeds the number of atomic particles in the entire universe!*

Question: Then is it true that humans only use a small amount of the brain?

This is not strictly true because every cell in the brain (if it is not dead) is active at all times. The statement is true in the sense that we only store a small fraction of the information the brain could hold. Also, there is a large amount of duplicated effort in the brain. Were it not for this, we could not afford to lose hundreds of neurons every day through aging.

Scientists have long been convinced that the brain is the organ of consciousness and the origin of action. But only in recent years have experimental techniques advanced enough to demonstrate this directly. To prove the point researcher José Delgado once entered a bullring with a cape and a radio transmitter. When the bull charged, Delgado stood his ground. At the last possible instant the speeding bull stopped short. Why? Because Delgado had used the radio transmitter to activate electrodes implanted in "control centers" of the bull's brain.

Physiological psychology *is the study of the way in which the brain and nervous system allow us to respond to the world and the effect that damage to these systems has on important psychological functions. The physiological psychologist tends to take a very* mechanistic *viewpoint, seeing humans and animals as complex biological machines whose behavior can be described in physical, mathematical, and chemical terms. For this single chapter we will do the same.*

Resources

Neurons—"Atoms" of the Nervous System

As physiological psychologist Paul MacLean has remarked, "The towering question before the world concerns whether man can master his brain and behavior before he has blown himself to smithereens through his mastery of physics and engineering." One of the most powerful keys to the understanding of the brain has been the study of individual nerve cells. Unlike other cells in the body, neurons are specially designed to conduct information. They are the basic units of the human "biocomputer."

Question: How can a living cell transmit information?

If we think of the nervous system as long "chains" of communicating cells, then neurons are the links. The "typical" neuron consists of four basic parts (Fig. 3-1). (1) The *dendrites* are a receiving area where information from other neurons is accepted. (2) The body, or *soma*, is a transition area in which incoming information is collected and combined. It also contains the genetic information and biological machinery that keeps the cell running. (3) When a sufficient level of activation has occurred in the soma, a *nerve impulse* travels down the *axon*. Axons are the real conducting area of the neuron. Although they are less than one-thousandth of an inch thick, axons may stretch several feet through the nervous system of an adult. Axons act like miniature cables carrying information from the sensory organs to the brain, from the brain to the muscles, or simply from one neuron to the next. (4) Finally, at the end of the axon we find an array of *terminal knobs* which lie in close proximity to the dendrites of other neurons. When a nerve impulse arrives, the terminal knobs release *neurotransmitters*. These are

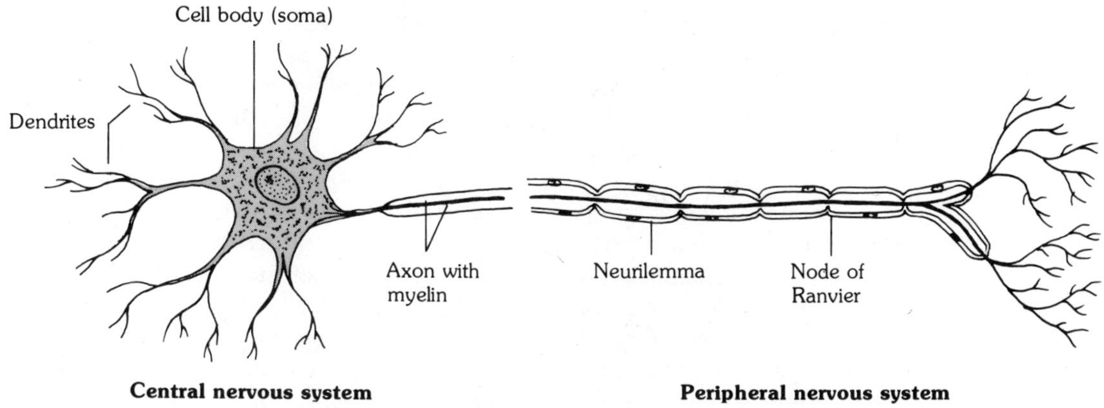

Fig. 3-1 A "typical" neuron, or nerve cell, showing several of its important features. The nerve impulse usually travels from the dendrites to the branching ends of the axon. The neuron shown here is a motor neuron. Motor neurons originate in the brain or spinal cord and send their axons to the muscles of the body.

chemicals that travel across the tiny space, or *synapse*, between two neurons (Fig. 3-2). Depending on the type of neuron, these chemicals pass on information by stimulating or inhibiting the activity of the next neuron. It can be seen that neurons transmit information through a combination of events occurring within and between cells.

Information in the environment exists as various forms of energy—light, heat, mechanical, and chemical. The sensory organs convert all information from the environment into a kind of "code" understood by all

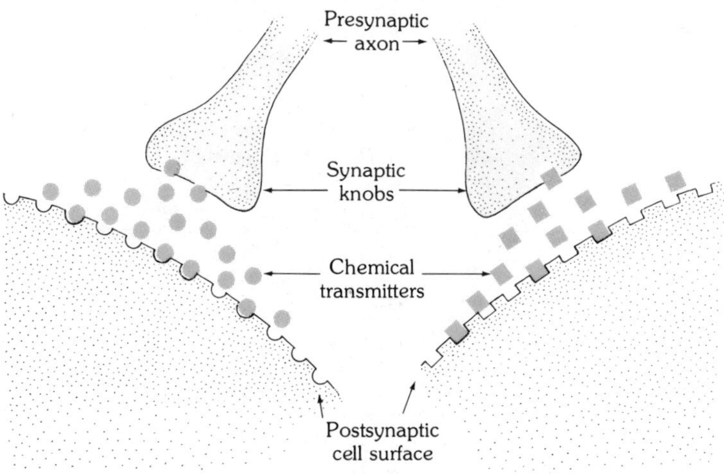

Fig. 3-2 A highly magnified view of a synapse. Transmitter chemicals cross the synapse (the distance is exaggerated here) to affect the next neuron. Transmitter chemicals vary in their effect: Some excite the next neuron, and some inhibit its activity.

parts of the brain and nervous system. The basic signal of this code is an *action potential,* the firing of a nerve impulse down the axon. Billions of nerve cells fire complex patterns of nerve impulses as the brain continuously receives, processes, and combines information.

Question: *Exactly what is an "action potential"?*

Each neuron can be thought of as a tiny biological battery ready to be discharged. Nerve cells are filled with and surrounded by a fluid containing dissolved chemicals, especially sodium and potassium (Fig. 3-3). These carry an electrical charge and are found in differing amounts inside and outside the cell. As a result, a tiny difference in electrical charge exists across the cell membrane (or "skin"). In humans, this electrical charge, called a *resting potential,* is about minus 70 millivolts (a millivolt is a millionth of a volt). A nerve impulse or action potential occurs when a brief flow of electrical current is caused by the movement of charged particles in and out of the cell. This discharge starts near the cell body and travels the length of the axon.

Question: *What triggers the action potential?*

Transmitter chemicals from other neurons cause the resting potential to increase or decrease. If a number of nerve impulses arrive together or in rapid succession, the collective effect changes the resting potential enough to reach the *threshold* for discharge and triggers a nerve impulse in the receiving cell. The existence of a threshold for firing makes the action potential an *all-or-nothing* event; it occurs completely or not at all. Notice, however, that there is a blending of information received from other cells before a neuron "decides" to send the message on.

In summary, the nerve impulse is basically an electrical event, while communication between neurons is primarily a chemical process. Human

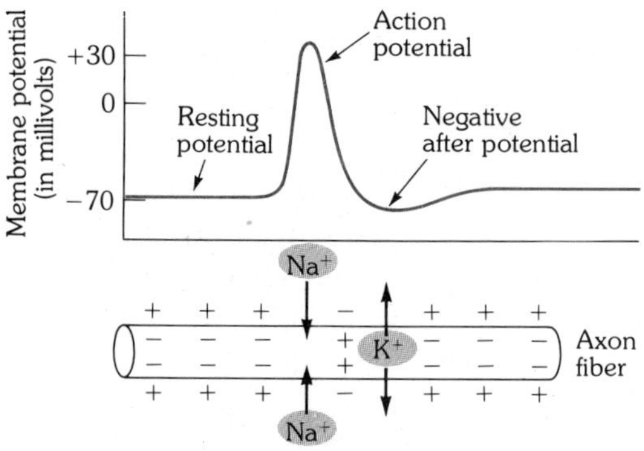

Fig. 3-3 Electrochemical changes in a nerve cell generate an action potential when sodium (Na^+) ions rush into the cell. After the action potential, an outward flow of potassium (K^+) ions restores the resting potential.

or animal behavior and experience can therefore be affected by altering the brain electrically (by applying brief shocks to specific brain areas) or chemically (by administering drugs).

From Neurons to Nerves

Question: Are neurons the same as nerves?

No. Like other cells in the body, neurons combine in groups to form tissues. These are assembled into larger structures like *nuclei* (collections of nerve cell bodies) or *nerves* (Fig. 3-4). Both the dendrites and the axons of neurons are considered *nerve fibers*. When nerve fibers are collected into larger bundles, a nerve is formed. Nerves, which act somewhat like electrical cables, run to and from the brain and spinal cord.

Nerve fibers may or may not have an outer coating of a fatty tissue called *myelin*. Myelin acts somewhat like a layer of insulation around the axon and increases the speed of the action potential. Nerve fibers outside the brain and spinal cord usually have a thin layer of living cells called the *neurilemma* wrapped around them. The neurilemma is important because it provides a "tunnel" through which crushed or cut nerve fibers can

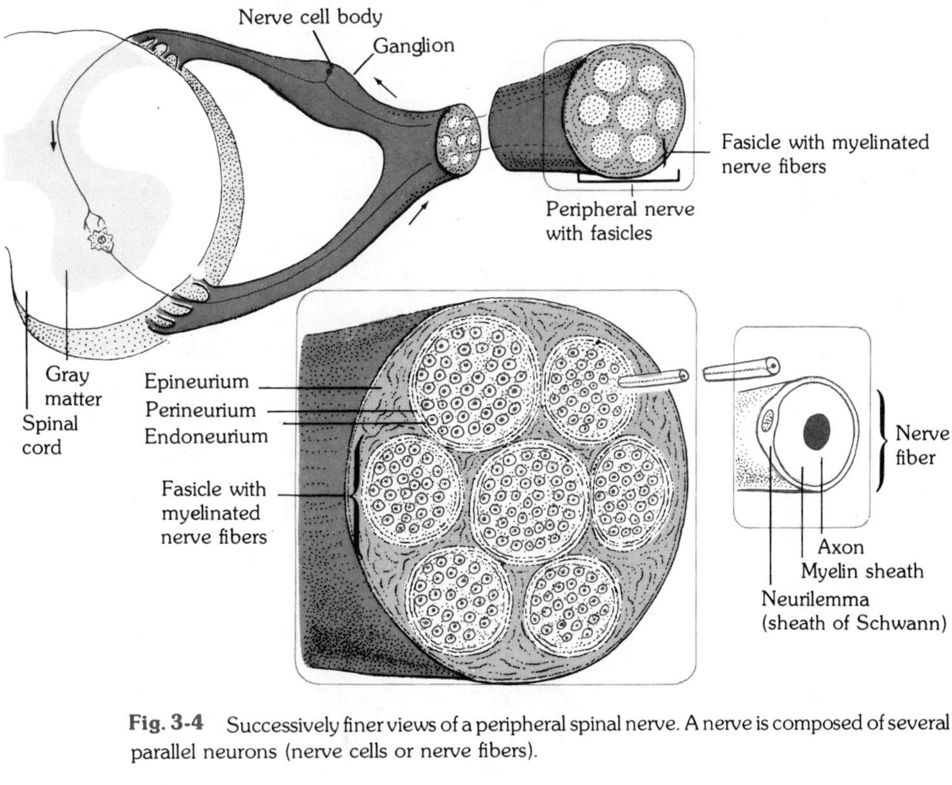

Fig. 3-4 Successively finer views of a peripheral spinal nerve. A nerve is composed of several parallel neurons (nerve cells or nerve fibers).

regenerate. If you were to accidentally cut the nerves in your finger, you could expect sensation to return at a rate of about 1 millimeter per day. If damage occurs within the brain or spinal cord, no regeneration is possible. Also, if the cell body of a neuron is destroyed anywhere in the nervous system, the damage is permanent. This is the case, for example, with infantile paralysis, in which the cell bodies of neurons sending axons to the skeletal muscles are destroyed (Wenger *et al.*, 1956).

There are three basic types of nerves: (1) nerves carrying information from the sensory organs to the brain called *afferent*, or *sensory*, nerves; (2) nerves carrying commands from the brain to muscles or glands called *motor*, or *efferent*, nerves; and (3) some mixed nerves which carry both sensory and motor information.

General Neuroanatomy—Wired for Action

Picture two people playing catch with a Frisbee. To an outside observer this appears to be an interesting but certainly not amazing activity. But consider what is going on inside the body. To launch the Frisbee on its flight or to anticipate its path for a catch, an incredible amount of information must be sensed, interpreted, and directed to countless muscle fibers. The neural circuits of the body are literally ablaze with activity. Let us consider in more detail the "wiring diagram" that makes this possible.

In action the nervous system is a single unified structure, but it may be divided into smaller parts to make it easier to study. As seen in Fig. 3-5, a distinction is made between the *central* and the *peripheral* nervous systems. The central nervous system (CNS) is composed of all nervous tissue encased by bone, or more simply, it is the brain and spinal cord. If you touch the back of your head and run your fingers down your spine you will feel the protective layer of bone around the CNS, the cranium for the brain and the vertebral column for the spinal cord.

Question: How are the CNS and the peripheral nervous system related?

The peripheral system consists of nerves which carry information to and from the CNS. The peripheral system is divided into two subparts: (1) the *somatic* system which conveys information from the sense organs and the skeletal muscles; and (2) the *autonomic* system which conveys information to and from the internal organs and glands of the body (see Fig. 3-6). The autonomic nervous system can be further divided into the *sympathetic* and *parasympathetic* branches, both of which are important in the control of emotional response.

The two autonomic branches of the nervous system have very different functions, even though they receive information from and direct the activities of the same organs and glands. The sympathetic branch responds during times of arousal or emotional upheaval to prepare the body for "fight or flight." In essence, it mobilizes the body's resources for action. The parasympathetic branch, on the other hand, is a "status quo" system. It is

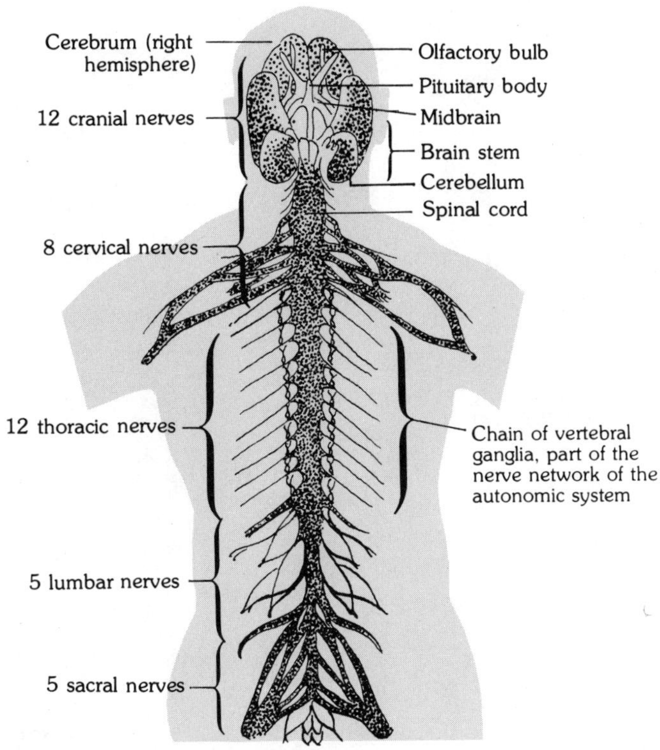

Fig. 3-5 The nervous system.

most active during periods of low arousal and has the role of maintaining vital functions like heart rate, breathing, and digestive processes at moderate levels. (See Chapter 13 for more information on the autonomic system.)

The Spinal Cord The spinal cord is an especially important structure since it acts like a cable system connecting the brain to other parts of the body. If you were to cut through the spinal cord, you would see columns of *white matter*—nervous tissue made up of the axons of neurons which leave the spinal cord at various points to form peripheral nerves. As you can see in Fig. 3-5, there are thirty pairs of *spinal nerves* leaving the spinal cord and one pair leaving the tip. The thirty-one pairs together with an additional twelve nerves which leave the brain directly (the *cranial nerves*), place the entire body in sensory and motor communication with the brain.

Question: How is this related to behavior?

Within the spinal cord itself, the simplest behavior sequence, a *reflex arc,* can be organized without any direct participation from the brain (see Fig. 3-7). Imagine that one of our Frisbee players steps on a thorn. Sensory information is *detected* by a *receptor cell* and carried to the spinal cord by

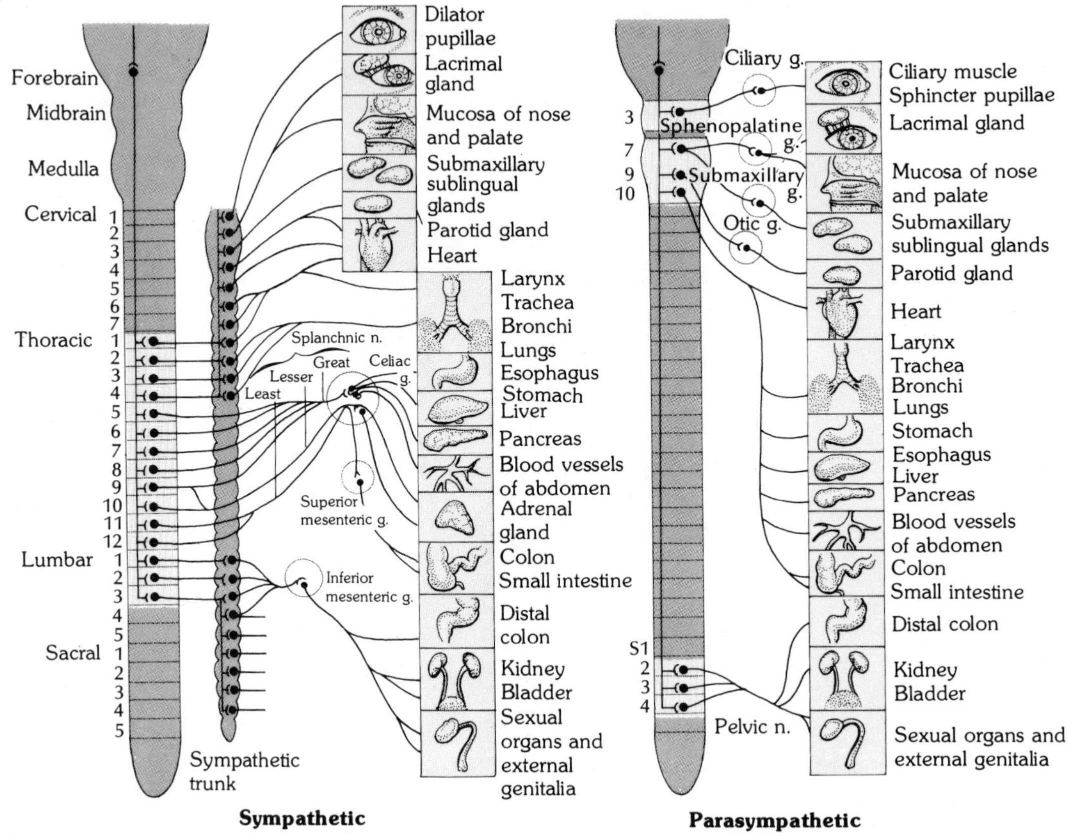

Fig. 3-6 Sympathetic and parasympathetic branches of the autonomic nervous system.

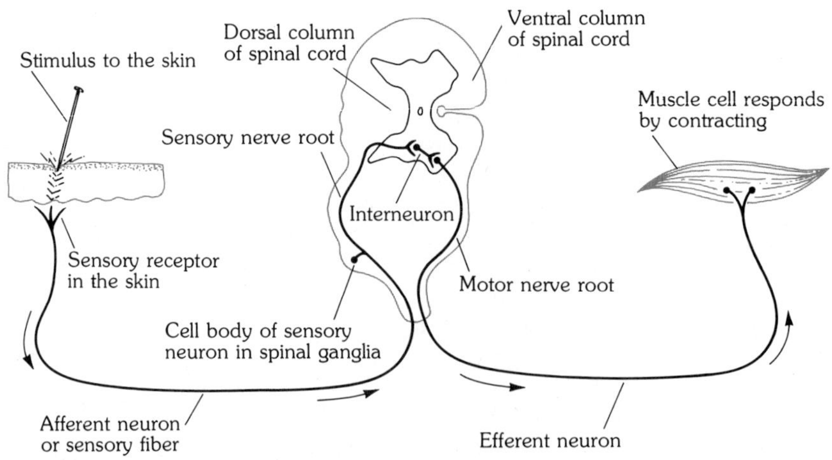

Fig. 3-7 A simple sensory-motor (reflex) arc. A simple reflex is set in motion by a stimulus to the skin (or other part of the body). The nerve impulse travels to the spinal cord and then back out to a muscle, which contracts. Reflexes provide an "automatic" protective device for the body.

a *sensory cell.* The sensory cell synapses with a *connector cell* in the spinal cord. The connector cell in turn communicates information to another connector cell (in this case, a motor neuron) that leads back to muscle fibers. The muscle fibers are made up of *effector* cells which contract and cause the foot to be withdrawn. Note that brain activity is not required for a reflex arc. It could even take place in a decapitated animal (or a headless Frisbee player, for that matter)!

In reality, more complex activity usually accompanies even a simple reflex. For example, muscles of the limb on the opposite side of the body must be activated in order to support the body when its weight is shifted. Even this can be carried out by the spinal cord, but it involves many more cells and several levels of the spinal nerves. Perhaps you have already realized how adaptive it is to have the spinal cord capable of responding on its own. Such automatic responding leaves the brain of our Frisbee ace free to deal with more important information—like the whereabouts of trees, lampposts, and attractive onlookers—as he is about to make a grandstand catch.

Learning Check

Before reading further, see if you can complete these sentences.

1. The ______________________ are receiving areas where information from other neurons is accepted.

2. The nerve impulse travels down the ______________.

3. The point of connection between two neurons is called a ______________.

4. The ______________ potential becomes an ______________ potential when a neuron reaches the threshold for firing.

5. Afferent nerves are also called ______________ nerves.

6. The somatic and autonomic systems are part of the ______________ nervous system.

7. The simplest behavior sequence is a ______________ ______________.

8. ______________ tissue is made up of effector cells.

Answers:

1. dendrites **2.** axon **3.** synapse **4.** resting, action **5.** sensory
6. peripheral **7.** reflex arc **8.** muscle

The Cerebral Cortex—My, What a Big Brain You Have!

In many respects humans are pretty unimpressive creatures. Fragile, weak, born naked and half-blind, humans are excelled by animals in almost every category of strength, speed, and sensory sensitivity. The one area in which humans excel is intelligence.

Question: Do humans have the largest brain?

Surprisingly not. Elephant brains weigh 13 pounds, and whale brains, 19 pounds. At 3 pounds, the human brain seems puny—until we figure the proportion of brain weight to body weight. We then find that an elephant's brain is 1/1,000 of its weight; the ratio for the whale is 1 to 10,000. The ratio for humans is 1 to 60 (Asimov, 1965).

So, compared to body size, humans have very highly developed brains. More importantly, as we move up the evolutionary scale there is an ever-increasing proportion of brain tissue devoted to the *cerebral cortex*. The cortex covers most of the visible portions of the brain with a mantle of *grey matter* (spongy tissue made up mostly of cell bodies and looking a little like a giant walnut). The cortex in lower animals is small and smooth; in humans it is the most prominent brain structure. Human intellectual superiority appears to be related to this *corticalization*, or increase in the size and wrinkling of the cortex. Also important is the fact that in humans there is an increase in the size of cortical *association areas* (more on this in a moment). These are areas that seem to be directly related to higher mental abilities like thinking, language, memory, and problem solving.

The cortex is composed of two sides, or *hemispheres*. Each hemisphere is a mirror image of the other, and the two hemispheres are interconnected through a large band of fibers called the *corpus callosum*. Surprisingly, the two halves control opposite sides of the body. The left side of the brain controls the right side of the body, and the right half of the brain controls the left body areas. Thus, if a person has an injury or a stroke which damages the right hemisphere, we can expect parts of the left side of the body to become paralyzed.

Maps of Reality The cerebral cortex can be divided into several distinct areas, or *lobes* (see Fig. 3-8).

Question: What is known about the function of the lobes?

The functions of various areas in each of the lobes have been "mapped" by clinical and experimental studies. Experimentally, the surface of the cortex can be activated by touching it with a small electrified needle or wire called an *electrode*. When this is done to a patient undergoing brain surgery (using only local painkillers), the patient can report what effect the stimulation has had. The functions of the cortex have also been identified by clinical studies of the changes in personality or behavior caused by diseases or injury of the brain. Let us consider the outcome of such studies.

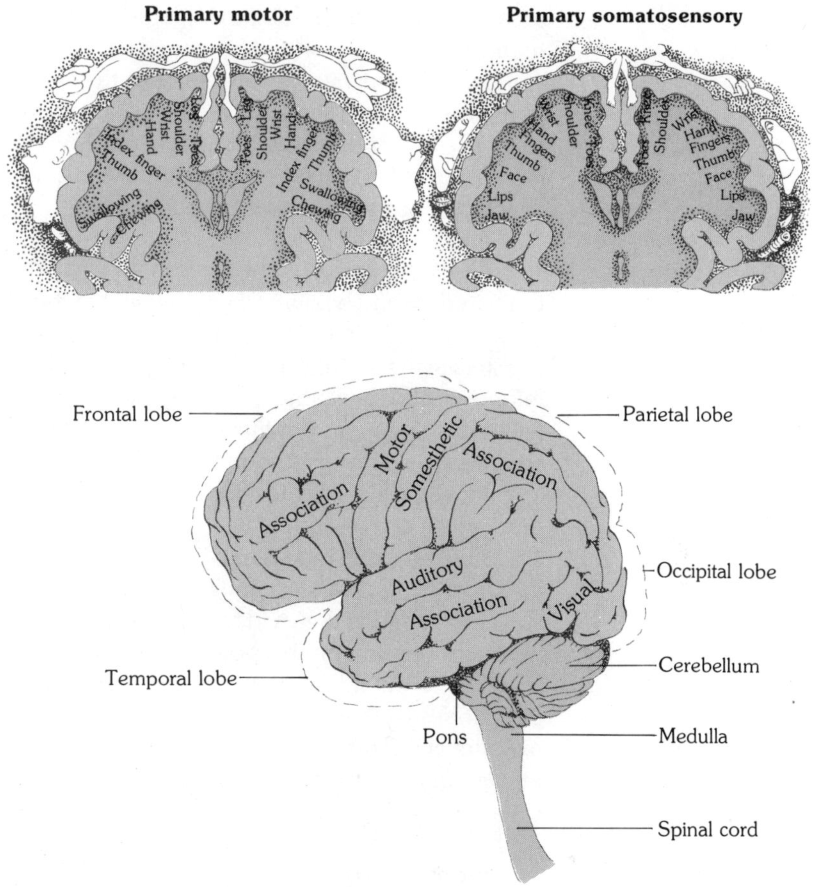

Fig. 3-8 This drawing shows the lobes of the cerebral cortex and the primary sensory, motor, and association areas on each. The top diagrams show (in cross section) the relative amounts of cortex "assigned" to the sensory and motor control of various parts of the body.

The Occipital Lobe The occipital lobe, which is located at the back of the brain, is the visual area of the cortex. Cells in the occipital cortex respond to signals from the eyes conveying information about the color, form, dimensions, and the distance of objects in the external world. Patients with *tumors* (a growth of cells which interferes with brain activity) in the occipital lobes experience a variety of visual problems. The most common impairments are blurred or double images, hallucinations or flashes of colored light, and blindness in portions of the visual field when damage is severe.

The Parietal Lobe The parietal lobe is located just above the occipital lobe. It wraps from the side of the brain to the inner surface on top. Touch, temperature, pressure, and other *somatic* (bodily) sensations are channeled to the *somesthetic* area on the parietal lobe. The correspondence between areas on the parietal lobe and parts of the body is not a perfect one. A *homunculus*, or distorted figure, can be used to depict the amount of brain tissue associated with various areas of the body. The distortion shows that, as a map of bodily sensations, the parietal lobe represents the sensitivity of body areas, not their size (see Fig. 3-8). For example, the lips are large on the homunculus because of their great sensitivity while the back and trunk, which are less sensitive, are much smaller.

The Temporal Lobes The temporal lobes are located on each side of the brain and extend below to the underside of the cortex. Auditory information projects directly to the temporal lobes, making them the site where hearing registers in the brain. If we were to stimulate the *primary auditory* area of the temporal lobe, our subject would experience a series of sounds increasing in pitch as we moved from the top to the bottom; stimulating in another direction, we would find that sound sensations would undergo an orderly change in loudness. This indicates that sound qualities are precisely mapped out on the surface of the cortex.

The temporal lobe is also associated with the storage of memories and the processing of smell stimuli. Stimulation of the temporal lobe in human subjects has led to the vivid recall of very old memories. (See Chapter 10 for more information on this point.) Brain surgeon Wilder Penfield (1975) has used the term "interpretative cortex" to describe the functions of the temporal lobes because he believes they relate incoming information to stored experiences. Tumors in the temporal lobe are associated with disordered recognition and memory, unusual dream states, and in some cases hallucinations of unpleasant odors.

The Frontal Lobes The frontal lobes perform a mixture of functions. An important area is the strip of tissue immediately in front of the parietal lobe. This is the *motor cortex*, which is responsible for directing the body's muscular responses. If the motor cortex is stimulated with a brief electrical current, muscular twitches will be observed in various parts of the body. By increasing the voltage or duration of current, larger groups of muscles can be made to contract, and movements such as rotation of the forearm or clenching of the fist will take place. Like the somesthetic area, the motor cortex corresponds to the importance of bodily areas, not to their size. The hands, for example, get more area than the feet (see Fig. 3-8).

Also related to the frontal lobes are behavioral functions of a more complex nature. When areas of the frontal lobes other than the motor cortex are removed, animals lose the ability to judge the passage of time, to hold the solution to a problem in mind, or to respond to emotionally unpleasant situations. Damage to the frontal lobes in humans tends to produce a decrease in emotionality and a general decrease in the ability to perform tasks requiring abstract thinking, reasoning, or planning (Thompson, 1967).

Question: The sensory and motor areas leave a lot of the cortex unaccounted for. What do the remaining areas do?

In the human brain, areas which are specifically sensory or motor in function make up only a small part of the cerebral cortex. All other areas (including parts of all the lobes previously described) have been collectively called the *association cortex.*

Associative Areas The association cortex seems to process and combine information from the various senses. When electrically stimulated, it yields responses more complex than simple sensory experiences or motor reactions. The production of vivid memories from the temporal lobe and the loss of complex skills after damage to the frontal lobes are excellent examples of the functions of the association cortex. Additional clues to the workings of the association cortex come from studies of humans with damage to other areas. Of special interest are *aphasias* (speech disturbances) and *agnosias* (the inability to identify objects). Aphasias result when there is damage to the speech areas of the frontal lobe. One region, known as Broca's area, is involved in the production of speech sounds. When Broca's area is damaged by disease or injury, it becomes impossible for an individual to speak, even though the speech of others can be understood. If the damage is more extensive and interferes with nearby language areas, spoken and/or written words cannot be understood.

Damage to the association areas does not interfere with the reception of sensory information, only with its recognition or interpretation. Thus, damage to the visual or touch association areas would result in agnosias in which a person could see, touch, and trace a form or object, but would be unable to name the object or identify its shape.

In summary, the cerebral cortex is an impressive living assembly of billions of sensitive cells and nerve fibers. The bulk of our conscious experience and understanding of the world can be traced directly to the sensory, motor, and association areas of the cortex and the complex lines of communication among them. The development of the cerebral cortex is pronounced in humans, making the human brain the most advanced and sophisticated among the species on earth. This, of course, is no guarantee that this marvelous instrument will be put to full use. Still, we must stand in awe of the potential it represents.

Learning Check

See if you can successfully match the following:

___ **1.** Corpus callosum	**A.**	Visual area
___ **2.** Occipital lobe	**B.**	Motor cortex and abstract thinking
___ **3.** Parietal lobe	**C.**	Speech disturbances
___ **4.** Temporal lobes	**D.**	Increase in proportion of cortex to other brain areas

___ **5.** Frontal lobes **E.** Bodily sensations

___ **6.** Association cortex **F.** Fibers connecting the cerebral hemispheres

___ **7.** Aphasias **G.** Cortex that is not purely sensory or motor in function

___ **8.** Corticalization **H.** Hearing

Answers: 1. F 2. A 3. E 4. H 5. B 6. G 7. C 8. D

The Subcortex—The "Animal" in Each of Us

Question: What do the brain areas below the cortex do?

A person can lose large portions of the cerebral cortex and still survive. As a matter of fact, if damage is limited to the less crucial areas of the cortex, little visible change may take place. Not so with the brain areas below the cortex. Most of these are so basic to normal functioning that damage may endanger a person's life. You may recall in the tragic assassination of Senator Robert Kennedy that the fatal bullet entered the lower part of his brain. As a result, Kennedy was unconscious throughout the period between the shooting and his death, and he had to be maintained on artificial respiration.

Question: Why are the lower brain areas so important?

Below the cerebral cortex and completely covered by it are structures that are collectively termed the *subcortex*. The subcortex can be divided into three general areas called the *brainstem*, or *hindbrain*, the *midbrain*, and the *forebrain.** Let us take a closer look at each of these areas to appreciate more fully their importance (see Fig. 3-9).

The Hindbrain As the spinal cord enters the skull to join the brain, it widens into the brainstem, consisting principally of the *medulla* and the *cerebellum*. The medulla contains centers important for the reflex control of vital life functions including heart rate, breathing, swallowing, and the like. For example, the medulla receives information about the carbon dioxide content of the blood and the tension of the muscles which expand the chest for breathing. Combining this information, the medulla *excites* the muscles so that you will inhale, then *inhibits* this excitement to cause exhalation. You

*The forebrain also includes the cerebral cortex which was discussed separately because of its size and importance.

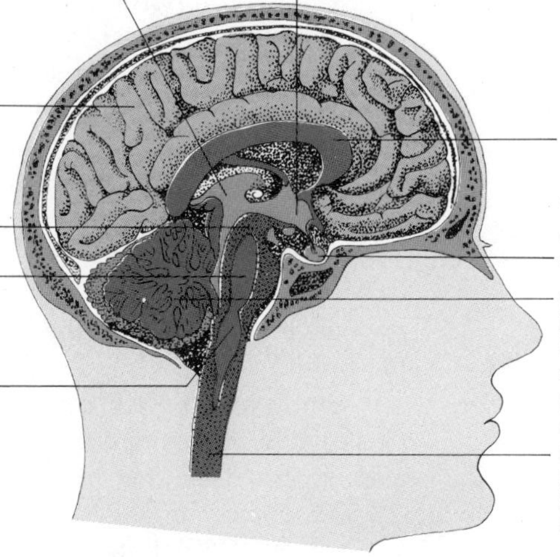

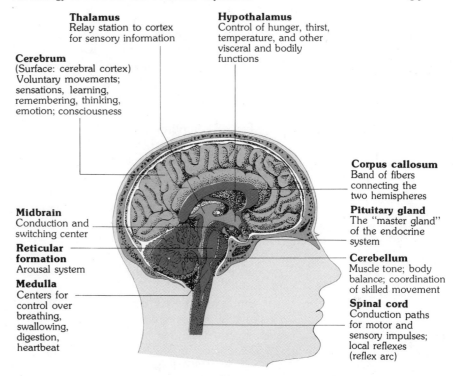

Fig. 3-9 This simplified drawing shows the main structures of the human brain and describes some of their most important functions.

can, of course, override this reflex by voluntarily holding your breath; but if you hold your breath long enough to pass out, the higher brain centers relinquish control, and you will once again begin reflex breathing. Various drugs, diseases, or injuries (a gunshot wound in Senator Kennedy's case) can interrupt the vital functions of the medulla enough to end or endanger life.

Also part of the hindbrain is the *cerebellum*, which looks like a smaller version of the cerebral cortex, and lies at the base of the brain. The cerebellum is closely connected to many areas in the brain and spinal cord and functions primarily to regulate posture, muscle tone, and muscular coordination.

Question: What happens if the cerebellum is injured?

Without the cerebellum, seemingly simple tasks like walking, running, or playing catch would be impossible. The importance of the cerebellum is indicated by the effects of a crippling disease called spinocerebellar degeneration. The first symptoms of this disease include tremor, dizziness, and muscular weakness. The disease then rapidly progresses to a point where affected persons undershoot or overshoot objects they are reaching for and have difficulty standing, walking, or even feeding themselves.

In a space within the medulla and brainstem is a *network* of fibers and cell bodies called the *reticular formation* (RF).

Question: *What does the reticular formation do?*

The RF is important for several reasons. First, it acts as a kind of central clearinghouse for most of the information coming to and from the brain. The RF helps direct incoming messages to the appropriate parts of the brain and outgoing messages to the appropriate parts of the body. Secondly, the reticular formation gives priority to some incoming messages while excluding others. This is basically what we mean by *attention*. Without the RF we would be overwhelmed with useless information from the environment. Third, and perhaps most importantly, the RF appears to be a general *activating system*. The sleepy driver who snaps to attention when an animal appears in the middle of the road can thank the RF for arousing the rest of the brain.

Studies of the RF originally indicated that destruction of the upper portions caused animals to enter a permanent coma resembling sleep. It was also observed that electrical stimulation of the same area would instantly awaken a sleeping animal (Moruzzi & Magoun, 1949; Lindsley, Bowden, & Magoun, 1949). Later studies have shown that when an animal is awake, stimulation of the reticular formation causes increased alertness, arousal, and scanning of the environment.

The Midbrain The midbrain mainly serves as a link between brain structures above and below it. Its two most important areas are the *superior colliculi*, which receive and process visual information, and the *inferior colliculi*, which do the same for hearing. In animals with highly developed vision or hearing these appear as large knobs on the midbrain.

The Forebrain Like gemstones of nerve tissue, two of the most important parts of the body lie buried deep within the very center of the brain. The *thalamus* and an area just below it called the *hypothalamus* are part of the forebrain.

Question: *How could these be any more important than other areas already described?*

The thalamus is a football-shaped structure that acts as a *final* "switching station" for sensory information on its way to the cortex. Not only does visual, auditory, taste, and touch information relay through the thalamus, it undergoes preliminary processing and analysis there as well. Injury to even small areas of the thalamus could cause deafness, blindness, or loss of any of the other senses.

The hypothalamus, which in the human is about the size of a thumbnail, has been implicated in the control of behaviors as diverse as sex, rage, temperature control, hormone release, eating and drinking, sleep, waking, and emotion. Because of its many connections with other areas of the cortex and subcortex, the hypothalamus has been called the "final common path" for all behavior. You might think of the hypothalamus as the last area in the brain where behaviors are organized or "decided on." (See Chapter 12 for a discussion of the role of the hypothalamus in hunger and thirst.)

The hypothalamus, parts of the thalamus, and several structures buried within the cortex have been collectively labeled the *limbic system*. Although the specific function of each of the parts of the limbic system is unclear, as a group they share an unmistakable role in the production of emotion and motivated behavior. Rage, fear, sexual response, and other instances of intense arousal have all been obtained from various points in the limbic system. In each case the response includes not only the internal bodily changes associated with the emotion, but also a complete set of visible behaviors. For example, cats made aggressive by electrical stimulation of the limbic system will crouch, hiss, expose their claws, lean forward, and tense their muscles—all characteristic of defense or attack.

One of the most exciting discoveries in physiological psychology occurred when it was found that animals could be trained to press a lever in order to receive an electrical stimulation of the limbic system as a reward (Olds & Milner, 1954). Since the original discovery, many additional areas of the limbic system have been shown to act as reward or "pleasure" centers in the brain. (See Chapter 9 for more information.) In addition, punishment, or "aversive," areas have also been found. When these areas are stimulated, animals show signs of discomfort and will work to turn off or avoid the stimulation. Since a great deal of human and animal behavior is directed by the pursuit of pleasure and the avoidance of pain, these discoveries continue to fascinate psychologists.

An Overview of the Brain

Given the amount of information covered in our journey through the brain, a short review seems in order. The three most basic functions of the brain are: (1) The brain must control vital bodily functions—regulating blood flow and respiration to keep up with changing bodily needs, for example. (2) Secondly, the brain must keep track of the external world by gathering and interpreting sensory information. It also must respond to this information by issuing motor commands to the muscles and glands. (3) More complex responses must be selected on the basis of current needs and past experience.

Each of these behavioral needs is met by the action of one or more of the three basic brain divisions (forebrain, midbrain, and hindbrain). Control of vital bodily needs is carried out by the hindbrain (with some indirect influence from the hypothalamus in the forebrain). Gathering sensory information and issuing motor commands takes place at all three levels of the brain. Response selection, learning, memory, and higher thought processes are controlled by the forebrain, particularly the cortex and the association areas (Schneider & Tarshis, 1975).

A final note of caution is also in order. For the sake of simplicity we have treated areas of the brain as if they were "centers" for the control of various functions. This is only a half-truth, since each area connects to many others. In reality the brain always functions as a unit. To say the least, it is much more complicated than implied here.

The Glandular System—Slow but Sure Messenger Service

The nervous system is not the only communication network in the body. The *endocrine system* is made up of a number of glands which pour chemicals directly into the bloodstream (see Fig. 3-10). These chemicals, called

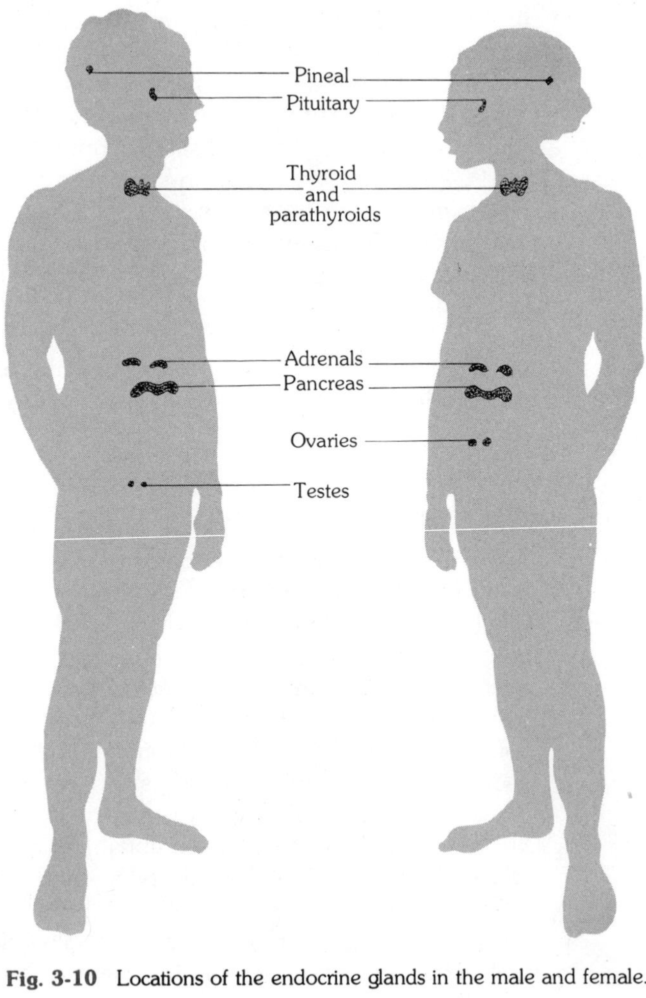

Fig. 3-10 Locations of the endocrine glands in the male and female.

hormones, are transported throughout the body where they affect bodily functioning and behavior.

Question: How do the glands affect behavior?

In humans, the size of the endocrine glands varies from person to person by a factor of about 3. In addition, the glands sometimes malfunction because of disease or injury. For these reasons, hormone output may vary considerably. In fact, it is occasional extremes of functioning that most dramatically reveal the importance of the glandular system. To answer your question, let us briefly consider some of the effects the more important glands have on the body and behavior.

The *pituitary* is a small grape-size structure hanging from the base of the brain. One of the most important roles of the pituitary is regulation of bodily growth. As a child's body grows, the pituitary secretes a hormone that regulates the rate of development. If too little *growth hormone* is secreted, a person may become a *dwarf*; too much produces a *giant*. Secretion of too much growth hormone toward the end of the growth period causes excessive growth of the arms, hands, feet, and facial bones. This condition, called *acromegaly*, causes a distortion in appearance that some people have used as the basis for successful careers as sideshow entertainers, wrestlers, and the like.

The pituitary also affects the functioning of other glands (especially the thyroid and adrenal glands) and controls such things as the release of hormones by the sex glands and production of milk during pregnancy. Because of its many effects, the pituitary is often called the "master gland."

Fig. 3-11 Underactivity of the pituitary gland may produce a dwarf; overactivity, a giant. (Photo courtesy of Circus World Museum, Baraboo, Wisconsin.)

The *thyroid gland* consists of tissue found in the neck on each side of the windpipe. The thyroid regulates *metabolism*—the rate of energy production and expenditure in the body—and can have a sizable effect on personality. A person with an overactive thyroid tends to be thin, tense, excitable, and nervous. An underactive thyroid in an adult can cause inactivity, sleepiness, slowness, and overweight. In infancy an underactive thyroid limits development of the nervous system and can bring about severe mental retardation (see Chapter 18).

When you are frightened or angry, a number of important changes take place in your body to prepare it for action: the heartbeat and blood pressure are raised; stored sugar is released into the bloodstream for quick energy; the muscles tense and receive more blood; and the blood is prepared to coagulate more quickly in the event of injury. These changes are brought about by the release of *adrenalin* and *noradrenalin* into the bloodstream. The *adrenal medulla* or inner core of the adrenal glands is the source of these hormones.

The *adrenal cortex* or outer layer of the adrenal glands produces a second set of important hormones called *corticoids*. These regulate salt balance in the body and are related to the body's ability to resist stress. They are also a secondary source of sex hormones (for a full discussion of the role of the sex glands in development see Chapter 25). The steroid drugs used (illegally) by weight lifters and other athletic competitors to increase strength and to "bulk up" are a synthetic version of one of the male corticoid hormones.

An oversecretion of the auxiliary sex hormones can cause *virilism*, in which a woman grows a beard or a man's voice becomes so low it is difficult to understand. Oversecretion in children may cause *premature puberty* resulting in full sexual development. One of the most remarkable cases on record is that of a five-year-old Peruvian girl who gave birth to a son (Strange, 1965).

In this brief discussion of the endocrine system we have considered only a few of the more important glands. Nevertheless, this should give you an appreciation of how completely your behavior and personality are tied to the ebb and flow of hormones in the body.

Learning Check

Test your comprehension with these questions. If you miss any, skim back over the preceding sections.

1. Three major divisions of the brain are the brainstem, or ________, the ________, and the ________.

2. Reflex centers for heartbeat and respiration are found in the (circle one): cerebellum, thalamus, medulla, RF.

3. The reticular formation has been called an ________ system.

4. The ________ is the final "switching station" for sensory information on its way to the cortex.

5. The ________ system is closely connected to emotion and motivated behavior.

6. Undersecretion from the thyroid would cause (circle one): dwarfism, giantism, overweight, premature puberty.

7. The body's ability to resist stress is related to the action of the adrenal ________.

Answers:
1. hindbrain, midbrain, forebrain **2.** medulla **3.** activating **4.** thalamus
5. limbic **6.** overweight **7.** cortex

Resources Summary

The brain and nervous system are made up of billions of interconnected cells called *neurons*. Neurons are arranged in long chains and pass information from one to another through *synapses*. The basic conducting structures of neurons are the *axons*, but *dendrites*, the *soma*, and the *terminal knobs* are also involved in communication. The firing of an *action potential* (nerve impulse) is basically an electrical event, whereas communication between neurons involves release of chemicals called *neurotransmitters*. *Nerves* are made of axons and associated tissues. Nerves may be *sensory* (afferent), *motor* (efferent), or *mixed*. Nerve tissue is subdivided into the *central nervous system* (the brain and spinal cord) and the *peripheral nervous system*, which includes the *sympathetic* and *parasympathetic* branches of the *autonomic* (involuntary) nervous system. The simplest behavioral sequence is a *sensory-motor arc* (reflex) involving a loop of *receptor* cells, *connector* cells, and *effector* cells.

The human brain is marked by advanced *corticalization*, or development of the *cerebral cortex*. The most basic functions of the lobes of the cortex are as follows: *occipital* lobe—vision; *parietal* lobe—bodily sensation; *temporal* lobe—hearing; *frontal* lobe—motor control and abstract thought. There are a number of *association* areas on the cortex that are neither sensory nor motor in function. These are related to more complex skills like language, memory, recognition, and problem-solving.

The *subcortex* includes a number of crucial brain structures. The *medulla* contains centers essential for reflex control of heart rate, breathing, and other "vegetative" functions. The *cerebellum* maintains coordination, posture, and muscle tone. The *reticular formation* directs sensory and motor messages and acts as an activating system for the brain. The *thalamus* conveys sensory information to the cortex and does some preliminary analysis. The *hypothalamus* is extremely important due to its influence over eating, drinking, and a number of other basic motives. The *limbic system*, which is made up of a number of structures, is the emotional system of the brain. The *endocrine system* serves as a *chemical* communication system in the body through its release of *hormones* into the bloodstream. The endocrine system influences behavior and even personality characteristics through its effect on bodily functioning.

Applications

In Search of the Mind

There will be a number of times in the chapters which follow when a knowledge of the brain and nervous system will add to your understanding of other topics, especially in the areas of motivation, emotion, and sleep. This may be the most pertinent application you will find for the preceding material.

For a more immediate application, let us consider an age-old question in the light of modern physiological research. Psychologists have long been interested in the relationship between "mind" and body. Actually, most psychologists have long since abandoned the term "mind" in favor of more specific terms, and physiological psychologists shrink back in horror at the mere mention of the word. Still, we cannot help but be interested in the role of the brain in producing "mind," "consciousness," or whatever we choose to call it.

As you already know, the cerebral cortex is divided into two hemispheres which control opposite sides of the body. In humans, the left side of the cortex (which controls the right side of the body) has been called the *major hemisphere* because it tends to be dominant over the right, or minor, hemisphere.* This, presumably, is why most people are right-handed. You might find it interesting to compare the two hemispheres by copying the design above, once with your right hand and once with your left.

*This relationship is usually reversed for a left-handed person.

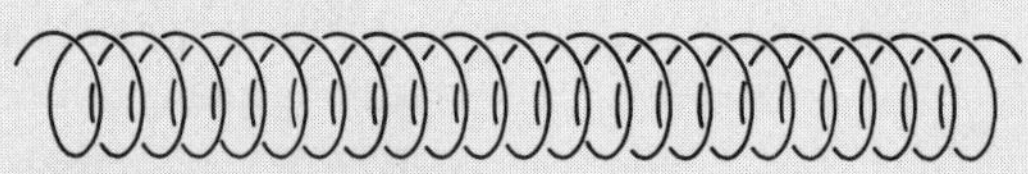

Right hand (left hemisphere)

Left hand (right hemisphere)

You should notice a definite superiority when your dominant hemisphere is controlling the movements.

The two hemispheres also show considerable difference in their function. The left hemisphere predominantly governs the ability to use language, to do mathematical computation, or to engage in other orderly or analytic acts. In contrast, the right hemisphere can only respond to the simplest elements of speech (but it does have other strengths). A variety of evidence suggests that the right hemisphere is superior at holistic, global, or relational tasks such as dance, arts, crafts, musical performance, recognition of faces, and the like (Ornstein, 1972).

Question: Aren't these functions as important as the ones controlled by the left hemisphere?

It depends. Commenting on the terms "major" and "minor," Robert Ornstein suggests that we label the left hemisphere "major" because we value logical analytic thought in our culture. However, if you are an artist or musician, then the right brain may be the "major hemisphere" from your point of view. Ornstein (1972) adds:

> If one is a wordsmith, a scientist, or a mathematician, damage to the left hemisphere may prove disastrous. If one is a musician, a craftsman, or an artist, damage to the left hemisphere often does not interfere with one's capacity to create music, crafts, or arts, yet damage to the right hemisphere may well obliterate a career.

Ornstein urges us to recognize that full use of the human brain should include taking advantage of the specialized skills of both hemispheres, by using both logic and intuition, for example.

Question: Is there any way to tell which hemisphere a person is using?

Researcher Marcel Kinsbourne (1972) believes that eye movements can reveal which hemisphere is being used. If a person is asked a verbal-analytical question (such as "multiply 12 by 7 and add 32 to the answer"), more eye movements are made to the right than if the question requires spatial visualization ("Are the eagle's wings spread on the back of a quarter?"). Thus, all other things being equal, a predominance of eye movements to the right indicates use of the left hemisphere while eye movements to the left correspond to right-hemisphere activity.*

Question: How does the difference between the hemispheres relate to the relationship between the brain and conscious awareness?

*Are your friends left-brained or right-brained?

Split Brains

Knowledge of the differences between the two hemispheres allows us to consider one of the most remarkable areas of research in physiological psychology. For several years Roger Sperry and his associates at the California Institute of Technology have been studying the effects of a radical form of brain surgery that *disconnects* the two cerebral hemispheres. The result of this "split-brain" operation is essentially a person with two brains in one body (Sperry, 1968).

The cerebral hemispheres have been disconnected in a number of animal experiments, but in humans the split brain has been observed only as a side effect of legitimate medical procedures. You will recall that the right and left hemispheres are connected by the corpus callosum. This is normally a beneficial arrangement because it allows sharing of the information and special skills of each side of the brain. However, in a person afflicted with severe epilepsy, the corpus callosum tends to involve the whole brain in seizure activity even if the disturbance was initially limited to one side. In an attempt to limit seizures in advanced cases of epilepsy, the corpus callosum is sometimes cut.

In both animals and humans, separation of the hemispheres has consistently resulted in a doubling of the realms of conscious awareness. As Sperry (1968) says:

> In other words, each hemisphere seems to have its own separate and private sensations; its own perceptions; its own concepts; and its own impulses to act. . . . Following the surgery, each hemisphere also has thereafter its own separate chain of memories that are rendered inaccessible to the recall processes of the other.

An example of the separate awareness of the two hemispheres would be this simple demonstration. If a split-brain subject were given a key (hidden from sight) to feel with his right hand, he could easily name what he had touched. However, if the left hand were given the key, the person would be unable to verbally describe the object. Since the verbal (left) hemisphere is no longer connected to the right, the speaking half of the brain is unaware of what is occurring in the other half. As another indication of dual consciousness, we could ask our subject to point (with the left hand) to an object corresponding to the hidden object felt by that hand. Even though the person cannot *say* what he felt, he can readily point to it (with his left hand).

Question: How does a split-brain person function after the operation?

Surprisingly, the split-brain individual acts quite normal in most situations because both halves of the brain have about the same experience at the same time. Also, if a conflict should arise, the dominant hemisphere tends to override the minor hemisphere. Split-brain effects only become apparent in specialized testing. For example, both eyes connect to both hemispheres. To get visual information to only one side of the brain, pictures must be flashed very briefly in either the right or left visual field. If this condition is met, truely fascinating situations develop. A dollar sign can be flashed to the right brain and a question mark to the left brain. If the person is asked to draw what he saw using the left hand (out of sight), he will draw the dollar sign. If he is then asked what he has drawn, he will say without hesitation that he drew a question mark (Sperry, 1968). In short, one hemisphere does not know what is happening in the other!

The superiority of the right hemisphere at spatial tasks provides another intriguing observation. A common test of spatial ability involves construction of a geometric design using a set of cubes. On this test the split-brain patient's left hand can typically perform quite well, but the right cannot. In addition, Ornstein (1972) reports that:

> Professor Sperry often shows an interesting film clip of the right hand attempting to solve the problem and failing, whereupon the patient's left hand cannot restrain itself and "corrects" the right—as when you know the answer to a problem and watch me making mistakes, and cannot refrain from telling me the answer.

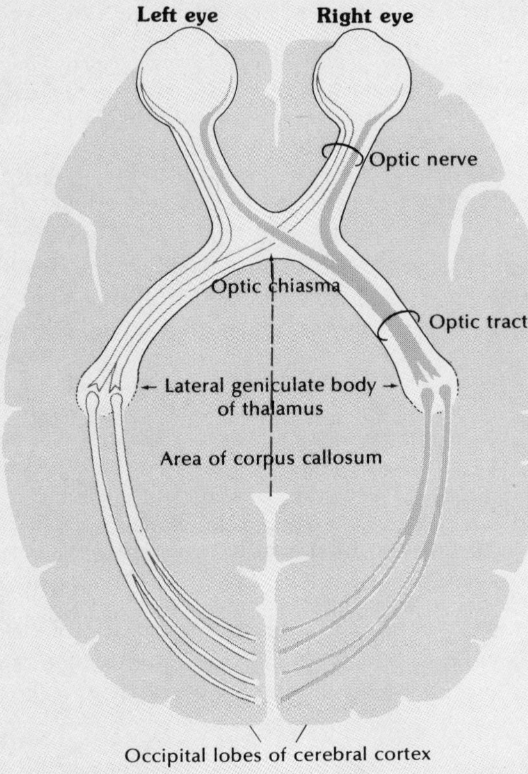

Fig. 3-12 Basic nerve pathways of vision. Notice that the left portion of each eye connects only to the left half of the brain; likewise the right portion of each eye connects to the right brain. When the corpus callosum is cut (in the area of the broken line), a split brain results, and visual information can be directed to only one hemisphere.

In other experiments, monkeys with split brains have been taught to perform two separate and conflicting tasks, one task being performed by each hand-eye-brain unit (Sperry, 1964). This has to be the ultimate case of the "right hand not knowing what the left hand is doing."

Mind and Brain Split-brain research is interesting and informative in its own right. But, more importantly, it seems (to this author, at any rate) to resolve many of the questions about what the "mind" is or where it is to be found. If dividing the brain produces two separate "minds" or spheres of consciousness, then it follows that consciousness is nothing more or less than the electrical and chemical activity of the brain. In humans, the terms "mind," "brain activity," and "consciousness" are simply different ways of describing the same set of events.

Does this diminish the almost miraculous nature of human consciousness? On the contrary, this view elevates the silent labor of billions of neurons to a level of respect usually reserved for the more spectacular wonders of nature. How does it feel to have the Eighth Wonder of the World inside your head?

Questions for Discussion

1. Growing knowledge of the brain has contributed to the development of a technique called ESB (electrical stimulation of the brain). ESB allows permanent alteration of the brain in humans without the limitations imposed by traditional methods of brain surgery. ESB has been used to alleviate medical problems (like brain tumors) and more recently to alter the personality of individuals who are uncontrollably aggressive or hostile. What limitations (if any) do you think should be imposed on such procedures? Why?

2. Dolphins, like humans, have very large brains in proportion to their body size. What differences do you think account for human intellectual superiority? (Or, as an alternative, do you think humans *are* intellectually superior to the dolphin?)

3. Do you think the distinction between right- and left-hemisphere functions is valid? For example, are there verbal skills involved in music, dance, or art?

4. What effect would you expect a drug to have if it raised the firing threshold for neurons? If it blocked passage of neurotransmitters across the synapse? If it mimicked the effect of a neurotransmitter? If it stimulated the RF? If it suppressed activity in the medulla?

5. What would be some of the possible advantages and disadvantages to having a "split brain"?

Suggestions for Further Reading

Delgado, J. *Physical Control of the Mind: Toward a Psychocivilized Society*. Harper & Row, 1969.

Eccles, S. J. C. (ed.) *Brain and Conscious Experience.* Springer-Vertag, 1966.

Gazzaniga, M. S. *The Bisected Brain.* Appleton-Century-Crofts, 1970.

Groch, J. *You and Your Brain.* Harper & Row, 1963.

Morgan, C. *Physiological Psychology*, 4th ed. McGraw-Hill, 1970.

Penfield, W., and T. Rasmussen. *The Cerebral Cortex of Man.* Macmillan, 1950.

Wooldridge, D. E. *The Machinery of the Brain.* McGraw-Hill, 1963.

The Sensory World and Reality

4

Chapter Preview

Sensory Deprivation—Life on a Sensory Diet

This chapter is a study of sensation. *Sensations are our link to the world "out there." When sensory organs turn information into nerve impulses—a "language" understood by the brain—the result is sensation.*

Question: What would happen if sensations were prevented from reaching the brain?

Prisoners, explorers, pilots, and truck drivers have at times "gone stir crazy," had "cabin fever," or have experienced dangerous lapses in awareness due to reduced stimulation. In addition, radar observers, radio monitors, truck drivers, and pilots sometimes experience bizarre sensations or see things that aren't really there. To find out why, D. O. Hebb and his associates paid volunteers $20 a day to undergo sensory deprivation. *Wearing goggles to prevent vision and listening to a constant "white" noise (which sounds like a waterfall), subjects spent several days in a small cubicle. Many participants looked forward to the experiment as a chance to do some deep thinking. In spite of this, few subjects endured more than two or three days of reduced stimulation without "pushing the panic button." Subjects lost track of time, had extreme difficulty concentrating, and experienced various perceptual distortions. Many of these reactions were anticipated, but not fully expected were the strange* hallucinations *reported by subjects.*

Question: What form did the hallucinations take?

Some subjects simply saw geometric shapes, had feelings of movement, heard music that wasn't there, or felt separated from their bodies. In other experiments, hallucinations during sensory deprivation have been more pronounced. A subject in one experiment screamed in panic: "There is an animal having a long slender body with many legs. It's on the screen, crawling in back of me!"

Subjects in an experiment performed by John Lilly (1956) were placed in a tank of warm water. There they floated for several hours wearing a face mask attached to a breathing apparatus. Subjects also wore darkened goggles and were, in effect, cut off from smell, touch, vision, hearing, and taste sensations. Under such severe conditions of sensory deprivation—with nothing coming in—subjects hallucinated within two or three hours. Lilly maintains that normal functioning of the brain and nervous system relies on adequate sensory stimulation. Without stimulation, it becomes increasingly difficult for a person to tell what is really "out there" and what is only "in his head." Sensation is obviously important. To find out more about sensation, read on!

Resources

Sensation and Reality

First, read the following directions for a simple experiment; then try it:

> Close your eyes for a moment. Then take your fingertips and press firmly on your eyelids. Apply enough pressure to "squash" your eye slightly. Do this for about thirty seconds and see what happens.

If you tried the experiment, you probably saw stars, checkerboards, and flashes of color. The reason for this is that the receptor cells at the back of the eye normally respond to light, but are also sensitive to pressure. You "fooled" the visual receptors into sending nerve impulses to the visual area of the brain. The intriguing thing about this is that you experience *light* sensations, not *pressure*. Early in psychology's history, physiologist Johannes Müller proposed the *doctrine of specific nerve energies* to explain this experience. Müller thought that sensory organs produce different kinds of "vibrations" in the nerves. Since we now know that receptors for all the senses—vision, touch, smell, taste, and hearing—produce the same kind of nerve impulses, Müller's concept has been replaced by that of *localization of function*.

Localization of function means that the sensation you experience depends on the area of the brain stimulated. For example, neurosurgeon Wilder Penfield has electrically stimulated the *visual area* in the brain of conscious human subjects. One subject's responses to such stimulation was that of "flickering lights," "colors," "a long, white mark," and other basic visual sensations (Penfield & Roberts, 1959).

Question: What is the point of this?

One point is that in the future it will probably be possible to route visual information to the brain of a sightless individual by artificial means. Re-

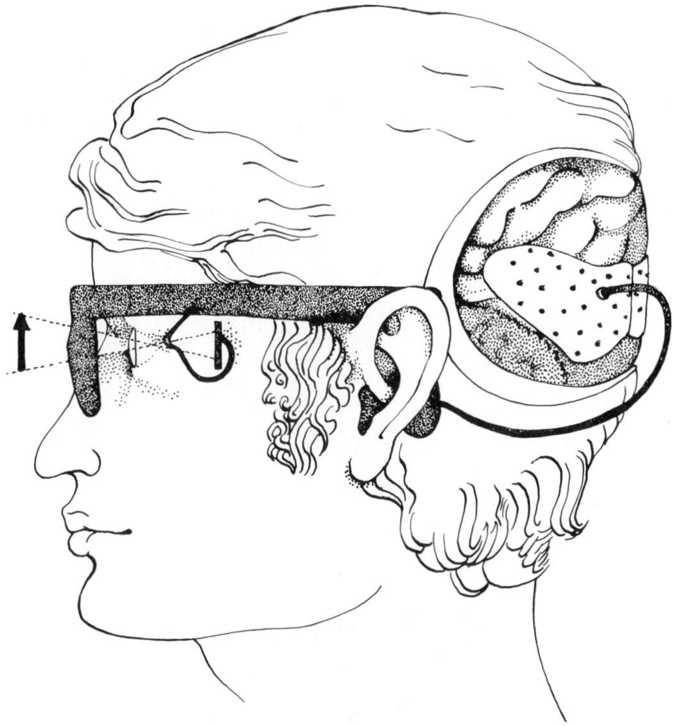

Fig. 4-1 Artist's concept of an artificial visual system. Images received by the artificial eye would be transmitted to electrodes implanted in the visual area of the brain (shown in cut-away view). The artificial eye, which operates like a television camera, might be placed in the eye socket as depicted in the drawing.

searchers are already working on a system that uses miniature television cameras to generate electrical signals which are then carried directly to the visual cortex of the brain via permanently implanted electrodes.

Another point is that our contact with "reality" is entirely dependent upon the way sensory systems are constructed and organized. We are surrounded by all kinds of energy: light, heat, mechanical vibrations, microwaves, and so forth. These energies affect us and convey information only if they reach the brain. But our sensory organs are capable of *transducing* (changing into nerve impulses) only a limited range of physical energies. Let us turn now to a look at the structures that connect us to the world of physical energies.

The Receptors—Private Line to Reality

The Somesthetic Senses Your awareness of your body and your ability to use it are strongly dependent upon the existence of the *somesthetic* (soma=body, esthetic=feel) senses. The somesthetic senses include the *skin senses* (touch), the *kinesthetic senses* (receptors in the muscles and joints that relay information on body position and movement), and the *vestibular senses* (receptors in the inner ear that signal balance—and cause motion sickness). Because of their importance, let us focus on the skin senses.

What we usually think of as touch is actually made up of five different sensations: touch, pressure, pain, cold, and warmth. A number of specialized receptor cells in the skin correspond roughly to each of the sensations (see Fig. 4-2).

Question: Does the number of receptors in an area of skin relate to its sensitivity?

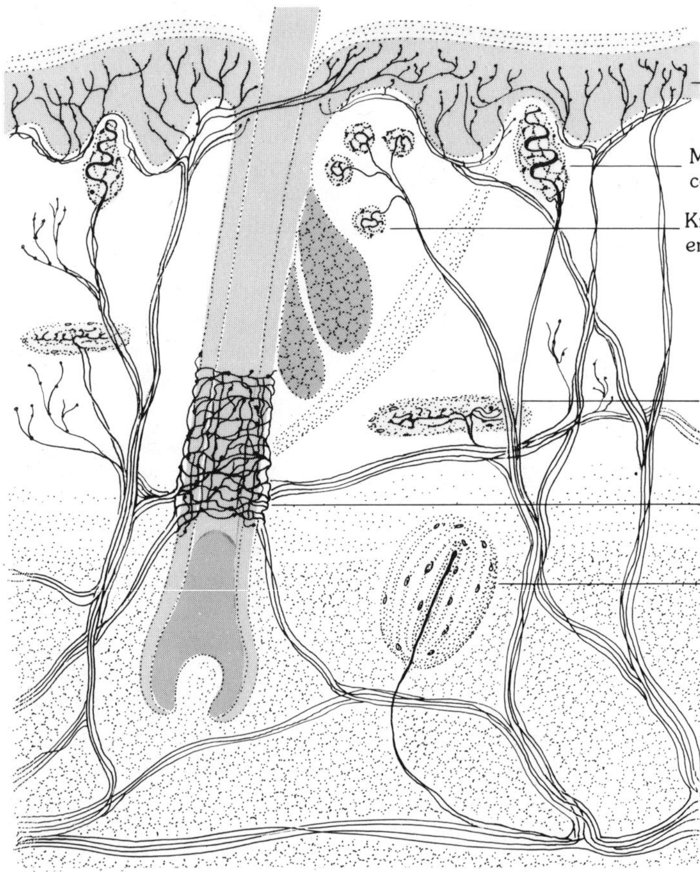

Fig. 4-2 The skin senses include touch, pressure, pain, cold, and warmth (and perhaps itching and tickling). This drawing shows some of the important sensory receptors. There is some specialization among them: The Krause bulbs are most sensitive to cold; Meissner's corpuscles, to touch; and Pacinian corpuscles, to pressure. Free nerve endings are receptors for pain and any of the other sensations.

Yes, the skin has been "mapped" by applying heat, cold, pressure, touch, or pain to points all over the body. This procedure shows that the skin receptors are found in varying concentrations and that the number of receptors corresponds to sensitivity. Important areas such as the lips, tongue, face, hands, and genitals are all quite sensitive.

Question: Are there more receptors for some sensations than for others?

Yes. Pain receptors are found in greater numbers than any of the others. Like the other skin senses, pain receptors vary in their distribution. Pinch the end of your nose, the back of your hand, or your shoulder, and you will experience differing amounts of pain.

Just as pain varies in parts of the body, so does it vary from person to person. Occasionally an individual is born with a complete insensitivity to pain. The history of one such individual, a twenty-two-year-old female college student, is typical. Since early childhood she experienced extensive burns, frostbite, deep cuts, and other serious tissue damage (McMurray, 1950). This points up the positive side of pain. Pain is an early warning system for tissue damage, and without it a person may be unable to detect or prevent injury.

The Sense of Smell Smell is a chemical sense, responding primarily to gaseous substances carried in the air. As air enters the nose, it passes over millions of nerve fibers embedded in the lining of the upper nasal passages. When airborne molecules pass over this area, nerve signals are generated and sent to the brain (see Fig. 4-3).

Question: How are different odors produced?

Scientists have noticed that molecules having a particular odor tend to have approximately the same shape. Specific shapes have been identified

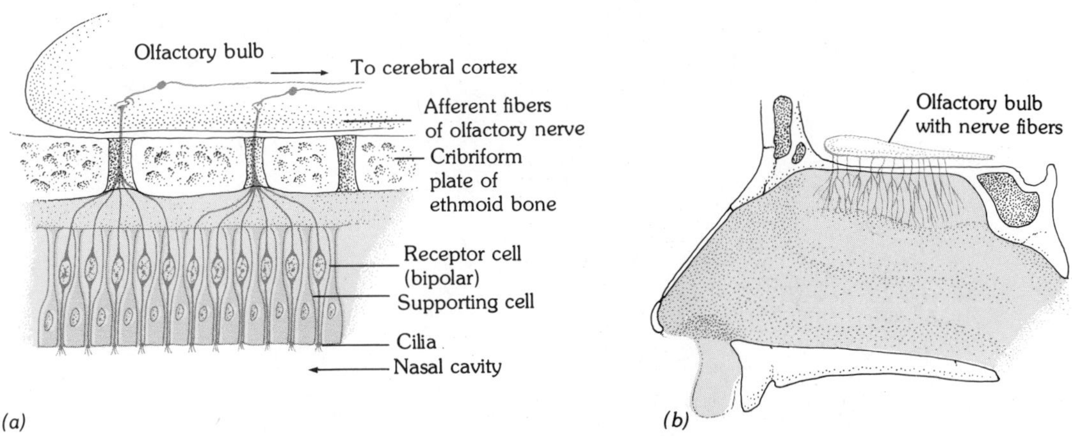

Fig. 4-3 Receptors for the sense of smell (olfaction). Olfactory nerve fibers respond to gaseous molecules.

for floral, camphoric, musky, minty, and etherish odors. It is currently believed that there are "holes" on the odor receptors having the same shape as the various molecules. Like a piece fit into a puzzle, a molecule produces an odor when it matches up with a hole of the correct shape.

Taste There may have been a time when taste was an important sense. In the dim past when most humans foraged for food, taste may have prevented an occasional poisoning. Now taste adds a joyous (but nonessential) dimension to the universal pastime of eating.

The primary receptor for taste is the *taste bud*, located mainly on the top of the tongue (see Fig. 4-4). As food is chewed, it dissolves and enters the taste bud, where it sets off a nerve impulse to the brain. Like the skin senses, taste receptors are not equally distributed. Look at Fig. 4-4, and you will see that some areas of the tongue are more sensitive to each of the tastes than the others. You will also notice that the only tastes listed are salty, sour, sweet, and bitter.

Question: *If these are the only tastes, how can there be so many different-tasting foods?*

Tastes seem more varied and complex than implied by the four taste qualities because we tend to include the sensations of texture, temperature, and smell along with taste. Smell is particularly important. Small bits of apple, potato, and onion taste almost exactly alike when the nose is plugged. It is probably no exaggeration to say that subjective taste is one-half smell. This is why food loses its "taste" when you have a cold.

Hearing Rock, classical, jazz, country, pop—whatever your musical preference, you have probably been transported at one time or another by the riches of sound. Hearing provides the brain with a wealth of information

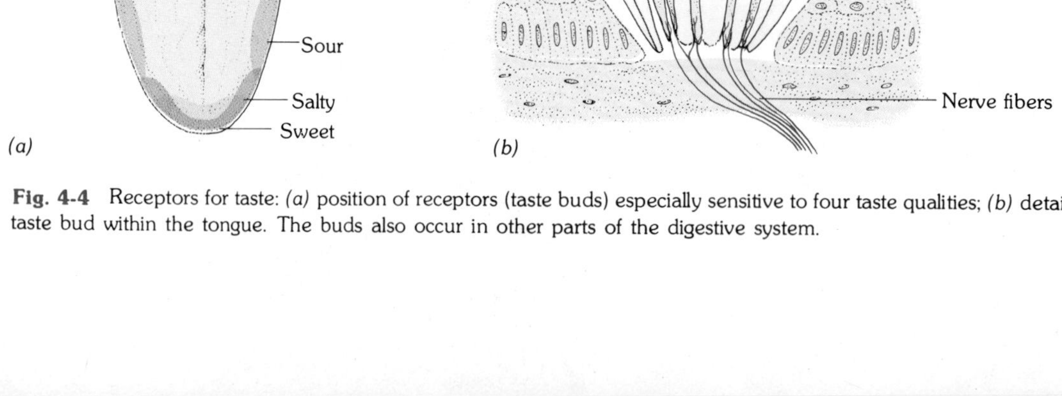

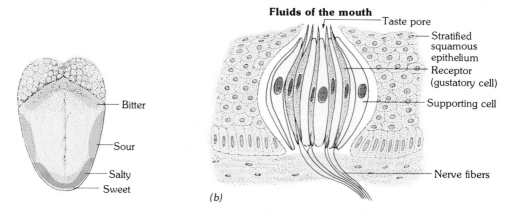

Fig. 4-4 Receptors for taste: *(a)* position of receptors (taste buds) especially sensitive to four taste qualities; *(b)* detail of a taste bud within the tongue. The buds also occur in other parts of the digestive system.

not available through the other senses, like the approach of an unseen car or the information conveyed by spoken language. Hearing is highly developed even at birth. A newborn baby will consistently look in the direction of a metal "cricket" snapped at various locations around the room.

Question: How are sounds transduced?

If you throw a stone into a quiet pond, a circle of waves will spread from it in all directions. In much the same way, sound travels as a series of invisible waves of *compression* (peaks) and *rarefaction* (valleys) in the air. Any object set in motion—a tuning fork, the string of a musical instrument, or the vocal cords—will produce *sound waves* as it vibrates (see Fig. 4-5). As these waves spread through the air, they collide with the eardrum, which is like a tight drumhead within the ear canal. The sound waves set the eardrum in motion, which in turn causes three small bones called the *auditory ossicles* to vibrate (see Fig. 4-6). The third ossicle is attached to a second membrane, or drumhead, called the *oval window*. As the oval window moves back and forth, it sets up waves in a fluid within the canals of the *cochlea*. The cochlea is really the organ of hearing since it is here that waves in the fluid are detected by sensitive cells which convert sound stimuli into nerve impulses to be sent to the brain.

Question: What causes deafness?

There are two principal types of deafness. *Conduction deafness* occurs when the auditory ossicles are immobilized by disease or injury. This reduces the transfer of vibrations from the eardrum to the inner ear. Conduction deafness can often be overcome through the use of hearing aids that make sounds much louder. *Nerve deafness* is a hearing loss resulting from damage to the auditory nerve. Hearing aids are of no help to a person with nerve deafness since auditory messages cannot reach the brain no matter how loud the sound. While we are on the topic of deafness, it should be

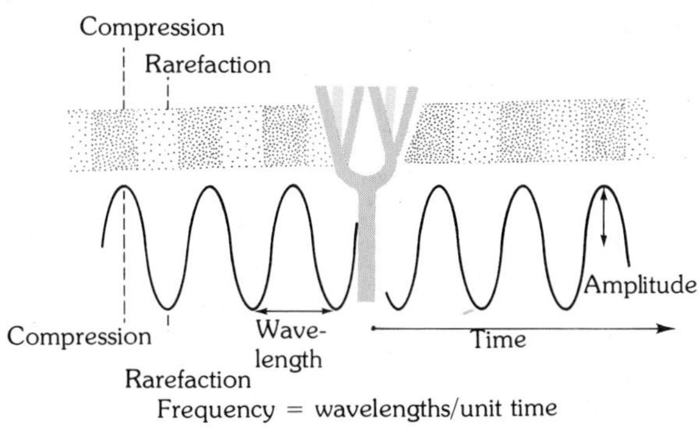

Fig. 4-5 The stimulus for hearing is waves of compression in the air or, more simply, vibrations. The frequency of sound waves determines their pitch. The amplitude determines loudness.

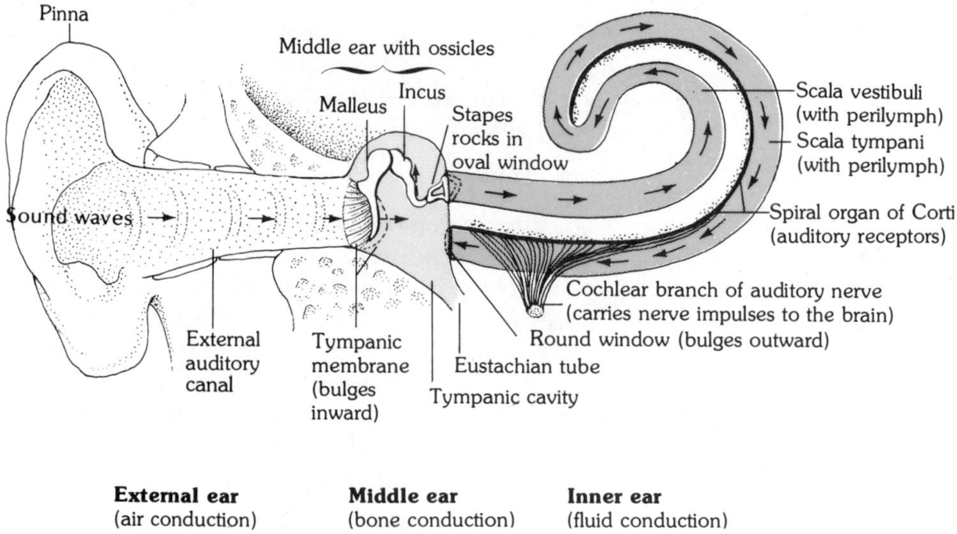

Fig. 4-6 Gross anatomy of the auditory system. The entire system is a mechanism for the transformation of physical pressure waves into nerve impulses.

noted that prolonged exposure to very loud sounds can cause permanent hearing loss. Figure 4-7 gives the approximate loudness rating of various sounds and identifies levels of potential danger.

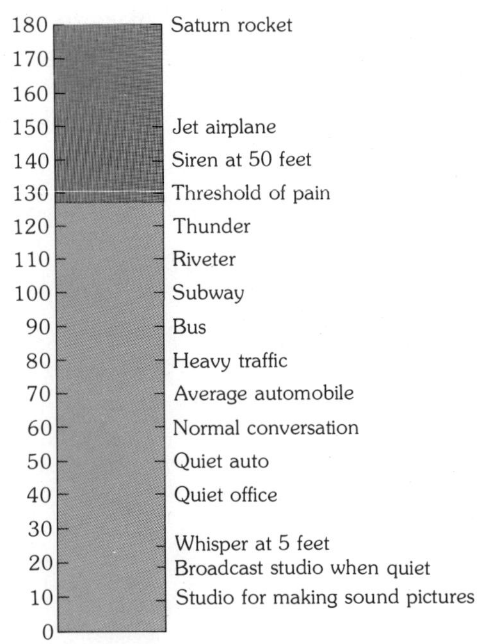

Fig. 4-7 The loudness of a sound is measured in decibels. For hearing, the absolute threshold is 0 decibels. Sound in the range of 110 decibels can be painful and if prolonged may damage the inner ear. Rock music, which may rate 120 decibels, is known to have caused hearing loss in musicians and may affect members of the audience as well. Sounds of 130 decibels pose an immediate danger to the hearing system.

Learning Check

1. The sensory organs are structures designed to ______________ physical energies into nerve impulses.

2. The skin senses are part of the ______________ senses.

3. The four basic taste sensations are ______________, ______________, ______________, and ______________.

4. The stimulus for the sense of smell is airborne ______________.

5. The true organ of hearing is the ______________.

6. Damage to the ossicles causes ______________ deafness.

Answers:

1. transduce **2.** somesthetic **3.** sweet, sour, salty, bitter **4.** molecules **5.** cochlea **6.** conduction

Vision—Window on the World

Question: Which of the five senses is most important?

Although there really isn't an answer to this question, one fact stands out clearly: approximately 70 percent of the information conveyed to the brain comes from vision. For this reason much more research has been focused on vision, and we will explore it in more detail than was afforded the other senses.

Dimensions of Vision The room in which you are sitting is filled with electromagnetic radiation: gamma rays, ultraviolet rays, infrared, FM, television, and shortwave broadcasts. What if you could see all of these radiations? Outlandish, you say? Not really, because light *is* electromagnetic radiation. Just as we can only hear sounds within a certain frequency range, we "see" only a small band of electromagnetic frequencies. The *visible spectrum* of colors is made up of light of various wavelengths. The spectrum starts at violet with a wavelength of 400 millimicrons. (A micron is a millionth of a meter; a millimicron is a thousandth of a micron.) Longer and longer wavelengths of light produce the colors blue, green, yellow, and orange until red, with a wavelength of 700 millimicrons, is reached. This physical property of light, its wavelength, corresponds to the psychological dimension of *hue*. Hue refers to the color of a stimulus. White light is made up of a mixture of frequencies from the entire spectrum. Colors are narrower "slices" of the spectrum. A very narrow band of wavelengths produces a color that is very *saturated* (or "pure").

Another dimension of vision is *brightness*. Brightness corresponds roughly to the total amount of light reflected from a surface, but like many other sensory experiences, brightness is not purely dependent on the physical stimulus. The psychological brightness of an object is greatly affected by the *context* in which it occurs (see Fig. 4-8).

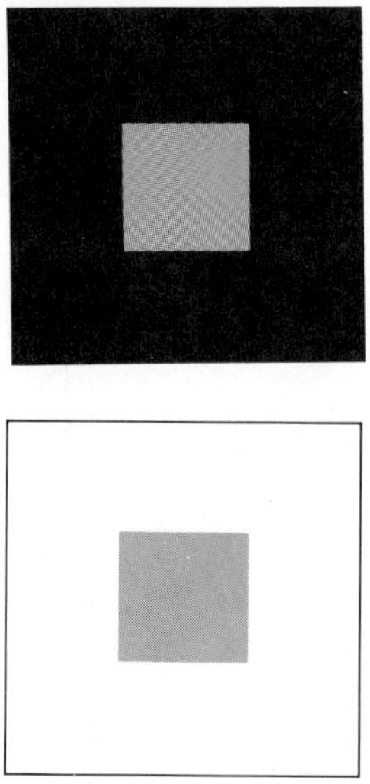

Fig. 4-8 Brightness is affected by context. The gray squares are equally bright but look different because of the background.

Structure of the Eye

Question: Is it true that the eye is like a camera?

If one is willing to push the issue a bit, the eye can be used as a camera. One nineteenth-century investigator briefly uncovered the eyes of a rabbit whose head was pointed toward a window. Immediately afterward he sacrificed the animal and "developed" its retina by placing the eye in alum solution. The retina clearly showed the image of the window! Since people had eyes before there were cameras, it may be more appropriate to say that the camera is like an eye. At any rate, the basic elements are similar. Both the eye and a camera have a transparent *lens* which focuses an image on a light-sensitive layer at the back of a closed space. In a camera this layer is the film, and in the eye it is a layer of cells sensitive to light called the *retina* (see Fig. 4-9).

Question: How does the eye focus?

There are other similarities between the eye and a camera. The lens in a camera focuses an image on the film. In a camera, focusing is accomplished mainly by changing the distance between the film and the lens. In the eye, it is accomplished when the lens changes shape. The lens is stretched or thickened by a series of muscles and ligaments which support it. This is called *accommodation*.

The shape of the eye also affects focusing. If the eye is too short, objects close to the eye cannot be focused, and *farsightedness* (hyperopia) results. If the eyeball is too long, subjects in the distance cannot be focused, resulting in *nearsightedness* (myopia). Another common visual problem accompanies aging. Sometimes with age the lens becomes less resilient and hence less able to accommodate. Since the lens must do its greatest bending to focus material close to the eye, the result is farsightedness. If a person is myopic because of the shape of his or her eyes and then develops *pres-*

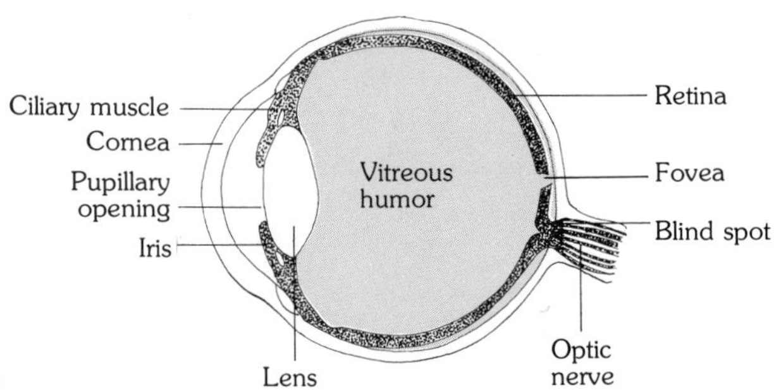

Fig. 4-9 The human eye, a simplified representation.

byopia because of aging, bifocal lenses may be required. Bifocals correct near vision *and* distance vision (see Fig. 4-10).

There is another correspondence between the eye and a camera. In front of the lens in both is a mechanism to control the amount of light entering. This is the *diaphragm* in a camera. In the eye it is the *iris*. The iris is very important to normal functioning of the eye. The retina adapts to changing light conditions, but does so very slowly. The iris makes immediate adjustments. Its largest opening is seventeen times larger than its smallest. Were this not the case, you would be blinded for quite some time when walking from a darkened room into bright sunlight or vice versa. The iris responds primarily to changes in light intensity; but interestingly it also responds to emotional states. When one is experiencing pleasant emotions, the iris *dilates*, causing the pupil to become large. Unpleasant emotions cause the pupils to *constrict*. Poets have long made note of this effect with phrases like: "Her eyes were limpid pools, wide with adoration," or "His eyes were pinpoints of hate." (The "bad guys" always have beady eyes!)

Only recently has this effect been studied and applied. Psychologist Eckard Hess has developed a technique he calls *pupilometrics* (Hess & Polt, 1960). Hess photographs the eyes as they respond to different stimuli (under controlled light conditions) and then measures the diameter of the pupil. In this way he can determine if one has responded pleasantly or unpleasantly to a stimulus. The eyes are apparently not only "windows to the soul" but also a door to the pocketbook. Pupilometrics has been used commercially to select pleasing packaging and effective advertisements, and many a poker game has been won by a seasoned gambler who has learned to watch the eyes of other players.

Rods and Cones At this point, our comparison between the eye and the camera breaks down. The eye is actually a very poor camera. First of all, the

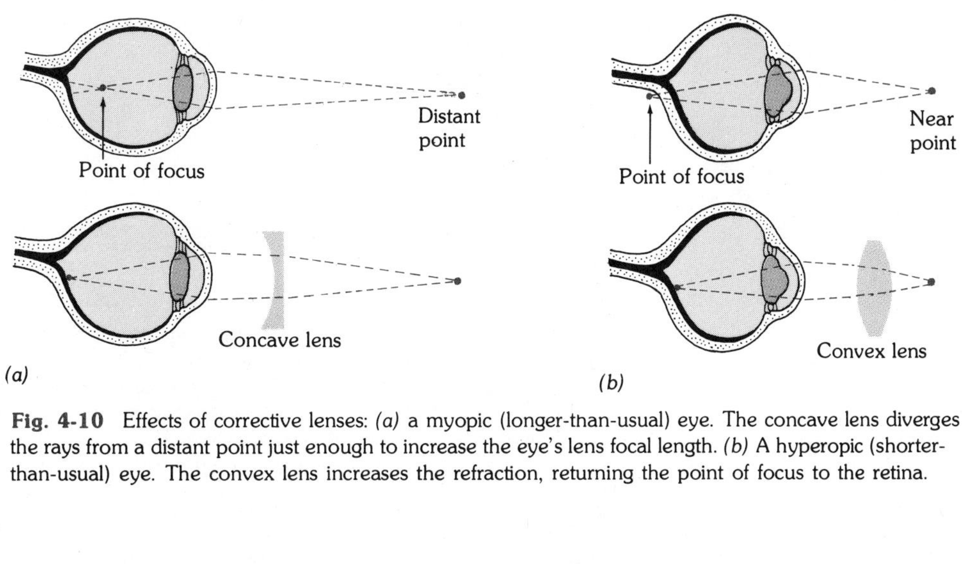

Fig. 4-10 Effects of corrective lenses: *(a)* a myopic (longer-than-usual) eye. The concave lens diverges the rays from a distant point just enough to increase the eye's lens focal length. *(b)* A hyperopic (shorter-than-usual) eye. The convex lens increases the refraction, returning the point of focus to the retina.

eye is equipped with two types of "film": receptor cells called *rods* and *cones*. These rods and cones look different and perform different functions. The cones, numbering about 6½ million in each eye, function in bright light to produce *color* sensations and to pick up fine details. By contrast, the rods, numbering about 100 million, function only in dim light and are capable of producing only sensations of *black*, *white*, and shades of *grey*. Also, the film is in backward compared to a camera. The visual receptors in the retina point toward the back of the eye, away from the light source. In addition, the film has a hole in it (there is a blind spot in the retina where there are no receptors); plus the image projected on the retina is upside down. And last, the eye shakes constantly, which would be disastrous for a camera. So much for the comparison of the eye with a camera! In spite of this, the eye is a magnificent *visual system*.

Question: Are there other differences between the rods and cones?

The cones are found mainly toward the center of the field of vision. In fact, there is a small cup-shaped depression in the middle of the retina (called the *fovea*) that is packed with pure cones. If you look at your thumbnail at arm's length, its image just about covers the fovea. *Visual acuity*—the ability to distinguish fine detail—is best when an image falls on the fovea and becomes weaker as one moves toward the edge of the eye. If you pick a letter on this page and stare at it, you will notice that you cannot read letters a few inches to either side without moving your eyes. The rods reach their greatest density about 20 degrees to each side of the fovea. In areas of the eye in which rods predominate, visual acuity is not as sharp. The rods, however, are unusually sensitive to movement. Try this demonstration:

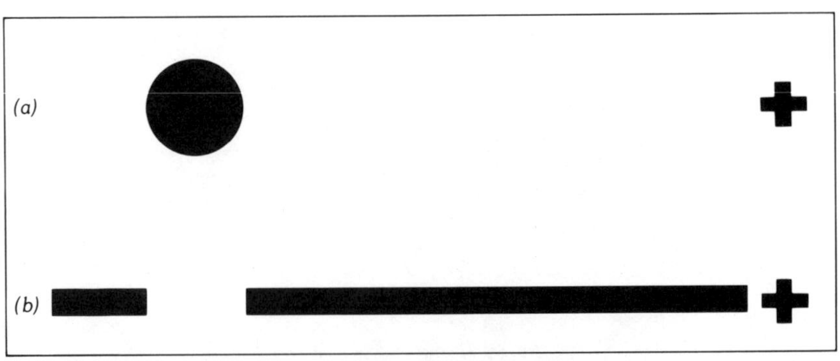

Fig. 4-11 Experiencing the blind spot. *(a)* With the right eye closed, stare at the upper right cross. Hold the book about 1 foot from your eye and slowly move it back and forth. You should be able to locate a position that causes the black spot to disappear. When it does, it has fallen on the blind spot. *(b)* Repeat the procedure described but stare at the lower cross. When the white space falls on the blind spot, the black line will appear to be continuous. This may help you understand why you do not usually experience a blind spot in your visual field.

> While staring straight ahead, hold your right hand out to the side of your head. It should be a foot or two out from your ear and at eye level. Pull your hand back behind the edge of your visual field. Now begin wiggling a finger and slowly move your hand forward. You should readily find a spot where you can detect *movement* without really being able to see your finger. If you move your finger a tiny bit farther forward you will, of course, be able to see it.

Night spotters in the military have long made use of a simple but important principle. Since the rods are more sensitive to dim light than the cones, and since they are most dense about 20 degrees to each side of the fovea, the best night vision is obtained by looking slightly to one side or the other of an object. With a little effort this can also be demonstrated:

> On a dark, moonless night, allow your eyes to slowly scan the sky until you find a star off toward the edge of your vision that is so dim that you can just barely see it. Now, if you look directly at the star (so that its image falls on the cones of the fovea), it should appear even dimmer and may actually disappear.

Color Vision—There's More to It than Meets the Eye

What would you say is the brightest color? Red? Yellow? Blue? Actually there are two answers to this question, depending on whether we are referring to the rods or the cones. The differing *maximal color sensitivity* of the rods and cones has important practical implications. The cones are most sensitive to wavelengths in the yellowish green region of the spectrum. In other words, if all possible colors were tested under conditions which ensured that they reflected the same total amount of light, then a yellowish green would appear *brightest* in the *daylight*. In recognition of this fact, you may have already seen a "day-glo" yellow firetruck or other emergency vehicle, and vests of this color are increasingly worn by roadside construction crews and hunters.

Question: To what color are the rods most sensitive?

The answer is surprising. If we were to test *only* the *rods* for sensitivity to different colors, we would find that *blue* is the brightest. Thus, at night and under other conditions of dim light when rod vision predominates, the brightest color is blue. Police and highway patrol cars in many states now have blue emergency lights for nighttime work. Also, you may have wondered why the runway lights at most airports are blue. It seems like a poor choice, but is actually the most visible to pilots.

Color Blindness and Color Weakness

Question: What is it like to be color blind? What causes color blindness?

A person who is completely color blind sees the world as if it were a black and white movie. How do we know? In a few rare cases people have been color blind in only one eye and can compare (Hsia & Graham, 1965).

Two colors of equal brightness look exactly alike to the color-blind individual. The color-blind person either lacks cones or has cones that do not function normally. Complete color blindness is frequently accompanied by visual *nystagmus*. This is a jerking eye movement which serves to repeatedly move the visual image off the inoperative fovea.

Total color blindness is rare. *Color weakness*, or partial color blindness, is more common. Approximately 8 percent of the male population (but less than 1 percent of women) are red-green color blind. (Another form of color weakness, involving yellow and blue, is extremely rare.) Red-green color blindness is a sex-linked trait and is almost always inherited from one's maternal grandfather. The red-green color-blind individual perceives both reds and greens as yellowish browns.

Question: Then how can they drive a car? Don't they have trouble with traffic lights?

The red-green color-blind individual has normal color vision for yellow and blue, and his acuity is normal. His principal problem while driving is to tell red lights from green. In practice this is not difficult. In the United States the red light is always on top, and the green light is brighter than the red. Also, in recognition of this problem, most modern traffic signals have a "red" light which has a background of yellow light mixed with it and a "green" light that is really blue green.

Question: How can a person tell if he is color blind?

A common test for color blindness is the *Ishihari* test. It consists of numbers composed of dots superimposed on a background that is also made up of dots. The numbers and background are different colors (red and green, for example). If a person is color blind, he sees only a collection of dots. If he has normal color vision, he can detect the presence of the number. You can test your own color vision by turning to Fig. 4-13.

Dark Adaptation—Let There Be Light!

Question: What happens to the eyes when they adapt to a dark room?

Dark adaptation, the increase in sensitivity to light that occurs when one spends time in the dark, is a striking event. Consider walking into a theatre. If you enter from a brightly lighted lobby, you practically have to be led to your seat. After a short time, however, you can see the entire room in perfect detail (including the couple kissing over in the corner). Studies of dark adaption show us that it takes about thirty-five minutes of complete darkness to reach maximum visual sensitivity. When dark adaptation is complete, the eye can detect lights 10,000 times weaker than those to which it was originally sensitive.

The fully adapted human eye is as sensitive to light as the eye of an owl, but its visual acuity (sharpness) is not as good. Before artificial illumination, changing from cone vision to rod vision occurred primarily at sunset, and gradual adaptation was adequate. Now we are often caught in states of temporary semiblindness. Usually this poses no danger, but it can. It takes a long time to dark adapt, but the process can be completely counteracted by just a few seconds exposure to bright light. Try this demonstration:

> Find a very dark room and spend fifteen or twenty minutes in it. At the end of this time, you should be able to see clearly. Now, close your left eye and cover it tightly with your hand. Turn on a bright light for one or two seconds and look at it with your right eye. With the light off again, compare the vision in your two eyes, first opening one and then the other. You will be completely blinded in your right eye.

This should be more than enough to convince you of the wisdom of the oft-repeated warning to avoid looking at the headlights of approaching cars during night driving.

Question: Is there any way to speed up dark adaptation?

The rods are insensitive to extremely red light. Submarines and airplane cockpits are illuminated with red light. So are the "ready rooms" for fighter pilots and ground crews. In each case this allows the people involved to perform their duties, to read, play cards, or whatever, and still be able to go out into the dark without the usual adaptation time. Since the red light doesn't stimulate the rods, it is as if they had already spent time in the dark.

Question: Can eating carrots really improve your vision?

Dark adaptation is based on *rhodopsin*, a reddish substance in the rods that bleaches (breaks down chemically) when struck by light. This is what causes the rods to generate nerve impulses. One of the breakdown products of rhodopsin is vitamin A. In the dark, rhodopsin recombines. As its concentration in the rods increases, sensitivity to light increases. Normal production of rhodopsin is dependent on an adequate intake of vitamin A. Therefore, if one is suffering from vitamin A deficiency, *night blindness* may result. Since carrots are an excellent source of vitamin A, they could improve night vision for someone suffering a deficiency, but not the vision of anyone with an adequate diet.

Learning Check

After such an extended discussion of vision you may find it helpful to review the questions below.

1. When the lens of the eye stretches or bends to focus, it is called ____________________.

2. When one is experiencing pleasant emotions, the iris ____________.

Unpleasant emotions cause the pupils to ____________________.

3. Rods function primarily in ________________ light; cones function in ________________ light.

4. When using the rods, the most visible color is ________________.

5. The ability to distinguish fine detail is called visual ____________.

6. The eyes become more sensitive to light at night due to the process of ________________.

Answers: **1.** accommodation **2.** dilates, constricts **3.** dim, bright **4.** blue **5.** acuity **6.** dark adaptation

Psychophysics—Testing the Limits

Question: *What is the quietest sound that can be heard? The weakest light that can be seen? The lightest touch that can be felt?*

Psychophysics is an attempt to answer these and similar questions. In psychophysics we relate changes in *physical* stimuli to *psychological* sensations. If we seek the absolute minimum amount of stimulation necessary for a sensation to occur, we are looking for the *absolute threshold.* Testing for absolute thresholds is a good indication of just how magnificently the senses link us to the world of physical energies. For example, the absolute threshold for loudness (as opposed to *pitch*) is so small that if your ears were more sensitive to sounds they would be less sensitive! That may sound contradictory, but under ideal testing conditions the eardrum must move a distance about equal to the diameter of a hydrogen atom (the smallest atom) before a sound is detected. If your ears were more sensitive than this, they would convert the random motion of air molecules into a constant hissing noise.

The absolute threshold for vision is equally spectacular. A *quantum* of light is the smallest possible particle or "package" of light energy, yet it only takes *3 quanta* of light striking the retina to produce a sensation. This is the equivalent of being able to see a single candle flame 30 miles away! Table 4-1 gives the approximate absolute thresholds for all five senses.

It is interesting to note that some sensory systems have upper limits as well as lower ones. Humans can hear sounds ranging in pitch from about 20 cycles (vibrations) per second to about 20,000 cycles per second. This is an impressive range, from the lowest ground-shaking rumble of a pipe organ to the highest squeak of a stereo tweeter. However, dogs and many other animals can hear sounds of much higher frequencies. Perhaps you have seen a "silent" dog whistle. These devices produce sounds above the limits of human sensitivity, but still within a dog's range. There is actually a sound present, but as far as a human is concerned, it doesn't exist.

Table 4-1 Absolute Thresholds

Sensory modality	*Absolute threshold*
Vision	Candle flame seen at 30 miles on a clear dark night
Hearing	Tick of a watch under quiet conditions at 20 feet
Taste	1 teaspoon of sugar in 2 gallons of water
Smell	1 drop of perfume diffused into the entire volume of a three-room apartment.
Touch	A wing of a bee falling on your cheek from a distance of 1 centimeter.

(from Galanter, 1962)

Perceptual Defense and Subliminal Perception

Question: Wouldn't the absolute threshold be different for different people?

Absolute thresholds not only vary from person to person, they also vary from time to time for a single person. The nature of the stimulus, the state of one's nervous system, and the costs of false "detections"—all affect the absolute threshold. The threshold can be raised (*perceptual defense*) or lowered (*perceptual vigilance*) by any of these factors. For example, perceptual defense was isolated in a series of experiments performed on the recognition of "dirty" and "clean" words (McGinnes, 1949). So-called dirty words such as "whore," "rape," "bitch," and "penis" were briefly flashed on a screen. It was found that these words took longer than "clean" words such as "wharf," "rope," "batch," and "pencil" to be recognized correctly. This particular experiment suffered from some methodological problems, but later experiments also suggest that the threshold for perception can be influenced by information that causes discomfort or embarrassment.

Question: Is this "subliminal" perception?

Yes, but here is a better example. In the late 1950s, the public was alarmed at reports of an "experiment" conducted by a commercial firm in a New Jersey motion-picture theater. During the showing of a regular movie, the words "Eat popcorn" and "Drink Coca-Cola" were flashed on the screen for 1/3,000 second every 5 seconds. Since the words were presented so briefly, these "ads" were *subliminal* (below the normal threshold for vision). During the six weeks that the messages were flashed on the screen, the firm recorded an increase of 57.5 percent in popcorn sales and an 18.1 percent increase in Coca-Cola sales. In the uproar that followed, some states rushed to pass laws forbidding the "invisible sell." But since then, subliminal advertising has been shown to be ineffective, and no laws were ever passed (Anastasi, 1964). The original "experiment" failed to take into account such factors as weather conditions, the time of year, the particular films shown, the makeup of the audience, or display procedures at the snack bar. To appreciate the importance of such factors, think of the effect the movie *Lawrence of Arabia* could have on beverage sales! Well-controlled laboratory experiments have shown that subliminal stimuli are basically weak stimuli. An advertiser would be better off using the loudest, clearest, most attention-demanding stimulus available. As psychologist Ann Anastasi puts it:

> So far there is no evidence that weak stimuli exert more influence on behavior than do strong stimuli. . . . When weak stimuli are employed . . . the probability of *misperception* increases. The advertiser who hopefully flashes the words "Buy Tasty Tea" on a motion picture screen may find that many subjects actually perceive "Burn Trashy Ties"—a suggestion they may feel strongly tempted to accept when opening Christmas packages (Anastasi, 1964).

Difference Thresholds

Another kind of threshold studied in psychophysics is the *difference threshold.* Here we are asking the question: "How much must a stimulus *change* (increase or decrease) before it becomes *just noticeably different?*" The study of just noticeable differences (JNDs) led to the discovery of one of psychology's first natural "laws." Called Weber's law, it can be roughly stated as: The amount of change in a stimulus necessary to produce a JND is a constant *proportion* of the original stimulus intensity.

Question: What does this mean in practice?

Let's take an example. Pretend that you are sitting in a room in which there are ten candles burning. Ten candles is the original stimulus intensity. Let's say that we begin lighting candles until the room becomes just noticeably brighter. If this takes three more candles, how many additional candles will we have to light in a room in which twenty candles are burning in order to cause a just noticeable increase in brightness? Your first guess may be three, but remember the JND is a *proportion*. We will have to light six candles if we start with twenty; nine if we start with thirty; and twelve if we start with forty. Here are Weber's proportions for some common judgments:

Pitch	1/333 (one-third of 1 percent)
Weight	1/53
Loudness	1/11
Taste	1/5

Notice the big difference in auditory sensitivity (pitch and loudness) compared to taste. Very small changes in hearing are easy to detect. A voice or a musical instrument that is off pitch one-third of 1 percent will be noticeable. For taste we find that a 20 percent change is necessary to produce a JND. If a cup of coffee has five teaspoons of sugar in it, one more

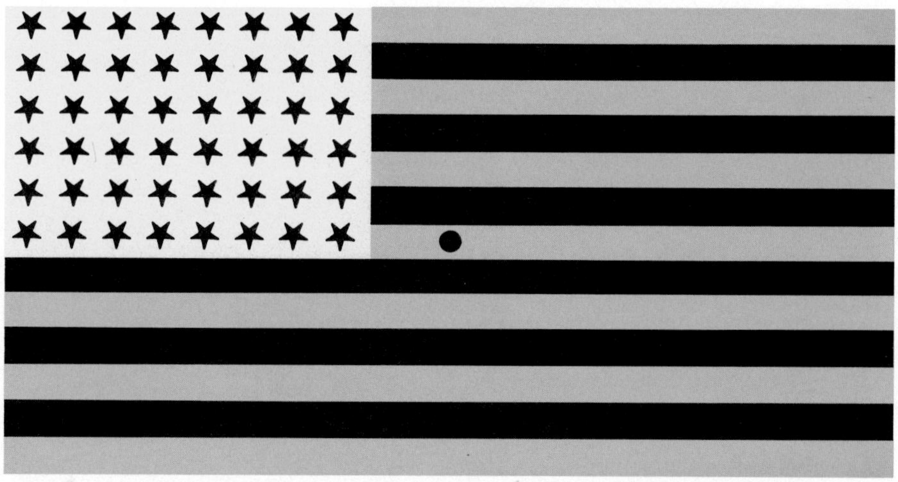

Negative afterimages. Stare at the black dot near the middle of the flag for at least thirty seconds. Then look immediately at the dot in the white space below the flag. You will see the American flag in its normal colors. Reduced sensitivity in yellow, green, and black receptors in the eye caused by prolonged staring results in the appearance of complementary colors. Project the afterimage of the flag on other (colored) surfaces to get additional effects.

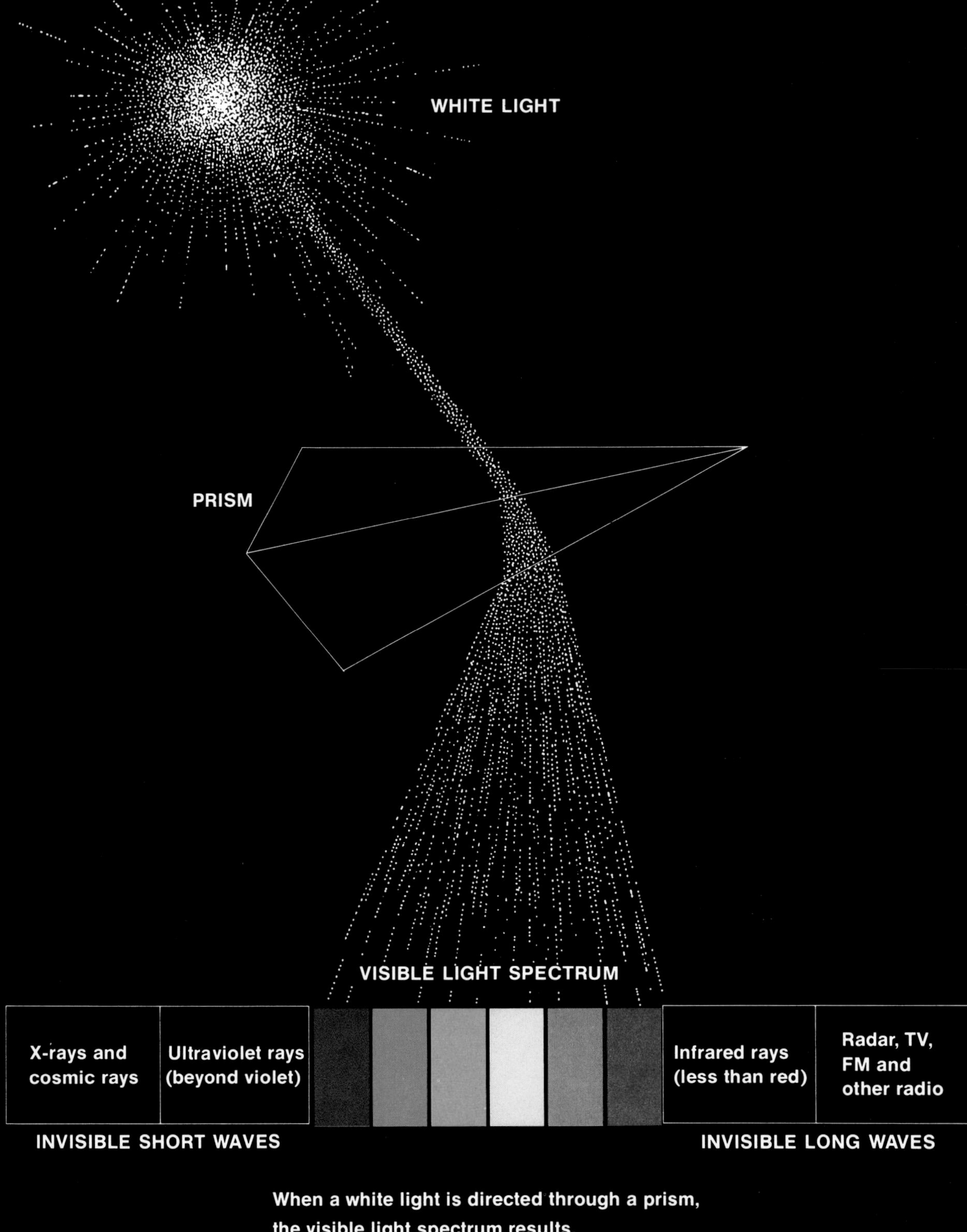
WHITE LIGHT
PRISM
VISIBLE LIGHT SPECTRUM
X-rays and cosmic rays
Ultraviolet rays (beyond violet)
Infrared rays (less than red)
Radar, TV, FM and other radio
INVISIBLE SHORT WAVES
INVISIBLE LONG WAVES
When a white light is directed through a prism, the visible light spectrum results.

Fig. 4-12 The visible spectrum.

ARE YOU COLOR BLIND?

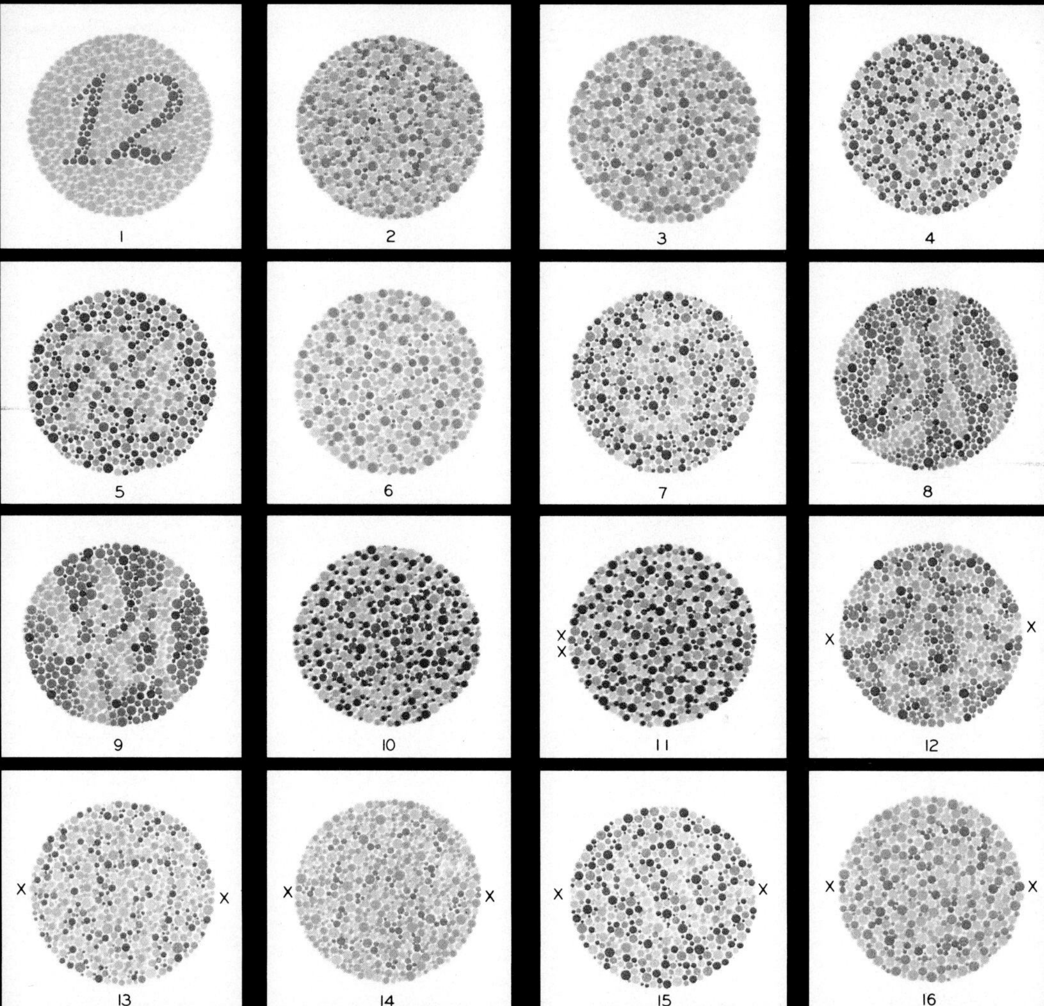

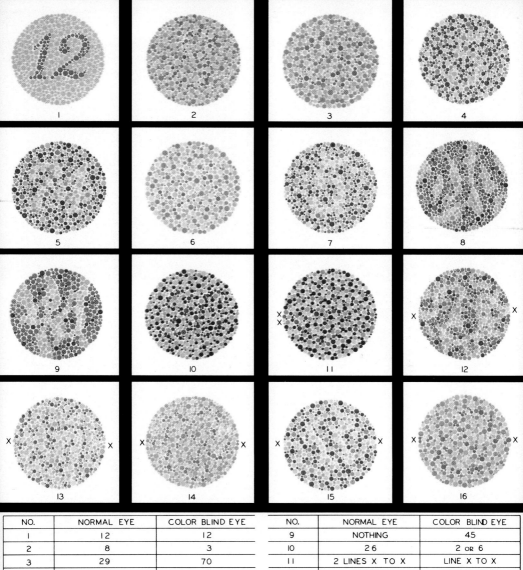

NO.	NORMAL EYE	COLOR BLIND EYE	NO.	NORMAL EYE	COLOR BLIND EYE
1	12	12	9	NOTHING	45
2	8	3	10	26	2 OR 6
3	29	70	11	2 LINES X TO X	LINE X TO X
4	5	2	12	NOTHING	LINE X TO X
5	74	21	13	LINE X TO X	NOTHING
6	45	NOTHING	14	LINE X TO X	NOTHING
7	5	NOTHING	15	LINE X TO X	NOTHING
8	NOTHING	5	16	LINE X TO X	LINE X TO X

Fig. 4-13 A test for color blindness.

Simultaneous contrast. The blue areas in this figure are printed with the same color ink, but contrasting backgrounds make them look like different shades. (Inmont Corporation.)

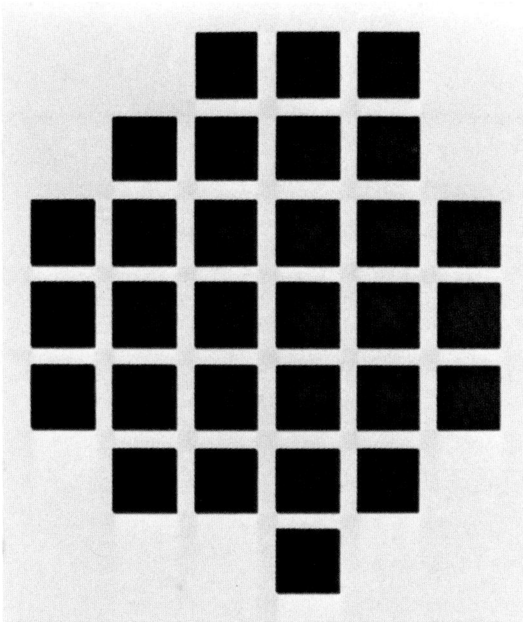

Retinal interactions. You will see flickering gray spots between the blocks of this pattern. This is caused by the influence of activity in surrounding areas of the retina. (Inmont Corporation.)

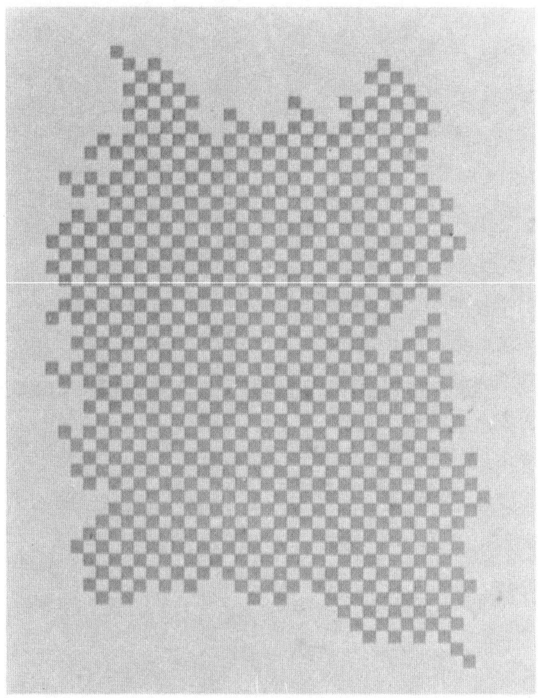

Additive fusion of color. At normal reading distance alternating squares of yellow and blue are seen. When viewed at a distance of 25 feet or more, the squares are fused into a uniform gray. This principle is sometimes used to blend colors in printing by mixing smaller dots of color. (Inmont Corporation.)

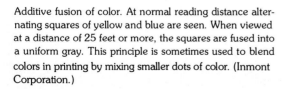

(one-fifth of 5) will have to be added before there is a noticeable increase in sweetness. It takes a lot of cooks to spoil the broth.

Weber's law is really just a rough approximation of the relationship between changes in stimuli and resulting judgments. When it is applied to other than pure sensory judgments, it is even more approximate. In spite of this, there is a lesson to be learned from it. Consider judgments of money, for instance. If you discovered that you had been overcharged $5 on the purchase of a shirt, would you return to demand your money? If you discovered that you had been overcharged $5 on the purchase of an automobile, would you return to demand your money? If your answer to the first question is yes, then rationally your answer to the second should be too. It may not be, however, since the larger base price of a car makes $5 seem a very small difference.

Sensory Adaptation and Selective Attention—Tuning In and Tuning Out

The sensations actually reaching the brain from any sensory system are greatly affected by *sensory adaptation* and *selective attention.* Let us take a brief look at each.

Sensory Adaptation Think about walking into a house where fried fish, sauerkraut, and head cheese was prepared for dinner. (Some dinner!) You would probably pass out at the door, yet people who have been in the house for some time will be unaware of the food odors due to *sensory adaptation.* Sensory adaptation refers to a decrease in sensory response that accompanies a constant or unchanging stimulus. Fortunately, the olfactory (smell) receptors are among the most quickly adapting. When exposed to a constant odor, they send fewer and fewer nerve impulses to the brain until the odor is no longer noticed. Adaptation to sensations of pressure from a wristwatch, bra, waistband, or glasses is based on the same principle.

Question: The eye gets more sensitive in dim light and less sensitive in bright light. Why doesn't vision undergo sensory adaptation like the sense of smell does? If you stare at something, it certainly doesn't go away.

The rods and cones, like other receptor cells, would respond less to a constant stimulus were it not for the fact that the eye normally makes thousands of tiny movements every minute. These movements are so small that they cannot normally be seen, but they nevertheless serve to shift visual images from one receptor cell to another and prevent sensory adaptation. Evidence for this comes from experiments in which subjects are fitted with a special contact lens that has a miniature slide projector attached to it (see Fig. 4-14). Since the projector follows the exact movements of the eye, an

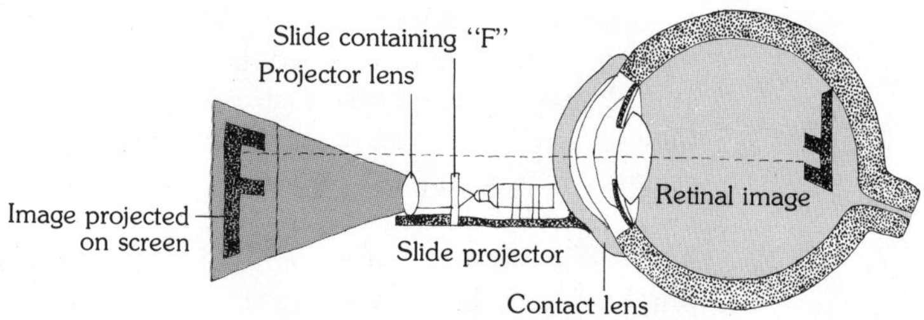

Fig. 4-14 Stabilized image. Miniature slide projector attached to contact lens moves each time the eye moves. As a result, the projected image always falls on the same area of the retina. Under these conditions, the image disappears after a few seconds. (After Cornsweet, 1970.)

image can be stabilized on the retina. When this is done, projected geometric designs fade from view within a few seconds (Pritchard, 1961).

Selective Attention Also dependent on the functioning of sensory systems is the so-called seat-of-your-pants phenomenon. As you sit reading this chapter, receptors for touch and pressure in the seat of your pants are sending nerve impulses to your brain. Even though these sensations have been present all along, you were probably not aware of them until just now. The seat-of-your-pants phenomenon is an example of *selective attention*. We are able to "tune in on" any one of the many sensory messages bombarding us while excluding others. Another familiar example of this is the "cocktail party effect." When you are in a group of people, surrounded by voices, you can still select out and attend to the voice of the persons with whom you are conversing; or if they get dull, you can eavesdrop on conversations all over the room. (Be sure to smile and nod your head occasionally!)

Question: What makes this possible?

Attention is probably based on a *central* (brain-centered) process of selecting messages, but evidence suggests that it may also rely on *gating* of nerve impulses outside the brain. For example:

> Psychologist Hernandez-Peon and his associates implanted recording electrodes in the cochlear nucleus of a cat. (The cochlear nucleus is the first major "relay station" for nerve impulses between the ear and the brain.) Next, a small metallic "cricket" or clicker was sounded, causing a burst of nerve activity in the cochlear nucleus. Then a live mouse (in a jar) was placed in front of the cat. While the cat's attention was shifted to the mouse, the clicker was sounded again. This time nerve activity was almost abolished by comparison to the first (Hernandez-Peon, Scherrer, & Jouvet, 1956).

Sensations other than hearing can also be gated this way. For instance, physiological psychologists Melzack and Wall (1965) are studying "pain gates" in the spinal cord. They have collected evidence that pain can be blocked when the pain gates are closed. Melzack and Wall believe that the ancient Chinese art of *acupuncture* can be explained this way: An acupuncturist's needles generate nerve impulses that close the gates to pain and

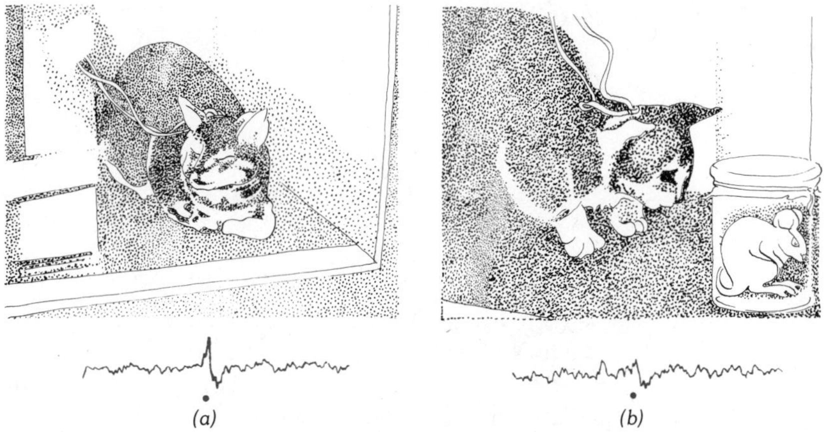

Fig. 4-15 Cat and mouse game. *(a)* When the cat is resting, a click produces the large response shown in the recording from the auditory nerve. *(b)* When the cat is attending to a mouse in a jar, the nerve-signal recording is much smaller. Apparently the click is not as loud to the cat.

prevent it from reaching the brain. (This is explained further in the "applications" section which follows.)

In combination with the sensory thresholds, sensory adaptation and selective attention show that what we experience as "reality" is only an edited and altered version of what's actually "out there." What you see may be what you get, but what you get isn't all there is!

Learning Check

1. Absolute thresholds (are constant/vary) from person to person.

2. A stimulus that causes discomfort or embarrassment may have to be viewed longer before it is perceived because of ______________ ______________.

3. JND stands for: ____________ ____________ ____________.

4. Sensory adaptation refers to an increase in sensory response that accompanies a constant or unchanging stimulus. T or F?

5. Selective attention refers to our ability to select what sensations we will receive. T or F?

6. Under no circumstance is vision subject to sensory adaptation. T or F?

Answers: **1.** vary **2.** perceptual defense **3.** just noticeable differences **4.** F **5.** T **6.** F

Resources Summary

We began this chapter by emphasizing the importance of sensation. *Sensory deprivation* studies indicate the brain ceases to function properly without adequate stimulation. The basic processes of *localization*, *sensory transduction*, *sensory adaptation*, *gating*, and *selective attention* emphasize that "reality" is changed each time sensory functions change. Each sensory system is highly specialized to convert a particular kind of physical energy into a code of nerve impulses. The five basic sensory systems are: the *somesthetic senses*, *smell (olfaction)*, *taste*, *hearing*, and *vision*. Of the five basic senses, vision is probably the most "important." Experiences generated by the eyes can be classified in terms of *hue*, *saturation*, and *brightness*. The eye itself is a marvel, combining *lens*, *iris*, and *retina* to code light into nerve impulses. Several facets of *color vision*, *rod* and *cone* function, and *visual acuity* were explored along with *color blindness* and *dark adaptation*. In each case, an understanding of vision has a number of practical applications. The topic of *psychophysics*, also covered in this chapter, helps us to understand the limits of our senses and how they vary in sensitivity.

Applications

Controlling Pain

The "resources" section of this chapter deals with useful information about several of the senses, particularly vision. Because so many applications have already been discussed, this will be a short section. Let's see if we can extend several of the ideas advanced in the chapter into an area of considerable interest: pain and its control.

In an individual with normal pain sensitivity, a number of psychological factors affect the amount of pain produced by a particular stimulus. The most important factors are: (1) *anxiety*, (2) *attention*, and (3) *control.*

Anxiety A consistent finding in studies of pain is that fear or high overall levels of anxiety increase pain (Barber, 1959). A dramatic reversal of this effect is the surprising insensitivity to pain displayed by soldiers wounded in battle. Being excused from further combat produces such relief that it leaves them insensitive to wounds that would agonize a civilian (Melzack, 1974).

Attention Pain, although it is an unusually persistent sensation, can be selectively "tuned out" (at least partially) just like any other sensation. Subjects in one experiment who were exposed to intense pain experienced the greatest pain relief when they were distracted by the task of viewing color slides and describing them aloud. They experienced the most pain when they paid careful attention to the pain stimulus and described their moment-to-moment reactions to it (Kanfer & Goldfoot, 1966). Distraction from a painful stimulus can take other forms. In another experiment it was found that thinking of pain as pleasurable (denying the pain) can also increase pain tolerance (Neufeld, 1970).

Control The more control one feels over a painful stimulus, the less pain experienced. For example, when subjects are allowed to terminate pain stimuli, to regulate them, or to administer them to themselves, pain is reduced (Staub et al., 1971).

Pain Relief

Question: How can these facts be applied?

In a sense they have already been applied to childbirth. "Natural" childbirth training, which emphasizes birth without drugs or painkillers, utilizes all three factors. In preparation for natural childbirth, the prospective mother learns in great detail what to expect at each stage of labor. This alleviates her fears and anxieties tremendously. During labor, she pays attention to important sensations indicating the progress of labor and adjusts her breathing accordingly. Her attention is directed to sensations other than pain. If she has learned a positive attitude toward all the sensations of the birth, pain takes on a more positive meaning.

Finally, because of her months of preparation and exercise and because of her active participation in the birth process, she feels *in control* of the situation.

Reduced anxiety, redirected attention, and added control can be applied to other painful circumstances. In any situation where pain can be anticipated (a trip to the doctor, dentist, and so on), lowered anxiety may be achieved by making sure that you are *fully informed.* Be sure that everything that will happen or could happen to you is explained, and fully discuss any fears you have. If you are physically tense, the use of relaxation exercises can help lower your level of arousal (relaxation techniques are described in detail in the Chapter 24 "applications" section. The desensitization procedure described in the same chapter may also help reduce anxiety).

Some dentists are equipped to help you shift attention away from pain. They use headphones which pipe a mixture of music and white noise to your ears. In other situations, shifting attention away from pain can be aided by focusing on some external object. Pick a tree outside a window, a design on the wall, or some other stimulus and examine it in great detail. Prior practice in meditation can be a tremendous aid to such attention shifts. (Meditation techniques are described in Chapter 6.)

Question: How can you increase control over a painful stimulus?

Practically speaking, the possibilities may be limited. You may be able to arrange a signal with a doctor or dentist that will give you control over whether a painful procedure will continue. A second possibility is more unusual. Ronald Melzack (mentioned earlier because his theory seems to explain how acupuncture alleviates pain) suggests that the sending of pain signals from the body to the spinal cord and brain involves passage through a series of "pain gates." These gates can be *closed* by stimulation of parts of the body other than the site of pain. Melzack believes that acupuncture stimulates large nerve fibers more than small fibers and causes the gates to be closed, thus blocking pain (Melzack, 1974).

Medical texts have long noted that intense surface stimulation of the skin can control pain from other sources. Physicians have found that a brief, mildly painful stimulus can relieve more severe pain. This effect, known as *counterirritation*, can be recognized in some of the oldest techniques used to control pain: applying ice packs, hot-water bottles, or mustard packs to other parts of the body (Melzack, 1974). This suggests a possibility for pain control that is based on increased control and counterirritation. If you pinch yourself, you can easily *create and endure* pain equal to that produced by many medical procedures (receiving an injection, having a tooth drilled, and so on). The pain doesn't seem too bad because you have control over it, and it is predictable. This fact might be used to *mask* one pain with a second painful stimulus that is under your control. For instance, if you are having a tooth filled, try pinching yourself, or digging a fingernail into a knuckle while the dentist is working. Focus your attention on the pain you are creating and increase its intensity anytime the dentist's work becomes more painful. This suggestion may not work for you, but casual observation suggests that it can be a useful technique for controlling pain in some circumstances. Generations of children have used it to take the edge off of a spanking.

Questions for Discussion

1. Is your brain sitting on a laboratory table somewhere? It is theoretically possible that your brain was donated to science some time ago. Let's say that it was preserved and recently reactivated and that a sophisticated computer is artificially generating patterns of nerve activity in the cortex by mimicking normal sensory messages in the nerves. These messages duplicate all of the sights, sounds, odors, and sensations of sitting and reading a book. If this were happening—right now—could you tell? Would you be able to discover you had no body? Defend your answer.

2. William James once said, "If a master surgeon were to cross the auditory and optic nerves, then we would hear lightning and see thunder." Can you explain what James meant?

3. Let's say that you would like to design a system that uses touch to convey "images" to a blind person. How would you proceed? What would be the advantages and disadvantages of using various body areas (hands, back, forehead, and so on)?

4. What changes would be likely to take place if the absolute thresholds for vision and hearing were changed so that we would see infrared and ultraviolet light and hear sounds up to 50,000 cycles per second? (Consider lighting systems, the design of stereo equipment, and so forth.)

5. In Zen Buddhism there is a familiar *koan*, or riddle, that says, "Last night I dreamt I was a butterfly. How do I know today that I am not a butterfly dreaming I am a man?" Can you relate this to the idea that we construct a version of reality out of the more basic world of physical energies surrounding us?

Suggestions for Further Reading

Case, J. *Sensory Mechanisms.* Macmillan, 1967.

Casey, K. L. "Pain: A Current View of Neural Mechanisms," *American Scientist*, vol. 61, March-April 1973.

Cornsweet, T. N. *Visual Perception.* Academic Press, 1970.

Geldard, R. F. *The Human Senses*, 2nd ed. Wiley, 1972.

Keller, H. *Story of My Life.* Airmont, 1970.

Mueller, C. G. *Sensory Psychology.* Prentice-Hall, 1965.

Senden, M. V. *Space and Sight.* Free Press, 1960.

5 Perception

Chapter Preview

Let There Be Light

What would it be like to have your vision restored after a lifetime of blindness? What would your first visual experience be like? Would you weep for joy at the wondrous world around you? In reality, a first look at the world can be disappointing. Usually nothing more than a blur is seen. A newly sighted person must learn *to identify objects, to read clocks, numbers, and letters, and to judge sizes and distances (Senden, 1960). Indeed, learning to "see" can be quite frustrating. Richard L. Gregory (1970) has described the experiences of Mr. S. B., a fifty-two-year-old cataract patient who had been blind since birth. After an operation restored his sight, Mr. S. B. had great difficulty learning to use his vision. For instance, for some time, Mr. S. B. could only judge distances in situations already familiar to him. One day he was found crawling out of the window of his hospital room. He wanted to go out to get a closer look at the automobile traffic on the street. His curiosity was understandable, but he had to be restrained. His room was on the fourth floor (Gregory, 1970).*

Eventually Mr. S. B. became so disillusioned by the difficulties of "seeing" that he began to spend his days sitting in complete darkness. He found darkness more comfortable than the flood of information pouring in through his eyes.

Sensory systems "boil down" information from the environment to bare essentials. Were it not for this, your brain would be confronted with so much information that, like Mr. S. B., you would have trouble using it. But getting information to the brain is not enough. What arrives is still a confusing and jumbled mass of sensations. Before information can be put in use, it must be organized. The process of assembling sensations into a usable mental representation of the world is called perception.

Perception is so automatic that we are rarely aware of it. To appreciate more fully this marvelous process, try to pretend that you are perceiving the world as Mr. S. B. did—for the first time.

Resources

Perceptual Constancies—Taming an Unruly World

Question: How could Mr. S. B. try to crawl out of a fourth-story window? Couldn't he at least tell distance from the size of the cars?

No, because using the size of an object to judge distance requires familiarity with the usual size of the object. If you hold your left hand a few inches in front of your eyes and your right hand at arm's length, the image made by your right hand is about half the size of your left. Still, because of the countless times you have viewed your hands from different distances, you know your right hand has not shrunk. Therefore, it must be more distant. This is called *size constancy*: The perceived size of an object remains the same even though the size of its retinal image changes.

Size constancy is greatly affected by past experience. For example, Turnbull (1961) tells of the time he brought a Pygmy from the dense rain forests of the Congo to the vast African plains. The Pygmy had no past experience with seeing objects at great distance. Hence, the first time he saw a herd of buffalo in the distance, he thought they were a swarm of insects. When he was told that they were buffalo he was insulted. "Do you think that I am ignorant?" he asked. Imagine his confusion when he was then driven toward the animals. He concluded that witchcraft was being used to fool him because the "insects" seemed to grow into buffalo before his eyes. Perhaps you have also experienced the failure of size constancy in unfamiliar situations. When viewed from an airplane, cars, houses, and people no longer seem normal in size and tend to take on a "cardboard-figure" quality.

A second important constancy is *shape constancy.* Shape constancy can be demonstrated by looking at this page in your book from directly overhead and then from an angle. Obviously, the page is rectangular, but most of the time the image actually reaching your eye is distorted. In spite of this, there is no tendency for you to assume the book changes shape when the image does.

In physical terms, brightness refers to how much light an object reflects. Under changing lighting conditions the same object reflects different total amounts of light. But because of *brightness constancy*, the psychological brightness of an object does not seem to change. In bright sunlight a white shirt reflects many times more light than it does in a dimly lit room, yet it looks as bright indoors as it did outside. This is because both indoors and out it reflects a larger *proportion* of light than surrounding objects.

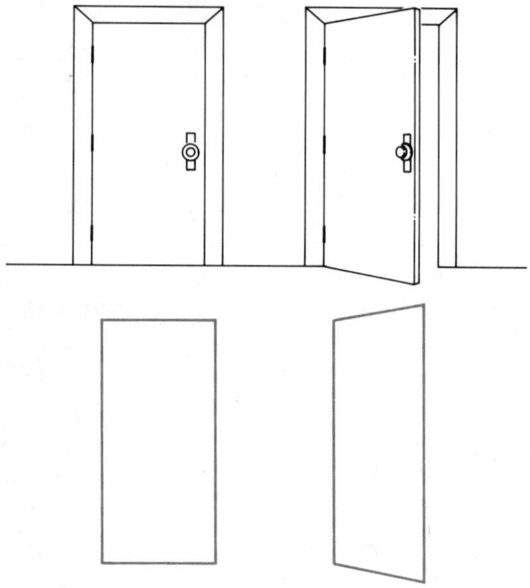

Fig. 5-1 Shape constancy. When the door is open, its image actually forms a trapezoid. It is perceived as a rectangle anyway.

To summarize, the energy patterns reaching our senses are constantly changing even when they come from the same object. Size, shape, and brightness constancy rescue us from a potentially confusing world in which objects would seem to shrink and grow, change shape as if they were made of rubber, and light up or fade like neon lamps. It is no coincidence that this describes the perceptions of people who have been subjected to sensory deprivation, have recently had their sight restored, or have taken drugs like LSD or mescaline. For different reasons, each of these interrupts normal perceptual constancy.

Depth Perception—What If the World Were Flat?

Before Columbus, many people considered the world flat. They were referring, of course, to the shape of the earth. But what if the visual world were flat? *Depth perception* is the ability to see three-dimensional space and to accurately estimate distances. Without depth perception you would be unable to successfully drive a car or ride a bicycle, play catch, shoot baskets, thread a needle, or simply navigate around a room. The world would look like a flat surface.

Question: Mr. S. B. had trouble with depth perception after his sight was restored. Does this mean that depth perception is learned?

Depth perception is partially learned and partially innate. The existence of a basic level of depth perception in human infants comes from work with the *visual cliff* (see Fig. 5-2). The visual cliff is basically a table covered with plate glass. One half has a sheet of patterned material placed against the underside of the glass. The other half of the glass has a piece of the same material placed several feet below. This makes the glass look like a tabletop on one side and a cliff or drop-off on the other. Infants aged from six to fourteen months were placed in the middle of the visual cliff. They had a choice of crawling to the "shallow" side or the "deep" side. (The glass prevented them from falling if they chose the deep side.) The majority of children chose the shallow side, refusing the deep side even when their mother tried to call them toward it. In other experiments baby chicks, goats, lambs, kittens, and rats were tested with similar results (Gibson & Walk, 1960). Thus, infants and newborn animals show evidence of depth perception.

Question: What factors allow us to see depth?

A number of *depth cues* combine to produce the experience of three-dimensional space.

Bodily Cues As their name implies, bodily cues for depth are "built into" an organism's visual system. One such cue is *accommodation.* The lens in

Fig. 5-2 Human infants and newborn animals refuse to go over the edge of the visual cliff. (Photo by Albert Fenn. Time-Life Picture Agency © Time, Inc.)

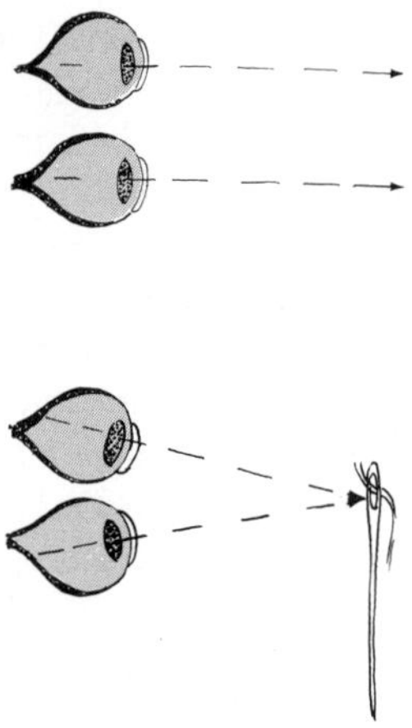

Fig. 5-3 The eyes must converge or turn in toward the nose to focus close objects.

each eye must *bend* more to focus objects close to the eye than at a distance. Sensations coming from the muscles which support the lens and alter its shape are channeled back to the brain. Differences in these sensations help us judge distances that fall within about 4 feet of the eye. Beyond 4 feet, accommodation contributes little to depth perception. Obviously, accommodation is more important to a watchmaker and a person trying to thread a needle than it would be to a basketball player or an airline pilot.

To find out what accommodation feels like, try this demonstration:

> Close your left eye. Hold the tip of a finger about 1 foot in front of your right eye. Bring the tip of your finger into sharp focus, then begin to move your finger in toward your eye, keeping it in focus until it is 1 or 2 inches from your eye. When your finger gets close, you should find that you will have to work to keep it in focus, and you will note a definite increase in tension within your eye.

A second bodily cue for depth is *convergence.* When you look at a distant object, the lines of vision from your eyes are parallel. When you look at something 50 feet or less in distance, your eyes must converge (turn in) to focus the object (see Fig. 5-3).

You are probably not aware of it, but whenever you estimate a distance under 50 feet (as when you approach a stop sign, play catch, toss horseshoes, and so forth), you are using convergence. Once again, information is fed to the brain by muscle sensations because convergence is controlled by a group of muscles attached to the eyeball. You can feel convergence by exaggerating it:

> Hold a finger at eye level 2 feet in front of your nose. Focus both eyes on the fingertip and slowly bring your finger toward your face. You will reach a point just before your eyes cross when convergence is so extreme that you can feel sensations from the muscles which control eye movement.

The most important source of depth perception is *retinal disparity.* Retinal disparity is based upon the simple fact that the eyes are about 2½ inches apart. Because of this, each eye receives a slightly different view of the world. When the resulting two images are *fused* into one overall visual image, a powerful sensation of depth occurs. Retinal disparity can be used to produce 3-D movies by filming with two cameras separated by several inches. The resulting images are simultaneously projected on a screen. The audience then wears glasses that filter out one of the images to each eye. Since each eye gets a separate image, realistic depth results when the images are fused. Try this demonstration of retinal disparity and fusion:

> Roll a piece of paper into a tube. Close your left eye. Hold the tube to your right eye like a telescope. Look through the tube at some object in the distance. Place your left hand against the tube halfway down its length and in front of your left eye. Now open your left eye. You should see a "hole" in your hand. You couldn't expect a professional photographer to do a better job of blending the two images than your visual system does automatically.

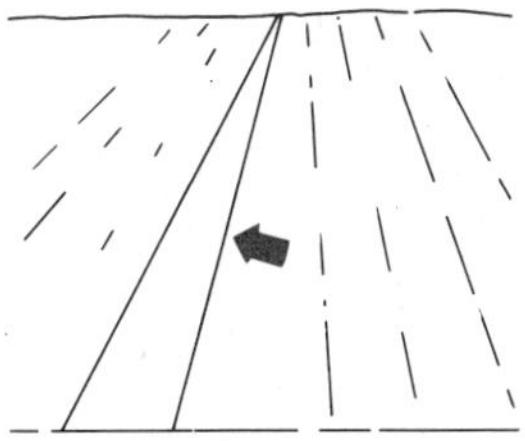

Fig. 5-4 Linear perspective.

Fig. 5-5 Relative size.

Fig. 5-6 Light and shadow.

Fig. 5-7 Overlap.

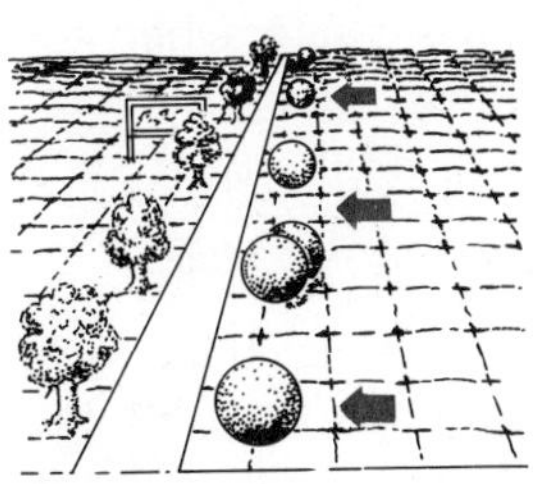

Fig. 5-8 Texture gradients.

Pictorial Cues for Depth—Three Dimensions from Two

Question: Can a person with one eye perceive depth?

Accommodation is a *monocular* depth cue (meaning it will work with one eye). Convergence and retinal disparity are *binocular* (two-eye) depth cues. A one-eyed person lacks convergence and retinal disparity, and accommodation is only helpful for judging small distances. This means that a person with only one eye will have restricted depth perception. Try driving a car or riding a bicycle some time with one eye closed. You will find yourself braking too soon or too late, and you will have difficulty estimating your speed. In spite of this, you will be able to drive, although with greater difficulty than usual. A person with one eye can even successfully land an airplane—a task strongly dependent on depth perception.

Question: How is it possible to see depth with one eye?

A good movie, painting, or photograph can create convincing sensations of depth by combining numerous *pictorial depth cues.* Pictorial cues will work on a flat surface to reproduce depth. They can also be used effectively by a one-eyed individual to accurately gauge depth.

Pictorial Depth Cues

1. *Linear perspective.* This refers to the apparent convergence of parallel lines in the environment. If you stand between two railroad tracks, they appear to come together in the distance. Since you know they are parallel, this implies great depth (see Fig. 5-4).
2. *Relative size.* If an artist wishes to depict two objects of the same size at different distances, he makes the more distant object smaller (see Fig. 5-5).
3. *Light and shadow.* Most objects in the environment are lighted in such a way as to create definite patterns of light and shadow. Appropriate distribution of light and shadow can give a two-dimensional design a three-dimensional feeling (see Fig. 5-6).
4. *Overlap.* Overlap (also known as interposition) describes a depth cue caused by one object partially blocking the view of another. Hold your hands up and have a friend try to tell from across the room which is nearer. Relative size will give him the answer if the difference between the two hands is large. But if one is only slightly closer to him than the other, he may have difficulty—until you slide one hand in front of the other. Overlap then removes any doubt (see Fig. 5-7).
5. *Texture gradients.* Changes in texture also contribute to depth perception. If you are standing in the middle of a cobblestone street, the street looks coarse near your feet, but the texture of the stones gets smaller and finer as you look off into the distance (see Fig. 5-8).
6. *Aerial perspective.* Smog, fog, dust, and haze add to the apparent depth of an object. Objects seen at great distance tend to be a hazy,

washed-out color, and lacking in detail due to aerial perspective. This is true even in clear air but is increasingly the case in our industrialized society. As a matter of fact, aerial haze is often most noticeable when it is missing. If you have traveled the wide open spaces of states like Colorado or Wyoming, you may have seen mountain ranges that looked only a few miles away, and then were shocked to find that you were actually viewing them through 50 miles of crystal-clear air.

7. *Relative motion.* Relative motion, also known as *motion parallax*, is one of the more important depth cues. When all else fails, motion parallax alone is enough to indicate depth in most situations. Relative motion can be seen by looking out a window and moving your head from side to side. You will notice that objects near you appear to move a sizable distance as your head moves. Trees, houses, and telephone poles at a greater distance appear to move slightly in relation to the background, and distant objects like hills, mountains, or clouds don't seem to move at all. Motion parallax accounts for much of the apparent depth of a good movie or animated cartoon. As a movie camera pans past objects, their relative motion is captured and transferred to the screen, duplicating what you would see if you were walking through the scene yourself. People who have lost vision in one eye depend heavily on motion parallax to enhance their remaining depth perception and often adopt more frequent head and eye movements to maximize this cue.

The Moon Illusion—Depth Cues in Action

Question: *How do the depth perception cues relate to daily experience?*

Like the bodily depth cues, you constantly use the pictorial cues to gauge depth and judge distances. This can be seen through an intriguing illusion. When the moon is on the horizon, it tends to look as large as a silver dollar. When it is directly overhead, it looks like a dime, very much smaller than it did earlier the same evening. Contrary to what some people believe, the moon's image is not magnified. If you measure the diameter of the image when it is on the horizon and measure it again overhead, you will find that it has not changed size. But the moon *looks* larger when it's low in the sky. This is because the *apparent distance* of the moon is greater when it is on the horizon and is seen behind houses, trees, telephone poles, foothills, and mountains.

Question: *But if it looks farther away shouldn't it also look smaller?*

Linear perspective, relative size, overlap, texture, aerial haze, and motion parallax all combine to make the moon appear more distant on the horizon. Overhead, all of these cues for distance are missing. Now, if one object is more distant than another but still makes the same size image as the nearer object, then the distant object must be larger. Since the moon makes the same size image on the horizon but seems farther away than when it is overhead, you compensate by perceiving it as larger on the horizon (Rock, 1962). You can prove this to yourself by removing the normal depth cues present when you look at a "harvest moon." Try looking at the moon through a rolled-up paper tube, or make your hands into a "telescope" and look at the next large moon you see. It will immediately "shrink" when viewed this way.

Learning Check

1. See if you can tell in your own words what the following terms refer to.

a. Size constancy ______________________________

____

b. Brightness constancy ______________________________

____

c. Depth perception ______________________________

____

2. List *at least* four pictorial depth cues: ______________________________

____

____

Answers: **1a.** The perceived size of an object remains the same even though the size of its retinal image changes. **1b.** Perception of brightness as the same even though the amount of light reaching the retina stays the same. **1c.** The ability to see three-dimensional spaces and accurately estimate distances. **2.** linear perspective, relative size, light and shadow, overlap, texture gradients, aerial perspective, relative motion

Perceptual Grouping—Bringing Order to Chaos

William James said that "to the infant the world is just a big, blooming, buzzing confusion." All infants are faced with the problem of making sense out of their perceptions. Gradually they become organized and perceptual constancies simplify their world.

Question: How are sensations organized?

The simplest organization is to group some sensations into an object or "thing" that stands out against some plainer background. *Figure-ground* organization is probably unlearned, since it is the first perceptual ability to emerge when a cataract patient regains sight (Hebb, 1949). To get a better idea of what figure-ground perception means, see Fig. 5-9. This is a reversible figure-ground design. You can see either a wine glass figure on a dark background or two human profiles on a white background.

Sensations other than vision also show figure-ground organization. For example, you may hear your own name as a figure when it is spoken against a background of conversation in a crowded room. Organization in hearing can even be reversible. Demonstrate this to yourself by quickly repeating the word "zero" aloud. You will hear the organization shift from "zero" to "rosey" and then back again. This exercise illustrates one of the principal problems involved in learning to understand a spoken foreign language.

Question: What causes sensations to become organized into a "figure"?

Even if you were looking at the world for the first time, we would expect the following factors to bring some order to your perceptions (refer to Fig. 5-10).

1. *Nearness.* Stimuli that are near each other tend to be grouped together (see Fig. 5-10*a*).
2. *Similarity.* "Birds of a feather flock together," and stimuli that are similar in size, shape, color, or form tend to be grouped together (see Fig. 5-10*b*).
3. *Continuation*, or continuity. Perceptions tend toward simplicity and continuity. In Fig. 5-10*c* it is easier to visualize a wavy line on a squared-off line than it is to see a complex row of shapes.

Fig. 5-9 A reversible figure-ground design. Do you see two faces in profile or a wine glass?

(a) Principle of nearness. Notice how differently a group of six can be perceptually organized, depending upon their spacing.

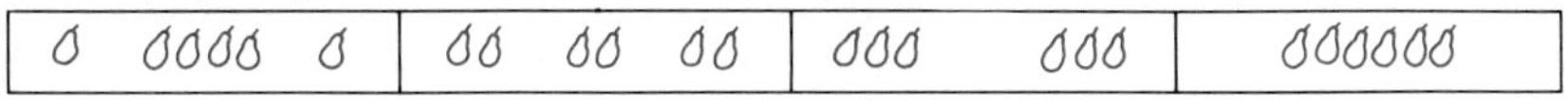

(b) Principle of similarity. In these examples, organization depends on similarity of *form.*

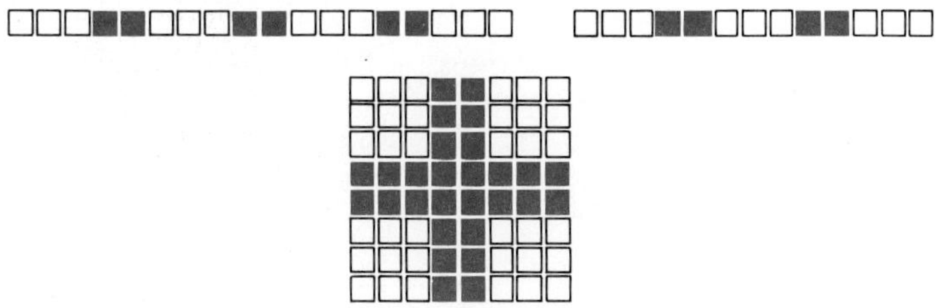

Similarity and nearness can be combined to produce new organization.

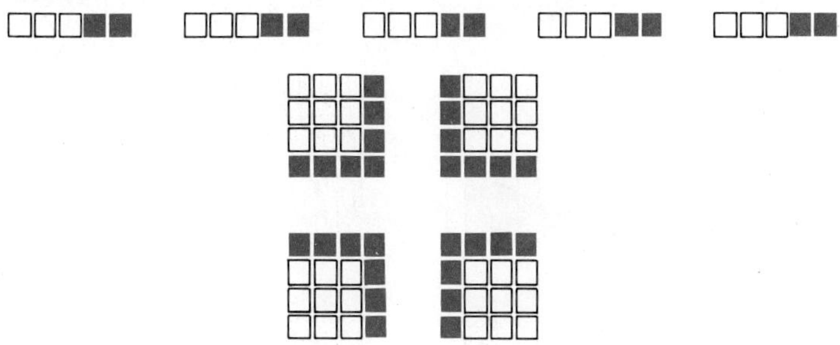

(c) Principle of continuity.

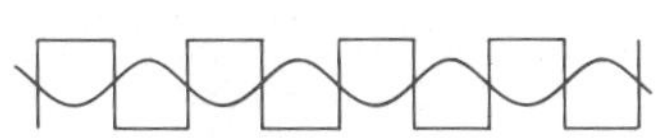

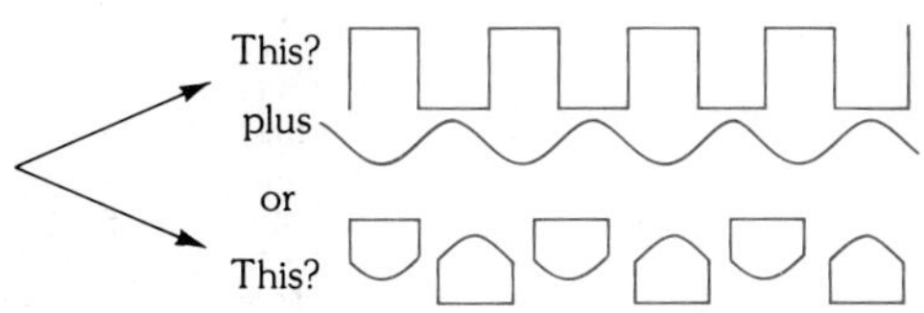

(d) Principle of closure.

Another example of closure

Fig. 5-10 Perceptual grouping illustrations.

4. *Closure.* Closure refers to the tendency to *complete* a shape so that it has a consistent overall form. Each of the shapes in Fig. 5-10*d* has one or more "gaps," yet each is perceived as a circle. The principles of perceptual organization were first explored by gestalt psychologists as a means of explaining why the "whole is not equal to the sum of its parts."

Organization of perceptions is not always simple or automatic. *Ambiguous* stimuli (stimuli that have no definite shape) allow more than one organization. A child staring at clouds may find dozens of ways to organize them into fanciful shapes and scenes. Even clearly defined stimuli may permit more than one interpretation. If you stare at Necker's cube (Fig. 5-11), you will see it change position in space.

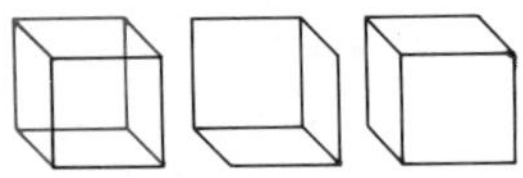

Fig. 5-11 The Necker cube. The design on the left can be seen as a three-dimensional cube projecting either up or down (like the cubes on the right). Staring at the cube changes its apparent position.

Figure 5-12 is another design with more than one possible organization.

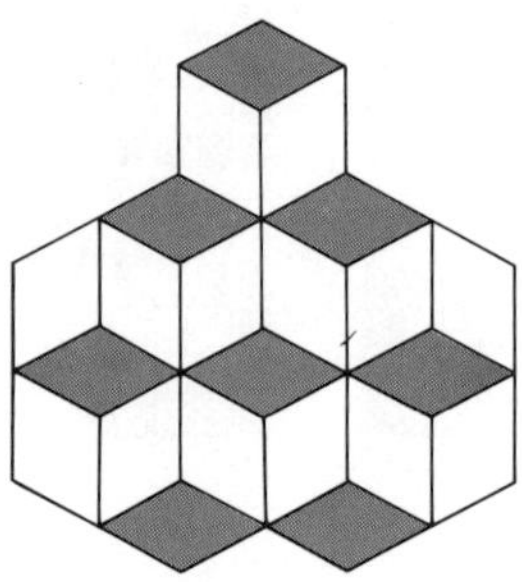

Fig. 5-12 How many blocks—six or seven?

Some designs defy consistent organization altogether. The "three-pronged widget" (Fig. 5-13) is one such "impossible" figure.

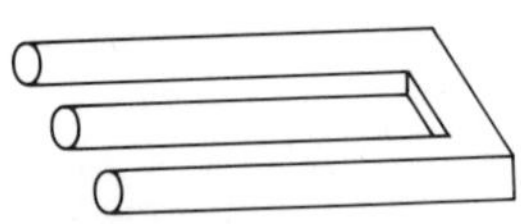

Fig. 5-13 An impossible figure—the "three-pronged widget."

Perceptual Habits—What If the World Were Upside Down?

The powerful role that learning and past experience play in perception can be seen in many ways. Stop for a moment and read aloud the short phrase in the triangles in Fig. 5-14.

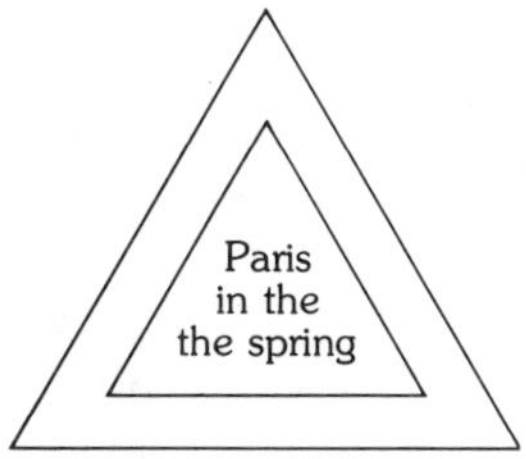

Fig. 5-14

Did you read "Paris in the Spring"? If so, look again. The word "the" appears twice in the phrase. Because of past experience with the English language, the repeated word is frequently overlooked. Language experience also plays a role in organization of the design pictured in Fig. 5-15.

Perceptual habits may become so ingrained that they lead us to distort or misperceive a stimulus. Magicians make use of perceptual habits when they use sleight of hand to distract an observer while performing a trick. Another kind of "magic" is related to consistency in the environment. It is usually safe to assume that the overall shape of a room is approximately that of a simple box. This need not be true, however. A decidedly lopsided room can be made to appear square by carefully distorting the proportions of the walls, floor, ceiling, and windows. One such room, called an *Ames room* after the man who designed it, presents a unique problem for the perceptual habits and organization of an observer.

Since the left corner of the Ames room is farther from a viewer than the right, a person standing in that corner looks very small whereas one standing in the right corner looks very large (see Fig. 5-16). If a person walks from the left corner of the room to the right, an observer is faced with maintaining shape constancy by perceiving the room as square or maintaining size constancy by refusing to see the person "grow." Most people choose shape constancy and see people "shrink" and "grow" before their eyes.

Question: To what extent do habits affect perception? Could an adult adapt to a completely new perceptual world?

Inverted Vision An answer to this question is offered by experiments in which people have worn lenses that invert visual images. In one such experiment a subject donned goggles that turned the world upside down and reversed objects from right to left. At first, even the simplest tasks—walking, eating, and so forth—became incredibly difficult. Imagine trying to reach for a door handle and watching your hand shoot off in the wrong direction.

Fig. 5-15 What do you see here?

Fig. 5-16 The Ames room. When the room is seen from the front, it looks normal. The diagram reveals its actual shape and shows why people appear to get bigger as they cross the room. (Photos © Baron Wolman.)

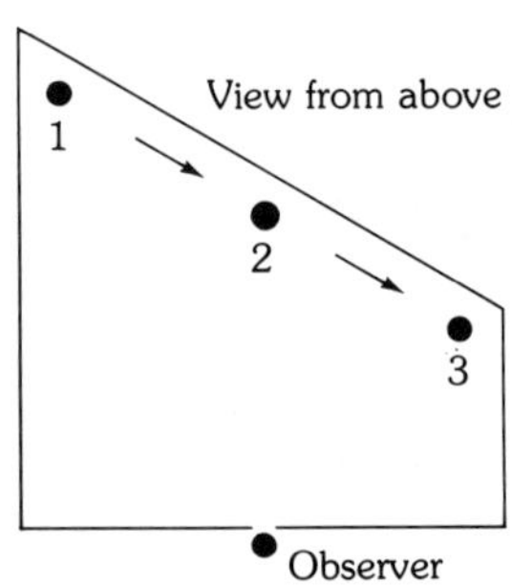

Subjects also reported that head movements seemed to make the world swing violently through space, causing severe headaches and nausea. Yet, incredible as it may seem, subjects eventually adapted completely to inverted vision. They could perform most activities and even began to consider their upside-down world "normal." So complete was their adaptation that they became completely disoriented when the goggles were removed, and for a time everything seemed upside down and backward again (Stratton, 1897). In more recent experiments subjects wearing inverting goggles have shown themselves capable of riding a bicycle, driving a car, and even flying an airplane after a few weeks of experience (Kohler, 1962). Such incredible perceptual adaptability seems to be related to superior human learning abilities. In experiments in which the eyes of goldfish have been surgically turned upside down, the fish swim in circles and rarely adapt (Sperry, 1956).

Categories Have you ever seen playing cards with a *red* ace of spades or a *black* four of hearts? Most of us have only had experience with cards on which spades and clubs are black, and hearts and diamonds, red. Psychologist Jerome Bruner used a *tachistoscope* (a device for projecting pictures for very short periods) to flash pictures of cards on a screen. He found that subjects misperceived cards that did not fit their expectations. For instance, a *red* six of spades would be misperceived as a normal six of hearts (Bruner & Postman, 1949). Bruner believes that perceptual learning builds up a set of *categories*. Experiences are then "sorted" into categories somewhat as if they were slots or "pigeonholes." Since subjects had no category for a red six of spades, they saw it as a six of hearts.

The categories used to organize perceptions are greatly affected by language. Benjamin Whorf (1940) has proposed that the words available to us in our language determine what we can perceive and remember. To an English-speaking person "rice" is simply rice. By contrast the Hanunoó people of the Philippine islands have names for ninety-two varieties of rice. This allows them to "see" differences in rice that would be difficult for us to detect or remember.

Question: But what difference does it make what you call something?

The effect of labels on perception can be seen very clearly in a study in which subjects were briefly shown a series of ambiguous figures (see Fig. 5-17). Each figure was given one of two labels. For half the subjects, the figures were described with the words in list I. Other subjects were given words in list II to describe the same figures. Later, subjects were asked to draw what they had seen. Compare their reproductions, and you will see that labels greatly affected what subjects "saw" and remembered.

Perceptual habits are responsible for a number of perceptual illusions. Size and shape constancy, habitual eye movements, continuity, and past experience combine in various ways to produce the illusions in Fig. 5-18.

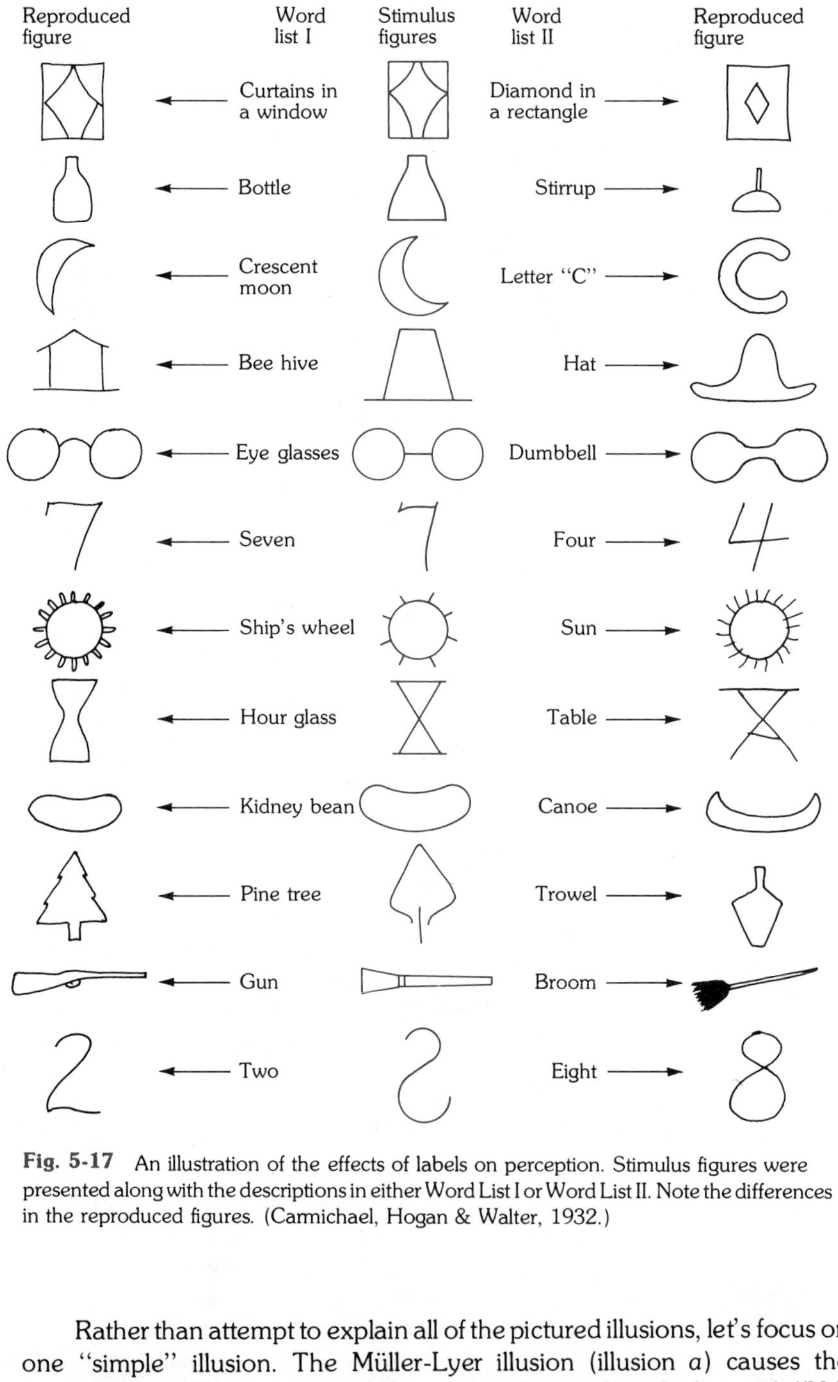

Fig. 5-17 An illustration of the effects of labels on perception. Stimulus figures were presented along with the descriptions in either Word List I or Word List II. Note the differences in the reproduced figures. (Carmichael, Hogan & Walter, 1932.)

Rather than attempt to explain all of the pictured illusions, let's focus on one "simple" illusion. The Müller-Lyer illusion (illusion *a*) causes the horizontal line with "arrowheads" to appear shorter than the line with "Vs" on each end. A quick measurement will show that they are the same length. How can we explain this illusion? Evidence suggests that it is based upon a

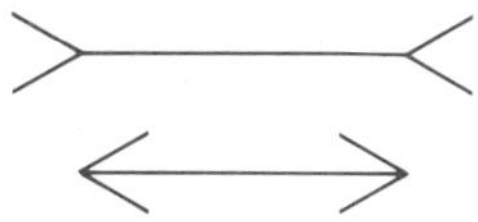

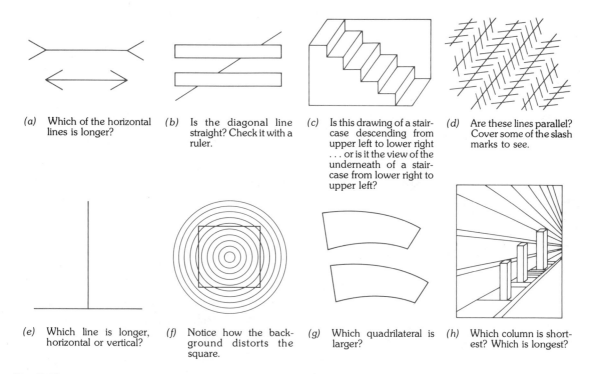

(a) Which of the horizontal lines is longer?

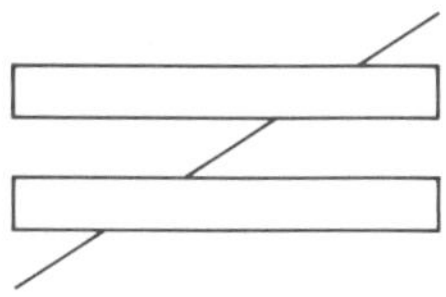

(b) Is the diagonal line straight? Check it with a ruler.

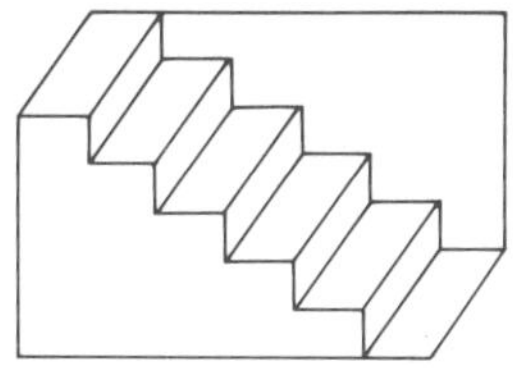

(c) Is this drawing of a staircase descending from upper left to lower right . . . or is it the view of the underneath of a staircase from lower right to upper left?

(d) Are these lines parallel? Cover some of the slash marks to see.

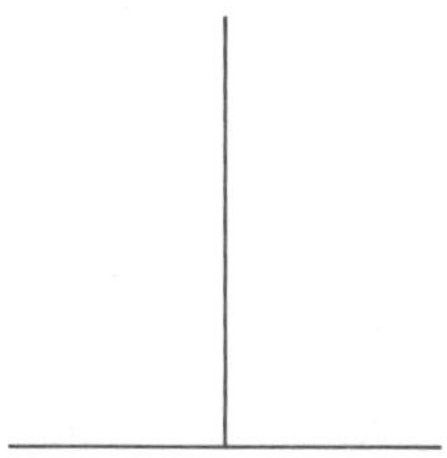

(e) Which line is longer, horizontal or vertical?

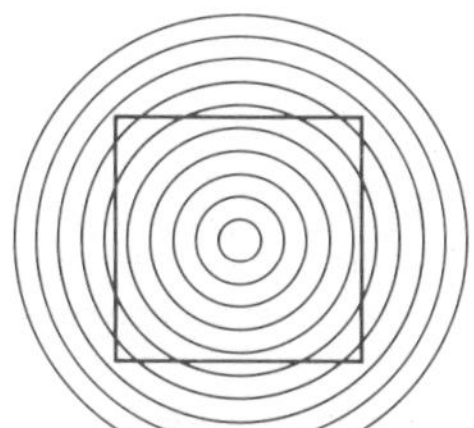

(f) Notice how the background distorts the square.

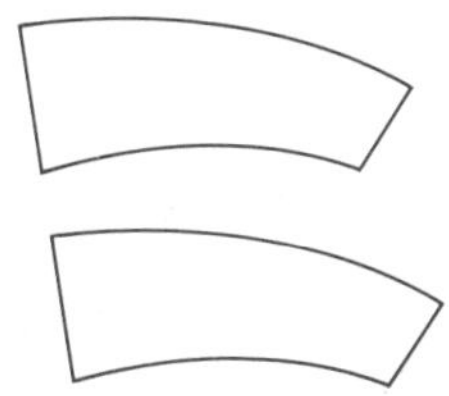

(g) Which quadrilateral is larger?

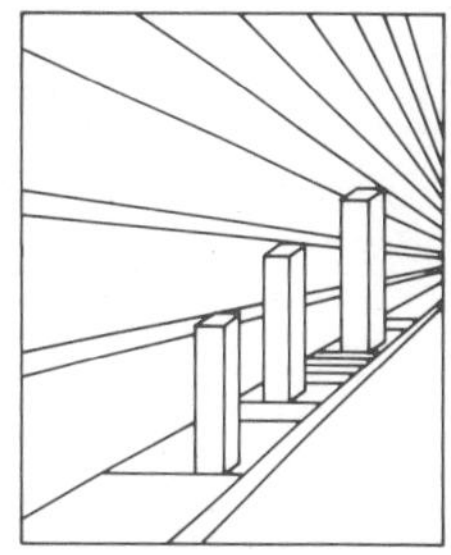

(h) Which column is shortest? Which is longest?

Fig. 5-18 Some interesting perceptual illusions.

lifetime of experience with the edges and corners of rooms and buildings. Richard Gregory (1970) believes you see the horizontal line with the "Vs" as if it were the corner of a room viewed from inside. (See illustration.) The line with "arrowheads," on the other hand, suggests the corner of a room or building seen from outside (see Fig. 5-19).

Earlier, in explaining the moon illusion, we said that if two objects make the same-size image but one is more distant than the other, the more distant object must be larger. (This is formally known as *size-distance invariance.*) Thus, if the V-tipped line looks farther away than the arrowhead-tipped line, you must compensate by seeing the V-tipped line as larger. This explanation of the Müller-Lyer illusion presumes that you have had years of experience with straight lines, sharp edges, and corners—a pretty safe assumption in our culture.

Question: Is there any way to prove that past experience causes this illusion?

If we could test someone who saw only curves and wavy lines as a child, we would know if experience with a "square" culture is important. Fortunately, in South Africa there is a tribe of people, the Zulus, who live in a "round" culture. In his daily life a Zulu rarely encounters a straight line:

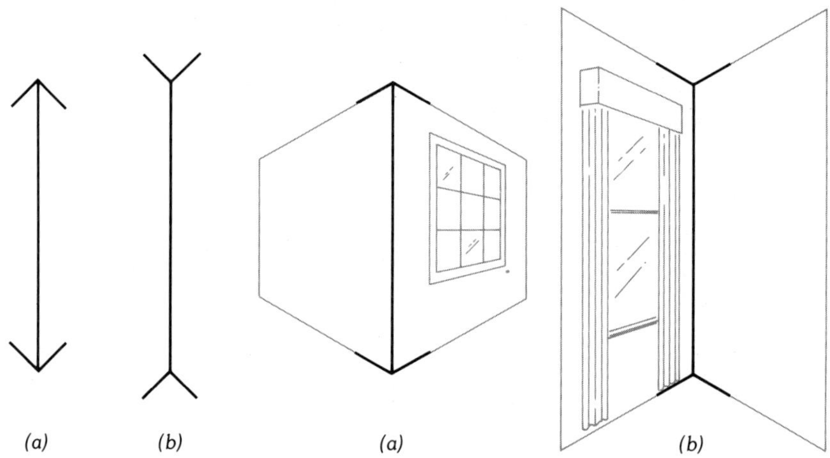

Fig. 5-19 Why does line *(b)* in the Müller-Lyer illusion look longer than line *(a)*? Probably because it looks more like a distant corner than a nearer one. Since the vertical lines form images of the same length, the more "distant" line must be perceived as larger.

Huts are shaped like rounded mounds and arranged in a circle, fields are plowed in curved lines, tools and toys lack straight edges, and there are no straight roads, square buildings, or edges.

Question: *What happens if a Zulu looks at the Müller-Lyer design?*

The typical Zulu does not experience the illusion. At most, he sees V-tipped lines as *slightly* longer than the other. This confirms the importance of past experience and perceptual habits in determining our view of the world.

Learning Check

1. Perceptual habits may become so ingrained that they lead us to distort or misperceive a stimulus. T or F?

2. Human ability to adapt to incredible perceptual changes is superior to other animals'. T or F?

3. Perceptual habits are responsible for a number of perceptual illusions. T or F?

4. "Size-distance invariance" refers to two objects making the same-size image when the distant object is larger. T or F?

Answers: 1. T 2. T 3. T 4. T

Adaptation Level—Medium Is the Message

Another factor affecting perception is the *context* in which a stimulus is judged. This fact hardly needs documentation. A man 6 feet in height will look "tall" when surrounded by individuals of average height and "short"

Fig. 5-20 Are the center dots in both figures the same?

among a group of professional basketball players. In Fig. 5-20, the center circle is the same size in both designs, but, like the man in different company, the circle takes on a different apparent size depending on one's frame of reference. The importance of context is also shown by Fig. 5-21. What do you see in the middle? If you read across, context causes it to be organized as a 13. Reading down makes it a B. Context may be thought of as a *frame of reference* or set of standards to which a stimulus is related.

If you were asked to lift a 10-pound weight, would you label it "light," "medium," or "heavy"? The answer to this question depends on what Harry Helson (1964) calls your *adaptation level.* This is your own personal "medium point" or frame of reference. If most of the weights you lift in day-to-day life *average* around 10 pounds, you will call a 10-pound weight "medium." If you are a watchmaker and spend your days lifting tiny watch parts, you will probably call a 10-pound weight "heavy." If you work as a furniture mover, your adaptation level will exceed 10 pounds, and you will call a 10-pound weight "light."

An indication of how broadly one's frame of reference affects judgments can be found in a study that asked people: "What is middle age?" A group of ten-year-olds said that "middle age" is thirty-six. Adults in their early twenties set "middle age" at forty-two, and a group of seventy-year-olds said fifty-two (Rethlingshafer & Hinckley, 1963)! Which is closest to your adaptation level?

Motives and Perception—May I Have Your . . . Attention!

You are being bombarded by sights, sounds, odors, tastes, and tactile sensations. Which are you aware of? The first stage of perception is *attention*—selection of incoming messages.

Very *intense* stimuli are attention getting. Stimuli that are brighter, louder, or larger tend to capture attention: A gunshot in a library would be hard to ignore. Big bright cars probably get more tickets than small dull ones. Raquel Welch has made a career out of the first principle of attention.

Repetitious stimuli, *repetitious stimuli*, *repetitious stimuli*, *repetitious stimuli*, *repetitious stimuli*, *repetitious stimuli* are also attention getting. A dripping faucet at night makes little noise by normal standards, but because of repetition it may become as attention getting as a single sound many times louder.

ATTENTION IS ALSO FREQUENTLY RELATED TO *contrast* OR *change* IN STIMULATION. Change is perhaps the most basic source of attention. We quickly *habituate* (respond less) to an unchanging stimulus. When you buy a new record album, it holds your attention all the way through, but as it becomes "old," a whole side may play without your really hearing it. Perhaps you have also noticed that you habituate to scenery along a familiar drive to work or to school. Only when a house is painted, a tree removed, or a billboard changed is attention aroused again.

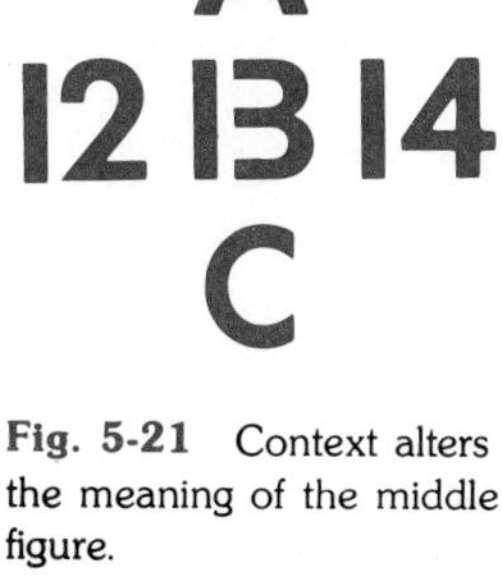

Fig. 5-21 Context alters the meaning of the middle figure.

Motives also play a role in directing attention. If you are riding in a car and are hungry, you will notice restaurants and billboards picturing food. If you are running low on gas, your attention will shift to gas stations. Advertisers, of course, know that their pitch will be more effective if it gets your attention. Ads are therefore loud, repetitious, and intentionally irritating. They are also designed to take advantage of two motives that are widespread in our society: *anxiety* and *sex*. Everything from mouth wash to automobile tires is merchandised using sex as a source of attention. It is difficult to ignore the double meaning underlying a stewardess seductively saying on national TV, "Hi, I'm Cheryl. Fly me!," or a man saying, "When I'm in the back seat with a chick, I just flick my Bic" (lighter). Many ads combine sex with anxiety. Mouth wash, deodorant, soaps, toothpaste, and countless other articles are pushed in ads that play on desires to be attractive or have "sex appeal" and to avoid embarrassment.

In addition to directing attention, motives may alter what is perceived:

> Ten-year-old children were tested with a device consisting of a knob that controlled the size of a spot of light projected on a screen. The children first looked at coins of different sizes and then adjusted the light until they thought it matched the size of the coin. All children over-estimated the size of the coins, but *poor* children *over-estimated* their size more than rich children (Bruner & Goodman, 1947).

Here is another example of motives affecting perceptions:

> Students from Dartmouth and Princeton colleges watched films of a rough game in which a popular Princeton player was injured. Princeton students saw the game as "rough and dirty" and 90% believed the other side started the rough play. Dartmouth students agreed that the game was rough but saw both sides as equally to blame. Princeton students believed the other team had committed twice as many penalties as their own team. Dartmouth students saw both teams as guilty of an equal number of penalties (Hastorf & Cantril, 1954).

Perceptual Expectancies—On Your Mark, Get Set

Question: What is a perceptual expectancy?

A runner in the starting blocks at a track meet is *set* to respond in a certain way. In perception, past experience, motives, context, or suggestion may create a *perceptual expectancy* that sets you to perceive in a certain way. If a car backfires, runners at a track meet may "jump the gun." As a matter of fact, we all frequently "jump the gun" when perceiving. We respond according to perceptual set by seeing what we expect to see. For example, let's say you are driving across the desert. You are very low on gas. Finally you see a sign approaching. On it are the words "FUEL AHEAD." You relax knowing you will not be stranded. But as you draw nearer, the words on the sign become "FOOD AHEAD." Most people have had similar experiences in which expectations altered their perceptions. To observe perceptual expectancies firsthand, perform the experiment described in Fig. 5-22.

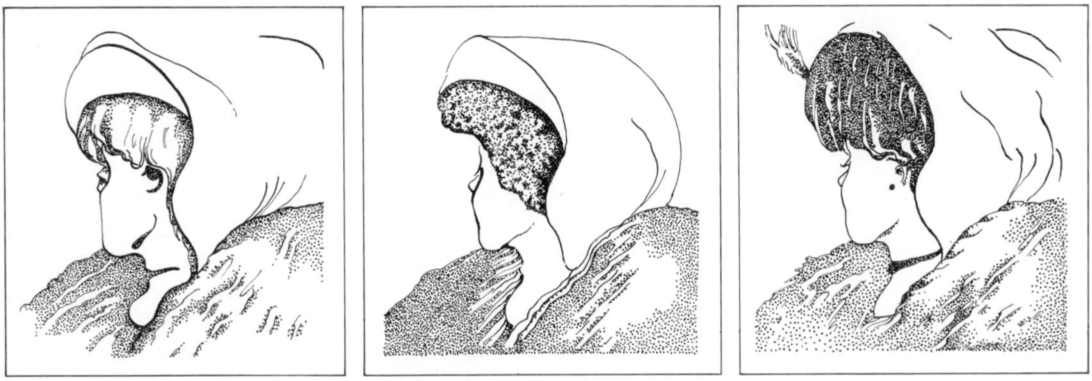

View I View II View III

Fig. 5-22 "Young woman/old woman" illustrations. As an interesting demonstration of perceptual expectancy, show some of your friends View I and some View II (cover all other views). Next show your friends View III and ask them what they see. Those who saw View I should see the old woman in View III; those who saw View II should see the young woman in View III. Can you see both? (After Leeper, 1935.)

Many perceptual expectancies are created by *suggestion*. This is especially true when one is perceiving other people. For example, a psychology professor once arranged an experiment in which a guest lecturer taught his class. Half the students in the class were given a page of notes that described the lecturer as a "rather *cold* person, industrious, critical, practical, and determined." The other students received notes describing him as a "rather *warm* person, industrious, critical, practical, and determined" (Kelley, 1950; italics added). Students who received the "cold" description perceived the lecturer as unhappy and irritable and didn't volunteer in class discussion. Those who got the "warm" description saw the lecturer as happy and good-natured, and they actively took part in discussion with him. Perhaps you have had a similar experience. If a friend introduces you to a person he has always described as "a little shy," "kind of wild," or "superfriendly," your first impressions of that person will probably be influenced by what you have been led to expect.

Resources Summary

Perception is the process of assembling sensations into a usable mental representation of the world. In vision, the image projected on the retina is constantly changing, but the external world appears stable and undistorted because of *size*, *shape*, and *brightness constancy*. *Depth perception* (the ability to perceive three-dimensional space) is present in rudimentary form at or soon after birth. Depth perception depends upon the *bodily cues* of *accommodation* (bending of the lens), *convergence* (an inward movement of the eyes), and *retinal disparity* (the difference in images received by each eye). A number of *pictorial cues* also contribute to depth perception. These are: *linear perspective*, *relative size*, *light and shadow*, *overlap*, *texture gradients*, *aerial haze*, and *relative motion* (or motion parallax).

The most basic organization of sensations is a division into *figure* and *ground* (object and background). A number of factors contribute to the organization of sensations. These are: *nearness*, *similarity*, *continuation* (or *continuity*), *closure*, and combinations of the preceding. The organization and interpretation of sensations are also greatly influenced by the development of *perceptual habits.* Studies of *inverted vision* suggest that even the most basic habits are subject to change. Among the most influential perceptual habits is the tendency to relate sensations to *verbal labels* or conceptual *categories.* Perceptual judgments are not made in a vacuum. They are almost always related to an internal frame of reference called the *adaptation level.* Attention is closely related to *stimulus intensity*, *repetition*, and *contrast* (or change). Attention and perceptual experience are also influenced by perceptual *sets*, or *expectancies.*

Applications

Fully Awake—Sensory Awareness

We have seen that "normal" perception is a selective construction that limits information available to us, makes the environment manageable, and our reactions to it more "automatic." Normally this is beneficial and aids survival in an incredibly complex sensory world. But simplified perception has its price. Aldous Huxley has described the human brain as a "reducing valve" which restricts perception to a mere trickle. Adult perception may become stale by comparison to the richness of childhood. Think of the first ice-cream cone you ever ate, the first time you saw a fire engine, rode in a car, touched snow, or smelled a rose. The Eastern philosophy of Zen asserts that most people live in the world of *maya*, or illusion, a world that is a mere shadow of the vividness and richness of reality. Zen masters claim that after they have seen a tree 500 times it is as vivid as the first.

While the average person has not reached perceptual restriction of the "If you've seen one tree, you've seen them all" variety, the fact remains that most of us tend to look at a tree and classify it into the perceptual category of "trees in general" without really experiencing the miracle standing before us.

Humanistic psychologist Abraham Maslow (1969) has studied the perceptual habits of people who are unusually aware, alive, open, and mentally healthy. He finds that these people are fully awake, that their perceptions are marked by:

1. Total immersion in the present.
2. A lack of self-consciousness.
3. A sense of timelessness.
4. "Innocence of vision" like that of an artist or child.
5. Freedom from selecting, rejecting, criticizing, evaluating. The person is aware of everything at once.
6. Surrender to the experience—it is accepted and trusted.

The kind of perception Maslow is describing is like that of a mother with her newborn infant, a child at Christmas, or two people in love.

Heightened awareness at an advanced level may be difficult to attain, but a valuable increase in awareness can be had rather easily.

One author has written of the value of such awareness in these terms:

> The heightening of the awareness of my sense impressions . . . appeared in retrospect to be most important. . . . there was a deeper sense of the uniqueness of each sound, sight, and touch, that was permanently satisfying.
>
> We are all unconscious artists, we weave the stuff of beauty from the properties and ingredients of matter (Shattock, 1958).

Question: How can awareness be improved?

It is important to realize that many perceptual habits that limit awareness serve no useful function. They are habits and nothing more. Any change in these habits will counteract the phenomenon of *habituation* and return to stimulus to full awareness. Psychologist Robert Ornstein makes this suggestion:

> A similar exercise attributed to Gurdjieff consists simply in maintaining continuous awareness of a part of one's body—an elbow, hand, leg. Another exercise of this tradition is to perform ordinary habitual actions slightly differently, such as putting shoes on in the opposite order, shaving the other side of the face first, eating with the left hand (if one is right-handed). These exercises can be seen as attempts to return habitual "automatic" action to full awareness (Ornstein, 1972).

In short, any change in perceptual habits can make an experience "new" and fresh again.

Attention is the second approach to heightened awareness. Attention can be voluntarily directed to sensations that are normally tuned out. Try letting your attention wander through your body at length; that is, take a "walk" through your body. What feelings are coming from your mouth, nose, shoulder, thigh, foot, scalp, palms, stomach, nostrils, eyes, and ears? Try another exercise in awareness with an apple. Examine the sheen of its surface. Look at the colors, feel its skin, smell it. Slowly bite into it. Savor its taste. Eat it slowly. Look at its texture. Examine the seeds. Eat all of it including the stem. How does an apple stem taste? (I've never tried one.)

The following quote summarizes the importance of attention:

> One day a man of the people said to Zen Master Ikkyu: "Master, will you please write for me some maxims of the highest wisdom?"
>
> Ikkyu immediately took his brush and wrote the word "Attention."
>
> "Is that all?" asked the man. "Will you not add something more?"
>
> Ikkyu then wrote twice running: "Attention. Attention."
>
> "Well," remarked the man rather irritably, "I really don't see much depth or subtlety in what you have just written."
>
> Then Ikkyu wrote the same word three times running: "Attention. Attention. Attention."
>
> Half-angered, the man demanded: "What does that word 'Attention' mean anyway?"
>
> And Ikkyu answered gently: "Attention means attention" (Kapleau, 1966).

To this we can add only one thought, provided by the words of poet William Blake: "If the doors of perception were cleansed, man would see everything as it is, infinite."

For Discussion

Eyewitness to a Murder

The following is a true account. Only the degree of exaggeration has been changed for educational purposes.

I was in a supermarket when suddenly a girl, about eight years old, came running around a corner. She looked back and screamed, "Stop! Stop! You're killing him! You're killing my father!" Naturally I was interested! I dropped my things and hurried in the direction from which the girl had come. As I turned the corner I was greeted by a grisly scene. I had never seen a murder before. There was a man stretched out on the floor with another on top of him. The guy on top was huge. He must have been 6 feet 6 inches tall and have weighed 300 pounds. He looked only half human. He had his victim by the throat and was beating his head against the floor. There was blood everywhere. I decided to do the right thing. I ran. . . .

By the time the store manager and I returned to the "scene of the crime," the police were just arriving. It took quite a while to straighten things out, but here are the facts that emerged: The "guy on the bottom" was a diabetic and had suffered an insulin reaction. As a result he passed out and hit his head as he went down. This caused the cut (actually quite minor) that accounted for the "blood everywhere." The "guy on top" had seen the first man fall and was trying to prevent him from further injuring himself while unconscious. He was also loosening the man's collar.

If I had never returned, I would have sworn in court that I had seen a murder. This perhaps is understandable. But what I will never quite recover from is the shock I felt when I met the "murderer." This is the man, you will recall, that I had seen a few moments before, in broad daylight, as a huge, vicious, horrible-looking creature. The man was not a stranger. He was a neighbor of mine. I had seen him dozens of times before. I know him by name. He is a rather small man.

Questions for Discussion

1. What perceptual factors were involved in the first version of the "murder" described above?
2. How did the girl affect what was seen?
3. How dependable do you think eyewitness testimony is in a courtroom?
4. Do you think your perceptions of an argument or fight with a friend, parent, or spouse are accurate? What factors might affect your viewpoint?
5. Have you ever had an experience similar to the one described?

Suggestions for Further Reading

Carraher, R. G., and J. B. Thurston. *Optical Illusions and the Visual Arts.* Van Nostrand Reinhold, 1968.

Forgus, R. L. *Perception.* McGraw-Hill, 1966.

Gregory, R. L. *Eye and Brain.* McGraw-Hill, 1966.

———. *The Intelligent Eye.* McGraw-Hill, 1970.

Hochberg, J. *Perception.* Prentice-Hall, 1964.

Locher, J. L. (ed.) *The World of M. C. Escher.* Abrams, 1971.

Altered States of Consciousness

6

Chapter Preview

Do You Believe in Magic?

In the quiet laboratories of Stanford Research Institute, one of America's largest think tanks, Uri Geller, an Israeli psychic, has agreed to demonstrate what he claims are his abilities to communicate by mental telepathy, to detect hidden objects, and to bend metal with "psychic energy." In the course of his testing Geller was able to:

> Select from a row of ten film canisters, the one which contained an object. This was done twelve times with different objects and without errors.
>
> Deflect a sensitive laboratory balance sealed inside a jar by passing his hand over it.
>
> Correctly guess the number that would come up on a die shaken in a closed box eight out of eight times.
>
> Reproduce drawings sealed in opaque envelopes.

Question: Was Geller cheating? Was he using some form of energy or some form of awareness beyond normal consciousness?

A partial answer to this and similar questions may be found in an examination of altered states of consciousness. *But before we delve into this intriguing topic, a word on normal consciousness is in order.*

Resources

Consciousness

Question: What is consciousness?

William James described consciousness as a "stream"—an ever-changing flow of awareness. When you are awake, consciousness includes a mixture of sensations from the external world, sensations generated by your own body, memories from the past, images and daydreams, and expectations about the future. But as James also noted:

> Our normal waking consciousness, rational consciousness as we call it, is but one special type of consciousness, whilst all about it, parted from it by the filmiest of screens, there lie potential forms of consciousness entirely different (James, 1958).

States of consciousness related to fatigue, delirium, hypnosis, meditation, drugs, and ecstasy differ significantly from what might be considered "normal" awareness. The sections which follow examine the nature and possible usefulness of several altered states of consciousness.

Extrasensory Perception (ESP)—Beyond Normal Awareness?

Parapsychology is the study of *psychic* phenomena (also known as *psi* phenomena). Psi events are those which lie outside normal experience and seem to defy accepted scientific laws.

Question: Do psychologists believe in ESP?

American psychologists as a group remain skeptical about ESP. However, many psychologists are seeking answers to the questions which surround psychic phenomena. Four major areas of investigation are:

1. *Clairvoyance.* The ability to perceive events or gain information in ways that appear unaffected by distance or normal physical barriers.
2. *Telepathy.* Extrasensory perception of another person's thoughts, or more simply, an ability to read someone else's mind.
3. *Precognition.* The ability to preceive or accurately predict future events. Precognition may take the form of *prophetic dreams* which foretell the future.
4. *Psychokinesis.* The ability to exert influence over inanimate objects by will power ("mind over matter"). If you are able to influence which face of a flipped coin comes up or move an object without touching it, then you have demonstrated psychokinesis.

Psychologists question the possibility of these four abilities for reasons detailed below.

Coincidence The difficulty of excluding *coincidence* from natural ESP occurrences is a serious problem. For example, ESP researcher J. B. Rhine (1953) describes a typical psychic experience: During the middle of the night, a woman away for a weekend visit suddenly had a strong impulse to return home. When she arrived she found the house on fire with her husband asleep inside. An experience like this is very striking, but it does not *prove* the existence of ESP. If, by coincidence, a "hunch" turns out to be correct, it may be *reinterpreted* as a premonition or case of clairvoyance. If it is not confirmed, it will simply be forgotten.

To avoid the problems of coincidence and after-the-fact reinterpretation of "natural" ESP events, Rhine has tried for years to study ESP more objectively. Many of Rhine's experiments make use of the *Zener cards* (see Fig. 6-1). In a typical clairvoyance test a subject attempts to guess the symbols on the cards as they are turned up from a shuffled deck. Pure guessing will produce an average score of five "hits" out of twenty-five cards. A person who consistently scores above this chance expectation is credited with ESP. Telepathy is tested when one person (the "sender") concentratés on a card and another person (the "receiver") tries to "read the mind" of the sender.

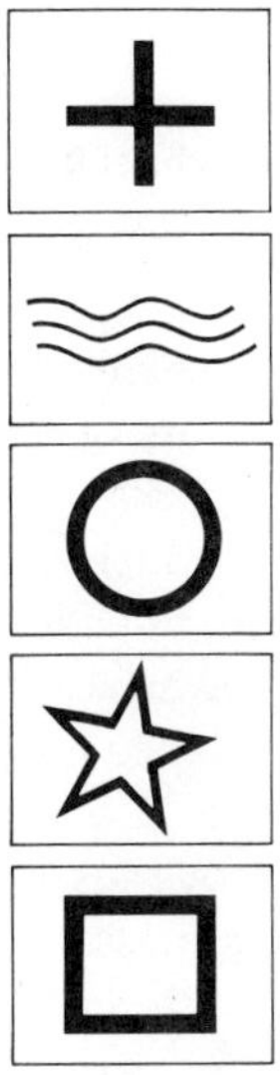

Fig. 6-1 ESP cards used by J. B. Rhine, an early experimenter in parapsychology.

Unfortunately, some of Rhine's most dramatic early experiments used badly printed Zener cards on which a faint outline of the symbols showed through the back. In other experiments, there is evidence that the experimenter knew which card was correct and unconsciously gave subjects cues with his eyes, facial gestures, or lip movements.

Statistics and Chance A second major criticism of ESP research focuses on *statistics* and the *consistency* of extrasensory skills. It is rare for a subject to be capable of maintaining ESP ability over any sustained period of time (Soal & Bateman, 1964). ESP researchers consider this an indication that parapsychological skills are very fragile and unpredictable. But critics argue that subjects who only temporarily show ESP have just received credit for a *run of luck*. When the run is over, it is not fair to assume ESP is temporarily gone. We must count *all* attempts.

Believers in ESP, such as ex-astronaut Edgar D. Mitchell, consider negative results in ESP tests to be the result of other factors: "The scientist has to recognize that his own mental processes may influence the phenomenon he's observing. If he's really a total skeptic, the scientist may well turn off the psychic subject" (*Newsweek*, March 4, 1974).

Skeptics and serious researchers in ESP both agree on one point. If psychic phenomena do occur, they cannot be controlled well enough to be used by entertainers. Stage ESP (like stage magic) is based upon a combination of sleight of hand, deception, and patented gadgets. A case in point is Uri Geller, a former nightclub magician who has "astounded" audiences from coast to coast with apparent feats of telepathy, psychokinesis, and precognition. Geller's performance in tests at Stanford Research Institute is described in the preview to this chapter. Not mentioned is what University of Oregon Professor Ray Hyman calls an "incredible sloppiness" in performance of these tests or the fact that Geller has been caught cheating at times (*Time*, March 4, 1974). *Time* goes on to note that:

> Unhappily for Geller, his powers have a tendency to vanish in the presence of sleight-of-hand men. On the *Tonight Show*, where Johnny Carson instituted airtight controls at Randi's [professional magician James Randi] suggestion, nothing that Geller attempted (during an embarrassing twenty minutes) seemed to work.

A good summary of the overall status of parapsychological research is provided by the remarks of Wayne Sage (1972): "Forty years of experiments in the telepathic, clairvoyant, and precognitive capacities of the human mind have left us no more certain, or uncertain, that such abilities even exist." Perhaps exciting discoveries in this realm of consciousness still await us. But, for now, it would seem that the best attitude toward ESP is to maintain an open mind while being carefully skeptical of evidence reported in the popular press or by researchers who are "true believers." Confirming and harnessing ESP could be one of mankind's greatest discoveries, but for the moment ESP offers little in the way of immediate usefulness.

Learning Check

Before reading on, answer the following questions about what you just read.

1. Name four areas of investigation in psychic phenomena where psychologists are seeking answers:

2. Psychologists must consider coincidence, statistics, and consistency when investigating extrasensory skills. T or F?

Answers: 1. clairvoyance, telepathy, precognition, psychokinesis 2. T

Hypnotism—Look into My Eyes

"Your body is becoming heavy. Your eyes are so tired you can barely keep them open. You feel warm and relaxed and very heavy. You are so tired you can't move. Relax. Sleep, Sleep, Sleep." These are the last words a book should ever say to you and the first a professional hypnotist might say.

Hypnotism, like ESP, has a certain aura of mystery surrounding it. Yet, unlike ESP, hypnosis is accepted by most psychologists as a scientifically valid phenomenon. Most would agree that hypnosis is a *trancelike, altered state of consciousness, characterized by narrowed attention and an increased openness to suggestion.*

Interest in hypnosis began in the 1700s with Franz Mesmer (whose name is the basis for the term *mesmerize*). Mesmer, an Austrian physician, believed that he could cure diseases by passing magnets over the body of an afflicted person. For a time mesmerism enjoyed quite a following. In the end, however, Mesmer's theories of "animal magnetism" were rejected by the medical profession, and he was branded a quack and a fraud. The term *hypnotism* was coined later by a respected English surgeon named James Braid. The Greek word *hypnos* means "sleep," and Braid used it to describe the sleeplike quality of the hypnotic trance. Today we recognize that hypnosis is *not* sleep, since EEG (brain-wave) recordings made during hypnosis are similar to those obtained when a person is awake. Hypnotism, as it is shown in movies and on television, and as it is used on the stage, bears little resemblance to the real thing.

Question: Can anyone be hypnotized?

Approximately eight people out of ten can be hypnotized, but only four out of ten will be good hypnotic subjects. If you are willing to be hypnotized, chances are good that you could be. Hypnotic susceptibility can be measured by making a series of suggestions to a person and recording the number of suggestions to which he or she responds. A typical hypnotic test is the Stanford Hypnotic Susceptibility Scale, shown in Table 6-1.

Question: How is hypnosis done? Could anyone be hypnotized against his will?

There are as many different hypnotic routines as there are hypnotists. The actual method of hypnotic induction doesn't seem to be too important. Common factors in all techniques are that they encourage a person (1) to

Table 6-1 Stanford Hypnotic Susceptibility Scale

Suggested behavior	*Criterion of passing (yielding score of +)*
1. Postural sway	Falls without forcing
2. Eye closure	Closes eyes without forcing
3. Hand lowering (left)	Lowers at least 6 in. by end of 10 secs.
4. Immobilization (right arm)	Arm rises less than 1 in. in 10 secs.
5. Finger lock	Incomplete separation of fingers at end of 10 secs.
6. Arm rigidity (left arm)	Less than 2 in. of arm bending in 10 secs.
7. Hands moving together	Hands at least as close as 6 in. after 10 secs.
8. Verbal inhibition (name)	Name unspoken in 10 secs.
9. Hallucination (fly)	Any movement, grimacing, acknowledgement of effect.
10. Eye catalepsy	Eyes remain closed at end of 10 secs.
11. Posthypnotic (changes chairs)	Any partial movement response
12. Amnesia test	Three or fewer items recalled.

(Adapted from Weitzenhoffer and Hilgard, 1959)

focus attention on what is being said, (2) to relax and feel tired, (3) to "let go" and accept suggestions easily, and (4) to use vivid imagination.

In advanced stages of hypnosis "reality testing" may be relaxed so that a partial suspension of normal "will power" is achieved. But at first one must cooperate willingly in order to become hypnotized. Many theorists feel that all hypnosis is really *self-hypnosis* and that the hypnotist simply serves as a guide to help the subject achieve an altered state of awareness that could be achieved alone.

Question: What does it feel like to be hypnotized?

You might be surprised at some of the actions you performed during hypnosis, and you might experience mild feelings of floating, sinking, anesthesia, or separation from your body. Personal experiences vary widely. However, in all but the deepest stages of hypnosis, people remain aware of what is going on.

Question: Could someone be made to perform an immoral act while hypnotized?

Generally speaking, a person will not do something when hypnotized that he or she would not normally do. However, a person who would not undress in public *might* undress if given the suggestion that he or she is at home alone and that it is bedtime (Eysenck, 1957). Also, hypnosis may *disinhibit* a person by providing an excuse to engage in prohibited behavior. If you were hypnotized and told to throw a cream pie in your teacher's face, you would probably comply because you could not be held responsible. After all, you were hypnotized, weren't you?

Question: What can be achieved with hypnosis?

A vast array of abilities has been tested for responsiveness to hypnotic suggestion. In some cases the evidence is incomplete or contradictory, but the following conclusions seem reasonably justified (Barber, 1970):

1. *Superhuman acts of strength.* Hypnosis has no more effect on physical strength than instructions that encourage a subject to make his or her best effort.
2. *Memory.* Memory per se cannot be improved through hypnosis, but motivation and attention in learning may be. In other words, you might be convinced through hypnosis that you are *extremely interested* in learning history, chemistry, or whatever so that your studying would be improved.
3. *Amnesia.* Hypnotic subjects can be instructed to forget what occurred during the trance. It is not clear, however, if they do forget or just can't or won't say what happened because of the suggestion that they would forget.
4. *Pain relief.* Hypnosis can relieve pain. Therefore, it can be especially useful in situations where chemical painkillers cannot be used, or are ineffective. One such situation is control of *phantom limb* pain. (Phan-

tom limb pains are recurring pains that amputees sometimes feel coming from the missing limb.)

5. *Age regression.* Through hypnosis subjects have been "regressed" to childhood. Some theorists feel that regressed subjects are only acting childlike and that nothing more than role playing is involved. Others consider hypnotic age regression fact and point out that in some extreme cases of age regression the *Babinski reflex* has reappeared. (The Babinski reflex is a spreading of the toes when the sole of the foot is stroked. It is only supposed to occur in early infancy.)
6. *Sensory changes.* Hypnotic suggestions concerning sensations seem to be among the most effective. Given the proper instructions, a person can be made to smell a small bottle of ammonia and respond as if it were a wonderful perfume.

Generally, hypnosis seems to have its greatest value as a tool for inducing relaxation, as a means of controlling pain, as an aid to maintaining motivation (to study, diet, quit smoking, and so forth), and as an adjunct to other forms of psychological therapy and counseling. The effects that can be obtained with hypnosis are useful, but seldom "amazing."

Stage Hypnotism

Question: *How do entertainers use hypnosis on stage to get people to do strange things?*

They don't. Little or no hypnosis is necessary to do a good stage hypnosis act. T. X. Barber, an authority on hypnosis, says that stage hypnotists make use of several characteristics of the stage setting to perform their act (Barber, 1970).

1. *Waking suggestibility.* We are all more or less open to suggestion, but on stage people are unusually cooperative because they don't want to "ruin the act." As a result, they will readily follow almost any instruction given by the entertainer.
2. *Selection of responsive subjects.* Participants in stage hypnotism must *volunteer* to come on stage. This alone ensures that participants are relatively uninhibited and ready to participate. Next the group is "hypnotized" *en masse* and anyone who doesn't succumb (go along) is eliminated.
3. *The hypnosis label disinhibits.* As we noted before, once a person has been labeled "hypnotized," he or she can sing, dance, act silly, or whatever without fear of embarrassment because being "hypnotized" takes away all personal responsibility for one's actions.
4. *The hypnotist as a "director."* After participants loosen up and respond to a few suggestions, they find that they are suddenly the star of the show. Audience response to the antics on stage brings out the "ham" in many participants so that all the "hypnotist" need do is direct the action.

5. *The stage hypnotist uses tricks.* Stage hypnosis is about 50 percent taking advantage of the situation and 50 percent deception. Here are several common deceptions:

> The hypnotist turns his microphone off and gives a participant *secret instructions*, like: "Sit in this chair. Close your eyes. Don't move until I tell you to." The hypnotist then waves his hand in front of the person's face and moves on as the audience is astounded by the way he "put that guy out."
>
> A disbeliever in the audience can be dealt with by use of the "hot ball" or a similar trick. The disbeliever is invited on stage and handed an ordinary-looking ball. He is then given suggestions that the ball is becoming so hot that he can no longer hold it. Soon he drops the ball and sheepishly returns to his seat as the audience laughs its approval. The trick? The ball has two compartments that contain chemicals that generate heat when mixed. As the hypnotist hands the ball to the skeptic, he turns it over, mixing the chemicals—and then watches the fun.
>
> One of the more impressive stage tricks is to rigidly suspend a person between two chairs and then to stand on the person's chest. This is astounding only because the audience does not question it. Anyone can do it as is demonstrated in the photographs and instructions in Fig. 6-2. Try it!

To summarize, hypnosis is real and is capable of causing a significant change in conscious experience. It is a useful tool that has been effectively applied in a variety of settings. The television or nightclub stage, however, is not one of these settings. Stage "hypnotists" entertain; they rarely hypnotize.

Learning Check

1. Hypnotism, unlike ESP, is accepted by most psychologists as a scientifically (valid/invalid) phenomenon.

2. Could someone be made to perform an immoral act while hypnotized?

____

____

3. Hypnosis seems to have its greatest value as a tool for inducing relaxation, as a means of controlling pain, as an aid to maintaining motivation, and as an adjunct to other forms of therapy and counseling. T or F?

4. Stage hypnotists entertain; they rarely hypnotize. T or F?

Answers: **1.** valid **2.** Generally speaking, no; however, hypnosis may provide an excuse to engage in prohibited behavior. **3.** T **4.** T

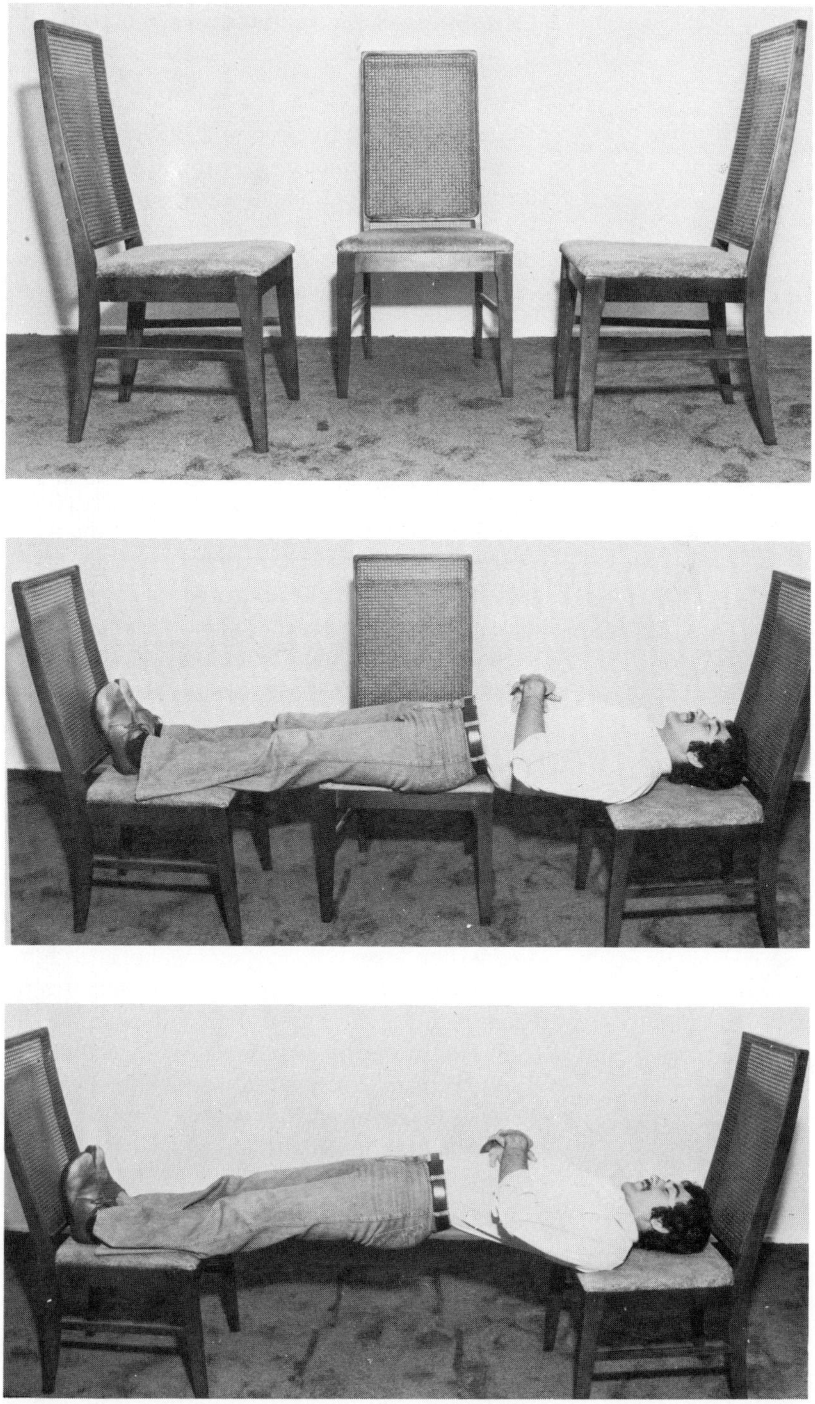

Fig. 6-2 Arrange three chairs as shown. Have someone recline as shown. Ask him to lift slightly and remove the middle chair. Accept the applause gracefully!

Drug-altered Consciousness

Alcohol, heroin, amphetamines, barbiturates, marijuana, cocaine, LSD, caffeine, nicotine. . . . The list of consciousness altering drugs—legal and illegal—available to anyone motivated enough to seek them out is extensive. The surest way to alter human consciousness is to administer a *psychoactive* drug. A psychoactive drug is a substance capable of altering attention, memory, judgment; time sense; feeling of control over one's actions; emotional mood or expression; and perception (by exaggerating sensations or causing hallucinations) (Ludwig, 1966).

Facts about Drugs Most psychoactive drugs can be placed on a scale ranging from *stimulation* to *depression*. Figure 6-3 shows the approximate relationships among various drugs and their effects on the central nervous system. A more complete summary and comparison of most of the psychoactive drugs currently available is reprinted on pages 140 and 141. Note that the drugs definitely capable of causing a *physical addiction* are: Heroin, morphine, codeine, methadone, barbiturates, and alcohol. Two drugs that *may* be physically addicting are tobacco and amphetamines. *All* of the drugs listed can lead to a *psychological dependence*, although the danger of abuse varies. The following discussion will focus on four types of drugs most frequently abused by college students.

Uppers—The Amphetamines *Amphetamines* form a large group of synthetic stimulants. Drugs commonly available in this group are *Dexedrine*, *Methedrine*, and *Benzedrine*. Amphetamines are widely prescribed by doctors to aid weight loss or to combat mild depression—both questionable practices in view of the fact that patients frequently learn to depend on amphetamines. Illicit use of amphetamines is widespread among individuals seeking an easy way to stay awake or to temporarily improve mental or physical performance. Truck drivers, athletes, factory workers, and students cramming for exams frequently abuse amphetamines for these purposes.

The most obvious abuse of amphetamines is that represented by the "speed freak," or habitual user. The speed freak takes amphetamines in large doses or injects Methedrine ("speed") directly into the bloodstream to produce euphoria, alertness, and a heightened sense of mental and physical energy and well-being.

The dangers in amphetamine usage are multiple. To stay "high," the true speed freak must inject more and more of the drug as his body develops a tolerance. The American Medical Association (1968) emphasizes that amphetamines speed the expenditure of bodily resources; they do not magically supply energy. Hence the aftereffects of an amphetamine high can be quite dangerous and uncomfortable. Possible effects include fatigue, depression, terrifying nightmares, confusion, and uncontrolled irritability and aggression. Repeatedly overextending one's body by speeding may lead to:

considerable weight loss, sores and non-healing ulcers, brittle fingernails, tooth grinding, chronic chest infections, liver disease, a variety of hypertensive disorders, and in some cases cerebral hemorrhage (Canadian Government's Commission of Inquiry, 1971).

Question: What is the meaning of the phrase "Speed kills!"?

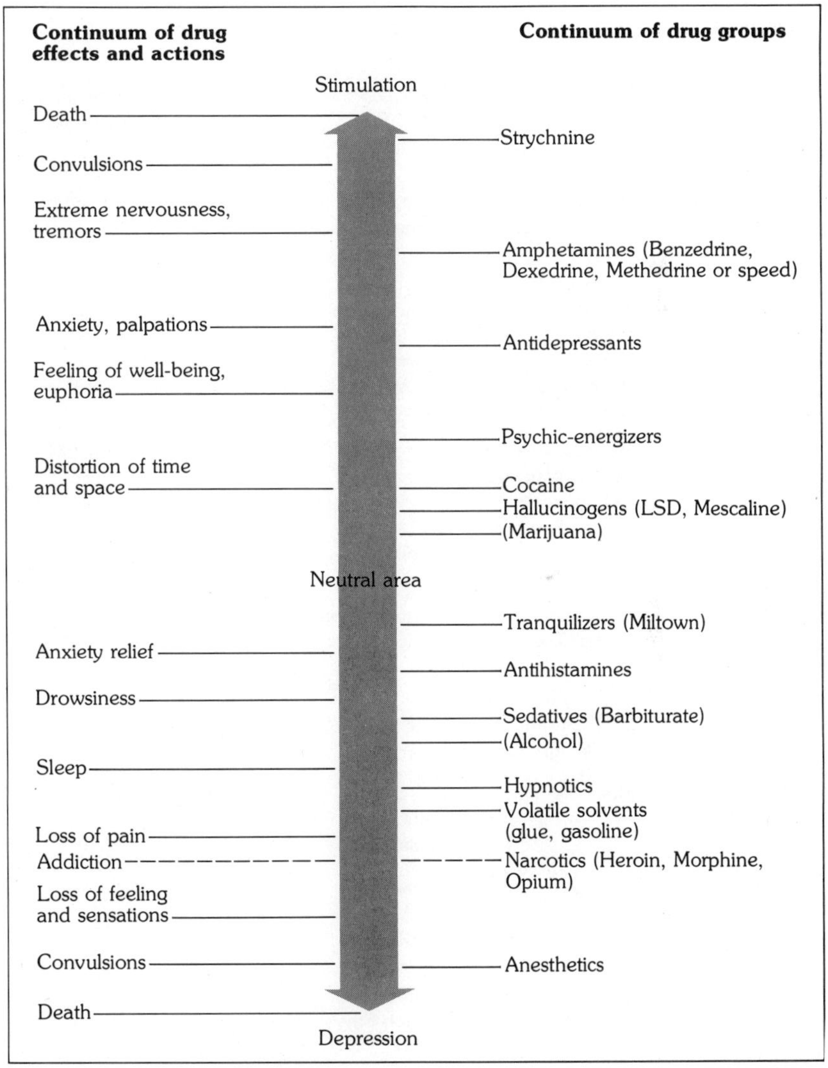

Fig. 6-3 Spectrum and continuum of drug action. All drugs can be placed on a continuum of stimulation-depression according to their effect on the central nervous system. (Robert W. Earle, Ph.D., Senior Lecturer, Department of Medical Pharmacology and Therapeutics, University of California at Irvine, California College of Medicine.)

Table 6-2 Facts about Drugs

Name	Slang name	Chemical or trade name	Source	Classification	Medical use	How taken
Heroin	H., Horse, Scat, Junk, Smack, Scag, Stuff	Diacetyl-morphine	Semi-synthetic (from morphine)	Narcotic	Pain relief	Injected or sniffed
Morphine	White stuff, M.	Morphine sulphate	Natural (from opium)	Narcotic	Pain relief	Swallowed or injected
Codeine	Schoolboy	Methyl-morphine	Natural (from opium), semi-synthetic (from morphine)	Narcotic	Ease pain and coughing	Swallowed
Methadone	Dolly	Dolophine, Amidone	Synthetic	Narcotic	Pain relief	Swallowed or injected
Cocaine	Corrine, Gold dust, Coke, Bernice, Flake, Star dust, Snow	Methylester of benzoy-leogonine	Natural (from coca, NOT cacao)	Stimulant, local anesthesia	Local anesthesia	Sniffed, in-jected, or swallowed
Marijuana	Pot, Grass, Tea, Hashish, Gage, Reefers	Cannabis sativa	Natural	Relaxant, euphoriant; in high doses, hallucinogen	None in U.S.	Smoked, swallowed, or sniffed
Barbiturates	Barbs, Blue devils, Candy, Yellow jackets, Phennies, Peanuts, Blue heavens	Phenobarbital, Nembutal, Seconal, Amytal	Synthetic	Sedative-hypnotic	Sedation, relief of high blood pressure, hy-perthyroidism	Swallowed or injected
Ampheta-mines	Bennies, Dexies, Speed, Wake-ups, Lid poppers, Hearts, Pep pills	Benzedrine, Dexedrine, Desoxyn, Methamphet-amine, Meth-adrine	Synthetic	Sympatho-mimetic	Relief of mild depression, control of ap-petite and narcolepsy	Swallowed or injected
LSD	Acid, Sugar, Big D, Cubes, Trips	D-lysergic Acid diethylamide	Semi-synthetic (from ergot alkaloids)	Hallucinogen	Experimental study of mental function, alcoholism	Swallowed
DMT	AMT, Business-man's high	Dimethyl-triptamine	Synthetic	Hallucinogen	None	Injected
Mescaline	Mesc.	3, 4, 5-tri-methoxyphen-ethylamine	Natural (from peyote)	Hallucinogen	None	Swallowed
Psilocybin		3(2-dimethyl-amino) ethylin-dol-4-oldihy-drogen phos-phate	Natural (from psilocybe)	Hallucinogen	None	Swallowed
Alcohol	Booze, Juice, etc.	Ethanol, Ethyl-alcohol	Natural (from grapes, grains, etc., via fer-mentation)	Sedative-hypnotic	Solvent, antiseptic	Swallowed
Tobacco	Fag, Coffin nail, etc.	Nicotiana tabacum	Natural	Stimulant-sedative	Sedative, emetic (nicotine)	Smoked, sniffed, or chewed

(Question marks indicate conflict of opinion. It should be noted that illicit drugs are frequently adulterated and thus pose unknown hazards to the user.)

Usual dose	Duration of effect	Effects sought	Long-term symptoms	Physical dependence potential	Mental dependence potential	Organic damage potential
Varies	4 hr	Euphoria, prevent withdrawal discomfort	Addiction, constipation, loss of appetite	Yes	Yes	No*
15 milligrams	6 hr	Euphoria, prevent withdrawal discomfort	Addiction, constipation, loss of appetite	Yes	Yes	No*
30 milligrams	4 hr	Euphoria, prevent withdrawal discomfort	Addiction, constipation, loss of appetite	Yes	Yes	No
10 milligrams	4-6 hr	Prevent withdrawal discomfort	Addiction, constipation, loss of appetite	Yes	Yes	No
Varies	Varied, brief periods	Excitation, talkativeness	Depression, convulsions	No	Yes	Yes?
1-2 cigarettes	4 hr	Relaxation; increased euphoria, perceptions, sociability	Usually none	No	Yes?	No
50-100 milligrams	4 hr	Anxiety reduction, euphoria	Addiction with severe withdrawal symptoms, possible convulsions, toxic psychosis	Yes	Yes	Yes
2.5-5 milligrams	4 hr	Alertness, activeness	Loss of appetite, delusions, hallucinations, toxic psychosis	No?	Yes	Yes?
100-500 micrograms	10 hr	Insightful experiences, exhilaration, distortion of senses	May intensify existing psychosis, panic reactions	No	No?	No?
1-3 milligrams	Less than 1 hr	Insightful experiences, exhilaration, distortion of senses	?	No	No?	No?
350 micrograms	12 hr	Insightful experiences, exhilaration, distortion of senses	?	No	No?	No?
25 milligrams	6-8 hr	Insightful experiences, exhilaration, distortion of senses	?	No	No?	No?
Varies	1-4 hr	Sense alteration, anxiety reduction, sociability	Cirrhosis, toxic psychosis, neurologic damage, addiction	Yes	Yes	Yes
Varies	Varies	Calmness, sociability	Emphysema, lung cancer, mouth and throat cancer, cardiovascular damage, loss of appetite	Yes?	Yes	Yes

*Persons who inject drugs under nonsterile conditions run a high risk of contracting hepatitis, abscesses, or circulatory disorders.

SOURCE: *Resource Book for Drug Abuse Education*, developed as a part of the Drug Abuse Education Project of the American Association for Health, Physical Education, and Recreation, and the National Science Teachers Association (NEA), 1969.

It should be obvious that amphetamines are dangerous drugs. Withdrawal from amphetamine addiction can be extremely painful (Grinspoon & Hedblom, 1972). But painful as withdrawal may be, it is not usually fatal. The real meaning of "Speed kills" lies in the fact that amphetamines can cause a loss of contact with reality known as *amphetamine psychosis*. Amphetamine psychosis is similar to extreme paranoia in which the individual feels threatened and suffers from delusions that someone is out to get him. Snyder (1972)[1] puts it this way:

> Acting on his delusions, the speed-freak may become violent—*to get them before they get me*. It is in this sense that the slogan SPEED KILLS is most accurate: more persons die from senseless and brutal violence associated with amphetamine delusions than from overdoses of the drug itself.

Question: How dangerous are downers?

Downers—Barbiturates Barbiturates are *sedative* drugs that produce a general depression of activity in the brain. They are used medically to calm patients or to induce sleep. In mild doses, barbiturates have an effect similar to alcohol intoxication, but an overdose can cause coma or death. Barbiturates combined with alcohol are particularly dangerous as the combined effects of the two drugs are multiplied by a *drug interaction* (one drug enhances the effect of another). Barbiturates are often taken in excessive amounts because a first dose may be followed by a second or third as the user becomes uninhibited or forgetful. Marilyn Monroe, Judy Garland, and a number of other well-known personalities have died of barbiturate overdoses. An overdose of barbiturates first causes unconsciousness and then so severely depresses activity in brain centers controlling heartbeat and respiration that death results.

The most frequently abused downers are the new short-acting drugs such as Seconals, Tuinals, Quaaludes, and Sopors. These seem to be preferred because they take effect quickly, and the "rush" of intoxication only lasts from two to four hours. All too often these short-acting capsules are gulped down with alcohol or added in uncounted quantities to a "spiked" punch bowl. It is no exaggeration to restate that mixing barbiturates with alcohol can be fatal.

Marijuana If you pick any twenty college students at random, approximately eight or ten will have tried marijuana. In the past few years, marijuana use has spread so widely (even into the suburbs) that some 20 to 30 million Americans are estimated to have tried it.

Marijuana and *hashish*, two drugs derived from the hemp plant *Cannabis sativa*, are the least toxic of the psychoactive drugs. Experts agree that *cannabis* is not addictive, does not lead to harder drugs, does not produce psychosis, illness, or death. In short, it is far less dangerous than two legal drugs—alcohol and tobacco.

[1]Copyright © 1971 Ziff-Davis Publishing Co. Reprinted by permission of *Psychology Today Magazine*.

Immediate Effects of Marijuana The physiological effects of marijuana usage involve mild stimulation of various pathways in the brain, slower reflexes, bloodshot eyes, increased appetite, and increased heart rate (Grinspoon, 1972). A variety of studies agree that the drug's typical psychological effects are: a sense of euphoria or well-being, relaxation, altered time sense, and impaired immediate memory. Most users accurately gauge intake of the drug so that the "high" attained remains pleasurable and controlled. Danger of overdose is very low, although extreme dosages can produce feelings of unreality, visual distortions, and sometimes hallucinations (National Institute for Mental Health, 1971). As a matter of fact, at moderate dosage levels it appears that a user must learn to experience any alteration in consciousness at all. Weil *et al.* (1968) found that inexperienced users report no effects with a mild dosage and that even with high dosages nonusers experienced very little change. Experienced users, on the other hand, got "high" with both mild and high dosages.

The effects of marijuana on driving performance have been measured on driving simulators using subjects in various stages of marijuana intoxication. Two early studies (Waller, 1971; Crancer *et al.*, 1969) found little interference in driving performance with marijuana (but significant deterioration for alcohol intoxication). These findings have been questioned by users and drug experts alike. It is generally agreed upon that marijuana *does* impair driving efficiency. Most arrests for marijuana possession occur when the user is stopped for a minor violation. Driving under the influence of any drug is dangerous.

Dangers of Marijuana Use It is difficult to form a final opinion on the dangers of marijuana use. Some researchers have charged that marijuana produces chromosomal, fetal, or brain damage, that it causes impotence in male users, and that it interferes with the body's natural immunity to diseases. However, each of these claims has been countered by evidence to the contrary (Hutman, 1975). Since evidence exists for each side, the questions of long-term mental and physical health hazards associated with chronic marijuana use are yet to be answered. In the meantime, there are three realistic liabilities associated with marijuana use. (1) In spite of the fact that marijuana is basically a mild drug, there is still a danger of psychological dependence associated with its frequent use. The danger is not so great as it is with alcohol, but frequent use of any drug as an escape from life's problems impedes emotional growth in much the same way that alcoholism does (Cohen, 1969). (2) *Heavy* use of marijuana is *at least* as damaging to the throat and lungs as cigarette smoking. In fact, there is some evidence to suggest that it does damage more quickly and that it can be carcinogenic (cancer producing) (Maugh, 1974a, b). This danger is reduced by the fact that few marijuana users smoke as frequently as the average cigarette smoker. Nevertheless, it is a finding of some importance. (3) Marijuana laws may not be realistic, but the fact remains that in most states possession or use of marijuana is a *felony*. In some cases the legal risks are truly staggering.

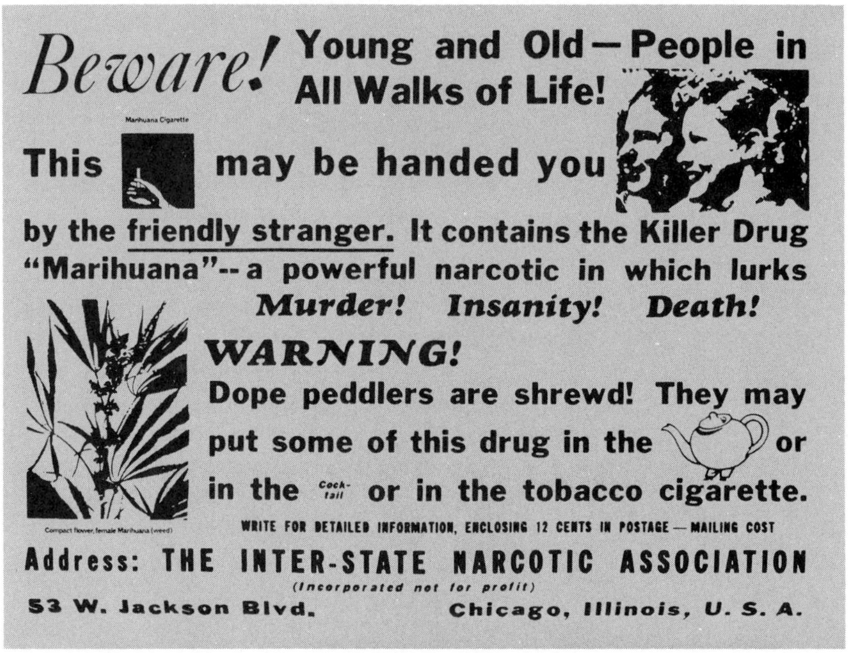

Fig. 6-4 An outdated antimarijuana poster demonstrates the kind of misinformation that has long been attached to this drug. Research is beginning to sort out what dangers (if any) are associated with continued use of marijuana.

Hutman (1975) notes that: "In Minnesota, a youth was given an indeterminant, 20-year maximum sentence for possession of 1/2800 of an ounce of pot. (Police had to vacuum the lining of his jacket to find it.)" Since penalties for possession are being reduced in many states, casual use of marijuana may not be a flirtation with a jail sentence. Still, costs can be high in terms of a future career, or employability. Answering yes to the question "Have you ever been arrested?" on job applications gets old quickly. A marijuana arrest can result in trading your hard work and education for a pleasure about as exciting as drinking a can of beer.

Alcohol Contrary to popular belief, alcohol is not a stimulant. The apparent gaiety at drinking parties is due to alcohol's effect as a central nervous system *depressant*. As Fig. 6-5 shows, small amounts of alcohol reduce inhibition and produce feelings of relaxation and euphoria. Greater amounts of alcohol cause progressively more dangerous impairment of brain function until the drinker loses consciousness.

Alcohol, America's favorite drug, generates America's biggest drug problem. Over 100 million Americans use alcohol, and an estimated 9 to 12 million of these have a life-impairing drinking problem. Of all drivers involved in traffic accidents resulting in death or bodily injury, 73 percent have blood alcohol levels of 0.2 percent or more (Cohen, 1970). It is probably no exaggeration to say of alcohol that, its abuse has killed more people, sent more victims to hospitals, generated more police arrests, broken up more marriages and homes, and cost industry more money than has the abuse of heroin, amphetamines, barbiturates and marijuana combined (Bengelsdorf, 1970).

Recognizing Problem Drinking Because alcohol abuse is such a common problem, it is important to recognize the danger signals of alcoholism.

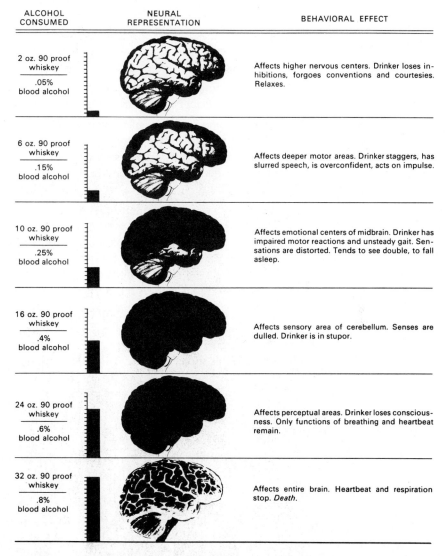

ALCOHOL CONSUMED	NEURAL REPRESENTATION	BEHAVIORAL EFFECT
2 oz. 90 proof whiskey / .05% blood alcohol	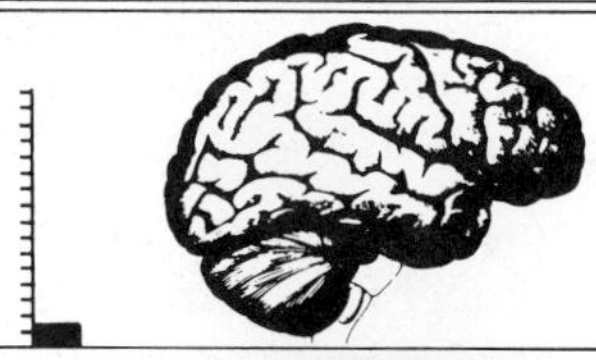	Affects higher nervous centers. Drinker loses inhibitions, forgoes conventions and courtesies. Relaxes.
6 oz. 90 proof whiskey / .15% blood alcohol	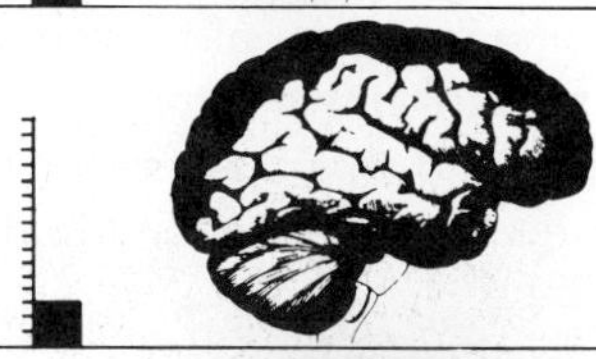	Affects deeper motor areas. Drinker staggers, has slurred speech, is overconfident, acts on impulse.
10 oz. 90 proof whiskey / .25% blood alcohol		Affects emotional centers of midbrain. Drinker has impaired motor reactions and unsteady gait. Sensations are distorted. Tends to see double, to fall asleep.
16 oz. 90 proof whiskey / .4% blood alcohol	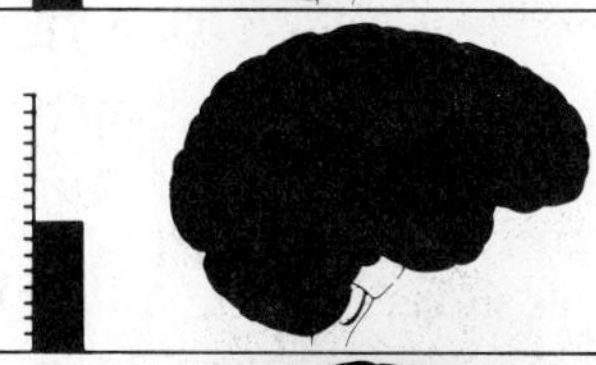	Affects sensory area of cerebellum. Senses are dulled. Drinker is in stupor.
24 oz. 90 proof whiskey / .6% blood alcohol	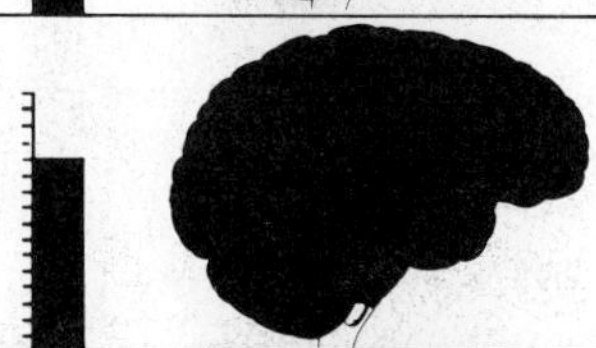	Affects perceptual areas. Drinker loses consciousness. Only functions of breathing and heartbeat remain.
32 oz. 90 proof whiskey / .8% blood alcohol	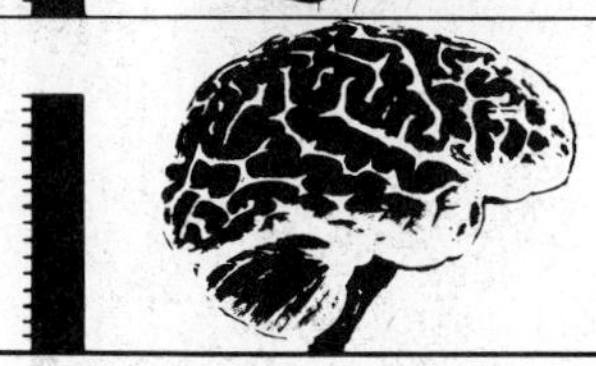	Affects entire brain. Heartbeat and respiration stop. *Death.*

Fig. 6-5 The behavioral effects of alcohol are related to blood alcohol content and the resulting suppression of higher mental functions. (From Jozef Cohen, *Eyewitness Series in Psychology*, p. 44. Copyright © by Rand McNally and Company. Reprinted by permission.)

Progression from a "social drinker" to a problem drinker to an alcoholic is often subtle. Coleman and Hammen (1974) and Jellinek (1960) have detailed steps in the development of a drinking problem:

1. *Initial phase.* Initially the social drinker begins to turn more frequently to alcohol to relieve tension or to feel good. Four danger signals in this period that signal excessive dependence on alcohol are:

   Increasing consumption. The individual drinks more and more and may begin to worry about his drinking.

   Morning drinking. Morning drinking is a dangerous sign particularly when it is used to combat a hangover or to "get through the day."

   Regretted behavior. The individual engages in extreme behavior while drunk that leaves him feeling guilty or embarrassed.

   Blackouts. Excessive drinking may be accompanied by an inability to remember what happened during intoxication.

2. *Crucial phase.* A crucial turning point comes as the person begins to lose control over his drinking. At this stage there is usually control over when and where a first drink is taken, but one drink starts a chain reaction leading to a second and a third, and so on.

3. *Chronic phase.* At this point the alcoholic drinks compulsively and continuously. He eats infrequently, becomes intoxicated from far less alcohol than before, and feels a powerful need for alcohol when he is deprived of it. His work, family ties, and social life all deteriorate. His self-drugging is usually so compulsive that when given the choice, the bottle comes before friends, relatives, employment, and self-esteem. He is an addict.

Treatment for alcoholism begins by sobering the person up and cutting off his supply. This produces all the symptoms of drug withdrawal and can be excruciatingly unpleasant for the alcoholic. The next step is to try to restore the alcoholic's physical health. Continued heavy use of alcohol usually causes severe damage to the body and central nervous system. Food, vitamins, and medical care cannot fully reverse this damage, but a reasonable state of health can be obtained. When he has "dried out" and his health has been restored, the alcoholic may be treated with tranquilizers, antidepressants, or psychotherapy.

Unfortunately, the success of these procedures has been limited. One lay-group approach that has been fairly successful is Alcoholics Anonymous, which functions on the premise that it takes a former alcoholic to understand and help a current alcoholic. AA's success rate may simply reflect the fact that members participate voluntarily, meaning they have admitted to themselves that they have a serious problem. Sadly, it seems that a problem drinker will often not admit his problem until he has really "hit bottom," but if he is willing, AA presents a practical approach to the problem.

Learning Check

1. Circle the letters of all the drugs listed below that are definitely known to be capable of causing a physical addiction:

a. Heroin
b. Morphine
c. Codeine
d. Methadone
e. Barbiturates
f. Alcohol
g. Tobacco
h. Amphetamines

2. Amphetamine psychosis is similar to extreme ________________ in which the individual feels threatened and suffers from delusions.

3. The combination of ________________ and alcohol can be fatal.

4. Which of the following is least physically dangerous?

a. Marijuana *b.* Alcohol *c.* Tobacco

5. Which of the following is the most dangerously abused?

a. Marijuana *b.* Alcohol *c.* Tobacco

Answers: **1.** all but *g* and *h* **2.** paranoia **3.** barbiturates **4.** *a* **5.** *b*

Resources Summary

States of awareness that differ from normal waking consciousness are called *altered states of consciousness*. Altered states are particularly associated with *ESP*, *hypnosis*, *psychoactive drugs*, and *meditation*.

Parapsychology, the study of ESP, has focused on four abilities: *clairvoyance*, *telepathy*, *precognition*, and *psychokinesis*. The existence of ESP is still debated because coincidence, inconsistency, statistical problems, deception, and sloppy research have invalidated many "proofs." Research is continuing. Stage mentalists do not use ESP in their acts.

Hypnotism is an altered state characterized by narrowed attention and increased suggestibility. Many of the effects of hypnosis are in doubt, but it does definitely seem capable of producing relaxation, controlling pain, maintaining motivation, and altering perceptions. Stage hypnotism makes use of deception and several characteristics of the stage setting to simulate hypnosis.

A *psychoactive drug* is a substance capable of altering functioning of the nervous system and brain in ways that alter consciousness. Most psychoactive drugs can be placed on a scale ranging from stimulation to depression. The *physically addicting* drugs are: heroin, morphine, codeine, methadone, barbiturates, alcohol, and maybe tobacco and amphetamines. All psychoactive drugs can lead to *psychological dependence*. The four drugs most frequently abused by college students are barbiturates, amphetamines, marijuana, and alcohol. The most dangerous and widely abused drug is probably alcohol. A crucial phase in the development of alcoholism occurs when one drink can start a chain reaction leading to more drinking.

Applications

An Alternative to Drugs—Meditation

One of the most popular forms of consciousness alteration has been reserved for the "applications" section of this chapter because of its high degree of usefulness. Transcendental meditation (TM for short) is a simple exercise that is capable of producing a highly relaxed, although wakeful, condition. Trained meditators claim that improved energy, concentration, memory, sexual response, and alertness come from regular meditation. Others refer to it as the "drugless high" (Campbell, 1974) because it makes them feel very relaxed and "at peace." Claims such as these may be exaggerated, but the fact remains that TM has no harmful effects and can be very beneficial.

In a study of the bodily changes that occur during TM, Wallace and Benson (1972) found that less oxygen is consumed, the heartbeat slows, respiration is reduced, and brain waves show a marked increase in alpha frequencies. These physiological changes are the *reverse* of what is observed when the body is subjected to stress. Hence it is believed that TM can be a highly valuable means of combating the stress of modern life.

Question: How is meditation done?

Transcendental meditation is the simplest of several styles of meditation. Because of its simplicity, it is easily learned. In one experiment (Maupin, 1965), college students were simply instructed to concentrate on breathing:

> While you are sitting let your breath become relaxed and natural. Let it set its own pace and depth if you can. Then focus your attention on your own breathing: the movements of your belly, not your nose or throat. Do not allow extraneous thoughts or stimuli to pull your attention away from your breathing. This may be hard to do at first, but keep directing your attention back to it. Turn everything else aside if it comes up (Maupin, 1965).

Not all subjects responded to this exercise, but at the end of a two-week period those who did reported that they had experienced deeply satisfying changes in consciousness. Their experiences included intense concentration, pleasant bodily sensations, and extreme detachment from outside worries and distractions.

If you would like to try the meditation exercise described above, set aside a few minutes twice each day. Begin by assuming a sitting or kneeling position on the floor. Keep your back straight and let your head tilt forward slightly. This position should be comfortable enough to allow relaxation without permitting sleep. What you are aiming for is summarized by Walpola Rahula:[2]

> At the beginning, you will find it extremely difficult to bring your mind to concentrate on your breathing. You will be astonished how your mind runs away. It does not stay. You begin to think of various things. You hear sounds outside. Your mind is disturbed and distracted. You may be dismayed and disappointed. But if you continue to practice this exercise twice a day, morning and evening, for about five or ten minutes at a time, you will gradually, by and by, begin to concentrate your mind on your breathing. After a certain period you will experience just that split second when your mind is fully concentrated on your breathing, when you will not hear even sounds nearby, when no external world exists for you (Rahula, 1959).

An alternative form of meditation you may want to try involves the use of a *mantra*. Mantras are smooth, flowing, words which are easily repeated. Instead of focusing on breathing, you can silently chant a mantra. Two widely used mantras are "Om" and "Om mani padme hum."* A mantra may be chanted anywhere, and, like breathing, it is basically used as a focus for attention. If other thoughts arise during meditation, one should return attention to the mantra as often as necessary to maintain meditation.

Meditation probably has its greatest value as a means of lowering stress in the body. But it has the added value of allowing a short "mental vacation" from the jarring clamor of the world and from the normal competition of thoughts and worries. Its simplicity is deceptive, and its benefits may take time to become noticeable. Meditation deserves a fair trial. Many people are finding it helpful, and you may too.

[2]Reprinted by permission of Grove Press, Inc.

*The principal claim of commercial meditation courses is that they offer a mantra tailored to the needs of each individual. Recent research (Benson, 1975) has shown that the same physical benefits accompany the use of *any* word or sound as a mantra.

For Discussion

Drug Abuse

Question: Why do people use drugs?

People seek drug experiences for a variety of reasons, ranging from curiosity and a desire to belong to a group to a search for meaning or an escape from feelings of inadequacy (Lipinski & Lipinski, 1970). Some observers believe that drug use is so deeply ingrained in modern society that "We are addicted to addiction. This is to say that, with few exceptions we subscribe to the premise . . . that life cannot be lived without drugs." We are so used to having our own way that we have come to believe "that we should be able to will ourselves to be calm, cheerful, thin, industrious, creative—and, moreover, to have a good night's sleep" (Farber, 1966). Farber believes that the medical profession, well meaning but misguided, has accepted these premises wholeheartedly, and unnecessarily encourages drug use. Indeed, one psychologist has observed:

> Depression, social inadequacy, anxiety, apathy, marital discord, children's misbehavior, and other psychological and social problems of living are now being redefined as medical problems, to be solved by physicians with prescription pads (Rogers, 1971).

Perhaps physicians and laymen alike can be partially excused for placing undue faith in the value of drugs because each is the target of multimillion-dollar advertising campaigns aimed at encouraging drug use. Even the lowly aspirin is now pushed as a means of relieving "nervous tension." Advertisements directed at physicians encourage overuse of drugs even more blatantly. An ad pictures a distraught mother with a child and asks: "Her kind of pressures last all day. . . . shouldn't her tranquilizer?" Another reads:

> School, the dark, separation, dental visits, monsters. The everyday anxiety of children sometimes gets out of hand.
>
> *A child can usually deal with his anxieties. But sometimes the anxieties overpower the child. Then he needs your help. Your help may include Vistaril* (Rogers, 1971).

Drugs, of course, have legitimate uses, and have alleviated much unnecessary suffering. The problem is that drugs strong enough to ease pain, induce sleep, end depression, or otherwise alter consciousness have a high potential for abuse.

Drug abuse and the legality of a drug are two relatively independent issues. This becomes clear when it is recognized that one of the most potent, destructive, and potentially dangerous drugs available is alcohol. It is estimated that 6 million Americans have a severe drinking problem. Another indication of the overuse of legally manufactured drugs can be found in the fact that in 1971 American drug companies produced *12 billion* legal amphetamine tablets, enough to supply every living American with thirty-five to fifty tablets (Grinspoon & Hedblom, 1972).

Facts such as these have led some observers to conclude that anyone who seeks drug-induced consciousness alteration will find a drug, legal or illegal, to achieve it. Psychiatrist Thomas Szasz (1972) believes that it is therefore futile for the government to attempt to "legislate morality" by regulating what drugs a person chooses to put into his or her body. Szasz suggests that current drug regulations have an effect similar to that produced by the prohibition of alcohol; that is, they encourage a black market, organized crime, disrespect for the law, and occasional poisonings from adulterated drugs. While it is true that illicit drug *use* is a "victimless crime," the fact remains that *abuse* of drugs—legal or illegal—represents a serious loss in terms of the productivity and mental health of self-drugged citizens.

Questions for Discussion

1. What drugs do you use? (Include caffeine, aspirin, and so forth.)
2. What drugs do your friends use?
3. What drugs do your parents use?
4. When and why do you use drugs?
5. What is your position on the legality and control of drugs?

Suggestions for Further Reading

Altered States of Awareness. Freeman, 1972.

Barber, T. *LSD, Marijuana, Yoga, and Hypnosis.* Aldine, Modern Applications of Psychology Series, 1970.

Castaneda, C. *The Teachings of Don Juan: A Yaqui Way of Knowledge.* Ballantine, 1971.

———. *A Separate Reality.* Simon and Schuster, 1971.

———. *Journey to Ixtlan.* Simon & Schuster, 1972.

———. *Tales of Power.* Simon & Schuster, 1974.

Huxley, A. *The Doors of Perception.* Harper & Row, 1970.

Ornstein, R. E. *The Psychology of Consciousness.* Freeman, 1972.

———, and C. Naranjo. *On the Psychology of Meditation.* Viking, 1971.

Tart, C. T. *Altered States of Consciousness.* Doubleday, Anchor Books, 1969.

7 Sleep and Dreaming

Chapter Preview

A Living Nightmare and Life Beyond Time

In January 1959, a New York disc jockey named Peter Tripp staged a "wakathon" in Times Square. Tripp went without sleep for 200 hours. Tripp's fight to stay awake was difficult from the beginning. After 100 hours, he began to have visual hallucinations. He saw cobwebs in his shoes, and a doctor's tweed coat became a suit of furry worms. When he crossed the street to a hotel to change clothes, a dresser drawer seemed to burst into flames. Tripp was convinced that the doctors monitoring his health were trying to "test" him by staging these strange occurrences.

After 170 hours, Tripp's agony had become almost unbearable. He struggled with the simplest thought and reasoning problems. His memory became quite poor. His brain-wave patterns looked like those of sleep. He was no longer sure he was himself and finally became convinced that the doctors were trying to send him to jail. By the end of 200 hours, Tripp was no longer able to distinguish between his waking nightmares, hallucination, and reality (Luce, 1965).

In a scene that could hardly be more removed from Peter Tripp's ordeal in Times Square, French scientist Michel Siffre entered Midnight Cave near Del Rio, Texas, on February 14, 1972 (Siffre, 1975). A small nylon tent deep within the cave became Siffre's home for the next 6 months.

Living alone within the unchanging depths of the cave, Siffre was completely isolated from clocks, calendars, the sun, the moon, and other reminders of time's passing. Siffre's ordeal—equal in many respects to

Tripp's—was undertaken to find what effect such isolation would have on the natural rhythms of human life.

While in the cave, Siffre lived by "cycles" rather than by days. A cycle was counted as the time from one awakening to the next. After each period of sleep, Siffre's "day" began with a call to members of an above-ground support crew. They in turn switched on the lights that illuminated Siffre's living area until he was again ready to sleep. When he felt that a "day" had passed, Siffre called the monitoring crew and had the lights turned off.

In addition to the scientific interest of Siffre's experience, there are practical concerns. For example, if two days could be perceived as one, the emotional strain associated with space flight, or the lengthy isolation of nuclear submarines, or a lonely radar outpost could be eased considerably.

In partial support of such possibilities, many of Siffre's days lasted well over 24 hours. At first he stayed very close to a 24-hour cycle, and overall his "days" averaged only 28 hours. But at several points Siffre's "days"—which seemed completely normal to him—lasted 35, 40, or even 50 hours. Siffre's longest cycle lasted an incredible 51¾ hours—about 18 hours of sleep and 33 awake.

Both of these men are voyagers into a realm that is at one and the same time familiar to us all and a source of great mystery. This chapter is a further investigation into sleep, dreaming, arousal, and points beyond.

Resources

Sleep—A Nice Place to Visit

The average person spends approximately twenty years of life in a strange state of semi-unconsciousness called sleep. Sleep is unique in many ways. It is not totally unconscious since dreams are often remembered, and thinking or problem solving may take place in dreams. It is not planless since some people can "set themselves" to awaken at a particular time. The sleeping individual is not completely unresponsive to the environment. A sleeping mother may ignore a jet rumbling by overhead but awaken at the slightest whimper of her child. As a matter of fact, some people can even perform simple tasks when asleep. In one experiment, subjects had to tap a switch each time a tone was sounded to avoid an electric shock. After some practice, all were able to continue doing this throughout the night without interrupting their sleep.

Because of its many contradictions, the phenomenon of sleep has always aroused curiosity. What do we know about this daily retreat from the world?

Question: How strong is the need for sleep? Could a person learn to do without sleep?

Sleep is only partially under voluntary control. You could choose, as Peter Tripp did, to stay awake for an extended period, but there are limits. Experimental animals that have undergone brain operations which prevent sleep fall into a coma and die after several days. In other experiments, animals have been placed on a treadmill above a tank of water. To avoid being dunked in the water, the animal must keep walking on the treadmill. This prevents normal sleep.

Many animals in this situation engage in *microsleep*. A microsleep is a momentary shift in brain activity to the pattern characteristic of sleep. Microsleeps occur in humans as well as animals. Perhaps you have realized at sometime during a monotonous late-night drive that several seconds have passed since you were last conscious of your surroundings. Many automobile accidents occur during such momentary lapses in consciousness caused by a microsleep.

Even if it were possible to survive without sleep, the psychological effects would be disastrous. As Peter Tripp found, moderate sleep deprivation causes lapses in the ability to think, reason, or concentrate (Murray, 1965). Longer periods without sleep may produce a temporary *sleep-deprivation psychosis* characterized by: loss of fine movements of the eyes, leading to staring; body tremors; sensations such as tingling and a feeling of "tightness" around the forehead; hallucinations of movement or vibrations in stationary objects, and visions of lacy designs like cobwebs. Advanced stages of sleep deprivation are marked by more exaggerated hallucinations, delusions, and confusion or disorientation (West *et al.*, 1962; Luby, 1962). Surprisingly, it does not seem necessary to completely make up for lost sleep. Most symptoms of sleep deprivation are completely removed by a single night's sleep.

Question: How much sleep is necessary?

Age is a large factor in sleep. Infants spend up to twenty hours a day sleeping. They tend to sleep in two- or four-hour cycles, which suggests that theirs is a "wakefulness of necessity" brought about mainly by needs for food and changing. With increasing age, most children go through a "nap" stage and eventually settle into a steady cycle of sleeping once a day (see Fig. 7-1). Some cultures, of course, have maintained the afternoon "siesta" as an adult pattern. Old age usually brings about a reduction in sleep time.

There is a great temptation to try to reduce sleep time. Buckminster Fuller, inventor of the geodesic dome, claims to have gone for long periods of time sleeping only two hours a day. Fuller had noticed that when a dog gets tired he simply lies down and sleeps. Fuller began sleeping whenever he felt like it. For him, this worked out to a half hour every six. Before you try the same thing, it should be noted that more formal studies of such schedules generally show them to be less efficient than sleeping once a day (Kleitman, 1961).

Question: If you sleep more than eight hours, does it mean you are unhealthy?

In the same way that individual needs for food differ, there is considerable variation around the eight-hour average for sleep. It is quite

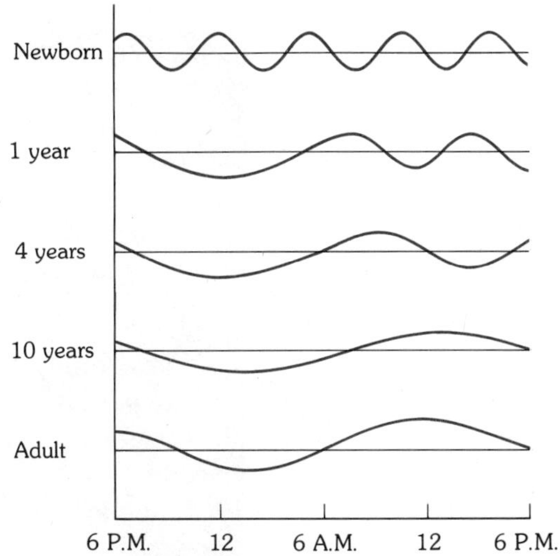

Fig. 7-1 Development of sleep patterns. Short cycles of sleep and waking gradually become the night-day cycle of an adult. (After Williams, 1964.)

normal for a healthy person to sleep as little as five hours per night or as much as eleven.

Most studies of sleep patterns show a consistent ratio of 2 to 1 between time awake and time asleep. This opens a more realistic possibility for altering sleep habits. As Michel Siffre (the temporary cave dweller) found, humans may be able to adapt to longer "days" than those typically imposed by the cycles of the sun. Other experiments (Kleitman & Kleitman, 1953) in which twenty-eight-hour days were set up indicate that younger subjects find it easier to adapt to longer cycles of sleep and waking, presumably because their sleep habits are less firmly established.

Stages of Sleep—The Nightly Roller-Coaster Ride

Question: What causes sleep?

Early conceptions of sleep linked it to fatigue. It was thought that some substance caused by fatigue must accumulate in the bloodstream and cause sleep. But studies of Siamese twins (individuals whose bodies are joined at birth) show that sleep is *not* caused by anything in the blood. One twin can frequently be observed sleeping while the second is awake (see Fig. 7-2). That sleep is more than a simple reaction to fatigue is also demonstrated by the well-rested student who must fight to stay awake during a boring lecture. In many ways the brain is as busy during sleep as it is during waking. Sleep is generated by activity in several important structures in the brain (hypothalamus, reticular formation, and cortex).

Question: What happens when you fall asleep?

The Stages of Sleep The changes that come with sleep can be measured through use of the EEG (electroencephalograph, or brain-wave machine). Except at death, the brain constantly gives off tiny electrical

Fig. 7-2 Siamese twins share the same blood supply, yet one head sleeps while the other is awake. (*Life Magazine* © Time, Inc., 1955.)

signals that can be amplified and recorded. When a person is awake and alert the EEG shows a pattern of small fast waves called *beta* (see Fig. 7-3). Immediately before sleep the EEG shifts to a different pattern of larger and slower waves called *alpha*. (Alpha waves also occur at other times when one is relaxed and thoughts are allowed to drift.) As the eyes close, breathing becomes slow and regular, the pulse rate slows, and body temperature drops.

Stage 1 As the person loses consciousness and enters *light sleep*, the heart rate slows even more. Breathing becomes more irregular; the muscles of the body relax (sometimes causing a reflex jerk). In Stage 1 sleep the EEG is made up of small, irregular waves with some alpha.

Stage 2 As sleep deepens, the EEG begins to show short bursts of activity called "sleep spindles" (see Fig. 7-3).

Stage 3 In Stage 3 a new brain wave called *delta* begins to appear. Delta waves are very large and slow. Delta waves signal deeper sleep and a further loss of consciousness.

Stage 4 About an hour after sleep begins, *deep sleep* is reached in Stage 4 when the brain-wave pattern becomes almost pure delta waves. In Stage 4, a person is in a state of nearly complete oblivion. If a loud noise awakens a person during Stage 4, he will emerge from sleep confused and will not remember the noise.

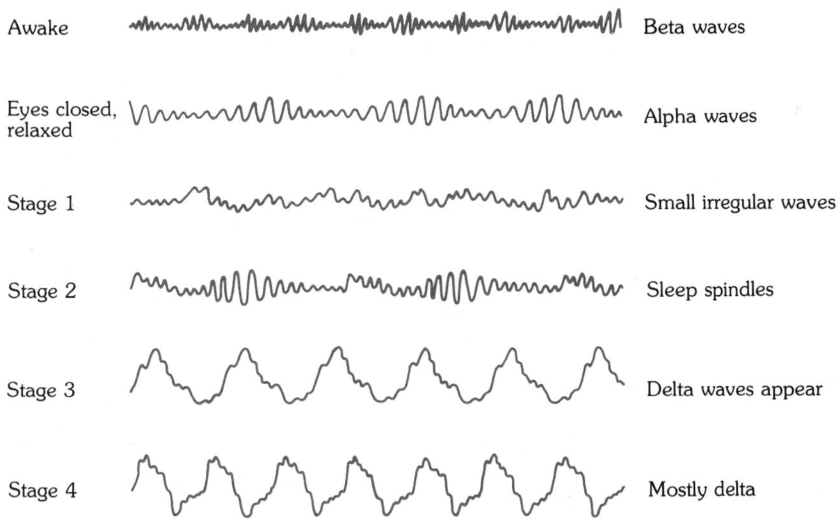

Fig. 7-3 Changes in brain-wave patterns associated with various stages of sleep.

After spending some time in Stage 4, the sleeper returns (through Stages 2 and 3) to Stage 1. This cycle of changes between deep sleep and light sleep is repeated four or five times per night.

With the discovery of sleep stages, it was almost immediately noticed that the eyes of a sleeper make rapid movements during each return to Stage 1. Subjects awakened at these times almost always report that they are dreaming. The two most basic states of sleep now appear to be rapid-eye-movement (or REM) sleep, and non-rapid-eye-movement (NREM) sleep (Oswald, 1962). NREM sleep is dream-free sleep made up of Stages 2, 3, and 4. NREM sleep is the deepest physical sleep. It increases with fatigue and exercise. REM, or Stage 1 sleep, totals only about 1½ hours per night, but because of its connection with dreaming it is every bit as important as NREM sleep.

Learning Check

See if you can answer these questions before reading on. Circle the correct response.

1. Visions of lacy designs and vibrations in stationary objects continue for many days after a sleep-deprived person returns to normal sleep. T or F?

2. Sleep represents a total loss of consciousness. T or F?

3. Adults need more sleep than children because they are more easily fatigued. T or F?

4. Younger subjects find it easier to adapt to longer cycles of sleep and waking. T or F?
5. Delta waves indicate a sleeper is in light sleep. T or F?
6. Dreaming occurs in light sleep. T or F?

Answers: 1. F 2. F 3. F 4. T 5. F 6. T

Dreaming—A Separate Reality

Modern sleep and dream research allow us to answer some age-old questions about dreams.

Question: Is it true that dreams are never in color?

About one dream in three is in color. There do not seem to be any important differences between colored and black and white dreams or the people who have them.

Question: Does everyone dream? Do dreams occur in an instant?

All people normally dream four or five times a night. The first dream lasts only about ten minutes. Dreams are spaced about ninety minutes apart, and each succeeding dream lasts a little longer. The final dream in the morning averages thirty minutes and may last as long as fifty. Dreams, therefore, occur in "real time"; they do not occur as a "flash" (Dement, 1960).

Question: If all people dream, why do some people say they don't?

Not all people remember their dreams. Subjects in dream research who had never before remembered a dream are often shocked by the vividness of their dreams when they are awakened during REM sleep.

Question: What happens to the body when a person dreams?

As discussed before, the brain returns to light sleep and rapid eye movements begin. Dream periods have been called *paradoxical sleep* because the sleeper looks like he is about to wake up but is actually harder to arouse. This may be because during REM sleep outside noises and other stimuli are incorporated into the dream. In one experiment subjects displaying REMs were sprayed with droplets of water. Of these subjects 42 percent reported dreams of rain, Niagara Falls, and so forth (Dement & Wolpert, 1958). In this sense, dreams may protect sleep.

Dreaming is a time of high emotion. The heart beats irregularly, and blood pressure and breathing fluctuates. Males usually have an erection, and females show signs of sexual arousal. This occurs for all dreams, not just those that are erotic. With all this emotional activity it might be expected that the muscles would be tense during dreaming. The reverse is true, however. Except for the eyes, the body becomes quite still during dreaming. It has been suggested that muscle relaxation may protect a person from acting out dreams.

Question: Does sleepwalking occur during dreaming?

Surprisingly, no. Sleepwalking and talking occur during Stages 3 and 4. This seems to be why sleep talking makes little sense and why a sleepwalker who is awakened is confused and remembers little (Jacobson *et al.*, 1965).

Stage 4 sleep is also the source of *night terrors*. Night terrors are severely frightening experiences that can be distinguished from the normal nightmare. A nightmare is simply a bad dream. *Nightmares* occur during REM sleep. They are usually very brief. The person awakens and remembers the bad dream in complete detail. During Stage 4 *night terrors*, a person experiences blind panic and may hallucinate frightening dream objects into the room itself. The attack may last fifteen or twenty minutes. When it is over, the person awakens drenched with perspiration, but has only a vague memory of the terror itself. Night terrors are more frequent in childhood, but continue to plague some adults throughout their lives (Kanner, 1957).

Question: How important are dreams? Are they essential for normal functioning?

To answer this question, dream researcher William Dement awakened subjects each time rapid eye movements and brain-wave changes signaled that they were dreaming. Subjects prevented from dreaming for several nights in a row showed an increasing need to dream. Dement only had to wake subjects four or five times the first night, but by the fifth night, twenty or thirty wakings were often necessary to prevent dreaming (Dement, 1960).

People deprived of dream sleep experienced memory lapses, difficulty concentrating, and became tense and anxious during the day. Subjects awakened an equal number of times during NREM sleep showed none of these effects. It appears that REM sleep and dreaming may be essential to keep the brain in good working order. People who are under stress spend more time in REM sleep (Hartmann, 1973).

The need for dreaming is also indicated by the *REM rebound effect*. After being deprived of REM sleep for several nights, a person will dream extra amounts on the first uninterrupted night of sleep. One researcher has used the REM rebound effect to link dreaming to schizophrenia. Schizophrenic patients deprived of REM sleep fail to show the rebound effect. This suggests that they may be discharging dream activity while awake. Perhaps the bizarre experiences of some disturbed individuals can be understood as the blending of dreams with normal daytime experiences (Zarcone, 1971).

Dreams and Beyond

Question: What do people usually dream about?

Calvin Hall, a noted authority on dreams, has collected and analyzed over 10,000 dreams. Hall (1966) found that most dreams are extensions of everyday experience. The favorite dream setting is familiar rooms in a house. Action usually takes place between the dreamer and two or three other people with whom the dreamer is emotionally involved—friends, enemies, parents, or employers. Actions in dreams are also predominantly familiar: running, jumping, riding, sitting, talking, and watching. About half of the recorded dreams had sexual elements. Dreams of flying, floating, and falling occur less frequently. Hall also found that if you're dreaming more now, you may be enjoying it less. Unpleasant emotions such as fear, anger, and sadness are more frequent in dreams than pleasant emotions.

Charles Tart (1969) has recently called attention to two types of dreaming that differ markedly from the normal dream. The first of these has been called the *"high" dream*. In the high dream, the individual dreams he or she has taken a psychedelic drug like LSD or mescaline and then experiences the sensory distortion, brilliant colors, and feelings of ecstasy that occur when a drug is actually taken. These are so vivid that the person may lose track of the fact that he or she is dreaming. Some prior experience with a psychedelic drug may be necessary for recognizing a high dream. It is, therefore, unclear how many people have had such experiences.

A second unusual form of dreaming, which may relate to the high dream, has been called the *lucid dream*. This is a dream in which the dreamer "wakes" from an ordinary dream and feels capable of normal thought and action *but* remains in the dream world. The lucid dream, in

Fig. 7-4 The elements of a dream are often distorted and incongruous. (Engraving by Anthony Willoughby.)

other words, seems to the dreamer as real as everyday experience. One author describes such a lucid dream:

> I dreamt that I stood at the table before a window. On the table were different objects. I was perfectly well aware that I was dreaming and I considered what sorts of experiments I could make. I began by trying to break glass, by beating it with a stone. . . . Yet it did not break. . . . Then I took a fine claret-glass from the table and struck it with my fist, with all my might, at the same time reflecting on how dangerous it would be to do this in waking life; yet the glass remained whole. But lo! when I looked back at it again after some time it was broken.
>
> It broke all right, but a little too late, like an actor who misses his cue. This gave me a very curious impression of being in a *fake-world* (van Eeden, 1913).

The lucid dream may also give rise to *out-of-body experiences* in which the dreamer perceives his sleeping body from a point of view outside his own physical body. The believability of out-of-body experiences has recently been enhanced by the work of Elizabeth Kübler-Ross. Kübler-Ross is an expert on death and the process of dying. (See Chapter 13.) Recently Kübler-Ross has interviewed a large number of people who have "died" and then been revived. Many report out-of-body experiences. In one such experience, a woman told of moving about the room and trying to tell doctors who were feverishly working over her body that it was all right to let her die!

Interpreting Dreams—Doorway to the Subconscious?

Sigmund Freud's book *The Interpretation of Dreams* (1900) opened a whole new world for psychological investigation. Prior to Freud, most psychologists considered dreams a meaningless carry-over of waking thoughts. By analyzing his own dreams, Freud saw that many represented *wish fulfillment*. Thus, a student who is angry at a teacher may dream of successfully embarrassing the teacher in class; a lonely man may dream of romance; or a hungry child may dream of food.

Not all wish fulfillment is so direct. Freud believed that the conscience relaxes during sleep, allowing dreams to fulfill or express *repressed*, or *unconscious*, desires or conflicts. Many such desires (particularly those associated with sex or aggression) are so threatening that they must be expressed in disguised form so as not to directly arouse the person's conscience. A woman sexually attracted to her best friend's husband might dream of stealing her friend's wedding ring and placing it on her own hand, an indirect representation of her true desires. (For a discussion of the use of dream analysis in psychotherapy see Chapter 23.)

To unlock dreams, Freud identified four *dream processes* which help disguise the hidden meaning of a consciously remembered dream. The first process is called *condensation*. Through condensation a single character in a dream may represent several people at once. A character in a dream that looks like a teacher, acts like your father, talks like your mother, and is dressed like your employer might be a condensation of prominent authority figures in your life. (It might also be someone on his way to a masquerade party!) A second means of disguising dream content is *displacement.* Through displacement the most important emotions of a dream may be redirected toward "safe" or seemingly unimportant images. A student angry at his parents might dream of accidentally wrecking their car instead of directly attacking them.

A third dream process is *symbolization*. This is one of the most controversial of Freud's ideas. Freud believed that dreams are usually expressed in images that are symbolic rather than literal in their meaning. The list below summarizes some common Freudian interpretations of dream symbols. You will notice that the interpretations strongly emphasize sexual motives and tend to be highly imaginative. Many psychologists reject such interpretations as misleading.

What did Freud see in dreams? Common Freudian dream interpretations and their symbols:

1. Parents—emperors, empresses, kings, queens
2. Children (brothers and sisters)—small animals
3. Birth—water
4. Death—journey
5. Nakedness—clothes, uniforms
6. Male genitals—sticks, umbrellas, poles, trees, anything elongated, pointed weapons of all sorts
7. Erection—balloons, airplanes, zeppelins, dreamer himself flying
8. Male sexual symbols—reptiles, fishes, serpent, hand or foot
9. Female genitalia—pits, hollow caves, jars, bottles, doors, ships, chests
10. Breasts—apples, peaches, other fruit
11. Intercourse—mounting a ladder or stairs, entering a room, walking down a hall or into a tunnel, horseback riding, and so forth

A process called *secondary elaboration* is the fourth method by which the meaning of dreams is disguised. Secondary elaboration is the tendency to reorganize a dream when remembering it. The story line of the dream is made more logical, and additional details are added to connect the jumbled dream images. You may be relieved to learn that Freud's is not the only approach to dream interpretation. Additional viewpoints are presented in the "applications" section of this chapter.

Our discussion of sleep and dreaming has led us from areas in which heavily documented laboratory research is available to the twilight zone of psychology. The future importance of altered states of consciousness in general and of dreaming and related experiences remains an exciting open question.

Learning Check

Match the following:

A. REM sleep **B.** NREM sleep

______ **1.** Dreams

______ **2.** Nightmares

______ **3.** Night terrors

______ **4.** Sleepwalking

______ **5.** Sleep talking

______ **6.** Signs of emotion and sexual arousal

______ **7.** Relaxed muscles, little movement.

8. People deprived of dream sleep:
a. Become tense and anxious during the day
b. Try to dream more frequently
c. Show a REM rebound effect
d. All of the above

9. In secondary elaboration a single dream character stands for many others. T or F?

Answers: **1.** A **2.** A **3.** B **4.** B **5.** B **6.** Usually A; night terrors are the exception where emotion is concerned **7.** A **8.** *d* **9.** F

Resources Summary

Sleep is essential for survival. Animals and people deprived of sleep experience involuntary *microsleeps*. Extended sleep loss may cause symptoms resembling psychosis. The amount of daily sleep decreases steadily from birth to old age. Sleep schedules show some flexibility, but eight hours remains the average under most conditions. Sleep is actively produced by brain structures. Sleep occurs in four stages. Stage 1 is "light" sleep, and Stage 4 is "deep" sleep. The sleeper alternates between Stages 1 and 4 (passing through 2 and 3) during sleep. Dreaming and rapid eye movements occur during Stage 1 sleep. Four to five dreams occur every night. Everyone dreams. Dreaming is coupled with emotional arousal but relaxed muscles. *Night terrors* (not the same as nightmares) occur during Stage 3 or 4 sleep. People deprived of dream sleep show emotional changes and dream more (the *REM rebound effect*) when allowed to sleep normally. Most dreams are about familiar settings, people, and actions. Two previously unrecognized forms of dreaming may be the "high dream" and the "lucid dream." Freud believed that dreams express unconscious wishes, impulses, or emotions. He believed the meaning of dreams is hidden by *condensation*, *displacement*, *symbolization*, and *secondary elaboration*.

Applications

Getting to Sleep

Question: What causes insomnia? Is there anything that can be done about it?

Most of us are victims from time to time of minor sleep disturbances. Some repeated insomniacs have been found to have a drop in blood sugar during the night. The restlessness and hunger this causes can be avoided by having a small snack before sleeping. More often, insomnia is caused by worry, stress, or excitement. This usually sets up a cycle in which arousal (from anxiety, excitement, or whatever) interferes with sleep; then frustration and anger resulting from the inability to sleep causes more arousal, which further interferes with sleep, which causes more frustration, and so on.

In one ingenious experiment, this cycle was broken by giving insomniacs fake drugs. The insomniacs were told that the side effects of the pills they were taking would be feelings of arousal and tension. Since they blamed their arousal on the pills instead of their inability to sleep, they relaxed and actually got to sleep sooner. This suggests that the best way to beat insomnia is to avoid fighting it. It is usually best to get up and do something useful or satisfying when you have difficulty sleeping (reading a textbook might not be a bad choice of useful activities).

Question: Why not just take a sleeping pill if you can't sleep?

Sleeping pills available without prescription have little or no sleep-inducing effect. Almost every other sleep drug known (particularly alcohol and barbiturates) suppresses dream sleep (Hartmann, 1966). The long-term effects of sleeping pills can, therefore, be very undesirable. Severe alcoholics who repeatedly go without REM sleep eventually have horrendous nightmares.

It is unfortunate that sleeping pills are most often used at times of depression, death, occupational change, or conflict. Each of these increases the amount of REM sleep necessary to restore brain functioning. The use of alcohol and barbiturates, therefore, becomes an especially poor way to get more "rest" at times of stress (Gresham, Webb & Williams, 1963).

Exploring Your Dreams

If Freudian dream interpretation were the only approach to understanding dreams, there would be little hope of successfully learning from your own dreams. According to Freud, the meaning of dreams is too deeply hidden. But there are other points of view. Dream theorist Calvin Hall (1966) prefers to think of dreams as plays and the dreamer as a playwright. Hall does admit that the images and ideas in dreams tend to be more *primitive* than those when one is awake. Nevertheless, much can be learned from a dream by simply considering the setting, cast of characters, plot, and important emotions portrayed. Another dream researcher, Rosslund Cartwright (1969), suggests that one's everyday dream life can be a source of varied experience and personal enrichment comparable to that brought about by positive experiences with psychedelic drugs. Cartwright encourages dream explorations as an avenue for personal growth.

Dream theorist Ann Faraday (1972) also believes in the value of studying one's own dreams. Faraday considers dreams a message *from* yourself *to* yourself. She suggests that the way to understand one's own dreams is to remember them, write them down, and look for the message they contain. Faraday offers several suggestions for catching dreams:

1. Keep a pen and paper or a tape recorder beside your bed.
2. Have a light handy.
3. Before retiring, consciously intend to remember your dreams.
4. If you rarely remember your dreams, you may want to set an alarm clock to go off two hours after you go to sleep. When the clock awakens you,reset it for two hours later, *etc*. One or more of these awakenings should occur during a dream.
5. Immediately record as many details of a dream as you can remember. Dream memories disappear quickly.

If you have trouble seeing the meaning of a dream, you may find a technique used by Fritz Perls helpful. Perls, the originator of gestalt therapy, considered most dreams a special message about what's missing in our lives, what we avoid doing, or feelings that need to be "reowned." Perls felt that dreams are a way of filling in gaps in personal experience (Perls, 1969). An approach that Perls found quite helpful in understanding a dream is to "take the part of" or "speak for" each of the characters and objects in the dream. This process of role playing may be clarified by the following excerpts from one of Perl's dream-work seminars. Linda, one of the participants, has just described dream images of a lake drying up and the animals in it dying. At the bottom of the lake she expects to find some treasure, but when she looks all she can find is an old license plate. Perls begins by asking her to play the license plate.

> I am an old license plate, thrown in the bottom of a lake. I have no use because I'm of no value—although I'm not rusted—I'm outdated, so I can't be used as a license plate.

Perls urges her to continue:

> Useless, outdated . . . the use of a license plate is to allow—give a car permission to go . . . and I can't give anyone permission to do anything because I'm outdated.

Next, Linda is asked to play the lake.

> I'm a lake . . . I'm drying up, and disappearing, soaking into the earth . . . (with a touch of surprise) *dying.* . . . But when I soak into the earth, I become a part of the earth—so maybe I water the surrounding area, so . . . even in the lake, even in my bed, flowers can grow (sighs). . . . New life can grow . . . from me (cries) (excerpted from Perls, 1969, pp. 86–87).

Thus we see that Linda's dream has expressed her fears of dying and being unwanted. Perls urges her to recognize that she can express the creative feelings in the dream and that she doesn't need a "license" to do so. It is obvious that she has learned something about herself through this exercise.

Using Your Dreams

> *There was a time when meadow, grove, and streams,*
> *The earth, and every common sight,*
> *To me did seem*
> *Apparelled in celestial light,*
> *The glory and the freshness of a dream.*
>
> William Wordsworth

History is full of cases where dreams have been a pathway to creativity and discovery. The chemist Friedrich Kekule von Stradonitz won a Nobel Prize for discovering that the molecules in the chemical benzene are arranged in a ring. His discovery came when he was awakened by a dream of a snake eating its own tail. As soon as Kekule woke from his dream, he knew the mystery of benzene's structure had been solved. The circle formed by the image of the snake had suggested to him that benzene was shaped like a ring.

Another Nobel Prize winner who had a dream breakthrough is Dr. Otto Loewi. Loewi had spent years on research relating to the chemical transmission of nerve impulses. A tremendous breakthrough in his research came when he dreamed of an experiment three nights in a row. The first two nights he woke up and scribbled the experiment on a pad, but the next morning he was unable to tell what the notes meant. On the third night he got up after having the dream, and instead of making notes went straight to his laboratory and performed the crucial experiment. Loewi later commented that if the experiment had occurred to him while awake he surely would have rejected it.

Loewi's experience gives some insight into the potential value of dreams for the production of creative solutions. The dream state is one of reduced inhibition and may be especially useful in solving problems that require a fresh point of view.

The likelihood of being able to take advantage of dreams for problem solving is improved if you "set" yourself before retiring by thinking intently about a problem you wish to solve. Try to steep yourself in the problem by stating it clearly and reviewing all relevant information. Then use Faraday's suggestions (listed in the previous section) to catch your dreams. While this cannot be guaranteed to produce a novel problem solution or a new insight, it is guaranteed to be an adventure.

Questions for Discussion

The following questions may be of interest for thought or classroom discussion.

1. How would your life change if you had to sleep fifteen hours per day? How would it change if you only needed two hours a day?
2. Would you give up sleep if you could?
3. Have you ever gone without sleep for an extended period, or have you had to adapt to an unusual sleep schedule? If so, what were your reactions? Your greatest difficulties?
4. Describe a recent dream you have had. How does it relate to your daytime experiences and feelings? What additional meanings can you find in it?
5. How important are your dreams to you? What value do they have? Do you think recording your dreams would be a worthwhile practice?
6. Have you ever solved a problem in your dreams? How much control do you have over what you dream?
7. You have a friend who claims never to dream. How could you realistically prove to your friend that he or she does dream?

Suggestions for Further Reading

Faraday, A. *Dream Power.* Coward, McCann, and Geoghegan, 1972.

Freud, S. *Interpretation of Dreams.* Hogarth, 1953.

Hall, C. *The Meaning of Dreams.* McGraw-Hill, 1966.

Hartmann, E. *The Biology of Dreaming.* Charles C Thomas, 1967.

Kales, A. (ed.) *Sleep: Physiology and Pathology.* Lippincott, 1969.

Kramer, M. (ed.) *Dream Psychology and the New Biology of Dreaming.* Charles C Thomas, 1969.

Luce, G. G., and J. Segal. *Sleep.* Coward-McCann, 1966.

Murray, E. J. *Sleep, Dreams, and Arousal.* Appleton-Century-Crofts, 1966.

Contents

Learning, Memory, and Thinking   Unit Three

Conditioning

8

Chapter Preview

What Did You Learn in School Today?

When the author was in college, students discovered an interesting "game" that could be played with the plumbing in the dorms. If a toilet was flushed while someone was taking a shower, the cold-water pressure dropped so much that it caused the shower suddenly to become scalding hot. Naturally, the shower victim screamed in terror as his reflexes caused him to leap back in pain. Soon it was further discovered that if several students flushed all *the toilets at once, the effects were multiplied many times over!*

Now, a flushing toilet has to be one of the world's most uninspiring stimuli. But for a time there was a whole crop of University of California, Riverside, students who jumped involuntarily whenever they heard a toilet flush. Their reaction was the result of a special form of learning called classical conditioning*. Details of how and why classical conditioning occurs are explored in this chapter.*

Consider another learning situation. Let's say that you are at school and that you are "starving to death." Locating a vending machine, you deposit your last dime to buy a candy bar. Your stomach growls in anticipation as you press the button, and . . . nothing happens. Being civilized and in complete control, you press the other buttons, try the coin return, and look for an attendant. Still nothing. Your stomach growls again. Being no longer either civilized or self-controlled, you give the machine a little kick (just to let it know how you feel). Then, as you turn away, the machine begins to whirr and out pops a candy bar plus 15¢ change. Once this happens, the chances are that you will repeat the "kicking process" in the future. If it pays off several times more, it may become a rather permanent habit. In this case, learning is based on instrumental conditioning, *also called* operant conditioning. *Although it may not yet be obvious, classical conditioning and instrumental conditioning are very different processes. These differences will be explained in this chapter.*

Resources

Classical Conditioning—How to Teach Your Little Brother to Salivate

Question: How was classical conditioning discovered?

At the beginning of the twentieth century, something happened in the lab of the Russian physiologist Ivan Pavlov that raised him to a position of international recognition. What happened was so unastounding that a lesser man might have ignored it: Pavlov's experimental subjects drooled at him!

Actually, Pavlov was studying the digestive process. In order to study and measure salivation, a part of the digestive process, he placed meat powder or some tidbit on a dog's tongue. After a time, Pavlov noticed that his animals were salivating *before* the food was placed in their mouths. Later, the dogs even began to salivate at the mere sight of Pavlov entering the room. Pavlov recognized that this was something more than misplaced affection. Salivation is normally a reflex (automatic, unlearned) response. Some form of learning had to be taking place in order for the animals to be salivating at the sight of food. Pavlov called this form of learning *conditioning*. Because of its importance in psychology's history, it is now called *classical conditioning.*

Question: Was Pavlov the first person to study conditioning?

The year before Pavlov began his studies of classical conditioning, an American graduate student, E. B. Twitmeyer, accidentally conditioned the patellar reflex, or knee jerk, of a human subject to the sound of a bell. Twitmeyer reported his discovery to other American psychologists, but he was ignored. "What could be important about a knee jerking when a bell rang?" they asked. Pavlov provided the answer. He spent forty years investigating and convinced others of its importance. This brought classical conditioning into the mainstream of psychology. Now the term *conditioning* has filtered into most people's vocabularies. In spite of this, few people really understand the process. Compare your understanding of conditioning with the information that follows.

Question: How did Pavlov study conditioning?

In Pavlov's classic experiments, a bell was rung immediately before meat powder was placed on a dog's tongue. The meat powder caused reflex salivation to occur. Many times the bell was rung before the meat powder was given to the dogs. Eventually, the bell alone began to produce salivation (see Fig. 8-1). (This was demonstrated by occasionally omitting the meat

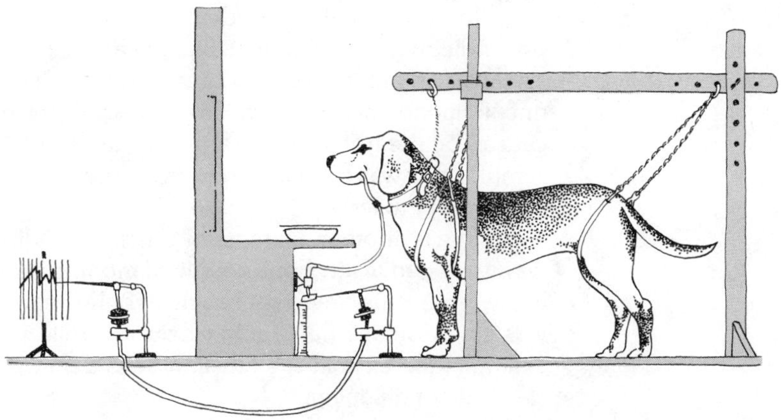

Fig. 8-1 Pavlov's conditioning apparatus. In Pavlov's early experiments, a tube carried saliva from the dog's mouth to a lever which activated a recording device (far left). The placing of a dish of food in front of the dog was paired with various other stimuli for conditioning.

powder after ringing the bell.) Pavlov labeled the bell a *conditioned* (meaning learned) *stimulus* (CS). The meat powder he called the *unconditioned stimulus* (UCS) because the dog did not have to learn to respond to it. Most unconditioned stimuli produce reflex responses. Since a reflex response is "built into" the nervous system, it is called an *unconditioned* (not learned) *response* (UCR). Salivation was the UCR in Pavlov's experiment. When the sound of the bell causes salivation without the appearance of the meat powder, salivation can no longer be called a simple reflex. It is therefore called a *conditioned* (learned) *response* (CR).

Question: Are all these terms and code letters really necessary?

In a word, yes. Pavlov's terminology helps us recognize the similarities that underlie different instances of classical conditioning. As an example, see if you can apply Pavlov's terms to explain the example of the shower and the flushing toilet:

1. What is the unconditioned (the unlearned) response? ____________

____

2. What is the unconditioned stimulus that causes the response? ______

____

3. What is the conditioned stimulus? ____________________

____

Now let's see if you understand the terms. In Fig. 8-2, example 1, the unconditioned, or unlearned, response was the jumping from the hot water. That was an unlearned, reflex response to the hot water. In example 2, the unconditioned stimulus was the hot water, or more specifically, the pain caused by the hot water. Example 3, the conditioned stimulus, that is, the stimulus that was conditioned to cause the person to jump, was the sound of the flushing toilet.

Here is another example of classical conditioning. A Vietnam veteran was wounded twice. For a couple of months after his return, he would dive to the ground anytime a car backfired or he heard a loud noise. His response was so automatic he couldn't help it. While this is a rather complicated example, the ex-soldier's reaction does demonstrate several other facts of classical conditioning:

Reinforcement The connection between a conditioned stimulus (CS) and a conditioned response (CR) must be *reinforced*, or strengthened. Conditioning is reinforced when the CS is followed by an unconditioned stimulus (UCS). In the case of the Vietnam vet, the loud noise of gunfire was the CS; the diving to the ground was the CR; and the UCS was the pain of being wounded. Of course, most people will jump at a loud noise, but in the case of the veteran, his extreme reaction of diving to the ground after a loud noise was reinforced because of its prior association with pain.

Extinction Since the veteran stopped diving to the ground after a few months, his conditioned response was apparently *extinguished*. Condition-

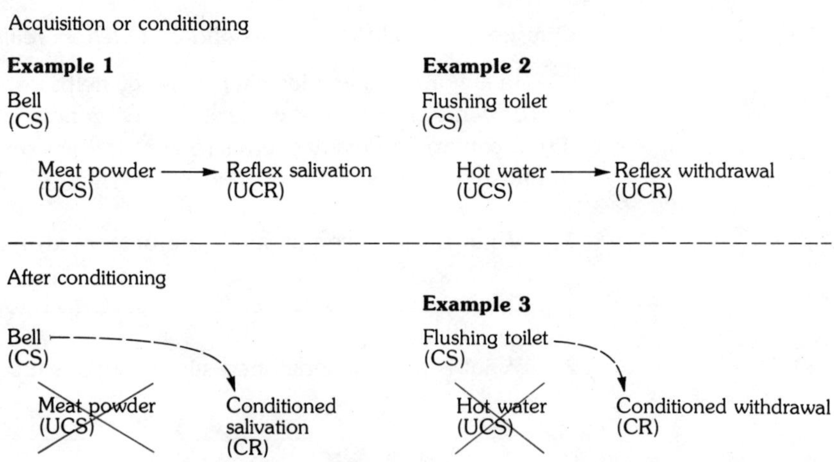

Fig. 8-2 The conditioning procedure.

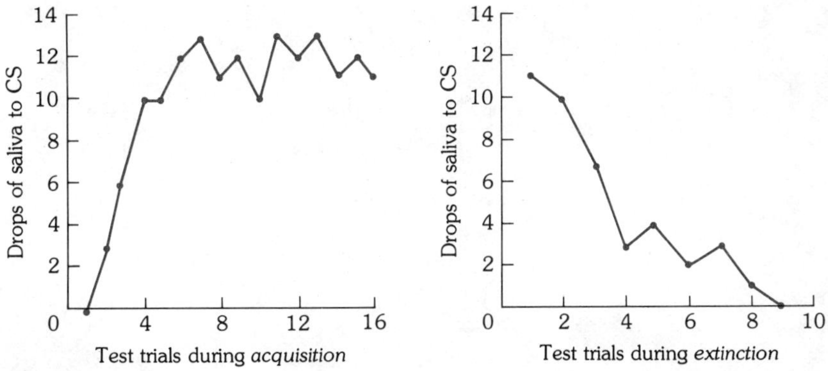

Fig. 8-3 Acquisition and extinction of a conditioned response. (After Pavlov, 1927.)

ing can not only cause us to acquire a response; it can also cause us to lose a response. Thus, conditioning is a reversible procedure. Since the CS (in the vet's case, a loud noise) is presented many times without being followed by a UCS (pain from being wounded), the CR grows weaker and disappears. This is called *extinction.*

Stimulus Generalization Once a person or an animal has been conditioned to respond to a particular CS, other stimuli similar to the CS may cause a response. This is called *stimulus generalization*. For example, when the Vietnam veteran dived to the ground when he heard any loud noise, he was generalizing his response to noises that sounded like gunshots.

American behaviorist John B. Watson demonstrated stimulus generalization in a classic experiment involving an eleven-month-old infant. In this case a loud noise was used as the unconditioned stimulus for a fear response in the infant.

> Watson wanted to see if fear caused by a loud noise could be transferred to other stimuli. An infant, Albert, was allowed to play with a furry white rat. Albert was unafraid of the rat and enjoyed playing with it. Henceforth, each time the rat was placed in front of Albert, an iron bar was struck with a hammer. This frightened and startled Albert. Soon Albert began to cry whenever the rat was placed in front of him (Watson & Rayner, 1920).

The rat, associated with loud noise, became a conditioned stimulus for fear. Once Albert had learned to fear the white rat, he transferred his fear to almost anything white and furry. He cried and was fearful when presented with a white rabbit, fluffy white toys, or wads of cotton. Albert might have even "freaked out" the first time he saw Santa Claus because he was removed from the experiment prior to the *extinction* procedures that were planned to reverse his fear. Do you know anyone named Albert who is afraid of Santa?

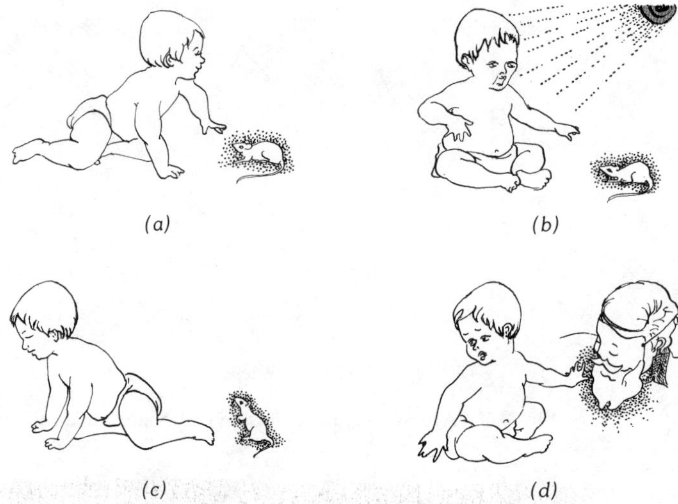

Fig. 8-4 After the white rat is associated with a loud frightening noise (in *b*), Albert develops a conditioned fear for the rat that generalizes to other white furry objects (like the man's beard in *d*).

Learning Check

Make certain you can answer these questions before continuing:

1. Strengthening a response to make it occur more is called:

____

2. Causing a person or animal to reverse or lose a conditioned response is called: ______________________________

3. When you react to a stimulus with the same response you have learned to give another similar stimulus, it is called: ________________

Answers: **1.** reinforcement **2.** extinction **3.** stimulus generalization

Classical Conditioning in Humans—Seen Any Good Movies Lately?

Question: How much human learning is based on classical conditioning?

Classical conditioning depends heavily on the existence of reflex responses. A *reflex* is a dependable, inborn stimulus-response connection. For example, pain causes a reflex action in parts of the body. The reflex of the eye to bright lights is the narrowing of the pupil. A puff of air to the eye causes an eye blink. Tart, acidic foods like pickles cause salivation. With humans it is entirely possible through conditioning to connect any of these reflex responses to a new stimulus. You could, if you wished, ring a bell, squirt pickle juice in your little brother's mouth, and establish conditioned salivation to the bell. However, in practice, simple conditioning of human reflexes doesn't happen very often.

Question: Then why bother talking about it?

Because more *subtle* kinds of conditioning greatly affect human behavior. For example, both physical and *emotional* responses may be classically conditioned to new stimuli. A common example of such "gut" conditioning is a *phobia*. A phobia is fear which persists even when no realistic danger exists. Because little Albert's conditioned fear of the white rat was not extinguished, he might have developed a lifetime phobia for anything white and furry. People who fear water, heights, thunder, automobiles, or Santa Claus often can trace their fear to one or two unfortunate experiences in which they were frightened, injured, emotionally upset, or subjected to pain while in the presence of the feared object or stimulus. A fear of water caused by a near drowning may spread through stimulus generalization to fears of boating or even bathing. These examples are called *conditioned emotional responses (CERs)* and play an important part in daily psychological functioning.

Vicarious, or Secondhand, Conditioning The importance of conditioned emotional responses (CERs) can be seen by a look at a recent experiment. Two groups of subjects were selected for the experiment. Subjects A were asked to watch while subjects B received painful, electric shocks. Actually, subjects B, unknown to subjects A, were only acting and pretending the shocks were painful. Each "shock" to subjects B was indicated by a signal light. Later, subjects A, after watching the light come on, were tested for emotional responses to the light. Even though they had never received a shock, subjects A showed GSR (galvanic skin response) changes when the light came on (Bandura & Rosenthal, 1966).

Question: What is the GSR?

The GSR measures change in electrical resistance of the skin. It is usually recorded from the palms of the hands, where sweating indicates emotional arousal. The experiment just mentioned shows that emotions displayed by others can cause a person to experience emotion vicariously, or secondhand. When you are watching a play or a movie, you often live vicariously, feeling the emotions, fears, and dangers of the players. The same thing happened in the experiment. Another person's emotional reactions to the "shocks" reinforced an emotional response to the light. When the light came on, subjects A reacted emotionally even though there was no real pain.

Vicarious classical conditioning, as it is called, probably plays a part in emotional reactions to many situations. For example, the movie *Psycho* temporarily made small motels and shower stalls conditioned fear stimuli for many people. The movie *Jaws* made ocean swimming a conditioned fear stimulus for others. If movies can affect us, the emotional reactions of parents, friends, and relatives might be even stronger. How, for instance, does a city child learn to fear snakes and to respond emotionally to mere pictures of them? Perhaps he has been told that "snakes are dangerous," but his *emotional response* has probably been learned by observing the negative reaction of others to snakes.

The emotional attitudes we have developed toward certain types of food, political parties, minority groups, escalators—whatever—is probably not only conditioned by direct experience but vicariously as well. Parents may do well to look in a mirror if they wonder how or where a child has "picked up" a particular fear or emotional attitude.

Learning Check

1. A ____________________ is a dependable, inborn stimulus-response connection.

2. CERs refers to ____________________

3. When a person reacts emotionally to the pain, fear, or joy of others, it is called ____________________

Answers:

1. reflex **2.** conditioned emotional response **3.** vicarious, or secondhand, conditioning

Instrumental Conditioning—Survival of the Fittest . . . Response

Question: What is instrumental conditioning, and how is it different from classical conditioning?

The basic principle of *instrumental conditioning* is simple. An act that is *instrumental* in producing reward tends to be repeated. Think of the earlier example of the vending machine. Since kicking the machine was immediately followed by reward, the odds that the "kicking response" would be repeated were increased. The idea that reward affects a response is certainly nothing new to parents (and other trainers of small animals). However, parents, as well as teachers, politicians, businessmen, foremen, and others, may use reward in ways that are haphazard, inexact, misguided, or *superstitious*.

Foremost among psychologists who have contributed to the precision of our understanding of instrumental learning is B. F. Skinner. Skinner prefers to call instrumental conditioning *operant conditioning* because learning occurs as an organism actively *operates* on the environment. In other words, operant responses are voluntary. Waving your hand to get attention in class or a dog sitting up for a bone are examples of voluntary operant responses. In classical conditioning, responses are *not voluntary*; they are learned reflexes, such as salivating at the sound of the bell.

Acquisition of an Operant Response Most laboratory research on operant conditioning takes place in some form of a "Skinner box," named after B. F. Skinner, who invented it for experiments in operant conditioning (see Fig. 8-5). A look into a typical Skinner box will clarify the process of operant conditioning.

Chapter 1
The Adventures of Mickey Rat

A hungry rat is placed in a small cagelike chamber. The walls are bare except for a metal lever and a tray from which food pellets may be dispensed (see drawing).

Frankly, there's not much to do in a Skinner box. This increases the chances that our subject will make the response we are interested in rewarding. Hunger also ensures that the animal will be actively emitting or giving off a variety of responses.

Now let's take another look at our subject.

Chapter 2
The Further Adventures of Mickey Rat

For a while our subject walks around, grooms, sniffs at the corners, or stands on his hind legs—all typical "rat behaviors." Then it happens; he places his paw on the lever to get a better view of the top of the cage. *Click!* The lever depresses, and a food pellet drops into the tray. Investigating the tray, he eats the pellet and then grooms himself. Up and exploring the cage again, he leans on the lever. *Click!* After a trip to the food tray, he returns to the bar and sniffs at it, then puts his foot on it. *Click!* Soon the rat's behavior has settled into a smooth pattern of frequent bar pressing.

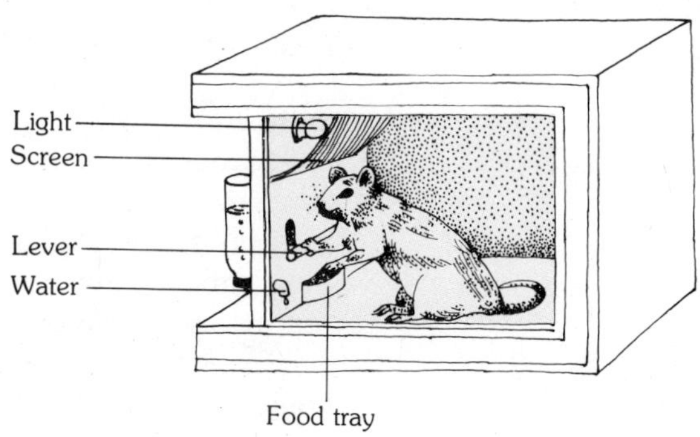

Fig. 8-5 The Skinner box. This simple device, invented by B. F. Skinner, allows careful study of operant conditioning. When the rat presses the bar, a pellet of food or a drop of water is automatically released.

Notice that the rat did not acquire a new skill in this situation. He already had the responses necessary to effectively depress the bar. Reward only alters how *frequently* he depresses the bar. Although he has not acquired any new responses, reward has caused him to put together existing responses into a consistent pattern or habit. This is operant conditioning.

Shaping Even when a simple response such as bar pressing is involved, it might be a long time before the rat accidentally made the response so that it could be rewarded. We might wait forever for more complicated responses to occur. For example, you would have to wait a long time for a duck to accidentally walk out of its cage, turn on a light, play "Yankee Doodle" on a toy piano, turn off the light, and walk back to its cage. If this is what you wanted to reward, you would never get the chance.

Question: Then how are the animals on TV and at amusement parks taught to perform complicated tricks?

The answer lies in *shaping*. Let's look again at our subject, Mickey Rat.

Chapter 3
Mickey Rat Shapes Up

Assume that the rat has not yet learned to press the bar. He also shows no signs of interest in the bar. Instead of waiting for the first accidental bar press, we can shape his behavior patterns. At first, we settle for just getting him to face the bar. Anytime he turns toward the bar, he is rewarded with a bit of food. Soon Mickey spends much of his time facing the bar. Next, we repeat the same process every time he takes a step toward the bar. When he turns toward the bar, then walks away, nothing happens. But when he faces the bar and takes a step forward, *click!* His responses are being shaped.

By changing the "rules" regarding what makes a successful response, the rat can gradually be trained to approach the bar and to press it. We can reward responses that come closer and closer to the final desired pattern until it occurs. The basic principle of shaping, then, is that gradual, or *successive, approximations* to the desired response are rewarded. Eventually, a long, complicated chain of responses can be maintained by one small reward at the end of the performance being taught. B. F. Skinner once taught two pigeons to play Ping-Pong in this way.

Extinction You might expect that a rat's bar-pressing response would immediately stop if food delivery was not made. However, the rat would stop pressing the bar, but not immediately. Just as the acquiring of an operant response takes time, so does extinction. Extinction refers to the same general phenomenon it did in classical conditioning. If a learned response is not reinforced, it gradually drops out of an organism's behavior.

Extinction may take a long time. In some cases animals will respond thousands of times without reward before giving up. Even after extinction seems complete, there may be a return of the previously rewarded habit. If a rat is removed from a Skinner box after extinction and given a short rest, he will begin pressing the bar when returned to the Skinner box.

Question: Does extinction take as long the second time?

If reward is still withheld, bar pressing will extinguish again, usually more quickly. This brief return of a habit following extinction is called *spontaneous recovery*. It seems to be very adaptive. The rat responds again in a situation that produced food in the past: "Just checking to see if the rules have changed!"

Learning Check

1. Instrumental, or operant, conditioning is different from classical conditioning in that operant conditioning is ________________, and classical conditioning is a ________________.

2. Changing the rules so that an animal (or person) is gradually trained to respond as you want it to is called ________________.

Answers: 1. voluntary, learned reflex 2. shaping

Stimulus Control—Putting Habits on a Leash

We have seen that a response followed by reward will be repeated. A second major principle of operant conditioning is that responses that are rewarded in a particular situation tend to come under the control of stimuli present in that situation. This is called *stimulus control*. Notice how this works with our friend Mickey Rat.

Chapter 4
The Return of Mickey Rat

> While learning the bar-pressing response, Mickey has been in a Skinner box illuminated by a bright light. During several training sessions, the light is alternately turned on and off. When the light is on, a bar press will produce food. When the light is off, bar pressing goes unrewarded. We soon observe that the rat presses vigorously when the light is on and ignores the bar when the light is off.

The stimulus which *follows* a response determines whether or not it will be repeated. This is the reinforcement principle. Stimuli which *precede* or come before a rewarded response control *when* and *where* it will occur. Evidence for stimulus control could be shown in the example above by turning the food delivery mechanism *on* when the light is *off*. A well-trained rat would never discover that the rules had changed.

Generalization Two other aspects of stimulus control are *generalization* and *discrimination*. Let's return to the example of the vending machine to illustrate these concepts. First, generalization.

Question: Is generalization the same in operant conditioning as it is in classical conditioning?

Basically, yes. Since rewarded responses come under the control of stimuli which precede them, stimuli similar to those which preceded reward also tend to *bring forth* a response. Assume, for instance, that you have been consistently rewarded for kicking one particular vending machine. Your "kicking response" tends to occur in the presence of that machine. It has come under stimulus control. Now let's say that there are three other machines on campus identical to the one that pays off. Because they are similar to the machine associated with reward, your kicking response will very likely transfer to them. If each of these machines has the same defect as the original and pays off in response to a kick, your kicking response may *generalize* to other machines on campus bearing only slight similarity to the original.

Question: What is discrimination?

Discrimination Generalization together with extinction give rise to discrimination. To discriminate means to respond differently to different stimuli. Because one machine rewarded your kicking response, you began kicking identical machines elsewhere on campus (generalization). Because these also paid off, you began kicking other machines on campus (more generalization). If kicking these other machines has no effect, the kicking response that generalized to them will extinguish due to nonreward. Thus, your response to machines of a particular size and color is consistently rewarded, whereas the same response to different machines is extinguished. You have learned to *discriminate* between stimuli that signal reward and nonreward, and your response patterns shift appropriately.

The Skinner box and vending machine examples we have discussed are simplified and unrealistic, but they convey the basic principles of operant conditioning. We will explore more realistic human and animal examples of these principles in the "applications" section of this chapter.

Partial Reinforcement—Las Vegas, a Human Skinner Box?

Serendipity (*n*): to discover one thing while looking for another.

B. F. Skinner, so the story goes, was studying operant conditioning when he ran short of food pellets. In order to continue, he arranged for a pellet to reward every other response. Thus began the formal study of *schedules of reinforcement*. Until now we have treated reward in operant conditioning as if it were continuous. *Continuous reinforcement* means that reward follows every response. This is fine for the laboratory, but has little to do with the real world where successful responses are more inconsistently and unpredictably rewarded. *Partial reinforcement* (reward which does not follow every response) may be administered in a number of patterns. Each has a characteristic effect on the rate at which a response is performed. In addition to these specific effects (to be explored in a moment), there is a general effect which accompanies any schedule of partial reinforcement: *Partial reinforcement while acquiring a response makes the response very resistant to extinction.* This is called the *partial reinforcement effect.*

Question: How does getting rewarded part of the time make a habit stronger?

If you have ever visited Las Vegas or a similar gambling mecca, you have probably been amused by the sight of row after row of people pulling slot machine handles. To get the flavor of what's happening here and to gain insight into partial reinforcement effects, imagine that you are making your first visit to Las Vegas and that you know nothing about slot machines. You put a nickel in a slot machine and pull the handle. Twenty-five cents in nickels spills into the tray. Taking one of your newly won nickels, you pull the handle again, and again there is a small payoff. Let's say this continues

Fig. 8-6 The one-armed bandit (slot machine) is a dispenser of partial reinforcement. (Photo by Elliot Erwitt, Magnum Photos, Inc.)

for fifteen minutes. Every pull is followed by a pay-off. Then someone notices the machine is defective, and without your knowing it turns off the payoff mechanism. Suddenly each pull of the handle is followed by nothing. Obviously you would pull several times more before giving up. However, when continuous reinforcement is followed by extinction, the message soon becomes clear enough: No more payoffs.

Contrast this with partial reinforcement. You begin by placing five nickels in the machine without a payoff. You are just about to decide that slot machines are not your game, but you have one more nickel. You stick it in, pull and handle, and . . . bingo! It returns $2 in change. After this, payoffs continue on a partial schedule; some are large, and some are small. All are unpredictable. Sometimes you hit two in a row, and sometimes twenty or thirty pulls go unrewarded. Now let's say the machine malfunctions, and, unknown to you, it will never pay off again. How many times do you think you would pull the handle this time before "handle pulling" is extinguished? Since you have developed the expectation that any play may be "the one," it will be hard to resist just one more play . . . and one more . . . and one more. Also, since acquisition on a schedule of partial reward includes long periods of nonreward, it will be harder to discriminate between conditions of reward and extinction.

Question: Do gamblers know about partial reinforcement?

Gambling odds are carefully selected so that in the long run the "house" always wins. If you play long enough, chance factors ensure that your losses will exceed your winnings. If one chooses to gamble, a sensible approach would be to decide how much you are willing to lose for "entertainment," and then quit when it is gone (or when you are ahead by some modest, predetermined amount). In practice, however, few people do quit, because before they reach their loss limit they have "won" several times on a schedule of partial reward. This is the "gambler's fallacy," and it has left many people penniless.

Schedules of Reinforcement

The patterns in which partial reward could be given are limitless. We will consider only the four most obvious possibilities.

Fixed Ratio (FR) During continuous reinforcement, every response is followed by reward. A simple variation would be to follow every other response with a reward. Likewise, we could follow every third, fourth, fifth, or *n*th response with a reward. Each of these possibilities is a fixed ratio (FR) schedule. The ratio of rewards to responses is fixed: FR_2 means every other response is rewarded, FR_3 means every third response is rewarded and so forth.

Question: What effect does a FR schedule have?

The most prominent characteristic of fixed ratio schedules is that they produce *extremely high rates of response.* A hungry rat on an FR_{10} schedule will run off ten responses as fast as he can, pause to eat his reward, and then will run off ten more.

Variable Ratio (VR) A variable ratio (VR) schedule is a slight variation on fixed ratio. Instead of rewarding, for example, every fourth response (FR_4), an organism on a VR_4 schedule gets rewarded on the average every fourth response. Sometimes a response must be made two times for a reward, sometimes five times, sometimes four, and so on. The actual number of responses necessary to produce reward varies, but it averages out to four (in this example). Variable ratio schedules also produce high response rates, although not quite as high as FR. Since reward is less predictable, VR schedules produce slightly greater resistance to extinction than fixed ratio schedules. Playing a slot machine is an example of behavior maintained by a variable ratio schedule of reward.

Fixed Interval (FI) Another way of dispensing partial rewards is to reward only the first response which occurs after the passage of a fixed amount of time. In other words, a rat on a $FI_{30\ second}$ schedule must wait thirty seconds after his last rewarded response before a bar press will pay off again. He can press the bar as often as he wants during the interval, but he will not be rewarded. FI schedules produce *moderate response rates* punctuated by spurts of activity mixed with periods of inactivity. Animals working on an FI schedule seem to develop a keen sense of the passage of time. For example:

Chapter 5
Mickey Rat—Again?

Mickey Rat, trained on a $FI_{60\ second}$ schedule, has just been rewarded for a bar press. What does he do? He saunters around the cage, grooms himself, hums, whistles, reads magazines, and polishes his nails. After fifty seconds, he walks to the bar and gives it a press—just testing. After fifty-five seconds have passed, he gives it two or three presses. Fifty-eight seconds, and he settles down to rapid pressing, fifty-nine seconds, sixty seconds, and he hits the rewarded press. After one or two more presses (unrewarded), he wanders off again for the next interval.

Question: How consistent is this pattern?

Periods of inactivity and bursts of response on a FI schedule are so consistent that they have been used in drug research to show that psychoactive drugs (like marijuana) can alter time sense in subjects (animals) who can't contaminate the findings with their expectations.

Variable Interval (VI) VI schedules are the logical variation of fixed interval. Here an organism is rewarded for the first response made after a variable amount of time has passed. A VI $_{30\ \text{second}}$ schedule means that reward follows an interval that *averages* thirty-seconds duration. VI schedules produce *slow steady rates* of response and tremendous resistance to extinction. When you dial a phone number and get a busy signal, reward (getting through) is on a VI schedule. You may have to wait thirty seconds or thirty minutes. If you are like most people, you will doggedly dial over and over again until you get a connection.

Learning Check

By now you should be so accustomed to answering the questions in these "learning checks," directions aren't necessary.

1. When responses are rewarded in a particular situation, they tend to come under the control of stimuli present in that situation. This is called

   ____

2. Two aspects of stimulus control are ____________________

   and ____________________________

3. To ____________________ means to respond differently to different stimuli.

4. When stimuli similar to those which preceded reward also bring forth a

   response, it is called ____________________

5. When a reward follows every response, it is called:

   ____________________________________;

   when a reward does not follow every response, it is called:

   ____________________________________.

Answers: **1.** stimulus control **2.** generalization and discrimination **3.** discriminate **4.** generalization **5.** continuous reinforcement and partial reinforcement

Resources Summary

Classical conditioning, studied by Pavlov, occurs when an *unconditioned* (unlearned) *stimulus* is preceded by a *conditioned stimulus*. The unconditioned stimulus causes a reflex called the *unconditioned* (unlearned) *re-*

sponse. If the conditioned stimulus is followed many times by the unconditioned stimulus, then the conditioned stimulus begins to produce a response by itself. This is called a *conditioned* (learned) *response*. When the conditioned stimulus is followed by the unconditioned stimulus, conditioning is *reinforced* (strengthened). When the conditioned stimulus is presented alone, conditioning is *extinguished* (weakened). Stimuli similar to the conditioned stimulus will also produce a response because of *stimulus generalization*. Emotional responses as well as simple reflexes can be conditioned. Conditioning can occur *vicariously* (secondhand).

Instrumental, or *operant*, *conditioning* occurs when a voluntary action is followed by *reward*, or *reinforcement*. Reinforcement increases the frequency of a response. Complicated operant responses can be learned by gradually *shaping* actions to a final desired pattern. If an operant response is not followed by reinforcement, it may *extinguish* (disappear). But after extinction seems complete, it may temporarily reappear (*spontaneous recovery*). Stimuli that precede a rewarded response tend to control the response on future occasions (*stimulus control*). Two aspects of stimulus control are *generalization* and *discrimination*. Rewards may be given *continuously* (after every response) or *partially*. Partial reward produces habits that resist extinction. Four of the best-known schedules of reward are: *fixed ratio*, *variable ratio*, *fixed interval*, and *variable interval*.

Applications

Conditioning in Everyday Situations

A technology of behavior is emerging. A later chapter of this book (Chapter 24) is devoted entirely to the application of conditioning principles to human problems. Conditioning principles are finding their way into business, education, industry, and the home. If you understand these principles, you will find frequent uses for them. It is impossible to detail all the possibilities, but a number of examples should extend your understanding.

Conditioning Pets One of the most common mistakes people make with pets (especially dogs) is beating them if they do not come immediately when called. Calling the animal then becomes a conditioned stimulus for fear and withdrawal. No wonder it disobeys when summoned on future occasions.

Question: How can conditioning be used to correct this?

Obviously the situation needs to be reversed. A "stop" command can be used to control an animal when it is running away, and return on command can be rewarded. A stop command can be used in conditioning a dog by attaching a 15- to 20-foot-long rope to the dog's collar. During training, if the dog walks or bolts beyond a radius of about 5 or 10 feet, take a firm grip on the rope, give the stop command, and begin walking away from the dog. When the dog hits the end of the rope it gives him a jolt (this will not hurt him and is not cruel). Very soon the stop command will bring the dog up short. The rope then becomes unnecessary.

An excellent way to train an animal to come on command is to give a distinctive call or whistle daily during feeding. This makes the signal a discriminative stimulus for reward (food). Effectiveness of the signal is greatly enhanced if it is also used at other times and in other settings and is followed first always, then frequently, then occasionally, with a little food. Ultimately, very few "bribes" will be necessary to maintain the effectiveness of the signal if it is conditioned on a partial schedule of reward. Later, petting and praise can be substituted for food.

Question: What can be done about an animal that begs at the table?

Pets beg at the table for only one reason. They have been rewarded occasionally for doing so. The problem is usually that the owner finds begging bothersome most of the time and seeks to discourage it by not rewarding it with food. But there is always that time when Fido is just too cute to resist. If the owner gives in then, begging has been rewarded on a partial schedule, which makes it very resistant to extinction. Also, persistence has been rewarded. If you don't want your pets to beg, never give in and reward them. If you want them to beg quietly, reward them after a period of silence, not after a particularly sorrowful plea, and then gradually extend the length of the silent period.

Conditioning in Industry Dr. Thomas Verhave, a psychopharmacologist at a major drug company, once initiated a program to teach pigeons to remove defective, dented, or double-capped capsules from an assembly line (Verhave, 1966). After watching a line of seventy women employees at the monotonous task of sorting capsules from a moving belt, Verhave was reminded of an experiment B. F. Skinner had carried out during World War II with pigeons. Skinner designed a guidance system for air-to-ground missles that was run by "feathered kamikazes." Using operant conditioning and discrimination training, Skinner taught pigeons to peck at targets projected on a screen (see Fig. 8-7). Three chambers, each housing a screen and one bird, comprised Skinner's "pigeon air guidance system." Pecks on the target were translated into mechanical guidance commands to the missile (Skinner, 1960). Skinner's system worked but was never adopted by the military. But Verhave was convinced that pigeons could be taught to be effective pill inspectors. He developed a device that rewarded pigeons for accepting good capsules and for rejecting defective capsules. Incorrect pecks at an illuminated screen received no reinforcement. Verhave's pigeons were performing at a 99 percent level of accuracy after only one week of training, but they were never put into full-time service because company executives feared that the public would not trust medicine inspected by pigeons. Maybe he should have used hawks?!

Conditioning in Business Perhaps the use of animals in industry will become more prevalent when it is recognized that they are often better capable of working in boring situations than are people. At the moment, most business and industrial applications of reinforcement principles focus on the effects of various bonuses, payment schedules, incentives, commissions, and profit-sharing plans on overall productivity. Before this trend, most people worked for either a straight salary or for an hourly wage. A straight salary can be thought of as a fixed interval schedule of reward. There is little relationship between the amount of effort expended from one paycheck to the next and the amount of pay. This is also partially true of an hourly wage. While it is true that more hours worked mean a larger paycheck, an employee gets paid the same amount for an hour of productive work as he or she does for an hour of goofing off. It can be very demoralizing to see others do less work and receive the same pay.

With these facts in mind, industrial psychologists have sought to make pay relate more directly to work output. The simplest alternative to hourly wages or salary is payment on a piecework (fixed ratio) basis. If an individual is paid a small amount for each item handled, pound picked, shirt sewed, or whatever, work output tends to be high because more items mean more pay. Piecework pay has something of a bad reputation because some employers pay so little on a per-item basis that tremendous amounts of work are necessary to earn a reasonable wage. But this need not be the case. For example, employees of a small

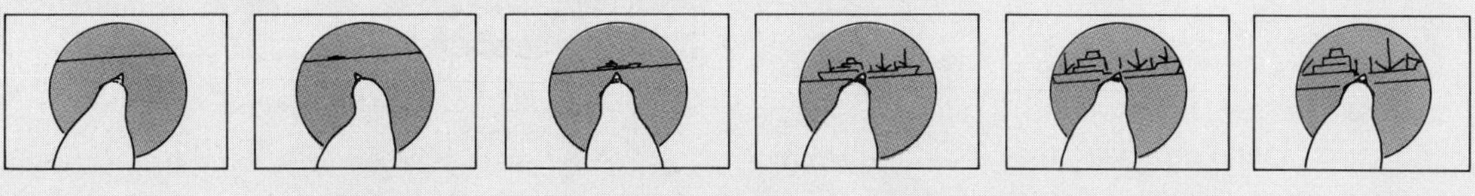

Fig. 8-7 Target practice for "feathered kamikazes." A trained pigeon guides a rocket to its target. Signals created by the pigeon's pecks modify the direction of the rocket until it is on target.

leather factory in Los Angeles are paid for making a prearranged number of items per week (billfold backs, handbag handles, and so on). Employees are allowed to work as many or a few hours per day as they choose, and they can work at any rate. This allows great flexibility for the workers. If they feel tired or want to chat, they work slowly. If they want a three- or four-day weekend, they work faster and longer. The company pays only for the work it gets, and the workers are paid fairly and have an unusually high level of freedom and responsibility.

The most widely used business adaptation of schedules of reinforcement is a combination of hourly wages and incentives for extra effort. Fixed interval rewards (hourly wage or salary) guarantee a good overall level of productivity and give workers a secure base pay, while fixed ratio rewards (incentives, bonuses, commissions, or profit sharing) tie extra effort to increased pay.

Conditioning and Children Children seem to have an almost endless craving for attention. This makes attention and approval from a parent a very powerful reinforcer.

Question: How does this affect a child?

Parents often unknowingly reinforce *negative attention seeking* in children. Generally, children are *ignored* when they are quiet or are playing constructively. They get attention as they get louder and louder, when they yell "Hey Mom!" at the top of their lungs, when they throw a tantrum, or "show off," or when they break something. Granted the attention they get is often a scolding, but it is still attention, and it still rewards negative attention seeking. To avoid this, the parent could ignore a child when he seeks attention this way. However, if attention seeking declines because it is not rewarded, some other behavior must be rewarded to take its place. Parents report dramatic changes in their children's behavior when they make a special effort to actively praise, attend to, or spend time with their children when they are quiet or playing constructively.

Question: What can be done about a child who throws tantrums in a store if she isn't allowed to buy candy?

Children are realists. If you say, "No, you may not buy candy" and stick to it, the child will get the message. Children can discriminate between what is said in a situation and the *actual* possibility of a reward. Children learn to throw tantrums with one parent but not the other; they learn to discriminate between parents' and grandparents' susceptibility to their requests; and they discriminate between a casual no and an angry no. The problem is that no occasionally becomes, "OK, but shut up!" If so, whining or crying has been rewarded on a partial schedule, and it will occur even more frequently in the future. Consistency is the key. If tantrums *never* pay off, they will be abandoned.

Question: But what if the tantrum is really embarrassing? Sometimes parents are willing to do anything to quiet the child.

Beginning a program of nonreward for tantrums may require considerable courage, but it does work. If you don't mind the idea of buying a treat, but dislike the tantrum, try requiring the child to "help" you in some (quiet) way as a condition for receiving the treat. If necessary, walk away from the child and return only when the child has quieted down; or leave the store with her when a tantrum starts and allow the child to return to the store when she has quieted down.

Conditioning Other Adults Students seldom realize how much power they have over teachers. Even tough-skinned veteran teachers are (believe it or not) still human and therefore sensitive to whether or not they are succeeding in class and being accepted by students. This fact can be used in a demonstration of the effects of reward on human behavior.

Shaping a Teacher

For this demonstration, approximately one half (or more) of the students in a classroom must partici-

> pate. First, a target behavior should be selected. This should be something like "lecturing from the right side of the room." (Keep it simple; teachers aren't too clever.) Begin training in this way: Each time the instructor turns toward the right side of the room or takes a step in that direction, participating students should look *really* interested. Also, smile, ask questions, and lean forward. If the teacher turns to the left or takes a step in that direction, participating students should lean back, yawn, check out their split ends, close their eyes, or generally look bored. Soon, without being aware of why, the instructor should be spending most of his or her time each class period lecturing from the right side of the classroom.

This little trick has been a favorite of psychology graduate students for decades. For a time, one of the author's professors delivered all his lectures from the right side of the room while toying with the venetian-blind cords. (We added the cords the second week!)

As was pointed out in the discussion of reinforcement with children, attention and approval are powerful rewards for human behavior. This is something to keep in mind when interacting with others.

Question: But how can this be applied?

An excellent example is provided by the work of two educators, Paul S. Graubard and Harry Rosenberg, who taught "incorrigible," "deviant," and "socially outcast" students to use reinforcement on classmates. They cite the example of Peggy, an attractive, intelligent student who was unable to make friends. Peggy encountered so much hostility that she was miserable and unhappy, and because of this did very poorly academically. When asked to name three other students she would like to have as friends, Peggy named three students who frequently insulted her. Here is how Peggy began to put into effect the reinforcement principles she had learned:

> I ignored Doris if she said anything bad to me. But when she said anything nice to me, I'd help her with her work, or compliment her, or sit down and ask her to do something with me. She's been increasingly saying nice things about me and now we can ride on the bus together, and she'll sit by me in class. I'll tell you that really helps me a lot.[1]

Peggy dealt with another student's hostility in the same way. Whenever Elwyn said something bad to her, she turned her back on him. But the first time he walked past her without saying something bad, she gave him a big smile and said, "Hi, Elwyn, how are you today?" The authors add that after Elwyn recovered from his initial shock, he grew to be Peggy's best friend.

The examples cited above should give you an idea of the value of understanding conditioning and of applying conditioning principles to everyday problems. Their successful use requires practice, but your efforts are sure to foster a deeper appreciation for their application. Give them a try!

Questions for Discussion

Here are some questions for thought or discussion.

1. Lately you have been getting a shock of static electricity every time you touch a door handle. You begin to notice a hesitation in your door-opening movements. Can you analyze this situation in terms of classical conditioning?
2. Over the years balloons have occasionally popped in your face when you were blowing them up. Now you squint and feel tense whenever you blow up a balloon. What kind of conditioning is this? What schedule of reinforcement has contributed to the conditioning? How could you extinguish the response?
3. You are in charge of a group of fifth-grade children that meets regularly for recreation. Other members of the group have excluded a younger girl and a very shy boy from activities. How could you use reinforcement principles to improve this situation? (Include techniques aimed at both the excluded children and the group.)
4. What role has reinforcement played in your selection of a major? Friends? A job? The clothes you wore to school today?
5. From your point of view, what would be the ideal way to be paid at a job? Should pay be weekly, hourly, daily? Should it be tied to work output? Should rewards other than money be offered?
6. If you owned a business what would you consider the ideal way to pay your employees?
7. Can you think of any situations in society in which rewards are haphazardly or inefficiently applied (for example, tax breaks for people who have children instead of for those who don't; better seats for those who "cut" in to line than for those who don't)?

Suggestions for Further Reading

Pavlov, I. *Conditioned Reflexes*. Clarendon Press, 1927.

Powers, R. B., and J. G. Osborne. *Fundamentals of Behavior*. West, 1976.

Reynolds, G. S. *A Primer of Operant Conditioning*. Scott, Foresman, 1968.

Skinner, B. F. *Behavior of Organisms*. Wiley, 1938.

———. *Walden Two*. Macmillan, 1960.

Learning

9

Chapter Preview

> . . . any subject can be taught effectively in some intellectually honest form to any child at any stage of development. —*Jerome Bruner*

Dr. Moore's "Learning Machine"

Teaching two- to five-year-olds how to read, write, type, and compose stories may sound like an impossible task. However, if the proper conditions for learning are created, it can become a reality. Dr. Omar Khayyam Moore of Yale University has designed a "responsive learning environment" to take full advantage of children's intellectual curiosity and creativity. In his lab children "play" with a "talking typewriter." A child's encounter with the talking typewriter begins the first time he presses a key. When he does, a letter appears on the paper and a voice names it through a loudspeaker. Surprised by this response, the child tries other keys. Soon the machine has captured the child's complete attention, and the connection between keys and letters begins to form.

After a number of sessions in which typing is fairly random, a new game begins. Whenever the child's attention begins to wander, a curtain is removed from a screen above the machine. A single letter appears and the letter is named over the loudspeaker. If the child returns to random key pressing, he finds that the keys no longer work—until he presses the key corresponding to the letter on the screen. When the child finds the right key, the correct letter is printed and a voice names it again. Then a new letter appears on the screen. Later, words appear. If the key for the first letter is pressed, a pointer moves to the second letter. When a child has correctly typed all three letters of a word like "dog," the machine pronounces the word, and a new word appears. Children rapidly go from random typing to reading and writing, and then they compose their own sentences and stories—all before age five! (Pines, 1963; Martin, 1969).

A child is allowed to spend no more than half an hour per day in Dr. Moore's lab. No one is required to stay, and no one forces a child to learn. However, most do stay, and they become completely lost in the joy of discovery. Think how this differs from the enforced boredom of many classrooms. Children, like all humans, have a tremendous curiosity and a staggering capacity for learning. In Dr. Moore's lab, children are not scolded, punished, rewarded, or urged. They learn because the environment is responsive *to their actions.*

It would be ideal if learning were always this spontaneous. Even when it is not, learning remains one of the most important topics in psychology. The ability to learn is every human's birthright. It is the key to adaptability in an ever-changing environment. In this chapter, several kinds of learning are described, and conditions that promote learning are explored.

Resources

What Is Learning?—Does Practice Make Perfect?

Many animals are born with built-in behavior patterns. When a *complicated pattern* of behavior is inborn, it may be referred to as *instinctual*, as in the case of the *maternal instinct* in many lower animals. A less controversial label describes any behavior that appears to be unlearned as *innate* (inborn). The simplest innate behavior is a *reflex*, but more complicated responses may be innate. The weaverbird, for instance, does not have to learn to tie the distinctive knot it uses when constructing a nest. In laboratory experiments, weaverbirds have been raised in total isolation from other members of their species for several generations. They still tie the knot on their first opportunity to build a nest.

Question: Do humans have instincts?

Humans have reflexes, but most psychologists reject the idea that people have instincts. In humans the capacity for learning is so advanced that the majority of our daily activities are either wholly learned or at least greatly affected by learning. Imagine what you would be like if you suddenly lost everything you have previously learned. What could you do? You would be unable to read, write, or speak. You couldn't walk, feed yourself, find your way home, drive a car, or "boogie." Needless to say, you would be totally incapacitated. (Dull, too!)

Question: Learning is obviously important. What's a formal definition of learning?

Learning is a relatively permanent change in behavior due to past experience. Notice that this definition *excludes* temporary changes caused by motivation, fatigue, maturation, disease, injury, or drugs. Each of these can change behavior, but none constitutes learning.

Question: Isn't learning the result of practice?

It depends on what you mean by practice. Merely repeating a response produces no learning. Practice must include some form of *feedback* (information about what effect a response has had) before learning will occur. In operant conditioning, food rewards are a form of feedback, but feedback need not be rewarding. Dr. O. K. Moore's "learning machine" does not reward children for correct responses, but since it provides feedback (also called *knowledge of results*, or KR), tremendous amounts of learning take place. The role of feedback can be seen in another example.

Imagine that you are given the task of throwing darts at a target. The dart must be thrown over a screen which prevents you from telling if you have hit the target. If you were allowed to throw 1,000 darts over the screen, we would expect no improvement because no feedback is provided. The importance of feedback is one of the most valuable lessons to be derived from psychological studies of learning. One can almost always increase the amount of feedback in a learning situation, and more feedback generally means more learning.

To return to our example, if the information "high or low, right or left" were provided after each throw of the dart, your score would improve immediately. If even more detailed feedback were provided (clock coordinates and number of inches from the target), your performance might equal that of someone practicing with a clear view of the target.

In learning to play a musical instrument, to sing, or to speak publicly, a tape recorder can be invaluable. In sports, videotape is being used to improve everything from tennis form to a pitcher's "pick-off move." The familiar game films in football are another form of feedback. Feedback is valuable academically too. When studying for a test, you can arrange to "take" the test several times before taking it in class. In other words, self-testing by the use of flash cards, workbooks, reviews, answering questions following chapters—all will help you to correct errors and speed up learning *before* the actual test in class. Studying for a test without feedback is like practicing for a basketball game by shooting baskets blindfolded.

Learning Check

Answer the following questions before reading on.

1. Learning is a relatively permanent change in behavior due to past experience. T or F?

2. Learning is the result of practice with feedback. T or F?

3. Most psychologists accept the idea that people have instincts. T or F?

Answers: 1. T 2. T 3. F

Biofeedback—Electronic Yoga?

Question: *What is "biofeedback"? Is it related to other kinds of feedback?*

An exciting recent psychological discovery is that humans can learn to control bodily activities formerly believed to be involuntary. For years, yoga and Zen masters have demonstrated extraordinary control over "involuntary" functions like heart rate, blood pressure, oxygen consumption, and temperature of parts of the body. Now, Western technology is showing that under the proper conditions anyone can learn to duplicate these "impossible" effects.

Question: *How is this possible?*

By applying the general principle of feedback to the control of bodily responses, we arrive at *biofeedback*. If I say to you: "Raise the temperature of your right hand," you probably couldn't because you wouldn't know when you were succeeding. However, your task could be made easier by attaching a sensitive thermometer to your hand. If the thermometer were wired so that an increase in temperature would activate a signal light, all you would have to do is try to keep the light on as much as possible. With practice you could then learn to raise your hand temperature at will.

Question: *How does the light help?*

Yoga and Zen masters use *meditation* to achieve this kind of control. Meditation makes the mind and body very "quiet" and allows a person to focus on tiny changes in bodily functioning. Biofeedback accomplishes the same thing by making bodily activities "louder." Bodily processes are monitored (usually electronically) and converted into a signal that provides the person with clear feedback about what his body is doing.

Question: *If you succeed at raising hand temperatures, what are you actually doing?*

You would probably find it difficult to describe what you had done. You might say, "I thought warm thoughts" or "I just had a feeling when the light was on and I kept trying to recapture that feeling." The point is when you are given feedback you can repeat whatever it was that you were doing, even if it was a very subtle mental state. Neal Miller and his research associates have found that almost any bodily function can be voluntarily controlled if feedback or reward follows change in the function.

In one typical experiment, Miller taught rats to change the speed of their heartbeat.

> Rats were temporarily paralyzed with a drug called curare. (Curare prevents the rat from affecting his heart rate by moving the voluntary muscles of his body.) Rats were given rewards in the form of electrical stimulation to a "pleasure center" in the brain. This is a very pleasant experience for an

animal and the rats quickly altered their heartrate to receive additional stimulation. The animals showed a 20% jump in heartrate during ninety minutes of training when small increases in heartrate were followed by reward. Rats rewarded for decreasing their heartrate showed a 20% drop (Miller & DiCara, 1967).

In other experiments, Miller and his associates have shown that rats can also learn to change their blood pressure, the blood flow to their stomach or kidneys, and the frequency of stomach contractions. They can even increase blood flow in one ear without affecting the other (Miller, 1969). Can you "blush" in your left ear?

Biofeedback and Medicine These findings have spurred research on applications of biofeedback to the treatment of psychosomatic diseases (diseases mainly caused by psychological factors). For example, Dr. Elmer and Alyce Green have had success in training people to prevent migraine headaches. Patients begin training with one temperature-sensitive electrode taped to a finger and another to the forehead. Patients learn to move the needle on a dial that registers the difference between hand and fore-

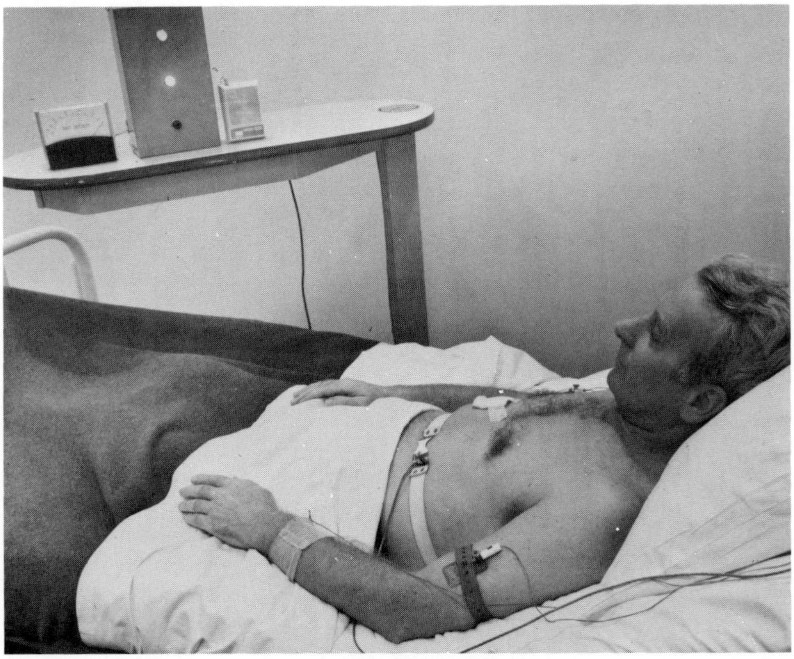

Fig. 9-1 A biofeedback session to control heart rate. A "traffic signal" (center box) of red, green, and yellow lights tells the patient to speed or slow his heartbeat. A buzzer sounds when the desired heart-rate change takes place. (Photo courtesy of the National Institute on Aging Gerontology Research Center.)

head temperature. This teaches them to redirect blood flow away from the head to their extremities. Since migraine headaches are caused by excessive blood flow to the head, biofeedback training equips patients to short-circuit headaches before they develop (Luce & Peper, 1971). Similarly, Arthur Shapiro (1969) has shown that through biofeedback people can learn to lower their blood pressure without the use of drugs. Biofeedback training has also been successfully applied to the control of muscular tension, irregular heart rate, and labor pains. It even shows promise for the control of some types of epilepsy.

Alpha Control Perhaps the most controversial use of biofeedback has been to control *alpha-wave* output of the brain. Alpha waves are one of several distinctive patterns of brain activity that can be recorded with the EEG (electroencephalograph, or brain-wave machine). Several years ago psychologist Joseph Kamiya developed a technique whereby subjects are signaled by a tone or light whenever they produce alpha waves (Kamiya, 1968). Subjects in alpha-control experiments report that high levels of alpha are accompanied by sensations of pleasure, relaxation, "passive alertness," or peaceful images. Some people have looked upon these findings as a potential avenue to "instant bliss," but evidence on the overall value of alpha training is still contradictory. It seems that the age of "electronic yoga" is not yet quite with us.

Learning Check

1. By applying the general principle of feedback to the control of bodily responses, we get what is called ______________________.

2. Research has shown that almost *any* bodily function can be voluntarily controlled if feedback or ______________________ follows change in the function.

3. It is possible to use biofeedback to control ______________ output of the brain.

4. Can you blush in your right ear? ______________________.

Answers: 1. biofeedback 2. reward 3. alpha wave 4. Answers will vary.

Reinforcement Revisited

"Responsive environments," feedback, and biofeedback are closely related to operant conditioning (discussed in Chapter 8) since learning in each case reflects the operation of the principle of reinforcement. Generally speaking, reinforcement is associated with pleasure, comfort, rewards, or feedback. Many reinforcers reduce pressing biological drives. Food, water, sex, and termination of a painful stimulus are all naturally rewarding. But reinforcement is not always this simple. Sometimes people or animals will work to *increase* the strength of a biological drive. Male rats will learn to cross an electrified grid to gain access to a sexually receptive female, even though they are removed before ejaculation (Sheffield *et al.*, 1951). This procedure would seem to increase the sex drive of the rat, but it is rewarding just the same.

As a practical "rule of thumb," psychologists define a *reinforcer* as any stimulus that increases the frequency of a response that it follows. *Positive reinforcers* (simple rewards) may be contrasted to *negative reinforcers*. A response that brings an end to discomfort (negative reinforcement) is just as likely to be repeated as one that produces pleasure (positive reinforcement). Note that negative reinforcement is not punishment since negative reinforcement strengthens a response. When dealing with humans, an effective reinforcer may be anything from an M&M to a pat on the back. In categorizing reinforcers, a useful distinction can be made between *primary reinforcers* and *secondary reinforcers*.

Primary Reinforcement *Primary reinforcers* are "natural," or unlearned, rewards that apply almost universally to a species. They are usually biological in nature and produce comfort or end discomfort. Food, water, and sex are primary reinforcers. There are also other less "natural" primary reinforcers. One of the most unusual (and powerful) forms of primary reinforcement involves direct stimulation of "pleasure centers" in the brain, (Olds and Olds, 1965).

Wiring a Rat for Pleasure

Use of brain stimulation for reward requires the permanent implantation of tiny electrodes in specific areas of the brain. A rat "wired for pleasure" can be trained to press the bar in a Skinner box to deliver electrical stimulation to its own brain. A rat will press the bar thousands of times per hour if each bar press is rewarded by brain stimulation. After fifteen or twenty hours of constant pressing, animals sometimes collapse from exhaustion. When they revive, they begin pressing again. If the reward circuit is not turned off, an animal may die of exhaustion while bar pressing.

Question: Has a human ever received brain stimulation?

Brain electrodes have been implanted in a few individuals suffering from psychosis, epilepsy, or constant pain. In some cases, patients have been given a small battery powered belt pack which allows them to press a button and deliver stimulation directly to pleasure centers in the brain anytime. Here is a description of one subject's reaction to brain stimulation:

> The patient, in explaining why he pressed the . . . button with such frequency, stated that the feeling was "good"; it was as if he were building up to a sexual orgasm (Heath, 1963).

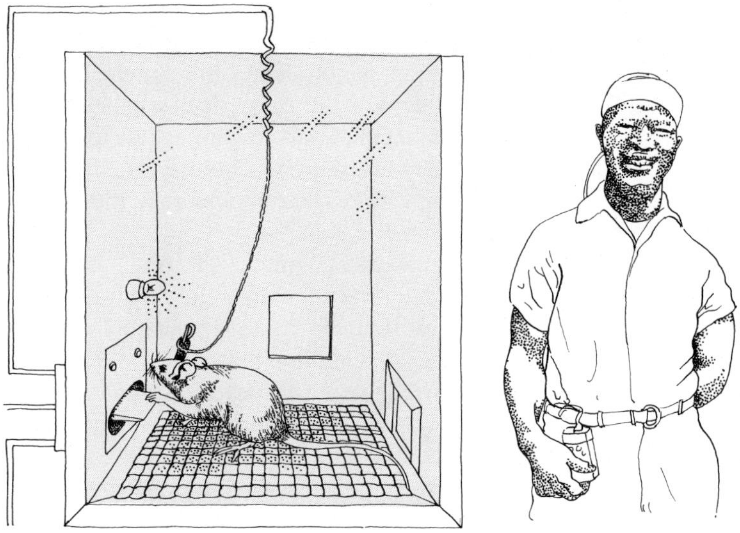

(a) (b)

Fig. 9-2 In the apparatus shown in *(a)*, the rat can press a bar to deliver mild electric stimulation to a "pleasure center" in the brain. Humans have also been "wired" for brain stimulation, as shown in *(b)*.

One shudders to think what might happen if brain implants were easy and practical to do. (They are not.) Every company from *Playboy* to General Motors would have a device on the market, and we would have to keep a closer watch on politicians than usual!

Secondary Reinforcers In some primitive societies, habits may still be acquired and maintained mainly by primary reinforcement. Most of us, however, respond to a much broader range of rewards. Money, praise, attention, approval, success, affection, and grades all serve as *learned*, or *secondary reinforcers*, in modern society.

Question: How does a secondary reinforcer become a reward?

A secondary reinforcer may simply be associated with a primary reward. Secondary reinforcement can be demonstrated experimentally in this way:

Chapter 1
Son of Mickey Rat

A rat caged in a Skinner box has learned through operant conditioning to press the bar for food pellets. Each rewarded bar press is also followed by a brief auditory tone. After a period of training in which bar pressing, food, and the tone are associated, the rat is moved to a new cage. This cage has no bar, but it does have a button mounted on the wall. If the rat pushes the button, the tone sounds, but no food is delivered. Even though primary reinforcement in the form of food is missing, the rat learns to press the button to turn on the tone. Because of its prior association with food, the tone has become a secondary reinforcer.

Secondary rewards may also gain their value more directly when they can be *exchanged* for primary rewards. Printed money obviously has little or no value of its own. You can't eat it, drink it, or sleep with it. However, it can be exchanged for food, water, lodging, and other . . . necessities.

In a series of classic experiments, chimpanzees were taught to work for *tokens*.

Chimps were first trained to put poker chips into a "Chimp-O-Mat" vending machine which dispensed a few grapes or raisins for each chip. Once the animals had learned to exchange tokens for food, they would learn new tasks to earn the chips and would also operate a device that required lifting a heavy weight to obtain them. Value of the tokens was maintained by occasionally allowing the chimps to use the "Chimp-O-Mat" to exchange chips for food (Wolfe, 1936; Cowles, 1937).

Fig. 9-3 Poker chips normally have little or no value for chimpanzees, but this chimp will work hard to earn them once he learns that the "Chimp-O-Mat" will dispense food in exchange for them. (Photo courtesy of the Yerkes Regional Primate Research Center.)

Money obviously gains its value as a reward because it can be exchanged for primary reinforcers. In the case of the chimpanzees, tokens which originally became valuable only because they could be exchanged for food took on new importance in the animal colony. It was observed that female chimps were strangely uninterested in the tokens, while the males continued to work hard to earn them. The explanation behind this mystery was reputedly discovered when an assistant returned to the lab late one night. It seems the male chimps were exchanging their hard-earned tokens for sexual favors from the females. The females then deposited the tokens in the "Chimp-O-Mat" to get food (Ruch, 1971).

Question: People sometimes hoard money even when all their needs are taken care of. Why is that?

Interestingly, the chimps also had a tendency to hoard tokens, even when they were hungry. These observations suggest that money may become a *generalized reinforcer*. At times its value seems to be almost independent of its connection to other rewards. In addition to being exchanged for primary rewards, money may form an avenue to other secondary reinforcers, such as prestige, attention, status, or power. This makes its value so general in our society that people sometimes pursue and hoard money just for the sake of having money.

Learning Check

1. A practical definition of a *reinforcer* is any stimulus that (increases/decreases) the frequency of a response that it follows.

2. There are two general kinds of reinforcers. ____________ reinforcers and ____________ reinforcers.

3. ____________ reinforcers are "natural," or unlearned rewards, such as food, water, and sex.

4. Money, praise, attention, approval, grades, and affection are all learned, or ____________, reinforcers.

5. Negative reinforcement increases the frequency of a response. T or F?

Answers: **1.** increases **2.** primary and secondary **3.** primary **4.** secondary **5.** T

Delay of Reinforcement—Are You Superstitious?

Reinforcement has its greatest effect on learning when the time lapse between a response and the reward which follows is short. This can be demonstrated in a simple experiment.

Chapter 2
In Which Mickey Rat II and Friends Get Delayed

Several groups of rats are trained to press the bar in a Skinner box for a food reward. For some of the animals a bar press is followed immediately by a food pellet. Other animals are trained with ever-greater amounts of delay between a bar press and a reward. When the delay reaches about fifty seconds, very little occurs. If delivery of the food pellet follows a bar press by more than about a minute and a half, no learning occurs (Perin, 1943).

If you wish to reward either an animal or a child for a correct response, reward will be most effective if it is given immediately after the response. This is also true of punishment. If you discover that your dog dug up and ate a tree in the yard while you were gone, it will do little good to punish him hours later. Likewise, the commonly heard childhood threat of "Wait 'til your father comes home, then you'll be sorry" does more to make Father an ogre than it does to effectively punish an undesirable response.

Superstitious Behavior A reward will reinforce not only the last response which precedes it, but also any other response that occurs shortly before the reward is given. This helps account for the learning of many human superstitions. If a golfer taps his club on the ground three times and then hits an unusually fine shot, the success of the shot rewards not only the correct swing but also the three taps. Animals undergoing operant conditioning often develop similar unnecessary habits. If a rat scratches its ear immediately before its first accidental bar press, it may continue to scratch its ear before each subsequent bar press. All the animal actually has to do to receive a food pellet is press the bar, but it may continue "superstitiously" to scratch its ear each time as if this were necessary.

Question: But if the superstitious behavior is unnecessary why does it continue?

Superstitious acts probably *appear* to pay off to the person or animal.

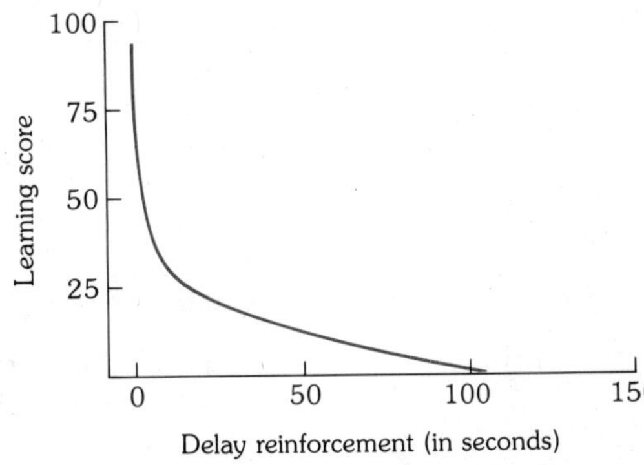

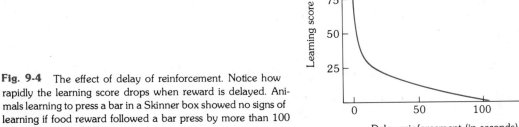

Fig. 9-4 The effect of delay of reinforcement. Notice how rapidly the learning score drops when reward is delayed. Animals learning to press a bar in a Skinner box showed no signs of learning if food reward followed a bar press by more than 100 seconds. (Perin, 1943.)

Chapter 3
Son of Mickey Rat in which Jonathan Livingston Pigeon Makes a Guest Appearance

A pigeon has been placed in a Skinner box. When it pecks at a lighted key, the pigeon is rewarded by food that drops into a feeder. The pigeon is allowed to peck at the key three times to obtain food. Then the key is disconnected from the food-delivery mechanism. At random intervals food falls into the tray as the pigeon continues pecking. *There is no connection between pecking and food*, but there *appears* to be. During twenty testing periods, twenty minutes in length, the pigeon made an average of 2,700 "superstitious" pecks (Neuringer, 1970).

Many human superstitions seem to be based on the same phenomenon. If you get the large half of a wishbone and have good fortune soon thereafter, you may credit the wishbone for your luck. If you walk under a ladder and then break a leg, you may avoid ladders in the future. Each time you avoid a ladder and nothing unusually bad occurs, your superstitious response is reinforced.

Question: What if you get the large half of a wishbone and nothing good follows? Wouldn't your superstitious belief in wishbones extinguish?

Perhaps you realized that in the example of the pigeon, superstitious key pecks are reinforced on what seems to be a schedule of *partial reward*. This makes superstitious behavior very resistant to extinction. Human belief in magic can also be interpreted along these lines. Primitive rituals to produce rain, ward off illness, or produce abundant crops very likely earned the faith of participants by occasionally appearing to succeed. Besides, better safe than sorry!

Learning Check

1. Reinforcement has its greatest effect on learning when the time lapse between a response and the reward which follows is long. T or F?

2. A reward will reinforce not only the last response which precedes it, but also any other responses that occur shortly before the reward is given. T or F?

3. Superstitions, because of a partial schedule of reward, are not very resistant to extinction. T or F?

Answers: 1. F 2. T 3. F

Punishment—Spare the Rod!

Question: Reinforcement strengthens a response. Does punishment weaken a response?

Common sense tells us that punishment abolishes undesired behavior. But punishment actually only temporarily *suppresses* a response. If the underlying habit is still reinforced, punishment will not reverse the learning process. A response temporarily suppressed by punishment will usually reappear later. If a child sneaks a snack from the refrigerator before dinner and is punished for it, he may pass up snacks for a short time. But since "snack sneaking" was also rewarded by the sneaked snack, the child will probably try again at a later date.

This fact has been demonstrated experimentally by arranging for rats to be slapped on the paw when they press the bar in a Skinner box. Two groups of well-trained rats were placed on extinction. One group was punished with a slap for each bar press, while the other was not. It might be expected that the slap would cause bar pressing to extinguish more quickly. This was not the case, however, as can be seen in Fig. 9-5. Punishment temporarily slowed responding, but did not cause more rapid extinction. Slapping the paws of rats or children has little permanent effect on the strength of habits.

Question: Then is punishment useless in the learning process?

Parents, educators, animal trainers, and the like have three tools available to control simple learning: (1) *Reward* strengthens habits; (2) *nonreward* causes them to be extinguished; (3) *punishment* suppresses a habit, but does not weaken it. These tools are used most effectively in combination. Punishment can be used as a means of *temporarily* suppress-

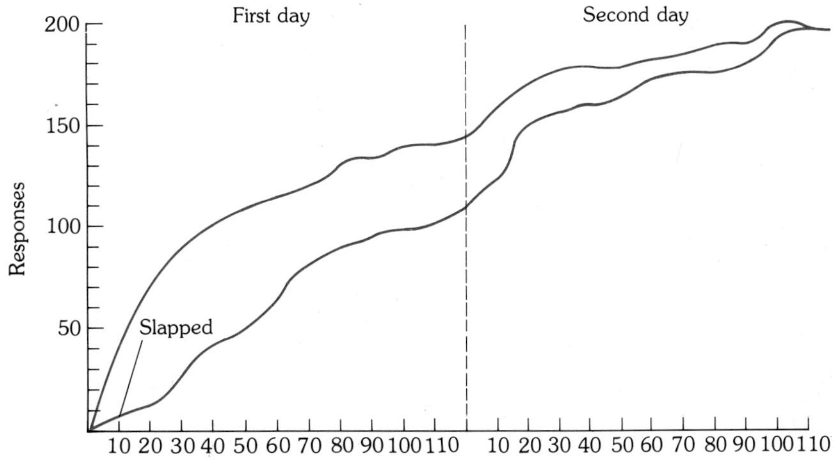

Fig. 9-5 The effect of punishment on extinction. Immediately after punishment, the rate of bar pressing is suppressed, but by the end of the second day, the effects of punishment had disappeared. (After B. F. Skinner, *The Behavior of Organisms*. © 1938. D. Appleton-Century Co., Inc. Reprinted by permission of Appleton-Century-Crofts.)

ing troublesome habits so that more desirable responses will occur. These can then be rewarded so that a new habit replaces the punished response. If reward is missing from the formula, punishment loses its effectiveness.

In a situation that poses immediate danger, such as when a child reaches for the top of a stove or a dog runs into the street, mild punishment may prevent disaster. Punishment in such circumstances is most effective when it produces responses *incompatible* with the undesirable response. If your dog chases cars, slapping him on the nose when he runs after one will be more effective than slapping him on the behind.

The most common error in the use of punishment is to rely on it exclusively as a means of training or discipline. The overall emotional adjustment of a child or a pet disciplined mainly by reward is usually superior to one disciplined mainly by punishment. Frequent punishment makes a person or an animal unhappy, confused, anxious, aggressive, and fearful of the source of punishment. Children who receive a lot of punishment from parents or teachers learn to dislike not only parents and teachers but also the activities associated with punishment (schoolwork or household chores, for instance) (Munn, 1969).

Another important reason for careful use of punishment is that it can greatly increase aggression. One researcher (Azrin *et al.*, 1965) has shown

Edict of Louis XI, King of France
A.D. 1481

"Anyone who sells butter containing stones or other things (to add to the weight) will be put into our pillory, then said butter will be placed on his head until entirely melted by the sun. Dogs may lick him and people offend him with whatever defamatory epithets they please without offense to God or King. If the sun is not warm enough, the accused will be exposed in the great hall of the gaol in front of a roaring fire, where everyone will see him."

Fig. 9-6 Punishment has long been used to suppress undesirable behavior.

that animals consistently react to pain by attacking whoever or whatever else is around. A common example of this effect is the faithful dog that nips its owner while undergoing a painful procedure at a veterinarian's office. We also know that one of the most common responses to frustration is aggression. Generally speaking, punishment is either painful or frustrating or both. Punishment, therefore, sets up a powerful learning environment for the promotion of aggression. When a child is spanked, he becomes angry, frustrated, and feels aggressive. What if he then goes outside and hits his little brother or the nextdoor neighbor? The danger is that if he does it may feel good because it releases his anger and frustration. If so, aggression has been rewarded and will tend to occur again in other frustrating situations. One study found that overly aggressive adolescent boys had been severely punished for aggression at home. Since aggression was suppressed at home, parents were frequently surprised to learn that their "good boys" were in trouble at school for fighting and other forms of aggression (Bandura & Walters, 1959). It would seem that the adage "Spare the rod and spoil the child" should be at least changed to "Use the rod sparingly or spoil the child" and perhaps to simply "Spare the rod."

Types of Learning—Verbal, Motor, and Cognitive

Question: Is all learning some form of classical, or operant, conditioning?

Our discussion has focused on conditioning because it is an important and basic form of learning. In later chapters memory, thinking, and problem solving will be discussed. For now, here are some additional forms of learning you should know about.

Verbal versus Motor Learning A distinction can be made between *verbal* learning and *motor* learning. Verbal learning involves the use of language or symbols. *Motor skills* are largely nonverbal. They can often be thought of as long *chains* of responses that are skillfully assembled into a smooth sense of habit. Typing, walking, pole-vaulting, shooting baskets, playing golf, driving a car, and skiing are all motor skills.

Question: What do you mean by a "chain of responses"?

Motor skills can be defined as "a sequence of habitual responses the order of which is partially or wholly determined by sensory feedback from preceding responses" (Gagné & Fleishman, 1959). This means that one response serves as a cue to produce the next response, which becomes the cue for the next, and so on. Chaining of responses will be quite familiar to anyone who plays a musical instrument. As a new piece of music is learned, a mistake on one or two notes part of the way through a piece usually brings the performance to a halt. The musician who "gets lost" must return to the beginning and try again (even if the music after the mistake is fairly well learned) because there has been a break in the chain of responses.

Motor skills tend to be retained considerably better than verbal learning. Figure 9-7 shows how much is remembered after the passage of varying amounts of time. People who learned a new motor skill (keeping a pointer on a rotating target) show very little forgetting after ten weeks without practice. Those who learned a list of nonsense syllables (nonexistent words like "jal," "mik," or "daf") remember very few at the end of the same period. Perhaps you have observed how well you can type (or roller-skate, swim, ride a bicycle, and so forth) after years without practice. Contrast this with the amount you remember from classes taken last semester. If motor skills underwent as much loss as verbal learning does, it would be disastrous to leave your car at a garage for two weeks. Your driving skills would be so shot by the time you picked up the car that you would be a menace to society on the way home!

Question: Why is there a jump in the motor skill curve after *practice has stopped?*

Improvement of a motor skill *after* practice is called *reminiscence*. Reminiscence probably reflects the absence of fatigue present at the end of practice. Since performance improves after a short rest, motor learning proceeds most efficiently when short practice sessions are alternated with long rest periods. This is called *spaced practice* (also called distributed practice by some), and it may be contrasted to *massed practice* in which one practice period follows the next in quick succession. Figure 9-8 shows this effect.

This suggests that you should keep practice sessions short and well spaced if you are learning to type, play a musical instrument, juggle, or some other motor skill. If you do, the same total amount of practice will produce more learning.

Here are three additional rules given by Gagné and Fleishman to aid motor-skill learning: (1) Practice should be as *lifelike* as possible so that artificial habits and "wrong" stimuli do not become part of the skill. A

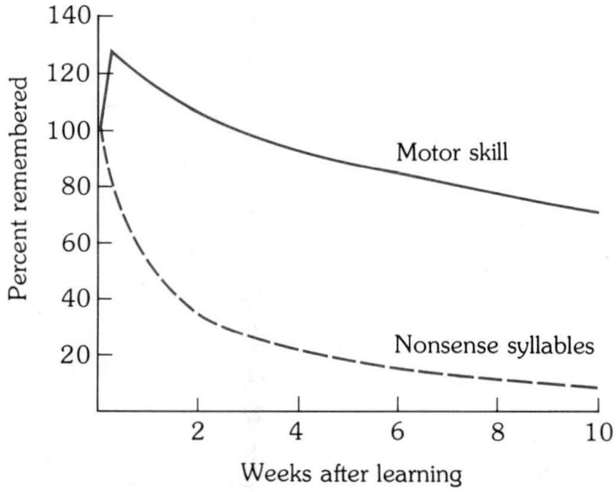

Fig. 9-7 The curves of forgetting for a simple motor skill and simple verbal learning. Notice that there is less rapid forgetting of the motor skill and that there is actually an improvement shortly after practice has ended. (After Leavitt & Scholsberg, 1944.)

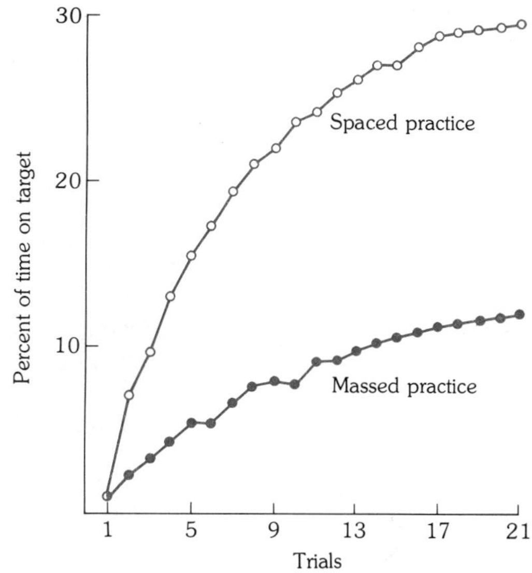

Fig. 9-8 Learning curves for massed and spaced practice. Subjects practiced keeping a pointer on a moving target. Each trial lasted 30 seconds. Some subjects had a 15-second rest period between trials (massed practice), and others, a 45-second rest (spaced practice). Learning with spaced practice was clearly superior. (From Bourne & Archer, 1956.)

competitive diver should practice on the board, not on a trampoline. If you want to learn to ski, practice on snow, not straw. (2) Someone experienced in the skill should direct attention to *correct responses* when they occur. If you want to learn to dance, it is important to know what a correct movement looks and feels like. In tennis, a correct serve is facilitated by making a "back-scratching" movement with the racket. (3) Learn *verbal rules* to back up motor learning. "In golf the feet should be at a right angle to the hole when putting." "To turn right when skiing, shift your weight to the left foot." Two additional principles are also helpful when developing a skill. (4) Begin by learning *units that can be practiced with some success.* When learning to play piano, simple sequences of notes and hand positions should obviously be mastered before more difficult passages. If you want to juggle, start with accurate tosses and catches before attempting more than one ball. (5) When possible, it is better to practice *natural units* rather than break the task into artificial parts. When learning to type, it is better to start with real words rather than exercises or nonsense syllables.

Cognitive Learning

Question: Is all learning just a connection between a stimulus and a response?

Classical and operant conditioning can be understood in such simple terms, but higher levels of learning cannot. *Cognitive learning* involves "knowing what leads to what." How do you navigate around the town you live in? Is it fair to assume that you simply learned what series of right and left turns to make at various intersections to get from one point to another? Actually, if you are new in a town, finding your way around may be temporarily accomplished at this level, but soon you develop an overall mental picture of how the town is laid out. This *cognitive map* (internal representation of relationships) allows you to take alternative routes to the same destination and to find your way there even after a few wrong turns or detours. Even when rats are tested there is evidence that they learn *where* food is to be found in a maze, not just which turns to make (Tolman, 1946). Undoubtedly much human learning begins at an associative level and gradually becomes more cognitive. When learning a foreign language, you may begin by associating English words to their foreign equivalents. Then, as you continue to learn, you will begin to gain an *understanding* of the overall structure and patterns of the new language.

Cognitive learning is closely related to another phenomenon known as *latent* (hidden) *learning*. Learning sometimes occurs with no obvious reinforcement at all.

Chapter 4
Mickey Rat II Learns Where the Action Is

> Two groups of rats are allowed to explore a maze. Rats in one group find food at the far end of the maze and soon learn to make their way rapidly through the maze when released. Rats in the second group are unrewarded and show no signs of learning. But later when these rats are given food, they run the maze as well as the rewarded group (Tolman and Honzik, 1930).

Although there was no outward sign of it, the unrewarded rats were learning their way around the maze.

Question: How did they learn if there was no reinforcement?

Many experiments have demonstrated that curiosity is a strong drive in animals as well as people. Monkeys have been known to solve puzzles after hours of playing with them simply to satisfy curiosity or end boredom (Harlow & Harlow, 1962). Apparently, the satisfaction of exploring the environment can be enough to reward learning. In humans, latent learning is probably related to higher level abilities like anticipation of future reward. If you give an attractive classmate a ride home, you may make mental notes about how to get to his or her house even if a date only seems to be a remote future possibility.

Learning Check

1. Punishment (does/does not) abolish undesired behavior that is also rewarded.

2. Circle the true statements below:

   a. Reward strengthens habits.

   b. Nonreward causes them to be extinguished.

   c. Punishment suppresses a habit but does not weaken it.

3. Verbal learning involves the use of ____________________ or ____________, while motor learning is largely ____________.

4. Learning that sometimes occurs with no obvious reinforcement is called ____________ learning.

Answers: **1.** does not **2.** a, b, c **3.** language or symbols, nonverbal **4.** latent

Modeling—Do as I Do, Not as I Say

A trip to the primate compound at any zoo is almost always rewarded by the opportunity to see monkeys imitating humans or each other. The higher you move in the animal kingdom, the more evidence you will find for learning through imitation. There can be little doubt that many human skills are learned by what Albert Bandura calls observational learning, *modeling*, or, simply, imitation. Modeling has a powerful effect on behavior. In one experiment children watched a movie in which an adult attacked a large blow-up "Bo-Bo" doll with a hammer. Later, when the

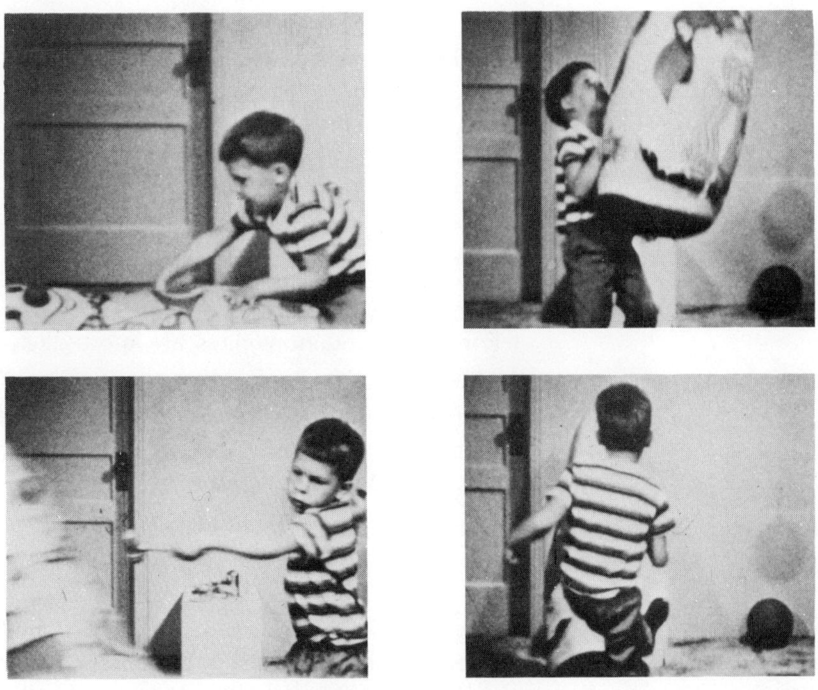

Fig. 9-9 A nursery school child imitates the aggressive behavior of an adult model he has just seen in a movie. (Photos courtesy of Albert Bandura.)

children were allowed to play with the doll, they also struck it with a hammer just as the adult model had done (Bandura, Ross, & Ross, 1963).

Question: Do children blindly imitate adults?

Observational learning equips a person to duplicate a response, but whether it is actually imitated depends on whether the model was rewarded or punished for what he did. Bandura and Walters (1963) summarize: "In addition, models who are rewarding, prestigeful, or competent, who possess high status, and who have control over rewarding resources are more readily imitated."

Among the adults highest in status in any child's world are his own parents. It can be frightening for a parent to realize how much children imitate adults. Through modeling a child learns not only attitudes, gestures, emotions, and other personality traits, but fears, anxieties, and bad habits as well. Consider a typical situation. Little Shawn-Erin-Ringo-Jeremy Jones has just been interrupted at play by his little brother. Angry and frustrated, he hits his little brother. This interrupts his father's TV program. Father promptly spanks little Shawn-Erin-Ringo-Jeremy, saying: "This will teach you to hit your little brother." And it will. Because of modeling effects, it is unrealistic to expect a child to "Do as I say, not as I do." The message the father has given the child is clear: "You have frustrated me; therefore, I will hit you." Is it any wonder that the child does the same when he is frustrated?

No Comment Necessary

Television as a model: TV violence during an average week

During an average week, TV programs contained over 600 acts of violence.

Ninety-five percent of televised cartoons contained violence.

In TV plays more than one-half of the major characters were responsible for inflicting violence on someone.

Foreigners and nonwhites are more likely to die on TV than are whites.

Forty percent of TV "lawmen" initiated violence, and seventy percent contributed to it. (U.S. National Commission on the Causes and Prevention of Violence, 1970.)

Resources Summary

Learning is a relatively permanent change in behavior due to past experience. Learning rarely occurs in the absence of *feedback* or *knowledge of results* (KR). A newly developed form of feedback with many promising applications is *biofeedback*. Biofeedback provides information about bodily processes that allows one to learn to control them voluntarily. *Reinforcement* (basically reward) may be *primary* (unlearned) or *secondary* (learned). Primary reinforcers are usually based on satisfaction of biological needs. Almost anything can become a secondary reinforcer through association with a primary reinforcer. Money is sometimes thought of as a *generalized* reinforcer.

Delay of reinforcement greatly reduces its effectiveness. A good deal of *superstitious* behavior can be traced to accidental reinforcement that appears to be occurring on a schedule of partial reward. Punishment can be quite effective for *suppressing* a response, but it does not appear to remove the underlying habit. Prominent among the undesirable side effects of punishment is its tendency to encourage aggression.

Several basic types of learning have been identified. These include: *verbal* learning, *motor* learning, and *cognitive* learning. Much human learning of all three types is based on the process of *observational learning* (essentially learning by imitation).

Applications

Everybody Has Them—Breaking Bad Habits

Question: How can I use learning principles to break a bad habit?

The following techniques have proved useful.

1. Try to discover what is reinforcing the habit and remove or avoid the reinforcement.

   Example: A student who developed a habit of taking longer and longer "breaks" when studying in the evening realized that his breaks usually were lengthened by TV watching. A chance to watch TV was also reinforcing more frequent "break taking."

   Comment: To improve his study habits he should resolve to stay out of the room where the TV is located until his work is done. Substituting a short walk for TV might be helpful.

2. Try to get the same reinforcement with new habits.

   Example: A young mother realized she was yelling at her children more often than she would like. This habit seemed to be reinforced by the periods of relative quiet that followed when she raised her voice.

   Comment: To avoid this habit, she should (as much as possible) ignore her children when they are noisy and make a special effort to praise them, show approval, and pay attention to them when they are playing quietly and constructively.

3. Make an incompatible response in the presence of stimuli that usually precede the bad habit.

   Example: A sprinter has developed a habit of "jumping the gun" at track meets and is frequently disqualified.

   Comment: The sprinter should prepare for meets by remaining in the blocks while his coach fires a starter's pistol several times.

   Example: A child has developed the habit of throwing her coat on the floor after coming in the front door. After being scolded, she would hang it up.

   Comment: The mother should recognize that scolding has become the cue for hanging the coat up. The girl should not just be scolded, but should put her coat on again, go outside, come in the door, and hang her coat up. Soon, coming in the door will become the cue for hanging the coat up.

4. Avoid cues that elicit the bad habit.

   Example: A housewife has begun to notice how much impulse buying she does at the grocery store. As a first step in avoiding this, she has begun to shop after she has had a meal because she has observed that hunger is a cue for food buying.

Comment: She should also make a shopping list and stick to it so that she only looks at items she intends to buy.

Example: A person who wants to cut down on smoking should remove as many cues for smoking as possible from his daily routine. He should remove ashtrays, matches, and extra cigarettes from the house and make an effort to avoid situations in which most of his smoking occurs; that is, stay away from other smokers, take a walk after a meal, and leave cigarettes at home.

The suggestions listed above are all to some extent included in a final general technique for breaking habits. This is called *negative practice*.

To make use of negative practice, you should deliberately repeat the bad habit until it becomes boring, painful, or produces fatigue. For example, if you have developed the habit of typing "hte" instead of "the," you should type "hte" 500 times in a row, saying to yourself "This is wrong" as you do so. If you have developed a habit of saying "you know" or "ah" too frequently when speaking, set aside fifteen minutes a day and repeat the error aloud over and over while thinking "I hate the way this sounds when someone else says it."

Throughout this chapter we have tried to emphasize the practical applications of learning theories to everyday problems. Many simple difficulties can be handled effectively without special training. If you have a really troublesome habit like overeating, excessive use of alcohol, cigarettes, or marijuana, you may find it most expedient to consult a professional counselor. Additional learning techniques for overcoming mild difficulties can be found in Chapter 24, "Behavior Modification," Chapter 12, "Motivation," and Chapter 8, "Conditioning."

Questions for Discussion

1. Can you think of anything you do that is not affected in some way by learning?
2. How could you include more feedback (or more immediate feedback) in your study habits?
3. Make a list of the reinforcers that have the greatest effect on your behavior. Which seem to exert the greatest influence, primary or secondary reinforcers?
4. How have your feelings and attitudes toward money been shaped by its status as a "generalized reinforcer"?
5. Do you consider classroom grades reinforcers or a form of threatened punishment (or both)? What change (if any) would you like to see in reinforcers available in the classroom?
6. Describe a superstitious behavior or ritual you have engaged in and explain how it might have been learned.
7. How would your life change if motor skills were as subject to loss as verbal learning?
8. Choose a bad habit you would like to break. How could the principles outlined above be applied to this habit?

Suggestions for Further Reading

Hill, W. F. *Learning*. Chandler, 1963.

Larsen, O. N. (ed.) *Violence and the Mass Media.* Harper & Row, 1968.

Logan, F. A. *Fundamentals of Learning and Motivation*. Brown, 1970.

Moore, O. K. "The Responsive Environments Laboratory," in Beatrice and Donald Goss (eds.), *Radical School Reform*, Chap. 15. Simon & Schuster, 1969.

Sahakian, W. S. *Psychology of Learning: Systems, Models, Theories.* Markham, 1970.

Whaley, D., *et al. Contingency Management*. $4.60 postpaid from Behaviordelia, P.O. Box 1044, Kalamazoo, MI 49001.

Memory

10

Chapter Preview

A Visit to the Realm of Past Memories

An electrode was placed at location number 11 on the patient's brain. The patient immediately said, "Yes, sir, I think I heard a mother calling her little boy somewhere. It seemed to be something that happened years ago. . . . It was somebody in the neighborhood where I live." The patient added that she seemed to be "somewhere close enough to hear." The electrode was moved to location number 13, and the patient exclaimed: "Yes, I hear voices. It is late at night, around the carnival somewhere—some sort of traveling circus. . . . I just saw lots of big wagons that they use to haul animals in." The electrode was then moved back to location number 11, and she said again, "Yes, I hear the same familiar sounds, it seems to be a woman calling, the same lady" (Penfield, 1958).

The statements above were made by a twenty-six-year-old woman undergoing brain surgery to relieve the symptoms of epilepsy. Because the operation used only local anesthetics, the patient was completely awake throughout. A part of the skull was removed, exposing the cerebral cortex (outer layer) of the living brain to view. This allowed the surgeon to electrically stimulate areas in the brain. When activated, some areas produced memories. This came as no surprise. What was surprising was the "realness" of the memories. It was as if the person were reliving the experience. Also, memories were retrieved that normally would have been considered permanently forgotten.

Question: Does this mean that every experience a person has ever had is recorded in memory?

No, that would be an exaggeration since some things are forgotten because they never get stored *in the first place. But the fact remains that few people make full use of their memory, and many memories that are stored are never* retrieved. *When you consider that the human brain records in a lifetime as many as 1 quadrillion separate bits of information (Asimov, 1967), it becomes clear that a person has enough room to store all the knowledge he or she could ever use.*

This chapter discusses memory, forgetting, and factors affecting both. As an inquiring person, you should find this material interesting and informative. Also included is a large section on improving your memory skills. As a student, you should find this section particularly useful. Almost anyone (including you) can learn to use his or her memory more effectively.

Resources

Measuring Memory—"The Answer Is on the Tip of My Tongue"

Question: *How is memory measured?*

Initially it might seem that you either remember something or you don't. But a moment of thought should convince you that this is not always true. While driving, have you ever found your way to a place to which you could not have given directions? Have you ever recognized someone you had only seen once before and thought was completely forgotten? In either case you have used a form of partial memory called *recognition*. Partial memory is also demonstrated by the *tip-of-the-tongue phenomenon*. This is the experience of having an answer or a memory just out of reach—on the "tip of your tongue."

In one study of partial memory, university students were asked to read the definitions of words like "sextant," "sampan," and "ambergris." When asked to give the defined words, students often drew a blank because these were words they had seen but rarely used. When students couldn't give the word, they provided whatever other information they could about it. It was found that students could often accurately guess the first and last letter and even the number of syllables of the word they were seeking. They were also able to give words that sounded like or meant the same as the defined word (Brown & McNeill, 1966).

Because memory is not an all-or-nothing process, there are several ways it can be measured. Four common techniques are: *recall*, *recognition*, *relearning*, and *redintegration*.

Recall To recall means to remember or reproduce important facts and information verbatim (word for word) without explicit cues or stimuli. For instance, if you study this passage until you can recite it without looking, then you will have recalled it. A type of recall is also required when you take an essay examination. Students often consider essay exams the most difficult test of memory because such exams offer no clues to help you

Fig. 10-1 Test-taking typically requires recall or recognition memory. (Photo by Marge Agin.)

remember what you studied. In order to show in your essay answer what you have learned, you must recall it.

Recognition If you were asked to write down all the facts you could remember from a class taken last year, it might be concluded that you remembered very little. However, a more sensitive testing procedure based on *recognition* could be used. For instance, you could be given a *multiple-choice* test covering the facts and ideas from the course. Since multiple-choice tests only require you to recognize the correct answer, you would probably find evidence that considerable learning had carried over. Similarly, if you were asked to describe the people you went to school with in the sixth grade or to recall their names, you could probably remember only a few. But if you were shown pictures or names of former classmates mixed with strangers, you would accurately *recognize* many more.

Because recall is so difficult, recognition memory is used by police departments to identify criminal suspects. Witnesses to a crime who disagree in their recall of the height, weight, age, eye color, or dress of a suspect often agree completely when they are given a chance to select the person from a group of photographs or a lineup.

Relearning In a well-known experiment on memory, a psychologist read a short passage in Greek to a child. This was done daily when the child was between fifteen months and three years of age. When he was eight, the child was asked if he remembered the Greek passage that was read to him when he was younger. The child showed no evidence of recall. He was then given selections from the passage he had heard and selections from other Greek passages to see if he could recognize the one he had heard. "It's all Greek to me!" he said, indicating that there was no recognition (and drawing a frown from everyone in the room). Had the investigator stopped here, he might have concluded that no memory remained. However, the child was then asked to memorize the original passage and several other passages of equal difficulty. This time his earlier learning became evident because he memorized the passage he had heard in childhood 25 percent faster than the other passages (Burtt, 1941).

Testing memory by *relearning* shows a *savings* in the time or effort necessary to remaster previously learned material. This is perhaps one of the best arguments in favor of taking a wide range of classes in school. It may seem that time spent learning algebra, geography, or a foreign language is wasted because so little is remembered a year or two later. But if you ever need these skills (for travel, employment, further education, and so forth), you will find that you can brush up on or relearn the necessary information in far less time than it took you to learn it originally.

Redintegration A fourth type of memory occurs when an entire past experience is reconstructed from one small recollection. This is called *redintegration* (ruh-din-tuh-gray-shun), and it almost always involves personal experiences rather than formal learning. You would probably experience redintegration after seeing a picture taken on your sixth birthday or your tenth Christmas. The limited memory cues provided by such a picture can unleash a whole flood of seemingly forgotten details and experiences. Many people find that redintegrative memories are especially

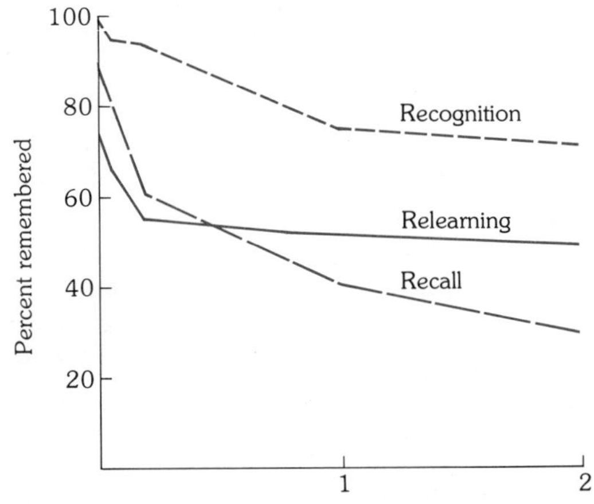

Fig. 10-2 Comparison of three measures of memory. Recognition memory shows less forgetting than recall after two days. In this example, relearning is somewhere in between, but it is often the most sensitive measure of the amount of information re tained. (After Luh, 1922.)

likely to be touched off by distinctive odors out of the past, from a farm visited in childhood, Grandma's kitchen, the seashore, a doctor's office, the perfume or after-shave of a former lover, and so on.

Learning Check

Before reading on, answer the following questions.

1. Four common techniques of measuring memory are ________, ________, ________, and ________.

2. Multiple-choice tests require the ________ technique.

3. Essay tests require the ________ technique.

4. A true-false quiz shows the "tip-of-the tongue" phenomenon in action. T or F?

Answers:

1. recall, recognition, relearning, redintegration **2.** recognition **3.** recall **4.** F

Eidetic Imagery—Is the Brain a Camera?

Question: What is a "photographic memory"? How is it different from the types of memory already described?

Eidetic (i-det-ik) *imagery*, known informally as photographic memory, occurs when a person has visual images clear enough to be "scanned" or retained for at least thirty seconds after viewing a picture. Eidetic imagery is more common during childhood. About five children in one hundred can give detailed descriptions and can answer questions about pictures they have viewed for only a few seconds. After looking at a photo, such a child can answer a question like, "How many buttons are on the policeman's coat?" by counting the buttons in his mental image. (To test your eidetic imagery, see Fig. 10-3.) Most eidetic skills disappear during adolescence and become quite rare by adulthood. This has led some psychologists to suggest that we all have "photographic memory" to a degree, but we trade it in for memorizing through language as we get older. Actually, this may not be too much of a loss, and it may be a mistake to envy the person with a photographic memory. The majority of eidetic memorizers have no better long-term memory than average.

A notable exception to this is reported by Russian psychologist A. R. Luria (1968). Luria studied a man (Mr. S) who had practically unlimited memory for visual images. Mr. S could remember almost everything that

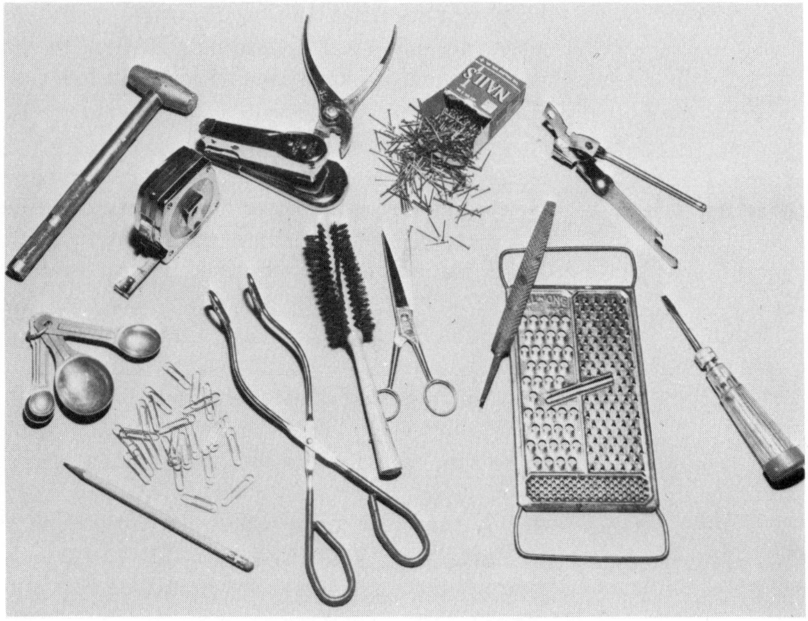

Fig. 10-3 Test your eidetic imagery. Look at this picture for about 30 seconds; then close the book and see how many objects you can list. (Hint: Do not name the objects as you look at them. This tends to place them in conventional memory and interferes with the use of eidetic images.) A person with good imagery will remember all or most of the items correctly. (Photo by Marge Agin.)

had ever happened to him with overwhelming accuracy and detail. When Luria tried to test Mr. S's memory by using longer and longer lists of words or numbers, he discovered that no matter how long the list Mr. S was able to reproduce it without error. Even when tested fifteen years later, Mr. S was still able to remember these lists. As fantastic as this might sound to a struggling student, Mr. S's memory caused great difficulty. He remembered so much that he could not separate what was important from the trivial. For instance, if he were tested on the contents of this chapter after reading it, he would remember not only every word, but all the images each word made him think of and all the sights, sounds, and feelings that occurred as he was reading. Finding the answer for one specific question, writing a logical essay, or even understanding a single sentence, therefore, became very difficult for him.

Short- and Long-term Memory—Do You Have a Mind Like a Steel Trap? Or a Sieve?

Question: *Why are some memories lost so quickly? For instance, why is it so hard to remember names a few minutes after you've been introduced to a group of people?*

Forgetting is the other side of the memory coin. As the case of Mr. S makes clear, there are advantages to being able to forget. Generally speaking, most forgetting occurs immediately after memorization. In a famous set of experiments, Herman Ebbinghaus (1885) memorized long lists of *nonsense syllables* (meaningless three-letter words, such as "gex," "cef," or "wol"). By waiting various amounts of time before testing himself, Ebbinghaus constructed a "curve of forgetting" (see Fig. 10-4). Notice that forgetting is rapid at first and then levels off to a slow decline. As a student, you should see that the less time there is between review for a test and the taking of the test, the less forgetting will occur. However, don't misinterpret this as a reason for cramming. The error most students make is to cram *only*. If you cram, you don't have to remember for very long, but you may not learn enough in the first place.

If you space your practice (see Chapter 9) by using short, daily study sessions and, in addition, cram or review before a test, you will get the benefit of good preparation and a minimum of time lapse. A study on retention done by H. F. Spitzer (1939) proved the value of spaced review or periodic studying. Students reviewed immediately after studying and then reviewed again several days later and a third time 63 days later. These students remembered over 30 percent more than students who did not review what they had learned.

The curve of forgetting only provides a general picture. To understand forgetting better, it must be recognized that there are at least two

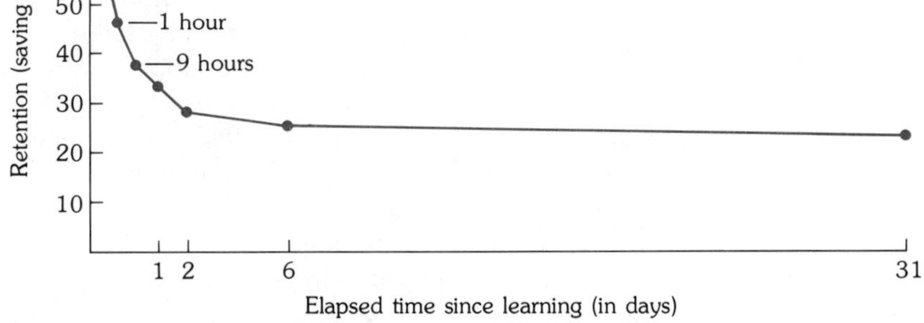

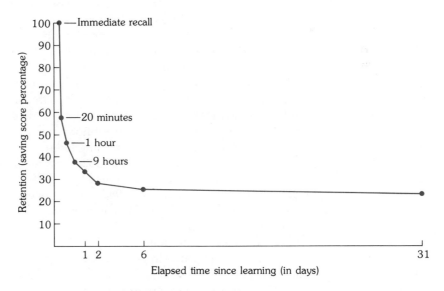

Fig. 10-4 The curve of forgetting. This graph shows the amount remembered (measured by relearning) after varying lengths of time. Notice how rapidly forgetting occurs. Material learned was nonsense syllables. Meaningful information is not forgotten so quickly. (After Ebbinghaus, 1885.)

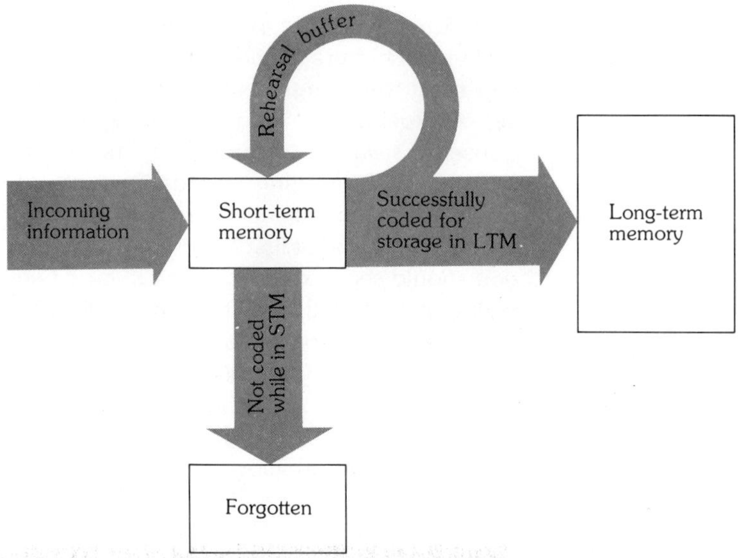

Fig. 10-5 Memory is thought to involve at least two steps. Incoming information is first stored in short-term memory. If it is not rapidly coded, it is forgotten. If it is transferred to long-term memory, it becomes permanently stored. Storage in STM can be prolonged by rehearsal.

basic memory systems. The first, called *short-term memory (STM)*, is used to hold information for very brief periods of time. This is the system used when dialing a phone number, remembering a name, or adding a column of numbers. Short-term memory can only hold a limited amount of information, and once information is removed from STM it is permanently lost. Generally this is an advantage. If most short-term memories were not erased, our minds would be cluttered with names, dates, telephone numbers, arithmetic sums, and other useless trivia (Miller, 1964). As you may have noticed when dialing a phone number, STM is very severely affected by any interruption or interference (Adams, 1967). You've probably had this experience. You look up a telephone number and walk to the phone repeating the number to yourself. You dial the number and get a busy signal. Returning a few minutes later, you find that you must look up the number again. This time as you are about to dial, someone asks you a question. You answer, turn to the phone, and find that you have forgotten the number.

Information that is important, useful, meaningful, or novel, may be transferred to the second memory system called *long-term memory (LTM)*. Long-term memory seems to be based on a separate system in the brain since it permanently records information and has a practically unlimited storage capacity. Evidence for this comes from the work of Wilder Penfield, a neurosurgeon who has found that vivid memories are brought out when the human brain is stimulated with an electric needle. (A description of Penfield's work is found earlier in the chapter preview.) Penfield reports that one patient heard familiar music so clearly that she thought a record player had been turned on nearby. Penfield believes that the nervous system retains a record of a person's past that is like "a continuous strip of movie film, complete with sound track" (Penfield, 1957).

The following questions and exercises will add to your understanding of long- and short-term memory.

Short-term Capacity

Question: How much information can be held in short-term memory?

Read the following numerals once. Then close the book and write as many as you can in the correct order.

8 5 1 7 4 9 3

If you were able to correctly repeat this series of seven digits, you have an average short-term memory.

Now try to memorize the following list of digits, reading them only once:

7 1 8 3 5 4 2 9 1 6

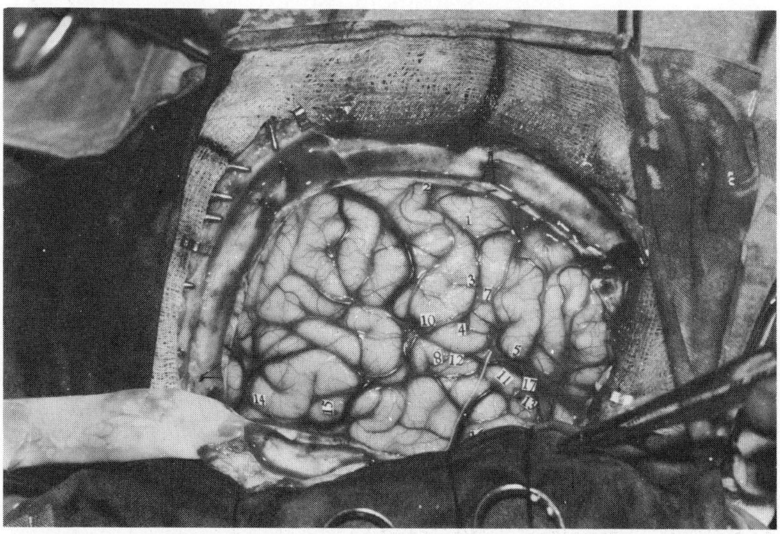

Fig. 10-6 Exposed cerebral cortex of a patient undergoing brain surgery. Numbers represent points at which stimulation produced memories. (From Wilder Penfield, *The Excitable Cortex in Conscious Man*, 1958. Courtesy of the author and Charles C Thomas, Publisher, Springfield, Illinois.)

This series was probably beyond your short-term memory capacity. Psychologist George Miller believes short-term memory capacity is limited by what he calls the "magic number" *seven* (plus or minus two) *bits* of information (Miller, 1956). When memorizing lists of random numbers like those above (*the digit-span test*), the average adult finds five digits child's play, six digits easy, seven difficult, and nine or ten impossible.

Coding Before we continue, try your short-term memory again, this time on letters instead of digits. Study the following letters for about 30 seconds. Then close your book and try to reproduce the entire letter square.

S A V A O
R E E E G
U R S Y A
O O D N S
F C N E R

Since this square contains twenty-five letters or separate "bits" of information, it should be beyond the seven-item capacity of STM. In spite of this, students are often able to memorize the square by converting the twenty-five individual bits of information into *five chunks* of information, making each line of letters into a nonsense word: "savao," "reeeg," "ursya," "oodns," and "fcner." If you saw this possibility, you probably were able to memorize the letter square. Look at the square again and you will notice that it can even be organized into *one* chunk well within anyone's memory capacity. If you read *up* the columns starting in the lower left corner, you will find the chunk: "Four score and seven years ago."

Coding information by organizing it into larger chunks is a key to increasing the efficiency of short-term memory (Sperling, 1967). The series of digits 1 4 9 2 1 9 7 6 is near the limit of STM capacity unles you recognize that the series can be chunked into two familiar dates: 1492 and 1976. As telephone numbers get longer, phone companies have found it useful to chunk numbers for customers by breaking them into an area code, a prefix, and then a short number.

Question: How long do short-term memories last?

Rehearsal Short-term *memory traces* appear to undergo very rapid decay or weakening. But short-term memories can be prolonged by *rehearsal*, that is, by mentally repeating the information over and over until it is used or until it is stored in long-term memory. If rehearsal is prevented, STM is incredibly short.

In one experiment subjects heard nonsense syllables like XAR followed by a number like 67. As soon as a subject heard the number, he would begin counting backwards by threes. (This prevented him from repeating the

> nonsense syllable.) Subjects were stopped after varying lengths of time and tested for recall of the last syllable they had heard. After only 18 seconds of delay, recall scores fell to zero (Peterson & Peterson, 1959).

After eighteen seconds without rehearsal, the short-term memory was gone forever! Keep this in mind in situations where you may only get one chance to hear information you want to remember. For example, if you are introduced to someone at a social gathering and his or her name slips out of STM, there is no way to retrieve it. To escape this awkward situation you might try saying something like, "I'm curious, how do you spell your name?" But unfortunately, the response to this strategy is too often an icy reply like, "B-O-B S-M-I-T-H, it's really not too difficult." To avoid embarrassment, pay careful attention to the name, repeat it to yourself several times, and try to use it in the next sentence or two—before you lose it.

Learning Check

Check your understanding of what you have just read by answering the following questions.

1. Eidetic memory refers to the so-called photographic memory.
T or F?

2. According to the Ebbinghaus "curve of forgetting," we forget slowly first and then a rapid decline occurs. T or F?

3. STM stands for ______________________________

4. LTM stands for ______________________________

5. If there is no rehearsal or mental repeating of the information desired to be learned, STM is incredibly short. T or F?

Answers: **1.** T **2.** F **3.** short-term memory **4.** long-term memory **5.** T

Interference and Inhibition—Why We Forget

Question: If long-term memories are permanent, why do we forget things?

As we have said, short-term forgetting occurs because information is no longer stored. Short-term memory can be thought of as a "leaky bucket": New information constantly pours in, but it rapidly escapes and is replaced by still-newer information (Miller, 1956).

At one time it was thought that long-term *memory traces* (changes in nerve cells in the brain) fade because of *disuse* and eventually become so weak that they can no longer be retrieved. A moment of thought will show that disuse fails to explain why some unused memories fade and others are carried for life. Another contradiction will be recognized by anyone who has spent time with the elderly. People growing senile may become so forgetful that they can't remember what happened a week ago. Yet at the same time your Uncle Oscar's recent memories are fading he may have vivid memories of trivial and long-forgotten events from the past. "Why, I remember it as clearly as if it were yesterday," he will say, not remembering that the story he is about to tell is the same one he told earlier the same day.

Question: Then what does cause forgetting of long-term memories?

A hint comes from an experiment in which college students learned lists of nonsense syllables. After studying, one group of students slept for eight hours and were then tested for memory of the lists. A second group remained awake for eight hours and went about their business as usual. When the second group was tested, they remembered *less* than the group that slept. This difference is based on the fact that new learning can *interfere* with previous learning (Shiffrin, 1970). If you think of the brain as a giant filing cabinet, this means that new learning displaces or covers up previous memories so that they become harder to locate (retrieve) even if they are still stored.

Question: What would happen if you could be placed in "suspended animation" immediately after learning?

Theoretically, any length of time could pass without the memory being lost. Without new memories to cause interference, it would be as if no time at all had passed. Of course, this experiment has not been

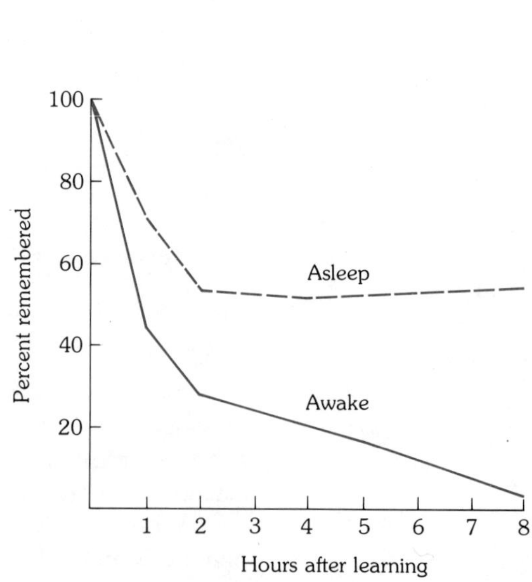

Fig. 10-7 The amount of forgetting after sleep or waking activity. Notice that sleep causes less memory loss than waking. (After Jenkins & Dallenbach, 1924.)

performed with humans, but something similar has been done with a rather interesting experimental subject, the common cockroach. If a cockroach is placed in a cold dark place, it enters a state resembling hibernation. This effect was used in a study in which two groups of cockroaches learned their way through a maze. One group was then allowed to wander around in a lighted cage doing all the things cockroaches normally do. The second group was placed in a darkened refrigerator. As predicted, the refrigerated cockroaches showed significantly better memory when they were later tested in the maze (Minami & Dallenbach, 1946).

Both the sleeping college students and the refrigerated cockroaches remembered more because *retroactive inhibition* was held to a minimum. Retroactive inhibition refers to the tendency for new learning to interfere with old learning. Avoiding new learning prevents retroactive inhibition from occurring. This doesn't exactly mean that you should sleep in your refrigerator after you study for an exam, but it does suggest that you should avoid learning material from other classes between your final study session and the exam.

A second basic type of interference is *proactive inhibition*. Proactive inhibition occurs when prior learning interferes with later learning. For instance, if you cram for a psychology exam and then later the same night cram for a history exam, your memory of the second thing studied (history) will be less accurate than it would have been if you had studied only history. (Due to retroactive inhibition your memory of the psychology will probably also suffer.) Proactive inhibition is especially likely to occur when old learning *conflicts* with new learning (Ceraso, 1967). Learning to back a car with a trailer attached is a good example. Normally when you are backing a car, the steering wheel is turned in the direction you want to go. Since this is the same as normal driving it is easily mastered. However, with a trailer attached, the steering wheel must be turned *opposite* from the direction you want the trailer to go. This causes established driving habits to interfere and makes learning to back a trailer difficult.

Old and new learning causes interference by *inhibiting retrieval*, not by *erasing* memories. A special form of memory inhibition is *repression*. Clinical psychologists believe that repressed memories are too painful to be brought to awareness. To a limited degree, ordinary memories may be repressed. The forgetting of past failures or embarrassments, a dental appointment, or the name of a person you dislike may be caused by repression. (See Chapter 15 for more information on repression.)

Learning Check

Before reading on, check your memory by defining these terms:

1. Memory traces: ______________________________

2. Retroactive inhibition: ______________________________

3. Proactive inhibition: ______________________________

4. Repression: ______________________________

Answers: **1.** changes in nerve cells in the brain **2.** tendency for new memories to interfere with old memories **3.** prior learning interferes with later learning **4.** holding back uncomfortable feelings or thoughts from consciousness

Memory Formation—Some "Shocking" Findings

Question: Why does a head injury cause amnesia?

A head injury may cause a "gap" in memories preceding the accident. *Retrograde amnesia*, as this is called, can be understood by recognizing that transferring memories from short-term storage to long-term storage takes a certain amount of time. The process of forming a long-term memory is called *consolidation* (John, 1967). You can think of consolidation as being somewhat like writing your name in wet concrete. Once the concrete is set, the information (your name) is fairly lasting, but while it is setting it can be wiped out (amnesia) or scribbled over (interference).

In one experiment on consolidation, a rat was placed on a small platform. Eventually the rat stepped down to the floor. When he did, he received a painful electric shock on his feet. After one shock the rat can be returned to the platform repeatedly, but he will not step down. Obviously the shock has been remembered. But what would happen if we prevented the memory of the shock from being stored? Interestingly, one means of preventing consolidation is to give the rat a different kind of shock called *electroconvulsive shock (ECS)* immediately after each learning experience (Jarvik, 1964). ECS is a mild electric shock to the brain. It does not harm the animal and is not painful, but it does destroy any memory that is being formed. If each painful shock (the one the animal remembers) is followed by ECS (which destroys memories during consolidation), the rat will step down from the platform over and over, each time getting shocked and then receiving ECS to erase the memory of the shocks. (See Chapter 22 for a discussion of the application of ECS to humans.)

Question: What would happen if the ECS were given several hours after the learning?

If enough time is allowed to pass between learning and the ECS, the memory is unaffected because consolidation has been completed. This is why people who have had head injuries usually only lose memories from immediately before the accident while older memories remain intact (Russell & Nathan, 1964). Likewise, you would forget more if you followed a study session with eight hours of waking activity and then eight hours of sleep than you would if you studied, slept eight hours, and then were awake for eight hours. In both cases sixteen hours have passed, but in the second instance forgetting is reduced because more consolidation has taken place before interference begins.

Question: What part of the brain causes consolidation?

Actually, many areas of the brain are responsible for memory, but of particular importance is the *hippocampus*. This structure, buried deep within the temporal lobes at each side of the brain, has recently been connected to long-term memory formation. Humans who have had the hippocampus damaged show a striking inability to store new memories. A patient described by Brenda Milner is typical. Two years after an operation that affected the hippocampus, a twenty-nine-year-old patient continued to give his age as twenty-seven and reported that it seemed that the operation had just taken place (Milner, 1965). His memory of events before the operation remained clear, but he found new learning almost impossible. When his parents moved to a new house a few blocks away on the same street, he could not remember the new address, and he was observed to read the same magazines over and over again without finding their contents familiar (Milner, 1965).

The Chemistry of Memory—Will We Eat College Professors?

Question: Can memory be improved with drugs?

The possibility of chemically improving memory has long intrigued both psychologists and the general public. We have known for some time that various stimulating drugs speed up consolidation if given just after learning. Note, however, that this only reduces the time during which interference can take place; it does not directly increase memory. Also, the drugs involved (metrazol, strychnine, nicotine, caffeine, and amphetamine) must be given in carefully controlled dosages, because at higher levels they *disrupt* memory or are poisonous (McGaugh, 1970).

Studies that focus on RNA (ribonucleic acid) probably hold the greatest promise for artificially improving memory. Since RNA is involved in protein production and other cell functions, a change in RNA structure is capable of altering the activity of individual nerve cells in the brain. Some psychologists now believe that *engrams*, or memory traces, are directly related to changes in RNA. An intriguing test of this possibility comes from work with planaria (flatworms). First, planaria were conditioned (using electric shock) to curl up or "skrunch" when a light came on. Then the planaria were cut in half and allowed to regenerate. (Planaria tails will grow new heads, and heads will grow new tails.) Half of the planaria pieces regenerated in plain water, and half regenerated in water containing an enzyme that destroys RNA. It was found that the heads that grew new tails all remembered the "skrunch response," but only those tails in plain water were able to transfer learning to their new heads* (McConnell, Jacobsen, & Kimble, 1959).

Fig. 10-8 A flatworm like those used in McConnell's study of "cannibal" worms and memory.

*The moral to this experiment seems to be: "If you're going to lose your head, lose it in plain water."

Question: Could RNA be used to transfer memories from one person to another?

The first planaria experiments have been very controversial because attempts to duplicate them have not always been successful. Transfer of memories from one animal to another through RNA has been even more controversial, but some experiments suggest this is possible. When it was discovered that planaria could be chopped up and fed to each other, "trained" planaria were fed to "untrained" planaria. The "cannibal worms" then showed evidence of learning (McConnell, 1962). In later experiments, RNA was extracted from the brains of trained rats, gerbils, or hamsters and injected into untrained animals. Injected animals then did better than controls on tasks originally learned by the trained animals (John, 1967).

Studies such as these have led to the tongue-in-cheek suggestion that we may be wasting a great natural resource: We should grind up the brains of retired college professors and feed them to promising young students! More seriously, it will be a long time before it becomes possible to take a memory pill or injection, and the possibility of a "French pill" or a "math pill" seems especially remote. The fact remains, however, that the future will probably see considerable cooperation among biochemists, psychologists, and educators in the search for the mechanisms of memory and that memory can and will be artificially enhanced.

Resources Summary

Memories vary considerably in strength. They may be revealed by *recall*, *recognition*, *relearning*, or *redintegration*. A specialized form of memory called *eidetic imagery* (photographic memory) may produce nearly complete recall for visual images. There are at least two memory systems called *short-term memory* (STM) and *long-term memory* (LTM).

Short-term memory is characterized by rapid forgetting (probably due to decay of the memory trace). It has an information capacity that averages seven items. "Chunking" and other forms of *coding* may extend the apparent limits of this seven-item capacity.

Forgetting of long-term memories cannot be explained by decay or disuse. Long-term memory appears to have a virtually unlimited capacity. Forgetting of long-term memories is best explained by the action of *interference*. Two kinds of interference are *retroactive inhibition* (new learning interferes with old) and *proactive inhibition* (old memories interfere with new). Retrieval of memories may also be caused by *repression*, the inhibition of painful or threatening memories.

Long-term memories must be *consolidated* to be permanently stored. Until they are consolidated, they are easily destroyed by *electroconvulsive shock* (ECS), head injuries, and so forth. Consolidation is most likely based on changes in RNA in nerve cells in the brain. The ability to form new memories is lost when an area in the brain called the *hippocampus* is injured.

Applications

How to Improve Your Memory

While you are waiting around for the development of a memory pill, let's focus on some ways of improving your memory right now.

Question: How much can memory be improved? What if I have a very poor memory?

No matter how good (or bad) your basic memory is, you could probably make much better use of the capacity you do have. As James Weinland (1957) has said, "A person is entitled to say that he has a poor memory only if he forgets many things that deeply interest him and that he has made an effort to remember." Weinland's point is aptly illustrated by the student who complains he can't remember facts in his classes, but who can remember the names of every part in an automobile, the names of all the players in the National Football League, and the cubic displacement and horsepower of every motorcycle sold in the United States.

In this and previous chapters, many factors affecting learning and memory have been mentioned. The list below summarizes these factors and some not previously discussed. You can improve your memory and study efficiency by controlling as many of these factors as possible.

Knowledge of Results Learning proceeds most effectively when feedback or knowledge of results allows you to check to see if you are learning. Feedback also helps you identify material that needs extra practice, and it can be rewarding to know that you have remembered or answered correctly. A prime means of providing feedback for yourself when studying is *recitation.*

Recitation Recitation means repeating to yourself what you have learned. If you are going to remember something, eventually you will have to retrieve it. Recitation forces you to practice retrieving information as you are learning. When you are reading a text, you should stop frequently and try to remember what you have just read by summarizing it aloud. In one experiment the best memory score of all was earned by a group of students who spent 80 percent of their time reciting and only 20 percent reading (Gates, 1958). Maybe students who talk to themselves aren't crazy after all!

Overlearning Numerous studies have shown that memory is greatly improved when study is continued beyond "bare mastery." In other words, after you have learned material well enough to remember it once without error, you should continue studying. Overlearning is your best insurance against "going blank" on a test because of nervousness or anxiety.

Selection The Dutch scholar Erasmus said that a good memory should be like a fisherman's net: It should keep all the big fish and let the little ones escape. If you boil down the paragraphs in most textbooks to one or two important terms or ideas, you will find your memorization chores more manageable and will probably remember more than you would if you tried to retain everything. Practice careful and selective marking in your texts and use marginal notes to further summarize ideas. Most students mark their texts too much instead of too little. If everything is underlined, you haven't been selective.

Spaced Practice Spaced practice is generally superior to massed practice. Four 15-minute study periods will produce more learning than a one-hour study session. Perhaps the best way to try to make use of this principle is to *schedule* your time. If the average student were to keep a totally honest record of his weekly activities, he would probably find that very few hours were spent really studying. To make an effective schedule, designate times during the week before, after, and between classes when you will study particular subjects. Then treat these times just as if they were classes you had to attend.

Organize Assume that you must memorize the following list of words: north, man, red, spring, woman, east, autumn, yellow, summer, boy, blue, west, winter, girl, green, south. This rather difficult list could be reorganized as follows: north, east, south, west, spring, summer, autumn, winter, red, yellow, green, blue, man, woman, boy, girl. This simple reordering made the second list much easier to learn when college students were tested on both lists (Deese & Hulse, 1967). In another experiment, students who made up stories using long lists of words to be memorized learned the lists better than those who didn't (Bower & Clark, 1969). Organizing class notes and outlining chapters can be very helpful when studying. It may even be helpful to outline your outlines, so that the overall organization of ideas becomes clearer and simpler.

Whole versus Part Learning If you had to memorize a speech, would it be better to try to learn it from beginning to end or in smaller parts like paragraphs? Generally it is better to practice whole packages of information rather than smaller parts. This is especially true for fairly short, organized information. An exception is that learning parts may be better for extremely long, complicated information. Try to study the largest *meaningful* amount of information possible at one time. It is also important to remember the *serial position effect*. This is the tendency to master material in the order: first, last, then middle. Since information in the middle is the last learned, it should be given special attention.

Sleep Remember that sleeping after study produces the least interference. Since you obviously can't sleep after every study session, or can't study everything just before you sleep, your study schedule (see above) should include ample breaks between subjects. Using your breaks and free time in a schedule is as important as living up to your study periods.

Review If you have spaced your practice and overlearned, review will be like icing on your study cake. Review shortly before an exam cuts down the time during which you must remember details that may be important for the test but not otherwise meaningful to you. When reviewing, hold the amount of new information you try to memorize to a minimum. It may be realistic to take what you have actually learned and add a little more to it at the last minute by cramming, but remember that more than a little new learning will confuse you and interfere with what you already know.

If you consistently use the principles reviewed above, you should get grades at least one step higher without increasing your study time, or you should get the same grades after spending less time. Give this an honest try, and we can almost guarantee these results. Besides, if you haven't adopted the SQ3R and LISAN techniques described in "The Psychology of Studying Psychology" in the beginning of this book, it might be time to give them a try.

For Discussion

Mnemonics—Memory Magic

Question: Some stage performers use memory as part of their acts. Do they have eidetic imagery?

Various "memory experts" entertain by giving demonstrations in which they memorize the names of everyone at a banquet, the order of all the cards in a deck, long lists of disconnected words, or other seemingly impossible amounts of information. These tricks are performed through the use of *mnemonics* (the first *m* is silent). Mnemonics refers to any kind of memory system or aid. Some mnemonic systems have become so common that almost everyone knows them. If you are trying to remember how many days there are in a month, you may find the answer by reciting "Thirty days hath September. . . ." Physics teachers often help their students remember the colors of the spectrum by giving them the mnemonic "Roy G. Biv": *r*ed, *o*range, *y*ellow, *g*reen, *b*lue, *i*ndigo, *v*iolet. The budding sailor who has trouble telling port from starboard may remember that port and left both have four letters or may remind himself, "I *left port*." And what beginning musician hasn't remembered the notes represented by the lines and spaces of the musical staff by learning "face" and "*e*very *g*ood *b*oy *d*oes *f*ine."

Mnemonic techniques are ways of avoiding *rote* learning (learning by simple repetition). The superiority of mnemonic learning as opposed to rote learning has been demonstrated many times. For example, Bower (1973) asked college students to study 5 different lists of 20 unrelated words. At the end of a short study session subjects were asked to recall all 100 items. Subjects using mnemonics remembered an average of 72 items, whereas a control group using simple or rote learning remembered an average of 28.

Stage performers rarely have a naturally superior memory. Instead, they make extensive use of memory systems to perform their feats. Few of these systems are of practical value to the student, but the principles underlying mnemonics are. By practicing mnemonics you should be able to greatly improve your memory with little effort.

The basic principles of mnemonics are:

1. *Use mental pictures.* There are at least two kinds of memory, *visual* and *verbal*. Visual pictures or images are generally easier to remember than words. Turning information into mental pictures is therefore very helpful (Paivio, 1969).
2. *Make things meaningful.* Transfer of information from short-term to long-term memory is aided by making it meaningful. If you encounter technical terms that have little or no immediate meaning for you, *give* them meaning, even if you have to stretch the term to do so. (This point is clarified by the examples below.)
3. *Make information familiar.* Connect it to what you already know. Another way to get information into long-term memory is to connect it

to information already stored there. If some facts or ideas in a chapter seem to stay in your memory easily, associate other more difficult facts with them.

4. *Form bizarre, unusual, or exaggerated mental associations.* When associating two ideas, terms, or especially mental images, you will find that the more outrageous and exaggerated the association, the more likely you are to remember it later.

A sampling of typical applications of mnemonics should make these four points clear to you.

Example 1 Let's say you have thirty new vocabulary words to memorize in Spanish. You can proceed by rote memorization (repeat them over and over until you begin to get them) or you can learn them with little effort through mnemonics. To remember that the word *pájaro* (pronounced pa-ha-ro) means bird, you can give the word familiar meaning and use mental images. *Pájaro* (to me) sounds like "parked car-o." To remember that *pájaro* means bird, I will visualize a parked car jam-packed full of birds. I will try to make this image as vivid and exaggerated as possible. I will picture the birds flapping and chirping and feathers flying everywhere. Perhaps I will also visualize my own car parked with a giant bird peeking out from inside. If you form similar images for the rest of the words on the list, you may not remember them all, but you will get most without any further practice. As a matter of fact, if you have formed the *pájaro* images just now, it is going to be almost impossible for you to ever see the word *pájaro* again without remembering that it means bird.

Question: What if I think pájaro *means "parked car" when I take my Spanish test?*

This is why you should form one or two extra images so that the important feature (bird, in this case) is repeated.

Example 2 Let's say you have to learn the names of all the bones and muscles in the human body for biology. You are trying to remember that the jawbone is the *mandible*. This one is easy because you can associate it to a *man nibbling*, or maybe you can picture a *man dribbling* a basketball with his jaw (make this image as ridiculous as possible). If the muscle name *latissimus dorsi* gives you trouble, familiarize it by turning it into "*the ladder misses the door, sigh*." Then picture a ladder glued to your back where the muscle is found. Picture the ladder leading up to a small door at your shoulder. Picture the ladder missing the door. Picture the ladder sighing like an animated character in a cartoon.

Question: This seems like more to remember, not less; and it seems like it would cause you to misspell things.

Mnemonics are not a complete substitute for normal memory; they are an aid to normal memory. Mnemonics are not likely to be helpful unless you make extensive use of *images*. Your mental pictures will come back to you very easily. As for misspellings, mnemonics can be thought of as a built-in hint in your memory. Often when taking a test, you will find that the slightest hint is all you need to remember correctly. A mnemonic image is like having someone leaning over your shoulder who says, "Psst, the name of that muscle sounds like 'ladder misses the door, sigh.' "

Here are two more examples to help you appreciate the flexibility of a mnemonic approach to studying.

Example 3 Your art history teacher expects you to be able to name the artist when you are shown slides as part of exams. Many of the slides you have only seen once before in class. How will you remember them? As the slides are shown in class, make each artist's name into an object or image. Then picture the object *in* paintings done by the artist. For example, Van Gogh you can picture as a *van* (automobile) *going* through the middle of each Van Gogh painting. Picture the van running over things and knocking things over. Or, if you remember that Van Gogh cut off his ear, picture a giant bloody ear in each of his paintings.

Example 4 If you have trouble remembering history, try to avoid thinking of it as something from the dim past. Picture each historical personality as a person you know right now (a friend, teacher, parent, and so on). Then picture these people doing whatever the historical figures did. Also try visualizing battles or other events as if they were happening in your town or make parks and schools into countries. Use your imagination.

Question: How can mnemonics be used to remember things in order?

Here are three techniques that are helpful.

1. *Form a chain.* To remember lists of ideas, objects, or words in order, try forming an exaggerated association (mental image) connecting the first item to the second, then the second to the third, and so on. To remember the following short list in order: elephant, doorknob, string, watch, rifle, oranges, picture a full-sized *elephant* balanced on a *doorknob* playing with a *string* tied to him. Picture a *watch* tied to the string, and a *rifle* shooting *oranges* at the watch. This technique can be used quite successfully for lists of twenty or more items. Try it next time you go shopping and leave your list at home.
2. *Take a mental walk.* Mnemonics were well known to ancient Greek orators, who would take a mental walk along a familiar path to associate ideas they wanted to cover in a speech to the images of statues found along the walk. You can do the same by "placing" objects or ideas along the way as you mentally take a familiar walk.
3. *Use a system.* Many times the first letter or syllables of words or ideas can be formed into another word that will serve as a reminder of order. "Roy G. Biv," cited above, is an example. As an alternative, learn the following: 1 is a bun, 2 is a shoe, 3 is a tree, 4 is a door, 5 is a

hive, 6 is sticks, 7 is heaven, 8 is a gate, 9 is a line, 10 is a hen. To remember in order, form an association between bun and the first item on your list, then form an association between shoe and the second item, and so on.

If you have never used mnemonics, you may still be skeptical, but give this approach a fair trial. Most people find they can greatly extend their memory through the use of mnemonics. You may want to discuss these ideas further with your instructor and classmates. Some possible questions follow.

Questions for Discussion

1. Have you ever used mnemonics without knowing it?
2. What other memory aids or strategies have you used or discovered?
3. Do you have any helpful examples to share with other students?
4. How could a person who doesn't have good mental images use mnemonics?

Suggestions for Further Reading

Adams, J. A. *Human Memory*. McGraw-Hill, 1967.

Hunter, I. M. L. *Memory: Facts and Fallacies*. Penguin, 1964.

Lindsay, P., and D. Norman. *Human Information Processing.* Academic, 1972.

Luria, A. R. *The Mind of a Mnemonist*. Basic Books, 1968.

Penfield, W. *The Excitable Cortex in Conscious Man.* Charles C Thomas, 1958.

Weinland, J. D. *How to Improve Your Memory*. Barnes & Noble, 1957.

Thinking, Problem Solving, and Creativity

11

Chapter Preview

Four Examples of Problem Solving

Item 1 *There was a flutter of feathers and then a pitiful thump as bird met glass. Apparently unhurt, the tiny hummingbird flew against the glass again and again. The bird had become trapped within a partially glassed-in porch. My sympathy must have equaled its frustration when I saw that freedom lay in the opposite direction, only a few feet behind the bird. It was totally exhausted when I carried it to safety and released it.*

Item 2 *A cat is placed in a cage. To escape, the cat must pull a latchstring on the door. Initially the cat ignores the string; instead, it tries to squeeze through the bars and randomly claws at them. By accident the cat claws at a loop on the end of the string. The door springs open, and the cat escapes. The cat is repeatedly made to solve this problem, and it pulls the string a little sooner each time. Eventually it pulls the string as soon as it is placed in the cage.*

Item 3 *A hungry chimpanzee is placed in a cage. Outside the bars and just beyond its reach is a banana. The chimp makes a few futile attempts to reach through the bars to get the banana. Then the chimp notices a stick lying on the floor of the cage. The chimp looks at the banana . . . then at the stick . . . then at the banana. Picking up the stick, the chimp smoothly and without further hesitation reaches out and rakes in the banana.*

Item 4 *Miguel Najdorf of Argentina is a grand-master chess player. In an exhibition, Najdorf once simultaneously played forty-five chess games.* It*

*To his relief, Najdorf was not placed in a cage for this exhibition.

is estimated that over 3,600 different positions arose during the evening of the exhibition. Of course, playing forty-five games at once is not too astounding for a chess master, but you must consider the manner in which the games were played: Najdorf was blindfolded (Hearst, 1969). (To be more accurate, he sat with his back to a room full of opponents and called out his moves!)

Thinking, problem solving, and creativity are the challenging topics of this chapter. It is hoped that the situations described above will whet your appetite for a better understanding of these topics. It is just such situations that have served as the raw materials from which much of our understanding of thinking has come.

Resources

What Is Thinking?—It's All in Your Head!

"What do you think?" "You're just not thinking." "Let me think about it." "I'll be thinking of you." It is little wonder that the term *thinking* is used in so many different ways. Thinking refers to many things: daydreaming, fantasy, problem solving, reasoning, free association, and dreaming (to name but a few). During most of your waking hours, you are engaged in some form of thought.

In its more advanced forms, thinking refers to the mental manipulation and combination of images, precepts, concepts, habits, words, and rules. Thinking is the basis for problem solving, creativity, intelligence, and learning which goes beyond simple conditioning.

Question: To what degree are animals capable of thought?

Thinking in Animals In its most basic form, thinking is the *internal representation* of external stimuli or situations. It can be easily demonstrated that many animals have this capacity.

Mickey Rat Plays the Old Shell Game

A hungry rat is allowed to watch as a light is turned on over one of three goal boxes. The rat has previously learned that the lighted box contains food. The light is turned off and after a delay the rat is released. Can it select the correct box? If the delay is brief, the answer is yes (Hunter, 1913).

Animals tested on similar *delayed-response* problems can generally maintain or *re-create* some kind of mental image long enough to make a correct choice. Rats are capable of responding up to ten seconds after the light has gone off. Dogs can delay five minutes, and higher animals can handle increasingly longer delays. As a human being, you could probably delay indefinitely if something of great value were placed behind one of the doors.

To a degree, animals are thinking when they engage in *trial and error learning.* The cat described in the chapter preview learned to pull the latchstring because correct responses were rewarded by release from the cage. Yet trial and error learning goes beyond simple operant conditioning. The cat appears to be actively searching for a way to escape and does not try all possible responses.

Testing various solutions to a problem by trial and error is a rather primitive form of thought, but it is an important one. Animals who show little variation in their responses or who have a limited capacity to internally symbolize (think about) their environment may be stymied by the simplest problem. You will recall that the hummingbird described earlier was unable to resolve a seemingly simple predicament. This behavior is typical of many lower animals. Often they will blindly try to get through a barrier that could be easily bypassed by temporarily moving *away* from the goal.

Question: The chimpanzee that used the stick to get the banana didn't use trial and error. Is that proof of more advanced thought?

German psychologist Wolfgang Köhler felt that problem solving of the type showed by the chimpanzee revealed a capacity for *insight.* Insight is a sudden reorganization of the elements of a problem whereby the solution becomes evident. While stationed on the Canary islands during World War I, Köhler performed a classic series of experiments with chimpanzees that gave further evidence of their capacity for intelligent problem solving.

One of Köhler's brightest subjects, a chimp named Sultan, was able to solve problems with such ease that Köhler challenged him with a *multiple-stick* problem. In this problem several sticks of increasing length were arranged between the cage and a banana (see Fig. 11-1). To reach the banana, Sultan had to use the first stick to retrieve the second stick (which was longer than the first). The second stick could be used to retrieve an even longer stick, which could then be used to reach the banana (Köhler, 1925).

Köhler noted that in the course of testing there were always long pauses during which Sultan scrutinized the surrounding area. These were followed by rapid solutions. Of course, it is possible that Sultan was only using *implicit* (unseen) trial and error to solve the problem. In other words, he may have been trying alternatives *symbolically* so that all but the correct response were discarded before he acted. But Köhler felt Sultan had actually perceived the relationship between elements of the problem (the shorter and longer sticks and the banana) and that his solutions were insightful.

Question: In the first chapter you said that it can be an error to attribute human characteristics to animals. Wasn't Köhler reading a lot into Sultan's ability?

It is quite possible that he was, but in the years since Köhler's work there has been a tremendous amount of additional research on the think-

Fig. 11-1 Psychologist Wolfgang Köhler felt that solution of a multiple-stick problem revealed a capacity for insight.

ing and problem-solving capacities of animals. Some of the most revealing research has centered on attempts to teach language to chimpanzees.

Talking Chimps Early experiments involving attempts to teach chimps to talk were a dismal failure. The world record for talking was held by Viki, a chimp who could say only four words ("mama," "papa," "cup," and "up") after six years of intensive training (Fleming, 1974; Hayes, 1951). Then there was a breakthrough. Beatrice Gardner and Allen Gardner of the University of Reno, Nevada, used a combination of operant conditioning and imitation to teach a female chimp named Washoe to use *American Sign Language* (ASL). ASL is a set of hand gestures used by the deaf (each gesture stands for a word).

Washoe's communication skills blossomed rapidly as her "vocabulary" grew. Soon she began to put together primitive sentence strings like: "Come-gimme sweet," "Out please," "Gimme tickle," and "Open food drink." She now has a vocabularly of about 175 signs and can construct six-word sentences. She has even tried to communicate with other chimpanzees through use of sign language (Gardner & Gardner, 1969).

Some critics are skeptical about Washoe's achievements since her arrangement of "words" is somewhat haphazard. Children quickly learn the difference between word orders like "Give me candy" and "Me give candy." An answer to this criticism has come from the work of David Premack (1970), who taught a female chimp named Sarah to use 130 "words" consisting of plastic chips arranged on a magnetized board (see Fig. 11-2).

Since the beginning of her training, Sarah has been required to use proper word order. She has learned to answer questions, to label things "same" or "different," to classify things by color, shape, and size, and to construct compound sentences. One of her most outstanding achievements is use of sentences involving *conditional relationships*: "If Sarah take apple, then Mary give Sarah chocolate"; "If Sarah take banana, then Mary no give Sarah chocolate."

Despite her achievements, by human standards Sarah's ability remains limited. The average three-year-old child can use about 1,000 words compared to Sarah's 130 (Lennenberg, 1969). Sarah also has a problem with accuracy, making errors from about 20 to 25 percent of the time (Lindesmith *et al.*, 1975). Because of such limitations some critics have labeled efforts to teach language to apes a waste of time. Nevertheless, this and similar research shows that primate *cognitive* (thinking) abilities go far beyond rote learning. Such research also promises to provide insights into the learning of language skills. These, in turn, may be useful for teaching language to autistic (emotionally disturbed) and severely retarded children.

Thinking in Humans Humans are capable of representational thought, trial and error problem solving, insight solutions, and, of course, many more advanced thinking processes. Blindfolded Miguel Najdorf's chess exhibition can be contrasted with Sarah's cognitive abilities to get an idea of the differences in thinking capacity between humans and animals.

Question: How do we represent things to ourselves for the purpose of thought?

Fig. 11-2 After reading the message "Sarah insert apple pail banana dish" on the magnetic board, Sarah performed the actions as directed. (After Premack & Premack. Copyright © 1972. Reprinted by permission of *Scientific American*.)

There are four basic *units* of thought. You will probably use all four to answer these questions:

1. To turn the hot-water faucet "on" in your kitchen, which direction do you turn the handle?
2. When it is fifteen minutes before eight o'clock, is the minute hand *above* or *below* the hour hand?
3. The opposite of "large" is "________________."

The internal representations you probably used are:

1. *Muscular responses.* On question 1 you may have found it helpful to make the movements you use to turn on the faucet.
2. *Images.* On both questions 1 and 2 you probably formed mental pictures of the faucet and the clock.

3. *Concepts.* Your answer to question 2 involved the concept of time, and the answer to 3, the concept of size.
4. *Language.* To summarize the outcome of your thinking, you had to translate your answers into words. In addition, you could have answered question 4 entirely on the basis of language, without using the other units of thought.

All four units are usually combined in situations requiring complex thought. Indeed, in some situations people need all the help they can get. Blindfolded chess players report that they use a combination of visual images, muscular sensations of "lines of force," concepts ("Game 2 is an English opening"), and the special notational system used by chess opponents to accomplish their seemingly impossible mental feats (Hearst, 1969). Because of their obvious importance, each of the units of thought is discussed in greater detail below.

Learning Check

Before you read further, it might be a good idea to check your progress by answering the questions below.

1. A ____________ ____________ problem can be used to show that animals are capable of representative thought.
2. Chimpanzees who appear to achieve insightful solutions to problems may only be using ____________ trial and error.
3. One of Sarah's most outstanding achievements has been the construction of sentences involving ____________ relationships.
4. List the four basic units of human thought: ____________, ____________, ____________, ____________.

Answers:

1. delayed response **2.** implicit **3.** conditional **4.** images, concepts, language, muscular responses.

Mental Imagery—Is One Picture Worth a Thousand Movements?

When we speak of images we are usually referring to a mental "picture," but images may involve the other senses as well. For example, your image of chocolate ice cream may include its taste and coldness along with its appearance; your image of a bakery may include its delicious odor; and your image of riding on a train could include sounds and a swaying motion. Some people tend to use more of one type of imagery than another. An artist might rely heavily on visual imagery, a musician, on auditory imagery, and an acrobat, on kinesthetic imagery. Other people experience a rare form of imagery called *synesthesia*, in which images cross normal sensory barriers. Experiencing sounds as colors is a common example of this effect. Despite these variations, it is generally accepted that most people experience images and that they can be an aid to thinking and problem solving.

Question: How are images used to solve problems?

Stored images can be used to bring prior experience to bear on problem solving. If you were given the question "How many uses can you think of for an old automobile tire?," you might begin by picturing all the uses you have already seen: as a swing, as a boat bumper on a pier, as soles for sandals, and so on. To generate more original solutions, *created images* may be used. Thus, an artist may completely picture a proposed sculpture before beginning work. Even in abstract subjects like science and mathematics, creative thought may rely on the use of imagery. Albert Einstein once reported that the basis for his thought was a kind of mental play in which muscular and visual images were associated and combined. Only in the later stages of his thought process were the results translated into language or mathematical symbols.

Question: I'm not sure I see how muscular responses relate to thinking.

It is somewhat surprising to recognize that we think with our bodies as well as our heads. Jerome Bruner (1966) believes that we often represent things in a kind of *muscular imagery* created by actions or *implicit actions*. For example, people who "talk" with their hands are using gestures to help themselves think as well as to convey meaning or to aid description. A great deal of information is contained in *kinesthetic* sensations (feelings from the muscles and joints). As one talks, these sensations help structure the flow of ideas. Another good way to see this happening is to ask someone who has participated in a sporting event to describe what took place. Along with a verbal description you will probably get an "instant replay" of many of the actions. Partially acting-out the "big plays" helps the person to think about and recapture the order of important events.

Question: A person can think while sitting perfectly still. Is any muscular imagery used under these circumstances?

Yes. One of the reasons thinking can be hard work is that it is accompanied by an undercurrent of muscular tension and activity throughout the body. In one classic study a subject was asked to imagine that he was hitting a nail with a hammer. As he did, there was a clearly recorded burst of activity in the muscles of his unmoving arm (Jacobson, 1932). Another study of muscular imagery employed deaf-mutes who were accustomed to using sign language for communication. When these subjects were asked to multiply and divide numbers in their heads, 80 percent showed increased muscular activity in their hands. Only 30 percent of a group of speaking subjects showed similar increases (Max, 1937).

Question: Is it possible to think without using muscle responses?

Apparently it is. An investigator once had himself injected with curare, a drug that paralyzes all the voluntary musculature. While he was paralyzed, he was asked to solve a number of problems and to answer questions. When the drug wore off, he gave his answers to the questions and reported that he had been completely capable of thought while immobilized (Smith *et al.*, 1947).

Concepts—"A Rose Is a Rose Is a Rose"

There was a time in your intellectual development when the words "stove," "chair," "bed," and "bottle" were the names of particular objects. Then, as your world enlarged and you experienced other objects with the same name, you began to develop *concepts*. A concept is a word or idea that represents a class of objects. Concepts provide a powerful tool for thought because they allow us to function on an *abstract* level—free from the details of a particular object or situation. *Concept* formation is part of the process whereby a child classifies and organizes experiences into meaningful categories. This is not by any means a simple process. Imagine a child learning the concept of "dog."

Dog Daze

A child and her father go for a walk. At a neighbor's house they see a medium-sized dog. The father says, "See the *dog*." As they pass the next yard the child sees a cat and says, "Dog!" Her father corrects her, "No that's a *cat*." The child now thinks, "Aha, dogs are large and cats are small." In the next yard she sees a Pekingese and says, "Cat!" "No, that's a dog," replies her father.

The child's confusion at this point is understandable. However, continued experience with *positive* and *negative instances* of the concept "dog" will eventually allow the child to recognize Great Danes and Chihuahuas as members of the same class.

Several general types of concepts have been identified. A *conjunctive concept* embraces a class of objects that have one or more features in common. For example, "iron" is hard, metallic, and magnetic. *Relational concepts* classify objects on the basis of their relationship to something else or on the basis of the relationship among features of an object. "Large," "above," "left," and "north" are all relational concepts. *Disjunctive concepts* refer to objects that have at *least one* of a number of features. For example, in the game of baseball a "strike" may be either a swing and a miss, a pitch down the middle, or a foul ball. Disjunctive concepts have an "either-or" quality that often makes them difficult to learn.

Question: How do concepts relate to thought?

Since concepts vary in their level of abstraction, simpler and more concrete concepts can be used to establish higher levels of meaning. This allows us to define and think about concepts that are not readily observable (such as, "truth," "beauty," "energy," or "algorithm"). Imagine how difficult it would be to establish the meaning of these concepts by merely pointing to positive and negative instances of each. In addition, you can use the conceptual meaning carried by familiar words to transfer meaning to words you may have never used before. For example: the mysterious sounding word *podbromhidrosis* simply means smelly feet; *galeanthropy* is the delusion that one has become a cat; and a *ballhooter* is a lumberjack who rolls logs down a hill! Transfer of conceptual meaning is the basis for most formal education. We are fortunate to be free of the inefficiency that would result if the meaning of a concept like "schizophrenia" had to be established by bringing dozens of disturbed persons to psychology class.

Generally speaking, concepts have two types of meaning. The *denotative* meaning of a word or concept is its explicit definition. The *connotative* meaning is its emotional or personal meaning. For example, the denotative meaning of the word "naked" (having no clothes) is the same for a nudist as it is for a movie censor, but we could expect their connotations to differ.

Question: Can you give a clearer statement of what a connotative meaning is?

Researcher Charles Osgood (1952) has used a method called the *semantic differential* to measure connotative meaning (see Fig. 11-3). Osgood found that when words or concepts are rated on a series of scales, most of their connotative meaning boils down to the dimensions: *good-bad*, *strong-weak*, and *active-passive*. Because concepts vary on these dimensions, words or phrases having approximately the same denotative meaning may be substituted to imply different connotations. For example, I am *conscientious*; you are *careful*; and he is *nit-picking*!

Language—What's in a Word?

Like fish who are unaware of water, we are so totally immersed in language that it is difficult to comprehend how essential it is. It has been estimated that between lectures, conversations, and reading assignments, the average student might easily be exposed to 190,000 words a day (Carroll, 1964). This flood of words, more than any other cognitive activity, is what separates humans from animals.

Question: I was under the impression that animals communicate. Don't they?

Blossom

Rounded								Angular
Strong								Weak
Smooth								Rough
Passive								Active
Large								Small
Hot								Cold
Bad								Good
Relaxed								Tense
Dry								Wet
Stale								Fresh

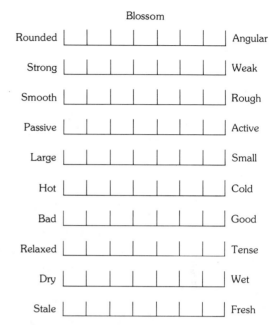

Fig. 11-3 This is an example of Osgood's semantic differential. Connotative meaning of the word "blossom" can be established by rating it on a number of scales. Mark your own ratings by placing check marks in the spaces provided. (From C. E. Osgood. Copyright © 1952 American Psychological Association. Reprinted by permission.)

As we have already seen, even spirited efforts to teach animals language have met with extremely limited success. This does not mean that animals don't normally communicate. They do. The cries, gestures, and mating calls of various animals can carry very specific information. Even the lowly honeybee can pass on fairly complex ideas about the location of nectar and pollen by performing an intricate "dance" (von Frisch, 1950). But animals do not use language to think, and their communication skills do not qualify as true language. Cries and gestures lack the essential hallmark of language: They are not *productive.*

Question: What do you mean by "productive"?

The great underlying strength of human language is that it can be used to generate new *possibilities*. Since words do not resemble the things they represent, they can be rearranged to produce new ideas and an infinite variety of meaningful sentences (Bruner, 1966). In fact, words can rather easily be arranged into sentences maybe no one has ever said before like: "Please feed me to the goldfish." Let us briefly investigate the properties of human language that make this possible.

Question: What does it take to make a language?

The Structure of Language First of all, a language must provide *symbols* which can be used to stand for objects and ideas. The symbols we call words are built out of *phonemes* (basic speech sounds) and *mor-*

phemes (speech sounds collected into meaningful units). The units of speech can be arranged into countless combinations. Consider the possibilities in just four morphemes: "reach," "to," "able," "un." From these we can make: "able to," "unable to," "reach to," "to reach," "able to reach," "unable to reach," "reachable," "unreachable," "reachable to," "unreachable to," "unto," "unto Able."

The second requirement of language is that it have a set of *rules* for the combination of symbols into phrases and sentences. The rules for structuring sentences are collectively called *grammar*. Grammar is particularly important to language because rearranging words almost always changes the meaning of a sentence: "Dog bites man" versus "Man bites dog." Also, the meaning of a sentence can be easily hidden by an ungrammatical arrangement: "Go you did why" versus "Why did you go?" (For more information on how people learn to use language, see Chapter 16.)

The third requirement of a language is that it be capable of conveying *meaning*. Study of the meaning of words and language is called *semantics*. It is in the area of meaning that the connection between language and thought becomes most evident.

Question: How important is language to the thinking process?

Language and Thought As we have already seen, thinking and language are not the same thing. Sometimes you will find yourself searching for a word to express an idea that exists as an image or a vague concept. Nevertheless, there is little doubt that human thought rests deeply on the use of language. Through language you can "talk to yourself," and you can *encode* the world into symbols that can be easily manipulated. Language is also important to thought because it makes the accumulated knowledge of past human experience available to present and future generations. This is unique among animal species.

Thought is also influenced by the meaning attached to words. Again we find that connotative and denotative meanings are important. Most of us would rather eat "prime beef" than "dead cow" even if they are the same thing. If you overhear a person saying that you are "heavy," should you be insulted because he or she thinks you are overweight or flattered because you are rated as an important person?

Semantic problems also arise when more than one language is involved. One investigator studied negotiations between French and American diplomats and found that misinterpretations of meaning were common. For instance, the verb "to compromise" has two meanings. In English its primary meaning is: to reach agreement, to adjust or settle differences. Its secondary meaning is: to suffer exposure, embarrassment, or loss of one's reputation. The order of these meanings is exactly the reverse in French. Is it any wonder that French diplomats reacted unpleasantly when the suggestion was made to "compromise"? (Klineberg, 1964).

Fig. 11-4 Human thought and the use of language are intimately interrelated. (Photo by David Powers, Jeroboam.)

Question: Then is it accurate to say that the language a person speaks affects thought?

Let's explore this question. How many words do you know for the term "camel"? In Arabic there are over 6,000 variations of the word "camel," but the only other English term is "dromedary." How many other words do you know for the term "snow"? If you are a skier, you may be able to add "hard pack," "powder," "kernel," and perhaps a few more, but this exhausts most of the possibilities. By contrast, Eskimos do not have a single word that refers only to snow; their language includes close to thirty terms for various kinds of snow and ice (Whorf, 1940). On the basis of such differences, linguist Benjamin Whorf has proposed the theory of *linguistic determinism* (sometimes referred to as the "Whorfian hypothesis").

The idea of linguistic determinism is simple but intriguing. Whorf feels that language is not only an instrument for reproducing ideas but also a *shaper* of ideas. Each culture prepares its members to think about particular topics by providing words with which to categorize experience. If you were to watch a parade of thirty camels and were questioned afterward about what you saw, you could be forgiven if you were only able to say "a bunch of camels." The English language does not equip you to easily encode the details of what you saw. In our culture the automobile has about the same importance that camels once had in Arabic culture. It would be rare for a person in our culture to look at thirty cars and not be able to remember the make, model, and special features of many of them. This reflects not only the importance attached to cars but also the language available to think about them.

Other differences in the way languages divide up experience make for some interesting comparisons. The Hopi have only one word referring to the concepts "insect," "airplane," and "aviator." The Navajos have only one word for "flint," "metal," and "knife." If these groupings seem strange, remember that it seems just as strange to an Eskimo when we call "snow" what they call *quali*, *kimoaqruk*, and *pukak*! Clearly, thought is intimately tied to and influenced by language.

Learning Check

See if you can answer these questions before reading more.

1. Synesthesia is the use of kinesthetic sensations as a vehicle for thought. T or F?

2. A "wog" is defined as anything that is small, blue, and hairy. "Wog" is a ______________ concept.

3. The connotative meaning of the word "naked" is "having no clothes." T or F?

4. True languages are ______________ because they can be used to generate new possibilities.

5. The basic speech sounds of a language are called ______________; the smallest meaningful units of speech are called ______________.

6. A generalized idea representing a class of objects is called a ______________.

Answers:

1. F **2.** conjunctive **3.** F **4.** productive **5.** phonemes, morphemes **6.** concept

Problem Solving—Getting an Answer in Sight

A good way to start off a discussion of problem solving is to solve a problem. Give this one a try.

> A famous ocean liner (the *Queen Ralph*) is steaming toward port at 20 miles per hour. It is 50 miles from shore when a seagull takes off from its deck and flies toward port. At the same instant a speedboat leaves port at 30 miles per hour. The bird flies back and forth between the speedboat and the *Queen Ralph* at a speed of 40 miles per hour. How far will the bird have flown when the two boats pass?

If you don't immediately see the answer to this problem, read it again. (The answer is revealed in the discussion below.)

We all do a tremendous amount of problem solving everyday. Problem solving can be as commonplace as figuring out how to make a non-poisonous meal out of the leftovers in the refrigerator or as significant as developing a cure for cancer. In either case we begin with an awareness that an answer probably exists and that by proper manipulation of the elements of thought a solution can be found. A number of different approaches to thinking and reasoning in problem solving can be identified.

Mechanical Solutions *Mechanical* solutions may be achieved by *trial and error* or by *rote*. If I have forgotten the combination to my bike lock, I may be able to discover it by trial and error. In an era of high-speed computers, many trial and error solutions are best left to machines. A computer could generate all possible combinations of the five numbers on my lock in just a split second. When a solution is achieved by rote, we mean that thinking has proceeded according to a learned set of rules. If you have a good background in mathematics, you may have solved the problem of the bird and the boats by rote. (I hope you didn't. There is an easier solution.)

Solutions by Understanding Many problems are unsolvable by mechanical means or by the use of habitual modes of thought. In this case a higher level of thinking based on *understanding* is necessary. A classic series of studies on this type of thinking has been performed by German psychologist Karl Duncker (1945). Duncker gave college students this problem:

> Given an inoperable stomach tumor and rays which at high intensity will destroy tissue (both healthy and diseased), how can the tumor be destroyed without damaging surrounding tissue? (Students were also shown the sketch in Fig. 11-5.)

Question: What did this problem show about problem solving?

Duncker asked the students to think aloud so that he could follow the course of their thinking. He found that there were two phases to successful problem solving. First, the student had to discover the *general properties*

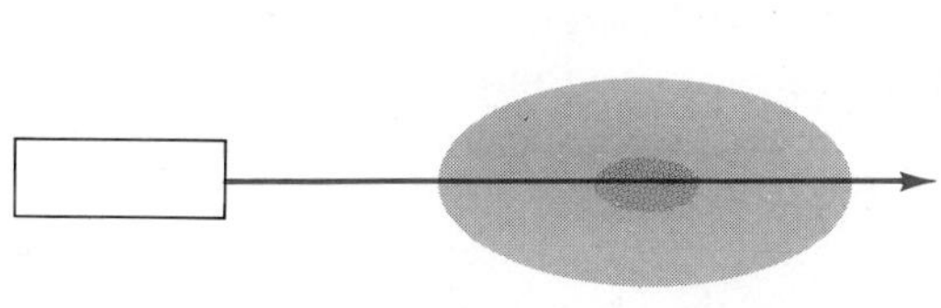

Fig. 11-5 A schematic representation of Duncker's tumor problem. The dark spot represents a tumor surrounded by healthy tissue. How can the tumor be destroyed without injuring surrounding tissue? (After Duncker, 1945.)

of a correct solution. This discovery was usually accomplished gradually, beginning with suggestions to desensitize surrounding tissue, to move the tumor toward the exterior, and so on. As soon as a student came to the realization that the intensity of the rays had to be lowered on their way to the tumor, a number of *functional* (workable) *solutions* could be proposed. This marked the second stage of problem solving during which a specific solution was selected. (The correct solution, of course, is to focus weak rays from several sources on the tumor or to rotate the person's body so that the exposure of healthy tissue is minimized.)

Solution by Insight You will recall that Köhler's apes sometimes showed *insight* in their problem solving. With humans we say that insight has occurred when an answer suddenly appears after a period of unsuccessful thought. An insight is usually so rapid and clear that one often wonders how such an "obvious" solution could have been missed. Perhaps you experienced insight when trying to solve the problem of the boats and the bird (above). Since the boats will cover the 50-mile distance in exactly one hour and since the bird flies 40 miles per hour, the bird will have flown 40 miles when the boats meet. No math is necessary if you have insight into this problem. We will return to the topic of insight in a moment. Let us turn now to consideration of factors which influence problem solving.

Functional Fixedness The ease with which a solution is achieved in problem solving is related to a variety of factors. These include complexity of the problem, novelty of the answer, motivation of the thinker, and prior experience with similar problems. In addition to these, there is a very important barrier to problem solving called *fixation*. Fixation is the tendency to get "hung up" on wrong solutions or to become blind to other alternatives. A prime example of fixation is *functional fixedness*. Functional fixedness is the inability to see new uses (functions) for familiar objects or for objects that have been used in a particular way.

Question: How does functional fixedness affect problem solving?

Karl Duncker, who originated the concept of functional fixedness, performed a clever study to demonstrate its operation. Duncker challenged students to mount a candle on a vertical board so that it could burn in the normal way. Duncker gave each student three candles, some matches, some cardboard boxes, some thumbtacks, and other items. Half of Duncker's subjects received these items *inside* the cardboard boxes. The others received all the items, including the boxes, laid out on a tabletop. Duncker found that when the items were in the boxes, solution of the problem was very difficult. This is because the boxes were seen as *containers*, not as items that might be part of the solution. (If you haven't guessed the solution, check Fig. 11-6.) Perhaps you have recognized that functional fixedness is a special case of the more general concept of perceptual sets (discussed in Chapter 5). This is a good reminder that the psychological

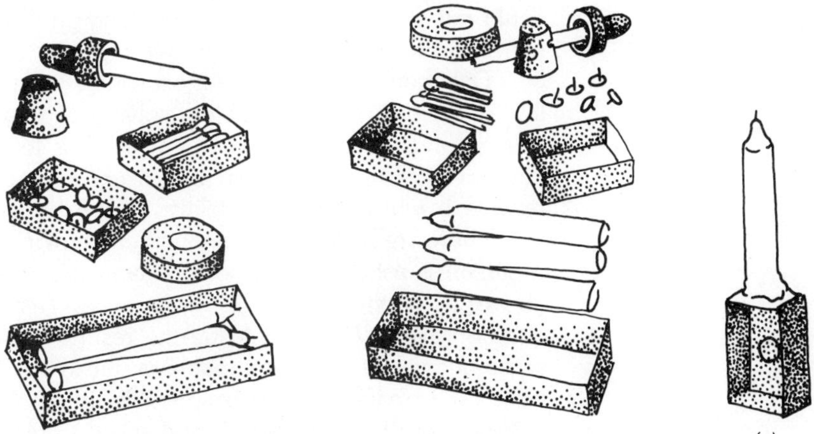

(a) (b) (c)

Fig. 11-6 Materials for solving the candle problem were given to subjects in boxes *(a)* or separately *(b)*. Functional fixedness caused by condition *(a)* interfered with solving the problem. The solution to the problem is shown in *(c)*.

processes of perception, learning, motivation, thinking, and so on, are thoroughly intermixed in real life. Psychologists treat them as separate topics only for convenience.

Creative Thinking—Fluency, Flexibility, and Originality

Question: What distinguishes creative thinking from more routine problem solving?

As we have noted, problem solving may be the result of thinking that is mechanical, insightful, or based on understanding. To this we can add that thought may be *inductive* (going from specific facts or observations to general principles) or *deductive* (going from general principles to specific situations). Thinking may also be *logical* (proceeding from given information to new conclusions on the basis of explicit rules) or *illogical* (intuitive, associative, or personal).

Creative thinking involves all these styles of thought (in varying combinations) *plus* fluency, flexibility, and originality (Guilford, 1950). The meaning of these terms can be illustrated by returning to an earlier example. Let's say that you would like to find a creative use (or uses) for the millions of automobile tires discarded each year. The creativity of your suggestions could be rated in this way: *Fluency* is defined as the total number of suggestions you are able to make. *Flexibility* is defined as the number of times you shift from one class of possible uses to another. *Originality* refers to how novel or unusual your suggestions are. By totaling the number of times you showed fluency, flexibility, and originality, we could rate the creativity of your thinking on this problem. Speaking more generally, we would be rating your capacity for *divergent thinking*.

Divergent thinking is the most widely used measure of creative problem solving. In routine problem solving or thinking, there is one correct answer and the problem is to find it. This leads to *convergent* thought (lines of thought converge on the correct answer). Divergent thinking is the reverse, in which many possibilities are developed from one starting place.

There are several tests of divergent thinking. In the *Unusual Uses Test* a person is asked to think of as many uses for an object (like the tires above) as possible. In the *Consequences Test* the object is to answer a question like: "What would be the results if everyone suddenly lost the sense of balance and were unable to stay in an upright position?" Subjects try to list as many reactions as possible. In the *Anagrams Test* subjects are given a word like "creativity" and asked to make as many new words as possible by rearranging the letters. Each of these tests can be scored for fluency, flexibility, and originality. (For an example of other tests of divergent thought see Fig. 11-7.)

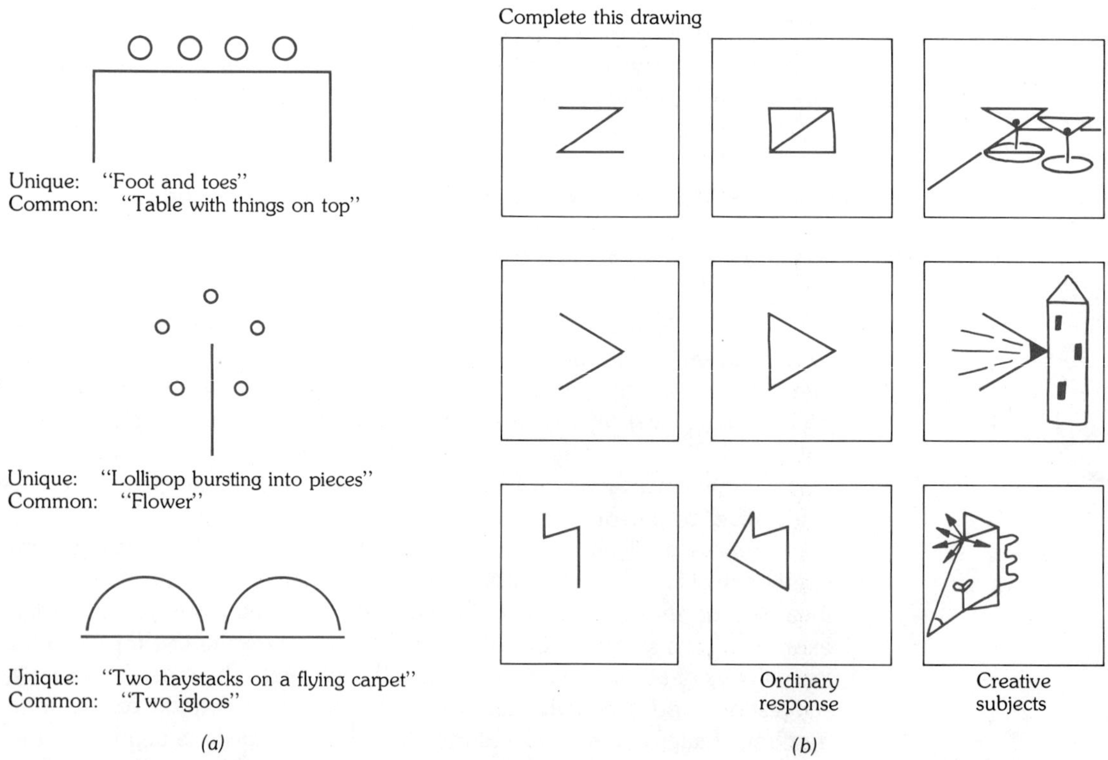

Fig. 11-7 Some tests of divergent thinking. Creative responses are more original and more complex. [*(a)* after Wallach and Kogan, 1965; *(b)* after Barron, 1958.]

Question: Isn't creativity more than divergent thought? What if a person comes up with a large number of useless answers to a problem?

A good question. Divergent thought is definitely an important part of creative thinking, but there is more to it. To be creative, the solution to a problem must be more than novel, unusual, or original. It must also be useful or meaningful, and it must meet the demands of the problem (MacKinnon, 1962). This is the dividing line between a "harebrained scheme" and a "stroke of genius."

Question: Is there any pattern to creative thinking?

Stages of Creative Thought The best summary of the sequence of events in creative thinking proposes five stages which usually occur:

1. *Orientation.* As a first step, the problem must be defined and important dimensions identified.
2. *Preparation.* In the second stage of creative thought, the person saturates himself with as much information pertaining to the problem as possible.
3. *Incubation.* Most major problems produce a period during which all attempted solutions will have proved futile. At this point problem solving may proceed on a subconscious level: While the problem seems to have been set aside, it is still "cooking" in the background.
4. *Illumination.* The stage of incubation is often ended by a rapid insight or series of insights. These produce the "Aha!" experience, often depicted in cartoons as a light bulb appearing over the thinker's head.
5. *Verification.* The final step is to test and critically evaluate the solution obtained during the stage of illumination. If the solution proves faulty, the thinker reverts to the stage of incubation.

Of course, creative thought is not always so neat. After studying Beethoven's notebooks, renowned conductor Leonard Bernstein had this to say about them: ". . . Beethoven struggled with all his force. The man rejected, rewrote, scratched out, tore up, and sometimes altered a passage as many as twenty times. . . . Beethoven's manuscript looks like a bloody record of a tremendous inner battle" (Pronko, 1969). Nevertheless, the stages listed are a good summary of the most typical sequence of events.

You may find it helpful to attach the stages to the following more or less true story. Legend has it that the king of Syracuse (a city in ancient Greece) once suspected that his goldsmith had substituted cheaper metals for some of the gold in a crown and had pocketed the difference. Archimedes, a famous mathematician and thinker, was presented with the problem of discovering whether or not the king had been cheated.

Archimedes began by defining the problem (orientation): "How can I determine what metals have been used in the crown without damaging it?" He then investigated all known methods of analyzing metals (preparation). All involved cutting or melting the crown, so Archimedes was forced to temporarily set the problem aside (incubation). Then one day as he stepped into his bath, Archimedes suddenly knew he had the solution (illumination). He was so excited he is said to have run naked through the streets shouting "Eureka, eureka!" (I have found it, I have found it!). On observing his own body floating in the bath, Archimedes realized that different metals would displace different amounts of water. All that remained was to test the solution (verification). Archimedes placed an amount of gold (equal to that given the goldsmith) in a tub of water. He marked the water level and removed the gold. He then placed the crown in the water. If it were pure gold, the crown would raise the water to exactly the same level. Unfortunately, the purity of the crown and the fate of the goldsmith are to this day unknown!

Learning Check

1. Insight is a form of mechanical problem solving. T or F?
2. The first phase of problem solving by understanding is to discover the general properties of a correct solution. T or F?
3. The term *fixation* refers to the point at which a helpful insight becomes fixed in one's thinking. T or F?
4. Functional fixedness is usually an aid to problem solving. T or F?
5. Fluency, flexibility, and originality are characteristics of convergent thought. T or F?
6. List the stages of creative thinking in the correct order:

______________________, ______________________,

______________________, ______________________.

Answers: **1.** F **2.** T **3.** F **4.** F **5.** F **6.** orientation, preparation, incubation, illumination, verification

Resources Summary

Thinking is the manipulation and combination of *internal representations* of external stimuli or situations. Animals reveal a capacity for thought through *delayed responding*, *trial and error learning*, and *insight* learning. The cognitive abilities of some higher animals are fairly advanced, as revealed by various attempts to teach language to chimpanzees. The basic units of human thought are: *muscular responses*, *images*, *concepts*, and *language*. Images may be *stored* or *created*. Muscular images are created by actions or implicit actions. Concepts are a generalized idea of a class of objects or events. Concepts may be classified as *conjunctive*, *disjunctive*, or *relational*. Concepts have two kinds of meaning. *Denotative* meaning is an explicit definition, and *connotative* meaning is emotional or personal.

One of the most powerful vehicles for thinking and the representation of concepts is *language*. A true language is *productive* and can be used to generate new possibilities. Language carries meaning by combining *symbols* according to a set of *rules*. The study of meaning is called *semantics*. Semantics greatly affects thinking. The idea that one's language can shape ideas is called *linguistic determinism*.

The solution to a problem may be arrived at *mechanically*, through *understanding*, or by *insight*. A person may be easily blinded to the solution for a problem by *fixation* or *functional fixedness*. Creative thinking involves *divergent thought* plus practicality or appropriateness. The typical stages of creative thinking are: *orientation*, *preparation*, *incubation*, *illumination*, and *verification*.

Applications

Difficulties in Thinking and Problem Solving

We all at one time or another experience difficulties in thinking and problem solving. The following may alert you to some of the more common problems.

Inadequate Information Albert Einstein passed on the credit for his contributions in physics by saying, "I have stood on the shoulders of giants." Einstein was simply pointing out that productive thought requires preparation and accurate information. Be sure in any problem-solving situation that you have the facts and that you are not overgeneralizing from limited personal experience or incomplete information.

Rigid Mental Set Try the problems pictured in Fig. 11-8. If you have difficulty, it is probably because you were limited by your mental set. (The answers to these problems along with an explanation of the sets which prevent their solution are found on page 262.) In addition to sets one brings to a problem, the problem itself may produce a set. A simple example of this is the following: "The name 'Polk' is pronounced 'poke,' the word 'folk' is pronounced 'foke,' and the white of an egg is pronounced ______?" Along the same line, you could be asked to find a hidden four-letter word in each of the following: GLONAQT, MXUELDE, BLUDLRL, GIUPLYL, DOESEAR. If you find GLONAOT (goat) in the first problem, MXUELDE (mule) in the second, BLUDLRL (bull) in the third, and GIUPLYL (gull) in the fourth, you may do the unnecessary work of finding "deer" in the last problem, which has two more direct answers in it: *does* or *sear*. It is a good idea to actively question the assumptions you are using in any instance of problem solving.

Problems with Logic A major thinking difficulty centers on the process of *logical reasoning*. Simple sequences of logical thought can be arranged as a set of *premises* (assumptions) and a *conclusion.* This format is called a *syllogism.* A syllogism can be evaluated for the *validity* of its reasoning and for the truth of its *conclusion*. It is entirely possible to draw true conclusions using faulty logic or to draw false conclusions using valid logic. The examples below show how this is possible.

Syllogism I

All humans are mortal. (Major premise)
All women are humans. (Minor premise)
Therefore, all women are mortal. (Conclusion)

Comment: As you can see from the diagram in Fig. 11-9, the logic of this syllogism is valid. Since our premises are true, this means the conclusion is true. The diagram shows all women included within the boundaries of mortals.

Syllogism II

All women are human.
All humans are mortal.
Therefore, all mortals are women.

Comment: In this example the conclusion drawn is false, because the reasoning is invalid. The diagram for syllogism I shows that all mortals are not women. Notice how little the syllogism has to be changed to produce a false conclusion. Now consider syllogism III.

Syllogism III

All psychologists are weird.
Mary is a psychologist.
Therefore, Mary is weird.

Comment: In this case the reasoning is valid, but the conclusion is false, because the first premise is false. All psychologists are *not* weird. (Honest!) Now let's consider one more syllogism.

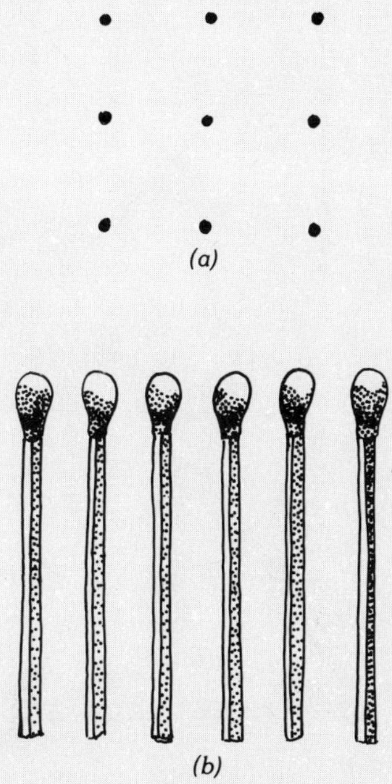

Fig. 11-8 *(a)* Nine dots are arranged in a square. Can you connect them by drawing four continuous straight lines (without lifting your pencil from the paper)? *(b)* Six matches must be arranged to form triangles. The triangles must be the same size, with each side equal to the length of one match. (The solutions to these problems appear on page 262.)

Syllogism IV

All ducks have wings.
All birds have wings.
Therefore, all ducks are birds.

Comment: This syllogism shows the importance of paying close attention to logic. The reasoning appears to be valid since the conclusion is true, but substitute "bats," or "airplanes," for "ducks" and see how the conclusion reads. It is a good idea to get in the habit of questioning the logic used by politicians, and advertisiers . . . and psychologists, for that matter!

Oversimplification It may be an oversimplification to say so, but oversimplification is another very basic source of thinking errors. There are two types of oversimplification that are particularly troublesome. The first is *all-or-nothing* thinking. Classifying things as absolutely right or wrong, good or bad, acceptable or unacceptable, or honest or dishonest prevents appreciation of the complexity of most life problems. The second problem is thinking in terms of *stereotypes*. Stereotypes are particularly troublesome when human relationships are involved. An overly sim-

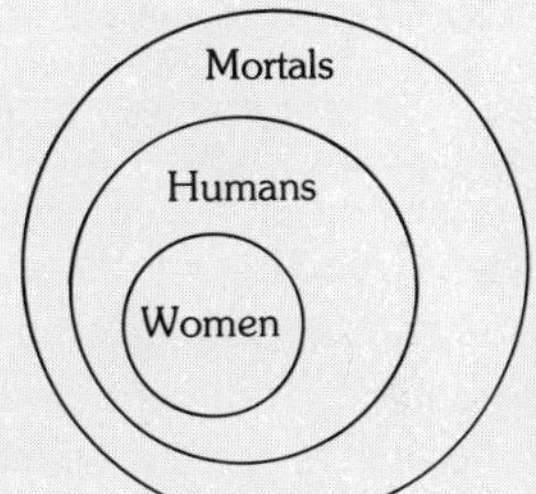

Fig. 11-9

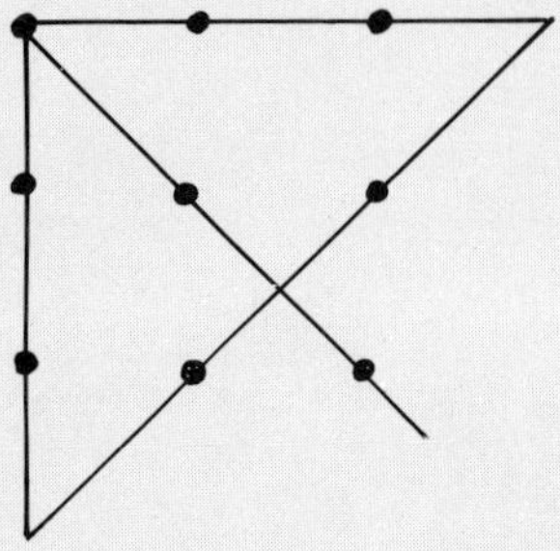

(a)

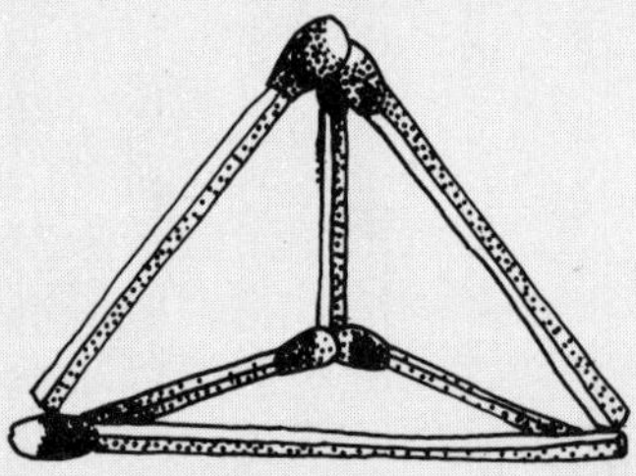

(b)

Fig. 11-10 Problem solutions. *(a)* The dot problem can be solved by extending the lines beyond the square formed by the dots. Most people assume incorrectly that they may not do this. *(b)* The match problem can be solved by building a three-dimensional pyramid. Most people assume the matches must be arranged on a flat surface.

plified, inaccurate, or rigid picture of men, blacks, women, Republicans, liberals, police officers, or any other group of people leads to muddled thinking about individual members of the group. Try to look for this and the other errors in your own thinking habits.

Enhancing Creativity—Brainstorms

Question: Is there any way to increase creativity in one's thinking?

Perhaps, but it cannot be overemphasized that "creativity" is often fostered by hard work and a prepared mind. Thomas Edison once explained his own creative accomplishments by saying, "Genius is 1 percent inspiration and 99 percent perspiration." In the real world, acts of "genius" often owe as much to persistence and dedication as they do to inspiration (Pronko, 1969).

Once it is recognized that "creativity" can be hard work, then something can be done to enhance it. Creativity relates directly to one's thinking habits, and like any ingrained tendency, thinking habits resist change. To enhance creativity, you must be prepared to cultivate actively a change in your thought patterns. Here are some suggestions on how to begin.

Brainstorming When a group of people are attempting to solve a problem, a technique called *brainstorming* has proved very effective (Haefele, 1962). Brainstorming makes use of the fact that much creative thought is built on divergent thinking. Participants are encouraged to produce as many ideas as possible by removing the threat of *evaluation*. Only *after* a brainstorming session is complete are ideas reconsidered and evaluated. The four basic rules of brainstorming might just as readily be applied to individual creative thinking as they are to group problem solving. Here they are:

1. Criticism of an idea is absolutely barred. All evaluation is to be deferred until after the session.
2. Modification or combination with other ideas is encouraged. Don't worry about giving credit for ideas or keeping them neat. Mix them up!
3. Quantity of ideas is sought. In the early stages of brainstorming quantity is more important than quality. Toss out lots of ideas.
4. Unusual, remote, or wild ideas are sought. Let your imagination run amuck!

As an aid to achieving steps 2, 3, and 4, you might find this list of suggestions helpful for encouraging original thought (adapted from Parnes, 1967).

1. *Consider other uses for all elements of the problem.* (This is designed to alert you to fixations that may be blocking creativity.)

2. *Adapt.* How could other objects, ideas, procedures, or solutions be adapted to this particular problem?
3. *Modify.* Imagine changing anything and everything that could be changed.
4. *Magnify.* Exaggerate everything you can think of. Think on a grand scale.
5. *Minify.* What if everything were scaled down? What if there were no differences between elements of the problem? "Shrink" the problem down to size.
6. *Substitute.* How could one object, idea, or procedure be substituted for another?
7. *Rearrange.* Break the problem into pieces and shuffle them.
8. *Reverse.* Consider reverse orders, opposites, and turn things inside out.
9. *Combine.* This one speaks for itself.

By making a habit of subjecting a problem to each of these procedures, you should be able to greatly reduce the chances that you will overlook a useful, original, or "creative" solution.

Questions for Discussion

As a basis for discussion, you might find it interesting to try answering these thinking and general information questions:

1. Argentinians do not have a fourth of July. T or F?

2. How many birthdays does the average person have? ________

3. A farmer had nineteen sheep. All but nine died. How many sheep did he have left? ________

4. It is not unlawful for a man living in Winston-Salem, North Carolina, to be buried west of the Mississippi River. T or F?

5. Some months have thirty days; some have thirty-one. How many months have twenty-eight days? ________

6. I have two coins which together total 55 cents. One of the coins is not a nickel. What are the two coins? ________

7. It would be far better to have an elephant eat you than a gorilla. T or F?

8. A hunter leaves home, walks 15 miles south, 10 miles west, and shoots a bear. He turns north, walks 15 miles, and is home. What is the color of the bear? ________

These questions are designed to cause some of the thinking problems discussed above. Check your answers and then see if you can identify the types of errors you made. If you made no errors, what problems did you avoid?

Answers: **1.** F. Of course they have a fourth of July. What would they do, go from the third to the fifth? **2.** One, celebrated each year. **3.** Nineteen: nine alive and ten dead. **4.** F. It is against the law to bury a living man anywhere. **5.** All of them. **6.** A half-dollar and a nickel. One of the coins is not a nickel, but the other one is! **7.** F. It would be better to have the elephant eat the gorilla. (Read it again.) **8.** White. The bear has to be a polar bear. The North Pole is the only place in the world you could walk 15 miles south, 10 miles west, and only have to walk 15 miles back home.

Suggestions for Further Reading

Barron, F. "The Psychology of Creativity." In *New Directions in Psychology*, vol. 2. Holt, 1965.

Bourne, L. E., B. R. Ekstrand, and R. L. Dominowski. *The Psychology of Thinking*. Prentice-Hall, 1971.

Carroll, J. B. *Language and Thought.* Prentice-Hall, 1964.

Koestler, A. *The Act of Creation.* Macmillan, 1964.

Singer, J. L. *Daydreaming: An Introduction to the Experimental Study of Inner Experience*. Random House, 1966.

Contents

Actions and Reactions

Unit Four

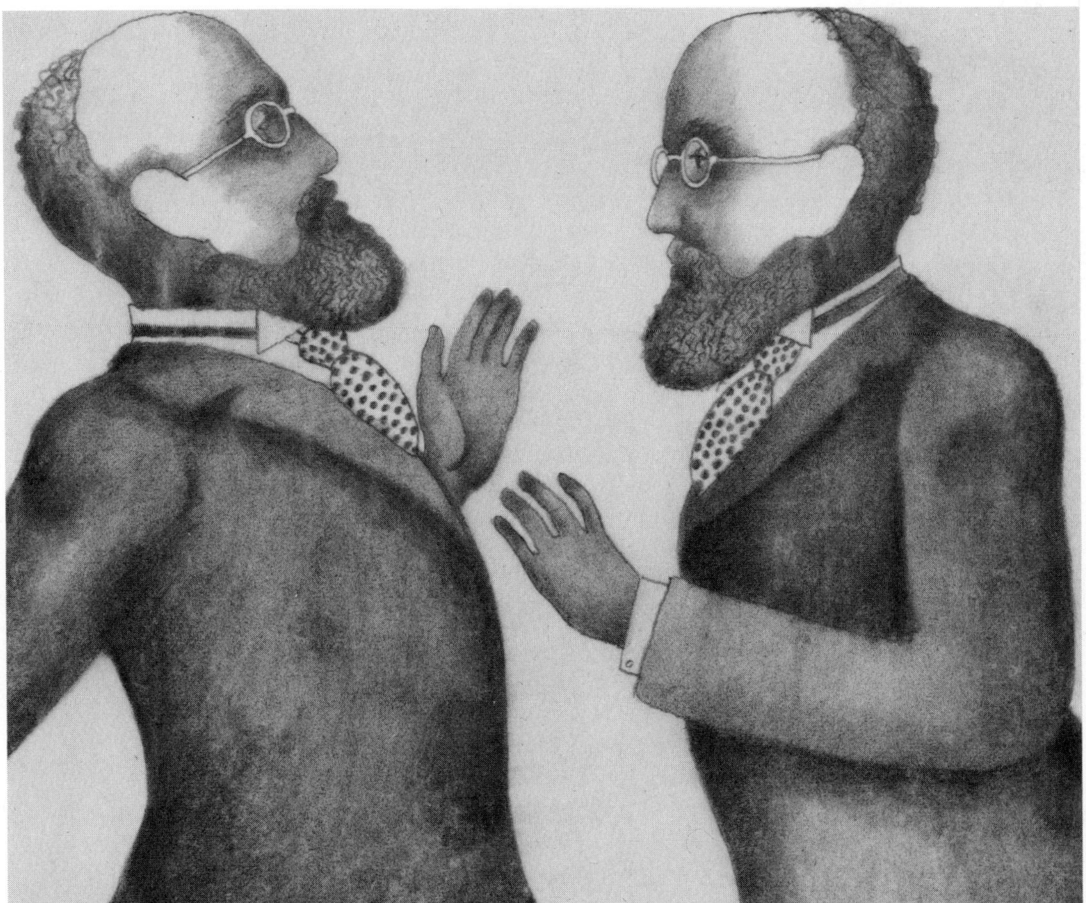

Motivation

12

Chapter Preview

The Ups and Downs of Human Motivation

Some Highs *Mt. Everest, the world's highest mountain, is located in the eastern Himalayas. Its Tibetan name means "Goddess-mother of the land." Its elevation is 29,141 feet. Above 22,000 feet the mountain is lifeless and hostile: granite cased in ice, howling winds that threaten frostbite and death from exposure, air so thin that climbers must carry oxygen with them. Climbers? But of course! What could be more characteristically human than responding to the challenge represented by the "summit of the world"? But such a goal is not easily won. It took years of planning and sacrifice and eighty days of brutal climbing before Sir Edmund Hillary of New Zealand and Tenzing Norgay, a Nepalese Sherpa, finally struggled the last agonizing yards to the summit on May 29, 1953.*

Of course, there are other ways to reach human heights. After earning doctorates in philosophy and theology, Albert Schweitzer returned to the university to obtain a medical degree. Then in 1913 he founded a hospital in equatorial Africa. For the remainder of his life he devoted his energies to tirelessly caring for the sick and injured who came to his hospital village. In 1952 he received the Nobel Peace Prize for his humanitarian work. Though certainly a "reward" for his work, this belated recognition had little to do with his dedication. From the moment he began his medical training, Schweitzer's one life goal was a selfless desire to aid and comfort those in greatest need.

And Some Lows *The reign of Adolf Hitler over Nazi Germany stands at the opposite end of the scale of human endeavors represented by the examples above. On Hitler's personal orders over 6½ million human lives were ended in the concentration camps run by the gestapo (state secret police). The motives for this slaughter are practically beyond the limits of comprehension.*

In an act equally beyond comprehension, Lee Harvey Oswald fired a bullet that killed then-president John F. Kennedy as his motorcade made its way through downtown Dallas on a fall afternoon in 1963. Why? We will never know, because Oswald was killed two days later.

Why? *Probably the most difficult question to answer in any study of human or animal behavior is the question "Why?" By raising the psychological question "why," we are asking for the causes of behavior, not simply for a description. If you are a fan of TV police dramas or of the mystery novel, you know that a case is solved only when a motive can be established. In attempting to answer the "why" questions in psychology, we will also be concerning ourselves with motives, but to a psychologist the term "motive" has a specialized set of meanings. The samples of behavior described above show some of the extremes and the complexities of human motivation that psychologists must attempt to explain. The pages which follow are an introduction to some of the concepts they have found useful.*

Resources

Motivation—Forces That Push and Pull

We move. Our behavior is directed toward different goals. Some goals are pursued more vigorously than others. The same goal may be pursued for different reasons, or different goals may be pursued for the same reasons. We use the concept of motivation to explain each of these basic aspects of behavior. To be more specific, motivation refers to "the dynamics of behavior, the process of initiating, sustaining, and directing activities of the organism" (Goldenson, 1970b).

Question: *Can you clarify that?*

Yes. Let's relate the concept of motivation to a simple sequence of activity:

> Liz is studying (psychology, of course) in the library. She begins to feel hungry and stops to check her pockets for a piece of gum. She resumes studying, but thoughts of food begin to interrupt her concentration. Her stomach growls. She feels restless and decides to buy an apple from a vending machine. The machine is empty, so she goes to the cafeteria. Closed. She returns to the library, packs up her books, and drives home where she prepares a meal and eats. At last her hunger is satisfied, and she again resumes studying.

Liz's food seeking was *initiated* by her bodily need for food; it was *sustained* because her need was not immediately met; and her activities were *directed* by possible sources of food.

A Model of Motivation Many motivated activities can be thought of as beginning with a *need*. The need which initiated Liz's search for food was a depletion of necessary substances within the cells of her body. Needs cause a psychological state or feeling called a *drive* to develop. (The drive is hunger, in Liz's case.) Drives activate a *response* (or a series of actions) designed to attain a *goal* that will relieve the need. Relieving the need temporarily ends the motivational chain of events. Thus, a simple model of motivation can be stated in this way:

NEED→DRIVE→RESPONSE→GOAL→GOAL ATTAINMENT (NEED REDUCTION)

Question: Why use the terms "need" and "drive"? Aren't they the same thing?

We need both terms to discuss motivation because the strength of needs and of drives may not be the same. If you were to begin fasting, your bodily need for food would increase daily, but you would probably find yourself less "hungry" on the seventh day of fasting than you were on the first. Your need increases, but the hunger drive comes and goes and may disappear at times.

Before we consider the preceding a complete model of motivation, let us observe Liz's eating behavior on another occasion:

> Liz has gone out to dinner at a fine restaurant. There she consumes soup, salad, a large steak, a large baked potato, one half of a freshly baked loaf of bread, two pieces of Italian cheesecake, and four cups of coffee. After the meal she remarks about her discomfort from having overeaten. Soon after Liz gets home, her roommate arrives with a strawberry pie. Liz exclaims that strawberry pie is her favorite dessert and proceeds to eat three good-sized pieces and has a cup of coffee to "wash it down."

Is this hunger? Certainly we can believe that Liz's extra-large meal was enough to satisfy her biological needs for food.

Question: What effect does this story have on the model of motivation?

This story illustrates that motivated behavior can be energized by external stimuli as well as by the "push" of internal needs. The "pull" exerted by a goal is called its *incentive value*. Some goals are so desirable (strawberry pie, for example) that they motivate behavior in the absence of internal need. Other goals are so low in incentive value that they will be rejected even though they might meet the internal need. Fresh, live grubs, for instance, are considered a delicacy in some parts of the world. Grubs are actually an excellent source of protein, but it is doubtful that the average American could eat them no matter how hungry he or she might be.

Fig. 12-1 Eating may be motivated by internal needs or by external incentives. (Photo by Peter Vilms, Jeroboam.)

In most instances it is helpful to recognize that actions are energized by a combination of internal needs *and* external incentives and that a strong state of need may make a less attractive incentive into a desirable goal. You may never have eaten a grub, but chances are good that you have eaten some pretty horrible "leftovers" when the refrigerator was bare. Incentives also help account for motives which do not seem to have any identifiable internal need; drives for success, status, or approval, for example.

This discussion may sound a long way from questions like: "Why do people climb mountains?" "Why is my aunt so mean?" or "Why do people skyjack airplanes?" (or rob banks, or batter children, or collect stamps). It is. Many of the "motivation" questions put to psychologists are really questions about personality, learning, adjustment, or other psychological processes.

As psychologists have studied it, motivation is a blending of biology and psychology. The psychologist would like to know how biological needs for the likes of food, water, air, or sleep are translated into the drives of hunger, thirst, and so on. Also of interest is the question of how we acquire more subtle needs for things like friendship, achievement, status, money, or knowledge.

Types of Motives For the purpose of study, motives can be divided into three major categories:

1. *Primary motives* are based on biological needs which must be met for survival. The most important primary motives are hunger, thirst, pain avoidance, and needs for air, sleep, elimination of wastes, and regulation of body temperature. Primary motives are unlearned.
2. *Stimulus motives* also appear to be innate, but they are not necessary for mere survival of the organism. Their purpose seems to be to provide useful information about the environment and stimulation to the nervous system. The stimulus motives include: activity, curiosity, exploration, manipulation, and physical contact.
3. *Learned*, or *secondary*, *motives* account for the great diversity of human activities suggested by the chapter preview. The most important secondary motives are related to acquired needs for affiliation (the need to be with others), approval, status, security, and achievement. The important motives of fear and aggression also appear to be subject to learning.

Primary Motives and Homeostasis—Keeping the Home Fires Burning

How important is food in your life? Water? Sleep? Air? Temperature regulation? For most of us, satisfying these biological needs is so habitual there is a tendency to overlook how much of our behavior they actually direct. But exaggerate any of these needs through famine, shipwreck, poverty, near-drowning, or exposure, and their powerful grip on behavior becomes evident. We are, after all, still animals in many ways. As Abraham Maslow has pointed out, biological needs tend to be *prepotent* (dominant) over psychological needs or motives. If your survival is threatened by starvation, lack of water, or a need for oxygen, you will probably set aside needs for prestige, achievement, approval, and the like, until your more pressing physical needs are met. The biological drives are essential because they maintain *homeostasis*, or bodily equilibrium (Cannon, 1932).

Question: What is homeostasis?

The term "homeostasis" means standing steady, or steady state. Within the body there are "ideal" levels for body temperature, concentration of various chemicals in the blood, blood pressure, and so forth. When the body deviates from these ideal levels, automatic reactions restore equilibrium. You might find it helpful to think of the homeostatic mechanisms as being similar in operation to a *thermostat* set at a particular temperature.

A (Very) Short Course on Thermostats

If room temperature falls below the level set on a thermostat, the heat is automatically turned on to warm the room. When the heat equals or slightly exceeds the ideal temperature, it is automatically turned off. In this way room temperature is maintained in a state of equilibrium hovering around the ideal level.

In the human body the first reactions to disequilibrium are also automatic. For example, if you become too hot, blood flow to body surfaces is increased, muscular activity is inhibited, and perspiring begins, thus lowering body temperature. Reactions such as these may take place without any awareness on your part. You become aware of the need to maintain homeostasis only when driven by continued disequilibrium to seek shade, warmth, food, water, and so forth.

Since hunger is one of the most interesting and completely understood of the primary drives, we will examine it in detail before returning to a discussion of biological drives in general. But before reading more, you may find it helpful to complete the learning check which follows.

Learning Check

1. Motives ____________, sustain, and ____________ activities.

2. Needs provide the ____________ of motivation, whereas incentives provide the ________.

3. Biological needs that must be met for survival generate ________ motives; learned motives are often referred to as ____________.

4. The maintenance of bodily equilibrium is called ____________.

5. A goal high in ____________ value may create a drive in the absence of any internal need.

Answers:
1. initiate, direct **2.** push, pull **3.** primary, secondary **4.** homeostasis **5.** incentive

Hunger—Pardon Me, That's Just My Hypothalamus Growling

Question: What causes hunger?

When you feel hungry, you probably associate a desire for food with sensations from your stomach. This, sensibly enough, is where the search for hunger began. In an early study, Cannon and Washburn (1912) decided to see if the contractions of an empty stomach cause hunger. To do this, Washburn trained himself to swallow a toy balloon. Once it was in the stomach, the balloon was inflated through an attached tube so that stomach contractions could be recorded (see Fig. 12-2). Cannon and Washburn observed that when Washburn's stomach contracted, he felt "hunger

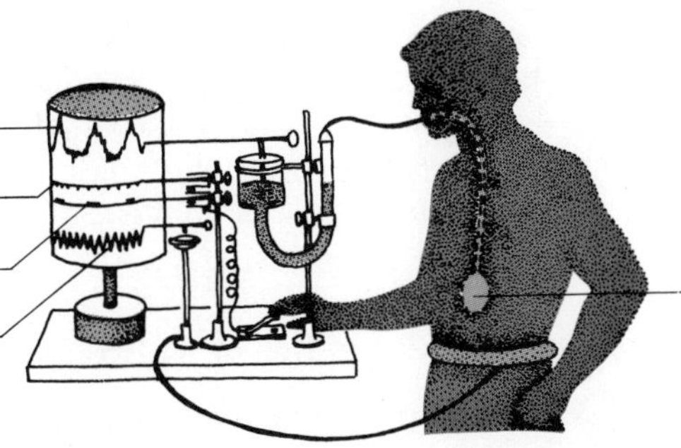

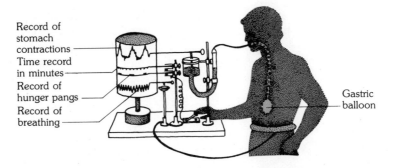

Fig. 12-2 In Cannon's early study of hunger, a simple apparatus was used to simultaneously record hunger pangs and stomach contractions. (After Cannon, 1934.)

pangs.'' They concluded that hunger is nothing more than stomach contractions.*

Later research has proved them wrong. Perhaps you already guessed that something more than the stomach is involved in hunger. Many people experience hunger as an overall feeling of weakness or ''shakiness'' that does not seem to be associated with the stomach. While it is certainly true that eating is limited when the stomach is distended (full), it can be shown conclusively that the stomach is not essential for experiencing hunger.

Question: How has this been demonstrated?

For one thing, cutting the sensory nerves from the stomach (so that stomach sensations can no longer be felt) does not abolish hunger. Even more convincing is the fact that there are a number of people who have had their stomachs removed surgically. These people continue to feel hungry and to eat regularly. It would seem that some *central* factor must be the cause of hunger. The most important factor now appears to be the level of sugar in the blood. If blood is transferred from a starving dog to one that was recently fed, the second dog will begin eating. (The reverse also holds true.) If insulin is injected in a human, it produces *hypoglycemia* (low blood sugar) and stimulates feelings of hunger and stomach contractions (Cofer & Appley, 1964).

Question: What part of the body is sensitive to changes in blood sugar?

Eating is primarily under control of the *hypothalamus*, a small structure in the center of the brain. Cells in the hypothalamus are sensitive to levels of sugar (and perhaps other substances) in the blood. One area in the hypothalamus has been identified as a *feeding center* that initiates eating. If this area is electrically stimulated, even a well-fed animal will immediately begin eating; if it is destroyed, the animal refuses to eat and

*This whole experiment is a study of motivation in itself: As a dedicated scientist, Washburn's thirst for knowledge was temporarily converted into a hunger for balloons!

will die if not force-fed (Avard & Brobeck, 1951). A second area of the hypothalamus seems to operate as a *satiety center* (or "stop center") for eating. If it is destroyed, dramatic overeating results. Rats with damage to this area overeat to the point of total obesity, sometimes getting so large that they can barely move. Some balloon up to weights of 1,000 grams or more (see Fig. 12-3). A normal rat weighs about 180 grams; picture a 180-pound man growing to a weight of 1,000 pounds to get an idea of what this means in human terms.

Question: Is this the cause of overeating in humans?

Obesity There are some striking similarities between the eating habits of overweight humans and those of animals with damage to the hypothalamus, but few instances of human overeating have been traced directly to physical problems. Other problems, however, have been identified. First of all, the obese seem to confuse hunger with other feelings. An overweight person is as likely to eat when aroused, angry, or depressed, as when hungry (Bruch, 1961). Secondly, the overweight are more sensitive than normal to *external* cues for eating and rely less than normal on internal feelings of hunger to regulate eating (Schachter, 1971).

The second cause of overeating is demonstrated by an experiment in which subjects were allowed to nibble on some crackers as they waited in a

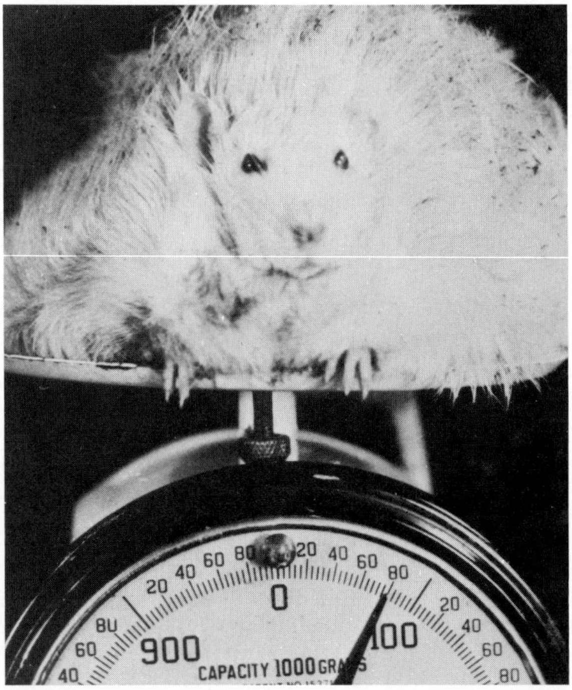

Figure 12-3 Damage to the hunger-satiety center in the hypothalamus can produce a very fat rat; a condition called hypothalamic *hyperphagia* (overeating). This rat weighs 1,080 grams. (The pointer has gone completely around the dial and beyond.) (Photo courtesy of Neal Miller.)

room. On the wall was a clock that could be adjusted to run fast or slow. When obese subjects were led to believe it was closer to mealtime than it actually was (fast clock), they ate more crackers than when they thought dinnertime was farther away than it actually was (slow clock). Subjects of normal weight decreased their eating when they thought it was closer to mealtime (Schachter & Gross, 1968). When the clock read five minutes after six, the reaction of fat subjects seems to have been, "Hmm, dinnertime, I must be hungry!"

Since eating in the overweight is largely under external control, it is also greatly affected by the attractiveness of food or the amount of effort necessary to obtain it. In one study, downgrading the taste of milkshakes at a girl's summer camp led to a greater decrease in milkshake drinking by overweight campers than it did in those of normal weight. Improving the taste led to greater increases in consumption by the overweight (Liebett, 1968). In another study, it was found that if shelling nuts was necessary before they could be eaten, only 5 percent of obese subjects ate them. When the nuts were preshelled, almost 100 percent of the obese subjects ate them. Subjects of normal weight ate about the same amount either way (Schachter, 1971). Unfortunately, reminders of food are everywhere in our society, and opportunities to eat are numerous. Overeating is very difficult to avoid for the person who is unusually sensitive to external signals for eating.

Other Factors in Hunger As the research on overeating suggests, "hunger" is affected by a number of factors in addition to actual bodily needs for food. Let us consider some additional topics of interest.

Cultural Factors Learning to think of some foods as desirable and others as revolting obviously has much to do with eating habits. In America we would never consider eating the eyes out of the steamed head of a monkey, but in Thailand this dish is considered a real delicacy. Many Americans still have trouble getting used to the thought of eating brain, cow's tongue, chocolate-covered grasshoppers, and caviar—all commonly accepted foods in other countries. By the same token, our willingness to consume large quantities of meat, to eat cows, and to cook fish would be considered barbaric in many cultures.

Taste Even tastes for "normal" foods may vary considerably. In one experiment it was demonstrated that the hungrier a person is, the more "pleasant" a sweet food tastes. However, when subjects were "full," they reversed their judgments and considered sweet foods to be "unpleasant" (Cabanac & Duclaux, 1970). It is also interesting to note that a *taste aversion* can be easily learned if a food causes sickness or if it simply precedes sickness caused by something else (Nachman, 1970). Not only will such foods be avoided, they can become positively nauseating for the person involved. A friend of the author's, who became ill after eating a cheese Danish (well, actually *several*), has never been able to come face to face with this delightful pastry again.

Question: *Sometimes you hear about pregnant women getting cravings for a particular food; does this actually occur?*

Specific Hungers Instances of food cravings reflect a combination of factors. There is evidence that both animals and people are able to develop *specific hungers* for nutritional substances lacking in their diet. For example, if animals are made ill by being deprived of vitamin B, they develop a marked preference for foods to which this essential vitamin has been added (Scott & Verrey, 1947). Similarly, it is possible that a pregnant woman who has food cravings could be responding to a nutritional need. This is not likely, however, since an expectant mother's diet is usually adequate. Such cravings are probably the result of expectations passed on as part of the lore about pregnancy.

Question: *Then do humans ever have specific hungers?*

There is some direct evidence of specific hungers occurring in humans, particularly in children. In one classic experiment on "self-selection" feeding, human infants were given a daily "cafeteria" choice of foods. Over a period of several months they selected a balanced diet, and their health and growth were normal (Davis, 1928). In fact, one child who began the study suffering from rickets voluntarily drank large amounts of cod-liver oil, and apparently cured himself of his nutritional disease. In similar fashion, malnourished children have been known to eat plaster from the walls in order to obtain the calcium it contains.

It should be noted, however, that the "wisdom of the body" is actually fairly limited. In the experiment described above, the babies could only select from nutritious foods. If candy had been a choice, they might not have done so well. Even by early childhood, learned food preferences tend to override specific hungers, so that poor diets of sweets and "junk-food" are not uncommon in our society.

Primary Motives Revisited—The Strange Case of Sex and Pain

The pattern of factors we have observed in the control of hunger is similar to that found for most of the other primary motives. For example, thirst is only partially related to dryness of the mouth and throat. When drugs are given to persons or animals so that their mouths remain constantly wet or dry, thirst and water intake remain normal. Like hunger, thirst appears to be controlled from the hypothalamus, where separate *thirst* and *thirst-satiety* centers are found. Also like hunger, thirst is strongly affected by individual learning and by cultural factors.

Question: *Is there such a thing as a "specific thirst"?*

In a sense there is. Before the body can retain water, minerals lost through perspiration (mainly salt) must be replaced. Thus when a person is really thirsty, a slightly salty liquid may be more satisfying than plain water. Among some of the people of the Sahara Desert, blood is a highly prized beverage, perhaps because of its saltiness.

The drives for food, water, air, sleep, and elimination are all fairly similar in that they are generated by a combination of activities in the body and the brain, are modified by learning and culture, and are influenced by external factors. Two of the primary drives are unlike the others. These are the drive to avoid pain and the sex drive. Each differs from the other primary drives in some interesting ways.

Question: How is the drive to avoid pain different?

Pain Drives like hunger, thirst, and sleepiness come and go in a fairly regular cycle each day. Pain, by contrast, is an *episodic* drive since it is aroused only when damage to the tissues of the body takes place. Most of the primary drives cause a person actively to seek a desired goal (food, drink, sleep, and so forth). The pain drive has as its goal the avoidance or elimination of pain. As we observed in an earlier chapter (Chapter 4), pain is a very useful motive since it helps protect the body from injury. However, under unusual circumstances the protective function of pain can be turned against a person. A prime example is the process of becoming addicted to a drug like heroin. Addiction rapidly locks the person into a cycle in which an injection of heroin is used to alleviate the painful symptoms of withdrawal, but at the same time the heroin relieves discomfort, it ensures that a number of hours later it will return. In a way we could say the drug addict has established a new biological motive.

The desire to end pain seems so basic that it may come as a surprise that avoiding pain appears to be partially learned. This was demonstrated by a study in which puppies were raised in total isolation. Each puppy was housed in a cage that prevented exposure to the normal bumps, bites, and other pains of "puppyhood." When the dogs had grown to maturity, they were tested for responses to pain. Dogs raised normally yelped and withdrew from pain, but the isolated group acted very strangely in response to it. For example, if a lighted match was held near a normal dog's nose, the dog avoided it. The isolated dogs acted like they either did not feel pain or did not know what to do about it, and sometimes pushed their noses toward the match (Melzack & Scott, 1957).* Thus, it can be seen that even a drive as basic as pain avoidance does not escape the effects of learning and experience.

The Sex Drive Sexual motivation is quite unusual by comparison to other biological motives. In fact, many psychologists do not think of sex as

*The author wishes to emphasize that in this and in other experiments in which animals are exposed to pain every effort is made to see that they are not mistreated.

a primary motive because sex (contrary to anything your personal experience might suggest) is not necessary for *individual* survival. It is necessary, of course, for the survival of humans and other creatures as a *group*.

In lower animals the sex drive is directly related to the action of hormones in the body. Females of the lower species are only interested in mating when their fertility cycle is in the stage of *estrus*, or "heat" (caused by secretion of the hormone *estrogen* into the bloodstream). Hormones are important in the male animal as well, and in most lower animals castration will abolish the sex drive. By contrast to the female, however, the normal male animal is always ready to mate. His sex drive is primarily aroused by the behavior of a receptive female. In animals, mating is therefore closely tied to the fertility cycle of the female.

Question: How much do hormones affect the sex drive in humans?

The connection between the sex drive and hormone cycles grows weaker as we ascend the biological scale toward humans. In humans the sex drive can be aroused at any time and by almost anything. Hormones do affect human sexual drives, but only to a limited degree. Human sexual behavior and attitudes are discussed in detail in Chapter 25. For now it is enough to note that the sex drive is *non-homeostatic*. Unlike drives for food, water, air, and so forth, the sex drive shows no clear relationship to deprivation (the amount of time since the drive was last satisfied). The sex drive is also unusual in that its arousal is as actively sought as its reduction. People rarely (if ever) read a book or see a movie because it makes them hungry or thirsty. They do not buy perfume because it makes others gasp for air, and they do not buy clothing because it makes them shiver or sweat. But each of these activities may be motivated by the arousal of the sex drive in oneself or the desire to arouse it in others. This quality of the sex drive makes it capable of motivating an unusually wide range of behaviors and accounts for its use to sell almost everything imaginable.

Learning Check

1. Centers for the control of hunger and thirst are found in the

____________________ of the brain.

2. According to Schachter's research, people who suffer from obesity have ravenous appetites and will eat almost anything. T or F?

3. If an animal is deprived of a necessary food substance, the animal

may develop a ____________ ____________ for foods containing the substance.

4. Pain avoidance is an ____________________ drive.

5. Sexual behavior in animals is largely controlled by ________ in the body.

Answers: **1.** hypothalamus **2.** F **3.** specific hunger **4.** episodic **5.** hormones

Stimulus Needs—Sky Diving, Horror Movies, and the Fun Zone

"Curiosity killed the cat," it is sometimes said, but nothing could be further from the truth. Curiosity plays a very important role in the survival of both animals and people. You have surely observed that animals devote large amounts of time and energy to investigating new or unusual objects in the environment. Drives for *exploration*, *manipulation*, or simply for *curiosity* seem to exist in most animals. As mentioned earlier in this chapter, such drives might be explained by the life-and-death necessity of keeping track of sources of food, danger, and other important details of the environment. However, the curiosity drives seem to go beyond such needs:

Monkey Business

One early researcher (Romanes, 1912) reported that one of his monkeys worked for two hours to open a trunk containing nuts. This activity took place

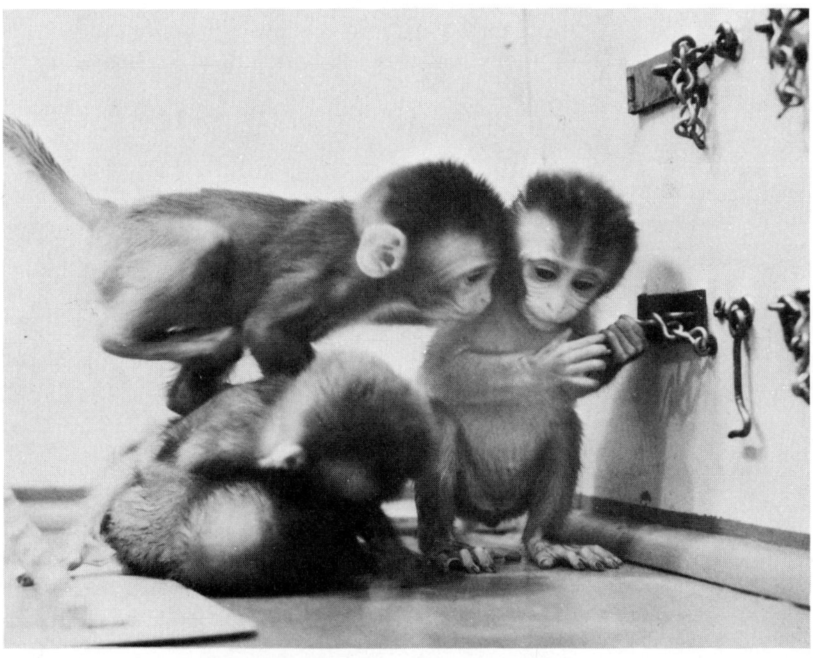

Fig. 12-4 Monkeys happily open locks that are placed in their cage. Since no reward is given for this activity, it provides evidence of the existence of stimulus needs. (Photo courtesy of Harry F. Harlow, University of Wisconsin, Primate Laboratory.)

while the monkey was surrounded by nuts left in plain sight. In another experiment, monkeys confined to a dimly lit box learned to perform a simple task in order to open a window that allowed them to view the outside world (Butler & Harlow, 1954). In still another experiment, monkeys quickly learned to solve a mechanical puzzle made up of interlocking metal pins, hooks, and hasps (Butler, 1954).

In each of these situations no reward was offered for exploration or manipulation. The monkeys seemed to be working for the sheer fun of it. Curiosity also seems to be a powerful drive in humans. Scientific investigation, intellectual curiosity, and other advanced activities may be an extension of this basic drive.

Closely related to the curiosity drive are needs for sensory stimulation. In the preview to Chapter 4, we discussed the effects of sensory deprivation. There we noted that hallucinations, discomfort, and a disruption of intellectual functioning take place when a person is deprived of normal sensory stimulation. The nervous system seems to require varied, patterned stimulation to respond normally. The drive for stimulation can even be observed in infants. When babies are shown patterns of varying complexity (see Fig. 12-5), they spend more time looking at complex patterns than at simpler ones (Berlyne, 1966). Indeed, human infants seem to have an almost limitless appetite for stimulation. They spend most of their waking hours tasting, touching, listening to, and visually exploring anything and everything in their immediate surroundings. By the time a child can walk, there are few things in the home that have not been tasted, touched, viewed, handled, or, in the case of toys, destroyed!

Question: Are the stimulus needs homeostatic?

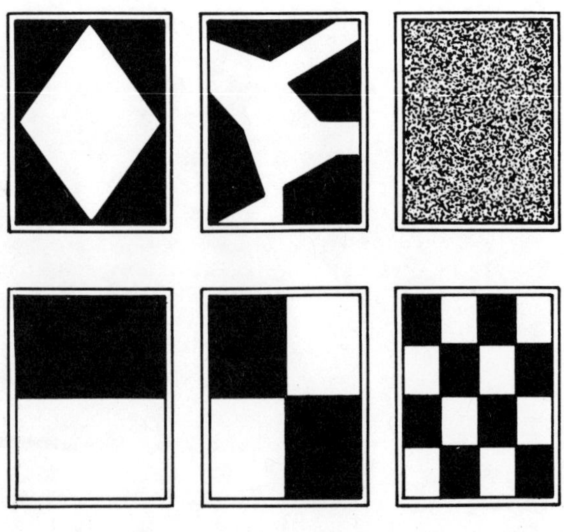

Fig. 12-5 Berlyne studied curiosity in infants by showing them these designs. Babies looked first at the more complex patterns on the right. (From *Science*, 153:25–33. Copyright © 1966 by the American Association for the Advancement of Science.)

Arousal Some psychologists would argue that they are not. However, by relating drives for stimulation and curiosity to the concept of homeostasis, we get a model of motivation that is very useful for understanding many human activities. This position, called the *arousal theory* of motivation, assumes that there is an ideal level of arousal for various activities and that individuals behave in ways that keep arousal near this ideal level (Hebb, 1966).

Question: *What do you mean by "arousal"?*

Arousal refers to variations in activation of the body and nervous system. Arousal is zero at death; it is low during sleep; it is moderate during normal daily activities; and it is high at times of excitement, emotion, or panic. Arousal theory assumes that an individual becomes uncomfortable when arousal is too low (as when a person is bored) or when it is too high (as might be the case during intense fear, anxiety, or panic). Curiosity and the drive to seek stimulation can be interpreted as an attempt to raise the level of arousal when it is too low.

The city dweller who visits the country complains that it is "too quiet" and seeks some "action." The country dweller finds the city "hectic," "frightening," or "too much" and seeks peace and quiet. The arousal theory of motivation also assumes that the ideal level of arousal varies from one person to the next and that individuals learn to seek a particular level of arousal. Most adults seem to vary their activities to maintain a comfortable level of activation. Music, parties, athletics, conversation, sleep, and a wide range of other activities may be mixed to keep arousal at moderate levels, thus preventing both boredom and overstimulation. Sometimes even extremely high levels of arousal may be desirable if they are brief or if they are under the individual's control. Sky diving, rock climbing, hang gliding, ski jumping, and other hazardous pursuits seem to be appealing because they temporarily raise arousal to very high levels which are followed by a satisfying return to normal. If you are a fan of horror movies or of carnival rides, your motives may be based on the same effect.

Question: *What is the ideal level of arousal?*

Performance of a task is usually best when arousal is moderate. Let's say that you have to take an essay exam in one of your classes. If you are sleepy or feeling lazy (arousal level too low), your performance will suffer. If you are in a state of anxiety or panic about the test (arousal level too high), you will also perform below par. This relationship between arousal and efficiency of behavior can be symbolized as an *inverted U function* (see Fig. 12-6). At very low levels of arousal the body is not sufficiently energized to perform effectively. With increased arousal, performance continues to improve up to the middle regions of the curve; then it begins to drop off as an individual becomes emotional, frenzied, or disorganized.

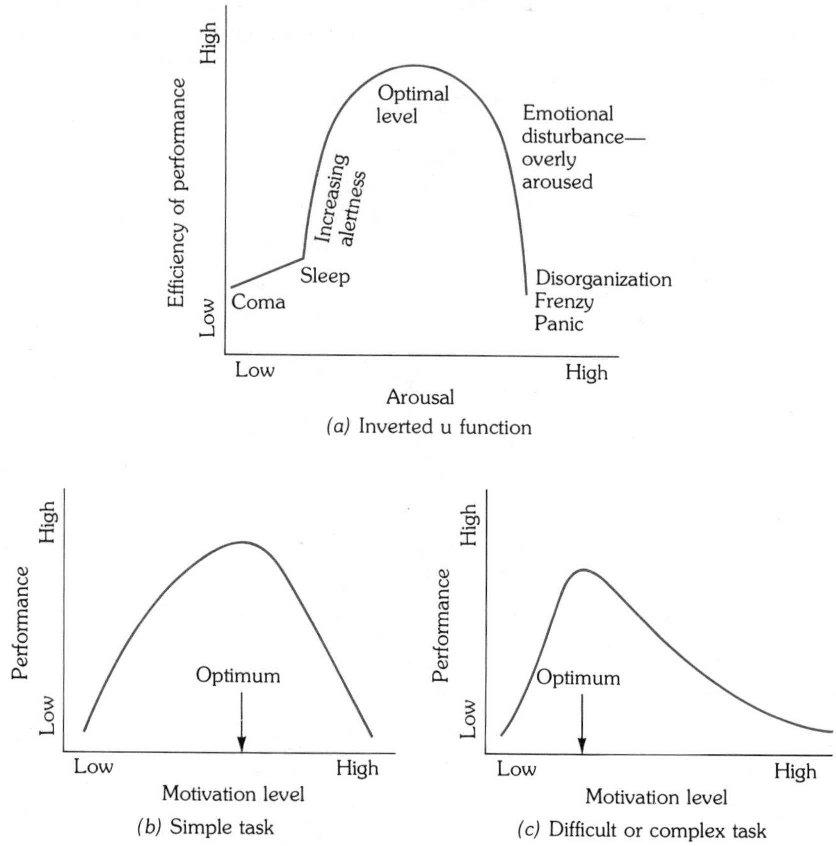

Fig. 12-6 *(a)* The general relationship between arousal and efficiency can be described by an "inverted u" curve. *(b)* The optimal level of arousal or motivation is higher for a simple task than for a complex task *(c)*.

Question: Is performance always best at moderate levels of arousal?

No, the optimal level of arousal depends on the complexity of the task to be performed. For simple tasks, greater activation runs little risk of disorganizing performance. If a task is relatively *simple*, the optimal level of arousal will be *high*. When a task is *difficult* or *complicated*, the best performance occurs at *low* levels of arousal. This relationship is called the *Yerkes-Dodson law* (see Fig. 12-6). It applies to a wide variety of tasks and to measures of motivation other than arousal.

Some examples of the Yerkes-Dodson law in operation might be helpful. At a track meet it is almost impossible for a sprinter to get too aroused for a race. The task is direct and uncomplicated: Run as fast as you can for a short distance. On the other hand, a golfer making the last putt in an important tournament and a basketball player making a game-deciding free throw face more sensitive and complex tasks. Excessive arousal is almost certain to hurt their performance. In school most students have had experience with "test anxiety" as a familiar example of the effects of excessive arousal on performance.

Social Motives—In Pursuit of Excellence

Competition and achievement are highly valued in American culture. In less industrialized nations, the desire to achieve may be minimal. Some of your friends are more interested than others in success, money, possessions, status, love, approval, grades, dominance, power, or belonging to groups. In each case we are referring to important individual differences in social motives or goals. Social motives help explain activities that seem removed from the satisfaction of biological needs. The accomplishments of men like Sir Edmund Hillary, Albert Schweitzer, or anyone who seeks excellence are best understood in terms of learned needs, particularly the need for achievement.

The *need for achievement* (nAch) is certainly not the only social motive of importance, but it is a dominant motive in American culture. To many people, being "motivated" means being interested in achievement. In other chapters of this text we will investigate the motives behind aggression, love, affiliation, and approval. For now, let us focus on the need for achievement.

Question: Is the need for achievement the same as the need for prestige?

The *need for prestige* is also important to many Americans. The symbols of status and prestige—automobiles, money, clothing, credit cards, and other material indications of wealth—are avidly sought by large segments of the population. Since material and financial success are highly valued, the desire for prestige and needs for achievement often become linked. But the need for achievement is not the same as the need for prestige. The need for achievement can be defined as a desire to meet some *internalized standard of excellence* (McClelland, 1961). The person with high needs for achievement strives to do well in any situation in which evaluation takes place. In a business setting this may lead to material wealth and prestige, but a person who is a high achiever in art, music, science, or amateur athletics may be striving for excellence without concern for material reward.

David McClelland (1955, 1958) and a number of other psychologists have been interested in the effects of high or low needs for achievement. To measure the need for achievement (nAch), McClelland used a series of pictures showing people in various situations related to work and school. People were asked to make up a story about each of the pictures. These were then scored for achievement-oriented imagery (references to striving, trying, success, and so forth). Using this simple measure, McClelland has found that he could predict the behavior of high and low achievers in

Fig. 12-7 Many human motives are acquired. (Photo by J. Berndt, Stock, Boston.)

many situations. In one study, for example, the occupations of college graduates were compared to their scores on a need for achievement test given in their sophomore year. Fourteen years after graduation, those individuals who scored high in need for achievement were more often found in entrepreneurial positions involving an element of risk and responsibility than those with low nAch (McClelland, 1965). McClelland has even related the achievement motive to the rise and fall of entire cultures. By studying achievement imagery in the literature of various cultures, he has shown that a rise in the achievement needs of a society precedes periods of growth, expansion, and prosperity, and a decline has been associated with the fall of civilizations (1961).

Characteristics of Achievers In front of you are five targets placed at various distances from where you are standing. You are given a beanbag to toss at the target of your choice. Target A, anyone can hit; target B, most people can hit; target C, some people can hit; target D, very few people can hit; target E is rarely if ever hit. If you hit A, you will receive $2; B, $4; C, $8; D, $16; and E, $32. You get only one toss. Which one would you choose? McClelland's research suggests that if you have a high need for achievement, you will select C or perhaps D.

Those high in nAch are *moderate* risk-takers. When faced with a problem or challenge, persons high in nAch avoid goals that are too easy because they offer no sense of satisfaction. They also avoid long shots because there is no hope of success or because if success occurs it will be due to luck rather than skill. Persons low in nAch select either sure things or impossible goals. Either way there is no risk of personal responsibility for failure. Desires for achievement and calculated risk taking are converted into successful performance of tasks in many situations. People high in nAch do better on various tasks in the laboratory. They are more likely to complete difficult tasks, they make better grades in high school and college, and they tend to excel in their chosen occupations.

Question: Why are some people high in achievement motivation and others low? How do people learn high needs for achievement?

The need for achievement has been related to variables such as social class, ethnic background, and religious affiliation. But the most direct factor in its development seems to be parental attitudes. Studies have shown that the mothers of boys with high needs for achievement tend to have higher expectations for their sons. They encourage greater independence early in life and tend to be warm, loving, supporting, and non-authoritarian. The formula for developing achievement seems to be a fairly demanding parent who encourages self-reliance and rewards independent behavior. Simply leaving a child to his or her own ends is not enough (Winterbottom, 1953, 1958).

Studies of needs for achievement have generally focused on males. Those involving female subjects have given less consistent results, and some researchers have uncovered evidence of a fear of success or a "desire to fail" in women subjects. For example, bright, successful undergraduate women at the University of Michigan were asked to enlarge upon the statement: "After first term finals, Anne finds herself at the top of her medical-school class" (Horner, 1969). Their responses were somewhat shocking:

> Anne is an acne-faced bookworm. . . . She studies twelve hours a day and lives at home to save money.
>
> Anne doesn't want to be number one in her class. . . . She feels she shouldn't rank so high because of social reasons. She drops to ninth and then marries the boy who graduates number one.
>
> Although Anne is happy with her success, she fears what will happen to her social life.[1]

When the women students completed the same statement, but with the name John substituted for Anne, their comments were rarely negative. It appears that many women in our society have been forced into the unfortunate position of seeing achievement and social acceptance as conflicting goals. Perhaps the women's movement and changing attitudes will help remove this unnecessary stumbling block from the paths of talented and aspiring women.

[1]Reprinted by permission of *Psychology Today Magazine*. Copyright © 1969 Ziff-Davis Publishing Co.

Learning Check

1. The curiosity drive includes needs for ______________ and ______________.

2. When a task is complex, the ideal level of arousal is ______________ when a task is simple, the optimal level of arousal is ______________.

3. The overall relationship between arousal and efficiency can be described as an ______________ ______________ function.

4. The need for achievement can be described as a desire to meet some internalized ______________ ______________.

5. People with high needs for achievement are attracted to "long shots" and "sure things." T or F?

Answers:

1. exploration, manipulation 2. low, high 3. inverted U 4. standard of excellence 5. F

Resources Summary

Motives initiate, sustain, and direct activities. Motivation typically involves the sequence: need, drive, response, goal, and goal attainment (need reduction). Behavior can be activated either by *needs* (push) or by *goals* (pull). The attractiveness of a goal is its *incentive* value. The three principal types of motives are: *primary* motives, *stimulus* motives, and *learned*, or *secondary*, motives. Most primary motives operate to maintain *homeostasis* in the body.

Hunger is influenced by such factors as fullness of the stomach, the taste of food, learning and cultural values, and other variables. The most direct control of eating is related to activity of the *hypothalamus*. Human obesity has been related to several problems including excessive sensitivity to external cues for eating. Lack of nutritional substances in the diet sometimes produces *specific hungers*.

Like hunger, thirst is affected by a number of factors including direct control by the hypothalamus. Pain avoidance is an unusual primary drive because it is *episodic*. Avoiding pain is partially learned. The sex drive is also unusual in that it is *non-homeostatic*.

The stimulus motives include drives for *exploration*, *manipulation*, *curiosity*, and needs for *sensory stimulation*. The stimulus motives appear to be innate. Drives for stimulation have been partially explained by the *arousal theory* of motivation, which states that an ideal level of bodily activation will be maintained if possible. Optimal performance at a task generally occurs at moderate levels of arousal. However, for simple tasks the ideal level may be higher, and for complex tasks it may be lower (*Yerkes-Dodson law*).

Social motives are learned, perhaps through association with primary motives. A large number of social motives have been identified and studied. One of the most prominent is the *need for achievement*. High needs for achievement are associated with a wide range of behavioral and personality characteristics.

Applications

We hope that the previous discussion will help you to understand better the operation of a number of basic motives. In this section we return to the topics of hunger and arousal for a look at some techniques for the control of each. Both are interesting topics, and the ideas described may prove useful to you. Let's begin with hunger.

Behavioral Dieting—Kicking the Food Habit

Most people today are aware that obesity may be hazardous to health, yet all around us are people who suffer from being overweight. The overweight run a high risk of developing heart and kidney diseases, of encountering dangerous complications in surgery, and of simply living fewer years than their slimmer neighbors. Before you count yourself out of this endangered group of people, consider this: Americans who are only 10 percent overweight eventually exhibit a 20 percent greater risk of dying before their time than do people of normal weight (Lappe, 1971). If you are not now overweight, perhaps you never will be. But the "battle of the bulge" is very common in our overfed culture, and chances are good that at some point you may need to control your weight.

Question: What can be done to control weight?

The basic approach for years has been to "diet"; that is, to restrict food intake drastically for a brief period. This, of course, is perfectly sensible in theory: You must eat less to lose weight. In practice, however, most people who lose weight by dieting regain it rapidly. What is really needed if one wishes to control weight is a complete overhaul of *eating habits* and control of the *external cues* for eating. The person who succeeds in changing eating habits can expect a permanent weight reduction. "Behavioral dieting," as this approach has been called, has repeatedly been proved superior to simple dieting for weight control. The following list is a collection of many of the behavioral techniques used to aid weight loss (compiled from Lake, 1973; Kiell, 1973; Mayer, 1968; and Trotter, 1974).

1. *Begin any weight control program with a physical checkup.* About 5 percent of all weight problems are physical.
2. *Learn your eating habits by observing yourself and keeping a "diet diary."* Begin by making a complete record of your eating habits for two weeks. Record where you eat, what you eat, and the feelings and events that occur just before and after eating. How do others around you respond to your eating? Is someone encouraging you to overeat?
3. *Count calories.* The only way to lose is to eat less, and calories allow you to keep an accurate record of your food intake.
4. *Develop techniques to control the act of eating.* Slow down, count your mouthfuls,

leave food on your plate, avoid eating alone (you're less likely to overeat in front of others).

5. *Learn to weaken your personal eating cues.* When you have learned when and where you do most of your eating, avoid these situations. Eat at other times and in other places. Be especially aware of the "night-eating syndrome." Most calories are consumed late in the day and at night. Keep food out of sight and find things to do to keep yourself busy during this dangerous period.
6. *Avoid snacks.* Buy only foods that require preparation, and fix only a single portion at a time. Delay the impulse to get a snack at least once, and several times if possible. Dull your appetite by having a cup of bouillon or a raw carrot.
7. *Exercise.* Physical activity burns calories. Stop saving steps and riding elevators. Add activity to your routine in every way you can think of.
8. *Get yourself committed to weight loss.* Involve as many people in your program as you can.
9. *Make a list of rewards you will receive if you change your eating habits and punishments that will occur if you don't.* You may find it helpful to set up specific rewards (see Chapter 24 for more details). Don't reward yourself with food.
10. *Chart your progress daily.* Record your weight, the number of calories eaten, whether you met your daily goal. (Set realistic goals by cutting down calories gradually. About a pound per week weight loss is realistic, but remember, you are changing habits, not just losing weight.)Take pride in your successes. Post your chart in a prominent place. This feedback on your progress is possibly the most important of all the techniques.

Be patient with this program. It takes years to develop eating habits. You can expect it to take at least several months to change them. If you are unsuccessful at losing weight with these techniques, you might find it helpful to seek the aid of a psychologist familiar with behavioral weight-loss techniques.

Body Rhythms and Arousal—Improving Your E.Q. (Efficiency Quotient)

Your body is a finely tuned instrument. Many of its functions are regulated by "internal clocks" that control a rhythmic cycle of changes every twenty-four hours. The cycles are called *circadian rhythms* (*circa* = about, *dia* = a day). An understanding of circadian rhythms and their effects can be quite useful.

Question: What kind of bodily changes are associated with these rhythms?

Almost a hundred bodily rhythms have been studied. The most important changes are in body temperature, blood pressure, urine volume, amino-acid level, and the activity of the liver and kidneys. These and a number of other bodily activities all reach a peak sometime during the day. Especially important is production of adrenalin, which causes general arousal, and is three to five times greater during the day (Luce, 1971). Most people have much more energy and are more efficient during their personal high point. The terms "day person" and "night person" are familiar references to such differences.

There are two major ways to make use of an awareness of circadian rhythms. The first is to learn your own personal high and low points. A good way to do this is to keep a log of your mood and energy level for each hour through the day. (See sample.) Do this for two weeks and then average your rating for each hour from early morning until bedtime. For increased efficiency, you can then schedule studying, chores, and recreation around your personal rhythms.

A second application is related to what has been called "time-zone fatigue" or "jet lag." It is a well-documented fact that businesspersons, dip-

Sample Body-Rhythm Log

Rating Scale: Mood: Very negative 1 2 3 4 5 Very positive
Energy: Very low 1 2 3 4 5 Very high

			Two-week average for:	
Time	*Mood*	*Energy level*	*Mood*	*Energy level*
8:00	3	2	3.2	2.5
9:00	3	3	3.0	3.1
10:00	4	3	3.4	3.6
Etc.			Etc.	

lomats, athletes, and other time-zone travelers frequently make errors or turn in poorer performances because their body rhythms have been temporarily disrupted. Even relatively minor changes in body rhythms cause a loss of efficiency as well as fatigue, irritability, nervousness, nausea, and a decline in mental agility.

Question: What does this have to do with those of us who are not world travelers?

There are few college students who have not at one time or another "burned the midnight oil," especially during a final-exam period. (Ah, there's a study in motivation!) During this or any other strenuous period, it is wise to remember the effects of disturbing bodily rhythms. Younger persons, of course, are less affected by disruptions, but everyone is susceptible, and any major deviation from your regular schedule of activities, sleep, and rest is likely to cost more than its worth. Often you can accomplish as much during one hour in the morning as you could have in three hours of work after midnight. The two-hours difference in efficiency might as well be spent sleeping. If you feel you must depart from your normal schedule, do it gradually over a period of days. If you can anticipate an upcoming body-rhythm change (when traveling, before finals week, or when doing shift work), adapt yourself to your expected schedule beforehand.

While you are learning to be aware of overall fluctuations in your level of arousal, it might also be helpful to pay attention to more specific variations. As pointed out earlier in the chapter, optimal performance at any task requires just the right amount of arousal. Simple tasks are performed best at high levels of arousal, and complex tasks, at moderate or low arousal. The athlete who "chokes up" or the student who "goes blank" in a test have both fallen prey to a too high level of arousal. On the other hand, the student who can't stay awake while studying suffers from a too low level of arousal.

There is no magic way of gaining control over your level of arousal, but by closely observing your own reactions, you should be able to make a list of things that consistently raise or lower arousal. These can then be used (within limits) to adjust your arousal level to a particular situation. The brief list below is offered as a starting place for constructing a list of your own.

Conditions that raise the level of arousal

- Vigorous physical exercise
- Pain or discomfort (uncomfortable chair for study, cold room, and the like)
- Mild hunger
- Fantasies about disaster, failure, anger, and so on (commonly referred to as getting "psyched up" in sports)

Conditions that lower the level of arousal

- Mild or repetitive exercise (walking, swimming, juggling)
- Voluntary relaxation (see Chapter 24 for instructions)
- Meditation, deep breathing
- Listening to soothing music
- Fantasies about previous successes, happy events, and pleasant surroundings

Questions for Discussion

1. Which of the primary drives do you consider the strongest? Why? Which occupies the greatest amount of your time and energies? How could the strength of the primary drives be established for animals?
2. Discuss some of the factors that contribute to overeating at Thanksgiving or a similar feast.
3. The sex drive is not essential for individual survival, and it can be easily interrupted by any of the other primary drives. Why do you think so much energy is directed toward sexuality in our culture?
4. In what ways have you observed the stimulus motives at work in human behavior? Does learning contribute to curiosity or needs for stimulation?
5. Does the American emphasis on competition (in your opinion) encourage achievement or discourage it? (Consider the effects, for example, when only one person can be considered the "winner" in many situations.)
6. How could you apply the concept of incentives to improve your motivation to study?
7. Have you experienced a major disruption of your body's circadian rhythms? What effect did this have on your functioning?

Suggestions for Further Reading

Berlyne, D. E. *Conflict, Arousal, and Curiosity.* McGraw-Hill, 1960.

Bindra, D., and J. Steward. *Motivation; Selected Readings.* Penguin, 1966.

Bolles, R. C. *Theory of Motivation.* 2nd ed. Harper & Row, 1975.

Mayer, J. *Overweight: Causes, Cost and Control.* Prentice-Hall, 1968.

McClelland, D. C. *The Achieving Society.* Van Nostrand, 1961.

Schachter, S. *Emotion, Obesity, and Crime.* Academic, 1971.

13 Emotion

Chapter Preview

Voodoo Death

In the reports of explorers and anthropologists, one finds occasional references to sudden death caused by "voodoo" or "magic." Few psychological phenomena spur more interest than these bizarre deaths. Here is an account of what happens in one tribe when a man discovers that he has been cursed by an enemy:

> He stands aghast, with his eyes staring at the treacherous pointers, and with his hands lifted as though to ward off the lethal medium, which he imagines is pouring into his body. His cheeks blanch and his eyes become glassy and the expression of his face becomes horribly distorted. . . . His body begins to tremble and the muscles twist involuntarily. He sways backwards and falls to the ground, and after a short time appears to be in a swoon; but soon he writhes as if in mortal agony, and, covering his face with his hands, begins to moan. . . . From this time onwards he sickens and frets, refusing to eat and keeping aloof from the daily affairs of the tribe. Unless help is forthcoming in the shape of a countercharm death is only a matter of a comparatively short time (Basedow, 1925; cited in Cannon, 1942).

This and other cases of voodoo death are difficult for those of us living in a modern society to believe. At first glance they seem to require a belief in the supernatural powers of magic. Actually, all they require is a belief in emotion. *Walter Cannon (1942), a well-known physiologist, studied a large number of voodoo deaths and concluded that they really do occur.*

Question: How could a voodoo curse cause death?

Cannon felt these deaths can be explained by changes in the body that accompany strong emotion. The person who has been cursed so completely believes he will die that he becomes terrified. Cannon believed the fear is so intense and lasting that it causes a heart attack or other bodily disaster.

More recent research suggests that Cannon's explanation was only partially correct. It now appears that such deaths are caused not by fear itself, but by the body's reaction *to fear. After a period of strong emotion, the parasympathetic nervous system normally restores balance to the body by reversing many of the changes caused by emotion. For example, during intense fear heart rate is increased by the sympathetic nervous system; to counteract this, the parasympathetic system later slows the heart. It is now believed that the cursed person's emotional response is so intense that the parasympathetic nervous system overreacts and slows the heart to a stop (Seligman, 1974). There is more to this story (as we will see in a later section of this chapter). For now, it is enough to say that emotions are not only the "spice of life." For some, they may be the spice of death as well.*

Resources

Dissecting an Emotion—How Do You Feel?

Have you ever seen a pound of anger, a quart of hate, or an ounce of joy? Of course, the question is ridiculous, yet we talk about emotions as if they were real "things." Rage, grief, ecstasy, joy, sadness, boredom—these and dozens of other terms are part of everyone's daily vocabulary. We use them so freely that it is easy to forget that emotions are *hypothetical constructs*. Like "personality," "intelligence," or "creativity," they cannot be observed directly. A person staring off into space might be bored, depressed, in love, or stoned (the last, by the way, is not an emotion). We usually must *infer* emotions from the actions and reactions of others (always a tricky business), or we must trust them to tell us how they feel. This and a number of other problems make the study of emotion difficult. The effort is worthwhile, however; emotions separate us from machines, plants, and pet rocks, and add an important dimension of meaning to human activities.

Parts of an Emotion There are a number of facets to any emotional experience. Consider the following vivid description of emotion from Dostoevsky's *Crime and Punishment*, in which Lizavita Ivanova is about to be murdered by the main character, Raskolnikov:

> . . . When she saw him run in, she trembled like a leaf and her face twitched spasmodically; she raised her hand as if to cover her mouth, but no scream came and she backed slowly away from him toward the corner, with her eyes

> on him in a fixed stare, but still without a sound, as if she had no breath left with which to cry out. He flung himself forward with the axe; her lips writhed pitifully like those of a young child when it is just beginning to be frightened and stands ready to scream.

Question: What does this tell us about emotion?

If you have ever experienced extreme fear like that described above, you will recognize that one part of any emotional experience is one's *subjective feelings*. Emotional feelings can be classified in terms of *intensity*, *pleasantness* or *unpleasantness*, and *complexity*. For example, joy is a simple, pleasant, and intense emotion. Jealousy is a complex, unpleasant emotion that may vary in intensity. Unfortunately, it is difficult to go beyond simple classification of subjective feelings because they are very difficult to describe. In one rather bizarre study, women were required to crush snails between their fingers and to describe their emotional reactions. The best they could do was to *name* their emotions (Coleman, 1949). Notice that Dostoevsky did not even try to describe the feeling of fear, only the reactions.

Emotional expressions are the second part of an emotion. When a person is afraid, we observe, as did Dostoevsky, that the person's hands tremble, her face contorts, and her posture becomes tense and defensive. Emotional expressions are particularly important for the study of emotion in animals, and the communication of emotion from one person to another.

Most people closely identify a pounding heart, sweating palms, "butterflies" in the stomach, and the like, with the experience of emotion. This is a valid observation since *physiological changes* taking place in the body are the core of fear, anger, joy, and other emotions. These changes, which are the third part of an emotion, include alterations in heart rate, blood pressure, perspiration, and other bodily "stirrings." Most of these reactions are caused by release of *adrenaline* (a general bodily stimulant) into the bloodstream and by actions of the nervous system.

Question: Are physical changes in the body different for different emotions?

There are differences, but they are minor. Your heart is as likely to pound during joy as it is during anger. This is why the fourth part of an emotion is important. Very basic to any emotional experience is the *interpretation* placed on it. This may be seen in some interesting ways. One is by the injection of adrenaline into laboratory subjects. This typically produces "cold emotions" in which the person feels "as if" he should be fearful, angry, or excited, but experiences no real emotion because he knows the drug caused these feelings (Marañon, 1924). A second example of the importance of emotional interpretations is provided by this case study:

Fig. 13-1 How accurately do facial expressions reveal emotion? After you have guessed what emotion these people are feeling, turn to page 307. (Photo courtesy of *The Record*, Hackensack, New Jersey.)

> Mister J. had recently suffered a divorce, lost his job, and had assumed responsibility for two small children. Mr. J. sought the aid of a psychologist during this stressful period of his life. The psychologist reports that he would occasionally get a call from Mr. J. asking for an appointment to discuss the onset of a deep depression. More often than not, Mr. J. would call back to cancel the meeting because his feelings of depression were a "false alarm." He had misinterpreted the fatigue and other early signs of a cold or flu as feelings of depression. In the context of his life situation it is easy to see how he might be mislead (Downey, 1976).

Theories of Emotion—Four Ways to Fear a Bear

Question: What causes emotion?

There are four major theories about what takes place when a person experiences an emotion. Let's take a brief look at each.

The Common Sense Theory of Emotion Common sense tells us that we see a bear, are frightened, and run (and sweat and yell). This is far too simple an explanation to satisfy any psychologist. Besides, it is wrong.

The James-Lange Theory (1884—1885) In the 1880s, American psychologist William James and Danish psychologist Carl Lange proposed a different version of the relationship between emotional feelings and bodily states. James and Lange suggested that "we are afraid of a bear because we run, or angry because we strike." In doing so, they turned the tables on our usual conception of emotion. Instead of assuming that bodily changes (such as increased heart rate) *follow* a feeling like fear, James and Lange assumed that bodily changes *precede* emotion. They argued that we see a bear, run, and *then* become conscious of fear. To support this idea, James pointed out that we often do not experience an emotion until after reacting. For example, imagine that you are driving and that a car suddenly pulls out in front of you. You swerve and skid to an abrupt halt at the side of the road. Only after you have come to a stop do you notice your pounding heart, rapid breathing, and tense muscles—and recognize your fear.

The Cannon-Bard Theory (1927) American physiologist Walter Cannon and his student Phillip Bard found a number of reasons to reject the James-Lange theory. While agreeing that the body becomes stirred up during emotion, Cannon and Bard noted that there are only slight differences in the physiology of various emotions. These differences are just not enough to allow for the rich and varied emotional life that humans experience. As a matter of fact, persons with spinal cord injuries still experience emotion, even though they may be unable to feel the normal sensations of physiological arousal (Hohmann, 1966).

Question: How do Cannon and Bard interpret emotion?

For the reasons above, and a number of others, Cannon (1932) proposed that emotional feelings and bodily arousal occur at the same time. In this version, seeing a bear activates the cortex, the thalamus, and the hypothalamus of the brain. Cannon believed the thalamus alerts both the hypothalamus and the cortex for action, but before the hypothalamus arouses the body, the cortex must give the go-ahead by deciding that the bear is dangerous. If the bear is seen as dangerous, bodily arousal, running, and feelings of fear will all be generated at once by brain activity.

Let us summarize: The commonsense theory of emotion is wrong. The James-Lange theory says emotion *is* bodily arousal and that the body must be aroused *before* an emotion is experienced. The Cannon-Bard theory moved emotions from the body to the head by saying that emotions are organized in the brain and that emotional feelings and bodily expressions occur simultaneously. There is a fourth possibility.

Schachter's Cognitive Theory of Emotion (1964) The previous theories are mostly concerned with emotion as physiological response. In Schachter's view, cognitive (mental) factors are also major determinants of emotions. According to Schachter, emotion is a combination of physical arousal and the *label* that is applied to that arousal. In other words, Schachter assumes that when a person becomes physically aroused, he has a need to interpret the arousal. The label (such as anger, fear, or happiness) he applies to his emotional feelings will be influenced by past experiences, the situation in which he finds himself, and the reactions of those around him.

To test this theory, Schachter and Singer (1962) injected subjects with the drug adrenaline. Subjects were misinformed about the drug they were receiving. Instead of adrenaline, they were told that they were receiving a vitamin being tested for its effects on vision. While this vitamin was supposedly taking effect, subjects were asked to wait in a room with another subject. The second "subject" was really an accomplice of the experimenters' who was trained to act very *happy* or very *angry*. As the adrenaline began to take effect, subjects found themselves in a room with someone who was joking, doodling, flying paper airplanes, and generally acting extremely happy *or* with someone who was acting very angry by criticizing the experimental questionnaire, complaining about the wait, and eventually stomping out of the room.

Fig. 13-2 Which theory of emotion best describes the reactions of these people? Given the complexity of emotion, each theory appears to possess an element of truth. (Photo courtesy of Marriott's Great America.)

Question: What does this have to do with the person's emotions?

Schachter and Singer were interested in what would happen when the adrenaline took effect and a subject began to feel aroused. Would the actions of the other "student" influence the emotions felt by the real subject? They found that if subjects were *correctly informed* about the effects of adrenaline (pounding heart, trembling hands), the antics of the actor had little effect on them. Informed subjects knew the drug had caused their unusual feelings. Those who were *uninformed* or *misinformed* (told that the drug would cause numbness and itching) were highly influenced by the "anger" and "happiness" conditions.

Faced with a stirred-up body and no explanation for the way they were feeling, subjects became happy or angry in accordance with the situation in which they found themselves. Schachter would predict, then, that if you met a bear, you would be aroused. If the bear seemed unfriendly, you would interpret his arousal as fear, and if the bear was throwing paper airplanes, you would be happy, amazed, and relieved!

Attribution We move now from fear of bear bodies to appreciation of bare bodies. Stuart Valins (1967) has added an interesting refinement to Schachter's theory of cognitive labeling. According to Valins, perception of emotion in any situation depends upon what you *attribute* your feelings of physical arousal to. To demonstrate attribution, Valins (1966) showed undergraduate male students a series of slides of nude females. While watching the slides, subjects heard an amplified heartbeat that they believed was their own. In reality they were listening to a recorded heartbeat carefully designed to beat *louder* and *stronger* when some (but not all) of the slides were shown.

After viewing the slides, subjects were asked to rate which they found most attractive. Students exposed to the false heart-rate information consistently rated slides that were paired with a "pounding heart" as the most attractive. In other words, when a subject saw a slide and heard his heartbeat become more pronounced, he attributed his "emotion" to the slide and his interpretation seems to have been "Now that one I like!" This and similar experiments make it clear that emotion is much more than just an agitated body. Perception, experience, attitudes, judgment, and many other more clearly "mental" factors also affect emotion.

Learning Check

Check your comprehension by answering these questions.

1. See if you can list the four components of an emotion. __________

____

2. Injection of adrenaline in laboratory subjects produces nonemotional physiological changes, described as ____________________.

3. According to the James-Lange theory of emotion, we see a bear, are frightened, and run. T or F?

4. The Cannon-Bard theory of emotion says that bodily arousal and emotional experience occur ______________________.

5. Schachter's theory of emotion emphasizes labeling and other ______________________ factors.

6. The example of the man who thought he was depressed when he was actually ill demonstrates Valin's concept of attribution. T or F?

Answers:

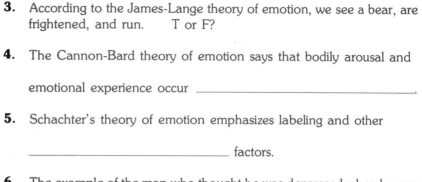

1. subjective feelings, emotional expressions, physiological changes, interpretation **2.** cold emotion **3.** F **4.** at the same time **5.** cognitive **6.** T. He *attributed* his feelings to his stressful circumstances.

Physiology and Emotion—Arousal, Sudden Death, and Lying

We have seen that emotion is part "mind" and part body or part intellectual and part "animal." To a large degree the physical aspects of emotion are innate or built into the body. The physical reactions of an African Bushman frightened by a wild animal and an urbane city dweller frightened by a prowler are quite similar. Unpleasant emotions produce especially consistent reactions. Among the most frequent are: pounding heart, muscular tenseness, irritability, dryness of the throat and mouth, sweating, "butterflies" in the stomach, frequent urination, trembling, restlessness, sensitivity to loud noises, and a large number of internal reactions (Shaffer, 1947). The consistency of these reactions is tied to the fact that they are caused by the *autonomic nervous system* (ANS). As you may recall from the discussion in Chapter 3, the reactions of the ANS are *automatic* and not normally under voluntary control. There are two divisions to the ANS, one called the *sympathetic* branch, and the other, the *parasympathetic* branch.

Question: What do these do during emotion?

The sympathetic branch prepares the body for emergency action—"fight or flight"—by arousing a number of bodily systems and inhibiting others. (Sympathetic nervous system effects are listed in Table 13-1.) These changes have a purpose. Sugar is released into the bloodstream for quick energy, the heart beats faster to distribute blood to the muscles, the unnecessary process of digestion is temporarily inhibited, blood flow in the skin is restricted to reduce bleeding, and so forth. Most of the sympathetic reactions increase the chances that a person or an animal will survive an emergency.

The actions of the parasympathetic branch generally reverse emotional arousal and calm and relax the body. After a period of high emotion, the heart is slowed, the pupils return to normal size, blood flow shifts away

Table 13-2 Sympathetic Nervous System Effects

Organ	*Parasympathetic system*	*Sympathetic system*
Pupil of eyes	Constricts to diminish light	Dilates to increase light
Tear glands Mucous membrane of nose and throat Salivary glands	Stimulate secretion	Inhibit secretion Causes dryness
Heart	Slowing, constriction of blood vessels	Acceleration, dilation of blood vessels to increase blood flow
Lungs, windpipe	Constrict bronchi of lungs to relax breathing	Dilate bronchi to increase breathing
Esophagus Stomach Abdominal blood vessels	Stimulate secretions and movement	Inhibit secretions and movements, diverts blood flow
Liver	Liberates bile	Retains bile
Pancreas	———	Releases blood sugar
Intestines	Stimulate secretion	Inhibit secretion
Rectum Kidney Bladder	Excitation, expulsion of feces and urine	Inhibition, retention of feces and urine
Skin blood vessels	Dilate, increase blood flow	Constrict, skin becomes cold and clammy
Sweat glands	Inhibit	Stimulated to increase perspiration
Hair follicles	Relaxed	Tensed to make hair stand on end (piloerection)

from the muscles and back to the internal organs, and so forth. In addition to restoring balance, the parasympathetic system helps build up and conserve bodily energy.

The parasympathetic system responds much more slowly than the sympathetic. This is why when you experience an emotion like fear, increased heart rate, muscular tension, and other signs of arousal do not subside until twenty or thirty minutes after the threat has passed.

As we noted in the chapter preview, the parasympathetic system may overreact during intense fear and in rare cases cause death. Voodoo curses are not the only cause of such deaths. There is evidence that in times of war the pressures of combat can be so intense that some soldiers literally die of fear (Moritz & Zamchech, 1946). Even in civilian life such deaths are apparently possible. In one case a terrified young woman was admitted to a hospital because she felt she was going to die. A backwoods midwife had predicted that the woman's two sisters would die before their sixteenth and twenty-first birthdays. Both died as predicted. The midwife also predicted that this woman would die before her twenty-third birthday. She was found dead in her hospital bed the day after she was admitted. It was two days before her twenty-third birthday (Zimbardo, 1975). The woman was a victim of her own terror.

Lie Detectors Because bodily changes caused by the autonomic nervous system are good indicators of emotion, a number of techniques for measuring them have been developed. One of the most interesting uses of these techniques is their application to the detection of lies. If you have not yet done so, there is a good chance you will take a "lie detector" test at some time in your life. Of course, this does not mean you are likely to become a criminal. It simply reflects the fact that a growing number of businesses and corporations in the United States are using lie detectors to screen potential employees and to maintain the honesty of current employees. There is reason to question such practices on the basis of both the accuracy and the ethics of "lie detection."

Question: What is a lie detector? Do lie detectors really detect lies?

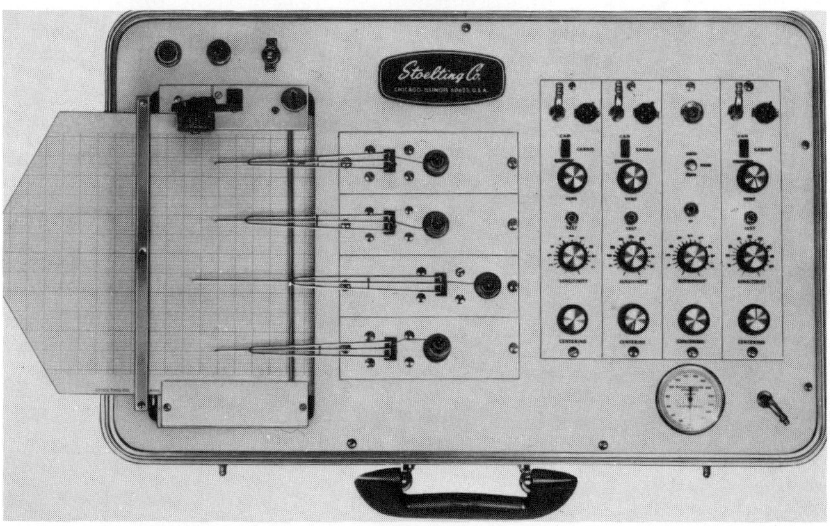

Fig. 13-3 A typical polygraph includes devices for the measurement of heart rate, blood pressure, breathing, and galvanic skin response. Pens mounted on the top of the machine make a record of emotional responses on a moving strip of paper. (Photo courtesy of the manufacturer, Stoelting Company, Chicago, Illinois.)

The lie detector is more accurately referred to as a *polygraph*. A polygraph (the word means many writings) is a portable device capable of drawing a record of changes in *heart rate*, *blood pressure*, *breathing rate*, and the *galvanic skin response* (GSR). (The GSR is recorded from the surface of the hand by electrodes that measure skin conductance or, more simply, sweating.) The polygraph has become popularly known as a lie detector because of its frequent use in criminology and job interviewing. To be more accurate, a polygraph is not a lie detector at all—it is a *nervousness* detector.

When attempting to detect a lie, the polygraph operator begins by asking a number of neutral (nonemotional) questions. ("What is your name? What did you have for lunch?" And so forth.) During this procedure a "baseline" or normal emotional responsiveness is established. Then more critical questions can be asked. ("Have you ever stolen money from an employer?" "Did you murder Hensley?") A person who lies will presumably become anxious or emotional when answering critical questions.

Question: Wouldn't a person be nervous just from being questioned?

Yes, but to minimize this problem, a skilled polygraph examiner asks a *series* of questions with critical items mixed among them. An innocent person may respond emotionally to the whole procedure, but supposedly only a guilty person will show increased response to key questions. For example, a suspected bank robber might be showed a picture and asked, "Was the teller who was robbed this person? Was it this person?" And so forth (Lykken, 1974). However, even when such precautions are taken, the polygraph can be quite inaccurate. Proponents of lie detection claim from 90 to 95 percent accuracy, but in one laboratory experiment, accuracy was lowered to 25 percent by subjects who intentionally thought exciting or upsetting thoughts during questioning. In another part of the same experiment accuracy was lowered to 10 percent by subjects who randomly tensed and released their toe muscles (reported by Smith, 1971).

It should also be noted that only a few states have passed laws requiring polygraph operators to be licensed. Many working polygraphers have had very limited training. Under these circumstances, some states have adopted a law forbidding employers to require job applicants to take a polygraph test as a condition of employment. The fact remains, however, that there is a good chance you will at some time be given a polygraph. The best advice under such circumstances is to remain calm and to actively challenge the outcome if the machine inaccurately questions your honesty.

Learning Check

See if you can correctly answer these questions:

1. Emotional arousal is closely related to activity of the ____________ nervous system.

2. The sympathetic system prepares the body for "fight or flight." T or F?

3. The parasympathetic system inhibits digestion and raises blood pressure and heart rate. T or F?

4. What bodily changes are measured by a polygraph? ____________

____

5. The polygraph is really a ______________________ detector.

Answers: **1.** autonomic **2.** T **3.** F **4.** heart rate, blood pressure, breathing rate, galvanic skin response **5.** nervousness or emotion

Development and Expression of Emotions—Feeling Babies and Talking Bodies

Question: How do emotions develop? Are some emotions more basic than others?

From his experiments with infants, John B. Watson identified three emotions that he considered unlearned. These are: *rage*, elicited in an infant by restricting movement; *fear*, elicited by loud noises, loss of support, and sudden shaking; and *joy*, elicited by stroking, tickling, and patting (Watson, 1930). Some authors have tried to explain more complex emotions as mixtures of these basic reactions. For example, a child about to eat a stolen cookie may be seen as having two combined emotions. On one hand, the pleasure of eating the cookie produces joy; on the other, the possibility of being punished causes fear. Combining the two feelings generates the emotion of guilt (Millinson, 1967). Likewise, we could consider feelings of jealousy to be a mixture of affection, anger, and fear.

Even the basic reactions of rage, fear, and joy take some time to develop. General *excitement* is the only emotional response a newborn infant experiences. However, as any parent can tell you, the emotional life of a baby blossoms rapidly. One researcher (Bridges, 1932) observed a large number of babies and found that all the basic human emotions (including those that are learned and those that are not) appear before age two. Bridges found that there is a consistent order in which emotions appear and that the first basic split in development is between pleasant and unpleasant emotions (see Fig. 13-4). Babies, in other words, rapidly become capable of letting others know what they like and dislike. (Prove this to yourself sometime by driving a baby buggy.)

Question: Are children more emotional than adults?

Studies have shown that the occurrence of temper tantrums declines drastically between infancy and adolescence and that emotional outbursts

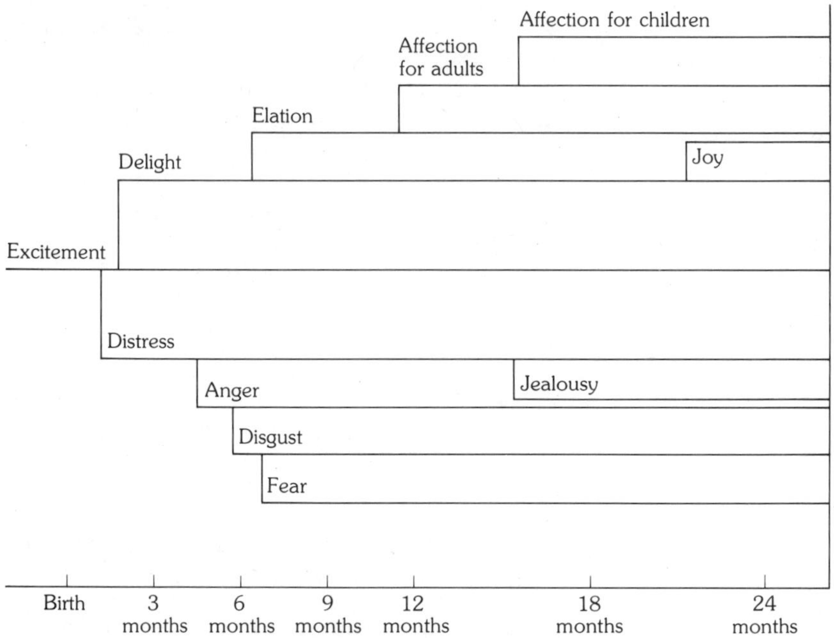

Fig. 13-4 In the human infant emotions are rapidly differentiated from an initial capacity for excitement. (After K. M. B. Bridges, 1932. Reprinted by permission of The Society for Research in Child Development, Inc.)

in general tend to become less intense as people grow older (MacFarlane *et al.*, 1954; Chown & Heron, 1965).

Question: Does this mean that people "mellow" as they age, or do they simply learn to suppress underlying emotions?

The answer is debatable, but some suppression undoubtedly does take place. For example, men and women show a difference in willingness to cry that is obviously learned. A little boy in our culture usually is encouraged to "be a man" by learning not to cry. This is unfortunate. It is pretty generally accepted by psychologists that free expression of emotion is essential for personal adjustment. Many males pay a high price for their "manhood" by denying themselves crying as an emotional outlet.

Emotional Expression Are human emotional expressions a carry-over from more primitive and animal-like stages of human evolution? Charles Darwin thought so. Darwin (1872) observed that tigers, monkeys, dogs, and human beings all bare their teeth in the same way during rage. Darwin believed that emotional expressions were retained during the course of human evolution because communicating one's feelings to others is an aid to survival.

Question: Then are emotional expressions the same for all people?

The most basic expressions appear to be fairly universal. Children who are born deaf and blind and who, therefore, have little opportunity to learn emotional expressions from others use the same facial gestures as others to display joy, sadness, disgust, and so on. In fact, the gestures of such children may be one of the few examples of "pure" emotional expression. By adulthood, most people have learned to carefully control facial expression so that many gestures become unique to various cultures. Among the Chinese, for example, sticking out the tongue is a gesture of surprise, not of disrespect or teasing. Despite cultural differences, basic facial reactions to happiness, pain, fear, and sadness are all fairly recognizable (Gitter *et al.*, 1972). It's also nice to note that a smile is the most universal and easily recognizable facial expression of emotion.

Body Language If a friend approached you and said, "Hey ugly, what are you doing?" would you be offended? Probably not, because such expressions are usually accompanied by a big grin. The facial and bodily gestures of emotion speak a language all their own and add an additional message to what is said verbally. The study of communication through body movement, posture, gestures, and facial expressions is called *kinesics* (informally referred to as "body language").

Question: What kinds of messages are sent with body language?

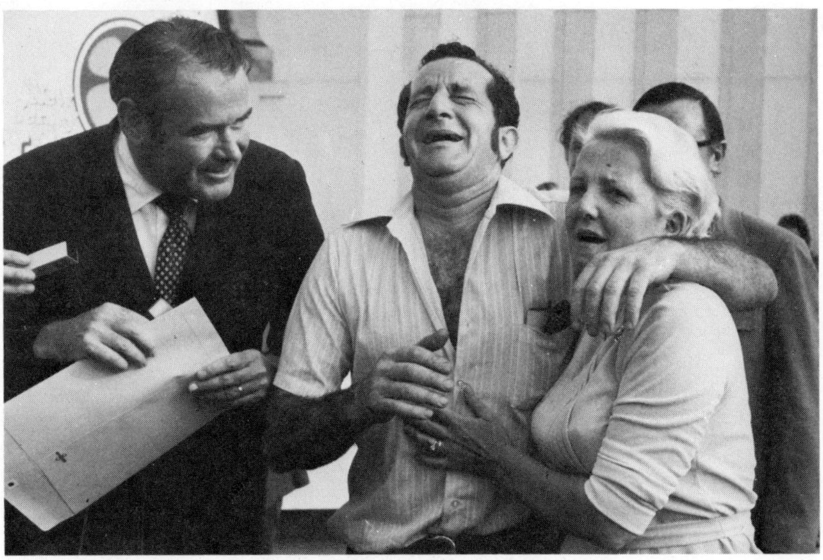

Fig. 13-5 Facial and bodily gestures do not always allow an observer to accurately "read" emotion. The agonized expression on the face of Frank De Vito is deceptive. Mr. De Vito and his wife have just learned that he has won $1 million in the New Jersey state lottery. (Photo courtesy of *The Record*, Hackensack, New Jersey.)

Most of the popular books on body language (for example, Fast, 1970) tend to list particular meanings for gestures. For example, a woman who stands rigidly, crosses her arms over her breasts, or sits with her legs tightly crossed is supposedly sending a "hands off" message. But researchers in the field of kinesics emphasize that gestures are rarely this fixed in meaning (Swensen, 1973). Being more realistic, we would say that an overall *emotional tone* is communicated.

Facial expressions accurately portray feelings of *pleasantness-unpleasantness*, *attention-rejection*, and *activation* (Schlosberg, 1954). By smiling when giving a friend a "hard time," you add the emotional messages of pleasantness and acceptance to the verbal insult and change its meaning. As they say in movie Westerns, it makes a big difference to "Smile when you say that, pardner."

Fig. 13-6 Emotions are often unconsciously revealed by gestures and body positioning. (Photo by Susan Miller.)

Other emotional feelings are telegraphed by the body. The most general seem to be *relaxation or tension* and *liking or disliking*. Relaxation is expressed by casual positioning of the arms and legs, leaning back (if sitting), and spreading the arms and legs. Liking is expressed mainly by leaning toward a person or object (Mehrabian, 1969). Since people learn to maintain much control over their facial gestures, body positioning can reveal feelings that would normally be concealed. Who do you "lean toward"?

Coping with Emotion—When Is Fear Healthy?

You have been selected to give a speech to 300 people; or, a physician has informed you that you must undergo a dangerous and painful operation; or, the one true love of your life walks out the door. What would your emotional response to these situations be? How do you cope with an emotional threat? According to Richard Lazarus (1968), there are two important steps in the process of coping with a threatening situation. The first is *primary appraisal* in which you decide if a situation is threatening or not. Then you make a *secondary appraisal* during which you choose a means of meeting the threat.

The emotional effects of appraising a threat have been demonstrated in a fascinating experiment performed by Joseph C. Spiesman and his associates (1964). These researchers used a graphic film called *Subincision* to stimulate emotional responses in volunteer subjects. Subincision is a ritual used to initiate adolescent boys into manhood in a primitive Australian tribe. The filmed procedure begins with three or four adults holding the boys down to prevent escape. Then a crude and obviously painful operation is performed in which the adolescent's penis is slit on the underside for its entire length. To add insult to injury, the operation is performed with a sharpened flintstone. Needless to say, American viewers respond emotionally to the gory details of this film.

The film was shown in four different versions to test the emotional effects of different appraisals. The first had no sound track. The second emphasized the painful and traumatic aspects of the operation. The third treated the operation in an intellectual and distant way. The fourth glossed over the threatening aspects of the operation and denied that it was painful.

Question: Did the sound tracks affect emotional reactions?

Recordings of heart rate and GSR showed quite clearly that appraisal of a situation affects emotional response. The film emphasizing traumatic aspects of the operation produced an increase in emotion over that caused by the silent film. On the other hand, the intellectual and denial sound tracks reduced emotion. The way a situation is "sized up" therefore becomes very important to coping with it. Public speaking, for instance, can be appraised as an intense threat, or as a chance to perform. Emphasizing the threat by imagining failure, rejection, or embarrassment obviously invites disaster. On the other hand, underestimating the threat of a situation can also create problems. The key to effectively appraising a threatening situation seems to be to achieve a realistic amount of fear. Either too much or too little reduces one's ability to cope.

Question: How could too little fear be a problem?

Irving Janis (1958) has studied the adjustment of people who must undergo major surgery. He found that *moderate* levels of fear were associated with better adjustment to the pain, helplessness, and vulnerability felt after the operations. People who showed little fear beforehand failed to do the "work of worrying" necessary for anticipating and rehearsing the approaching discomforts. Those who showed extreme fear were adversely affected because they added emotional upheaval to the stress of surgery. Fear appears to be a very useful emotion, but only when it is in proportion to the amount of threat.

Learned Helplessness—Is There Hope?

Question: What would happen if a person appraised a threatening situation as hopeless?

Bruno Bettelheim (1960), who survived imprisonment in Nazi concentration camps, has described a reaction he calls "give-up-itis." Many of the prisoners felt so helpless that they developed a "zombie-like" detachment that made them into "walking corpses." Martin Seligman (1974) has described a similar reaction in Vietnam prisoner of war camps. Seligman reports the case of a young marine who had adapted unusually well to the stresses of being a POW. His health was apparently related to a promise made by his captors that if he would cooperate he would be released on a certain date. As the date approached, his spirits soared. Then came a devastating blow. He had been deceived. There was never any intention of releasing him. He immediately lapsed into a deep depression, refused to eat or drink, and died shortly thereafter.

Examples such as these are admittedly extreme, but they demonstrate once again the power of emotions. Recent attempts to understand such events have focused on the concept of *learned helplessness*.

Learned helplessness has been demonstrated in the laboratory with animals tested in a shuttle box. If placed in one side of a divided box, dogs will quickly learn to leap to the other side to escape an electric shock. If they are given a warning before the shock occurs (for example, a light dims), most dogs will learn to avoid the shock by leaping the barrier before the shock arrives. This is true of most dogs, but not those who have learned to feel helpless.

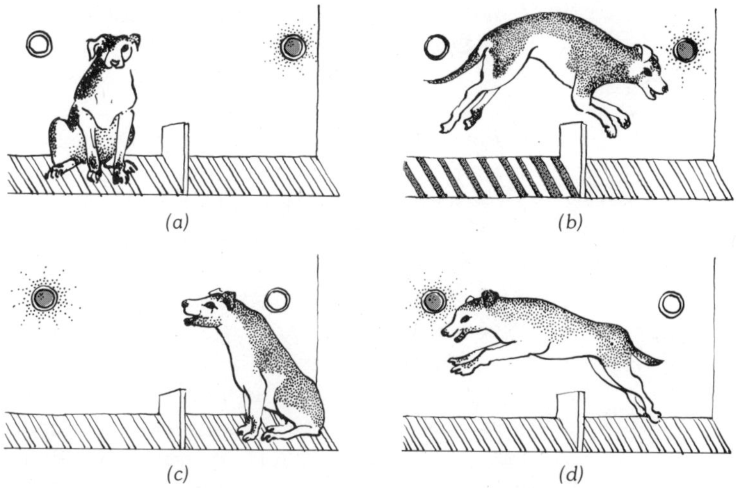

Fig. 13-7 In the normal course of escape and avoidance learning a light dims shortly before the floor is electrified *(a)*. Since the light does not yet have meaning for the dog, it receives a shock (noninjurious, by the way) and leaps the barrier *(b)*. Dogs soon learn to watch for the dimming of the light *(c)* and to jump before receiving a shock *(d)*. Dogs made to feel "helpless" rarely even learn to escape shock, much less to avoid it.

Question: How is a dog made to feel helpless?

Before being tested in the shuttle box, some dogs were placed in a harness (from which they could not escape) and were given several painful shocks. The animal was helpless to prevent these shocks (Overmier & Seligman, 1967). When placed in the shuttle box, these dogs reacted to the first shock by crouching, howling, and whining. None tried to escape. They helplessly resigned themselves to their fate—after all, they had already learned that there was nothing they could do about shock.

Martin Seligman (1972) believes that the concept of learned helplessness applies to human behavior as well as it does to animals. As an example, Seligman describes the fate of Archie, a fifteen-year-old boy. For Archie, school has been an unending series of shocks and failures. Other students treat him like he's stupid; in class he rarely answers questions because he doesn't know some of the words. He feels knocked down every direction he turns. These may not be electrical shocks, but they are certainly psychological "shocks," and Archie has learned to feel helpless to prevent them. When he leaves school his chances of success will be poor. He has learned to passively endure whatever shocks life has in store for him.

Seligman has also noted the similarity between learned helplessness and depression. Depression is one of the most widespread emotional problems in the United States today.

Question: Does Seligman's research give any clues about how to "unlearn" helplessness?

Hope With dogs, the most effective technique has been to forcibly drag them away from the shock into the "safe" compartment. After this is done several times, the animals regain "hope" and feelings of control over the environment. Just how this can be accomplished with humans is a question for further research. It seems obvious, however, that someone like Archie would benefit from an educational program that would allow him to "succeed" repeatedly.

We might even be able to "immunize" people against helplessness and depression by giving them experience at mastering seemingly impossible challenges. The Outward Bound schools, in which people pit themselves against the rigors of mountaineering, white-water canoeing, and wilderness survival, might serve as a model for such a program.

As a final note, the value of hope should not be overlooked. As fragile as this emotion seems to be, it is a powerful antidote to depression and helplessness. As an individual, you may find hope in religion, nature, human companionship, or even technology. Wherever you find it, remember its value: It is among the most important of all human emotions.

Learning Check

1. The only recognizable emotional response in a newborn baby is fear. T or F?

2. Some facial expressions of emotion appear to be innate. T or F?

3. A formal term for "body language" is ________________.

4. Depression in humans is similar to learned ________________ observed in animal experiments.

5. List the three emotions that John B. Watson considered innate:

____

Answers:

1. F. Excitement is the first response. **2.** T **3.** kinesics **4.** helplessness **5.** fear, rage, joy

Resources Summary

The four major parts of an emotion are: *subjective feelings*, *emotional expressions*, *physiological changes* in the body, and *interpretation* of the emotion. Psychologists have advanced three major theories about what takes place during emotion. The James-Lange theory says that emotional experience follows the bodily reactions of emotion. The Cannon-Bard theory says that bodily reactions and emotional experience occur at the same time and that emotions are organized in the brain. Schachter's cognitive theory emphasizes the importance of labels or interpretations applied to feelings of bodily arousal. Also important is the process of *attribution*, a term referring to the emotional effects of associating bodily arousal with a particular person, object, or situation.

Physical changes which accompany emotion are caused by the action of *adrenaline*, a hormone released into the bloodstream, and by the *autonomic nervous system* (ANS). The *sympathetic* branch of the ANS is primarily responsible for arousing the body, the *parasympathetic* branch, for quieting it. The *polygraph* or "lie detector" measures emotion by monitoring heart rate, blood pressure, breathing rate, and the galvanic skin response (GSR). The accuracy of the polygraph as a lie detector has been challenged by recent research.

Emotions develop from the general excitement observed in newborn babies. Three of the basic emotions—fear, rage, and joy—may be unlearned. Basic emotional expressions like smiling, frowning, or baring one's teeth when angry may also be unlearned. However, unlearned expressions are modified by learning and cultural factors. Bodily gestures ("body language") also express emotion, mainly by communicating *emotional tone* rather than specific messages.

The *appraisal* of a situation greatly affects emotional response to it. Appraisal of threat is particularly related to fear reactions. Moderate amounts of fear may be helpful in a stressful situation. The concept of *learned helplessness* has been used to explain failure to cope with a threatening situation.

Applications

Coping with Death—A Problem for Everyone

There are a number of situations in each person's life that are heavily charged with emotion. The second most difficult to handle is probably the death of a close friend or relative; the first is one's own impending death.

Death is a topic of importance to us all. The statistics on death are very convincing: 1 out of 1 dies. In spite of this, there tends to be a conspiracy of silence surrounding the topic of death. Perhaps this is because most of us would rather not be reminded of our ultimate demise. Modern medical practice and the funeral industry have also served to insulate most people from contact with death. As a result, most of us are poorly informed about a process that is as basic as birth.

We have seen in this chapter that it is very valuable to understand one's own emotions and those of others. With this in mind, this section is devoted to an investigation of emotional responses before, during, and after death.

Fears of Death

Fears of death are not so extensive as might be supposed. In a public opinion poll of 1,500 adults, only about 4 percent showed evidence of directly fearing their own death (Kastenbaum & Aisenberg, 1972). Those fears which do exist apparently change with age. Hall (1922) found that younger individuals fear the *occurrence* of death, whereas older people fear the *circumstances* of death. In another study, elderly patients were rated for signs of fear before death. It was found that feelings of acceptance, anticipation, and, in some cases, apathy, far outnumbered instances of fear before death.

These findings seem to indicate a general lack of fear about death, but there is another possible interpretation. It may be more accurate to say that they reflect a deeply ingrained tendency to deny the reality of death. The mere fact that death has been something of a taboo subject suggests that underlying fears do exist. When *Psychology Today* surveyed its readers on the subject of death, it was found that less than one-third of those who replied grew up in families in which death was openly talked about (Schneidman, 1971). The average person's exposure to death unfortunately consists of the artificial and obviously unrealistic portrayals of death on television. It has been estimated that by the time a person is fourteen years old, he or she will have witnessed 18,000 T.V. deaths. With almost no exceptions these will have been *homocides*, not deaths due to illness or aging (Tobin, 1972).

The Stages of Death

A more direct indication of emotional responses to death comes from the work of Elizabeth Kübler-

Ross (1969). Kübler-Ross, a *thanatologist* (one who studies death), has spent hundreds of hours at the bedsides of the terminally ill. She has found that the dying person tends to go through a series of emotional stages in order to prepare for death. The five basic steps are:

1. *Denial and isolation.* The initial reaction to impending death is an attempt to deny its reality and to isolate oneself from all information confirming that death is really going to occur. Initially the person may be convinced that "It's all a mistake," that lab reports or x-rays have been mixed up, or that a physician is in error. This may proceed to attempts to ignore or avoid any reminder of the situation.
2. *Anger.* In this stage the dying individual says, "Why me?" As he faces the ultimate frustration of having everything he ever valued stripped away, the person's anger spills over into rage or envy toward those who will continue living. Even good friends may temporarily become enemies because of their health.
3. *Bargaining.* During this period the person bargains with himself or with his God. The person says, "Just let me live a little longer and I'll do anything to earn it." Individuals may bargain for time by trying to be "good" ("I'll never smoke again"), by righting past wrongs, or by praying that if they are granted more time they will dedicate themselves to their religion.
4. *Depression.* As death draws nearer and the person begins to recognize that it cannot be prevented, feelings of futility, exhaustion, and deep depression set in. The person recognizes that he will be separated from friends, loved ones, and the familiar routines of life, and this causes a profound sadness.
5. *Acceptance.* Assuming that death is not sudden, many people eventually reach a stage during which they calmly accept death. The person is neither happy nor sad, but is at peace with himself. This is usually a quiet time when the struggle with death has been resolved. The need to talk about death is ended, and silent companionship from others is frequently all that is desired.

Not all terminally ill individuals experience all these stages, and the stages may not always occur in this order. Also, not everyone reaches a stage of acceptance when dying. Some people fight it to the end. Individual styles of dying vary greatly according to psychological maturity, religious orientation, age, occupation, the attitudes of relatives, and so forth. Nevertheless, Kübler-Ross' is the best available summary of emotional reactions to death.

Question: How can I make use of this information?

This information can be put to use in a number of ways. First of all, it can help both the dying individual and survivors to recognize and to cope with periods of depression, anger, denial, and bargaining. Secondly, it is helpful to realize that close friends or relatives of the dying person may go through many of the same emotional stages before or after the person's death.

Perhaps the most important thing to recognize is that the dying person has a need to share feelings with others and to discuss death openly. Too often the dying person feels isolated and separated from others by the wall of silence erected by doctors, nurses, and family members. Adults tend to "freeze up" with a dying person, saying things like, "I don't know how to deal with him." Understanding what the dying person is going through may make it easier for you to offer support at this important time. A simple willingness to be with the person and to honestly share his or her feelings can help bring dignity, acceptance, and meaning to the difficult process of dying.

Bereavement After a friend or relative has died there is generally a period of grief. Grief is such a consistent reaction to the loss brought by a death that even animals have been observed to grieve for a lost mate (Averill, 1968). Grief normally begins with an initial period of numbness and shock. This may be accompanied by an inability to accept the loss and, sometimes, anguished outbursts of anger. In our culture, funeral services frequently serve as useful outlets for grief by encouraging the release of emotions. The first intense emotions of grief then give way to days, weeks, or sometimes months of depression. This period may be marked by feelings of apathy and futility, by insomnia, a loss of appetite, and similar signs of depression.

Most psychologists consider the emotional reactions of grief an essential part of adjustment to the loss of a friend or relative. In fact, a person who avoids this "grief work" by suppressing emotions may later experience a much more severe and lasting depression.

Question: How can normal grief be distinguished from unhealthy depression?

This is a rather difficult judgment to make because it is related to many psychological dimensions. Practically speaking, a useful answer can be found in a list of ten "danger signals" compiled by the National Association for Mental Health to help people distinguish normal depression from reactions that require professional help. Here is the list:

1. A general and lasting feeling of hopelessness and despair.
2. Inability to concentrate, making reading, writing, and conversation difficult. Thinking and activity are slowed because the mind is absorbed by inner anguish.
3. Changes in physical activities like eating, sleeping, and sex. Frequent physical complaints with no evidence of physical illness.
4. Loss of self-esteem, which brings on continual questioning of personal worth.
5. Withdrawal from others due to immense fear of rejection.
6. Threats or attempts to commit suicide, viewed as a way out of a hostile environment and a belief that life is worthless.
7. Hypersensitivity to words and actions of others and general irritability.
8. Misdirected anger and difficulty in handling most feelings. Self-directed anger because of perceived worthlessness may produce general anger directed at others.
9. Feelings of guilt in many situations. A depressed person assumes he is wrong or responsible for the unhappiness of others.
10. Extreme dependency on others. Feelings of helplessness and then anger at the helplessness.

No single item (except number 6) necessarily indicates dangerous depression, but if several are observed, it should be assumed that it would be wise to seek professional help. This scale, of course, applies to instances of depression other than those caused by bereavement and may be used as a general guide for judging the severity of depression.

Questions for Discussion

1. Do you consider yourself more or less emotional than average? What role has learning played in the development of your emotional life? (Consider the influence of family, friends, and culture.)
2. In what ways have emotions contributed to your enjoyment of life? In what ways have they caused problems for you?
3. There is an element of truth to each of the theories of emotion. Which seems to apply best to your own emotional experience?
4. What would be the advantages and disadvantages of being emotionless? (You might use Mr. Spock from "Star Trek" as a model for answering this question.)
5. Does a person have the right to commit suicide? Should a person with a terminal illness have the right to request euthanasia (induced painless death)? Should extraordinary medical procedures be used to prolong the life of a dying individual? What do your answers reveal about your attitudes toward death?
6. Did you learn "body language" from your parents? How similar are your facial and hand gestures to theirs?
7. In what ways do schools, parents, and the government encourage feelings of helplessness? In what ways do they (or could they) add to feelings of confidence, competence, or "hope"?

Suggestions for Further Reading

Darwin, C. *The Expression of Emotions in Man and Animals.* Chicago University Press, 1965 (first published in 1872).

Kübler-Ross, E. *On Death and Dying.* Macmillan, 1969.

Mandler, G. "Emotion." In *New Directions in Psychology*, vol. 1. Holt, 1962.

Mark, V. H., and F. R. Ervin. *Violence and the Brain*. Harper & Row, 1970.

Seligman, M., "Fall into Helplessness," *Psychology Today* (June) 1973, pp. 43—48.

Schachter, S., and J. E. Singer. "Cognitive, Social, and Physiological Determinants of the Emotional State," *Psychological Review* (**69**), 1962, pp. 379—399.

14 Frustration, Conflict, and Stress

Chapter Preview

How to Build a Human Time Bomb

When he was arrested, John was sitting atop a 3-ton bulldozer staring into space. Behind him lay a mile-long path of destruction, for John had cut a broad, straight path through yards, roads, and fields. Trees and fences fell before his blade. The path led back to his house where the dozer was usually kept. Why did he do it? John explained that his father had denied him use of the family car that morning. Hours later, his anger reached the exploding point. . . .

Question: What would cause someone to react so drastically to a family disagreement?

In John's case the answer is that he was frustrated—*very frustrated! How does it feel to be frustrated? Try the following and see.*

> Get a small rubber band (the size found on newspapers) and stretch it across the back of your hand as pictured. Twist it once and be sure to push it down tightly on your thumb and little finger. Now try to remove the rubber band using only the hand it is on. Do not rub your hand against another object and do not use your other hand or your fingernails.

If you are temporarily unsuccessful at this task, you will have some idea of what mild frustration feels like.

Perhaps you have been as frustrated as John must have been when he climbed into the driver's seat. For example, picture yourself looking for a parking place in a crowded lot. Imagine that you are late for a test and have already been delayed by an irritating traffic jam. After fifteen minutes

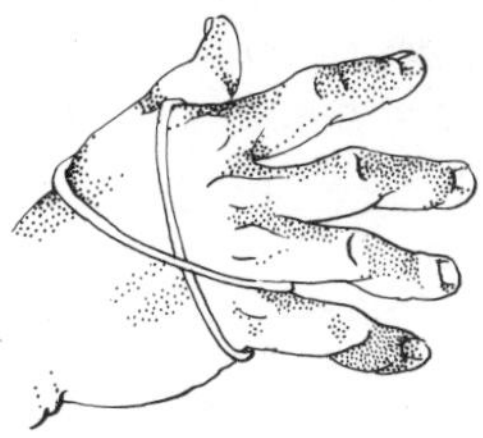

Fig. 14-1

of frantic searching, you finally spy an empty space, but as you start toward it, a Volkswagen darts around the corner and into the space. A car behind you begins to honk impatiently. Your car's radiator boils over. In such a situation you might be seized by an overwhelming desire to run *over anything in sight—other cars, pedestrians, lamp posts, trees, and flower beds. Few people actually carry out such impulses, but the feeling is common. Aggressive urges frequently accompany frustration.*

Question: Is frustration the same as anger?

No. Frustration can be defined as a negative emotional state that occurs when one is prevented from reaching a goal. John's desire to use the family car was blocked *by his father. You were probably at least temporarily frustrated in your attempt to remove the rubber band, and in the imaginary parking lot, the goal of finding a parking space was blocked by the presence of other cars.*

This chapter will discuss frustration and some of the strategies people adopt to deal with it. We will also discuss some common forms of conflict. *Conflicts develop when a person has two or more competing or contradictory motives or goals. Choosing between college and work, marriage and single life, or study and failure are examples of conflicts many students face.*

Frustration and conflict are two principal causes of stress. *Stress occurs when demands are placed on an organism to* adjust or adapt. *Stress is a normal part of life, but when it is severe or continues for long periods, it can do tremendous damage to one's body. Therefore, the last section of this chapter focuses on ways for you to avoid or cope with frustration, conflict, and stress.*

Resources

Sources of Frustration—Blind Alleys and Lead Balloons

Question: What causes frustration?

Obstacles of many kinds cause frustration. These may be *internal, external,* or *personal. External* frustration is based on conditions outside of the individual which impede progress toward a goal. All of the following are external frustrations: getting stuck with a flat tire, having a marriage proposal rejected, finding the cupboard bare when you go to get your poor dog a bone, finding the refrigerator bare when you go to get your poor tummy a T-bone, finding the refrigerator gone when you return home, being chased out of the house by your starving dog. In other words, external frustrations are based upon *delay, failure, rejection, loss,* and other direct blocking of motives. The amount of frustration experienced usually *increases* as the *strength, urgency,* or *importance* of the blocked motive increases. An escape artist submerged in a tank of water and bound with 200 pounds of chain could be expected to become *quite* frustrated by the jamming of a trick lock. Another aspect of frustration is summarized by the old phrase "the straw that broke the camel's back." *Repeated* frustrations can accumulate in their effect until a small irritation unleashes an unexpectedly violent response. The boy who bulldozed the countryside probably had been frustrated many times before in dealings with his father.

Personal frustrations are based on an individual's personal characteristics. If you are 4 feet tall and aspire to be a professional basketball player, you very likely will be frustrated. If you want to go to medical school, but can only earn D grades when working at your fullest capacity, you will likewise be frustrated. In both examples, frustration is ultimately based on personal limitations, although the resulting failures may be *experienced* as externally caused frustration. External and personal frustration may be distinguished from *internal* frustration. Internal frustrations usually take the form of *conflict*. Since conflict is discussed below as a separate topic, we turn now to the general question of how people react to frustration.

Reactions to Frustration—Irresistible Force Meets Immovable Object

Question: Does frustration always cause aggression? Aren't there other reactions?

Although aggression is a common response to frustration (Miller, 1941), there are several others. The first response is usually *persistence*, characterized by more *vigorous efforts* and more *variable responses*. For example, if you put your last dime in a vending machine and find that pressing the button has no effect, you will probably press harder and faster (vigorous effort) and then you will press all the other buttons (varied response). Persistence may help you to get *around* a barrier and to achieve your goal. However, if the machine *still* refuses to deliver or to return your dime, you may become aggressive and kick the machine (or at least tell it what you think of it). Notice that many sports are based on the connection between frustration and aggression. For example, football is based on placing a barrier between the ball carrier and a goal. Millions of Americans derive great secondhand joy out of seeing a football player aggressively *break through* the opposing team's line to make the goal.

Increased persistence can be very adaptive. Overcoming a barrier ends the frustration and satisfies the need or motive directed toward the goal. The same is true of aggression which removes or destroys a barrier. A primitive man who is parched with thirst but separated from a waterhole by a menacing animal may ensure his own survival by attacking the animal. In modern society direct aggression is seldom acceptable. If you encounter a long line at the drinking fountain, aggression is hardly an appropriate response. Since aggression is disruptive and generally discouraged, it is frequently *displaced*.

Question: How is aggression displaced? Does displaced aggression occur often?

Direct aggression toward a source of frustration may be impossible or it may be too dangerous. If one is frustrated by one's boss at work or by a teacher at school, the cost of direct aggression may be too high (loss of a job or failure of a needed class). Instead, the aggression may be displaced or *redirected* toward whoever or whatever is available. Targets of displaced aggression tend to be "safer" or less likely to retaliate than the original source of frustration. Attacking the helpless countryside when the real source of frustration is one's father is a clear case of displaced aggression. Sometimes long *chains* of displaced aggression can be observed, in which one person displaces aggression to the next. For instance, a businessman who is frustrated by high taxes reprimands an employee, who swallows his anger until he reaches home and then yells at his wife, who in turn yells at the children, who then tease the dog; the dog chases the cat, who later knocks over the canary cage.

Psychologists attribute much of the hostility and destructiveness in our society to displaced aggression. Urban ghetto areas that have been rocked by riots are filled with people who live daily with high levels of frustration brought on by poverty and social inequalities. In many communities across the nation the result of such long-term frustration has been displaced aggression on a grand scale, with anything and everything serving as potential targets for attack and destruction.

Another form of displaced aggression is *scapegoating*. A scapegoat is a person (or a group of people) toward whom displaced aggression is

"Bills, bills, bills! I'll remember this when it comes time for your Christmas tip."

Fig. 14-2 (*The Better Half* by Barnes, reprinted courtesy of the Register and Tribune Syndicate, Inc.)

habitually directed. For example, during and before World War II, Hitler used the Jews in Germany as scapegoats. Hitler blamed Germany's problems on the Jews and encouraged the German people to vent their frustrations through hatred of the Jews. Another disturbing example of displaced aggression on a large scale is the fact that in the United States between 1880 and 1930 there was a strong correlation between the price of cotton and the number of lynchings of blacks in the South. As the price of cotton went down (and frustration increased), the number of lynchings increased (Dollard *et al.*, 1939).

Question: I have a friend who dropped out of school and joined the French foreign legion. He seemed very frustrated before he quit. What type of response to frustration is this?

Another major reaction to frustration is *escape* or *withdrawal*. It is unpleasant to be frustrated. If other reactions do not reduce feelings of frustration, a person may try to escape. Escape may mean actually leaving a source of frustration (dropping out of school, quitting a job, leaving an unhappy marriage), or it may mean *psychologically* escaping. Two common forms of psychological escape are *apathy* (pretending not to care) and the *use of drugs* like alcohol, marijuana, or narcotics.

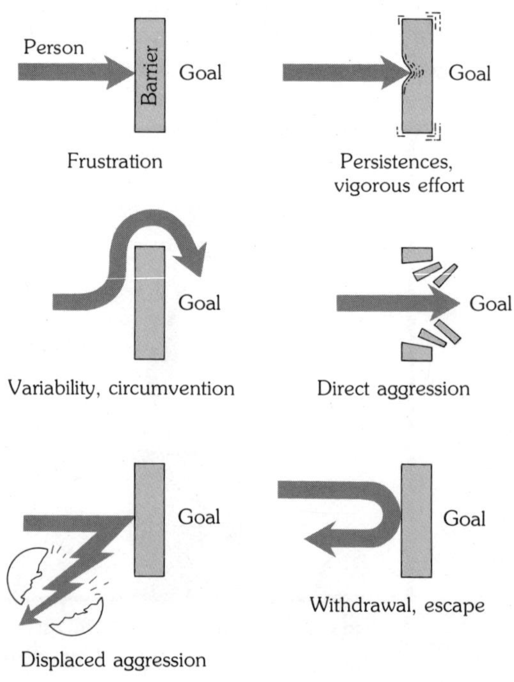

Fig. 14-3 Summary of reactions to frustration.

Learning Check Be sure you can answer these questions before continuing.

1. When progress toward a goal is blocked, the resulting emotion is called ____________________.

2. Delays, rejection, and losses are sources of what kind of frustration? ____________________.

3. Scapegoating is based on ____________ ____________.

4. Sampson Goliath is 7 feet tall and weighs 300 pounds. He has failed miserably in his aspirations to become a jockey. The source of his frustration is mainly ____________________.

5. As a reaction to frustration, apathy may be viewed as a form of ______________________________.

Answers: 1. frustration 2. external 3. displaced aggression 4. personal 5. escape or withdrawal

Conflict—Yes-No-Yes-No-Yes-No-Yes-No-Yes-No . . . Well, Maybe

Conflict is a special kind of frustration. When an individual must make a decision between *incompatible* or *contradictory* needs, desires, motives, wishes, or external demands, he experiences conflict. There are three basic forms of conflict, each with its own characteristics (Lewin, 1935).

Approach-Approach Conflicts The simplest conflict comes from having to choose between two *positive* or desirable alternatives. Choosing between tutti-fruity-coconut-mocha-champagne-ice and orange-marmalade-peanut-butter-coffee-swirl at the ice-cream parlor may throw you into a temporary conflict, but if you really like both choices, your decision will be quickly made. Even when more important decisions are involved, approach-approach conflicts tend to be the easiest to resolve. The old fable about the mule who died of thirst and starvation while standing between a bucket of water and a bucket of oats is obviously unrealistic. When both alternatives are positive, the scales of decision are easily tipped one direction or the other.

Avoidance-Avoidance Conflicts Double avoidance conflicts are based on being forced to choose between two *negative* or undesirable alternatives. A person in a double avoidance conflict is "caught between the devil and the deep blue sea" or "caught between the frying pan and the fire." In real life, double avoidance conflicts involve choosing between things like birth control and religious belief, studying and failure, unwanted pregnancy and abortion, the dentist and tooth decay, a monotonous job and poverty.

Question: Suppose I don't object to abortion. Or suppose that I consider any pregnancy sacred and not to be tampered with.

Notice that these examples can only be defined as conflicts on the basis of an individual's own needs and values. If a woman wants to terminate a pregnancy and has no personal objection to abortion, she experiences no conflict. If she would not consider abortion under any circumstances, there is no conflict.

Double avoidance conflicts often have a "damned if you do, damned if you don't" quality. In other words, both choices are negative, but *not choosing* is impossible or equally undesirable. For example, many people complain that in political elections neither candidate is a good choice, but not voting is worse. A more dramatic example of this aspect of double avoidance conflict is illustrated by the plight of a person trapped in a hotel fire, twenty stories from the ground. Should the person jump from the window and almost surely die on the pavement? Or should he try to dash through the flames and almost surely die of smoke inhalation and burns? When faced with a choice like this, people tend to *vacillate* or waver between the two alternatives. In his hotel room, a trapped individual may first think about the window, approach it, but then back away after looking down twenty stories. Next he may try the door and back away as the heat singes his hair and smoke billows in.

The individual in a double avoidance conflict vacillates between the alternatives but seldom resolves the conflict. Sometimes people pull out of the situation entirely. This is called "leaving the field," and it is another form of escape. In the example of the hotel fire, the individual cannot leave the field (unless he can fly), but many times one can. The author recently talked to a student who could not attend school unless he worked. However, if he worked he could not earn passing grades. His solution after much vacillation? He joined the navy.

Approach-Avoidance Conflicts Approach-avoidance conflicts are also difficult to resolve. In some ways they are more complex than double avoidance conflicts because people seldom escape them. A person in an approach-avoidance conflict is "caught" because he is simultaneously attracted to and repelled by the same activity or goal. Attraction keeps the person in the situation, but its negative aspects keep him in conflict. For example, a high school student arrives to pick up his date for the first time. He is met at the door by her father who is a professional wrestler—7 feet tall, 300 pounds, and entirely covered with hair. The father gives the boy a crushing handshake and growls that he will break him in half if the girl is not home on time. The student considers the girl attractive and has a good time. But does he ask her out again? It depends on the relative strength of his attraction and his fear. Almost certainly he will feel *ambivalent* about asking her out again, knowing that another encounter with her father is involved.

Ambivalence (mixed positive and negative feelings) is a central characteristic of approach-avoidance conflicts. Ambivalence is usually translated into *partial approach* (Miller, 1944). Since our student is still attracted to the girl, he may spend time with her at school and elsewhere, but may not actually date her again. Some more realistic examples of approach-avoidance conflicts are: planning marriage to someone your parents strongly disapprove of, wanting to be an actor but suffering stage-fright, wanting to buy a car but not wanting to be tied to monthly pay-

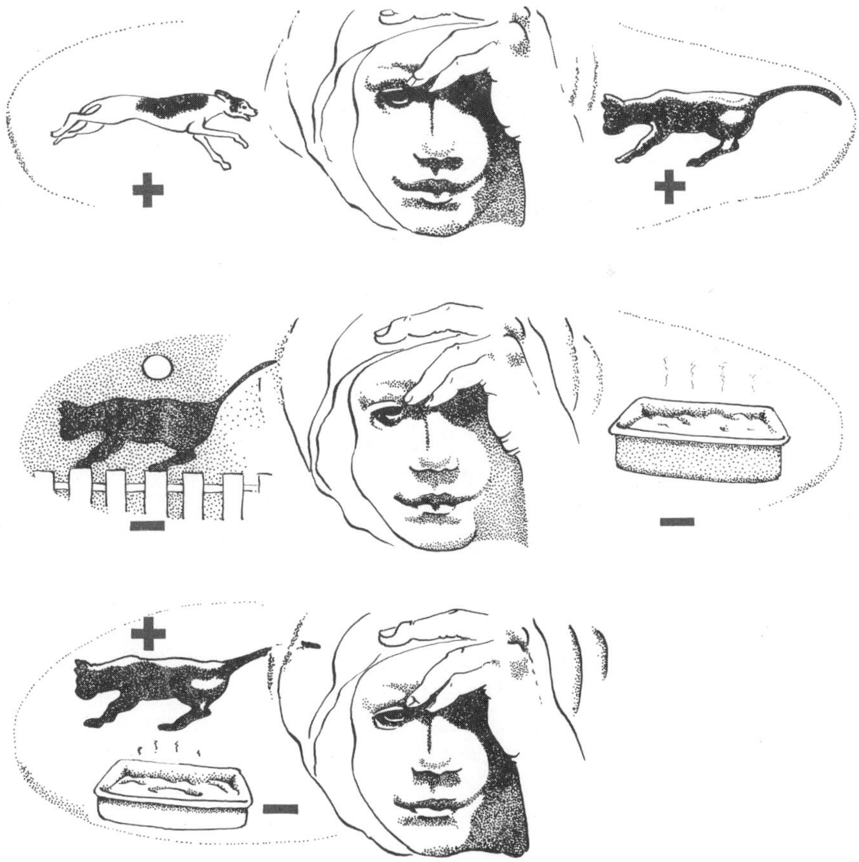

Fig. 14-4 Three basic forms of conflict.

ments, wanting to eat when overweight, and wanting to go to school but hating to study. Many of life's important decisions have approach-avoidance dimensions.

Learning Check

1. Conflict is related to the presence of contradictory ____________ or an attempt to reach contradictory ____________.
2. The easiest conflict to resolve is an ____________ conflict.
3. The type of conflict characterized by vacillation is ____________ conflict.
4. Approach-avoidance conflicts produce mixed feelings called ____________.

Answers:

1. motives, goals 2. approach-approach 3. avoidance-avoidance 4. ambivalence

Stress—Invisible Killer on the Loose

Question: What do air traffic controllers, hard-driving businesspersons, and "executive" monkeys have in common?

Ulcers! Several years ago a psychologist investigated the effects of stress by studying monkeys who were subjected to electric shock. The monkeys were shocked in pairs so that when one received a shock, the other did too. One monkey in each pair differed from the other in one important regard. One was made an "executive" who could turn off or postpone the shock by depressing a lever every few seconds. The other had no control over the shock. The executive monkeys were very good at their task and over a period of weeks very few shocks were actually administered. However, the additional *psychological stress* of responsibility caused the executive monkeys to develop stomach ulcers. The nonexecutive monkeys, who received exactly the same number of shocks, were unaffected by the *physical stress* of the shocks (Brady, 1958). Air traffic controllers and pressured businesspersons are representative of the growing number of occupations associated with high ulcer rates. Like the executive monkeys, humans also develop ulcers when subjected to prolonged psychological stress.

Ulcers are considered a *psychosomatic* disorder (*psyche* = mind, *soma* = body). In psychosomatic diseases psychological stress causes

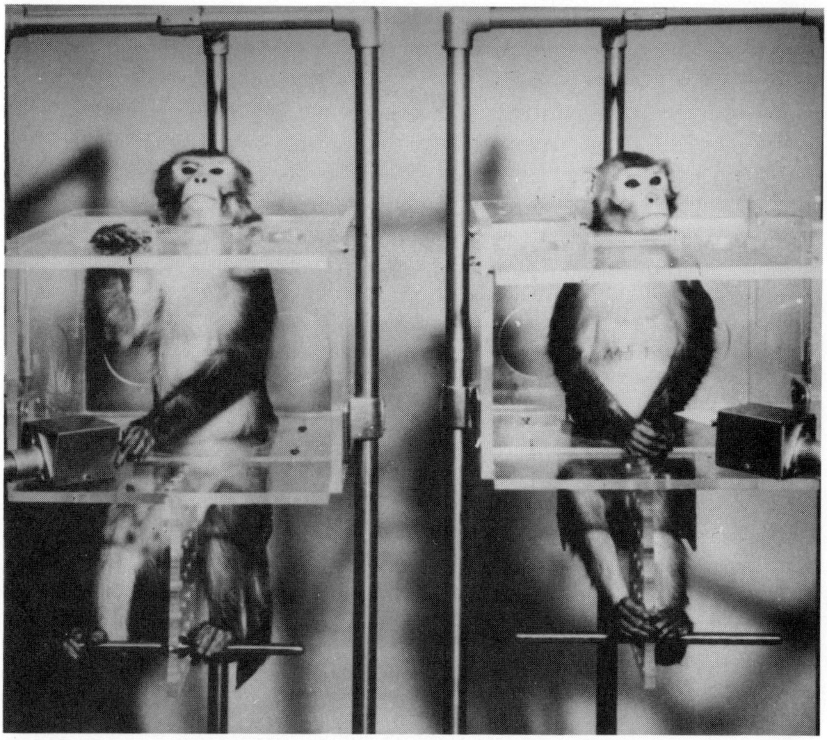

Fig. 14-5 The "executive" monkey on the left has control over the electrical shocks received by both monkeys. The monkey on the right has no control. Which monkey gets ulcers? (See text.) (Photo courtesy of Joseph Brady.)

actual damage to the tissues of the body. Psychosomatic problems are not the same as *hypochondria*. Hypochondriacs suffer from imaginary diseases. There is nothing imaginary about a bleeding ulcer. A severe case could be fatal.

Question: *What diseases are psychosomatic ? Who gets them?*

The major psychosomatic illnesses are stomach ulcers, essential hypertension (high blood pressure), asthma, migraine headaches, and eczema (skin eruptions). These represent only the most obvious problems. It is estimated that one-half of all patients who go to see a doctor either have a psychosomatic problem or have a problem complicated by psychosomatic symptoms.

Question: *How do you get a psychosomatic disorder? How can stress, particularly psychological stress, cause* physical *damage?*

The answer seems to lie in the body's defenses against stress. During strong emotion the body prepares for peak output—for fight or flight—and undergoes significant changes. The nature of these changes has been studied by Hans Selye (Selye, 1953). Selye noticed that the initial symptoms of almost any trauma (disease, poisoning, infection, or injury) were the same. The symptoms are headache, fever, fatigue, aching muscles and joints, loss of appetite, and lack of energy. Selye reasoned that any stress can cause what he calls the *general adaptation syndrome* (G.A.S.). The G.A.S. is simply a consistent pattern of stages that one's body goes through as it reacts to stress. The first stage is called the *alarm reaction*. During this stage the body mobilizes its defenses against stress. A rapid change in hormone output from the adrenal glands causes the symptoms described above. If stress continues, the second stage, called the *stage of resistance*, begins. At this point the body's defenses are stabilized and symptoms disappear. However, this outward appearance of normality is maintained at a high price, because resistance to other stressors is decreased. If stress continues, the *stage of exhaustion* may be reached. In this stage the body's resources are exhausted and a psychosomatic disorder, organ failure, or complete collapse results.

Learning Check

1. Ulcers developed by executive monkeys are an example of a ______________ disorder.
2. The first stage of the G.A.S. is called the ______________ reaction.
3. Hypochondria refers to illness based upon ______________ symptoms.

Answers: 1. psychosomatic 2. alarm 3. imagined

Resources Summary

Frustration is a negative emotion which occurs when progress toward a goal is blocked. Frustration may be based on *internal*, *external*, or *personal* sources. Major reactions to frustration include *persistence*, *aggression*, *displaced aggression*, and *escape* or *withdrawal*. A special form of frustration is *conflict*. Conflict occurs when one must choose between contradictory alternatives. The three major forms of conflict are *approach-approach*, *avoidance-avoidance*, and *approach-avoidance*. Approach-approach conflicts are the easiest to resolve. Avoidance-avoidance conflicts are difficult to resolve, and are characterized by *vacillation* and *escape*. Approach-avoidance conflicts are difficult to resolve and are characterized by *ambivalence* and *partial approach*. Frustration and conflict are two frequent sources of *stress*. When stress is intense or prolonged, it may cause bodily damage in the form of ulcers and other *psychosomatic* problems. The body reacts to stress in a series of stages called the *general adaptation syndrome* (G.A.S.). The stages of the G.A.S. are *alarm*, *resistance*, and *exhaustion*. Bodily damage occurs if the stage of exhaustion is reached.

Applications

Dealing with Stress

Question: How do I know if I am subjecting myself to too much stress?

Psychologists Thomas Holmes and Minoru Masuda have proven something that physicians have suspected for a long time: Stressful events reduce the body's natural defense mechanisms against disease (Holmes & Masuda, 1972). They have found that disaster and sorrow often lead to illness. More surprising is the finding that almost any major *change* in one's life requires adjustment and increases susceptibility to illness and accident. Holmes and his associates have developed a rating scale to help determine the potential health hazards one faces when stresses accumulate. They call this the Social Readjustment Rating Scale (SRRS). It is reprinted in Table 14-1. The effect of life events is expressed as life crisis units (LCUs). As you read the scale, notice that a positive life event may be as costly as a disaster. Marriage rates 50 life change units, even though it is usually considered a happy event. Notice also that many items read "Change in. . . ." This means that an improvement in life conditions is as costly as a deterioration.

To use the scale, add up the LCUs for all life events you have experienced during the last *two* years and compare the total to these standards:

0 to 150	No significant problems
150 to 199	Mild life crisis (33 percent chance of illness)
200 to 299	Moderate life crisis (50 percent chance of illness)
300 or over	Major life crisis (80 percent chance of illness)

When the LCU total exceeds 300 points there is an 80 percent chance of illness or accident in the near future. A high LCU score should be taken seriously. It would be a good idea to total your LCUs once a year and to make adjustments in your life-style when the score goes over 300. Remember, "To be forewarned is to be forearmed."

Question: What can be done about a high score?

A high LCU score is a signal that additional stress should be avoided. The easiest way to achieve this is to make as few additional changes as is practical. Added responsibilities should be avoided and existing responsibilities reduced if possible. The one change that can be made safely is to include more rest and unpressured relaxation in your daily schedule.

Question: What can be done psychologically to

Table 14-1 Social Readjustment Rating Scale The Social Readjustment Rating Scale lists significant life events and offers a rating of their contribution to susceptibility to illness.

Rank	*Life event*	*Life crisis units*	*Rank*	*Life event*	*Life crisis units*
1	Death of spouse	100	23	Son or daughter leaving home	29
2	Divorce	73	24	Trouble with in-laws	29
3	Marital separation	65	25	Outstanding personal achievement	28
4	Jail term	63	26	Wife begins or stops work	26
5	Death of a close family member	63	27	Begin or end school	26
6	Personal injury or illness	53	28	Change in living conditions	25
7	Marriage	50	29	Revision of personal habits	24
8	Fired at work	47	30	Trouble with boss	23
9	Marital reconciliation	45	31	Change in work hours or conditions	20
10	Retirement	45	32	Change in residence	20
11	Change in health of family member	44	33	Change in school	20
12	Pregnancy	40	34	Change in recreation	19
13	Sex difficulties	39	35	Change in church activities	19
14	Gain of new family member	39	36	Change in social activities	18
15	Business readjustment	39	37	Mortgage or loan less than $10,000	17
16	Change in financial state	38	38	Change in sleeping habits	16
17	Death of close friend	37	39	Change in number of family get-togethers	15
18	Change to different line of work	36	40	Change in eating habits	15
19	Change in number of arguments with spouse	35	41	Vacation	13
20	Mortgage over $10,000	31	42	Christmas	12
21	Foreclosure of mortgage or loan	30	43	Minor violations of the law	11
22	Change in responsibilities at work	29			

Adapted with permission from "Social Readjustment Rating Scale," by T. H. Holmes and R. H. Rahe, *Journal of Psychosomatic Research*, 1957. Reprinted with permission from Pergamon Press, Ltd.

avoid psychosomatic illness or illness made more likely by life crises and stress?

The research of two noted cardiologists provides a partial guide. Meyer Friedman and Ray Rosenman have studied the personality characteristics of people who are especially prone to suffer heart attack. They find a consistent pattern of destructive habits summarized in the self-identification test which follows.

1. (You) have a habit of explosively accentuating various key words in your ordinary speech even when there is no need for such accentuation.
2. (You) *always* move, walk, and eat rapidly.
3. (You) feel an impatience with the rate at which most events take place.
4. (You) frequently strive to think of or do two or more things simultaneously.
5. (You) almost always feel vaguely guilty when you relax and do absolutely nothing for several days.
6. (You) attempt to schedule more and more in less and less time and in doing so make fewer and fewer allowances for unforeseen problems. This causes a *chronic sense of time urgency* (adapted and shortened from Friedman & Rosenman, 1974).

In summary, coronary-prone people "push" themselves and create a constant sense of frustration and conflict. The best way to avoid the destructive stress this produces is to try to adopt behavior that is the opposite of that listed above.

For Discussion

A psychologist studying frustration placed rats on a small platform at the top of a tall pole. Then he forced them to jump off the platform toward two elevated doors, one locked and the other unlocked. If the rat chose the correct door, it swung open and he landed safely on another platform. If he chose the locked door, he bounced off it and fell into a net far below. The problem of choosing the open door was made unsolvable and very frustrating by randomly alternating which door was locked. After a time, most rats adopted a *stereotyped* response. That is, they chose the *same door* every time. This door was then *permanently locked.* All the rat had to do was to jump to the other door to avoid a fall, but time after time the rat bounced off the locked door (Maier, 1949).

Question: Isn't this an example of persistence?

No, there are important differences between stereotyped responses to frustration and persistence. Think of the struggle an infant undergoes when learning to walk. For an adult a corresponding amount of frustration would be overwhelming. The typical adult can stand to "fall on his face" just so often. If you were to approach learning a foreign language, or an equally difficult task with a willingness to "fail" as much as a child does when learning to walk, you would almost surely be a success. Persistence does pay off. But all too often people are not persistent enough because they fear failure. Fear of failure may *ensure* failure. However, persistence that is not *flexible* can lead to "stupid," stereotyped behavior like that of a rat on a jumping stand. It is important when dealing with frustration to know when to quit and establish a new direction.

Here are some suggestions to help you avoid needless frustration.

1. Try to identify the source of your frustration. Is it internal, external, or personal?
2. Is the source of frustration something that can be changed? How hard would you have to work to change it? Is it under your control at all?
3. If the source of your frustration can be changed or removed, are the necessary efforts worth it? The answers to these questions help determine if persistence will be futile. There is value in learning to accept gracefully those things which cannot be changed.

It is also important to distinguish between *real* barriers and *imagined* barriers. All too often we create our own imaginary barriers. For example:

> Anita wants a part-time job to earn extra money. At the first place she applied she was told that she didn't have enough "experience." Now she complains of being frustrated because she wants to work but cannot. She needs "experience" to work, but can't get experience without working. She has quit looking for a job.

Is Anita's need for experience a real barrier? Unless she applies for *many* jobs it is impossible to tell if she has overestimated its importance. For her the barrier is real enough to prevent further efforts, but with persistent looking she might locate an "unlocked door." If a reasonable amount of persistence does show that "experience" is essential, it might be obtained in other ways—through temporary volunteer work, for instance.

Question: How can I handle conflicts more effectively?

Most of the suggestions just made also apply to conflict. However, here are some additional things to remember when you are in conflict or must make a difficult decision.

1. Don't be hasty when making important decisions. Take time to collect information and to weigh pros and cons. Hasty decisions are often regretted. Even if you do make a faulty decision, it will trouble you less if you know that you did everything possible to avoid a mistake.
2. Try out important decisions *partially* when possible. If you are thinking about moving to a new town, try to spend a few days there first. If you are choosing between colleges, do the same. If classes are in progress, sit in on some. If you want to learn to skin-dive, rent equipment for a reasonable length of time before buying.
3. Look for workable compromises. Again it is important to get all available information. If you think that you only have one or two alternatives and they are undesirable or unbearable, seek the aid of a teacher, counselor, minister, or social service agency. You may be overlooking possible alternatives that these people will know about.
4. When all else fails, make a decision and live with it. Indecision and conflict exact a high cost. Sometimes it is best to select a course of action and to stick with it unless it is *very obviously* wrong *after* you have taken it.

In class you may want to describe some of the frustrations and conflicts you have experienced and how you handled them. Prepare to discuss frustrations and conflicts you have resolved unusually effectively or that you could have improved on. Do you have some additional hints to share with other students?

Questions for Discussion

1. How could you reduce conflict or avoid an unfortunate decision in the following situations: choosing a school to attend, choosing a major, deciding about marriage, choosing a job, buying a car?
2. Calculate your life-change score. If your score is elevated, what could you do to reduce the chances of illness? If it is low, what could you do to put more excitement in your life?! Can you see any relationship between previous periods of illness and the number of life changes that preceded them?
3. What do you consider the most prominent sources of stress in our society? What do you think should or could be done to combat these stresses?

4. Defend or deny the following statement (attributed to Professor P. T. Barnumandbailey Circuits): "Television is the opiate of the people. If all the TV tubes in the U.S. suddenly went blank, the mental health of the nation would crumble because people could no longer escape their problems by watching television."

5. How could you best deal with the following sources of frustration: delays, losses, lack of resources, failure, rejection?

6. "Erhard Seminars Training" is a pop psychology organization that teaches "graduates" that "What is, is, and what isn't, isn't." What are the values and limitations of adopting this outlook toward failures and frustrations?

Suggestions for Further Reading

Dollard, J., *et al. Frustration and Aggression.* Yale University Press, 1939.

Lazarus, R. S. *Psychological Stress and the Coping Process.* McGraw-Hill, 1966.

Levi, L. *Society, Stress, and Disease.* Oxford University Press, 1971.

Maier, N. R. F. *Frustration.* Ann Arbor Paperbacks, 1961.

Selye, H. *The Stress of Life.* McGraw-Hill, 1956.

Toffler, A. *Future Shock.* Random House, 1970.

15 Psychological Defense

Chapter Preview

Freudian Slips

Shortly after he became president, Gerald Ford was speaking at an awards luncheon of the National Collegiate Athletic Association. Ford said that the athletic director of a college and the president of the United States have a great deal in common. He added: "We both buy aspirin by the six-pack—and we both have a certain lack of performance *in our job." Ford's speech was supposed to read: "We both have a certain lack of* permanence *in our jobs."*

In his book entitled Psychopathology of Everyday Life *(1938), Sigmund Freud analyzed hundreds of similar slips of the tongue. For example, he recalls the day the president of the Austrian assembly announced at the opening of a meeting: "Gentlemen, I declare this meeting closed!" Freud also tells of the reserved society matron who stated at a gathering, "Men have it easier than women. All a man must have is his* five *straight limbs."*

Speech blunders, or "Freudian slips" as they are sometimes called, are frequently comical because they reveal motives or feelings that are opposite to a person's public image. Such errors are seldom detected by those who make them. Freud was among the first to point out that thoughts, images, or motives that make us uncomfortable tend to be blocked from awareness. This process of blocking or avoiding anxiety gives rise to what are called psychological defense mechanisms. *Defense mechanisms are habitual and unconscious techniques used to reduce or avoid anxiety or the awareness of something unpleasant. They help us to deny or distort the real sources of anxiety and maintain an idealized self-image so that we can live with ourselves.*

Defense mechanisms are almost always to some extent self-deceptive. Often they create large "blind spots" in a person's personality, as when an extremely stingy person fails to recognize that he is a "tightwad." Everyone has at one time or another used defense mechanisms. If you don't recognize the behavior of many of your friends and relatives (and yourself) in this chapter, then you're probably defending!

Resources

Denial—Say It Isn't So

One of the most primitive defense mechanisms is *denial*. Denial means to protect oneself from an unpleasant reality by refusing to accept it. Denial is closely associated with death, illness, and similar painful and threatening experiences. For instance, if you were informed that you have only three months to live, what would be your first reactions? They would probably include thoughts like: "Aw, come on, someone must have mixed up the x-rays," or "The doctor must be mistaken," or simply, "It can't be true!" Similar denial and disbelief are common reactions to the unexpected death of a friend or relative: "It's just not real. I don't believe it. I just don't believe it!"

Denial sometimes protects us from encounters or experiences that might psychologically harm or overwhelm us. The protective function of denial can best be illustrated by one of the most overwhelming encounters with death or disaster yet experienced by humans. At 8:15 A.M. on August 6, 1945, an atomic bomb fell on the city of Hiroshima, Japan. Most people within 2,000 yards of the point of impact remember only a sudden sensation of searing heat, followed by unconsciousness. Interviews held years later by Robert Lifton show that those who survived awoke to a scene of death that took on a dreamlike quality:

> There were dead bodies everywhere. . . . There was practically no room for me to put my feet on the floor. . . . At that time I couldn't figure out the reason why all these people were suffering, or what illness it was that had struck them down. . . . There was no light at all, and we were just like sleepwalkers.

The city of Hiroshima was totally destroyed. A young university professor recalls:

> Everything I saw made a deep impression—a park nearby covered with dead bodies waiting to be cremated. . . . The most impressive thing I saw was some girls, very young girls, not only with their clothes torn off but with their skin peeled off as well. . . . My immediate thought was that this was like the Hell I had always read about.

Lifton claims that humans are unable to remain open to emotional experiences of this intensity for any length of time. Survivors were initially horrified when they saw corpses scattered in strange array or the extremely disfigured faces and rotting flesh of other survivors. But as they saw more and more, they felt nothing. Lifton suggests that denial in this case was so complete that it should be called *psychological closure* (Lifton, 1963).

Denial also may be used as a defense against lesser disasters. When someone ignores the warning pains from a decayed tooth or the first signs of an illness, it is a form of denial. The husband or wife who is blind to obvious indications that the partner is having an affair is also using denial. So too is anyone who claims: "I'm never going to get old" or "I never use denial."

Learning Check Before reading more, write a brief description of denial: ____________

____

____

____

____

(Check your definition against that given above.)

Repression—Out of Sight, But Not Out of Mind

Freud noticed that his patients had tremendous difficulty recalling shocking or traumatic events from childhood. It seemed that powerful forces were holding these painful memories from awareness. Freud called this *repression*. Apparently, we protect ourselves by repressing thoughts or impulses that are painful or threatening. Feelings of hostility toward a loved one, the names of disliked people, and past failures and embarrassments are common targets of repression.

Question: If I try to forget a test I have failed, am I repressing it?

Repression can be distinguished from *suppression*. If you are consciously trying to put something out of mind, you are suppressing it. This is usually a little like trying not to think of pink elephants. Remembering *not* to think of pink elephants ensures that you *will* think of pink elephants. When repression actually occurs, it is unconscious. For instance, you may discover that you have completely forgotten a dental appointment *after* it is too late to keep it. Memories of dentists and pain caused you to repress or forget the dental appointment. Here's another example. Someone points out that you seem to dislike your father. Suddenly you recognize that you really do dislike him, but had never noticed it before. Freud considered the awareness of repressed feelings and memories very important because he felt that they continue to influence our personalities even though repressed feelings are unconscious.

Learning Check See if you can describe repression in *your own words*: ______________

____

____

____

(Check your definition in the preceding section.)

Reaction Formation—Repression with a Twist

Reaction formation is a defense in which impulses are not only repressed, they are also held in check by exaggerated opposite behavior. For example, a mother who unconsciously resents her children may, through reaction formation, become overprotective and overindulgent to an exaggerated degree. Her real thoughts of "I hate them" and "I wish they were gone" are replaced by "I love them" and "I don't know what I would do without them." The mother's hostile impulses are traded in for "smother love" so that she will not have to admit her dislike of her children. The basic idea is that an unacceptable feeling or impulse is so threatening that it is not enough simply to repress it. The individual goes overboard to act out a behavior opposite from the real impulse or feeling.

Question: What if the mother really loves her children?

You mean, how can reaction formation be distinguished from real motives? Exaggeration is the key to making this distinction. Perhaps you've met John "Don Juan" Jones, a middle-aged man who is threatened by repressed feelings of impotence. He makes a pass at every woman he meets and brags loudly to anyone who will listen about his sexual conquests. Then there's Jock E. Strap who has repressed feelings of inadequacy and is extremely threatened by any sign of "weakness." He has become what he considers to be an example of "all-American manhood," yet even the "sweat set" finds it difficult to take him seriously.

The excessive quality of behavior caused by reaction formation is also seen in this excerpt from a news article:

> Birmingham, England (AP)—Melinda Hertel, sweet sixteen and miniskirted, slammed her desk shut, pulled her hat on over her long brunette hair and walked out of school on strike. The reason: Melinda doesn't want boys sharing her lessons.
>
> "I'll not go back until I get a promise that I'll be put in an all-girl class."
>
> "Sixteen-year-old boys have one aim in life. That's to get a girl in the back row of the pictures with them."
>
> "We all know what they want. They will be trying to chat me up, distracting me from lessons and trying to give me a baby."

"I wear miniskirts because it is the fashion—not because I want some stupid boy gazing at my legs in class."

"I'm just not interested in boys, school romances or going steady," she added. "I've no intention of allowing any boy near me until I'm at least twenty-one."

The lady doth protest too much. It would appear that Melinda is threatened by her own attraction to boys.

Learning Check In reaction formation, impulse are held in check by ______________ ____behavior.

(Answer is found in the first sentence of the preceding section.)

Fantasy—Now Showing: Wild Adventures and X-Rated Escapades

Has your reading of this chapter been interrupted by a daydream? Even if you are able to read without such interruptions, odds are that you rarely get through a lecture without some daydreaming. Daydreaming is one of the most common forms of *fantasy*.

Question: How is fantasy used as a defense?

In fantasy, frustrated or "unacceptable" needs and motives may be freely expressed. As a matter of fact, daydream topics can indicate which of a person's needs are being frustrated. One study showed that during a thirty-day period, male undergraduate students daydreamed about vocational success most often, followed by sexual fantasies, fantasies about money or possessions, and the achievement of mental feats. Female undergraduates reported sexual fantasies most often, followed by fantasies of vocational success, fantasies about money or possessions, and fantasies about physical attractiveness (Shaffer & Shoben, 1956).

In another study, P. Cameron and his associates found that students attending a lecture spend nearly one-fourth of the lecture time daydreaming about sex. I'm sure you can guess who gets the starring role in the fantasies (Cameron *et al.*, 1968). It is interesting that both of these studies show a marked absence of daydreams about food. Actually this is not too surprising in a society that places heavy emphasis on success, money, status, and sexuality.

Question: Would the fantasies of a starving person be different?

Most people are rarely frustrated by lack of food. When they are, a corresponding shift in their fantasy life occurs. In a study carried out during World War II by Keys and his associates, thirty-two conscientious objectors volunteered to go on a semistarvation diet for six months. By the end of the twenty-fifth week, food dominated their thoughts, talk, and daydreams. Some men even hung pictures of attractive cuts of meat or chocolate cake on the walls instead of pictures of pretty girls (Keys *et al.*, 1950).

Question: Is fantasy unhealthy?

Fantasy is valuable as an outlet for frustrated motives. For example, after losing an argument, you might find yourself going over the conversation of the argument in fantasy, only this time you get to say all the clever things you should have said in reality at the time of the argument. Fantasy can be particularly valuable in situations too dangerous to allow the direct expression of impulses. For instance, if you are sexually attracted to a married friend or angry at a teacher or if you have a momentary urge to kill the fool in front of you on the highway, the substitution of fantasy for action may prevent a disaster. In such cases, fantasy is healthy.

Daydreams have been called the "nursery of great achievement." Fantasies can help define future plans and aspirations as one tries on various roles, life-styles, and possibilities. Your fantasies about the wonderland which awaits you after college probably provide day-to-day motives to continue working in a system that offers few immediate rewards.

Fantasy itself is seldom harmful, but secondary fear or guilt caused by fantasy may be. Let's say that a child has been scolded by his mother. Angry, the child daydreams about his mother dying. Under normal conditions such a fantasy would be short-lived and of little importance. But imagine what might happen if the mother were killed in an accident the next day. The child's guilt would be overwhelming. Along the same lines, we have seen that sexual fantasies *per se* are a normal occurrence. They are unhealthy only if they cause guilt or distress. Fantasies also become a problem when they are too often used as an escape from reality. If you spend so many waking hours in a dream world that you are unable to pass your classes, you are no longer just having fantasies. You are being "had" by fantasies!

Learning Check

1. Fantasy is rarely related to frustrated motives. T or F?

2. One of the most common forms of fantasy is ________________.

Answers: 1. F 2. daydreaming

Regression—About Face!

Regression is another form of escape from anxiety, an escape into the past.

Question: How can you escape into the past?

Fig. 15-1 (Photo by Marge Agin.)

There are several levels of regression. In extreme cases regression takes the form of a return to earlier periods of growth. Dinello (1967) has described a seventeen-year-old youth who regressed to the infantile state and began wearing a diaper. Regression on this scale in adults is abnormal and unusual. In children it is fairly common. Most parents who have a second child have had to put up with at least some regression by the older child. Frustrated by a new rival for attention, an older child may regress to childish speech, bed-wetting, or infantile play after the new baby arrives.

However, regression is usually less severe. The child at summer camp who gets homesick and longs for the security of familiar surroundings is undergoing mild regression. An adult who throws a temper tantrum or a married adult who "goes home to mother" is also regressing.

In its broadest meaning, regression refers to any return to earlier, less demanding situations or habits. Good examples of mild forms of regression can be observed on college campuses the last week or so before final exams. Touch football games, Frisbee matches, the throwing of paper airplanes, and other playful activities blossom as students begin to feel the pressure of exams. They represent the tendency to regress or avoid reality. Even nostalgia for the "good old days" is a form of regression. For some, the "old days" look less stressful than the present. But most who have tried have found that "you can't go home again" in the truest sense. The people and places from the past that looked so good are usually disappointing when revisited.

Learning Check

Define regression: ______________________________

____

____

(Check your definition against the one above.)

Projection—All the World's a Movie Screen

Projection, another defense mechanism, is an unconscious process that protects us from accepting traits in ourselves that consciously we would find unacceptable.

Question: How does projection work?

A person who is *projecting* unconsciously transfers his or her own shortcomings or unacceptable impulses to others. By exaggerating these unacceptable traits in others, the individual lessens his or her own failings.

Question: Can you give some examples?

The author once worked for a very greedy shop owner who was dedicated to separating every customer from as much money as possible, often by sharp and deceptive practices. This same man considered himself a pillar of the community and a good Christian. How did he justify to himself his greed and dishonesty? He believed that everyone who entered his store was bent on cheating him anyway they could. In reality, few, if any, of his customers shared his motives, but he projected his own greed and dishonesty to them.

Another example of projection can be seen in a quote from Adolf Hitler describing Winston Churchill:

> For over five years this man has been chasing around Europe like a madman in search of something he could set on fire. Unfortunately he again finds hirelings who open the gates of their country to this international incendiary.

Here is a classic case of Hitler projecting on Churchill the very traits for which Hitler is known.

Projection occurs on many levels. Unreasonable jealousy, for instance, is often based on projection. The husband who unfairly accuses his wife of flirting assumes that she is attracted to other men because he is attracted to other women but can't admit it. He may even imagine his wife has been unfaithful to justify his own extramarital affair. At a more commonplace level, we find that an aggressive driver seems to notice nothing but aggressive drivers on the road. An unfriendly person complains that his neighbors are unfriendly wherever he lives. Along the same lines, a dishonest college student will usually convince himself that everyone else cheats, too.

Perhaps the most common example of projection is an experience everyone has had: Some days *everyone* you meet is friendly and in a good mood, while on other days *everyone* is unfriendly and unhappy. What's happening is that you probably are projecting your own feelings to those around you. The chances of everyone you meet being in a good or a bad mood simultaneously are rather slim. Obviously, the change is in you.

Learning Check See if you can define projection:

____

____

____

(Check your answer above.)

Isolation and Intellectualization—Logic-Tight Compartments

Question: I've been thinking about the greedy store owner. I knew a guy like that. In church every Sunday, he was a model of the golden rule. But during the week his motto seemed to be, "Do unto others before they do unto you." How can someone be so inconsistent?

Isolation is a defense sometimes used to maintain one's self-image. Through isolation, conflicting attitudes are separated into logic-tight compartments.

Question: What is a "logic-tight compartment"?

This is a descriptive phrase used when contradictory or opposite attitudes seem to be locked away from contact with each other. Even forceful, logical argument is not enough to make such a defensive individual see his inconsistency. Anyone who can say: "I can't stand hostile people. Everytime I meet a hostile person I get so angry I'd like to kill him" is using isolation. When you hear a person say: "America, the land of freedom, equality, and opportunity for all—and we don't want any damned foreigners is here messing it up," that person is also using isolation. Isolation tends to be associated with a rigid personality structure.

Much more widely used as a defense mechanism is *intellectualization.*

Question: Is intellectualization still a form of isolation?

Yes, but it's more subtle and sophisticated. Intellectualization means to remove or isolate emotion from a situation by talking about it formally, intellectually, or "at a distance." For example, the author once overheard (the author is an incurable eavesdropper) a woman discussing a divorce. The first impression was that she was a counselor or a social worker talking about a case in which she was involved. Only after several minutes of conversation did it become clear that *she* was being divorced! Also, classroom discussions about death, abortion, sexuality, and other sensitive topics lean heavily toward intellectualization. Participants talk intellectually with a matter-of-fact tone that carefully avoids emotion. A striking example of intellectualization and isolation is provided by Bluestone and McGahee (1962). Their study of prisoners awaiting execution showed a pattern in which the prisoners felt as though everything were happening to someone else, and as if they were watching, unemotionally, from a distance.

Learning Check

1. It is sometimes said that isolation involves use of ______________ ______________ compartments.

2. Define intellectualization: ______________________________

____

(Check your answers against the previous discussion.)

Rationalization—Sour Grapes and Sweet Lemons

Every teacher is familiar with a rather amazing phenomenon that occurs whenever a test is scheduled. On the day of the exam, an incredible wave of disasters seems to sweep through the city. An amazing number of mothers, fathers, sisters, brothers, aunts, uncles, grandparents, friends, relatives, and pets become ill or die. Motors suddenly fall out of automobiles. Books are lost or stolen. Alarm clocks roll over and ring out no more.

The making of excuses comes from a natural tendency to explain one's behavior. When the explanations offered are reasonable, rational, and convincing—but not the real reasons—we say a person is *rationalizing*. Rationalization unconsciously provides us with reasons for behavior we ourselves find somewhat questionable. Here is a typical example of rationalization. A student who fails to turn in an assignment made at the beginning of the semester explains:

> My car broke down two days ago and I couldn't get to the library until yesterday. Then I couldn't get all the books I needed because some were checked out, but I wrote what I could. Then last night, as the last straw, the ribbon in my typewriter broke, and since all the stores were closed I couldn't finish the paper on time.

"Grapes! What a treat these will be."
"Oh, well, they're probably sour anyway."

Fig. 15-2 The fable of the fox and the grapes.

If asked why he left the assignment until the last minute (the real reason for its being late), the student would probably launch into another set of rationalizations. If these are questioned, the student will probably become emotional as he is forced to see himself without the protection of his rationalizations.

Sour grapes and *sweet lemons* reactions are two familiar variations of rationalization. The term "sour grapes" derives from one of Aesop's fables. After trying repeatedly to get some grapes that are too high to reach, a fox tells himself, "They're probably sour anyway." Many of life's disappointments are softened by similar rationalization. If you are not invited to a party, you will probably tell yourself, "It would have been dull anyway. I'm not missing anything." When applying for a job, you get enthusiastic about it. But when the position goes to someone else, you mentally review its bad points and decide it would have been a sour experience. You rush to a sale to pick up an advertised bargain and find the item sold out and conclude, "It must have been crummy to sell that cheap anyway."

"Sweet lemons," of course, is the reverse of sour grapes. Here a person convinces himself that an undesirable situation is really positive. Let's say that you selected four colleges that you thought you might like to attend. Let's further assume that the only school which admitted you, or which you could afford, was the last choice on your list of four. Once you realize that particular college is the only one you will be able to attend, you will probably begin unconsciously forming a list of positive points so that you can convince your friends (and yourself) that what you got is what you want. The anxiety which follows most major decisions or commitments is usually followed by sweet-lemon rationalization. Talk to someone who has just bought a car or a house, selected a college major, accepted a job, become engaged to be married, or started time payments on a set of encyclopedias. You will find that even the slightest hint of skepticism on your part will unleash a flood of sweet-lemon rationalization.

Learning Check

1. Define rationalization: ______________________________

____

____

2. Two common variations of rationalization are ______________

and ______________________________.

(Check your answers in the material above.)

Defenses—Some General Comments

Question: When are defense mechanisms unhealthy?

It is difficult to state a general rule, but when defenses begin costing a person more than they return in protective benefits they become undesirable. A person who overuses defense mechanisms is less adaptable because he or she uses great amounts of energy to maintain an unrealistic self-image:

> Frank is a frail, skinny, high school student. He is relatively unpopular and has no close friends. He has been unable to distinguish himself in sports, academics, or other pursuits. A few years ago he began repressing strong feelings of inferiority and adopted a loud overbearing manner. He has gained a reputation for bragging and puffery that further hurts his acceptance among fellow students. Projecting his own hostility and resentment at being rejected, he is developing an increasingly sour view of other people. He has convinced himself that he avoids others, not they him. He has recently taken up reading psychology books and uses the jargon to intellectualize and rationalize his own failures and as a means of maintaining a feeling of superiority over others. He spends a great deal of time fantasizing about the future he foresees for himself as a great psychologist but has isolated these expectations from his poor grades which he blames on "lousy teachers."

We all know Frank. It requires little insight to see that he is struggling and that his defenses have become a trap which prevent him from overcoming his weaknesses.

Question: All of the defense mechanisms described seem pretty undesirable. Do they have a positive side?

Defense mechanisms serve the purpose of protecting us from anxiety. They may help prevent a person from being overwhelmed by a temporary threat and may provide time for us to learn to cope with continuing threats. If you have recognized some of your own behavior in the preceding pages, it is hardly a sign that you are hopelessly defensive. Most people make occasional use of defense mechanisms.

There are two defense mechanisms that have a decidedly more positive quality to them. These are *compensation* and *sublimation*.

Compensation—"I Was a 97 Pound Weakling"

Compensation is a form of behavior whereby a person tries to make up for some personal defect or fault. *Compensatory reactions* are defenses against feelings of inferiority. A person who has a deficiency or weakness (real or imagined) may go to unusual lengths to overcome the weakness or to compensate for it by excelling in other areas. Two of the better known "muscle men" in America are Jack LaLanne and Charles Atlas. Both made successful careers out of body building, in spite of the fact that they were thin and sickly as young men. Perhaps it would be more accurate to say *because* they were thin and sickly. There are dozens of examples of compensation at work. A childhood stutterer may excel in debate at college. Franklin D. Roosevelt's outstanding achievements in politics came after he was stricken with polio. As a child, Helen Keller was unable to see or hear, but she became an outstanding thinker and writer. Eric Kloss, Doc Watson, Ray Charles, Stevie Wonder, Jose Feliciano, and a number of other well-known musicians are blind.

If compensation is directed at overcoming the "deficiency" itself, it may be constructive. However, this is not always the case, and sometimes the desire to prove one's adequacy becomes so overpowering that it controls a person's behavior to the exclusion of other pursuits. It has been suggested that Napoleon and Hitler were both small men who sought power to prove that they were really "big." More commonly, a student who feels physically inferior may throw himself into school so deeply that a completely unbalanced (and unsatisfying) life-style is created. A person who feels unloved may eat too much. A woman who feels unattractive may compensate by self-destructive promiscuous sex. In its mildest form, compensation gives rise to undesirable attempts to build oneself up by bragging or by cutting others down with criticism and thinly disguised insults.

Learning Check Compensation is usually a defense against feelings of ________________.

(Check the previous discussion for the answer.)

Sublimation—Refined Sex

Freud coined the term *sublimation* to describe what he considered the most mature of the defense mechanisms. Sublimation is defined as working off frustrated desires (especially sexual desires) in substitute activities that are constructive and accepted by society. Freud believed that art, music, dance, poetry, scientific investigation, and most other creative activities represent a rechanneling of sexual energies into productive and acceptable behavior. He believed that almost any strong desire can be sublimated. For example, Freud (1910a) considered Leonardo da Vinci's *Madonna and Child with St. Anne* (see Fig. 15-3) the result of sublimation: Leonardo had two mothers, his true mother from whom he was separated at a tender age and a loving stepmother. Freud points out that it is quite unusual for St. Anne, Mary, and Jesus to be portrayed as a trio and for a mature Mary to be sitting on her mother's lap reaching out for the child on the ground. Freud interprets the painting as an expression of Leonardo's childhood love for his two mothers.

Desires less pleasant than love can also be sublimated. Helene Deutsch (1965) tells about the inhabitants of a small university town who

Fig. 15-3 Leonardo's *Madonna and Child with St. Anne.* (Courtesy Alinari-Art Reference Bureau.)

awoke to the horrifying discovery that all the loose dogs in a certain part of town had lost their tails during the night. It was later learned that some medical students had gotten drunk at a party and that one of them had the inspiration to cut off the dogs' tails as a "joke." Deutsch points out that this student's sadistic urges later found constructive sublimation in medicine when he became one of the most famous surgeons in the world. By sublimating, a very aggressive person may find social acceptance as a professional soldier, boxer, or football player. Greed may be refined into a successful business career. Lying may be sublimated into storytelling, creative writing, or politics.

Sexual motives appear to be the most easily and widely sublimated. Freud would have had a field day with such modern pastimes as surfing, motorcycle riding, drag racing, and dancing to or playing rock music, to name but a few. People enjoy each of these activities for a multitude of reasons, but it is hard to overlook the rich, sexual symbolism possible in each.

Question: What do you mean?

It is difficult to ignore the significance of thousands of adolescent boys sitting in the water with a long phallic symbol between their legs trying to achieve the ultimate in surfing, which is to "get locked into a hot tube." The pelvic movements of rock musicians and those of rock dancers are also obviously sexual expressions. These comments are not intended to be crude or to embarrass, but simply to point out the symbolic nature of much human behavior and the possibilities for sublimating sexual energies.

Resources Summary

Defense mechanisms are habitual and unconscious strategies used to deny, distort, or counteract sources of anxiety and to help maintain an idealized self-image.

Do-It-Yourself Summary Below you will find a list of definitions for all the defense mechanisms discussed in this chapter. In the spaces provided, write in the correct term to fit the definitions. The terms are all listed below.

Terms used to define defense mechanisms: *Rationalization*, *fantasy*, *sublimation*, *repression*, *reaction formation*, *regression*, *projection*, *denial*, *isolation*, *compensation*, *intellectualization*.

1. ______________________ Protecting oneself from an unpleasant reality by refusing to perceive it.

2. ______________________ Preventing painful or dangerous thoughts from entering consciousness.

3. ______________________ Preventing dangerous impulses from being expressed by exaggerating opposite behavior.

4. ______________________ Fulfilling frustrated desires in imaginary achievements.

5. ______________________ Retreating to an earlier level of development or to earlier less demanding habits or situations.

6. ______________________ Attributing one's own shortcomings or unacceptable impulses to others.

7. ______________________ Separating contradictory or opposite attitudes into logic-tight compartments.

8. ______________________ Separating emotion from a hurtful, threatening, or anxiety-provoking situation.

9. ______________________ Justifying one's own behavior by giving reasonable and "rational" but false reasons for it.

10. ______________________ Counteracting a real or imagined weakness by emphasizing desirable traits or by seeking to excel in other areas.

11. ______________________ Working off frustrated desires in substitute activities that are constructive or socially accepted.

Check your answers to make sure you have a correct summary.

Answers: **1.** denial **2.** repression **3.** reaction formation **4.** fantasy **5.** regression **6.** projection **7.** isolation **8.** intellectualization **9.** rationalization **10.** compensation **11.** sublimation

Applications

Avoiding Defensiveness—Self-Disclosure

Psychological defenses are basically dishonest. They are used when it becomes necessary to distort information to fit the picture we have of ourselves. Heavy reliance on psychological defenses is also costly, and defensiveness breeds more defensiveness. As psychologist Sidney Jourard puts it:

> The greater the discrepancy between my unexpurgated real self and the version of myself that I present to others, the more dangerous will other people be for me. If becoming known to another person is a source of danger, then it follows that merely the presence of the other person can serve as a stimulus to evoke anxiety, heightened muscle tension, and all the assorted visceral changes which occur when a person is under stress (Jourard, 1959).

Question: How can a person avoid defensiveness?

Your most frequently used defenses are usually unconscious. This makes overcoming defensiveness difficult, but an effort to cultivate habits of greater honesty with oneself can lead to greater self-acceptance and can help eliminate the need for defensiveness. A valuable step in the direction of greater honesty with oneself is what Jourard calls "self-disclosure"—being open and honest with others.

> Self-disclosure, letting another person know what you think, feel or want, is the most direct means . . . by which an individual can make himself known to another. . . . Self-disclosure is both a symptom of personality health . . . and at the same time a means of ultimately achieving healthy personality (Jourard, 1959).

Question: If I wanted to practice self-disclosure, how would I do it?

Make a daily effort to share your thoughts, fears, failings, embarrassments, desires, dreams, or fantasies with someone else. Tell someone you trust something about yourself that you've never told anyone before. At first you may have to force yourself to disclose yourself more openly. However, as you make an effort to reveal things about yourself that you would normally hide, your defenses will relax and you will find your personality becoming freer as you learn to accept yourself and your feelings.

You will be surprised. Frequently you will tell someone what you consider a dark secret about yourself, and that person will say, "Yes, I know that, I've noticed it in you many times." Others sometimes see us more objectively than we do ourselves. Another common reaction will be, "Yes, I've felt that way too." You will be surprised at what a *relief* it is to reveal things you thought were embarrassing or secret feelings to trusted others. Try it.

Questions for Discussion

The psychological defense mechanisms are intriguing because they are so readily observed in everyday life. The following questions may stimulate further thought or discussion about psychological defenses.

1. Have you encountered any particularly clear examples of the use of defense mechanisms? Describe some of the defenses you have recognized in yourself and others.
2. The defenses in this chapter were described in psychodynamic terms, that is, in terms of the balance of forces within the personality. Can you advance a learning-theory explanation for any of the defenses? (Hint: Think in terms of avoidance learning and the rewards connected with defensive responses.)
3. Do you think there is any danger in self-disclosure? Can self-disclosure be overdone?
4. Watch your local paper for examples of defense mechanisms. Share these with the class. Do other class members agree with your labeling of the defense involved? Do you think the psychological defenses can be realistically separated into as many terms as used in this chapter?
5. What are the advantages and disadvantages of using defense mechanisms?
6. Do you think it would be possible for a person to be completely free of defense mechanisms? How could you distinguish a person low in defensiveness from a person pretending to be psychologically honest?

Suggestions for Further Reading

Freud, S. "The Psychopathology of Everyday Life." In *The Basic Writings of Sigmund Freud.* Random House, 1938.

Jourard, S. *Disclosing Man to Himself.* Van Nostrand, 1968.

Mahl, G. F. *Psychological Conflict and Defense.* Harcourt Brace Jovanovich, 1971.

Perls, F. *Gestalt Therapy Verbatim.* Real People Press, 1969.

Contents

Human Development and Personality

Unit Five

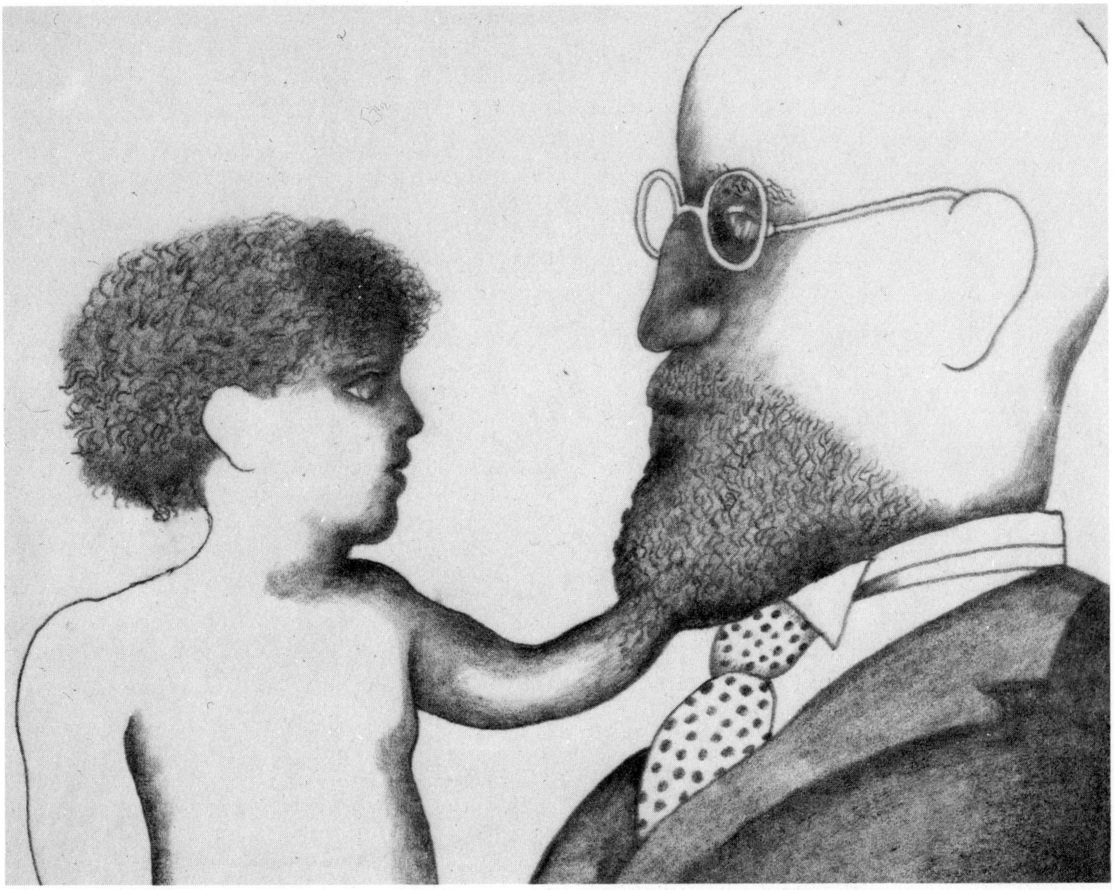

Human Development

16

Chapter Preview

Alien Minds

You may not have noticed. Not everyone has. There are alien creatures among us. More arrive daily. They look a lot like you and me . . . but they're smaller . . . and they think differently. They speak in strange patterns and they ask many questions. It's obvious they are trying to understand how we live. Their goal is to inhabit the planet earth in our place. Who are these creatures and where are they from? You need not be alarmed; they come not from outer space, but from inner space. They are the product of a biological union—of life perpetuating life. They are children.

There are a number of reasons for studying children. At a practical level, parents and educators need accurate information to promote full development of a child's potentials. In personal terms, the study of children helps answer the question "How did I become the person I am today?" At the theoretical level we recognize that adult personality is closely tied to the child in each individual's past. This alone makes the study of children rewarding, but there is another reason. Children are not just "little adults." Their understanding of the world is qualitatively different from yours and mine. Entry into a child's circle of awareness has much of the intrigue of meeting a person from another culture. It might even be compared to an encounter with an "alien mind." In short, children are extremely interesting creatures, and a tremendous amount of psychological research has focused on them.

Question: What branch of psychology studies children?

The study of children is the heart of developmental psychology. *However, you should recognize that developmental psychologists are interested in every stage of life from "the womb to the tomb." Developmental psychology can therefore be described as the* study of progressive changes in behavior and abilities from conception to death. *In this chapter you will find discussion of a number of general principles of development, including an account of the far-reaching effects of events in the first years of life. Perhaps learning about development will contribute to your development. Find out by reading more!*

Resources

The Newborn Baby—The Basic Model Comes with Options

At birth the human *neonate* (newborn) is completely helpless and will die if he is not cared for. He has only a limited sensitivity to pain and cannot lift his head, turn over, or feed himself. Does this mean he is inert and unfeeling? Definitely not! The neonate is more sensitive and responsive than many people realize. He responds readily to light, sounds, tastes, and touch. He will, in fact, follow a moving object with his eyes and will turn in the direction of sounds. A number of adaptive *reflexes* can also be observed. An object pressed to his palm will be grasped with surprising strength. Indeed, the *grasping reflex* is so strong that many infants can hang by their hands if lifted. This may improve the infant's chances for survival by reducing the possibility of falling. Another adaptive reflex can be demonstrated by touching the baby's cheek. Immediately he will turn toward your finger as if searching for something.

Question: How is this turning adaptive?

The *rooting reflex*, as this is called, helps the infant find a bottle or breast. When a nipple touches the infant's mouth, the *sucking reflex* helps him to obtain the food he needs. Also of interest is the *Moro reflex*. If the baby's head is allowed to drop or if he is startled by a loud noise or other frightening stimulus, he will make movements similar to an embrace. These have been compared to movements used by baby monkeys to cling to their mother. It is left to the reader's imagination to decide if there is any connection.

Question: How much intelligence does a newborn have?

Child psychologist Jerome Bruner believes babies are smarter than most people think. Bruner cites an experiment in which three- to eight-week-old babies showed signs of understanding that a person's voice and body are connected. If a baby heard his mother's voice coming from where she was standing, he remained calm. If her voice came from a loudspeaker several feet away, the baby became agitated and began to cry. In another experiment, six-week-old infants were placed in a "baby theater," where they were allowed to watch a movie while sucking on a pacifier. The movie was out of focus, but the pacifier controlled the projector. Babies quickly learned to suck faster on the pacifier to bring the movie into clearer focus. The babies seemed to have grasped the significance of their actions. Bruner considers this an indication that the human mind is quite active from birth onward (Pines, 1970).

Another look into the private world of the infant can be drawn from tests of infant vision.

Question: How is it possible to test a baby's vision?

Working with infants always requires imagination because of their inability to talk. To test infant vision, Robert Fantz (1963) invented a device called a "looking chamber." A child is placed on his back inside the chamber so he is facing a lighted area above. Next, two objects are placed in the chamber. By observing the movements of the infant's eyes and the images reflected from their surface, it is possible to tell what the infant is looking at. Fantz found that three-day-old babies preferred complex patterns like checkerboards and bull's-eyes to simpler colored rectangles.

Of greater interest was the finding that infants spend more time looking at a human face pattern than at a scrambled face or a colored oval. When real human faces were used, Fantz found that familiar faces were preferred to unfamiliar faces. This changes at about age two, when unusual objects begin to hold greater interest for the child. For instance, Jerome Kagan (1971) showed three-dimensional face masks to two-year-olds and found they were fascinated by a face with eyes on the chin and a nose in the middle of the forehead. Kagan believes their interest came from a need to understand why the scrambled face differed from what

Fig. 16-1 Infants within Fantz's chamber looked at the simple face longer than the scrambled face, and at both faces longer than the design on the right. (Photo courtesy of David Linton.)

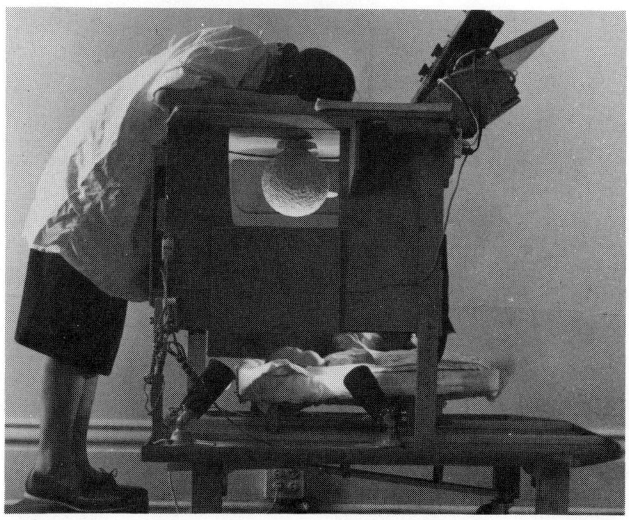

they had come to expect. We therefore see a progression in the infant's interest in the world. At first, bright and complex patterns catch his eye; next there is a preference for the familiar; following that is an interest in the unusual. We also know that the infant develops an intense early interest in the human face.

Perhaps the most striking characteristic of the human infant is the dazzling speed with which he is transformed from a helpless baby to an independent person. Early growth is extremely rapid. By the third year of life, the child stands, walks, talks, explores, and has a unique personality. At no other time after birth does development proceed more rapidly. During this period there is a fascinating interplay of forces shaping the child's development, most importantly, heredity and environment.

Heredity and Environment—The Nature of Nurture and the Nurture of Nature

Question: Which has a greater effect on development, heredity or environment?

For many years psychologists debated—sometimes heatedly—the relative importance of "nature" versus "nurture" in determining behavior. The potent effects of heredity ("nature") certainly cannot be denied. At the moment of conception, when a sperm and egg unite to make a new organism, an incredible number of personal characteristics and developmental patterns are determined. For example, there are about 1 million different species of animals on earth. The mere fact that heredity "programs" a growing bundle of cells to become a fish, a bird, an ape, a hamster, or a person has obvious implications for the course of development. In addition, each person receives a totally unique biological inheritance from his or her parents.* It has been estimated that the genetic information carried in the 46 *chromosomes* of a single human cell would fill a thousand 600-page books if translated into words. These "hereditary instructions" control development throughout life by affecting growth rates and the timing of puberty and aging. In addition, heredity determines sex, eye and skin color, body size and shape, height, intelligence (to an extent), athletic potential, and a host of other details. (Score 1 for those who favor heredity as the more important factor.)

Does this mean "nurture" takes a back seat in development? Consider Aldous Huxley's (1965) dramatic summary of the influence of environment:

> Anatomically and physiologically man has changed very little during the last twenty or thirty thousand years. The native or genetic capacities of today's

*An exception to this statement is the case of identical twins. Since they develop from a single fertilized egg, identical twins have identical heredity.

> bright city child are no better than the native capacities of a bright child born into a family of Upper Paleolithic cave-dwellers. But whereas the contemporary bright baby may grow up to become almost anything—a Presbyterian engineer, for example, a piano-playing Marxist, a professor of biochemistry who is a mystical agnostic and likes to paint in water-colors—the Paleolithic baby could not possibly have grown into anything except a hunter or food-gatherer.[1]

(Score 1 for the environmentalists!)

The outcome of this debate (we have only viewed an opening round) is recognition that *both* heredity and environment are important. The two are, in fact, inseparable. As a person grows there is a constant interplay or *interaction* between the forces of nature and nurture. Heredity shapes development by providing a framework of personal potentials and limitations that are altered by learning, nutrition, disease, culture, and other environmental factors.

Question: How soon after birth do hereditary differences appear?

They appear immediately. Infants are unique individuals from the time of birth. Jerome Kagan (1969) found that newborn babies differ in activity, irritability, distractability, and other aspects of *temperament*. Another careful study found that babies could be reliably separated into three categories: "easy children" (about 40 percent of those observed), "difficult children" (about 10 percent), and "slow-to-warm-up children" (about 15 percent). The remaining children did not fit neatly into one category (Thomas *et al.*, 1968). "Easy children" are those who are relaxed and agreeable. Such children adapt well to their surroundings. "Difficult children" tend to overreact to most situations. They are moody, intense, easily angered or frustrated, and prone to tantrums. By contrast, the "slow-to-warm-up child" is restrained and unexpressive. These children are slow to react and might be described as "shy" or withdrawn.

Because of such inborn differences, babies rapidly become *active participants* in their own development. Growing infants change the environment at the same time they are changed by it. For example, Amy is an "easy" baby who smiles frequently and is easily fed. This encourages touching, feeding, and affection from her mother. The mother's responses, in turn, reward Amy and cause more smiling and other positive reactions. A *relationship* has been established between mother and child. Of course, this can also work in reverse, as when a "difficult" baby angers or frustrates his parents and becomes more difficult due to their reactions.

We might say, then, that four factors combine to determine a person's *developmental level* at any stage in life. These are: *heredity*, *environment*, the individual's own *behavior*, and the passage of *time* (which allows the first three factors to operate).

[1]From "Human Potentialities" by A. Huxley. In R. E. Farson (Ed.) *Science and Human Affairs*. Palo Alto, California; Science and Behavior Books, 1965.

Maturation—Heredity at the Helm

In some areas of development the effects of heredity outweigh those of environment. For example, one classic study concerned this question: "If a baby is not allowed to practice crawling or walking early in life, will he walk at the same age as an unrestrained child?" To obtain an answer, Dennis (1940) studied Hopi Indian children who were kept on cradle boards for the first nine months of life. According to tradition, these children were firmly bound to a board for most of each day. As a result they got little or no practice at sitting, creeping, or walking. Nevertheless, they learned to walk at about the same age (fifteen months) as unrestrained children. The age at which a child learns to walk is more the result of *maturation* than of learning.

Question: What, specifically, is maturation?

Maturation refers to growth and development of the body and the nervous system. Maturation underlies the *orderly unfolding* of many basic responses. For instance, the strength and coordination needed for sitting appears before that needed for crawling. Therefore, children almost universally sit before they crawl (and crawl before they stand, stand before they walk, and so on) (see Fig. 16-2). In general, increased muscular control proceeds from "head to toe" and from the center of the body to the extremities.

The development of *language* is also closely tied to maturation. By one month of age, the infant can control crying enough to use it as an attention-getting device, and parents can tell the nature of the infant's needs from the tone of the crying. By the time a child is six months old, the nervous system has matured enough to allow the child to grasp objects, to smile, laugh, sit up, and to *babble*. The babbling stage is marked by a continuous outpouring of connected and repeated language sounds.

At about one year of age the child can stand alone for a short time and can respond to words like "No" or "Hi." Soon afterward, the first connection between words and objects is formed, and the child may address his parents as "Mama" or "Dada." Between the ages of 1½ and 2 years, the child becomes able to stand and walk alone. By this time his vocabulary may include from two dozen to 200 words. These are arranged into simple two-word sentences called *telegraphic speech*: "Want Teddy," "More milk," "Mama gone." From this point on, growth of the child's vocabulary and language skills proceeds at a phenomenal rate. By first grade, the child can understand around 8,000 words and can use about 4,000.

Question: It's easy to see that maturation is important, but isn't language also learned?

It is, of course. Imitation of adults and rewards for correctly using words (as when the child asks for food) are quite important. But the rapid

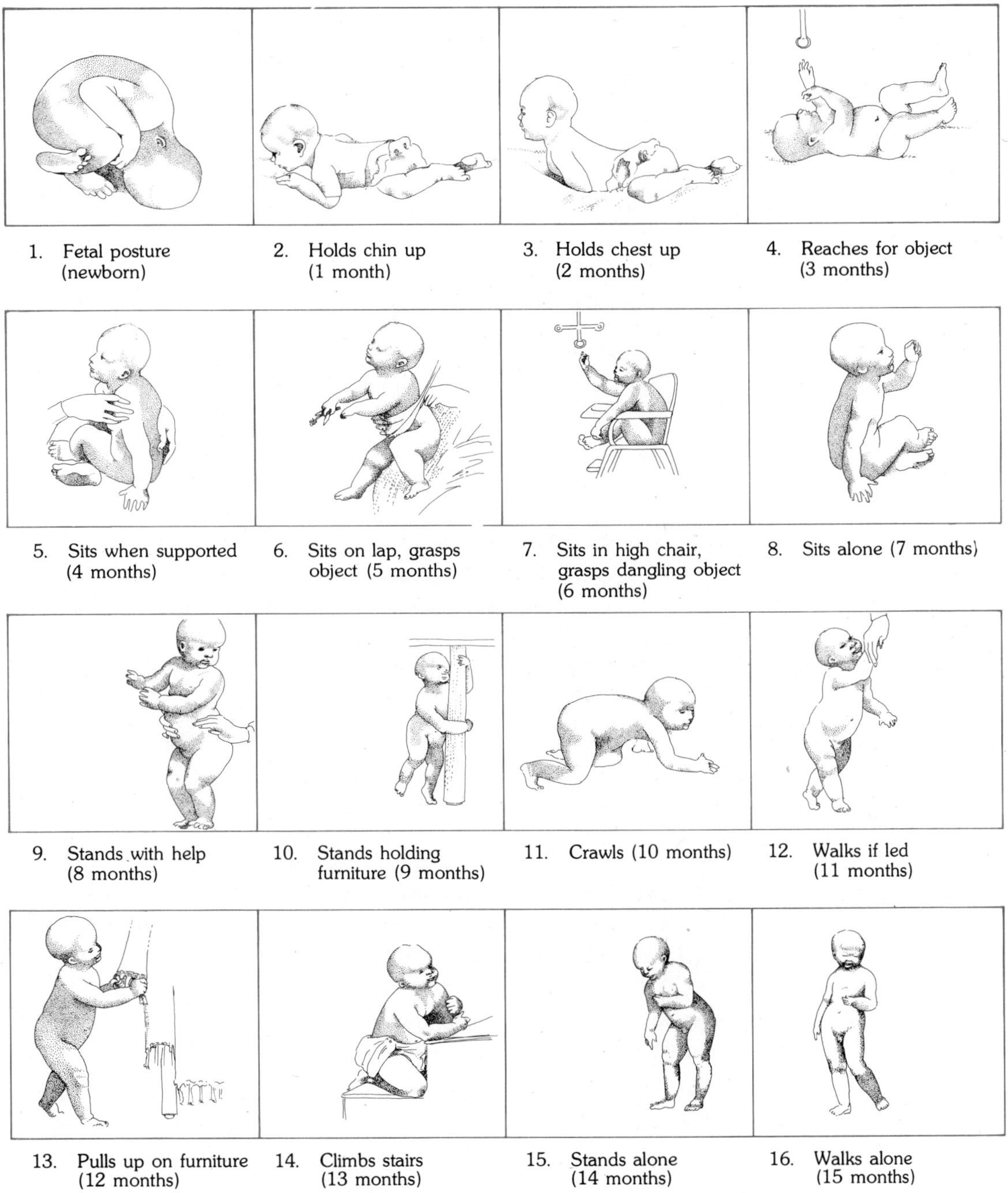

Fig. 16-2 Most infants follow an orderly pattern of motor development. Although the order in which children progress from one stage to the next is similar, there are large individual differences in the age at which various stages are reached. The ages listed are averages. (Based on Shirley, 1933 and Frankenburg and Dodds, 1967.)

rate of language development suggests that something more must be involved. *Psycholinguists* like David McNeill (1966) and Noam Chomsky (1968) believe that humans have a *biological predisposition* to develop language. They consider this universal, like the infant's predisposition to walk upright when sufficiently mature.

Maturation also has a very dramatic effect on the pace of learning other basic skills. This is demonstrated by the following experiment (Kellogg & Kellogg, 1933):

Donald's Strange Sister

When Donald was nine months old, his parents brought a seven-month-old chimp home to be raised as one of the family. Every effort was made to treat Donald and Gua (the chimp) like brother and sister. For the next eight months they were treated as much alike as possible and received equally affectionate care and training. During this time, Gua rapidly surpassed Donald in learning many "civilized" acts (such as drinking from a cup, using a spoon, responding to spoken instructions, and maintaining bowel and bladder control). By the time Donald was about 18 months old, however, Gua's superiority came to an end as Donald began to use language. From this time on, he excelled Gua in everything but physical strength.

Gua's early superiority is easily explained. A chimp has only about one-third the life span of a human and matures much more rapidly. Gua's rapid maturation gave her an early "edge" in learning. Notice, however, that her abilities quickly hit a peak, whereas Donald's continued to improve as he matured. Notice also the importance of Donald's inherited potential for learning language.

Readiness Other studies have shown that maturation creates a condition of *readiness* for learning. The principle of readiness (also known as the "principle of motor primacy") states, "Until the necessary physical structures are mature, no amount of practice will be sufficient to establish a skill." It is impossible, for instance, to teach a child to walk or to become toilet trained before he has matured enough to control the necessary muscles. The parent who tries to force a child to learn a skill for which he is not yet ready invites failure and runs the risk of needlessly frustrating the child.

Question: Then are there definite ages at which children become ready to learn particular skills?

Readiness is not an all-or-nothing effect. Training that comes too early will be unsuccessful; training that is only a little early may succeed, but will be inefficient; and training when a child is maturationally ready produces rapid learning. This progression can be seen in an experiment in which a group of two- and three-year-old children were given twelve weeks of special practice at learning to climb a ladder (to reach a tabletop covered with toys). By the end of the 12-week period, the children had become good climbers. At this point, children in a second group (matched in age with the first group) were given practice at ladder climbing (Hilgard, 1932).

Question: Did it take the second group 12 weeks to learn to climb?

No, the second group caught up to the first after just one week. Even though they missed out on the previous 12 weeks of practice, their bodies had continued to mature. Hence, they learned more rapidly and efficiently when given the chance.

Many parents are anxious to see their children move through the developmental stages, and there is always a temptation to try to "hurry" a child along. However, it is valuable to recognize that much unnecessary grief can be avoided by respecting a child's own particular rate of maturation. The parent who successfully toilet trained an eighteen-month-old child in eight trying weeks might have easily done the same thing in two or three weeks by waiting until the child was twenty months old to begin.

Learning Check

Complete the following statements.

1. Robert Fantz has used a ______________ ______________ to test infant vision.

2. Individuals are ______________ ______________ in their own development.

3. As a person grows, there is a constant ______________ between the forces of heredity and environment.

4. The emergence of behavior primarily under the control of heredity is called ______________.

5. The "principle of motor primacy" is also known as ______________.

6. Heredity, environment, the individual's own behavior, and the passage of time combine to determine a person's ______________ ______________.

Answers: **1.** looking chamber **2.** active participants **3.** interaction **4.** maturation **5.** readiness **6.** developmental level

Early Environment—As the Twig Is Bent

Environment obviously begins to modify development immediately after birth, but it may come as a surprise that the prenatal environment is also important. Normally we think of the *intrauterine environment* of the womb as highly protected and stable. In general, it is; but a number of conditions can affect the fetus before birth. If a mother's health or nutrition is poor, if she contracts certain diseases such as German measles or syphilis, uses drugs, or is exposed to x-rays, the fetus may be harmed. Drugs are particularly troublesome. Smoking can elevate or lower the heart rate of the unborn child, and a mother who smokes heavily is more likely to give birth to an underweight baby. If the mother is addicted to morphine or heroin, the child may be born with an addiction.

Question: Is it true that a mother's emotions can affect the fetus?

Psychological stress experienced by the mother may have an effect because adrenaline released into the mother's bloodstream is transferred to the fetus. Difficult births are also associated with measurable differences after birth. There is no truth, however, to stories about babies' acquiring fears, a taste for a particular food, an interest in music, and so on, because the mother ate the food, listened to music, or was frightened while pregnant.

In later years, a child's environment expands to include the effects of culture, subculture, family, school, television, and peers. Immediately after birth and for the first few years, the most important influences come from an infant's caretakers. The quality of "mothering" is therefore of prime importance. One revealing study of *maternal influences* began with selection of children who were unusually competent (A children) or who had a low degree of competence (C children). As increasingly younger children were observed, it became apparent that A and C patterns were already set by age three. To learn how this was possible, children under three and their mothers were observed at home (White & Watts, 1973). On the basis of several years of research, five types of mothers were identified (Pines, 1969).

Fig. 16-3 Mothering makes a difference. (Photo by Marge Agin.)

1. The "super mother" occasionally goes out of her way to provide an educational experience for her child, yet accepts the child as he is. There appears to be a balance between activities initiated by the mother and by the child. The "super mother" produces an A child—competent in most areas of development.
2. The "smothering mother" pushes the child and constantly orders him around. The child's present level of ability is never accepted as adequate. This produces a child of A intellectual ability, but one who is immature and shy.
3. The "almost mother" waits for the child to lead in most situations and seems to have difficulty understanding and meeting his needs. The typical outcome is a B child of above-average competence who has some difficulty in dealing with the environment.
4. The "overwhelmed mother" spends little time with her child. The child spends much of his time sitting or doing nothing and may be cared for by brothers or sisters. The mother has difficulty meeting the problems of daily living, and the entire home tends to be disorganized. This produces a C child of average or below-average competence.
5. The "zoo-keeper mother" gives her child good physical care, but interacts with him very little. This mother's child-care routines are rigid and highly structured. She tends to produce a C child who approaches problems inflexibly (summary adapted from Lugo & Hershey, 1974).

Although not yet confirmed by others, these findings support two beliefs long held by developmental psychologists: first, that mothering *does* make a difference and, second, that early development has lasting effects on a person.

Critical Periods in Development—Mother Goose and Motherless Monkeys

Question: Why do experiences early in life have such lasting effects?

Part of the answer lies in the existence of *critical periods* for acquiring particular behaviors. A critical period is a time when certain events must occur for a person (or an animal) to develop normally. This can be seen very clearly in the case of some animals. To illustrate, Konrad Lorenz, an ethologist who studies animal behavior, once became curious about why baby geese follow their mother. The obvious explanation seemed to be, "It's instinctive," but Lorenz showed otherwise.

Mother Lorenz

Normally the first large moving object a baby goose sees is its mother. Lorenz hatched geese in an incubator so the first moving object they saw was Lorenz. From then on, these baby geese followed Lorenz. They even reacted to his call as if he were their mother (Lorenz, 1937).

Fig. 16-4 "Mother" Lorenz leads his charges on a stroll. The goslings have imprinted on Dr. Lorenz because he was the first moving object they saw after they hatched. (Photo by Thomas McAvoy, Time-Life Picture Agency © Time, Inc.)

It can be seen that the response pattern of "mother-goose following" is not automatic. It is established during a critical period by the essential experience of seeing a large moving object. The rapid and early establishment of a permanent behavior pattern of this type has been called *imprinting*.

In most birds, the critical period for imprinting is very brief. For instance, Hess (1959) found that if ducklings are not allowed to imprint on their mother or some other object within 30 hours after hatching, they never will.* In many animals, imprinting and other events taking place during a critical period have lifelong consequences:

The Goose's Revenge

Imprinting normally serves the useful purpose of attaching an immature animal to its mother. It also guides the selection of a mate of the same species

*Ducklings have been imprinted on decoys, rubber balls, wooden blocks, and a number of other unlikely objects.

at sexual maturity. When Lorenz's geese reached sexual maturity, Lorenz became the object of their mating ritual. Part of this ritual involves stuffing worms into the mouth of the intended mate—as a surprised Lorenz learned while asleep on the lawn one day (proving, perhaps, that it's not nice to fool Mother Nature)!

Question: Does imprinting occur in humans?

True cases of imprinting are limited to birds and other animals (Hess, 1959). However, human infants form an *emotional attachment* to their *primary caretakers* (usually parents), and there is a critical period during which this must occur for healthy development (Bowlby, 1969, 1973). Until babies are about six months old, they show no more attachment to parents than they do to strangers. After this period they begin to display *stranger anxiety* and show other signs of having learned to fear the unfamiliar (Scott, 1967). Attachment probably serves the same purpose for a human infant as it does for baby animals; that is, it keeps the infant close to its parents and increases its chances of survival.

Research with rhesus monkeys suggests that, like imprinting, infant attachments have lasting effects. Harry Harlow (1966, 1967) has shown that baby monkeys separated from their mothers and raised in isolation become troubled adult animals. Among other things, these "motherless monkeys" never develop normal sexual behaviors, and they make very poor mothers if mated. They are coldly rejecting or indifferent to their babies and may brutalize or injure them. It has been suggested that human parents who abuse, reject, or physically injure their children may be displaying a similar pattern. Most abusive parents were themselves rejected or mistreated as children.

Meeting a baby's *affectional needs* appears to be as important as meeting more obvious needs for food, water, and physical care. Rejection or social deprivation during infancy can result in a lasting inability to form deep emotional attachments to others. Therefore, an important *developmental task* of the first year of life is creation of a bond of trust and affection between the infant and at least one other person. Parents are sometimes afraid of "spoiling" a baby with too much attention, but for the first year or two this is nearly impossible. As a matter of fact, a later capacity to experience warm and loving relationships may depend on it.

Question: Are there other critical periods?

Psychologists are just beginning to explore the full range of critical periods in human development. It is well known, for example, that if a person waits until adulthood to learn a second language, it becomes virtually impossible to achieve an authentic native accent. In general, reaching maximum ability in artistic, athletic, musical, or language skills requires practice that begins at an early age. A case in point is the success of Russian athletes who are selected early and rigorously trained throughout childhood. The work and theories of Japanese music teacher Shinichi

Suzuki are also highly suggestive. Using scaled-down instruments, Suzuki has taught children as young as three years old to play the violin. By age six, these children have spent half their lives playing Bach, Handel, Mozart. By age ten, many are so phenomenal that serious adult students envy their ability.

In many ways it would be accurate to say that all of infancy is a *relatively critical period* in development. While we must wait for further research on variables affecting the kinds of skills described above, one area is fairly well understood. The effects of early stimulation and deprivation are discussed in the following section.

Deprivation and Enrichment—A Practical Definition of Tender Loving Care

News item: "Wild Child Raised by Apes Found in Africa." Over the years there have been several reported discoveries of "feral children." These are children who have supposedly grown up in the care of animals and who act like animals when found. Actually, there is little documented evidence that such children have existed, but we needn't go this far afield for proof of the destructive effects of early *deprivation*. There are numerous confirmed cases of children who have spent the first five or six years of life in closets, attics, and other restricted environments. When discovered, these children are usually mute, severely retarded, and emotionally damaged. Special efforts to teach such children to speak and to function normally have met with only limited success.

Question: What aspects of such experiences are responsible for the damage done?

One of the earliest hints came when psychoanalyst René Spitz (1945) compared two groups of infants. One group was made up of healthy and lively babies in an institution Spitz called the "nursery." In the "foundling home" was a second group of babies who suffered from a condition called *hospitalism*. This is a pattern of deep depression marked by weeping and sadness, long periods of immobility or mechanical rocking, and a lack of normal response to other humans. The foundling home also had an unusually high rate of infant deaths, and development of the living babies was severely retarded.

By comparing conditions at the two institutions, Spitz found some striking differences. At the nursery, each baby had a separate attendant; at the foundling home, there were eight babies to a nurse. Spitz considered the "wasting away" of the foundling home babies a result of *anaclitic* (dependency) depression. In other words, he emphasized the fact that babies in the nursery had dependable "mother figures," whereas those in the foundling home had one-eighth of a nurse each. More recent research suggests that another factor was of greater importance. More than anything else, the "wasted" babies lacked *perceptual stimulation*. All were well cared for physically, but they were kept in bare rooms, in cribs with white sheets hung on the sides. The infants could only see the blank ceiling, and their only contact with others came during a few brief periods each day when they were quickly fed or changed. To put it mildly, there was *nothing happening* for these children: no change, no input, no cuddling, no attention, and, most of all, no stimulation. This was deprivation in the fullest sense of the word.

Experiments with animals have confirmed the destructive effects of a lack of stimulation in infancy. For example, monkeys raised in darkness for the first three months of life are unable to use their vision properly when brought into the light (Riesen, 1965). Also revealing is the research of Harry Harlow. As mentioned earlier, Harlow separated infant rhesus monkeys from their mothers at birth. The real mothers were replaced with "surrogate (artificial) mothers"—essentially dummies of approximately the

Fig. 16-5 An infant monkey clings to a cloth-covered surrogate mother. Baby monkeys become attached to the cloth "contact-comfort" mother but not to a similar wire mother. This is true even when the wire mother provides food. (Photo courtesy of Harry Harlow, University of Wisconsin Primate Laboratory.)

same size and shape as real monkeys. Some of the surrogates were made of cold, unyielding wire, and others were covered with soft terry cloth. When the infants were given a choice between the two mothers, they consistently chose to spend most of their time clinging to the cuddly terry cloth mother. This was true even when a bottle was mounted in the wire mother, making it the source of food.

The "love" and attachment displayed toward the cloth mothers was identical to that shown toward natural mothers. When frightened by rubber snakes, wind-up toys, and other "fear stimuli," the infant monkeys ran to their cloth mothers and clung to them for security (Harlow & Zimmerman, 1958). Harlow has concluded that one of the most important dimensions of early stimulation is *contact comfort*, supplied by touching, holding, and stroking an infant. Harlow's findings may be inconclusive where humans are concerned, but other findings back them up. For example, one researcher found that just 20 minutes of extra touching a day could affect the developmental rate of infants in an institution (Casler, 1965).

For many psychologists, the concept of contact comfort has become part of the rationale for advocating breast feeding of infants. Breast feeding almost guarantees a baby will receive an adequate amount of touching and handling. In addition, the breast-feeding mother produces *colostrum* rather than milk for the first few days after birth. Colostrum is a fluid rich in proteins that carries antibodies from the mother to the newborn and helps to prevent certain infectious diseases.

Question: What about the mother who can't breast-feed or who prefers not to?

The advantages of breast feeding are not overriding. If a mother is aware of the importance of touching and cuddling and makes an effort to provide it, bottle feeding is in no way psychologically inferior to breast feeding. In fact, a mother's warmth or coldness, relaxation or tension, and acceptance or rejection have more to do with the effects of feeding than does the choice of breast or bottle (Heinstein, 1963).

Enrichment If too little stimulation limits development, can an abundance of stimulation enhance it? A number of attempts to answer this question have made use of *enriched environments*. An enriched environment is one that has been deliberately made more novel, complex, and richly stimulating. Enriched environments for infants may be the "soil" from which brighter children grow. To illustrate, let us begin with an experiment in which rats were raised in an enriched environment (Kretch *et al.*, 1962):

Building Bigger and Better Brains

To begin with, infant rats were divided into two groups. One group was raised in *stimulus-poor* conditions. These animals were housed in adequate but

> unstimulating cages with gray walls that contained nothing to explore or investigate. The second group was housed in a sort of "rat wonderland." The walls of this *stimulus-enriched* environment were decorated with colored patterns, and the cage was filled with platforms, ladders, and cubbyholes to be explored. When the rats reached adulthood, they were tested for ability to learn mazes. The stimulated rats dramatically out performed their deprived relatives. In addition, later tests showed that the stimulated rats had brains that were larger and heavier with a thicker cortex.

It is a long leap from rats to people, but it is hard to overlook the significance of an increase in brain size caused by sensory stimulation. If stimulation can enhance the "intelligence" of a lowly rat, it is reasonable to assume that human infants also benefit from stimulation.

Question: Is there any evidence that this is actually the case?

As might be expected, it is much harder to prove that such things occur in humans. In Chapter 18, you will find a full discussion of the effects of environment on intelligence. For now, let us examine one case of enrichment applied to humans.

Infants like to reach out and touch things, but normally it takes about five months after birth for this skill to develop. In an experiment conducted at a state hospital, newborn infants were given several kinds of extra stimulation each day for several months (White & Held, 1966):

> Each child in the stimulus enrichment condition was handled an extra fifteen minutes daily; each was placed in a position that allowed visual exploration outside the crib; white crib sheets were replaced by patterned sheets with colorful animal designs; and a collection of bright and colorful objects was hung over each child's crib.

As limited as these changes may seem, they caused "visually directed reaching" to occur an average of a month and a half early. This may not sound like an earth-shaking improvement in adult terms, but to an infant it represents a substantial acceleration of development.

This is only one of many experiments showing a positive relationship between stimulation and improvements in various abilities, particularly those that might be labeled "intellectual." Most people recognize that babies need lots of "tender loving care" where physical needs are concerned. But as the previous discussion shows, a complete definition of tender loving care should include a baby's psychological needs as well. It would be a good idea to place stimulation, affectionate touching, and personal warmth high on any list of infant needs.

Learning Check

The preceding sections of this chapter contain a large amount of information. Check your comprehension by answering the questions below. Skim back over the material if you miss any.

1. A duckling can be imprinted after the critical period has passed if the environment is enriched. T or F?

2. The development of stranger anxiety in an infant corresponds to formation of an attachment to parents. T or F?

3. A baby's affectional needs can be met by supplying adequate food, water, and physical care. T or F?

4. Harlow's "motherless monkeys" became attached to the surrogate mother that fed them. T or F?

5. René Spitz attributed hospitalism to anaclitic depression. T or F?

6. Bottle feeding prevents a mother from providing an adequate amount of contact comfort for an infant. T or F?

7. The intrauterine environment has little effect on a person's development. T or F?

8. The "super mother" goes out of her way to provide educational experiences, but accepts the child as he is. T or F?

Answers: 1. F 2. T 3. F 4. F 5. T 6. F 7. F 8. T

Cognitive Growth—How Do Children Learn to Think? How Do Children Think to Learn?

Question: How much does a child's intelligence differ from that of an adult?

From the standpoint of maturation, it is estimated that 50 percent of adult intelligence is developed by age four and 80 percent by age eight (Bloom, 1964). These figures are somewhat deceptive because a child's intelligence differs from that of an adult in *quality* as well as quantity. Generally speaking, a child's thinking is *less abstract* than that of an adult. Children use fewer generalizations, categories, or principles and tend to base their understanding of the world on particular examples, tangible sensations, and concrete objects.

An indication of the concrete nature of thinking in very young children is their failure to recognize the permanence of objects. Older children and adults realize that an object that is out of sight still exists. With a very young child, "out of sight" can literally mean "out of mind." If a ball rolls behind something while a four- or five-month-old child is playing with it, the child behaves as if the ball has ceased to exist and stops looking for it.

Long after children have discovered the permanence of objects, their thinking remains concrete in other ways. For example, before age six or seven, children are unable to make *transformations*. If you show a child a short, wide glass full of milk and a tall, narrow glass (also full), the child will

Fig. 16-6 Children under age 7 intuitively assume that a volume of liquid is increased when it is poured from a short, wide container into a tall, thin one. (Photo by Marge Agin.)

tell you the taller glass contains more milk. Children will tell you this even if you allow them to watch as you pour milk from the short glass into an empty, tall glass. They are not bothered by the apparent transformation of the milk from a smaller to a larger amount. They respond only to the fact that "taller" seems to mean "more." After about age seven, children are no longer fooled by this situation. Perhaps this is why seven has been called the "age of reason." From seven on, we see a definite trend toward more abstract thought (Elkind, 1968).

Question: Is there any pattern to the growth of intellect in childhood?

According to Swiss psychologist and philosopher Jean Piaget (1951, 1952), there is more than a pattern. Piaget believes all children pass through a definite series of *stages* in their intellectual development. For many years Piaget has studied thinking differences between children and adults. Many of his first observations were based on "naturalistic experiments" using his own children as subjects.* In Piaget's experiments a child is presented with certain problems to be solved (the milk-glass problem is a good example). Piaget has found that certain problems can be solved

*It is tempting to imagine that Piaget's illustrious career could very well have been launched one day when his wife said to him, "Watch the children for a while, will you, Jean?"

before others and that the ability to solve some problems is a *prerequisite* for solving others. Piaget's theories have had a profound effect on our thinking about children. The following is an abbreviated summary of what he has found.

The Sensorimotor Stage (0–2 Years) In the first two years of life a child's intellectual development is largely *nonverbal*. The child is mainly concerned with learning to coordinate appropriate movements with information from the senses. At first, the infant must rely on reflexes to guide responses, but soon movements become *purposeful*. The infant can voluntarily reach out to touch or grasp an object and begins actively to explore the environment. Also important at this time is gradual emergence of the concept of *object permanence*. At about a year and a half, the child begins to pursue disappearing objects. By age two the child can anticipate the movement of an object behind a screen. When watching an electric train, for example, the child looks ahead to the end of a tunnel rather than staring at the spot where the train disappeared. In general, these developments indicate that the child's conceptions are becoming more *stable*. Objects cease to appear and disappear magically, and a more orderly and predictable world replaces the confusing and disconnected sensations of infancy.

The Preoperational Stage (2–7 Years) During the preoperational period the child is developing an ability to think *symbolically* and to use language. A casual conversation with a child in this stage might leave you impressed with his surprisingly grown-up statements. But the child's thinking is still very *intuitive*. (Do you remember thinking as a child that the sun and the moon followed you when you took a walk?) In addition, the child's use of language is not as sophisticated as it might seem. Children have a tendency to confuse words with the objects they represent. If the child calls a toy block his "car" and you use it to make a "train," he may be upset. To the child, the name of an object is as much a part of the object as its size, shape, and color. This seems to underlie a preoccupation with name calling. To the preoperational child an insulting name may hurt as much as "sticks and stones."*

During the preoperational stage, the child is also quite *egocentric*, meaning he is unable to take the viewpoint of other people. His ego seems to stand at the center of his world. To illustrate, show the child a two-sided mirror and then hold it between the two of you so the child can see himself in it. If you ask him what he thinks *you* can see, he imagines that you see *his* reflected image instead of your own. The child's limited and egocentric conception of the world is also demonstrated by the following (Laurendeau & Pinard, 1962):

*I am reminded of one rather protected youngster who was angered by her older brother. Searching for a way to retaliate against her larger and stronger foe, she settled on "You panty-girdle!" It was the worst thing she could think of.

Adult: Why is it dark at night?
Child: Because if you don't sleep, Santa Claus won't give you any toys.
Adult: Where does the dark come from at night?
Child: Well, bandits they take something or mother pulls down the blinds and then it's very dark.

The concept of egocentrism helps us to understand why children can seem exasperatingly selfish or uncooperative at times. A child who blocks your view by standing in front of a television set assumes that you can see if he can. If you ask him to move so you can see, he may move so that he can see better!

The Concrete Operational Stage (7–11 Years) An important development during this stage is mastery of the concept of *conservation*. A child has learned the concept of conservation when he understands that rolling a ball of clay into a "snake" does not increase the amount of clay and that pouring liquid from a tall, narrow glass into a shallow dish does not reduce the amount of liquid. In each case the volume remains the same despite a change in shape or appearance. The original amount is "conserved."

During the concrete operations stage, a child's thought begins to include the concepts of time, space, and number. Categories and principles are used, and the child can think logically about concrete objects or situations. Another important development at this time is the ability to reverse thoughts or operations. Lack of *reversibility* is illustrated by this conversation with a four-year-old (Phillips, 1969):

"Do you have a brother?"
"Yes."
"What's his name?"
"Jim."
"Does Jim have a brother?"
"No."

Reversibility of thought allows the older child to recognize that if $4 \times 2 = 8$, then 2×4 does, too. Younger children must memorize each relationship separately.

The Formal Operations Stage (11 Years and Up) Sometime after about the age of eleven, the child begins to break away from concrete objects and specific examples. Thinking is based more on *abstract principles*. The child can think about his thoughts and becomes less egocentric. The older child or adolescent also gradually becomes able to consider *hypothetical possibilities*. For example, if you ask a younger child: "What do you think would happen if it suddenly became possible for people to fly?" he will respond, "But people can't fly." The older child is able to consider the possibilities and to discuss their implications. The stage of formal operations represents attainment of full adult intellectual ability.

The older adolescent is capable of inductive and deductive reasoning and can conceptualize mathematics, physics, philosophy, psychology, and other theoretical and abstract systems. From this point on, improvements in intellectual ability are based on the accumulation of knowledge, experience, and wisdom rather than on an enlargement of basic thinking capacity.

Learning Check

1. List Piaget's four stages of cognitive growth in their order of appearance. ______________________________

____

____

2. In which stage does object permanence develop? ______________________________

____

3. Mastery of the concept of conservation occurs in which stage? ______

____

4. In general, a child's thinking is less ______________ than that of an adult.

Answers: **1.** sensorimotor, preoperational, concrete operational, formal operations **2.** sensorimotor **3.** concrete operational **4.** abstract

Resources Summary

Even at birth the human neonate is sensitive and responsive. In addition to having a number of reflexes, the newborn is capable of altering simple actions to make changes in the environment. Infants are aware of their surroundings and prefer to look at some things more than others. Early development is extremely rapid. *Heredity* and *environment* interact with the effects of an infant's *own behavior* and the passage of *time* to determine *developmental level.*

The effects of heredity are clearly evident in the process of *maturation*. Maturation has a marked effect on motor development, language acquisition, and the pace of early learning. Maturation also creates a state of *readiness* for the development of many skills.

The effects of environment begin before birth in the *intrauterine* environment and continue throughout life. *Maternal influences* are particularly important during the first few years of life. Environmental influences are magnified during certain *critical periods* in development. Human emotional attachments are associated with a critical period similar to that seen in animal *imprinting*. Early *deprivation* involving insufficient *affection* or *perceptual stimulation* can have lasting ill effects on a child. *Contact comfort* seems to be an essential ingredient of healthy stimulation in infancy. There is evidence that *enriched environments* may encourage optimal development.

The intellect of a child is less abstract than that of an adult. Jean Piaget believes that the growth of intellect goes through a fixed progression of *cognitive stages*. The stages and their approximate age ranges are: *sensorimotor* (0–2), *preoperational* (2–7), *concrete operations* (7–11), and *formal operations* (11–adult).

Applications

Making the Most of a Magic Time of Life

Many applications of the ideas presented in this chapter are self-evident. A few bear additional emphasis or extension.

Maturation It is valuable to remember that individual differences in maturation rates are the rule in human development. Aware parents recognize the difference between the *statistical* child and the *particular* child. Developmental norms specifying ages at which particular abilities appear are based on *averages*. There is always a wide range of normal variation around each average. Thus, it is reasonable to expect plateaus, reversals, and periods of rapid advancement in the development of a particular child. This applies not only to the appearance of motor skills like crawling and walking but also to language development and the stages of cognitive development described by Piaget. In all areas of development the uniqueness of a child should be respected. This means resisting the temptation to compare the child to others, particularly in the child's presence. Each child is an individual and should be judged as such.

Enrichment As we have already emphasized, babies need stimulation. By keeping this need in mind, parents can do much to provide opportunities for varied sensory experience during infancy. A baby should be surrounded by colors, music, people, and things to see, taste, smell, and touch. Babies are not vegetables. It makes perfect sense to talk to an infant, to take him outside, to hang mobiles over his crib, or to rearrange his room weekly. The possibility of providing too much stimulation is remote. Most parents could put far more imagination into attempts to enrich an infant's surroundings than they typically do.

Question: Are such measures useful only during infancy?

Definitely not. Enriching the environment at any stage of childhood appears to be well worth the effort. As a matter of fact, Jerome Kagan has recently reported that stimulation in later childhood can have a greater effect on intellectual development than previously believed possible. Kagan studied babies in a primitive Guatemalan village who were raised in darkened huts. Without the benefit of even a moderate amount of stimulation, these children were severely retarded by age two. Yet by age eleven they had become beautiful children—gay, alert, and active (Kagan & Klein, 1973). The rich stimulation of village life during later childhood was enough to reverse the effects of early deprivation. Kagan relates this to a serious error he believes we make in this country. He points out that most of our schools tend to decide at an early age that some children have potential and that others do not. Those who seem bright and promising are more often exposed to stimulating and enriching experiences than those who do not. In this way, schools may needlessly perpetuate the effects of a poor start in life.

Question: In general, what kinds of experiences are most likely to encourage intellectual development?

Piaget's theory suggests that the ideal is to provide experiences that are only slightly novel, unusual, or challenging. A child's intellect develops through a process of *accommodation*. Old concepts and thinking habits become obsolete and are adapted or discarded to fit new demands. To stretch a child's intellect, demands must be made, but experiences that are too far beyond the familiar may cause frustration and withdrawal. Therefore, gradually expanding beyond a child's current level of comprehension is usually most productive.

Piaget's work also shows the importance of relating to a child on the right level. If you give a physical explanation when a very young child asks, "Why does the sun come up in the morning?," you may have missed the point. Answering in terms of the child's egocentric viewpoint is more likely to be meaningful. An answer like, "So that you will know it's time to get up" is completely satisfactory for a young child. Later, explanations can be made increasingly abstract and accurate.

It is also valuable to remember that children are newcomers to language. Many of the "silly" things children say have meanings that become apparent only to the adult patient enough to look for them. For example, language expert S. I. Hayakawa (1965)[2] relates this incident:

> Once when our little girl was three years old, she found the bath too hot and said, "Make it warmer." It took me a moment to figure out that she meant, "Bring the water more nearly to the condition we call warm." It makes perfectly good sense if you look at it that way.

[2]From "The Use and Misuse of Language" by S. I. Hayakawa. In R. E. Farson (Ed.) *Science and Human Affairs.* Palo Alto, California; Science and Behavior Books, 1965.

Intellectual growth is encouraged when a child feels free to express ideas and feels understood when he does.

Question: Are there any guidelines for relating to children at the right level?

In a delightful book entitled *Using Psychology*, Morris Holland offers some suggestions about how best to relate to children at different stages of intellectual development. The following points are drawn from his discussion (Holland, 1975).

1. *Sensorimotor stage (0–2).* Active play with a child is most effective at this stage. Encourage explorations in touching, smelling, and manipulating objects. "Peekaboo" is a good way to establish the permanence of objects.
2. *Preoperational stage (2–7).* Although the child is beginning to talk to himself and to act out solutions to problems, touching and seeing things will continue to be more useful than verbal explanations. Concrete examples will also have more meaning than generalizations. The child should be encouraged to classify things in different ways. Learning the concept of conservation may be aided by demonstrations involving liquids, beads, clay, and other substances.
3. *Concrete operational stage (7–11).* Children in this stage are beginning to use generalizations, but they still require specific examples to grasp many ideas. Expect a degree of inconsistency in the child's ability to apply concepts of time, space, quantity, and volume to new situations.
4. *Formal operations stage (11–adult).* At this point, it becomes more realistic to explain things verbally or symbolically to a child. Helping the child to master general rules and principles now becomes productive. Encourage the child to create hypotheses and to imagine how things "could be."

Keeping this general outline in mind should help you adjust to the changing patterns of intellect displayed by developing children.

Questions for Discussion

1. In what ways is it accurate to treat children as "little adults"? In what ways is it inaccurate?
2. Do you think an infant would be more or less likely to survive if maturation proceeded from toe to head and from the extremities inward?
3. How many ways can you think of for an infant to reward its mother and for the mother to reward the infant?
4. What types of toys would you select for an infant or young child? Do you think simple toys or elaborate toys would be best? Why? Would your choice change for an older child? Why?
5. How has heredity affected your development? How has environment affected you?
6. How would child rearing be different if parents had to teach children deliberately to walk or to talk?
7. If you were the director of an orphanage or a similar institution, what steps would you take to ensure the normal development of infants in your care?

Suggestions for Further Reading

Ambron, S. *Child Development.* Dryden, 1975.

Developmental Psychology Today. CRM, 1971.

Ginsburg, H., and S. Opper. *Piaget's Theory of Intellectual Development: An Introduction.* Prentice-Hall, 1969.

Lugo, J. O., and G. L. Hershey. *Human Development.* Macmillan, 1974.

Millar, S. *The Psychology of Play.* Penguin Books, 1968.

Staats, A. W. *Child Learning, Intelligence, and Personality: Principles of a Behavioral Interaction Approach.* Harper & Row, 1971.

Whiting, J., and I. Child. *Child Training and Personality.* Yale University Press, 1953.

Special Problems in Development

17

Chapter Preview

Life with Billy

By the time he was five, Billy's "record" read like a script of a parent's worst nightmare. Billy threw uncontrollable temper tantrums and never seemed to sleep. At age five Billy had not learned to talk. He got into closets and tore up his mother's evening dresses and urinated on her clothes. He smashed furniture and spread soap powder and breakfast food all over the floors. He tripped a maid at the head of the stairs and then lay on the floor doubled up with laughter. He attacked his mother at every opportunity, once going for her throat with his teeth. He tried to stuff his baby brother in a toy box. When Billy's parents bought him a doll they called by the baby's name, they began finding the doll pushed head down in the toilet bowl. Billy refused to eat anything but cold, greasy hamburgers from a certain drive-in. To get through a week his parents were forced to buy the hamburgers by the sack and hide them around the house so Billy wouldn't eat them all at once. When his parents went out driving they had to detour around drive-ins to prevent Billy from frothing at the mouth and trying to jump out the window (Moser, 1965). Billy, you may note, was not an average five-year-old.

Question: *What was his problem!?*

Billy was an autistic child. *His problem is rare. Few children get off to as bad a start in life as Billy. Nevertheless, every individual faces certain challenges and problems on the path to healthy development. Some obstacles, like toilet training or establishing an identity, can be considered universal. Others are specialized problems. In either case, the challenges of development extend far beyond childhood and on into old age. In this chapter we will examine some of the special problems presented by each stage of life. Be alert for information pertinent to your own life. Be alert for Billy, too. You'll meet him again later in the chapter.*

Resources

The Cycle of Life—Rocky Road or Garden Path?

If you pride yourself on being "one of a kind," you have good reason. There is no such thing as a "typical person" or a "typical life." Nevertheless, there are certain broad similarities in the universal *life stages* of infancy, childhood, adolescence, young adulthood, middle adulthood, and old age. Each stage represents a milestone in physical maturation and psychological development, and each confronts a person with a new set of *developmental tasks* to be mastered. These are skills that must be acquired or personal changes that must take place for optimal development.

In an influential book entitled *Childhood and Society* (1963), personality theorist Erik Erikson suggests that we also face a specific *psychosocial* dilemma, or "crisis," at each stage of life. According to Erikson, resolving these crises creates a new balance between a person and the social world. An unfavorable outcome throws one off balance and makes it harder to deal with later crises. A string of "successes" produces healthy development and a satisfying life. Those who are plagued with unfavorable outcomes may experience life as a "rocky road."

Question: What are the major developmental tasks and life crises?

This is a broad question requiring several pages for an answer. Read on!

Developmental Tasks and Life Crises—A Lifetime in a Nutshell

Countless details must be ignored to condense the events of a lifetime into a few pages. Much is lost, but the net effect is a clearer picture of an entire life cycle. Actually, when we speak of a cycle of life, we really mean two cycles in one. Erikson (1964) has noted that these are "the cycle of one generation concluding itself in the next and the cycle of individual life coming to a conclusion." From either perspective, the healthy development of past, present, and future generations is deeply interrelated. A single lifetime represents but one link in a chain of humanity stretching into this planet's uncertain future. Let's examine the events of a "typical" life.

Early Childhood, 0–6 Years Author James Coleman (1969, p. 80) summarizes the developmental tasks of the early childhood period as:

> Acquiring a sense of trust in self and others. Developing healthy concept of self. Learning to give and receive affection. Identifying with own sex. Achieving skills in motor coordination. Learning to be member of family group. Beginning to learn physical and social realities. Beginning to distinguish right and wrong and to respect rules and authority. Learning to understand and use language. Learning personal care.[1]

Question: Are there any life crises during this period?

Erikson emphasizes three critical themes in early childhood development.

Stage One, First Year of Life: Trust versus Mistrust During the first year of life children are completely dependent on others for safety and comfort. Erikson believes that a basic attitude of *trust* or *mistrust* is formed at this time. Trust is established by regular satisfaction of a baby's needs. Babies given adequate warmth, touching, love, and physical care learn to view the world as a safe and dependable place. Mistrust is caused by inadequate or unpredictable care and by parents who are cold, indifferent, or rejecting. Basic mistrust may become the core of later insecurity, suspiciousness, or inability to relate to others.

Stage Two, 1–3 Years: Autonomy versus Shame and Doubt Stage two is the age of exploration. Muscular development allows a child to take charge of his or her own behavior. Growing independence is expressed by climbing, touching, exploring, and a general desire to do things for oneself. Parents help their children develop a sense of *autonomy* when they encourage them to try new skills and reassure them if they fail. Consistent *overprotection* may limit development by denying opportunities for self-direction. Teasing and ridicule also create problems. The child's first crude efforts to do things often result in spilling, falling, wetting, and other "accidents." Erikson feels that parents who make fun of their children cause them to feel ashamed of their actions and to doubt their abilities. Thus, feelings of *shame* and *doubt* are the unfavorable outcome of this stage.

Stage Three, 3–5 Years: Initiative versus Guilt In stage three the child moves from simple self-control to an ability to take initiative. Through play the child learns to plan, undertake, and carry out a task. Parents reinforce *initiative* by giving freedom to play, to ask questions, to use imagination, and to choose activities. The child may be emotionally handicapped by parents who criticize severely, discourage play, or ridicule questions. In this case, children learn to feel that their play, ideas, or questions are silly or stupid and become *ashamed* of them. They also learn to feel *guilty* about

[1]From *Psychology and Effective Behavior* by James C. Coleman. Copyright © 1969 by Scott, Foresman and Company. Reprinted by permission.

Fig. 17-1 According to Erikson, children aged three to five face an important conflict between initiative and guilt. (Photo by Optic Nerve, Jeroboam.)

the activities they initiate when these activities seem to be a nuisance to parents.

Middle Childhood, 6–12 Years Many of the events of middle childhood are symbolized by that fateful day when you made your first trip to school. With dizzying speed your world expanded beyond the bounds of the family, and you were confronted with a whole series of new challenges.

Question: What are the developmental tasks of middle childhood?

The major tasks are:

> Gaining wider knowledge of physical and social world. Building wholesome attitudes toward self. Learning appropriate masculine or feminine role. Developing conscience, morality, scale of values. Learning to read, write, calculate, other intellectual skills. Learning physical skills. Learning to win and maintain place among age-mates. Learning to give and take, and to share responsibility (Coleman, 1969, p. 80).

The years from 6 to 12 are very industrious years for a child. It is just this quality that Erikson considers essential for healthy development.

Stage Four, 6–12 Years: Industry versus Inferiority Erikson describes the elementary school years as the child's "entrance into life." Children begin to learn skills valued by society, and success or failure can have lasting effects on feelings of adequacy. Children develop a sense of *indus-*

try if they win praise for building, painting, cooking, reading, studying, and other productive activities. If a child's accomplishments are regarded as messy, childish, or inadequate, feelings of *inferiority* result. For the first time, teachers, classmates, and adults outside the home become as important as parents in shaping attitudes toward oneself.

Adolescence, 12–18 Years Adolescence is a turbulent time for most persons in our culture. Caught between childhood and adulthood, the adolescent faces some unique problems. The tasks of this period can be described as:

> Developing a clear sense of identity and self-confidence. Adjusting to body changes. Developing new, more mature relations with age-mates. Achieving emotional independence from parents. Selecting and preparing for an occupation. Achieving mature values and social responsibility. Preparing for marriage and family life. Developing concern beyond self (Coleman, 1969, p. 80).

Question: Which of these tasks does Erikson consider most important?

Stage Five, Adolescence: Identity versus Role Confusion Erikson considers a need to answer the question "Who am I?" the primary crisis during this stage of life. Mental and physical maturation brings to the individual new feelings, a new body, and new attitudes. The adolescent must build a consistent *identity* out of self-perceptions and relationships with others. Conflicting experiences as a student, friend, athlete, worker,

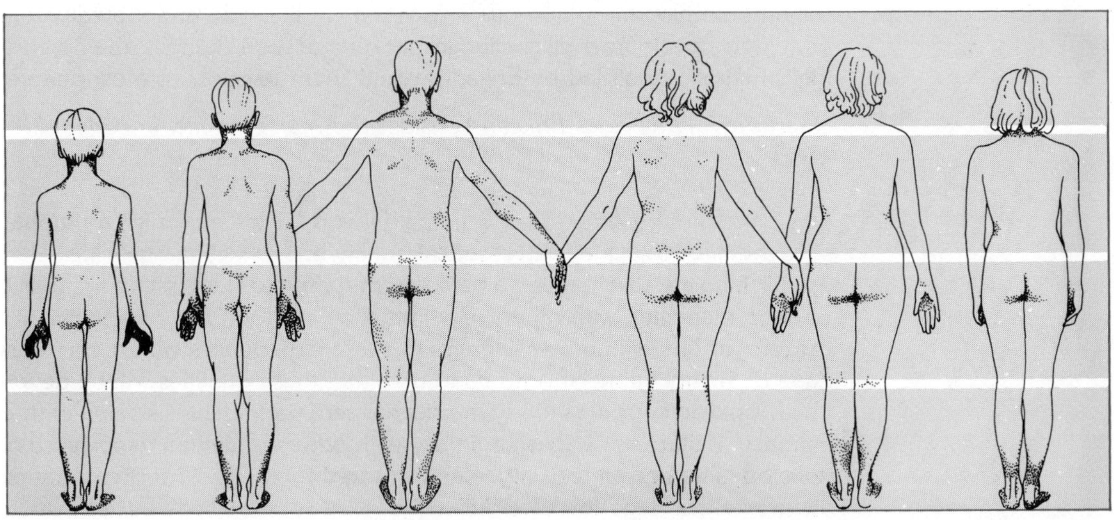

Fig. 17-2 Dramatic differences in physical size and maturity are found in adolescents of the same age. The girls pictured are all thirteen; the boys sixteen. Maturation that occurs earlier or later than average undoubtedly affects the "search for identity." (From J. M. Tanner. Copyright 1973 by Scientific American, Inc. All rights reserved.)

son or daughter, lover, and so forth, must be integrated into a unified sense of self. Failure to develop identity causes *role confusion* and leaves the person unsure about who he is and where he's going.

Role confusion may cause the person to seek identity by emulating musicians, athletes, leaders of religious groups, or media heroes. Role confusion may also underlie a tendency to overidentify with a clannish group and to reject anyone who looks or acts different. Despite these excesses, the search for identity is also a basis for healthy explorations in religion, philosophy, psychology, ecology, politics, human rights, and other areas of personal relevance. In many cases, making vocational plans helps a person define an identity.

Early Adulthood, 18–35 Years The developmental tasks of early adulthood are:

> Seeing meaning in one's life. Getting started in an occupation. Selecting and learning to live with a mate. Starting a family and supplying children's material and psychological needs. Managing a home. Finding a congenial social group. Taking on civic responsibility (Coleman, 1969, p. 80).

Question: Is it fair to say that these are essential for healthy development?

Certainly these tasks reflect the expectations of our culture and the lives of the vast majority of Americans. However, with the rapid changes taking place in this country, they do not apply to all segments of the population. For example, many young adults are deferring marriage in favor of less binding relationships, and those who marry are having fewer children. Communal living, extended educational goals, alternatives to full-time employment, and other variations in life-style undoubtedly generate new developmental challenges. In spite of such changes, the psychological crisis pinpointed by Erikson would seem to apply to most people.

Question: What does Erikson consider the major conflict in early adulthood?

Stage Six, Young Adulthood: Intimacy versus Isolation Erikson emphasizes the need to achieve an essential quality of *intimacy* in one's life. After establishing a stable identity, a person is prepared to share meaningful love or deep friendship with others. By "intimacy" Erikson means an ability to care about others and a willingness to share experiences with them. Marriage or sexual intimacy is no guarantee that these qualities will be developed. Erikson considers many marriages mere partnerships lacking in true intimacy. Failure to establish intimacy with others leads to a deep sense of *isolation*. The person feels alone and uncared for in life. This circumstance often sets the stage for later difficulties.

Middle Age, 35–60 Years Many researchers now believe that personality development continues until at least age 50.

Question: Do you mean that a 20-year-old has a partially developed personality?

No, certainly by age 20 we would say that a person has a fully formed personality. It's just that the demands placed on an individual in later years are quite different and require continued personal change. A summary of the demands of middle age reads:

> Achieving full civic and social responsibility. Relating to oneself and to one's spouse as a person. Establishing adequate financial security for remaining years. Developing adult leisure-time activities, extending interests. Helping teen-age children become responsible and happy adults. Adjusting to aging parents. Adjusting to physiological changes of middle age (Coleman, 1969, p. 80).

Successful adjustment during middle age centers on a conflict summarized by Erikson's seventh stage of development.

Stage Seven, Middle Adulthood: Generativity versus Stagnation According to Erikson, an interest in guiding the next generation, called *generativity*, is the main source of balance in mature adulthood. In general this means caring about oneself, one's children, and the future. Generativity may be achieved by guiding one's own children or by helping other children (as a teacher, clergyman, or coach might do). It may also be achieved through productive or creative work. In any case, a person's concern and energies must be broadened to include the welfare of others and society as a whole. Failure in this is marked by a stagnant concern with one's own needs and comforts. Life loses meaning, and the person feels bitter, dreary, and trapped.

Later Life In some cultures the aged are respected and revered. In our culture considerable value is placed on youthfulness. This orientation adds an important psychological dimension to the difficulties of aging. Ilya Ehrenburg (1968) expresses the problem in an examination of his own reactions to aging:

> For the past fifteen years or so, I have been learning how to be an old man. This is not nearly as easy as I thought when I was young. I used to think that desires die down along with the possibilities of satisfying them; but then I began to understand that the body ages before the spirit, and that one has to learn to live like an old man.

Acceptance of the aging process is not the only developmental task of later life. Others are:

> Adjusting to decreasing physical strength. Adjusting to retirement and reduced income. Adjusting to death of spouse and friends. Meeting social and civic obligations within one's ability. Establishing an explicit affiliation with age group. Maintaining interests, concern beyond self (Coleman, 1969, p. 80).

While Erikson acknowledges the difficulties, he sees the major challenge of aging in broader terms. As in the earlier stages, Erikson's last stage of development emphasizes a psychological crisis that must be resolved successfully.

Question: What is Erikson's last stage?

Stage Eight, Late Adulthood: Integrity versus Despair Because old age is a time of reflection, a person must be able to look back over the events of a lifetime with a sense of acceptance and satisfaction. According to Erikson, the previous seven stages of life become the basis for successful aging. The person who has lived richly and responsibly develops a sense of *integrity*. This sense allows aging and death to be faced with dignity. If previous life events are viewed with regret, the elderly person falls into *despair*. In this case, there is a feeling that life has been a series of missed opportunities, that one has failed, and that it is too late to reverse what has been done. Aging and the threat of death then become a source of fear and depression.

In this brief overview we have seen that the successful life begins with learning to trust others and ends with trusting oneself and one's life: The circle closes; the cycle is complete. This description may not be an exact map of your future, but it reflects the life events of many people. Anticipating some of the typical trouble spots may help you to prepare for them. You may also be better prepared to understand the problems and perspectives of friends and relatives at various stages of the life cycle. The remaining pages of this chapter are devoted to discussion of specialized problems in development.

Learning Check

Since Erikson's eight life stages are scattered through the previous pages you might find it helpful to summarize them. Complete this do-it-yourself summary to check your recall of the stages. Compare your answers to those listed below to make sure you have a correct summary.

Stage	Crisis	Favorable outcome
First year of life	**1.** ______ vs. **2.** ______	Faith in the environment and in others
Ages 1–3	Autonomy vs. **3.** ______	Feelings of self-control and adequacy
Ages 3–5	**4.** ______ vs. guilt	Ability to begin one's own activities
Ages 6–12	Industry vs. **5.** ______	Confidence in productive skills, learning how to work
Adolescence (ages 12–18)	**6.** ______ vs. role confusion	An integrated image of oneself as a unique person
Early adulthood (ages 18–35)	Intimacy vs. **7.** ______	Ability to form bonds of love and friendship with others
Middle adulthood (ages 35–60)	Generativity vs. **8.** ______	Concern for family, society, and future generations
Late adulthood	**9.** ______ vs. **10.** ______	Sense of dignity and fulfillment, willingness to face death

Answers: **1.** trust **2.** mistrust **3.** shame or doubt **4.** initiative **5.** inferiority **6.** identity **7.** isolation **8.** stagnation **9.** integrity **10.** despair

Problems of Childhood—When Is Stress a Strain?

Question: *Is it possible for problems in development to start with birth?*

Birth is presumably quite stressful. From the warm and protected confines of the womb, a baby is forcefully thrust into a cold, noisy world. The new arrival is greeted with glaring lights, booming voices, cutting of the umbilical cord, and a swift slap on the bottom. According to French obstetrician Frederick Leboyer, these events make birth a needlessly traumatic experience. In his book *Birth without Violence* (1975), Leboyer advocates a system that purportedly makes birth pleasant for both mother and baby. Delivery takes place in a silent, dimly lit room. Immediately after birth the baby is placed on its mother's stomach and gently massaged. After several minutes of soothing, the umbilical cord is cut and the baby is bathed in warm water. Leboyer claims that babies delivered in this way are healthier, happier, and less anxious than those subjected to birth procedures he considers "cruel."

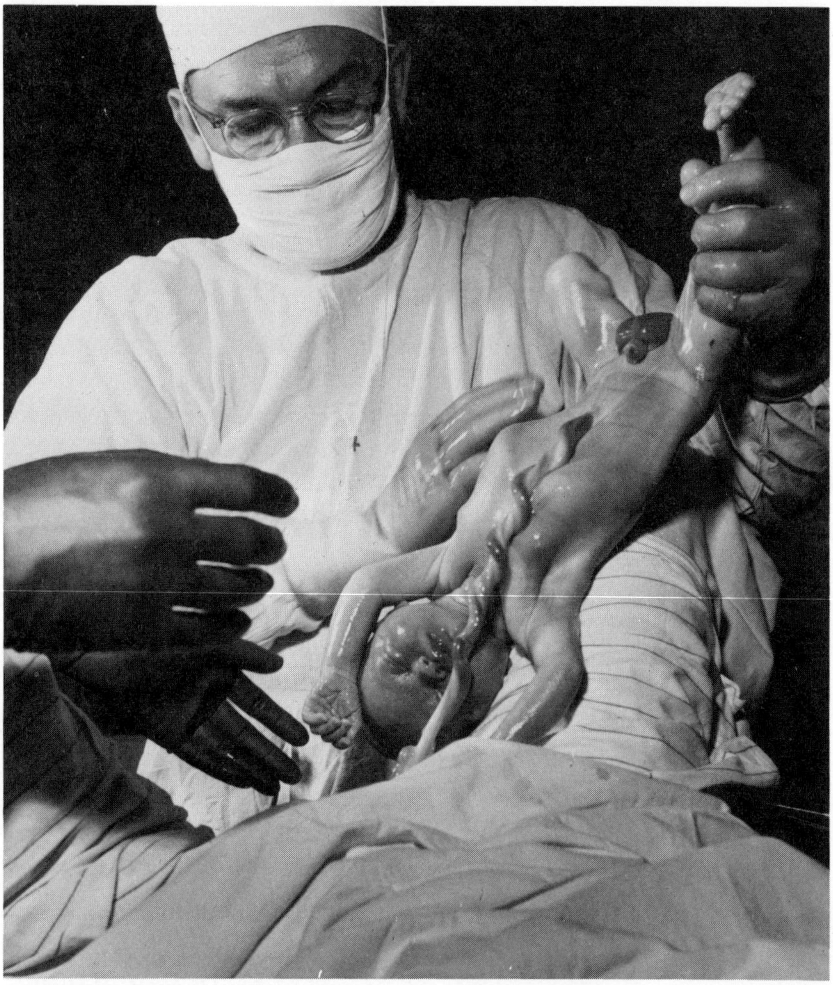

Fig. 17-4 Does the manner in which an individual is born have psychological significance? (Photo by Wayne Miller, Magnum.)

From a medical standpoint other obstetricians have been skeptical of Leboyer's methods. Many feel that his ideas may actually be dangerous. For example, delay in cutting the umbilical cord may increase chances of infection or other complications. Still, "gentle" birth has an intuitive appeal to many parents, and to date Leboyer has delivered well over 1,000 babies by his method.

Questions can also be raised about Leboyer's approach on psychological grounds. Leboyer's basic assumption seems to be that stress is bad. Is this true? How much stress is normal or healthy in infancy and childhood? Contrary to what common sense might suggest, a moderate amount of stress during infancy may be beneficial.

The Mickey Rat School of Hard Knocks

When baby rats were subjected to handling, mild electric shocks, or frightening rides in a bottle washing machine, they opened their eyes sooner, gained weight faster, and grew larger than their nonstressed littermates (Levine, 1969). The stressed rats were also more active as adults and were less timid and emotional when placed in stressful situations (Dennenberg, 1967).

These effects are apparently due to stimulation of the body's adrenal-pituitary system. As noted in the previous chapter, stimulation during infancy is generally beneficial. The benefits apparently extend to moderately stressful stimulation.

Question: Can we really conclude by observing rats that moderate stress is acceptable for humans?

Perhaps not, but there is evidence of similar effects in humans. One study of several cultures concerned the fate of children subjected to stressful rituals like piercing of the ears, nose, or lips. It was found that stressed children averaged over 2 inches taller as adults than those who escaped the rituals (Landuet & Whiting, 1964).

These observations raise questions about the psychological benefits of completely avoiding stressful stimulation. A certain amount of stress in childhood is not only inevitable, but possibly desirable. Certainly this does not mean that parents should go out of their way to stress a child. It does mean that overprotection (sometimes called "smother love") should be avoided. The urge to protect a child is difficult to resist at times. However, if no immediate danger is present, it is reasonable to let children get stuck in trees, make themselves dizzy, squabble with neighbor children, and so forth. Getting into a few scrapes can help prepare a child to cope with later stresses.

Question: How can you tell if a child is being subjected to too much stress?

Normal Childhood Problems Child specialists Chess, Thomas, and Birch (1965) have listed a number of difficulties experienced at times by almost every child. These can be considered normal reactions to the unavoidable stress of growing up.

1. All children experience occasional *sleep disturbances*, including wakefulness, frightening dreams, or a desire to get into parents' bed.
2. *Specific fears* of the dark, dogs, school, or of a particular room or person are also common.
3. Most children will be *overly timid* at times, allowing themselves to be bullied by other children into giving up toys, a place in line, and the like.
4. Temporary periods of *general dissatisfaction* may occur when nothing pleases the child.
5. Children also normally display periods of *general negativism* marked by tantrums, refusal to do anything requested, or a tendency to say no on principle. Negativism is particularly characteristic of two-year-olds, and may be a sign of growing independence.
6. Another normal problem is *clinging*, in which the child refuses to leave the side of his mother or to do anything on his own. Clinging is especially common among three-year-olds.
7. Development does not always advance smoothly. Every child will show occasional *reversals* or *regressions* to more infantile behavior.

Two additional problems common to the elementary school years are *sibling rivalry* and *rebellion*. Where there is more than one child in a family, it is normal for a certain amount of jealousy or rivalry to develop between brothers and sisters. Sibling rivalry can be minimized by parents who avoid "playing favorites" and who resist the temptation to compare one child to another. Most schoolchildren are also at times rebellious against the rules and limitations of the adult world. For many children, the company of peers offers a chance to "let off steam" by doing some of the things the adult world forbids. Being messy, noisy, hostile, or destructive is normal when engaged in to a moderate degree.

It is important to keep in mind that "normal problems" can signal a more serious disturbance if they are displayed for prolonged periods or if they become exaggerated. Problems of a more serious nature are identified in the following section.

Significant Childhood Problems—Off to a Bad Start

Although severe emotional disturbances affect only a minority of children, the number involved is larger than most people realize. A report of the President's Joint Commission on the Mental Health of Children (1970) estimated that .6 percent of our children are psychotic; about 2 or 3 percent are severely disturbed; and an additional 8 to 10 percent are neurotic. This means that one child in ten has a serious emotional problem.

Question: What is the nature of these problems?

Toilet-Training Disturbances Difficulty sometimes centers on toilet training or bowel and bladder habits. The two most common problems are *enuresis* (lack of bladder control) and *encopresis* (lack of bowel control). Enuresis is more common than soiling and is many times more common among males than females. Both wetting and soiling seem to be a means of expressing pent-up aggression felt toward parents or a means of retaliating against parental demands the child considers unfair.

Feeding Disturbances Feeding disturbances take a variety of forms. The disturbed child may vomit or refuse food for no reason or may drastically overeat or undereat. Overeating may be encouraged by an overprotective mother who compensates for feeling unloved by showering the child with "love" in the form of food. Some parents may overfeed a child because they consider a fat baby healthy or desirable. Whatever the source, the overfed child develops conflicts that have lifelong consequences. Even by early childhood, obesity may result in exclusion from active social life with playmates. Later, guilt, disappointment, and anxiety are common.

Serious cases of undereating are called *anorexia nervosa* (nervous loss of appetite). Anorexia nervosa is most common among adolescent females, where it may represent conflict about developing sexual maturity. As a childhood problem, undereating appears related to the fact that eating is a *social event* that can become an arena for conflicts; that is, refusal to eat may be a way of gaining attention, or of doing battle with parents.

Speech Disturbances The two most common speech problems are *delayed speech* and *stuttering*. Delayed speech is generally discovered by the time a child starts school. The child may fail to learn language because of a general lack of stimulation. Other possible causes are parents who discourage the child's attempts to grow up and interference caused by the stress of separation from the mother, hospitalization, or birth of a sibling. Stuttering is a complex problem that is rarely physical in origin. Stuttering may reflect tension or frustration in the child or it may merely be a learned response. In either case, parents often react with obvious emotion to the appearance of a "speech disorder." Their reaction can add considerably to the child's feelings of anxiety or inadequacy and thus perpetuate the problem.

Learning Disorders A child may experience difficulties in learning for many reasons. One of the most significant problems is *hyperactivity*. The hyperactive child is constantly in motion and cannot concentrate. The hyperactive child's excess activity is especially troublesome in school. The child talks rapidly, cannot sit still, rarely finishes work, acts on impulse, and cannot pay attention. These characteristics severely limit the child's ability to learn.

Question: What causes hyperactivity?

The causes of hyperactivity are still something of a mystery. Some have suggested that factors as different as fluorescent lighting in the classroom and artificial dyes and flavorings in the diet may be to blame. The most widely accepted theory is that hyperactivity is the result of *minimal brain damage*. Experts who support this theory link hyperactivity to limited or previously undetected damage to the brain, possibly occurring at birth. When there does seem to be a definite physical cause for hyperactivity, medication can be quite successful in controlling it. The drugs used are typically stimulants like amphetamine. It may seem a contradiction, but giving a hyperactive child a stimulant lengthens his attention span and reduces overactivity.

Childhood Autism Childhood autism is a problem that affects 1 in 2,500 children, boys four times more often than girls. Autism is one of the most severe childhood problems. The autistic child is totally locked into a private world and appears to have no need for affection or contact with others. Autistic children do not even seem to know or care who their parents are. In addition to being extremely isolated, the autistic child typically has a host of other problems. The child may throw gigantic temper tantrums. Sometimes these include self-destructive behavior like head banging or biting shoulders and hands. Language learning is usually so retarded that the child is mute. If they speak at all, autistic children often infuriatingly parrot back everything said. These children also engage in frequent repetitive actions like rocking, flapping their arms, or waving their

Fig. 17-5 The autistic child seems lost in his own world. (Photo courtesy of Benhaven.)

fingers in front of their eyes. Additionally, the child may show no response to an extremely loud noise (sensory blocking) or may spend hours watching a water faucet drip (sensory "spin-out") (Ferster, 1961, 1968).

Question: Do parents cause autism?

Some experts have laid the blame for autism on parents who were too detached or uninterested in the child during infancy. Autism can be viewed as the ultimate example of failure to establish trust and attachment during the first months of life. However, this view can be unfair to parents who may not really be to blame. There is reason to doubt that the actions of parents fully explain the occurrence of autism. The autistic child often seems to be different as soon as birth. Even as babies these children seem aloof and do not cuddle or mold to their parent's arms. Many parents with autistic children also have normal children and feel that the autistic child was not treated differently as a baby. Observations such as these suggest that some constitutional abnormality may be involved, but the true causes of autism remain a mystery.

Question: Can anything be done for an autistic child?

An approach called *behavior modification* has been remarkably successful in combating autism when treatment is begun early. Behavior modification is essentially the application of learning principles to human problems (see Chapter 24 for more information). Billy (the child described in the chapter preview) was one of the first patients in an extraordinary program for the autistic. Billy was selected for the program, designed by Dr. Ivar Lovaas at U.C.L.A., because of his appetite for hamburgers. The process of teaching Billy to talk illustrates one aspect of the program.

Teaching Billy to talk began with his learning to blow out a match—making a sound like "who." Each time he made the "who" sound, Billy was rewarded with a bite of one of his beloved hamburgers. Next he was rewarded for babbling meaningless sounds. If he accidentally said a word, he was rewarded. After several weeks, he was able to say words like "ball," "milk," "mama," and "me." By a painstaking continuation of this process, Billy was eventually taught to talk. Notice that this process is basically an example of *operant shaping*, discussed in an earlier chapter. In a behavior modification program, each of the autistic child's other maladaptive behaviors is attacked using combinations of reward and punishment. Strangely enough, one of the most disturbing autistic behaviors is the easiest to control. Lovaas and others have found that following actions like head banging by punishment can bring a swift end to self-destructive behavior (Lovaas, 1965, 1966).

Autism and other severe childhood problems represent a monumental challenge to the ingenuity of psychologists, educators, and parents. Great strides have been made in the last few years, however, and there is reason to believe that in the future even more help will be available to children who get a bad start in life.

Learning Check

See if you can answer these questions before you continue reading.

1. When baby rats are subjected to moderate stress, they lose their appetite and become weak and sickly. T or F?
2. Children of other cultures who take part in stressful childhood rituals average over 2 inches taller as adults than children who do not. T or F?
3. Negativism is especially characteristic of five-year-olds. T or F?
4. Sleep disturbances and specific fears can be a sign of significant childhood problems when they are prolonged or exaggerated. T or F?
5. A moderate amount of sibling rivalry is considered normal. T or F?
6. Encopresis is the formal term for lack of bladder control T or F?
7. The hyperactive child is lost in his own private world. T or F?

Answers: 1. F 2. T 3. F 4. T 5. T 6. F 7. F

Special Problems of Adulthood—A Second Look at Adult Life Stages

Erikson's life stages and the developmental tasks associated with them summarize many of the major psychological events of adulthood. However, many psychologists have felt a need for additional information on the typical problems of adulthood. Recent research has identified several important substages in adult development not discussed by Erikson. One of the most informative accounts of these substages is based on the research of Roger Gould (1975), a psychiatrist interested in adult personality.

Question: What personality changes and psychological developments can a person look forward to in adulthood?

Gould's research reveals that the most common developments are as follows.

Ages 16–18: Escape from Dominance Ages 16 to 18 are marked by a struggle to escape from parental dominance. Efforts to do so cause considerable anxiety about an uncertain future and conflict about continuing dependence on parents.

Ages 18–22: Leaving the Family The majority of people break away from their families in their early 20s. Leaving home is usually associated with building new friendships with other adults. These friends serve as substitutes for the family and as allies in the process of breaking ties.

Ages 22–28: Building a Workable Life The trend in the mid-20s is to seek mastery of the real world. Two dominant activities are striving for accomplishment (seeking competence) and reaching out to others. Note that the second activity corresponds to Erikson's emphasis on seeking intimacy at this time. Married couples in this age group tend to place a high value on "togetherness."

Ages 29–34: Crisis of Questions Around the age of 30 many people experience a major life crisis. The heart of this crisis is a serious questioning of what life is all about. Assurance about previous choices and values wavers. Unsettled by these developments, the person actively searches for a style of living that will bring meaning to the second half of life. Marriages are particularly vulnerable during this time of dissatisfaction. Extramarital affairs and divorces are common symptoms of the midlife crisis.

Ages 35–43: Crisis of Urgency People of ages 35–43 are typically beginning to become more aware of the reality of death. Having a limited number of years to live begins to exert pressure on the individual. Attempts to succeed at a career or to achieve one's life goals become intensified. Generativity, in the form of nurturing, teaching, or serving others, helps alleviate many of the anxieties of this stage.

Ages 43–50: Settling Down The urgency of the previous stage gives way to a calmer acceptance of one's fate in the late 40s. The predominant feeling is that the die is cast and that former decisions can be lived with. Those who have families begin to appreciate their children as individuals and ease up on their tendency to extend their own goals to their children's behavior.

Age 50 and Up: Mellowing After age 50 a noticeable mellowing occurs. Emphasis is placed on sharing day-to-day joys and sorrows. There is less concern with glamor, wealth, accomplishment, and abstract goals. Many of the tensions of earlier years give way to a desire to savor life and its small pleasures.

After age 50 the problems an individual faces in maintaining a healthy and meaningful life are complicated by the inevitable process of aging. How unique are the problems of old age and how severely do they challenge the need to maintain integrity and personal comfort? You will find some answers in the next section.

Aging—Will You Still Need Me When I'm 64?

In the 1800s the average life expectancy was 36 years. By 1900 it was 49 years. In 1951 the United States average was 69 years, and in 1970 it had become 70 years. There is little doubt that future improvements in medical care will bring even longer life (Hellman, 1971). As the number of people reaching advanced age continues to climb, psychologists have shown increased interest in the problems of aging. They have good reason. Currently there are an estimated 21 million Americans over the age of 65, and the aged are the fastest growing segment of society. By the year 2,000 there will be some 30 million persons aged 65 and older.

Question: What is life like for the aged?

As was noted earlier, the elderly experience problems in many areas: housing, leisure, retirement, sexuality, finances, and so forth. Many problems center on the physical changes of aging. For most women, the first real encounter with aging is the *menopause*. At menopause monthly menstruation ends, and a woman is no longer able to bear children. At the same time, hormone levels in the body change—sometimes causing drastic alterations in mood or appearance. Many women find this change as difficult to adjust to as adolescence. Some postmenopausal women become deeply depressed as they face the unavoidable fact that they are becoming "old." Males do not experience any abrupt physical change comparable to menopause. Just the same, declining vigor and changing physical appearance may also bring self-doubts and depression to the male.

For those who are still young the prospect of physical aging may be the largest threat of old age. How reasonable are fears of physical and mental deterioration? As we have noted, physical aging is a source of legitimate concern for the elderly. However, it is a misconception to believe that the aged are all sickly, infirm, or senile. Only about 5 percent of the elderly are in nursing homes. As for the possibility of mental

Fig. 17-6 Is "oldness" a social convention? Do the needs of "old people" differ from those of the young? (Photo by Bill Stanton, Magnum.)

deterioration, Dr. Alex Comfort (1976) comments: "The human brain does not shrink, wilt, perish, or deteriorate with age. It normally continues to function well through as many as nine decades." As a *gerontologist* (one who studies aging), Comfort estimates, "Only 25 percent of the disability of old people is medical. The remaining 75 percent is social, political, and cultural." Comfort charges that "oldness" is merely a social convention which expels people from useful work. Comfort believes that retirement, which usually cuts income in half at a set age, is just another name for dismissal and unemployment.

Despite the obvious problems of aging, it is a myth to assume that growing old is awful. In one study, Bernice Neugarten (1971) examined the lives of 200 people between the ages of 70 and 79. She found that 75 percent were satisfied with their lives after retirement. Other myths about aging identified by Neugarten are:

1. Old persons generally do not become isolated and neglected by their families. Most *prefer* to live apart from their children.
2. Old persons are rarely placed in mental hospitals by uncaring children.
3. Old persons who live alone are not necessarily lonely or desolate.
4. Few elderly persons ever show signs of senility or mental decay, and few ever become mentally ill.

In short, most of the elderly studied by Neugarten were integrated, active, and psychologically healthy.

Dr. Comfort (1976) may have best put the problems of aging into perspective by listing the needs of the elderly. Comfort says that as an "old" person you will need four things: dignity, money, proper medical services, and useful work. These are exactly the things you have always needed.

Learning Check

Check your comprehension with these questions.

1. The principal crisis in the 35–43 age range is a questioning of life values and choices. T or F?

2. An important development for people aged 16–18 is escape from parental ______________.

3. The average male experiences the menopause between age 45 to 50. T or F?

4. An expert on the problems of aging is called a ______________.

Answers: **1.** F. This occurs at about age 30. **2.** dominance **3.** F. Males do not experience menopause or anything directly comparable. **4.** gerontologist

Resources Summary

According to Erikson each life stage provokes a specific *psychosocial crisis*. In order of occurrence these are: trust versus mistrust, autonomy versus shame and doubt, initiative versus guilt, industry versus inferiority, identity versus role confusion, intimacy versus isolation, generativity versus stagnation, and integrity versus despair. Erikson's stages supposedly occur in an invariant order, and success at later stages depends on the outcome of earlier stages. In addition to the dilemmas identified by Erikson, we recognize that each life stage requires successful mastery of certain *developmental tasks*.

There is evidence that a moderate amount of stress in childhood is not only normal, but perhaps beneficial to development. Few children go through childhood without experiencing some of the normal problems of growing up: negativism, clinging, rebellion, and so forth. More significant problems affect about 1 child in 10. Major areas of difficulty are toilet training, feeding, speech, and learning. Childhood autism is representative of some of the more severe disorders that may occur. Some cases of autism are being treated successfully by use of behavior modification techniques.

Certain relatively consistent events mark adult development in our society. These range from escaping parental dominance in the late teens to a noticeable mellowing in the 50s. Old age presents a number of specialized problems. However, many of the problems of the elderly are not unique to their age group. Aging is a challenge, but it is far from awful. Most elderly persons are satisfied with their lives.

Applications

Parenting

Raising children draws many of the problems of development into a single arena. When parenting is effective, both adult and child benefit. When parents fail to give their children a good start in life, everybody suffers—the child, the parents, and society as a whole. What does it take to be a good parent? In the previous chapter, emphasis was placed on promoting a child's intellectual development. This is a worthwhile goal, but is it enough? Developmental psychologist Edward Zigler (1973) has observed in *Human Behavior Magazine*:

> Thousands of bright children have opted for a life of drugs and apathy; others wander our nation aimlessly. . . . Too many children doubt their own worth. . . . Too many of our children feel that the most affluent and democratic society in the history of man has little to offer them, and that they have little to offer it.

Healthy development requires emotional and social competence as well as intellectual ability. In addition to the skills needed for achievement, effective parents give their children a capacity for love, joy, and fulfillment.

Question: What can parents do to promote healthy development in their children?

Much of the answer can be found in two key areas of parent-child relationships. These are *communication* and *discipline*. In each area parents can set an example of tolerance, understanding, and acceptance that goes beyond their traditional role as mere dispensers of "dos" and "don'ts."

Discipline

One of the lasting myths about parenthood is belief that "Love is all a parent has to give a child." No psychologist would deny that love is essential for healthy development, but *discipline* can be of equal importance. Parents with unmanageable, delinquent, or unhappy children often can honestly claim that they have given them lots of love. Yet when parents fail to provide a framework of guidelines for behavior, children become antisocial, aggressive, and insecure. Parents who allow themselves to be dominated or manipulated create lifelong patterns of manipulation and self-serving behavior in the child.

Question: Does this mean that discipline should be strict and unbending?

No. The family need not be made into a military boot camp. Effective discipline can be quite permissive. It is important to remember that rules about the proper time and place to engage in toilet functions, restraints on natural impulses for sex and aggression, and numerous other parental curbs on behavior are frustrating to children. The problem in providing adequate discipline is to socialize a child without undue frustration and without destroying the bond of love and trust between parent and child.

Question: How can a balance be maintained?

Many experts are advocating a new style of child rearing that recognizes a child's psychological needs. The core of this approach is a special form of permissiveness. Dr. Haim G. Ginott (1965) in his highly acclaimed book *Between Parent and Child* explains:

> The essence of permissiveness is the acceptance of children as persons who have a constitutional right to have all kinds of feelings and wishes. . . . All feelings and fantasies, all thoughts and wishes, all dreams and desires, are accepted, respected, and may be permitted expression. . . . Overpermissiveness is the allowing of undesirable acts. Permissiveness brings confidence and an increasing capacity to express feelings and thoughts. Overpermissiveness brings anxiety and increasing demands for privileges that cannot be granted (pp. 110-111).

In other words, discipline should give children freedom to express their deepest feelings through speech and actions. This does not mean freedom to do entirely as one pleases. It means the child has room to move about freely *within* well-defined limits. Of course, individual parents may choose limits that are more or less "strict." But this choice is less important than the consistency of parental standards. *Consistent* discipline gives a child a sense of security and stability; inconsistency makes the child's world seem unreliable and unpredictable.

Question: How can limits best be maintained?

Parents tend to base discipline on one or more of the following techniques: *power assertion, withdrawal of love, or child management* (Coopersmith, 1968; Hoffman, 1970). "Power assertion" refers to physical punishment or to a show of force in which parents take away toys or privileges. As an alternative, some parents may temporarily withdraw love by refusing to speak to a child, by threatening to leave, by rejecting the child, or by otherwise acting like the child is temporarily unlovable. Management techniques combine praise, recognition, approval, rules, reasoning, and the like to encourage desirable behavior. Each of these approaches can effectively control a child's behavior, but their side effects differ considerably.

Question: What are the side effects?

Power-oriented techniques, particularly harsh or severe physical punishment, are associated with fear, hatred of parents, and a lack of spontaneity and warmth. Severely punished children also tend to be defiant, rebellious, and aggressive.

Withdrawal of love, which is a major middle-class mode of discipline, produces children who tend to be self-disciplined. We might say that such children have developed a good conscience. They are often described as "model" children or as unusually "good." But as a side effect they are also frequently anxious, insecure, and dependent on adults for approval.

Management techniques also have their limitations. Most important is the need to carefully adjust them to a child's level of understanding. Younger children may not always see the connection between rules, explanations, and their own behavior. In spite of this limitation, management techniques receive a big plus in an important area of child development. Psychologist Stanley Coopersmith (1968) has found a direct connection between parental styles of discipline and a child's *self-esteem.*

Question: What is self-esteem?

By "self-esteem" we mean a quiet confidence that comes from regarding oneself as a worthwhile person. Many theorists consider high self-esteem essential for emotional health. Individuals with low self-esteem have a low estimation of their value as people. This attitude has a negative effect on many of their activities and their relationships with others.

Coopersmith divided boys into groups having

high or low self-esteem. He then investigated the child-rearing attitudes and practices of the boys' parents. He found that low self-esteem was related to the use of physical punishment or withholding of love. High self-esteem, by contrast, was related to management techniques which emphasized strict and consistent discipline coupled with high parental interest and concern for the child. In general, it appears that parenting which minimizes physical punishment and avoids unnecessary withdrawal of love is most effective.

Question: Are you saying that physical punishment and withdrawal of love should not be used?

Most parents have used each of the three major types of discipline at one time or another, and each has its place. Coopersmith's findings simply suggest that physical punishment and withdrawal of love should be used with caution. In using these two forms of punishment, the following guidelines should be observed.

1. Separate disapproval of the act from disapproval of the child. Instead of saying, "I'm going to punish you because *you are bad*," say, "I'm upset about *what you did*."
2. Punishment should never be harsh or injurious to a child. Don't physically punish a child while you are angry. Also remember that giving a child the message "I don't love you right now" can be more painful than any spanking.
3. Punishment is most effective when it is administered immediately. This statement is especially true for younger children.
4. Spanking and other forms of physical punishment are not particularly effective for children under age two. The child will only be confused and frightened. Spankings also become less effective after age five because they tend to humiliate the child and breed resentment.
5. Reserve physical punishment for situations that pose an immediate danger to the younger child, for example, when a child runs into the street.

After age five the most effective form of discipline is management techniques. Especially useful are psychological techniques which emphasize communication.

Communication Between Parent and Child

When clear communication is maintained between parent and child, many discipline problems can be avoided before they develop. Dr. Haim Ginott (1965) has suggested that it is essential to make a distinction between a child's feelings and a child's behavior. Since children (and parents, too) do not choose how they will feel, it is important to allow free expression of feelings. The child who learns to regard some feelings as "bad," or unacceptable, is being asked to deny a very real part of his experience. Ginott encourages parents to teach their children that all feelings are appropriate, and only actions are subject to disapproval. Many parents are unaware of just how often they block communication and the expression of feelings in their children. Consider this typical conversation excerpted from Ginott's book (pp. 29-30, 1965):

Son: I am stupid, and I know it. Look at my grades in school.
Father: You just have to work harder.
Son: I already work harder and it doesn't help. I have no brains.
Father: You are smart, I know.
Son: I am stupid, I know.
Father: *(loudly)* You are not stupid!
Son: Yes, I am!
Father: You are not stupid. Stupid!

By debating with the child, the father misses the point that his son *feels* stupid. It would be far more helpful for the father to encourage the boy to talk about his feelings.

Question: How could he do that?

He might say, "You really feel that you are not as smart as others, don't you? Do you feel this way often? Are you feeling bad at school?" In this way the child is given an opportunity to express his emotions, and he feels understood. The father might conclude the conversation by saying, "Look, son, in my eyes you are a fine person. But I understand how you feel. Everyone feels stupid at times."

Communication with a child can also be the basis of effective discipline. Dr. Thomas Gordon (1970), a child psychologist who has developed a program called Parent Effectiveness Training (PET), offers a useful suggestion. Gordon believes that parents should send "I" messages to their children, rather than "you" messages.

Question: What's the difference?

"You" messages take the form of threats, name-calling, accusing, bossing, lecturing, or analyzing. Generally, "you" messages tell a child what's "wrong" with him. An "I" message is a form of communication in which you tell a child what effect his behavior has had on you. To illustrate the difference, consider this example. After a hard day's work, Susan wants to sit down and rest a while. She begins to relax with a newspaper when her five-year-old daughter starts banging loudly on a toy drum. Most parents would respond with a "you" message:

"You go play outside this instant." (bossing)

"Don't ever make such a racket when someone is reading." (lecturing)

"You're really pushing it today, aren't you?" (accusing)

"You're a spoiled brat." (name-calling)

"Do you want me to swat you?" (threatening)

Gordon suggests sending an "I" message like, "I am very tired, and I would like to read. I feel upset and can't read when you make so much noise." This forces the child to accept responsibility for the effects of her actions. If this doesn't curb misbehavior, the consequences can also be stated as an "I" message: "If you keep banging on that drum, I will have to put it away." If the child makes more noise, then she has caused the toy to be put away. If she takes it outside, then she has decided to do so. Both parent and child have been allowed to maintain a sense of self-respect and self-worth, and a needless clash has been averted.

Only two additional points on communicating with children need be noted. They are: "Listen more than you talk"; and "Live the message you wish to communicate."

For Discussion

There are probably as many philosophies on how to raise children as there are parents in the world. Here is the viewpoint of poet and mystical philosopher Kahlil Gibran:

> Your children are not your children.
> They are the sons and daughters of Life's longing for itself.
> They come through you but not from you,
> And though they are with you yet they belong not to you.
> You may give them your love but not your thoughts,
> For they have their own thoughts.
> You may house their bodies but not their souls,
> For their souls dwell in the house of tomorrow, which you cannot visit, not even in your dreams.
> You may strive to be like them, but seek not to make them like you. . . .[2]

In parenting there is a constant tension between the need to give a child guidance and the need to give freedom for individual growth. Gibran obviously advocates a permissive, "hands off" approach to raising children. Elsewhere it has been charged that permissiveness and a lack of parental leadership are the source of many of our society's social ills. In view of what you now know about the whole cycle of human development, which of Gibran's statements do you agree with? Which do you disagree with? Why?

Questions for Discussion

1. Describe an incident from your own childhood that you consider growth-promoting. Describe an incident that set you back or had a negative effect on you. How do these incidents differ?
2. Were you physically punished as a child? What is your attitude toward physical punishment now? Would you use physical punishment on your own children?
3. In what ways do parents add to the conflicts of young adults who are seeking independence?
4. Do you know a person who seems to have "flunked" one or more of Erikson's developmental stages? What effect has this had on the person's subsequent development?
5. Anthropologist Margaret Mead has charged, "We have become a society of people who neglect our children, are afraid of our children." Do you agree?
6. Do we need a "children's liberation movement" to establish the civil rights of children? (Keep in mind that few parents show their children the courtesy they show strangers.)

[2]Reprinted from *The Prophet.* Copyright 1923 by Kahlil Gibran. Renewal copyright 1951 by Administrators C.T.A. of Kahlil Gibran Estate, and Mary G. Gibran. Reprinted by permission of publisher Alfred A. Knopf, Inc., New York, N.Y.

7. If you could choose to remain a particular age, which would you choose? Why? What are your attitudes toward old age?

Suggestions for Further Reading

Bettelheim, B. *The Empty Fortress: Infantile Autism and the Birth of the Self.* Free Press, 1967.

Chess, S., A. Thomas, and H. G. Birch. *Your Child Is a Person: A Psychological Approach to Parenthood without Guilt.* Viking, 1965.

Comfort, A. *A Good Age.* Crown, 1976.

Erikson, E. *Childhood and Society.* 2nd ed. Norton, 1963.

Ginott, H. G. *Between Parent and Child.* Macmillan, 1965.

Gordon, T. *P. E. T.: Parent Effectiveness Training.* Wyden, 1970.

Kimmel, D. C. *Adulthood and Aging.* Wiley, 1974.

Where to Write for Information

Autism: The National Society for Autistic Children, 101 Richmond Street, Huntington, W. Va., 25701.

Hyperactivity: H.E.W., Office of the Secretary, Secretary's Committee on Mental Retardation, Washington D.C., 20201.

Learning Disorders: National Association for Children with Learning Disabilities, 5225 Grace Street, Pittsburgh, Penn., 15236.

Individual Differences in Intelligence

18

Chapter Preview

What Day Is It?

Ask George in which recent years April 21 fell on a Sunday. Without hesitation he will answer: "1968, 1963, 1957, 1946." Surprisingly this gives only the slightest hint of his skill. If encouraged, George will go back as far as 1700—with complete accuracy! His "calendar calculations" cover a range of at least 6,000 years, extending centuries beyond present perpetual calendars. With equal ease he can identify February 15, 2002, as a Friday or August 28, 1591, as a Wednesday.

Question: Is he a genius?

George's abilities are all the more amazing in view of the fact that he is mentally retarded and cannot add, subtract, multiply, or divide even simple numbers (Horwitz et al.*, 1965). George is an "idiot savant," a person of subnormal intelligence who shows highly developed mental ability in one or more very limited areas.*

Question: How could he be retarded and have this ability both at the same time?

The striking contrast between George's general retardation and incredible mental ability serves as a fitting introduction to the challenge psychologists have faced in their efforts to define and measure intelligence. Quite frankly, we are still searching for definitive answers to questions like these: "Is intelligence a general trait or a specific skill?" "Is intelligence determined by the genetic 'wheel of fortune' or is it nurtured by environment?" "Is it possible to construct an intelligence test that is fair to all people?" "How important is intelligence for 'success'?" Because our understanding of intelligence is undergoing rapid change, we cannot hope to give final answers.

For the sake of clarity, this chapter is divided into two distinct parts. In the resources *section we will assume that intelligence can be measured, and we will use measurements as a way of answering a number of questions about intelligence. In the* applications *section we will consider some of the questions that have been raised about intelligence tests and the meaning of their results.*

Resources

Defining Intelligence—Intelligence Is . . . It's . . . You Know, It's . . .

The existence of individual differences is a basic psychological fact. With over 3 billion human beings on earth, still no two are exactly alike. Even identical twins have different fingerprints and voiceprints. Many personal qualities might be measured, but one of the most intensely studied has been *intelligence*. Much of the interest in intelligence stems from its seemingly pervasive relationship to ability in many areas.

Like so many important concepts in psychology, intelligence cannot be observed directly: It has no mass, occupies no space, and is invisible. Nevertheless, we feel certain it exists. Consider the following two individuals:

> When she was fourteen months old, Anne H. wrote her own name. She taught herself to read at age two. At age five she astounded her kindergarten teacher by walking into class with a stack of encyclopedias—which she proceeded to read. At ten she breezed through an entire high school algebra course in 12 hours.
>
> At age ten Billy A. can write his name and can count, but he has trouble with simple addition and subtraction problems and finds multiplication impossible. He has been held back in school twice and is still incapable of doing the work his eight-year-old classmates find easy. His teachers have suggested that he be transferred to a special educational program for slow learners.

Anne is considered a genius; Billy, a slow learner. There seems little doubt that they differ in intelligence.

Question: Wait! Anne's ability is obvious, but how do we know that Billy isn't just lazy?

This dilemma is precisely the one that Alfred Binet faced in 1904. The minister of education in Paris had given Binet the task of devising a way to distinguish slower students from the more capable (or the capable but lazy). In a flash of brilliance, Binet and an associate assembled a test consisting of "intellectual" questions and problems. Next, they established which questions an "average" child could answer at each age. Children low in intellectual ability were identified by below-par performance on the test.

Binet's approach gave rise to modern intelligence tests and at the same time launched 70 years of debate that has often been heated and at times bitter. Part of the debate is related to the basic difficulty of defining intelligence.

Question: Is there an accepted definition of intelligence?

Most psychologists would probably agree with David Wechsler's general description of *intelligence* as the: *global capacity of the individual to act purposefully, to think rationally, and to deal effectively with the environment*. Beyond this, there is so much disagreement that many psychologists simply accept an *operational* definition* of intelligence as "that which an intelligence test measures."

Question: Isn't the operational definition circular?

Not completely. By selecting items for an intelligence test a psychologist is saying in a very direct way: "This is what I mean by intelligence." A test that measures memory, reasoning, and verbal fluency offers a very different definition of intelligence than one that measures strength of grip, length of the nose, or age in days. Later in this chapter we will consider the question of whether intelligence tests are *valid*. (A test is valid if it measures what it claims to measure.) For now, let us take a practical approach to the definition of intelligence by examining the features of tests currently in use.

Testing Intelligence—Making the Invisible Visible

The Stanford-Binet American psychologists recognized the usefulness of Binet's test and in 1916 revised it at Stanford University. After several more revisions, the *Stanford-Binet Intelligence Scale* is still widely used. The Stanford-Binet assumes that intellectual ability in childhood improves with increasing age. As a result, the Stanford-Binet is really a set of increasingly difficult tests, one for each age group.

The age-ranked questions of the Stanford-Binet allow a person's *mental age* to be determined. For example, at ages eight or nine, very few children can define the word "connection." At age ten, 10 percent can. At age thirteen, 60 percent can. In other words, the ability to define "connection" indicates mental ability comparable to that of the average thirteen-year-old and gives a mental age of thirteen (on this single item). Table 18-1 is a sample of items that persons of average intelligence can answer at various ages.

*We would say that a concept has been defined "operationally" when the procedures used to measure it have been specified.

Table 18-1 Sample Items from the Stanford-Binet Intelligence Scale

Two years old	On a large paper doll, points out the hair, mouth, feet, ear, nose, hands, and eyes. When shown a tower built of four blocks, builds one like it.
Three years old	When shown a bridge built of three blocks, builds one like it. When shown a drawing of a circle, copies it with a pencil.
Four years old	Fills in the missing word when asked, "Brother is a boy; sister is a ______." and "In daytime it is light: at night it is ______." Answers correctly when asked, "Why do we have houses?" "Why do we have books?"
Five years old	Defines *ball*, *hat*, and *stove*. When shown a drawing of a square, copies it with a pencil.
Nine years old	Answers correctly when examiner says, "In an old graveyard in Spain they have discovered a small skull which they believe to be that of Christopher Columbus when he was about ten years old. What is foolish about that?" Answers correctly when asked, "Tell me the name of a color that rhymes with head." "Tell me a number that rhymes with tree."
Adult	Can describe the difference between laziness and idleness, poverty and misery, character and reputation. Answers correctly when asked, "Which direction would you have to face so your right hand would be toward the north?"

(Terman & Merrill, 1960.)

Mental age gives a good indication of one's actual abilities, but it says nothing about whether overall intelligence is high or low. To know the meaning of mental age, *chronological* age (age in years) must also be considered. Mental age can then be related to chronological age to yield an *IQ*, or *intelligence quotient*. IQ is defined as mental age (MA) divided by chronological age (CA) and multiplied by 100:

$$\frac{\text{MA}}{\text{CA}} \times 100 = \text{IQ}$$

An advantage of the IQ is that it allows comparison of intelligence among children with different combinations of chronological and mental ages. A ten-year-old child with a mental age of twelve has an IQ of 120:

$$\frac{(\text{MA})\quad 12}{(\text{CA})\quad 10} \times 100 = 120\ (\text{IQ})$$

A second child having a mental age of twelve but with a chronological age of twelve would have an IQ of 100:

$$\frac{(\text{MA})\ 12}{(\text{CA})\ 12} \times 100 = 100\ (\text{IQ})$$

The IQ shows that the younger child is brighter than his twelve-year-old friend, even though their intellectual skills are actually the same. Notice that IQ equals 100 when MA = CA. An IQ of 100 is therefore defined as average intelligence, and an IQ over 100 indicates above-average intelligence. IQ scores below 100 occur when age in years exceeds mental age, as would be the case for a fifteen-year-old with a MA of twelve:

$$\frac{12}{15} \times 100 = 80$$

Question: How old does a child have to be before the IQ becomes stable?

IQ scores do not become dependable until about age six (Cronbach, 1970). After this, intelligence tests are quite *reliable.** The average change in IQ on retesting is approximately five points in either direction. During intellectual development children may show small increases, declines, or fluctuations in tested intelligence. There is no typical pattern, but the fact remains that changes are usually quite small.

Question: How much does aging affect the IQ?

Since IQ reflects education, maturity, and experience as well as native intellectual capacity, studies of IQ change have shown a gradual increase in intellectual ability until somewhere between the ages of 20 and 30. After age 30, there is a gradual decline (Wechsler, 1958). Other studies have shown little or no change in intelligence due to aging. (Owens, 1953, 1966). More recent findings clarify the situation by suggesting that only certain kinds of intellectual abilities are affected by aging. When general information or comprehension is emphasized, there is little decline until advanced age. Tests or test items requiring speed, rapid insight, or perceptual flexibility show earlier losses and a rapid decline after middle age (Baltes & Schaie, 1974). Perhaps the most intriguing link between IQ and aging is the observation that impending death may be signaled by significant changes in brain function. Certain intellectual skills have been shown to decline abruptly about five years before death, even when the person appears to be in good health (Jarvik *et al.*, 1973).

Question: Is the Stanford-Binet the only intelligence test?

*The *reliability* of a test may be defined in various ways. In this case, we refer to the consistency of the test. If a person receives approximately the same score when taking the same test on different occasions, then the test is considered reliable.

The Wechsler Test A widely used alternative to the Stanford-Binet is the *Wechsler Adult Intelligence Scale*, or *WAIS*. This test also has a form adapted for use with children, called the *Wechsler Intelligence Scale for Children* (*WISC*). The Wechsler tests bear an overall similarity to the Stanford-Binet, but differ in some important respects. The WAIS was specifically designed to test adult intelligence, and both the WISC and the WAIS rate *performance* (nonverbal) intelligence in addition to *verbal* intelligence. The Stanford-Binet only gives one overall IQ, whereas the Wechsler tests can be broken down to reveal strengths and weaknesses in various areas. Overall IQ scores on the WAIS and WISC are always calculated directly without using the concept of mental age. The intellectual skills revealed by the Wechsler tests and some sample items are listed in Table 18-2.

Table 18-2 Sample Items Similar to Those Used on the WAIS.

Verbal Subtests	**Sample Items**
Information	How many wings does a bird have? Who wrote *Paradise Lost*?
General Comprehension	What is the advantage of keeping money in a bank? Why is copper often used in electrical wires?
Arithmetic	Three men divided eighteen golf balls equally among themselves. How many golf balls did each man receive? If two apples cost 15¢, what will be the cost of a dozen apples?
Similarities	In what way are a lion and a tiger alike? In what way are a saw and a hammer alike?
Vocabulary	This test consists simply of asking, "what is a ______?" or "what does ______ mean?" The words cover a wide range of difficulty or familiarity.
Performance Subtests	**Description of Item**
Picture Arrangement	Arrange a series of cartoon panels to make a meaningful story.
Picture Completion	What is missing from these pictures?
Block Assembly	Copy a design with blocks.
Object Assembly	Put together a jigsaw puzzle.
Digit Symbol	

1	2	3	4
X	III	I	0

Fill in the symbols:

3	4	1	3	4	2	1	2

(Courtesy of The Psychological Corporation.)

Group Tests Both the Stanford-Binet and the Wechsler tests are *individual intelligence tests* that must be administered by a specially trained tester. Other tests of intelligence have been designed for use with large groups of people. *Group intelligence tests* are usually in paper-and-pencil form and require the examinee to read, to follow instructions, and to solve problems of logic, mathematics, or the visual arrangement of figures. The first group intelligence test was the *Army Alpha*, developed for use in classifying World War I military inductees. If you have been wondering if you have ever taken an intelligence test, the answer is probably yes. The Scholastic Aptitude Test (SAT), the American College Test (ACT), and the College Qualification Test (CQT) are all group tests that can be used to estimate a person's intelligence as well as his or her chances for college success.

Learning Check

Check your comprehension before you continue reading.

1. The first successful intelligence test was developed by ________.

2. If we define intelligence as "that which an intelligence test measures," we are using:
a. a circular definition
b. an abstract definition
c. an operational definition
d. chronological age as the definition of intelligence

3. IQ is defined as $\frac{(\quad)}{(\quad)} \times 100$

4. Ability to answer general information and comprehension questions shows the most rapid decline during aging. T or F?

5. The WAIS is a group intelligence test. T or F?

Answers: **1.** Alfred Binet **2.** c **3.** $\frac{(MA)}{(CA)} \times 100$ **4.** F **5.** F

Variations in Intelligence—The Numbers Game

Based on observations of a large number of randomly selected people, the classifications shown in Table 18-3 have been established for various IQ ranges. A look at the percentages reveals a definite pattern. The distribution of IQs approximates a *normal* (bell-shaped) curve in which the major-

Table 18-3 Distribution of Adult IQ Scores on WAIS

IQ	*Verbal Description*	*Percent of Adults*
Above 130	Very superior	2.2
120—129	Superior	6.7
110—119	Bright normal	16.1
90—109	Average	50.0
80—89	Dull normal	16.1
70—79	Borderline	6.7
Below 70	Mentally retarded	2.2

(Wechsler, 1958)

ity of scores fall close to the average and relatively few at the extremes. Figure 18-1 graphically shows this characteristic of measured intelligence.

Question: On the average, do males and females differ in intelligence?

IQ does not give a definite answer to this question since intelligence test items are selected to be equally difficult for both sexes. It seems safe to assume that men and women do not differ in overall intelligence, and no significant IQ difference has been found. However, tests like the WAIS allow a comparison of the intellectual strengths and weaknesses of men and women. Here a difference does emerge: Women perform better on test items that require verbal ability, vocabulary, and rote learning; men are best at items that require visualization of spatial relationships and arithmetic reasoning (Wechsler, 1958). It is not clear whether these differences are genetic or the result of differences in experience associated with sex roles. In any case, differences in male and female skills balance out in general intelligence.

Question: How much do variations in intelligence affect success in school, jobs, and other undertakings?

IQ differences of a few points tell little about intellectual potential. But when a broader range of scores is considered, meaningful differences emerge. The correlation between IQ and school grades is .50—a sizable association. Furthermore, the average IQ of high school graduates is approximately 110; college graduates average 120; and persons who attain the Ph.D. or other advanced degrees average 130 (Cronbach, 1970). As one might expect, there is also a relationship between IQ and job classification. Persons holding "high-status"* positions average much higher IQs than those in "lower status" occupational settings. For example, accountants average about 120 in IQ and miners about 90 (Anastasi & Foley, 1958). It is important to note, however, that there is a consider-

*The term high-status is used to refer to the traditionally higher paid business and professional occupations.

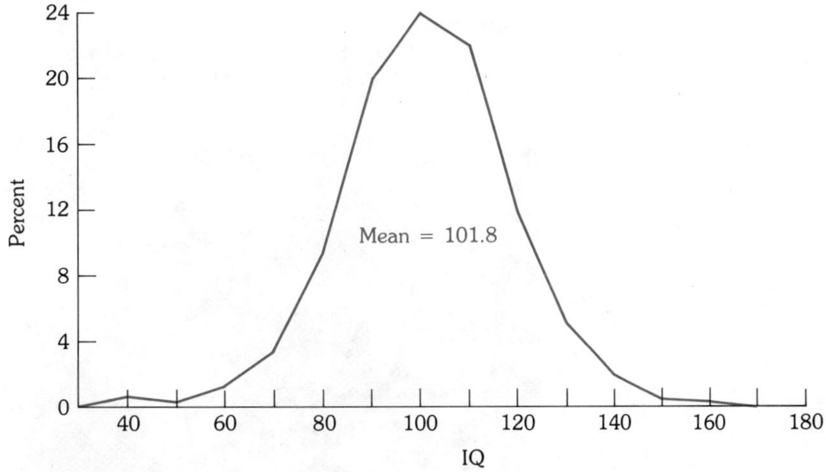

Fig. 18-1 Distribution of Stanford-Binet Intelligence Test scores for 3,184 children. (After Terman and Merrill, 1960.)

able range of IQs in all occupations. There are many people of high intelligence who, because of choice or circumstance, will be found in "low-ranking" occupations.

It is tempting to interpret the association between IQ and occupation as evidence that high-status jobs require more intelligence. This is dangerous because intelligence tests as a rule require the same types of mental gymnastics as are necessary for success in school. Since higher status jobs often require an academic degree, the apparent connection between IQ and job status may be misleading. Selection procedures for professional jobs appear to be biased in favor of a particular type of intelligence, namely, the kind measured by intelligence tests.

When variations in IQ are extreme—below 70 or above 130—influences on adjustment and one's potential for success become unmistakable. Only 4½ percent of the population score in these ranges, but this translates to about 9 million people in the United States who are exceptional by way of having very high or very low IQs. Discussions of the mentally gifted and the mentally retarded follow.

The Mentally Gifted—Is Genius Next to Insanity?

Question: How high is the IQ of a genius?

Only about 1 percent of the population scores above 140 on IQ tests. A person scoring this high is at least "gifted" and, depending on the standards used, may be considered a "genius." (Some psychologists reserve the term "genius" for even higher IQs.) The association between high IQ and works of genius is unmistakable. One interesting study estimated the

Fig. 18-2 John Kirtley belongs to Mensa, an international organization of exceptionally intelligent people. Although his IQ is 174, John prefers to do custodial work, feeling that his unusual intellect would be "used" by his employers if he pursued a technical occupation. (Wide World Photos, Inc.)

IQs of famous historical figures by noting the age at which they learned to read, used certain words, or had mastered certain problems. (Table 18-4.)

To study the intellectually gifted more directly, Lewis Terman selected 1,500 children with IQs of 140 or more. By following the development of this gifted group into adulthood, Terman identified a number of popular misconceptions about genius.

Misconception: The gifted tend to be peculiar, socially backward people.

Fact: On the contrary, Terman's gifted subjects were socially well adjusted and showed above-average leadership capacity.

Misconception: "Early ripe means later rot": The gifted tend to fizzle out as adults.

Fact: This is false. When retested as adults, Terman's subjects again scored in the upper IQ ranges.

Misconception: The very bright are usually physically inferior "egg-heads" or weaklings.

Fact: This is also a misconception. As a group, the gifted were above average in height, weight, and physical appearance.

Misconception: The highly intelligent person is more susceptible to mental illness ("Genius is next to insanity").

Fact: Terman demonstrated conclusively that the gifted have better than average mental health records, indicating a greater *resistance* to mental illness.

Misconception: Intelligence has nothing to do with success, especially in practical matters.

Fact: The later success of Terman's subjects was the most striking finding of the study. As a group, they were considered to be very successful. The number who had completed college, earned advanced degrees, or held professional positions was much higher than average. Many had received special recognition for outstanding achievement such as being listed in *Who's Who* or *American Men of Science.* By average age of forty the gifted group was responsible for the production of dozens of books, thousands of scientific articles, and hundreds of short stories and other publications (Terman & Oden, 1959).

Question: Were all of the gifted children superior as adults?

No, remember that high IQ reveals *potential*. It is not a guarantee of success. Some of the gifted had committed crimes, were unemployable, or were poorly adjusted. You have probably known people of high intelligence who seemed to be adversely affected by their intellectual gifts. Overall, however, Terman's study makes it clear that the very bright tend to be superior in many ways. (Frustrating, isn't it?)

Table 18-4 The Estimated IQs of Famous Men

John Quincy Adams	165
Francis Bacon	145
Samuel Taylor Coleridge	175
René Descartes	150
Charles Dickens	145
Benjamin Franklin	145
Thomas Jefferson	145
John Stuart Mill	190
Wolfgang Amadeus Mozart	150
Daniel Webster	145
William Wordsworth	150

(From Cox, 1926.)

High intelligence is not without its problems, particularly in childhood. The gifted child may rapidly become bored in a classroom designed for average children. Boredom can lead to behavioral problems or clashes with teachers who consider the gifted child a show-off or smart aleck. The extremely bright child may also find the company of his or her classmates less stimulating than that of older children or adults. In recognition of these problems many school systems now provide special programs and classes for "MGM" children (Mentally Gifted Minors).

Mental Retardation—A Difference That Makes a Difference

An individual with intellectual abilities significantly below average is termed *mentally retarded*. An IQ of 70 or below has traditionally been the dividing line between normal intelligence and retardation. Below an IQ of 70, additional distinctions may be made as shown in Table 18-5.

Question: Are the retarded usually placed in institutions?

No, total care is only necessary for the profoundly retarded. The *severely* and *moderately* retarded are capable of mastering basic language skills and routine self-help skills. Many become self-supporting by working in a "sheltered workshop" (a special simplified work environment). The *mildly* retarded benefit from carefully structured and supervised education. As adults, they are capable of living alone and may marry (although they tend to have difficulties with many of the demands of adult life) (Suinn, 1975).

It is important to realize that the mentally retarded have no handicap where feelings are concerned. They are sensitive to rejection and are easily hurt by teasing or ridicule. Likewise, they respond warmly to love and acceptance. Professionals working with the retarded emphasize their rights to self-respect and to a place in the community. This is especially important during childhood, when the support of others adds significantly to the person's chances of becoming a well-adjusted member of society.

Question: What causes mental retardation?

Clear causes cannot always be found, but most cases of retardation can be traced to one or more of the following conditions:

Table 18-5 Terms Used to Describe Mental Retardation

IQ Range	*Degree of Retardation*	*Educational Classification*
70—84	Borderline	Slow learner
55—69	Mild	Educable retarded
40—54	Moderate	Trainable retarded
25—39	Severe	Trainable retarded
Below 25	Profound	Total-care group

(Adapted Kessler, 1966.)

Fig. 18-3 This youngster is a participant in the Special Olympics—an athletic event for the mentally retarded. It is often said of the Special Olympics that, "Everyone is a winner—participants, coaches, and spectators." (Photo courtesy of Paul Shanklin, *Goleta Valley Today*.)

1. *Birth injuries* are a relatively rare but significant problem.
2. *Disease or infection* contracted by the mother before birth or the child shortly after birth can cause retardation. German measles contracted by the mother during pregnancy is especially dangerous.
3. *Deprivation in infancy*, in the form of malnutrition or an extremely unstimulating environment, has been linked to retardation.
4. In some cases, definite *genetic abnormalities* can be identified.

In addition to these general problems, there are several distinctive forms of retardation that deserve special mention.

Phenylketonuria (PKU) PKU is a genetically inherited lack of an important bodily enzyme, which causes the buildup of phenylpyruvic acid (a destructive chemical) in the body. PKU is now easily detected in babies by medical testing during the first month of life. It can usually be controlled by a special diet.

Microcephaly Microcephaly means small-headedness. The microcephalic suffers a rare abnormality in which the skull is extremely small or fails to grow. The brain is forced to develop in a severely limited space, causing severe retardation that usually requires the individual to be placed in an institution. The microcephalic is typically affectionate, well behaved, and easy to work with.

Hydrocephaly Hydrocephaly (water on the brain) is caused by excess production of cerebrospinal fluid within the brain. Accumulation of this fluid forces the brain against the skull, grossly enlarging the head and damaging brain tissue. There has been limited success in controlling hydrocephaly with drugs and surgical procedures to drain off the excess fluid.

Cretinism Cretinism is a form of retardation that develops in infancy due to insufficient secretion of thyroid hormone. In some parts of the world cretinism is caused by too little iodine in the diet (iodine is necessary for normal thyroid function). Widespread use of iodized salt makes this cause of the condition rare in the United States. Cretinism causes stunted physical and intellectual growth that cannot be corrected unless detected early. Fortunately, it is easily and routinely detected in infancy and may be treated by thyroid hormone replacement.

Mongolism Mongolism (also referred to as *Down's syndrome*) causes moderate to severe retardation and a very short life expectancy. The most distinctive features of mongolism are almond-shaped, slanted eyes and an overly large, protruding tongue. It is now known that the mongoloid has an extra chromosome; the cells of normal individuals have 46 chromosomes, whereas the mongoloid has 47. The cause of the extra chromosome is unknown, but an important factor seems to be the age of the mother. Mothers between the ages of 20 and 24 have about 1 chance in 8,000 of giving birth to a mongoloid child. After age 45 the odds increase to approximately 1 in 600. This rather significant increase in risk is a factor to be considered in family planning. There is no cure for mongolism, although the mongoloid child is usually loving and responsive to attention and with training can make limited progress.

Learning Check

1. The distribution of IQs approximates a ______________ (bell-shaped) curve.
2. The association between IQ and "high-status" jobs proves that "high-status" jobs require more intelligence. T or F?
3. Women tend to excel on test items that require verbal ability, vocabulary, and rote learning. T or F?
4. Only about 6 percent of the population score above 140 on IQ tests. T or F?
5. An IQ score below 90 indicates mental retardation. T or F?

Match

6.	______ PKU	**A.**	Too little thyroid hormone
7.	______ Microcephaly	**B.**	Very small brain
8.	______ Hydrocephaly	**C.**	47 chromosomes
9.	______ Cretinism	**D.**	Lack of an important bodily enzyme
10.	______ Mongolism	**E.**	Excess of cerebrospinal fluid

Answers: **1.** normal **2.** F **3.** T **4.** F **5.** F **6.** D **7.** B **8.** E **9.** A **10.** C

Hereditary and Environmental Factors—The Nature and Nurture of Intelligence

Question: Is intelligence inherited?

In a classic study of genetic factors and learning ability, Tryon (1929) managed to breed separate strains of "maze-bright" and "maze-dull" rats. Tryon began by testing a large number of animals in a maze. The brightest rats from this group were selected and interbred, and the dullest were likewise mated. This procedure was continued for several generations until separate strains of exceptionally "bright" and unusually "stupid" rats emerged. At this point, the dullest "super rat" was brighter than the brightest rat in the dull group. This and similar studies of *eugenics* (selective breeding for desirable characteristics) raise the question of the relative importance of heredity and environment in determining human intelligence.

You may have casually observed that there seems to be a close relationship between the intelligence of parents and their children or between siblings in the same family.

Question: Does this prove that intelligence is hereditary?

No, because brothers, sisters, and parents share similar environments as well as similar heredity. By making comparisons more formally, hereditary and environmental factors in intelligence become clearer. As Table 18-6 shows, the similarity in IQ among relatives grows in direct proportion to their closeness on the "family tree."

An especially interesting comparison can be made for siblings, fraternal twins, and identical twins. *Fraternal twins* result when two separate eggs are fertilized at the same time. Fraternal twins are no more alike genetically than ordinary siblings, but their IQs are more alike because of the greater similarity of their childhood environment. *Identical twins*, who develop from a single egg, have *identical* heredity and similar environment and, as a result, nearly identical IQs. The interplay of heredity and environ-

Table 18-6 Correlations* Between Intelligence Test Scores for Persons with Varying Degrees of Genetic Similarity

Identical twins	.90
Fraternal twins	.65
Siblings	.50
Parents and their children	.50
Cousins	.25
Grandparent-grandchild	.15
Unrelated children	.00

*A correlation of 0.0 indicates no relationship between two measures. A correlation of 1.0 means that a perfect association exists.

(Based on Hunt, 1961, p. 8.)

ment is also revealed by comparing identical twins raised together to those raised apart. As we have noted, the correlation of IQs for identical twins raised together is .90. If they are raised apart (so that their childhood environments are less similar), the correlation drops to .80.

On the basis of such comparisons, some psychologists attribute as much as 80 percent of intelligence to the effects of heredity. Heredity is clearly important, but this figure may be an exaggeration. Large environmental effects can also be demonstrated. In one study, striking increases in IQ were observed when children were moved from an orphanage to more stimulating environments. Twenty-five children, all considered mentally retarded and unadoptable, were moved to an institution where they received personal attention from adults. Later, these supposedly retarded children were adopted by parents who gave them love, a family, and a stimulating environment. The IQs of the children showed an average gain of 29 points. For one child, the increase was an amazing 58 points. A second group of initially less "retarded" children who remained in the orphanage *lost* an average of 26 IQ points (Skeels, 1966)! The importance of environment is also shown by a study of black children who moved from the South to a northern city. The children were observed to gradually increase in IQ as they were exposed to the educational and environmental advantages of the city (Lee, 1951).

Many of the findings concerning heredity, environment, and intelligence can be summarized in these terms: Inherited intellectual potential may be compared to a rubber band that is stretched by outside forces. A longer rubber band may be stretched more easily, but a shorter one can be stretched to the same length if enough force is applied (Stern, 1956). Of course, a superior genetic "gift" may allow for a higher maximum IQ, but in the final analysis intelligence reflects development as well as potential, nurture as well as nature.

Learning Check

1. Selective breeding for desirable characteristics is called ____________.

2. The greatest similarity in IQs is observed for:
a. parents and their children
b. identical twins
c. fraternal twins
d. siblings

3. Intelligence is entirely hereditary. T or F?

4. Except for slight variations in testing, IQ cannot be changed. T or F?

Answers: **1.** eugenics **2.** b **3.** F **4.** F

Resources Summary

Intelligence refers to one's general capacity to act purposefully, think rationally, and deal effectively with the environment. In practice, intelligence is often *operationally defined* as "that which an intelligence test measures." The first practical intelligence test was assembled by Alfred Binet. A modern version of Binet's test is the Stanford-Binet Intelligence Scale. A second major intelligence test is the Wechsler Adult Intelligence Scale (WAIS). The WAIS measures both *verbal* and *performance* intelligence. Intelligence tests have also been produced for use with groups. *Group* tests include the *Army Alpha*, the *SAT*, the *ACT*, and the *CQT*.

Intelligence is expressed in terms of an *intelligence quotient* (IQ). IQ is defined as mental age (MA) divided by chronological age (CA) and then multiplied by 100. IQ becomes fairly stable at about age six. The peak of intellectual ability apparently occurs between twenty and thirty years of age.

The distribution of IQ scores approximates a *normal curve*. There are no overall IQ differences between males and females, but intellectual strengths have been noted for each. IQ is strongly related to school grades and levels of academic achievement. There is also an association between IQ and job status, but this may be artificial. People with IQs in the "gifted" or "genius" range tend to be superior in many respects. The term "mentally retarded" is applied to those whose IQ falls below 70. Chances for successful adjustment are related to the degree of retardation. Retardation may be caused by *birth injuries*, *disease*, *deprivation*, or *genetic abnormalities*. Five specialized forms of retardation are: *phenylketonuria* (PKU), *microcephaly*, *hydrocephaly*, *cretinism*, and *mongolism* (*Down's syndrome*).

Studies of *eugenics* in animals and familial relationships in humans demonstrate that intelligence is partially determined by heredity. However, environment is also important, as revealed by drastic changes in tested intelligence brought about by stimulating environments. Intelligence reflects the combined effects of both heredity and environment on development of intellectual abilities.

Applications

Intelligence in Perspective—Are Intelligence Tests Intelligent?

Almost everyone has some curiosity about how they would score on an intelligence test. If you would like to get a rough estimate of your IQ, take the following self-administered test.

Dove Counterbalance Intelligence Test

Time limit: 5 minutes

Circle the correct answer.

1. T-bone Walker got famous for playing what?

a. trombone
b. piano
c. T-flute
d. guitar
e. "hambone"

2. A "gas head" is a person who has a ____.

a. fast-moving car
b. stable of "lace"
c. "process"
d. habit of stealing cars
e. long jail record for arson

3. If you throw the dice and 7 is showing on the top, what is facing down?

a. 7
b. snake eyes
c. boxcars
d. little joes
e. 11

4. Cheap chitlings (not the kind you purchase at a frozen-food counter) will taste rubbery unless they are cooked long enough. How soon can you quit cooking them to eat and enjoy them?

a. 45 minutes
b. two hours
c. 24 hours
d. one week (on a low flame)
e. one hour

5. Bird or Yardbird was the jacket jazz lovers from coast to coast hung on ________.

a. Lester Young
b. Peggy Lee
c. Benny Goodman
d. Charlie Parker
e. Birdman of Alcatraz

6. A "handkerchief head" is:

a. a cool cat

b. porter
c. an Uncle Tom
d. a hoddi
e. a preacher

7. Jet is ______________.

a. *an East Oakland motorcycle club*
b. one of the gangs in *West Side Story*
c. a news and gossip magazine
d. a way of life for the very rich

8. "Bo Diddly" is a ______________.

a. game for children
b. down-home cheap wine
c. down-home singer
d. new dance
e. Moejoe call

9. Which word is most out of place here?

a. splib
b. blood
c. gray
d. spook
e. black

10. If a pimp is up tight with a woman who gets state aid, what does he mean when he talks about "Mother's Day"?

a. second Sunday in May
b. third Sunday in June
c. first of every month
d. none of these
e. first and fifteenth of every month

11. How much does a "short dog" cost?

a. 15¢
b. $2
c. 35¢
d. 5¢
e. 86¢ plus tax

12. Many people say that "Juneteenth" (June 10th) should be made a legal holiday because this was the day when:

a. the slaves were freed in the United States
b. the slaves were freed in Texas
c. the slaves were freed in Jamaica
d. the slaves were freed in California
e. Martin Luther King was born
f. Booker T. Washington died

13. If a man is called a "blood," then he is a ______________.

a. fighter
b. Mexican-American
c. Negro
d. hungry hemophile
e. red man or Indian

14. What are the Dixie Hummingbirds?

a. a part of the KKK
b. a swamp disease
c. a modern gospel group
d. a Mississippi Negro paramilitary strike force
e. deacons

15. The opposite of square is ______________.

a. round
b. up
c. down
d. hip
e. lame

Answers: **1.** *d* **2.** *c* **3.** *a* **4.** *c* **5.** *d* **6.** *c* **7.** *c* **8.** *c* **9.** *c* **10.** *c* **11.** *c* **12.** *b* **13.** *c* **14.** *c* **15.** *d*

If you scored 14 on this exam, your IQ is approximately 100, indicating average intelligence. If you scored 11 or less you are mentally retarded. With luck and the help of a special educational program, we may be able to teach you a few simple skills!

Question: Isn't this test a little unfair?

No, it is *very unfair*. It was constructed by black sociologist Adrian Dove as "a half serious attempt to show that we're just not talking the same language." Dove tried to slant his test as much in favor of urban black culture as he believes the typical intelligence test is biased toward a white middle-class background. Dove's test is a thought-provoking reply to the fact that black children in the United States score an average of about 15 points lower on standardized IQ tests than do white children. By reversing the bias, Dove has shown that intelligence tests are not equally valid for all groups. As Kagan (1973) has commented, "If the Wechsler and Binet scales were translated into Spanish, Swahili, and Chinese and given to every ten-year-old in Latin America, East Africa, or China, the majority would obtain IQ scores in the mentally retarded range." Certainly we cannot believe that children of different cultures are all retarded. The fault must lie in the test. In recognition of this problem, some psychologists are trying to develop "culture-fair" tests that will not disadvantage certain groups. (For a sample of culture-fair test items, see Fig. 18-4.)

Biased tests are not the only IQ issue blacks have confronted. Arthur Jensen, writing in the *Harvard Educational Review*, has claimed that the lower IQ scores of blacks can be primarily attributed to "genetic heritage." It is important to note that few psychologists support this conclu-

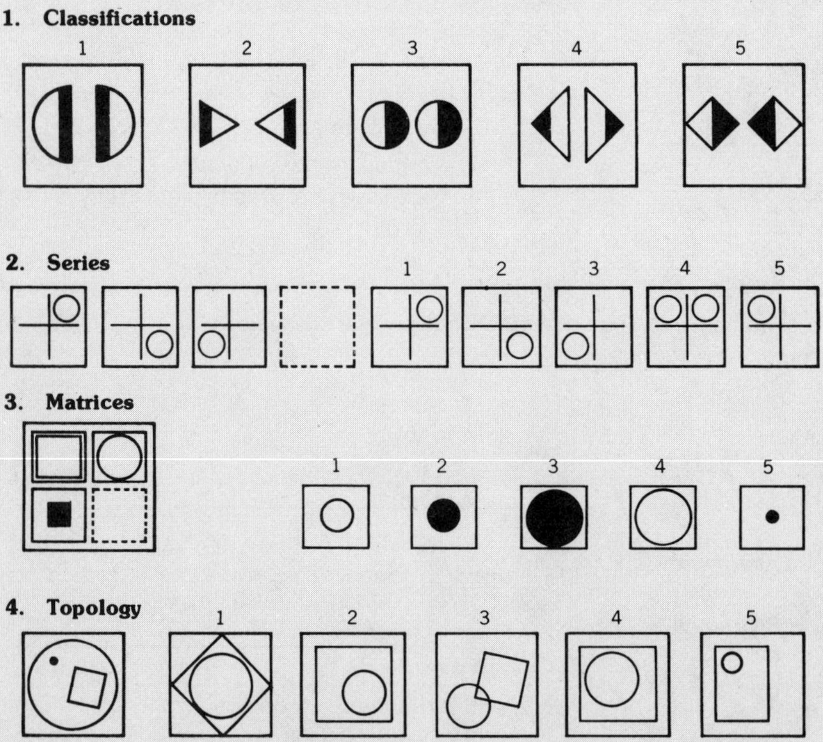

Fig. 18-4 Sample items from a culture fair test. **1.** Which pattern is different from the remaining four? (Number 3.) **2.** Which of the five figures on the right would properly continue the three on the left, i.e., fill blank? (Number 5.) **3.** Which of the figures on the right should go in the square on the left to make it look right? (Number 2.) **4.** At left, the dot is outside the square and inside the circle. In which of the figures on the right could you put a dot outside the square and inside the circle? (Number 3.)

sion, and a number of arguments have been advanced against it.

First, it is no secret that as a group blacks in the United States are more likely than whites to live in environments that are physically, educationally, and intellectually impoverished. Second, even if we assume that the gap in IQ between blacks and whites is hereditary, it is small enough to be corrected by environment. Jensen's reply to this claim is that special educational programs like Head Start have proved incapable of narrowing the IQ gap. But it is essentially ridiculous to expect that a brief summer program or a few hours a day are enough to counteract the differences in educational and environmental advantages of blacks and whites.

Third, Jensen confuses *racial* and *hereditary* differences. Many blacks in the United States have as few as 10 percent "black genes," and some whites have as many as 75 percent "black genes." "Race" in the United States is a *social* concept, not a biological reality.

Perhaps the most devastating criticism of Jensen is that his logic is faulty. Consider this example: Corn comes in different varieties selectively bred to grow to a certain height. If we plant tall and short varieties side by side in the same field, we will observe a genetically determined difference in their height at maturity. But what if we take corn (all the same variety) and plant half in a fertile field and half in poor soil? Again we observe a difference in maximum height, but this time it is obviously a mistake to assume that it is genetically caused.

Only when black children are raised in exactly the same surroundings as white children can hereditary factors be clearly assessed. Along this line, a recent study looked at the fate of black children adopted by white families. These children had IQ scores averaging 106, which is comparable to the national average for white children (Scarr-Salapatek & Weinberg, 1975). It is not clear if the black children were actually "brighter" as a result of this experience or if they were just better prepared to take a "white" test. The fact remains, however, that when an equal opportunity for intellectual development is capable of closing the IQ gap, then the genetic position must be abandoned.

Questioning the Concept of IQ— Beyond the Numbers Game

Blacks are not the only segment of the population with reason to question the validity of intelligence testing and the role of heredity in determining intelligence. The clarifications won by blacks extend to others as well. Consider the nine-year-old child confronted with this question on a classroom-administered intelligence test: "Which of the following does not belong with the others? Field hockey, pool, football, or baseball." If the child misses the question, does this reveal a lack of intelligence? It can be argued that an intelligent choice could be based on any of these alternatives: "Field hockey is played mostly by girls; pool isn't a team sport; football isn't played with a stick or bat; baseball doesn't involve putting the ball into a goal" (Sheils & Monroe, 1976).[1] The parents of a child who misses this question may have good reason to feel angry since educational systems tend to classify children and then make the classification stick.

Recent public concern has led some states to outlaw use of intelligence tests in public schools. Criticism of intelligence testing has also come from the academic community. Harvard University psychologist David McClelland (1973) believes IQ is of little value in predicting real competence to deal effectively with the world. McClelland concedes that IQ predicts school performance, but when he compared a group of college students with straight A's to another group with poor grades, he found no differences in later career success.

The application of the preceding discussions to your personal understanding of intelligence can be summarized in this way: Intelligence tests are a two-edged sword. We have learned much from their use, yet they have the potential to do great harm. In the final analysis, it is important to remember that creativity, motivation, physical health, mechanical aptitude, artistic ability, and numerous other qualities not measured by intelligence tests contribute to the achievement of life goals. Also remember that *IQ* is *not intelligence*. IQ is an *index* of intelligence (as defined by a particular test). Change the test and you change the score. An IQ is not some permanent number stamped on the forehead of a child that forever determines potential.

For Discussion

Let us end on an optimistic note. Rather than getting caught in the debate about hereditary and environmental factors in intelligence or the validity of intelligence tests, some psychologists and educators are seeking ways to teach necessary intellectual skills to all children. In some cases their success has been striking. One experiment divided 40 children from extremely disadvantaged (slum) families into two groups. Children in the control group received no extra attention or training. Beginning shortly after birth, the experimental group was given a wide variety of stimulation to develop perceptual, motor, and language abilities. At age two the children were placed in small classes with other children and several teachers. Each child received lots of teacher attention and exposure to a broad range of topics and thinking exercises. When tested at age 5½ the average IQ for the control group was about 95; the average for the experimentals was 124 (reported by Whimbey, 1974). These results should be encouraging to everyone interested in the fulfillment of human potentials.

Questions for Discussion

1. In what ways might our society encourage the development of different intellectual skills in males and females?
2. Do you know your IQ? Would you like to know it? Why?
3. What advantages or disadvantages would you expect to be associated with knowing your own IQ? With having a teacher know your IQ? With your parents knowing your IQ?
4. How might public education be restructured to encourage full intellectual development for all children? How might grading be changed to reflect broader definitions of intelligence?
5. How would you feel about the application of eugenics to human reproduction? Can you think of circumstances under which you would or would not consider it acceptable?
6. Should standardized intelligence testing be outlawed in public schools? Why or why not?

Suggestions for Further Reading

Cronbach, L. *Essentials of Psychological Testing.* 3rd ed. Harper & Row, 1970.

Garcia, J. "IQ: The Conspiracy," *Psychology Today* (April) 1972, pp. 40–43.

Kamin, L. J. *The Science and Politics of IQ.* Erlbaum/Wiley, 1974.

Rosenthal, R. and L. Jacobson. *Pygmalion in the Classroom.* Holt, 1968.

Sarason, S., and J. Doris. *Psychological Problems in Mental Deficiency.* 4th ed. Harper & Row, 1969.

Terman, L. M., and M. H. Oden. *The Gifted Group at Midlife.* Stanford University Press, 1959.

Wallach, M., and C. Wing. *The Talented Student: A Validation of the Creativity-Intelligence Distinction.* Holt, 1969.

Personality: Traits, Types, and Testing

19

Chapter Preview

The Extra Dimension

"*Lunar IX* to Mission Control, over."

"Mission Control, go ahead."

"This is Colonel Willis. Please inform Colonel Rapp that I am beginning a sleep cycle."

"Mission Control, this is Colonel Rapp. Please tell Colonel Willis that if he would work more and sleep less, we would be on schedule."

"Now just a minute, Rapp, you're the one who held up the meteorological report, not to mention the. . . ."

This imaginary conversation between two feuding astronauts illustrates the importance of personality. Despite our advanced technology, the human dimension still determines success or failure in many situations. It is said, for instance, that the most dangerous part of an automobile is the "nut at the wheel." Similarly, the human element will remain when the engineering problems of extended space flight are solved: Can humans withstand prolonged confinement without serious personality clashes? Clearly, space travelers will have to be selected carefully for maturity, stability, and compatibility.

Of course, personality is also an issue in our daily lives. Selecting a mate, choosing friends, getting along with co-workers, voting for a president, and numerous other activities raise questions about personality. But what is personality? How does it differ from temperament, character, or attitudes? Can personality be measured? How stable are personality characteristics? These and related questions are the concern of this chapter.

Resources

Do You Have Personality?

"Jim's not handsome, but he has a great personality." "My father's business friends think he's a nice guy, but they never see him at home where his real personality comes out." "The twins are such a paradox. They have completely different personalities." Statements like these are made so effortlessly and with such authority that we often believe people know what personality is. But when questioned, many people stammer and finally say something about "charm," "charisma," "character," or simply that some people have "more personality" than others. If you have used the term "personality" in such ways, you have given it a different meaning than a psychologist would. To a psychologist it makes little sense to ask: "Do I have personality?" or to proclaim, "She has lots of personality." In psychological terms everyone has personality.

Question: Then how do psychologists use the term?

Since personality is an *hypothetical construct,** psychologists give it different meanings. However, most regard personality as a person's *unique* and *enduring behavior patterns*. In other words, personality refers to the consistency in what a person is, has been, and will become. It also refers to the singular combination of talents, attitudes, values, hopes, loves, hates, and habits that mark each person as unique.

Question: How is psychologists' use of the term different from the way most people use it?

Many people confuse personality with *character*, which is personality evaluated. If by saying someone has "personality" you mean that he is friendly, enthusiastic, moderate, honest, open, or loving, you are really referring to character. Having "lots of personality" is a matter of taste, not amount. In some cultures, a person with "good character" is fierce, aggressive, and competitive. In other cultures, cooperation, humility, and restraint are valued. Thus, while everyone in a particular culture has personality, not everyone has character—or at least not good character. (Do you know any good characters?)

An additional distinction can be made between personality and *temperament*. Temperament is the "raw material" from which personality is formed. Temperament refers to physique and the hereditary aspects of one's emotional nature: sensitivity, strength and speed of response, prevailing mood, and fluctuations in mood (Allport, 1961).

Personality is very difficult to study because it cannot be directly observed. The remainder of this chapter is devoted to discussion of techniques and approaches that have been helpful in attempts to pin down this elusive concept.

*An explanatory concept that is not directly observable.

Fig. 19-1 Does this man have personality? Do you? (Photo by Anna Kaufman Moon, Stock, Boston.)

Personality Types—Which Are You?

The study of personality *types* is a natural extension of interest in personality. We often speak of the hot-tempered redhead, the executive type, the athletic type, the motherly type, the strong, silent type, and the like. Informal conceptions of personality types abound.

Question: How valid is it to speak of personality "types"?

Psychologists have been hesitant to adopt most type systems because they oversimplify personality. Consider the idea, first proposed by Swiss psychiatrist Carl Jung, that a person is either an *introvert* (shy, self-centered person) or an *extravert* (bold, outgoing person). These terms have become so widely accepted that many people think of themselves and their friends as belonging to one category or the other. However, the wildest, wittiest, most party-loving "extravert" you know is introverted at times, and extremely introverted persons are assertive and sociable in some situations. Rather than classify people, it may make better sense to rate them in degrees of introversion or extraversion. Yet, even if this is done, we will find that most people fall somewhere in the middle, between the extremes.

Despite their faults, type systems reflect a natural tendency of people to group one another into categories when they perceive similarities between them. For example, popular stereotypes in our culture hold that fat people are good-natured, warm-hearted, and lazy. Thin people are supposedly tense, ambitious, and quiet. Those with a muscular build are considered aggressive, adventurous, and self-reliant (Wells & Siegel, 1961).

Question: Is there really any connection between body build and personality?

To answer this question, let us examine one well-known system of personality types.

Body Type and Personality In ancient Greece, the famous physician Hippocrates proposed that an abundance of certain "humors" or fluids in the body affected personality. Hippocrates believed, for example, that a person with an excess of "black bile" was prone to sadness and depression. Courage and vitality, he believed, were linked to the blood, anger and irritability to "yellow bile," and listlessness to "phlegm." A modern outgrowth of Hippocrates' thinking is the constitutional theory of William Sheldon. Sheldon's theory is basically an attempt to verify the popular body-personality stereotypes we have just mentioned.

Sheldon (1954) carefully analyzed body dimensions of thousands of male college students and concluded that physique can be described as a combination of three basic components: *endomorphy*, *mesomorphy*, and *ectomorphy*. Endomorphy is characterized by a fat, soft, round body structure. (Sheldon noted that endomorphs float in water!) Mesomorphy is marked by a robust development of muscles, bones, and ligaments. This gives the body a hard, muscular, or angular appearance. (Mesomorphy is not necessarily an athletic body. A "walking muscle" might be a more apt description.) Ectomorphy is characterized by underdeveloped muscles and bones. The ectomorph is flat-chested, thin, fragile, and linear. (But he has a large head!)

Question: How can I tell if I am an endomorph, mesomorph, or ectomorph?

You are probably none of these. "Pure" examples of each physique are rare. The average person's *somatotype* (body type) is a mixture of all three components. In rating body structure, a number from 1 to 7 is assigned to each dimension. The average person is rated around 4 on each (see Fig. 19-2).

Question: What connection did Sheldon find between body type and personality?

Sheldon compared ratings on 60 personality characteristics with the three body types. Three personality types emerged: *viscerotonia*, *somatotonia*, and *cerebrotonia*. Viscerotonia combines sociability, tolerance, and goodwill with a love of eating, sleeping, and physical comfort. Somatotonia is characterized by assertiveness, boldness, energy, aggression, a callous attitude toward the feelings of others, and a love of physical exercise. The cerebrotonic individual is self-conscious, shy, sensitive, nervous, and has a need for privacy and intellectual stimulation.

It may come as no surprise to learn that Sheldon found a strong association between endomorphy and viscerotonia, mesomorphy and somatotonia, and ectomorphy and cerebrotonia. These associations are exactly what would be expected on the basis of stereotyped images of fat, muscular, and skinny persons. But before you leap to conclusions about yourself or your friends, bear in mind that most people are a mixture of the three body types.

Few psychologists expected the strong association between body build and personality found by Sheldon. Many have criticized Sheldon for allowing the possibility of bias to enter his research methods. In most of Sheldon's research the same person rated a subject on both body type and personality, allowing ratings to be influenced by preconceptions about fat, muscular, or thin persons.

Question: Is there a relationship between body type and personality, then, or isn't there?

When studying personality development we must not overlook the possible influence of body configuration. For example, an endomorphic person may become jovial and socially skillful to compensate for being overweight in a culture that prizes slimness and muscular development. Or perhaps the "jolly, fat man" is simply living up to the stereotyped expectations of others. It is also possible that people with a particular body type are more likely to succeed at certain activities. The muscular mesomorph's

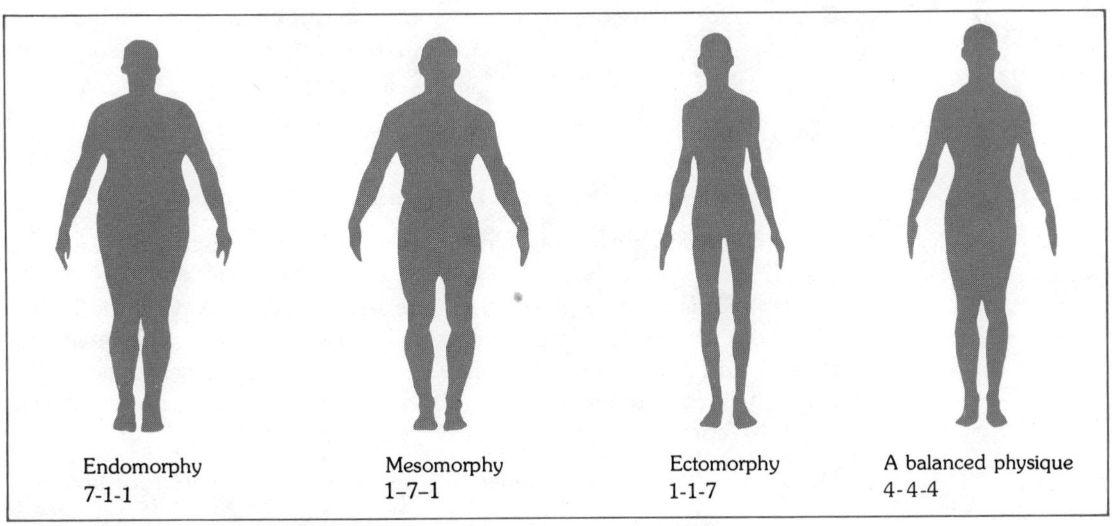

Fig. 19-2 Sheldon's somatotype system. 1–7–1 type might be a Sumo wrestler or an olympic weight lifter. "Twiggy" is a 1-1-7 type, Jackie Gleason a 7-1-1 type.

boldness could reflect more frequent success at bullying others, for example.

Despite such possibilities, it now seems unlikely that connections between physique and personality are as direct or clear-cut as Sheldon claimed. Although more recent research partially supports the body-personality relationships reported by Sheldon, the associations are usually quite weak (Cortes & Gatti, 1972). In summary, it seems fair to conclude that body type plays a role in personality formation, but rarely is it a central or determining factor. It would appear to be as big a mistake to judge people by their bodies as it is to judge books by their covers.

If you have resisted the idea of putting yourself in an all-or-nothing category, be it introvert, extravert, endomorph, athletic type, studious type, or whatever, then you may be more comfortable with a *trait* approach to personality.

Learning Check

1. ______________________________ is personality evaluated.

2. All people can be classified as either introverts or extraverts. T or F?

Match in accordance with Sheldon's theory:

3. ______ Endomorphy **A.** Cerebrotonia

4. ______ Mesomorphy **B.** Somatotonia

5. ______ Ectomorphy **C.** Viscerotonia

Answers: 1. Character 2. F 3. C 4. B 5. A

The Trait Approach—Personality as Consistency

How many words can you think of to describe the personality of a close friend? You should have little trouble making a long list: Over 18,000 English words refer to personal characteristics (Allport & Odbert, 1936). Many of these words describe personality *traits*. Traits are relatively permanent and enduring qualities that a person shows in most situations. For example, if you are usually optimistic, reserved, or friendly, these qualities might be considered stable traits of your personality.

Question: What if I am sometimes pessimistic, uninhibited, or shy?

The first three characteristics are still traits as long as they are most *typical* of your behavior. Let's say Ima Student approaches most situations with optimism but has a habit of expecting the worst each time she takes a test. If her pessimism is limited to this situation or to a few others, it is still accurate and useful to describe her as an optimistic person.

In general, the trait approach attempts to specify those traits which best describe a particular individual. Take a moment to check traits in Table 19-1 that you feel are descriptive of your personality. Are the traits you checked of equal importance? Are some stronger or more basic than others? Do any overlap? For example, if you checked "dominant," did you also check "confident" and "bold?" Answers to these questions would interest a *trait theorist*. To understand personality, trait theorists attempt to classify traits and to reduce them to a manageable number by discovering which are most basic.

Question: Are there different kinds of traits?

Classifying Traits Gordon Allport (1961), a psychologist who has written extensively about personality traits, identifies several types of traits. *Common traits* are those shared by most members of a culture. Common traits reveal similarities among people of a particular national origin or linguistic background, but they tell us little about individual members of a culture. Since we know that no two people are exactly alike, we must also consider unique personal characteristics, or *individual traits*.

If the difference between common traits and individual traits is unclear, consider this illustration: Each person's hand is unique in the details of its shape (individual traits), but in an anatomy class we can still describe the characteristics of "hands in general" (common traits). Thus, Allport felt that by studying traits we could discover what is true of personalities in general at the same time that we could improve our understanding of

Table 19-1 Adjective Checklist

Check the traits you feel are characteristic of your personality. Are some more basic than others?

aggressive	organized	ambitious
confident	loyal	generous
warm	bold	cautious
sensitive	mature	talented
sociable	busy	funny
dominant	dull	accurate
humble	uninhibited	future-oriented
thoughtful	serious	helpful
orderly	anxious	comforming
liberal	curious	optimistic
meek	neighborly	passionate
kind	compulsive	honest
cheerful	emotional	good-natured
clever	calm	reliable
jealous	religious	nervous

individual personalities. The study of personality in general has been called the "nomothetic approach," and the detailed study of a single individual, the "idiographic approach."

Allport also made a distinction between *cardinal* traits, *central* traits, and *secondary* traits. Cardinal traits are so basic that all of a person's activities can be traced to existence of the trait. It is said, for instance, that an overriding factor in the life of Albert Schweitzer was "reverence for every living thing." Likewise, Abraham Lincoln's personality was dominated by the cardinal trait of honesty. According to Allport, few people have cardinal traits.

Question: How do central and secondary traits differ from cardinal traits?

Central traits are the basic building blocks that make up the core of personality. Allport found that a surprisingly small number of central traits is sufficient to capture the essence of a person. College students asked to write a short description of someone they knew well mentioned an average of only 7.2 central traits (Allport, 1961). In contrast, secondary traits are less consistent and less important aspects of a person. For this reason, any number of secondary traits could be listed in a personality description. Secondary traits include such things as food preferences, attitudes, political opinions, and reactions to particular situations. In Allport's terms, a personality description might therefore include:

Name: Jane Doe
Age: 22
Cardinal traits: None
Central traits: Possessive, autonomous, artistic, dramatic, self-centered, trusting
Secondary traits: Prefers colorful clothes, likes to work alone, politically liberal, always late, and so forth

Source Traits A second major approach to the study of personality traits is illustrated by the work of Raymond B. Cattell (1965). Cattell was dissatisfied with merely classifying traits. Instead, he wanted to reach deeper into personality to learn how traits are organized and interrelated. Cattell began by studying characteristics making up the visible portions of personality. He called these *surface traits*. Through use of questionnaires, direct observation, and life records, Cattell assembled data on the surface traits of a large number of people. He then noted that surface traits often appear in *clusters*, or groupings. In fact, some traits appeared together so often they seemed to represent a single more basic trait. By use of a sophisticated statistical technique, Cattell narrowed surface traits down to a list of sixteen underlying *source traits*. Cattell considers this the number of traits necessary to adequately describe an individual personality.

Cattell's list of source traits also forms the basis of a personality test called the *Sixteen Personality Factor Questionnaire* (often referred to as the *16 PF*). Like many personality tests of its type, the 16 PF can be used to produce a *trait profile*. A trait profile is a graphic representation of the scores obtained by an individual on each trait. Trait profiles can be very helpful for obtaining a "picture" of an individual personality or for making comparisons between the personalities of two or more persons (see Fig. 19-3).

The Trouble with Traits Let's say you have observed that a friend seems to be aggressive in many situations. Someone asks why your friend seems so aggressive. You explain that aggressiveness is a trait of his personality. Have you actually explained his behavior? Let's review the logic involved. How do we know your friend has the trait of aggressiveness? Because he acts aggressively. And why does he act aggressively? Because he has the trait of aggressiveness. And how do we know he has this trait? Because he acts aggressively. And why does he act aggressively? Without going any further, the *circularity* of a trait approach to personality can be easily seen. Traits are a good way to describe personality, but they do little to explain behavior. For this reason, many psychologists have shown

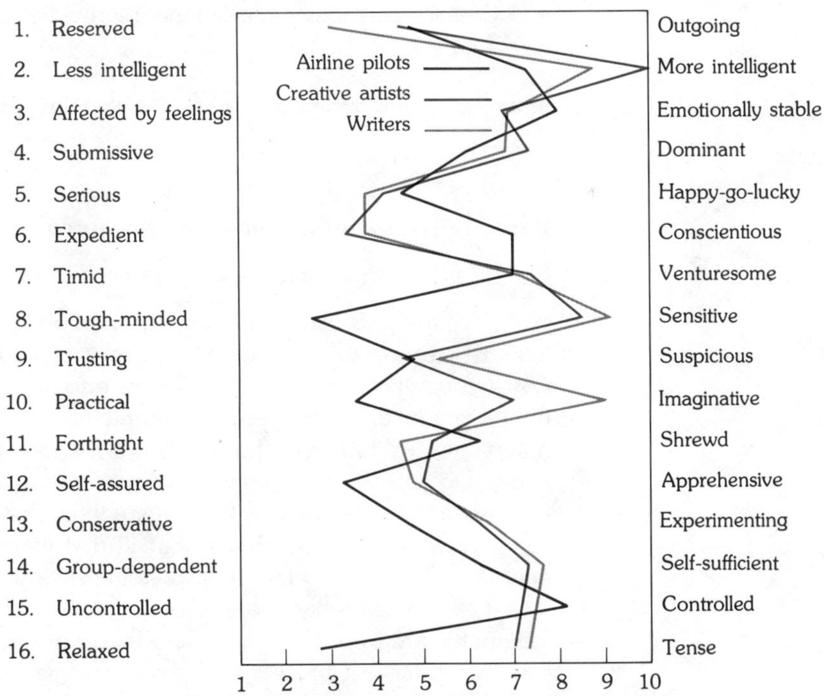

Fig. 19-3 The 16 source traits measured by Cattell's 16PF are listed above. Scores can be graphed as a profile for an individual or a group. Profiles above are group averages for airline pilots, creative artists, and writers. Notice the similarity between artists and writers and the difference between these two and pilots. (After Cattell, 1973.)

interest in developing models or theories of personality. (A discussion of personality theories is found in the next chapter.)

Perhaps the greatest value of the trait approach is the refinement it has brought to personality measurement and testing. To adequately study traits, psychologists have found it necessary to develop a variety of means for assessing personality. The resulting techniques have been of tremendous value in research, industry, education, and clinical work.

Learning Check

1. According to Allport, few people have __________ traits.

2. Cental traits are those shared by most members of a culture. T or F?

3. When surface traits occur in clusters they reflect existence of underlying __________ traits.

4. Cattell's personality questionnaire provides ratings on 16 surface traits. T or F?

Answers: 1. cardinal 2. F 3. source 4. F

Personality Assessment—Psychological Yardsticks

Question: How is personality "assessed"?

Psychologists use interviews, observation, questionnaires, and projective tests to measure personality. Each is a refinement of more informal ways of judging others. At one time or another you have probably "sized up" a potential date, friend, or employer by engaging in conversation (interview). Perhaps you have asked a friend, "When I am delayed I get angry. Do you?" (questionnaire). Maybe you watch your professors when they are angry or embarrassed to learn what they are "really" like (observation). Or possibly you have noticed that when a person says, "I think people feel. . . ," he may be expressing his own feelings (projection).

It can be seen that everyone engages in personality assessment. If our judgments are important, as in choosing a roommate or a spouse, errors can be costly. As professionals, psychologists also make judgments of personality that are costly when in error. Understandably, they have had an interest in improving the accuracy of personality assessment. Let's see what they have learned.

The Interview A very direct way to learn about a person's personality is to engage in conversation. An interview is described as *unstructured* if the conversation is informal, and the interviewee is allowed to determine what subjects are discussed. In a *structured interview* information is obtained by asking a series of planned questions.

Question: How are interviews used?

Interviews are used to identify personality disturbances, to select persons for employment, college, or special programs, and for research on the dynamics of personality. Interviews also provide information for counseling or therapy. For instance, a counselor might ask a depressed person: "Have you ever contemplated suicide? What were the circumstances?" The counselor might then follow by asking: "How did you feel about it?" or, "How is what you are now feeling different from what you felt then?" One advantage of interviewing is that is flexible, and it uncovers feelings. In addition, it allows observation of a person's tone of voice, hand gestures, posture, and facial expressions. These "body language" cues may add completely new meaning to what is said, as when a person claims to be "completely calm," but trembles uncontrollably.

Interviews give rapid insight into personality, but they are subject to certain limitations. For one thing, interviewers can be swayed by preconceptions. A person identified as a "housewife," "college student," "high school athlete," or "ski bum" may be misjudged because of an interviewer's attitudes toward a particular life-style. Secondly, the interviewer's own personality may cause him to accentuate, overlook, or distort qualities of the interviewee. A third problem is the tendency of interviewees to be influenced by actions of the interviewer.

Question: How is that possible?

An interviewer's approval, expressed by nodding or smiling, and his disapproval, expressed by frowning or silence, affects what is said in an interview (Greenspoon, 1955). The situation is complicated by the tendency of interviewers to smile and talk more with persons of the opposite sex. It is also known that younger persons are less likely to say "unacceptable" things to an older interviewer and that blacks tend to give more "proper" responses to white than to black interviewers (Rosenthal, 1969). If you are young, black, and female, your chances of being accurately interviewed may be pretty low.

A final problem in interviewing is the *halo effect*. The halo effect is a tendency to generalize a favorable or unfavorable impression to unrelated details of personality. A person who is likable or physically attractive may be rated more mature, intelligent, or adjusted than he or she actually is. The halo effect is something to keep in mind when interviewing for employment. First impressions do make a difference.

Even with their limitations, interviews are a respected method of personality assessment. In many cases interviews are an essential step to additional personality testing and to counseling or therapy.

Direct Observation and Rating Scales Are you fascinated by bus depots, airports, subway stations, or other public places? Many people relish a chance to observe the behavior of others. When used as an assessment procedure, direct observation is a simple extension of this natural interest in "people watching." For instance, a psychologist might arrange to observe a disturbed child playing with other children. By careful observation the psychologist will identify personality characteristics and clarify the nature of the child's problems.

Question: Wouldn't observation be subject to the same problems of misperception as an interview?

Yes, misperceiving can be a difficulty. Because of it, *rating scales* are sometimes used (see Table 19-2). Rating scales limit the chance that some traits will be overlooked while others are exaggerated. Perhaps they should be standard procedure for choosing a roommate, spouse, or lover!

A specialized form of direct observation is called *situational testing*. Situational tests are based on the premise that the best way to learn how a person reacts to a certain situation is to simulate that situation. Situational tests expose a person to frustration, temptation, pressure, boredom, or other conditions capable of revealing personality characteristics. One of the most ambitious examples of situational testing was devised by the Office of Strategic Services (OSS) during World War II. The OSS was a forerunner of the CIA, and its agents were involved in dangerous and demanding espionage.

Question: How were OSS candidates tested?

Candidates were tested under conditions requiring the same skills of leadership, tolerance for stress, and ability to cooperate needed for success as a spy. Some of the tests were both diabolical and ingenious. For example:

Lesson 1: Never Trust Another Spy

> In one test, a candidate and two "helpers" were required to build a tower out of heavy logs. Soon after the trio started work the candidate's troubles began. One of the helpers knocked down part of the structure; the other followed instructions improperly; both repeatedly insulted the candidate. The whole scene soon began to look like something from a slapstick movie.

What was happening? In reality the "helpers" were *observers* trained to sabotage the efforts of the candidate. The "helpers," of course, recorded each candidate's reactions. Some candidates decided to work alone or stalked off in disgust. Others patiently attempted to work with the two "clowns" assigned to help. What would have been your reaction?

Table 19-2 Sample Rating Scale Items

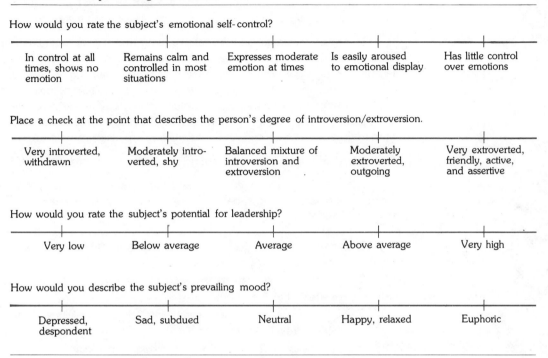

How would you rate the subject's emotional self-control?

In control at all times, shows no emotion	Remains calm and controlled in most situations	Expresses moderate emotion at times	Is easily aroused to emotional display	Has little control over emotions

Place a check at the point that describes the person's degree of introversion/extroversion.

Very introverted, withdrawn	Moderately introverted, shy	Balanced mixture of introversion and extroversion	Moderately extroverted, outgoing	Very extroverted, friendly, active, and assertive

How would you rate the subject's potential for leadership?

Very low	Below average	Average	Above average	Very high

How would you describe the subject's prevailing mood?

Depressed, despondent	Sad, subdued	Neutral	Happy, relaxed	Euphoric

Personality Questionnaires Most personality questionnaires are paper-and-pencil tests requiring people to answer questions about themselves. As measures of personality, questionnaires are more *objective* than interviews or observation. Questions, administration, and scoring are all standardized so that scores are unaffected by the opinions or prejudices of the examiner. The best-known and most widely used objective test of personality is the *Minnesota Multiphasic Personality Inventory* (usually referred to as the MMPI). The MMPI is composed of 550 items to which a subject must respond "true," "false," or "cannot say." Items include statements such as:

> Everything tastes the same.
> There is something wrong with my mind.
> I enjoy animals.
> Whenever possible I avoid being in a crowd.
> I have never indulged in any unusual sex practices.
> Someone has been trying to poison me.
> I daydream often.[1]

[1]Reproduced by permission. Copyright 1943, renewed 1970 by The University of Minnesota. Published by The Psychological Corporation, New York, N.Y. All rights reserved.

Question: How can these items show anything about personality? For instance, what if a person has a cold so that "everything tastes the same"?

The answer to a single item tells nothing about personality. A person who agrees that "everything tastes the same" might indeed have a cold. It is only through *patterns* of response that personality dimensions are revealed. Items on the MMPI were selected for their ability to correctly identify persons with particular psychiatric problems. If a series of items is consistently answered in a particular way by depressed persons, it is assumed that others who answer the same way are also prone to depression.

Question: What personality dimensions are measured by the MMPI?

The MMPI was designed to measure ten major aspects of personality. Each is represented by a separate subscale on the test. The subscales and their interpretations are:

1. *Hypochondriasis.* Reflects exaggerated concern about one's physical health.
2. *Depression.* High scorers are marked by feelings of worthlessness, hopelessness, and pessimism.
3. *Hysteria.* Reflects somatic complaints related to psychological disturbances (psychosomatic problems).
4. *Psychopathic deviancy.* Shows a disregard for social and moral standards and emotional shallowness in relationships.
5. *Masculinity/femininity.* Indicates degree of traditional "masculine" aggressiveness or "feminine" sensitivity.
6. *Paranoia.* Indicates extreme suspiciousness and feelings of persecution.
7. *Psychasthenia.* Suggests presence of irrational fears (phobias) and compulsive (ritualistic) actions.
8. *Schizophrenia.* Reflects withdrawal, unusual and bizarre thinking or actions.
9. *Hypomania.* Suggests emotional excitability, manic moods or behavior, and excessive activity.
10. *Social introversion.* High score indicates a tendency to be socially withdrawn.

After the MMPI is scored, results are charted as an MMPI profile (see Fig. 19-4). By comparing a person's profile to scores produced by normal adults, various personality disorders can be identified. The most common interpretation is that neurotics (persons with mild emotional disturbances) score high on scales 1–3; psychotics (severely disturbed persons) score high on scales 6–9; and antisocial or delinquent persons score highest on scale 4.

Question: How accurate is the MMPI?

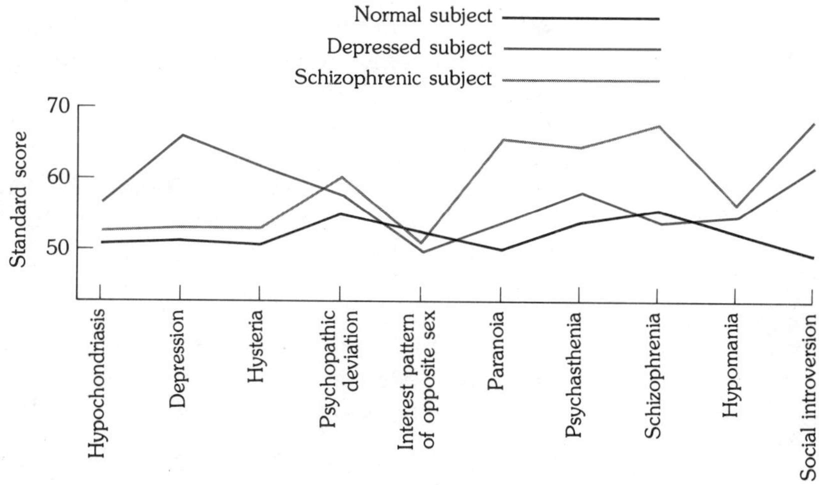

Fig. 19-4 An MMPI profile showing hypothetical scores indicating normality (black line), neurotic (colored line), and psychosis (gray line).

The accuracy of the MMPI or any other personality questionnaire rests on the assumption that a person is willing to tell the truth about himself. Because of the importance of this assumption, the MMPI has an additional "Lie Scale" to detect attempts of subjects to make themselves look better (or worse) than they really are. An elevated score on the Lie Scale may cause results on the remainder of the test to be discounted. This supposedly makes the MMPI a difficult test to fake. However, the Lie Scale alone is not enough to ensure accuracy of the results. If MMPI scores were used as the only basis for classifying a person as neurotic, severely depressed, or schizophrenic, a large number of normal people would be incorrectly labeled (Cronbach, 1970). Fortunately, such judgments usually take into account information from interviews or other sources.

Projective Tests of Personality—Inkblots and Thematic Plots

Projective tests are a very different approach to personality assessment than the techniques already discussed. Interviews, observation, rating scales, and inventories typically provide information on overt or observable traits. By contrast, projective tests are designed to uncover deep-seated or *unconscious* wishes, thoughts, and needs.

Question: How is a test able to do that?

As a child you may have delighted in finding faces and objects in cloud formations. Or perhaps you have learned something about a friend's personality from his reaction to a movie or a painting. If so, you will have some insight into the rationale for constructing and interpreting projective tests. A projective test provides an *ambiguous stimulus* that the subject must describe or about which he must make up a story. Describing an unambiguous stimulus (a picture of an automobile, for example) tells little about your personality. But when you are faced with an unstructured stimulus or situation, you must organize and interpret what is seen in terms of your own life experiences. Everyone sees something different in a projective stimulus, and what is seen presumably reveals inner workings of the personality.

Since projective tests have no right or wrong answers, the ability of subjects to fake or "see through" the test is greatly reduced. Moreover, projective tests can be an unusually rich source of information, since responses are not restricted to simple true/false or yes/no answers.

Question: Is the inkblot test a projective technique?

The Rorschach Inkblot Test The inkblot test, or Rorschach, is one of the oldest and most widely used projective tests. Developed by Swiss psychologist Hermann Rorschach in the 1920s, it consists of a set of ten standardized inkblots. These vary in color, shading, form, and complexity.

Question: How does testing take place?

First, the subject is shown each blot and asked to describe what she sees in it (see Fig. 19-5). Later the psychologist may return to a blot, asking the subject to identify specific sections of it, to elaborate on previous descriptions, or to suggest a completely new story about it.

Scoring the Rorschach is complex. A subject's responses are scored in terms of three major categories: (1) *location*, indicating whether a response was to the blot as a whole or to specific parts; (2) *determinants*, indicating

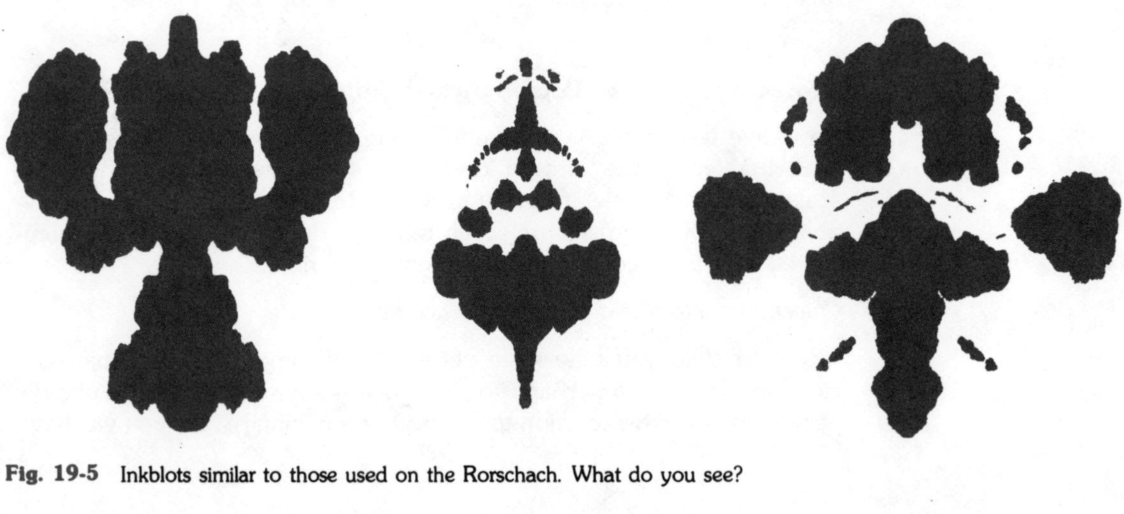

Fig. 19-5 Inkblots similar to those used on the Rorschach. What do you see?

whether the subject's response was determined by shape, color, or texture of the blot; and (3) *content*, consisting of the description or story given to the blot. Obvious differences in content like "blood dripping from a dagger" versus "flowers blooming in a field" are important for identifying a subject's conflicts and fantasies. But, surprisingly, content is considered less important than location, determinants, and organization of responses. These factors allow a psychologist to view the ways in which a subject perceives the world and to detect disorders in personality function.

The Thematic Apperception Test Another popular projective test is the Thematic Apperception Test, or TAT, developed by Harvard psychologist and personality theorist Henry Murray.

Question: How does the TAT differ from the Rorschach?

The TAT consists of 20 sketches depicting various scenes and life situations (see Fig. 19-6). The subject is shown each sketch and is asked to make up a story about the people in it. Later the subject is shown each

Fig. 19-6 This is a picture like those used for the Thematic Apperception Test. If you wish to simulate the test, tell a story that explains what led up to the pictured situation, what is happening now, and how the action will end.

sketch a second or, perhaps, a third time and asked to elaborate on previous stories or to construct new stories for each.

The term "apperception" means "readiness to perceive"; the word "thematic" refers to the existence of themes or recurring plots. When a subject tells a story about a TAT card, the tester gets a view of deep-rooted fantasies, thoughts, and conflicts by analyzing the themes underlying the subject's perceptions.

Question: How is the TAT scored?

Scoring of the TAT is restricted to analysis of the content of the stories. In particular, the psychologist is concerned with what the basic issues are in each story: Interpretation focuses on how people feel, how they interact, what events led up to the incidents depicted in the sketch, and how the story will end. A simpler method of interpreting the TAT is to score the frequency with which particular themes, motives, or traits appear in the entire series of stories. Thus, a psychologist might note how often a client mentions marriage problems, unsatisfying relationships with parents, or anxieties about sexual matters. The psychologist might also count the number of times the central figure in each story is angry, overlooked, apathetic, jealous, or threatened.

Question: How accurate are projective tests?

Limitations of Projective Testing Although projective tests have been popular with clinical psychologists, their *validity* is considered lowest among tests of personality. (Recall that a test is valid when it measures what it claims to measure.) Because of the subjectivity involved in scoring, *reliability* (consistency) of judgments among different users of the TAT and Rorschach is also low. Note that after the subject interprets an ambiguous stimulus, the scorer must interpret the subject's ambiguous responses. In a sense, the interpretation of a projective test may be a projective test for the scorer! In addition, themes revealed by projective tests are not necessarily courses for action. In fact, they may reflect what a subject has seen in books or movies rather than his own thoughts and motives.

Despite the drawbacks of projective tests, many psychologists attest to their value, especially as part of a battery of tests and interviews. It is said that in the hands of a skillful and experienced clinician, projective tests are helpful in the detection of major conflicts and in making decisions about the goals of therapy. Moreover, since projective tests are unstructured, they may be more effective for getting clients to talk about anxiety-provoking topics than are the direct questions of inventories and interviews.

Learning Check

1. Planned questions are used in a ______________________ interview.

2. The halo effect is the tendency of an interviewer to influence what is said by the interviewee. T or F?

3. Which of the following is considered the most objective measure of personality: rating scales, personality questionnaires, projective tests, the TAT?

4. Situational testing allows direct ______________________ of personality characteristics.

5. Delinquents typically score highest on which MMPI scale: depression, hysteria, psychopathic deviancy, hypomania?

6. The use of ambiguous stimuli is most characteristic of: interviews, projective tests, personality inventories, direct observation?

7. The content of one's responses to the MMPI is considered an indication of unconscious wishes, thoughts, and needs. T or F?

8. OSS candidates were selected through use of situational tests. T or F?

Answers: **1.** structured **2.** F **3.** personality questionnaires **4.** observation **5.** psychopathic deviancy **6.** projective tests **7.** F **8.** T

Resources Summary

Personality is made up of one's unique and enduring behavior patterns. *Character* is personality evaluated. *Temperament* refers to the hereditary and physiological aspects of one's emotional nature.

A basic approach to the study of personality is classification into *types*. Jung's concept of the *introvert* and the *extravert* are an example of this approach. One well-known type system is Sheldon's somatotype theory. Sheldon linked body types to personality types in this way: endomorphy-viscerotonia, mesomorphy-somatotonia, and ectomorphy-cerebrotonia.

The *trait* approach attempts to specify qualities of personality that are most enduring or characteristic of a person. Allport makes useful distinctions between *common* traits and *individual* traits and among *cardinal*, *central*, and *secondary* traits. A second trait approach, developed by Cattell, attributes visible or *surface* traits to the existence of underlying *source* traits. When traits are measured and graphically presented, a *trait profile* is produced.

Accurate *assessment* of personality is of great importance to psychologists. To improve accuracy, a number of techniques are used. The *interview* provides much information but is subject to numerous limitations. *Direct observation*, sometimes involving *situational tests* or rating scales, allows assessment of a person's actual behavior. *Personality questionnaires* are self-report or paper-and-pencil tests. They are quite objective, but their accuracy and validity are open to question.

Projective tests ask a subject to project thoughts or feelings to an ambiguous stimulus or unstructured situation. The *Rorschach*, or *inkblot*, *Test* is a well-known projective technique. A second is the *Thematic Apperception Test* (TAT). The validity and reliability of projective tests are quite low. Nevertheless, projective techniques are considered useful by many clinicians.

Applications

Personality Testing and You—Evening the Odds

Humorist Art Buchwald (1965) once lampooned personality questionnaires by writing his own test. Here is a sample of his items:

> *Answer:* "Yes," "No," or "Don't bother me, I can't cope!"
>
> I would enjoy the work of a chicken flicker.
> My eyes are always cold.
> Frantic screams make me nervous.
> I believe I smell as good as most people.
> Most of the time I go to sleep without saying good-bye.
> I use shoe polish to excess.
> The sight of blood no longer excites me.

Buchwald's questions may seem ridiculous, but they are not very different from the real thing. Psychologist Frank McMahon once described personality test questions as a "smoke screen against logic."

Not all psychologists share McMahon's feelings, and most are well aware of a test's limitations. If psychologists were the only persons giving these tests there would be few problems. However, many organizations, including businesses, routinely use personality tests, and errors or abuses sometimes occur. Consider this example:

> Elizabeth has worked for almost 10 years as a nurse's aide. Recently she applied to a college nursing program. Elizabeth had no doubts about her preference for a career in nursing or her previous satisfaction with nursing duties. As part of the selection procedures for the nursing program, she took a personality test. Incredibly, the results showed her to be ill-suited for a nursing career.

Question: Could the test be right?

Given Elizabeth's obvious suitability for a nursing career, the test results appear to be in error. How did this happen? Perhaps Elizabeth simply misunderstood the questions. A personality test can be viewed as a paper-and-pencil interview in which the "interviewee" is not clear what he is saying about himself.

To avoid the problems of traditional tests, McMahon (1964) constructed an "above-board" test in which the meaning of questions is clearly stated. For example, the true-or-false question: "Some people have it in for me" is followed by: "If True, 'I can't seem to get them off my mind,' True or False." Wider adoption of this approach to testing might help avoid problems like that Elizabeth encountered. In the meantime, a case can be made for removing some of the mystery from personality testing. As a "consumer" of psychological services or a seeker of employment, you have a right to understand personality tests. An unusual score may eliminate an otherwise qualified person from consideration for a program or a position.

Question: How can I avoid some of the pitfalls in test taking?

How to Take Personality Tests In *The Organization Man*, William Whyte (1956) suggests that the basic idea to keep in mind when taking a personality test for employment is, "You don't win a good score: you avoid a bad one." Whyte also gives specific suggestions and offers some sample questions:

1. Have you enjoyed reading books as much as having company in?
2. Do you sometimes feel self-conscious?
3. Does it annoy you to be interrupted in the middle of your work?

Comment Questions like these relate to social introversion or extraversion. It is neither necessary nor advisable to try to "fool" a test by presenting a false picture of yourself. But beware of extremes. If you agree exclusively with out-going or introverted statements, you will portray yourself as an excessively shy or brash person.

4. I often get pink spots all over.
5. The sex act is repulsive.
6. Strange voices speak to me.

Comment It should be obvious that the preceding are dangerous questions. They were originally designed to detect psychiatric problems. Agreement with even a few such statements will produce an "abnormal" profile.

7. Prostitution should be state supervised.
8. Modern art should not be allowed in churches.
9. It is worse for a woman to have extramarital relations than for a man.

Comment Opinion questions of this type yield a measure of how liberal or conservative your views are. If you are applying for a job or are in doubt, keep your replies in line with moderate attitudes.

Underline the word you think goes best with the word in capitals:

10. GRASS (green, mow, lawn, court)
11. NIGHT (dark, sleep, moon, morbid)
12. NAKED (nude, body, art, evil)

Comment The safest response to word-association items is the most run-of-the-mill connection (the first choice in each of the preceding). Unless the test is one of creativity, this is not the time to show off the uniqueness of your personality. It should be obvious that the last choice in each sample item has "trouble" written all over it.

13. When you look at a great skyscraper, do you think of:
    a. our tremendous industrial growth?
    b. the simplicity and beauty of the structural design?
14. Who helped mankind most?
    a. Shakespeare
    b. Sir Isaac Newton

Comment Items of this type measure the relative importance you attach to certain values, such as esthetic, economic, religious, social, or theoretical. Selecting a in 13 will increase your economic score; b reveals esthetic interests. There are no right answers to such questions except in terms of the type of position or program for which you are applying.

General Comments Remember that many of the more sophisticated personality tests have subscales sensitive to test-taking attitudes. Inconsistency, lying, or "faking good" (trying to answer questions as if you are nothing less than the ideal, all-American, healthy personality) will invalidate the test results. For this reason, it is recommended that you avoid trying to create a false impression. The suggestions above are given to help you recognize that a personality test can be a type of interview. As is true in any other interview, your interests are best served when you present an accurate and balanced picture of yourself. The preceding discussion in no way prepares you to "cheat" on personality tests. Rather, it is intended to alleviate the anxiety and misunderstanding associated with their use.

Question: But couldn't accuracy of the tests be undermined if everyone were aware of the intent of the questions?

On the contrary, there is evidence that accuracy of test predictions may be *improved* when you "put your best foot forward." Floyd Ruch (1967) reports studies of firemen, nurses, air force officers, and dental students given instructions to answer as they thought they should for the job they were seeking. These frank instructions produced test scores which predicted success more accurately than scores obtained with standard instructions to "tell the truth." Testing this way seems to tap social skills necessary for assuming a new occupational role.

Question: What if I am not hired, accepted to a program, or given a promotion because of my score on a personality test?

The U.S. Supreme Court handed down a decision in 1971 limiting the use of tests as conditions of employment or promotion. If you think a test was unfair you may have a case. More importantly, it should be recognized that errors can occur even when a test is fair and properly administered. The American Psychological Association recommends that an employee or potential employee should have the right to review and appeal personnel decisions in which test results play a part. In short, if you feel you were inaccurately rated by a personality test, you should challenge it.

For Discussion

Birth Order—Personality by Position?

Without exception you are one of the following: the oldest or only child in your family, a middle child, or the youngest. If you had it to do over again, which would you choose to be? Your answer could depend on the personality traits you would most like to have. Birth order, or *ordinal position*, in a family can leave a lasting imprint on adult personality.

Question: *What traits are associated with birth order?*

The clearest differences are between *firstborn* and *later-born* children. The firstborn seem to have a higher chance of achieving eminence than later-born. Freud, Kant, Beethoven, Dante, Einstein, and a disproportionately large number of other eminent men and women were firstborn children (Harris, 1964). Firstborns have better high school and college grade averages. More firstborns become National Merit Scholars, and more are medical students or graduate students. Of the last 36 presidents, 20 were firstborn, as were most of this country's astronauts. More firstborns are listed in *Who's Who in America* (Harris, 1964; Hilton, 1967). In short, firstborns tend to be high achievers—responsible, hardworking, and self-disciplined.

Before congratulating yourself on being a firstborn or lamenting that you are not, consider this: firstborns are also shyer, more conforming, and more likely to be anxious under stress than later-born persons (Schachter, 1959).

Question: *What are the strengths of later-born persons?*

Later-born persons tend to excel in social relationships. They are affectionate, friendly, and at ease with others. Youngest children also tend to be more original and creative than firstborns.

Question: *How does birth order influence personality?*

Parental Attitudes The answer seems to lie in the "emotional set" parents bring to each child. Because they are first on the scene, oldest children often get more attention, praise, and concern than later children. The first child is talked to more, spanked more, and more protected. The firstborn is also more likely to be a planned child, and is breast-fed longer (Sears, Maccoby, & Levin, 1957). This pattern of behavior and attitudes seems to benefit the firstborn, who come to think of themselves as important persons. High parental expectations for the firstborn are then translated into high self-expectations.

A principal disadvantage of being firstborn is that inexperienced parents are more anxious and inconsistent. As a result, firstborns develop higher levels of anxiety and a tendency to conform to adult values. Parents consistently report that they used lighter discipline and were more relaxed with second or later children. The youngest child in a family is particularly prone to be pampered and to have fewer responsibilities than did older brothers and sisters.

At this point it should be emphasized that birth-order effects can be stated only as broad patterns. Being a first or later-born child does not mean that your personality will fit the preceding descriptions. Countless factors, including the number of children in a family, their sex, age differences, and the ages of parents, can modify birth-order effects.

Question: How important are the age and sex of other children in the family?

Sibling Effects The effect of siblings (brothers and sisters) on one's development is obviously important. In fact, at least one theorist has suggested that siblings are as important as parents in shaping some aspects of personality. Walter Toman (1970) believes brothers and sisters often turn to each other when parents cannot fill all their psychological needs. Thus, your relationship with brothers and sisters may have served as a training ground for adult attitudes and relationships. According to Toman (1970), the following are common patterns:

Oldest Brother of Brother(s) This individual is aggressive, assertive, and a perfectionist. He gets along well with other males and might be described as a "man's man."

Oldest Brother of Sister(s) This person is most at ease with women. He therefore prefers women as friends and work partners. He does not consider himself "one of the boys" or a leader of men.

Oldest Sister of Sister(s) She is a competent and efficient worker who prefers a position of leadership. She may be somewhat dominant or commanding and thus unhappy when not in charge.

Oldest Sister of Brother(s) Men play an important role in her life. She relates easily to her husband if married and enjoys directing and advising children. She is independent, practical, and achieving.

Youngest Brother of Brother(s) He is a great lover of attention. He can be an imaginative and creative worker, but is also erratic and unproductive at times. He is rarely a leader.

Youngest Brother of Sister(s) He seems to have learned how to charm others into catering to his needs. Women adore him.

Youngest Sister of Sister(s) Like the youngest brother of sisters, she is charming, but also more flighty, emotional, and adventurous. Her lack of experience with males may cause difficulties if she marries.

Youngest Sister of Brother(s) She gets along well with males, particularly those who favor a traditionally "feminine" woman. Men consider her a good sport, but women may not always like her.

Like all generalizations, these descriptions apply more to some people than to others. Do you know people who seem to fit Toman's descriptions, or who seem to contradict them? To what extent do they apply to you? If you consider both birth-order and sibling effects, does a more accurate description of your personality result?

Questions for Discussion

1. Are birth-order and sibling effects an example of personality typing? To what extent do they oversimplify matters?
2. Is Toman's theory of sibling effects subject to the fallacy of positive instances? (See Chapter 2.)
3. Have you ever been interviewed or given a personality test? How accurate did you consider the resulting assessment of your personality?
4. Under what circumstances would you consider a personality test an invasion of privacy?
5. If you could select only three personality traits, which would you consider most basic? Why?
6. If you were selecting candidates for an extended space flight, how would you make your choices? What could be done to improve the accuracy of your judgments of candidates' personalities?
7. Do you think there is such a thing as "national character"? That is, do Germans, French, Americans, Canadians, and so forth, have common traits?
8. Do you know anyone who seems to have a cardinal trait? What do you think are central traits of your personality? Secondary traits?
9. Do you think animals have personalities? Defend your answer.

Suggestions for Further Reading

Allport, G. W. *Pattern and Growth in Personality*. Holt, 1961.

Cattell, R. B. *The Scientific Analysis of Personality*. Penguin, 1965.

Cronbach, L. J. *Essentials of Psychological Testing*, 3d ed. Harper & Row, 1970.

Guilford, J. P. *Personality*. McGraw-Hill, 1959.

Harris, I. D. *The Promised Seed: A Complete Study of Eminent First and Later Sons*. Free Press, 1964.

20 Theories of Personality

Chapter Preview

Eels, Cocaine, Hypnosis, and Dreams

One of his earliest scientific discoveries was the location of the testes in a species of eel. Later he made a discovery he believed would ensure his greatness. He obtained some cocaine and began to study its value as a medicine. Soon he was convinced that it was a wonder drug. He proclaimed, "I took coca again and a small dose lifted me to heights in a wonderful fashion. I am just now busy collecting the literature for a song of praise to this magical substance." (Jones, 1953, p. 84). His infatuation with cocaine came to a rapid end when he prescribed it to aid a friend addicted to morphine: The friend developed a double dependency. His next experiment was with hypnosis, but he abandoned it when it did not meet his needs. At age 44, rejected by friends, and virtually unknown in intellectual circles, he published his first book, a masterwork entitled The Interpretation of Dreams *(1900). Less than 1,000 copies were sold.*

Question: Who are you talking about?

The hero of this little essay is no less than the best known of all personality theorists, Sigmund Freud. Volume after volume followed Freud's initial work until he had built a monumental theory of personality and profoundly influenced the course of modern thought. Other theorists owe a debt to his pioneering efforts.

As there are literally dozens of personality theories, we cannot hope to do more than introduce the reader to the most influential. For clarity, we will confine ourselves to the following perspectives: (1) psychoanalytic theory, (2) behavioristic theory, and (3) humanistic theory.

Resources

My life has been aimed at one goal only; to infer or to guess how the mental apparatus is constructed and what forces interplay and counteract in it (Sigmund Freud).

Psychoanalytic Theory—The Battle Within

Psychoanalytic theory grew out of the clinical study of disturbed individuals. Sigmund Freud, a Viennese physician, became interested in personality and the treatment of mental disorders when he determined that many of his patients' problems were without physical cause. Starting about 1890 and continuing until he died in 1939, Freud evolved a theory of personality that is more complex than a short description can show. We will consider only its main features.

Question: How did Freud view personality?

The Structure of Personality Freud conceived of personality as a dynamic system of energies directed by three structures: the *id*, the *ego*, and the *superego*. Each is a complex system in its own right, and behavior in most situations involves the activity of all three.

The Id The id is made up of inherited biological instincts and urges present at birth. It is self-serving, irrational, impulsive, and totally *unconscious*. The id operates on the *pleasure principle*, meaning that pleasure-seeking impulses of all kinds are freely expressed. If everyone's personality were solely under control of the id, the world would be chaotic beyond belief. Newborn infants are sometimes described as "all id" since they desire immediate satisfaction of their needs.

Freud thought of the id as a wellspring of energy for the entire psyche, or personality. This energy, called *libido*, derives from the *life instincts* (called Eros), which promote survival and underlie sexual desires. Freud also postulated a *death instinct* (Thanatos), which he deemed responsible for aggressive and destructive urges. Most id energies are directed toward discharge of tensions associated with sex and aggression.

The Ego The ego, sometimes described as the "executive," draws its energy from the id. The id is like a blind king whose power is awesome but who must rely on others to carry out his orders. The id can only produce mental images of things it desires (called "primary process thinking"). The ego wins power to direct the personality by matching the desires of the id with external reality.

Question: Are there other differences between the ego and the id?

Yes. In contrast to the id, which operates on the pleasure principle, the ego is directed by the *reality principle* (which involves delaying action until it is appropriate). The operation of the reality principle results in "secondary process thinking," which is basically realistic problem solving. The ego is thereby the system of thinking, planning, and deciding. It is in conscious control of the personality.

Question: What is the role of the superego?

The Superego The superego acts as a judge or censor for the thoughts and actions of the ego. One part of the superego, called the *conscience*, represents all actions for which a person has been punished. If you act contrary to standards of the conscience, you are punished internally by *guilt* feelings. The *ego-ideal* represents all behavior one's parents approved or rewarded. The ego-ideal is a source of goals and aspirations. When its standards are met, *pride* is felt. By these processes, the superego acts as an "internalized parent" to bring behavior under control. In Freudian terms, a person with a poorly developed superego will be a delinquent, criminal, or antisocial personality. In contrast, an overly strict or repressive superego will cause inhibition, rigidity, or intolerable guilt.

Question: How do the id, ego, and superego interact?

The Dynamics of Personality It is important to recognize that Freud did not envision the id, ego, and superego as parts of the brain, or as "little men" running the human psyche. In reality they are distinct and conflicting psychological processes. Freud theorized a delicate balance of power among the three. For example, the demands of the id for immediate gratification frequently conflict with the superego's moral restrictions. Perhaps the role of each division of the personality can be clarified by an example.

Freud in a Nutshell

Let's say you are sexually attracted to someone. The id clamors for immediate satisfaction of its sexual desires but is opposed by the superego (which finds the very thought of sexual behavior appalling). The id says, "Now, now, now!" The superego icily responds, "Never!" And what does the ego say? The ego says, "I have a plan!"

To be sure, the oversimplification is drastic, but it captures the essence of Freudian personality dynamics. In its attempts to reduce tension, the ego could initiate actions leading to friendship, romance, courtship, and marriage. If the id is unusually powerful, the ego may direct an attempted seduction. If the superego is dominant, the ego may be forced to *displace* or *sublimate* sexual energies to other activities (sports, music, dancing, pushups, cold showers . . .). According to Freud, similar internal struggles and redirection of energies typifies most personality functioning.

Fig. 20-1 Freud considered personality an expression of two conflicting forces, life instincts and the death instinct. Both are symbolized in this painting by Allan Gilbert.

Question: Is the ego always caught in the middle?

Basically yes, and the pressures on it can be quite strong. In addition to meeting the conflicting demands of the id and superego, the overworked ego must deal with external reality. When the ego is threatened or overwhelmed, the person feels anxiety. Impulses from the id that threaten a loss of control cause *neurotic anxiety*. Threats of punishment from the superego cause *moral anxiety*. Each person develops habitual ways of reducing these anxieties, and many resort to use of *ego-defense mechanisms* to lessen internal conflicts (see Chapter 15).

Levels of Awareness A major principle of psychoanalytic theory is that behavior is often an expression of unconscious forces within the personal-

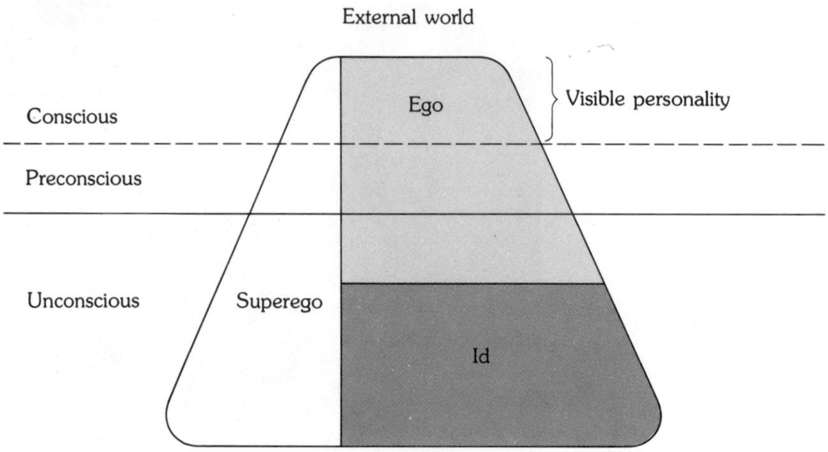

Fig. 20-2 The approximate relationship between the id, ego, superego, and levels of awareness.

ity. The unconscious includes repressed memories and emotions as well as the instinctual drives of the id. Although they are below the level of awareness, unconscious thoughts, feelings, or impulses may slip into behavior in disguised or symbolized form. For example, if you meet someone you would like to know better, you may unconsciously leave a book or a jacket at his or her house to ensure another meeting.

Question: Earlier you said the id is completely unconscious. Are the actions of the ego and superego unconscious?

At times, yes, but they also operate on two other levels of awareness, the conscious and the preconscious (see Fig. 20-2). The *conscious* level includes everything we are aware of at a given moment: thoughts, perceptions, feelings, and memories. The *preconscious* contains material that can be readily brought to awareness. If you stop to think about a time when you have felt angry or rejected, you will be moving this memory from the preconscious to the conscious level of awareness. Another illustration of the levels of awareness is found in the operation of the superego. At times we consciously attempt to live up to moral codes or standards; at other times a person may feel guilty without knowing why. Psychoanalytic theory attributes the latter instances to unconscious workings of the superego.

Learning Check

1. List the three divisions of personality postulated by Freud:

____

2. Which division is totally unconscious? ____________________

3. Which division is responsible for moral anxiety? ______________

Answers: 1. id, ego, superego 2. id 3. superego

Learning Theories of Personality— Habit I Seen You Somewhere Before?

Question: How do behaviorists approach personality?

In an earlier chapter we described John B. Watson's classic experiment with Albert, the infant who learned to fear a white rat. It could be said that fear of small, furry, white objects became a "trait" of Albert's personality. This example strikes to the heart of learning theories of personality. The behaviorist position is that personality is no more (or less) than a collection of learned behavior patterns and habitual responses. "Personality," like other learned behavior, is acquired through the effects of classical and operant conditioning, reinforcement, extinction, generalization, and discrimination.

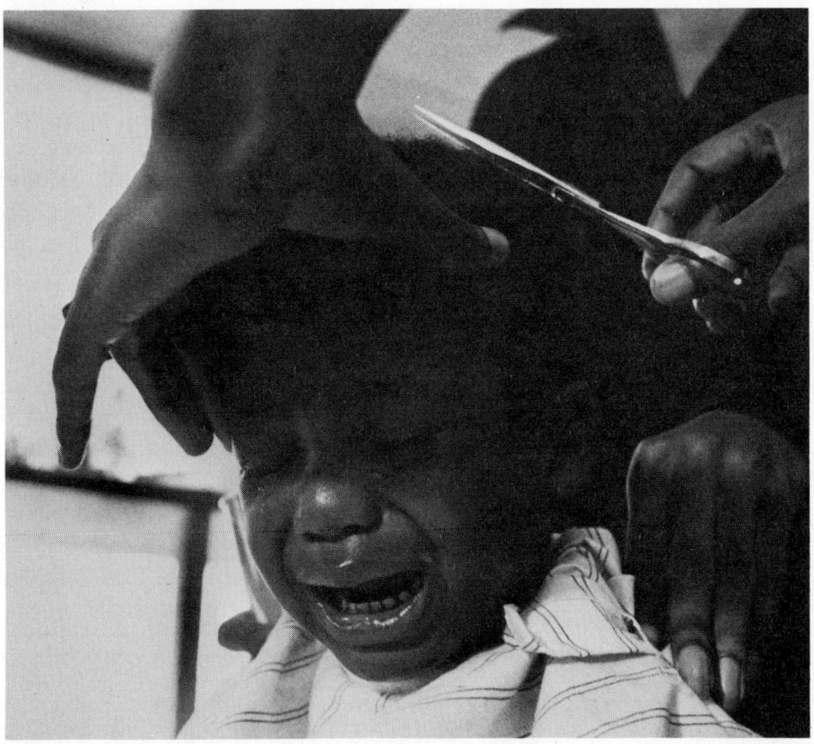

Fig. 20-3 The behaviorist views personality as a collection of habits. This boy may be learning to respond with anxiety to new or unexpected events. (Photo by Chester Higgins, Ralpho/Photo Researchers, Inc.)

Some psychologists carry the behavioral analysis of personality even further. *Social learning theorists* (who emphasize the importance of social relationships and observational learning) reject the idea that personality is made up of consistent traits. They would contend, for instance, that there is no such thing as a trait of "honesty" (Bandura, 1973; Mischel, 1968).

Question: *Certainly some people are honest while others are not. How can honesty not be considered a trait?*

A social learning theorist would agree that some people are *more often* honest than others, but would hold that honesty is a response to *specific situations*. It would not be unusual, for example, to find that a person honored for returning a lost wallet has cheated on his income tax (or his wife). If such inconsistency seems unlikely, consider this: In a classic experiment on honesty, children were "tempted" by opportunities to fake the solution to a puzzle, to cheat at games, to steal money, to copy answers on a test, and so forth. It was found that children who were honest in some situations were dishonest in others (Hartshorne & May, 1928). A child who would not cheat might steal or vice versa. If you were to ask a social learning theorist: "Are you an honest person?" his reply might be: "In what situation?"

A more extreme view of personality is held by radical behaviorist B. F. Skinner, who has said: "Intelligent people no longer believe that men are possessed by demons . . . but human behavior is still commonly attributed to indwelling agents" (Skinner, 1971, p. 5). For Skinner, "personality" is a convenient fiction we invent to pretend we have explained behavior that is actually controlled by the environment. Skinner believes that everything a person does is ultimately based on past and present rewards and punishments. Perhaps Skinner's point of view has been shaped by his environment.

Question: *How do learning theorists view the structure of personality?*

The Structure and Dynamics of Personality Learning theorists John Dollard and Neal Miller (1950) consider *habits* the basic structure of personality. As for the dynamics of personality, Dollard and Miller believe habits are governed by four elements of the learning process: *drive*, *cue*, *response*, and *reward*. A drive is any stimulus strong enough to goad a person to action (hunger, pain, lust, frustration, fear, and so on). Cues are signals from the environment that guide responses so they are most likely to bring about reinforcement (reward).

Question: *I'm not sure I see the connection to personality.*

An example may clarify this viewpoint. Let's say a child is frustrated by an older brother who takes a toy from him. A number of responses are open to the child. He can throw a temper tantrum, hit the older brother, tell Mother, and so forth. The response selected depends on available cues and the previous effects of each response. If telling Mother has paid off in the past, and she is present, this may be the immediate response. If a different set of cues exists (if Mother is absent or if the older brother looks particularly menacing), some other response may be selected. To an outside observer the child's actions seem to reflect his personality. To the learning theorist they are a direct reaction to the combined effects of drive, cue, response, and reward.

Social learning theory adds the concept of *self-reinforcement* to the behavioristic view of personality dynamics. We all evaluate our own actions and may reward ourselves with special privileges or treats when the evaluation is positive. Thus, habits of self-praise or self-reproach become an important dimension of personality. Self-reinforcement might be considered the behaviorist's equivalent of the Freudian superego.

Humanistic Theory—New Images

Humanism is a reaction to the pessimism of psychoanalytic theory and the mechanism of learning theory. At its core is a new image of what it means to be human. Humanists reject the Freudian view of personality as a battleground for biological instincts and unconscious forces. They view people as unique and set apart from the rest of the animal kingdom. Humanists also oppose the mechanical, "thing-like" overtones of the behaviorist viewpoint. We are not, they say, merely a bundle of moldable responses; instead, we are creative beings capable of making responsible choices. The humanistic viewpoint leads to a greater emphasis being placed on immediate *subjective experience* than on prior learning.

Fig. 20-4 Humanists consider self-image a central determinant of behavior and personal adjustment. (Photo by Roger Lubin, Jeroboam.)

Humanists tend to be optimistic in their belief that people are motivated not merely to survive, but to strive for *self-actualization* (fulfillment of potential). Humanists feel that personal growth and harmonious functioning occur when people are realistically in touch with themselves and others.

Question: Who are the major humanistic theorists?

There are many psychologists whose theories fall within the humanistic tradition. Of these, the best known are Carl Rogers and Abraham Maslow. Let's sample the ideas of each.

Carl Rogers' Self Theory Carl Rogers is a contemporary psychotherapist who, like Freud, based his theory on clinical experience. Unlike Freud, who portrayed the normal personality as "adjusted" to internal conflict, Rogers sees greater possibility for inner harmony. The *fully functioning person*, he says, is one who has achieved an openness to feelings and experiences and has learned to trust inner urges and intuitions (Rogers, 1961). Rogers feels this is most likely to occur when a person receives ample amounts of love and acceptance from others.

Personality Structure and Dynamics Rogers' theory of personality centers on the concept of the *self*, a flexible and changing perception of personal identity that emerges from the *phenomenal field.*

Question: What is the "phenomenal field"?

The phenomenal field is the person's total subjective experience of reality. The self is made up of those experiences identified as "I" or "me" that are separated from "not me" experiences. Much human behavior can be understood as an attempt to maintain consistency between one's *self-image* and actions. For example, an individual who thinks of herself as a kind and considerate person will act accordingly in most situations.

Question: Let's say I know a person who thinks she is kind and considerate, but she really isn't. How does this fit Rogers' theory?

According to Rogers, experiences that match the self-image are *symbolized* (admitted to consciousness) and contribute to gradual changes in the self. Information or feelings inconsistent with the self-image are said to be *incongruent*. It is incongruent, for example, to think of yourself as a considerate person if others frequently mention your rudeness. It is also incongruent to pretend you are kind when you are feeling callous or to say you are not angry when you are seething inside.

Experiences seriously incongruent with the self-image can be threatening, and they are often distorted or denied conscious recognition. Blocking, denying, or distorting experiences prevents the self from changing and creates a gulf between the self-image and reality. As the self-image grows more unrealistic, the *incongruent person* becomes confused, vulnerable, dissatisfied, or seriously maladjusted (see Chapter 21).

When a person's self-image is consistent with what he really thinks, feels, does, and experiences, he is best able to actualize his potentials. Rogers calls this *congruence*. Instead of becoming a rigid source of threat, the self-image of a *congruent person* is flexible, and it realistically changes as new experiences occur. Rogers also considers it essential to have congruence between the self-image and the *ideal self*. The ideal self is similar to Freud's ego-ideal. It is an image of the person you would most like to be.

Question: Is it really incongruent to not live up to one's ideal self?

Rogers is aware that we never fully attain our ideals, but the greater the gap between the way you see yourself and the way you would like to be, the greater the tension and anxiety experienced. The Rogerian view of personality functioning can therefore be summarized as a process of maximizing potentials by accepting information about oneself as realistically and honestly as possible.

Abraham Maslow and Self-actualization Maslow's research on the characteristics of self-actualizers (described in Chapter 1) is only one of his many contributions to personality theory. On the basis of his work on self-actualization, Maslow proposed that there is a *hierarchy* of human needs. By this he meant that some needs are more basic or powerful than others. Think for a moment about the needs that influence your behavior. Which seem strongest? Which do you spend the most time and energy satisfying? Now look at Maslow's hierarchy (Fig. 20-5).

Note that physiological needs are at the bottom. Since these are necessary for survival, they tend to be *prepotent* (dominant) over the higher needs. It could be said, for example, that "to the starving man, food is god."

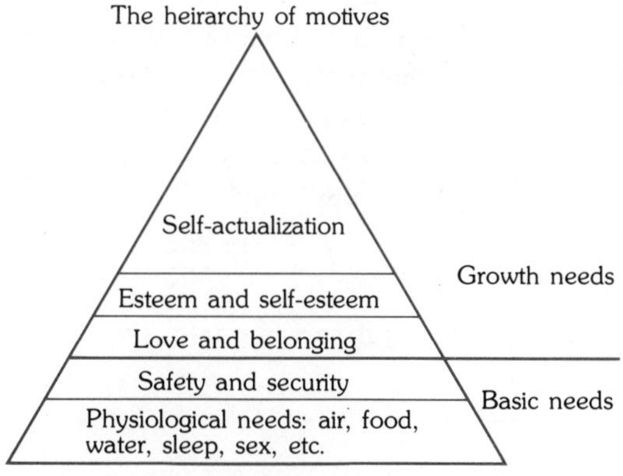

Fig. 20-5 Maslow felt that lower needs in the hierarchy are dominant. Basic needs must be satisfied before growth motives are fully expressed. Desires for self-actualization are reflected in various meta-needs (see text).

Only when the physiological needs are met do higher needs become important. This statement is also true of needs for safety and security. Until there is a minimum amount of order and stability in a person's life, he may have little interest in higher pursuits. For this reason, Maslow described the first two levels of the hierarchy as *basic needs*. Higher, or *growth needs*, include love and belonging (family, friendship, and so forth) and needs for esteem and self-esteem (recognition and self-respect).

Question: The need for self-actualization is listed at the top of the hierarchy. Does that mean it is the weakest need?

Although Maslow felt that a desire for self-actualization is universal, he saw it as fragile and easily interrupted by lower needs. Only when the lower needs are under control and regularly satisfied can the highest levels of motivation emerge.

Question: How are needs for self-actualization expressed?

Maslow called the less powerful but humanly important actualization motives *meta-needs*. Maslow (1970) lists these meta-needs:

1. Wholeness (unity)
2. Perfection (balance and harmony)
3. Completion (ending)
4. Justice (fairness)
5. Richness (complexity)
6. Simplicity (essence)
7. Aliveness (spontaneity)
8. Beauty (rightness of form)
9. Goodness (benevolence)
10. Uniqueness (individuality)
11. Playfulness (ease)
12. Truth (reality)
13. Autonomy (self-sufficiency)
14. Meaningfulness (values)

Maslow said there is a need to move up the hierarchy to the meta-needs. A person whose basic needs are met but whose meta-needs are unfulfilled falls into a "syndrome of decay" and experiences despair, apathy, and alienation.

Question: How many people are motivated by meta-needs?

Maslow estimated that only about one person in ten is primarily motivated by self-actualization needs. Most are more concerned with esteem, love, or security. Perhaps this is because incentives and rewards in our society are slanted to encourage conformity, uniformity, and security in schools, jobs, and relationships. When was the last time you met a meta-need?

Learning Check

1. Social learning theorists relate personality "traits" to

____

2. Dollard and Miller consider cues the basic structure of personality. T or F?

3. Humanists emphasize subjective experience and innate drives for self-actualization. T or F?

4. A close match between the self-image and the ideal self creates a condition called incongruence. T or F?

5. Self-actualization is a prepotent need. T or F?

6. Security is a (circle one) basic, growth, meta-need.

Answers: 1. specific situations 2. F 3. T 4. F 5. F 6. basic

Personality Development—Goldilocks and the Three Theories

Every society must bring about the *socialization* of its children by teaching them language, customs, rules, roles, and morals. The job of preparing children for participation in society is typically placed in the hands of parents. This arrangement is convenient and fateful. While socializing children, parents impart something of their own personality to a child.

Question: How does this occur? What factors are most influential in the development of adult personality?

Each theory offers a different version of the important events in personality formation. Let's begin with a look at the psychoanalytic viewpoint.

A Freudian Fable? Freud theorized that the core of personality is formed before age six in a series of *psychosexual stages*. His account holds that childhood urges for erotic pleasure have lasting effects on development. Freud's emphasis on infantile sexuality is one of the most controversial aspects of his thinking. However, Freud used the term "sex" very broadly to mean any pleasurable activity.

Freud identified four psychosexual stages, the *oral*, *anal*, *phallic*, and *genital*. At each stage a different part of the body becomes an *erogenous zone* (an area capable of producing pleasure). Each then serves as the principal source of pleasure, frustration, and self-expression. Freud believed that many adult personality traits can be traced to *fixations* in one or more of the stages.

Question: What is a fixation?

A fixation is an unresolved conflict or emotional hang-up caused by overindulgence or frustration. A description of the psychosexual stages shows why Freud considered fixations important.

The Oral Stage During the first year of life, most of the infant's pleasure comes from stimulation of the mouth. If a child is overfed or frustrated, oral traits may be created. Adult expressions of oral needs include gum chewing, nail biting, smoking, kissing, overeating, and alcoholism.

Question: What if there is an oral fixation?

Fixation early in the oral stage produces an *oral-dependent* personality. The oral-dependent person is gullible (he swallows things easily!), passive, and needs lots of attention (he wants to be mothered). Frustrations later in the oral stage cause aggression in the form of biting. Fixation here causes the *oral-aggressive* adult to be argumentative ("biting sarcasm" is his forté!), cynical, and exploitive of others.

The Anal Stage Between the ages of one and three, the child's attention shifts to the process of elimination. When his parents attempt to toilet train him, the child can gain approval or express rebellion or aggression by "holding on" or "letting go." Therefore, harsh or indulgent toilet training may establish such responses as personality traits. Freud characterized the *anal-retentive* (holding-on) personality as obstinate, stingy, orderly, and compulsively clean. The *anal-expulsive* (letting-go) personality is disorderly, destructive, cruel, or messy.

The Phallic Stage Freud theorized that between the ages of three and six increased sexual interest causes the child to become physically attracted to the parent of the opposite sex. In males this generates the *Oedipus conflict*, in which the boy feels rivalry with his father for the affection of the mother. Freud felt the male child feels threatened by the father (specifically, the boy fears castration). To alleviate his anxieties, the boy must *identify* with the father. Identification causes him to take on the father's values and to form a conscience.

Question: What about the female child?

In a counterpart to the Oedipus conflict called the *Electra conflict*, the girl loves her father and competes with her mother. However, according to Freud, the girl's identification with the mother is more gradual and less effective in creating a conscience. Freud believed that females already feel castrated and so are less driven to identify with their mothers than boys are with their fathers. This particular aspect of Freudian thought has been thoroughly (and rightfully) denounced by modern feminists. It is probably best understood as a reflection of the times in which Freud lived.

Question: What is the "phallic personality" like?

Adult characteristics of the *phallic personality* are: vanity, exhibitionism, sensitive pride, and narcissism (self-love).

The Genital Stage According to Freud, the last stage of personality formation comes after a long period of *latency* during which psychosexual development is temporarily interrupted. The genital stage begins at puberty and is marked by a growing capacity for mature and responsible social-sexual relationships. The genital stage culminates in hetereosexual love and the attainment of full adult sexuality.

Critical Comments As bizarre as Freud's developmental theory might seem, it has been influential for several reasons. First, it pioneered the idea that the first years of life help shape adult personality. Second, it identified feeding, toilet training, and early sexual experiences as critical events in personality formation. Third, Freud was among the first to propose that development proceeds through a series of stages. (Erik Erikson's psycho-*social* stages are a modern extension of Freudian thinking.)

Question: Is the Freudian view of development widely accepted?

Despite its contributions, Freud's theory remains controversial, and few psychologists embrace it without reservation. In some cases Freud was clearly wrong. His portrayal of the elementary school years (latency) as free from sexuality and unimportant for personality development defies belief. His idea of the role of a stern or threatening father in the development of a strong male conscience has also been challenged. Studies show that an affectionate and accepting father is more likely than a stern one to create a strong conscience in a son (Mussen et al., 1969; Sears et al., 1957). Freud also overemphasized sexuality in personality development; other motives and cognitive factors are of equal importance. Many more criticisms could be listed, but the fact remains that there is an element of truth to much of what Freud said.

Question: How do learning theorists account for personality development?

Behavioristic Views of Development Many of Freud's major points can be restated in terms of modern learning theory. Miller and Dollard (1950) agree with Freud that the first six years are crucial for personality development, but for different reasons. Rather than thinking in terms of psychosexual urges and fixations, they ask: "What makes early learning experiences so lasting in their effects?" Their answer is that childhood is a time of urgent and tearing drives, powerful rewards and punishments, and crushing frustrations. Also important is *social reinforcement* based on the effects of attention and approval from others. These forces combine to shape the core of personality.

Miller and Dollard consider four situations of critical importance. These are: *feeding*, *toilet* or *cleanliness training*, *sex training*, and *anger* or *aggression training*.

Question: Why are these of special importance?

Feeding serves as an illustration. If a child is fed when he cries, he is encouraged to actively manipulate the environment. The child allowed to cry without being fed learns to be passive. Thus, a basic active or passive orientation toward the world may be established by early feeding experiences. Feeding can also affect later social relationships since the child learns to associate satisfaction and pleasure, or frustration and discomfort, with the presence of others.

Toilet and cleanliness training can be a particularly strong source of emotion for both parents and children. Parents are usually aghast the first time they find a child smearing feces about with gay abandon. Their reaction is often sharp punishment, and that of the child, frustration and confusion. Many attitudes toward cleanliness, conformity, and bodily functions are formed at such times. Studies also show that severe, punishing, or frustrating toilet training can have undesirable effects on personality development (Sears et al., 1957). Toilet and cleanliness training therefore demand patience and a sense of humor.

Question: What about sex and anger training?

When, where, and how a child learns to express anger and aggression is of obvious importance. Since many of the most important factors are discussed elsewhere (see Chapter 9), we will focus on sex training.

Becoming Male or Female From birth onward, children are identified as boys or girls and encouraged to learn sex-appropriate behavior. Two

Fig. 20-6 Adult personality is influenced by identification with parents. (Photo by David Powers, Jeroboam.)

processes that contribute greatly to personality development in general, and particularly to sex training, are *identification* and *imitation*. Identification refers to the child's desire to be like adults he or she admires or is dependent on. Many of a child's "male" or "female" traits come from conscious or unconscious attempts to pattern behavior after that of the same-sex parent. Identification, in other words. encourages imitation.

Question: How is imitation different from other kinds of learning?

Albert Bandura and others have shown that learning takes place vicariously as well as directly (Bandura, 1965). This means we can learn without direct reward by observing and remembering the actions of others. But imitation of actions depends on their outcome. For example, boys and girls have equal opportunities to observe adults and other children acting aggressively. However, girls are less likely than boys to imitate aggressive behavior because they rarely see female aggression rewarded or approved. It can be seen that many arbitrary dimensions of "maleness" or "femaleness" are perpetuated at the same time sexual identity is established.

A Humanistic View of Development Why do mirrors, photographs, tape recorders, and the reactions of others hold such fascination and threat for most people? Carl Rogers would say it is because they provide information about one's self. The development of a self-image is highly dependent on information from the environment.

Question: How does development of the self contribute to later personality functioning?

Rogers holds that positive and negative evaluations by others cause a child to develop internal standards of evaluation called *conditions of worth.* In other words, we learn that some actions win our parents' love and approval while others are rejected. Learning to evaluate some experiences or feelings as "good" and others as "bad" is directly related to a later capacity for *positive self-regard.* To think of himself as a good, lovable, or worthwhile person, the individual's behavior and experiences must meet his conditions of worth. The problem, however, is that this can cause incongruence by leading to the denial of many legitimate feelings and experiences. To put it simply, Rogers sees many adult adjustment problems as an attempt to live by the standards of others. He believes congruence and self-actualization are encouraged by substituting *organismic valuing* for conditions of worth. Organismic valuing is a direct, gut-level response to life experiences that avoids the filtering and distortion of incongruence.

Learning Check

1. Freud's version of personality development is based on the concept of

______________________________ stages.

2. Arrange these stages in the proper order: phallic, anal, genital, oral.

____

3. Freud considered the anal-retentive personality obstinate and stingy. T or F?

4. Which of the following is not a critical learning situation in the behaviorist theory of personality formation (circle correct answer)? feeding, sex training, language training, anger training

5. Behavioristic theories emphasize identification and ______________

______________________________.

6. Rogers considers acceptance of conditions of ______________ a troublesome aspect of development of the self.

Answers:

1. psychosexual 2. oral, anal, phallic, genital 3. T 4. language training
5. imitation 6. worth

Personality Theories—Overview and Comparison

Question: Which personality theory is right?

Each theory has made significant contributions to our understanding of personality by meaningfully organizing observations of human behavior. Nevertheless, none of the major theories can be fully proved or disproved. (If a theory could be proved true it would no longer be a theory. It would be a law.) At the same time that theories are neither true nor false, their implications or predictions may be. The best way to judge a theory, then, is in terms of its *usefulness* for explaining behavior, for stimulating research, and for suggesting ways of treating psychological disorders. Each theory has fared differently in these areas. A few brief comments on each follow.

Psychoanalytic Theory By present standards, psychoanalytic theory seems to overemphasize biological instincts and an unnecessarily dim view of human potential. To a large extent these distortions have been corrected by Freud's followers (referred to as *neo-Freudians*). Carl Jung, Alfred Adler, Otto Rank, Karen Horney, Erich Fromm, Erik Erikson, and many other personality theorists have extended and elaborated psychoanalytic theory far beyond its original scope.

Freud has also been criticized for overemphasizing sex and aggression. Perhaps he can be excused for this. Freud's views of human nature were highly influenced by the social climate in which he lived. Most of the patients who ended up on his couch had problems directly related to the strict morals and rigid rules of Victorian Vienna. Freud honestly tried to describe what he observed, but what he saw does not fully apply to modern men and women.

Question: What about the theory's value for explanation, research, and treatment?

One of the most telling criticisms of Freudian theory is that it can be used to explain any psychological event *after* it has occurred, but it offers little help in predicting future behavior. For this reason, many psychoanalytic concepts are difficult or impossible to test empirically. Most of the research inspired by psychoanalytic theory has been restricted to case studies and clinical observations.

As previously noted, Freudian theory suggests a treatment procedure for psychological disorders. This is one of the areas in which the theory has been most useful. Freudian concepts of unconscious motivation, repression, ego-defense, and childhood conflicts have found their way into the thinking of many psychotherapists. This aspect of psychoanalytic theory is examined in greater detail in Chapter 23.

Behavioristic Theory Learning theories have provided a good framework for personality research. Of the three major perspectives, the behaviorists have made the best effort to rigorously test and verify their concepts. Their emphasis on conditions under which behaviors are learned has led to the development of effective methods for modifying maladaptive behavior (see Chapter 24).

Question: What are the criticisms of behavioristic theories?

Learning is obviously important in most areas of human functioning. However, behavioristic theories tend to underestimate the importance of temperamental, emotional, cognitive, and subjective factors in personality. Moreover, proponents of the trait approach have been critical of the tendency of behavioral theories to deny consistencies in behavior. Although many responses are undoubtedly situational, unique and enduring personality traits also seem to exist. Within its scope behavioristic theory is masterfully effective in accounting for human behavior. The most valid criticism that can be raised against it is that it can be a narrow approach to the rich textures of human experience.

Humanistic Theory A great strength of the humanists has been their willingness to investigate areas of importance ignored by other viewpoints. Their stress on the positive dimensions of human experience has helped restore balance to psychological thought. As Maslow put it: "Human nature is not nearly as bad as it has been thought to be. . . . It is as if Freud supplied us the sick half of psychology and we must now fill it out with the healthy half" (1968, pp. 4–5).

Question: How does humanistic theory measure up as a basis for research?

The chief criticism of humanistic theory in this respect lies in the impreciseness of its concepts. For example, what really is "self-actualization"? Can it be measured? Are the characteristics of self-actualizers open to debate? Imprecise concepts have not completely prevented humanists from carrying out research, but their approach generally tends to be more philosophical than empirical. The real strength of this perspective is the encouragement it gives for self-examination and personal growth. The humanistic emphasis on self-awareness, experiencing, and free emotional expression underlies many of the new growth-oriented psychotherapies.

Summary In the final analysis we need the concepts of all three perspectives (and those discussed in the previous chapter) to account adequately for the complexities of personality. There is an element of truth to each view, and a balanced picture emerges only when all are considered.

Resources Summary

We depart from our usual format in this summary to get a better overview of the three major perspectives on personality.

Theory	*View of Human Nature*	*Is Behavior Free or Determined?*	*Principal Motives*	*Personality Structure*
Psychoanalytic	Negative	Determined	Sex and aggression	Id, ego, superego
Behavioristic	Neutral	Determined	Drives of all kinds	Habits
Humanistic	Positive	Free choice	Self-actualization	Self

Theory	*Role of Unconscious*	*Conception of Conscience*	*Developmental Emphasis*	*Barriers to Personal Growth*
Psychoanalytic	Maximized	Superego	Psychosexual stages	Unconscious conflicts; fixations
Behavioristic	Minimized	Self-reinforcement	Critical learning situations; identification and imitation	Maladaptive habits
Humanistic	Minimized	Ideal self; valuing process	Development of self-image	Conditions of worth; incongruence; basic needs

Applications

The Search for Self-actualization

> Some people fear finding themselves alone—and so they don't find themselves at all (André Gide).

> What a man can be, he must be. This need we may call self-actualization (Abraham Maslow).

Self-actualization is a concept that has reappeared several times in this book. Perhaps you have been attracted to the promise it holds for personal growth. Self-actualizers lead rich, creative, and fulfilling lives.

Question: What steps can be taken to promote self-actualization?

Promoting self-actualization is more difficult than might be imagined. Many people are caught in a struggle for survival or security and never get a chance to develop their potentials fully. Others show little interest in personal growth or in the qualities Maslow described. Moreover, Maslow made few specific recommendations about how to proceed. Nevertheless, a number of helpful suggestions can be gleaned from his writings (Maslow, 1954, 1967, 1971).

Steps toward Self-actualization There is no magic formula for leading a more creative life. Knowing or even imitating the traits of unusually effective people cannot be counted on to promote self-actualization. Self-actualization is primarily a *process*, not a goal or an endpoint. As such, it requires hard work, patience, and commitment. Here are some ways to begin.

Be Willing to Change Begin by asking yourself: "Am I living in a way that is deeply satisfying to me and which truly expresses me?" If not, be prepared to make changes in your life. Indeed, ask yourself this question often and accept the need for continued change.

Take Responsibility You can become an architect of self by acting *as if* you are *personally* responsible for every aspect of your life. Shouldering responsibility in this way is not totally realistic, but it helps end the habit of blaming others for your own shortcomings. This attitude is illustrated by a young woman who realized in a counseling session: "I can't depend on someone else to *give* me an education. I'll have to get it myself" (Rogers, 1962).

Examine Your Motives Self-discovery involves an element of risk. To learn your strengths, limitations, and true feelings, you must be willing to go out on a limb, speak your mind, and take some chances. Fears of failure, rejection, loneliness, or disagreement with others are a tremendous barrier to personal change. If most of your behavior seems to be directed by a desire for "safety" or "security," it may be time to test the limits of these needs. Try to make each life decision a choice for growth, not a response to fear or anxiety.

Experience Honestly and Directly Wishful thinking is another barrier to personal growth. Self-actualizers trust themselves enough to accept all kinds of information without distorting it to fit their fears and desires. Try to see yourself as others do. Be willing to admit, "I was wrong" or "I failed because I was irresponsible." This basic honesty can be extended to perception in general. Try to experience the world as you did when you were a child: fully, vividly, and directly. Try to see things as they are, not as you would like them to be.

Make Use of Positive Experiences As a "rule of thumb," growth-promoting activities usually "feel good." Perhaps you have felt unusually alert and alive when expressing yourself through art, music, dance, writing, or athletics. Or perhaps life seems especially rich when you are alone in nature, surrounded by friends, or when you are helping others. Whatever their source, Maslow considered "peak experiences" temporary moments of self-actualization. Therefore, you might actively repeat activities that have caused feelings of awe, amazement, exaltation, renewal, reverence, humility, fulfillment, or joy.

Be Prepared to Be Different Maslow felt that everyone has a potential for "greatness," but most fear becoming what they might. Much of this fear is related to the fact that actualizing potentials may place you at odds with cultural expectations or with others who are important in your life. As part of personal growth, be prepared to be unpopular when your views don't agree with others. Trust your own impulses and feelings; don't automatically judge yourself by the standards of others. Accept your uniqueness: As one young woman put it, "I've always tried to be what others thought I should be, but now I'm wondering whether I shouldn't just see that I am what I am (Rogers, 1962).

Get Involved Maslow found with few exceptions that self-actualizers tend to have a mission or "calling" in life. For these people "work" is not done just to fill deficiency needs, but to satisfy higher yearnings for truth, beauty, brotherhood, and meaning. Many of the things you do may be motivated by more commonplace needs, but you can add meaning to these activities by endeavoring to work hard at whatever you do. Get personally involved and committed. Turn your attention to problems outside yourself.

Slow Down Try to avoid hurrying or overscheduling your time. Self-awareness takes time to develop, and a certain amount of leisure is essential for contemplation and self-exploration. Time pressures tend to force a person to rely compulsively on old habits.

Start a Journal Although this suggestion does not come from Maslow's writings, it is a valuable means of promoting self-awareness. Many people find a journal provides the kind of information necessary to make growth-oriented life changes. A journal should include a description of significant events in your daily life. In addition, thoughts, feelings, fears, wishes, frustrations, and dreams should be recorded. Some find it useful to write dialogues in their journal in which they speak to parents, teachers, lovers, objects, and so forth. Review and reread your journal periodically. You will find it is easier to learn from an event after it has "cooled off" and you can view it objectively.

Assess Your Progress Since there is no final point at which one becomes self-actualized, it is important frequently to gauge your progress and to renew your efforts. Boredom is a good sign you are in need of change. If you feel bored at school, at a job, or in a relationship, consider it a challenge or an indication that you have not taken responsibility for personal growth. A situation is only as "boring" as you allow it to be. Almost any activity can be used as a chance for self-exploration if it is approached creatively.

What to Expect As has already been noted, growth-promoting activities are usually personally satisfying.

Question: Are there other signs that one is moving in the right direction?

Yes, there should be a noticeable improvement in the quality of your daily life and a greater acceptance of yourself and of others. You should feel more confident and should carry out daily routines with less strain or conflict. These changes do not happen overnight, and your first steps toward self-actualization may be threatening at the same time they are exhilarating. Positive changes can also be quite subtle. An idea of what to expect is provided by the words of Henry David Thoreau. After he had spent two years in the wilderness at Walden Pond, Thoreau had this to say about his experience:

> I learned this, at least, by my experiment: that as one advances confidently in the direction of his dreams, and endeavors to live the life which he has imagined, he will meet with a success unexpected in common hours. He will put some things behind, will pass an invisible boundary; new universal and more liberal laws will begin to establish themselves around and within him. . . . The laws of the universe will appear less complex, and solitude will not be solitude, nor poverty, poverty, nor weakness, weakness.

For Discussion

Moral Development—Values and Personality

A person with a terminal illness is in great pain and pleading for death. Should extraordinary medical procedures be used to keep him alive? If a friend of yours desperately needed to pass a test and asked you to help him cheat, would you do it? Questions such as these have more to do with personality than you might suspect. We have already seen that personality theories use some concept of conscience in their explanations of behavior. By conscience, we typically mean a system of *moral values* for evaluating one's own behavior. For many, conscience is simply an internal source of reward (pride) and punishment (guilt). But according to researcher Lawrence Kohlberg, conscience is only one of several ways in which moral values are represented in the personality. Kohlberg (1963, 1969) believes there are higher levels of moral development and that these are acquired in a fixed series of stages.

Question: What does he base this belief on?

To study moral development, Kohlberg posed *moral dilemmas* to children of different ages. Here is one of the dilemmas he used (Kohlberg, 1969; adapted):

> A woman was near death from cancer, and there was only one drug that might save her. It was discovered by a druggist who was charging 10 times what the drug cost him to make. The sick woman's husband could only get together $1,000, which was half of what the drug cost. He asked the druggist to sell it cheaper or to let him pay later. But the druggist said no. So the husband got desperate and broke into the man's store to steal the drug for his wife. Should he have done that? Was it actually wrong or right? Why?

Each child was asked to say what action should be taken by the husband. Choices the children made were interesting, but the reasons they gave to back them up were of greater importance. By classifying the reasons given, Kohlberg identified three levels of moral development. At the first, or *preconventional level*, moral thinking is determined by the consequences of actions (punishment, reward, or exchange of favors). In the second, or *conventional level* of morality, actions are directed by a desire to conform to the expectations of others or to uphold socially accepted rules and values. The third, or *postconventional level* represents advanced moral development. Behavior at this level is directed by self-accepted moral principles. In addition to the three levels, Kohlberg identified six stages of moral development.

Kohlberg's Stages of Moral Development

Preconventional

Stage 1. *Punishment orientation.* In this stage actions are evaluated in terms of possible punishment, not goodness or badness. Obedience to power is emphasized.

Stage 2. *Pleasure-seeking orientation.* Right action is determined by one's own needs. Concern for the needs of others is largely a matter of "You scratch my back and I'll scratch yours," not of loyalty, gratitude, or justice.

Conventional

Stage 3. *Good boy/good girl orientation.* Good behavior is that which pleases others in the immediate group or which brings approval. The emphasis is on being "nice."

Stage 4. *Authority orientation.* Upholding law, order, and authority, doing one's duty, and following social rules are emphasized.

Postconventional

Stage 5. *Social-contract orientation.* Support of laws and rules is based on rational analysis and mutual agreement. Rules are recognized as open to question, but are upheld for the good of the community and in the name of democratic values.

Stage 6. *Morality of individual principles.* Behavior is directed by self-chosen ethical principles that tend to be general, comprehensive, or universal. High value is placed on justice, dignity, and equality.

Examples of reasoning at each stage

Stage 1. "He shouldn't steal the drug because he could get caught and sent to jail" (avoiding punishment).

Stage 2. "It won't do him any good to steal the drug because his wife will probably die before he gets out of jail" (self-interest).

Stage 3. "He shouldn't steal the drug because others will think he is a thief. His wife would not want to be saved by thievery" (avoiding disapproval).

Stage 4. "Although his wife needs the drug, he should not break the law to get it. Everyone is equal in the eyes of the law, and his wife's condition does not justify stealing" (traditional morality of authority).

Stage 5. "He should not steal the drug. The druggist's decision is reprehensible, but mutual respect for the rights of others must be maintained" (social contract).

Stage 6. "He should steal the drug and then inform the authorities that he has done so. He will have to face a penalty, but he will have saved a human life" (self-chosen ethical principles).

Question: Does everyone eventually reach stage 6?

Kohlberg found that people advance through the stages at different rates and that many people fail to reach the "principled" stages of morality. The self-interested stages (1 and 2) are most characteristic of young children and older delinquents. Conventional group-oriented morals of stages 3 and 4 are characteristic of older children and most of the adult population. Kohlberg estimates that postconventional morality, representing self-direction and higher principles, is characteristic of only about 20 percent of the adult population. Possibly from 5 to 10 percent of the population consistently operates at stage 6.

Morality in the Real World To illustrate the importance of moral development as a personality characteristic, let us compare two very different individuals. First let's apply Kohlberg's analysis to statements attributed to Nazi officer Adolf Eichmann, accused of sharing responsibility for the deaths of millions of Jews in Germany during World War II:

> In actual fact, I was merely a little cog in the machinery that carried out the directives of the German Reich [stage 1]. It was really none of my business [stage 2]. Yet what is there to "admit"? I carried out my order [stage 1] (Kohlberg, 1969, p. 177).

Compare this to the words of Mahatma Gandhi, the famous leader who protested British rule of India. Gandhi once addressed a British court:

> Nonviolence is the first article of my faith. It is also the last article of my creed. But I had to make a choice. I had to either submit to a system which I considered had done irreparable harm to my country, or incur the risk. . . . I am here, therefore, to invite and cheerfully submit to the highest penalty that can be inflicted upon me for what in law is a deliberate crime and what appears to me to be the highest duty of a citizen.

Gandhi, like other great leaders (Lincoln, Martin Luther King), was clearly operating at stage 6.

Moral development is a promising topic for additional psychological study. Kohlberg has recently embarked on research into the possibility of teaching higher levels of morality. Although Kohlberg's definition of morality is open to debate, his research appears to be a worthwhile endeavor. Many of the problems facing us today—overpopulation, environmental destruction, crime, prejudice—are essentially problems of individual conscience.

Questions for Discussion

1. How did you answer Kohlberg's moral dilemma? Do you think your answer reflects the role of moral reasoning in your personality?
2. Kohlberg says moral reasoning is a stable personality characteristic; social learning theory says honesty is situational. Which do you think is right? Why?
3. Do you think higher levels of moral reasoning can be taught without specifically teaching moral values?
4. What level of moral reasoning is most frequently displayed by the characters in TV dramas, comedies, or commercials?

5. Do you think the "draft dodgers," antiwar activists, or conscientious objectors of the 1960s were acting in self-interest or at higher levels of morality?
6. Can you describe an action you performed recently that seems to represent operation of the id, ego, or superego? How would a behaviorist or a humanist interpret the same event?
7. Can you cite a behavior or an experience that seems to support the existence of the unconscious or of unconscious motivation?
8. Can you cite observations that support Freud's scheme of psychosexual stages? Can you cite observations that contradict it?
9. Is "Mr. Clean" an anal-retentive?
10. As a child who did you identify with? What effect did this have on your personality?
11. Freud thought that adolescent males who clash with adult male authority figures (teachers, ministers, policemen, and so forth) are experiencing a carry-over of the Oedipus conflict. What do you think?
12. What experiences have you had that have contributed to personal growth? What experiences set you back or were otherwise negative in their effects? Which personality theory best explains the differences between these experiences?

Suggestions for Further Reading

Fadiman, J., and R. Frager. *Personality and Personal Growth.* Harper & Row, 1976.

Freud, S. *An Outline of Psychoanalysis.* Norton, 1949.

Hall, C. S., and G. Lindzey. *Theories of Personality*, 2nd ed. Wiley, 1970.

Maddi, S. R. *Personality Theories: A Comparative Analysis.* Dorsey, 1968.

Pervin, L. A. *Personality: Theory, Assessment, and Research.* Wiley, 1970.

Contents

Abnormal Behavior and Psychotherapy

Unit Six

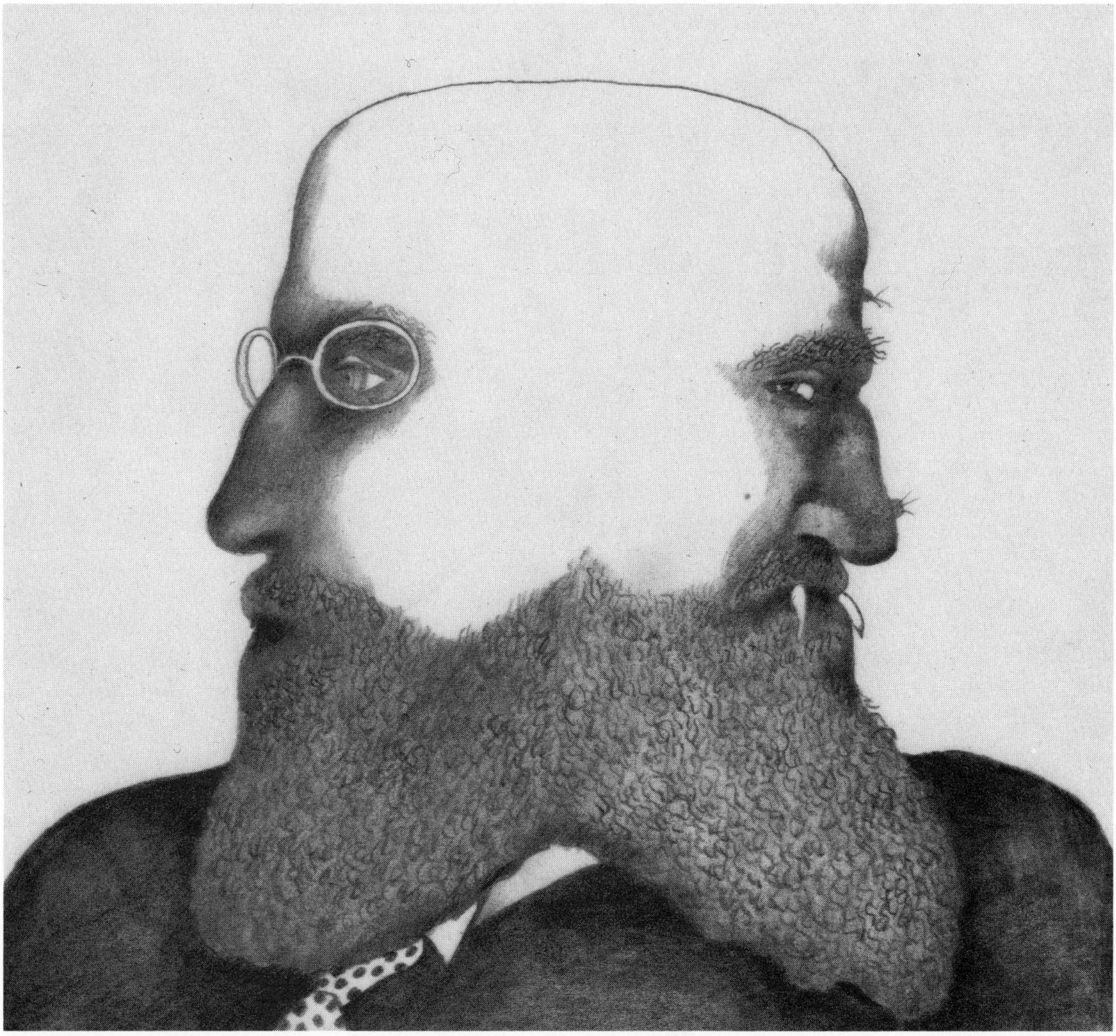

Neurosis and the Unhealthy Personality

21

Chapter Preview

Catch-22: A Practical Definition of "Crazy"

"Can't you ground someone who's crazy?"

"Oh, sure, I have to. There's a rule saying I have to ground anyone who's crazy."

"Then why don't you ground me? I'm crazy. Ask Clevinger."

"Clevinger? Where is Clevinger? You find Clevinger and I'll ask him."

"Then ask any of the others. They'll tell you how crazy I am."

"They're crazy."

"Then why don't you ground them?"

"Why don't they ask me to ground them?"

"Because they're crazy, that's why."

"Of course they're crazy." Doc Daneeka replied. "I just told you they're crazy, didn't I? And you can't let crazy people decide whether you're crazy or not, can you?"

Yossarian looked at him soberly and tried another approach. "Is Orr crazy?"

"He sure is," Doc Daneeka said.

"Can you ground him?"

"I sure can. But first he has to ask me to. That's part of the rule."

"Then why doesn't he ask you to?"

"Because he's crazy," Doc Daneeka said. "He has to be crazy to keep flying combat missions after all the close calls he's had. Sure, I can ground Orr. But first he has to ask me to."

"That's all he has to do to be grounded?"

"That's all. Let him ask me."

"And then you can ground him?" Yossarian asked.

"No. Then I can't ground him."

"You mean there's a catch?"

"Sure there's a catch," Doc Daneeka replied. "Catch-22. Anyone who wants to get out of combat duty isn't really crazy."

There was only one catch and that was Catch-22, which specified that a concern for one's own safety in the face of dangers that were real and immediate was the process of a rational mind. Orr was crazy and could be grounded. All he had to do was ask; and as soon as he did, he would no longer be crazy and would have to fly more missions. Orr would be crazy to fly more missions and sane if he didn't, but if he was sane he had to fly them. If he flew them he was crazy and didn't have to; but if he didn't want to he was sane and had to. Yossarian was moved very deeply by the absolute simplicity of this clause of Catch-22 and let out a respectful whistle.

"That's some catch, that Catch-22," he observed.

"It's the best there is," Doc Daneeka agreed.[1]

This excerpt from Joseph Heller's novel Catch 22 *captures the ambiguities presented by the classic question "What is normal?" In the 1800s doctors and laymen alike used such terms as "crazy," "insane," "cracked," and "lunatic" quite freely. The "insane" were considered bizarre and definitely different from you or me. Today our understanding of "mental illness" or emotional disturbance is becoming increasingly sophisticated. Drawing lines between normal and abnormal and between pathological and healthy can be accomplished only by taking into consideration some complex issues.*

In this chapter and the next we will summarize some of the major psychological disturbances and the characteristics which distinguish them.

Resources

Psychopathology—Defining Major Psychological Problems

Mental health problems are more common than many people suspect. Here are the facts on psychopathology:

- Nearly half of all hospital beds in all types of hospitals are occupied by the mentally ill.
- 1 out of every 10 children born will experience either a major or a minor mental disorder.
- 1 out of every 100 persons will become so severely disturbed as to require hospitalization (Joint Commission on Mental Illness and Health, 1961).

A tremendous variety of problems comes under the general heading of *psychopathology*. Psychopathology may be defined as *the inability to behave in ways that foster the well-being of the individual and ultimately of*

[1]*Catch 22*, copyright © 1955, 1961 by Joseph Heller. Reprinted by permission of Simon and Schuster, Inc.

society. This definition covers not only obviously maladaptive behavior like drug addiction, compulsive gambling, or loss of contact with reality but also any behavior that interferes with personal growth and self-fulfillment (Coleman, 1972).

Psychological problems are grouped into broad categories of maladaptive behavior. The most widely accepted system of classification lists four major types of problems: personality disorder, psychosomatic illness, neurosis, and psychosis.

A *personality disorder* is a maladaptive personality trait that dominates the individual. Alcoholism, drug addiction, and sexually deviant behavior are all common personality disorders. Typically, the person who has a personality disorder cannot or will not change his destructive behavior.

Psychosomatic illness was discussed in Chapter 14. You will recall that the term "psychosomatic illness" refers to actual physical illness in which psychological processes have played a causal role (ulcers, asthma, and high blood pressure, for example).

Neurosis is primarily a disorder in which high levels of anxiety (basically inappropriate fear) cause personal discomfort and the development of self-defeating and maladaptive behavior patterns. Although a person may be considerably incapacitated, in neurosis there is no loss of contact with reality, and hospitalization is rarely required.

Psychosis is the most severe psychopathology and often requires hospitalization. In psychosis the person has lost contact with reality: He can no longer tell the difference between what is fantasy and what is real. In addition, there is usually a major deterioration in ability to control thoughts and actions.

Fig. 21-1 Psychosis is a severe mental disorder that frequently requires hospitalization. (Photo by John Launois, Black Star.)

Question: Is psychosis the same as insanity?

No. Psychosis is a psychiatric term which describes a particular form of psychopathology. *Insanity* is a *legal* term. Insanity refers to legal responsibility for one's actions or to the legal designation required for involuntary commitment to a mental institution. Insanity is usually established through the testimony of psychiatrists who serve as expert witnesses in a court of law.

Normality—What Is Normal?

Setting aside certain behaviors or certain people as psychologically unhealthy raises the age-old issue of what is normal. Defining normality can be a tricky business. We might begin by saying that *subjective discomfort* is characteristic of psychopathology; that is, the unhealthy personality will be marked by unhappiness, anxiety, depression, or other signs of emotional upset.

Question: But couldn't a person be psychotic without feeling subjective discomfort?

Yes, a problem with this definition is that a person's behavior might be quite maladaptive without producing subjective discomfort. A psychotic displaying obviously bizarre and maladjusted behavior might report that he feels "on top of the world." It could be said, additionally, that a *lack* of discomfort may indicate a problem. If a person were to show no signs of grief or depression in response to the death of a friend or loved one, we would suspect psychopathology just as surely as we might if grief continued for months. In practice, subjective discomfort accounts for most instances in which a person makes a decision to voluntarily seek professional help.

Some psychologists have tried to define normality more objectively by using *statistics*. For example, since we know that anxiety is a characteristic of neurosis we could devise a test to learn how many people show low, medium, or high levels of anxiety. Usually the results of such a test will fall into a *normal** (bell-shaped) *curve* (see Fig. 21-2). Notice that most people's scores are in the center region of such a curve. Those people who deviate from the average by being anxious all of the time (high anxiety) might be considered abnormal. Incidentally, a person who never feels anxiety might also be considered abnormal.

Question: Then a statistical definition of abnormality tells us nothing about the meaning of a deviation from the norm?

Right, it is as statistically "abnormal" (unusual) for a person to score above 145 on an IQ test as it is to score below 55, but only in the second case would we consider the score "abnormal" or undesirable.

*Normal in this case is a statistical concept referring only to the shape of the curve.

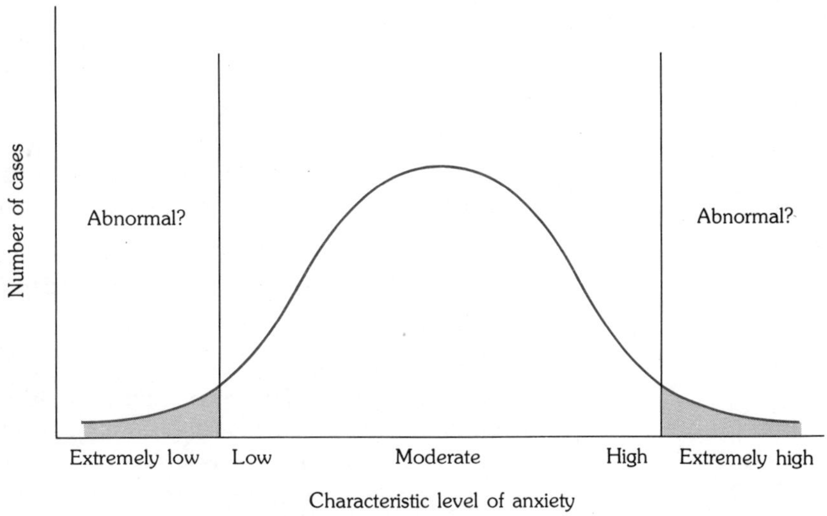

Fig. 21-2 The number of people displaying a personal characteristic may help define what is statistically abnormal.

Another major problem with a statistical definition is the question of *where to draw the line* between normality and abnormality. To take a new example, we could undoubtedly calculate the average frequency of sexual intercourse for persons of a particular age, sex, and marital status. Obviously a person who feels driven to seek sexual release dozens of times a day has a problem. But as we move back toward the norm we face the statistical problem of drawing lines. How often must an otherwise normal behavior occur before it becomes abnormal?

Social nonconformity may also serve as a basis for judgments of normality. Abnormal behavior can sometimes be viewed as a failure in *socialization*. Here we refer to the person who has not adopted the usual minimum rules for social conduct or who has learned to engage in socially destructive or self-destructive behavior. This form of nonconformity must be carefully distinguished from that of the individual who is nonconforming because of high levels of creativity or a unique life-style. It should be noted also that adherence to social norms is no guarantee of freedom from psychopathology. In some cases neurosis takes the form of rigid conformity.

Before any behavior can be defined as normal or abnormal we must consider the *context* in which it occurs. Is it abnormal for a grown man to remove his pants and expose himself to another man or woman in a place of business? It depends on whether the other person is a bank clerk or a physician! Almost any imaginable behavior can be considered normal in some context as the following example indicates:

> In mid-October, 1973, an airplane carrying a rugby team called the "Old Christians" crashed in the snowcapped Andes of South America. Incredibly, 16 of the 45 people who had been aboard at the time of the crash survived 73

days in deep snow and subfreezing temperatures. They were forced to use extremely grim measures to do so—they ate the bodies of those who had died in the crash (adapted from *Time*, Jan. 8, 1973).

One of the most influential contexts in which any behavior is judged is that of culture. In some cultures it is considered normal to believe that plants and trees are inhabited by spirits; or to defecate or urinate in public; or to appear naked in public. In our culture each of these behaviors would be considered unusual or abnormal.

Question: If abnormality is so hard to define how are judgments of psychopathology made?

It should be clear at this point that all definitions of abnormality are *relative*. Yet, in spite of the great difficulty of formally defining abnormality, we do know that psychological disturbances occur and that they must be identified. In practice, the judgment that a person needs help usually occurs when the person *does something* (hits a person, hallucinates, stares into space, collects rolls of toilet paper, and so forth) that *annoys or gains the attention* of a person in a *position of power* (an employer, teacher, parent, spouse, or the person himself) who then *does something* about it. (A policeman may be called, the person may be urged to see a psychologist, or a relative may start commitment proceedings.)

The sections which follow continue our discussion of normality by describing in greater detail some of the psychological problems already mentioned. You will find short sections on the often misunderstood personality disorders of sexual deviance and psychopathy and an extended discussion of neurosis. Before you read further see if you can answer these questions.

Learning Check

1. What percentage of hospital beds are occupied by the mentally ill?

10% 25% 50% 75% 90%

2. In neurosis the person has lost contact with reality. T or F?

3. Statistical definitions of abnormality avoid the problems of other approaches. T or F?

4. The normality of any behavior must be judged in relation to the

______________________ in which it occurs.

Answers: **1.** 50% **2.** F **3.** F **4.** context or culture

The Antisocial Personality—Rebel without a Cause

A major failure in socialization may produce an *antisocial* or *sociopathic* personality. The sociopath (also sometimes called a *psychopath*) is a person who seems to lack a *conscience*. The sociopath is selfish, impulsive, unable to feel guilt, manipulative, lacking in moral values, and emotionally shallow. Of particular importance are the sociopath's lack of a sense of responsibility, a general disregard for the truth, and a lack of a sense of shame (Cleckley, 1964).

Question: Are sociopaths dangerous?

Sociopaths are rarely the crazed murderers that have been portrayed on TV and in movies. It is true that many sociopaths are delinquents or criminals who may pose a threat to the general public. But sociopaths like Charles Manson, whose "family" of followers committed the grisly Tate-LaBianca murders, are quite unusual. Most sociopaths create a very good first impression and are frequently described as "charming." Their lying, self-serving manipulation, and lack of dependability only gradually become evident to their "friends." As Harold Greenwald comments:

> Usually when we talk about the psychopath we are talking about the *unsuccessful* psychopath. The reason why we generally do not discuss the successful psychopath is because we would then have to discuss many of the rulers of the world. . . . Many of the symptoms . . . such as lack of morals and apparent lack of guilt, exist widely among people of power and influence (Greenwald, 1967; quoted in *Psychosources*, 1973).

Many successful businesspeople, entertainers, politicians, and other "normal" individuals reveal sociopathic leanings through their willingness to use other people coldly for their own ends.

Question: What causes sociopathy?

There is usually a history of emotional deprivation and disregard during the sociopath's childhood which prevents the development of concern for the feelings of others. In addition, adult sociopaths have been tested in situations in which they must learn to avoid an electric shock. Under these and similar circumstances they show much less anxiety than normal (Lykken, 1957; Schachter & Latané, 1969). The sociopath might therefore, be described as emotionally *cold*. He simply doesn't feel normal pangs of conscience, guilt, or anxiety. His coldness seems to account for an unusual ability to lie, cheat, or steal calmly.

Question: Can sociopathy be treated?

Sociopathy is rarely treated with any success since the sociopath manipulates therapy as he might any other situation. If it is to his advantage to act "cured," he will do so, but he then returns to former patterns of behavior at the first opportunity.

Sexual Deviance—Trench Coats, Whips, Leathers, and Lace

Sexual deviance, like any form of deviance, implies a departure from accepted standards of proper behavior. By the most strict standards (including the law in some states), any sexual activity other than face-to-face heterosexual intercourse between married adults is "deviant." But public standards and behavior found privately acceptable by consenting adults are often at odds. By private standards, oral-genital contact, masturbation, and premarital sex can no longer be considered sexual deviations. From a psychological point of view, the mark of true sexual deviations is that they are compulsive, destructive, or bizarre, or they cause guilt, anxiety, or discomfort for one or both participants. Deviations fitting this definition are related to a wide variety of behaviors including *pedophilia* (sex with children), *bestiality* (sex with animals), *incest* (sex with blood relatives), *fetishism* (sexual arousal associated with inanimate objects), *exhibitionism* (displaying the genitals), *voyeurism* (viewing the genitals of others), *transvestism* (achieving sexual arousal by wearing clothing of the opposite sex), *sadism* (inflicting pain as part of the sex act), and *masochism* (receiving pain as part of the sex act).

Question: Isn't homosexuality a deviation?

Recently the American Psychiatric Association removed male homosexuality and female lesbianism from its list of sexual deviations. This was done mainly in recognition of the fact that few homosexuals are disturbed by their sexual orientation *per se*. If they suffer from any maladjustment, it is usually due to the pressures of rejection by family, employers, or society in general. The gay person is basically comfortable with his or her attraction to members of the same sex.

Sexual deviation is a highly emotional subject for many people. As a result, many misconceptions about sexual deviance have developed. Coleman (1972) lists the following as major *misconceptions*:

1. *Sexual offenders are typically homicidal sex fiends.* Actually only about 5 percent of all convicted sex offenders inflict physical injury upon their victims.
2. *Sexual offenders are oversexed from exposure to pornography.* Most offenders are *undersexed*—more inhibited than average and less exposed to pornography.
3. *Sexual offenders suffer from glandular imbalance.* Not so. Human sexual patterns are learned.
4. *Sexual offenders typically progress from minor to more serious sex crimes.* This progression is rare. Usually the person persists in one sexually maladaptive activity.
5. *Sexual offenders are usually repeaters.* Sex offenders have one of the lowest rates of repeated offences.

The picture of sexual deviance that most often emerges is one of sexual inhibition and immaturity in which some relatively infantile sexual expression (like exhibitionism or pedophilia) is selected as a sexual outlet because it is less threatening than normal sexuality. The sexual offender is more to be pitied than feared. A notable exception to this is the problem of *forcible rape*. Many psychologists no longer think of rape as an exclusively sexual act. Rather, it is an act of brutality or aggression based on the need to debase others. Many rapists are sociopathic persons who impulsively take what they want without concern for the feelings of the victim or guilt about their deed. Many others harbor deep-seated resentment toward or outright hatred of women. The women's movement has drawn attention to the fact that, as an act of aggression, rape is a logical extension of sexist attitudes.

Learning Check

1. The sociopathic personality is often described as having no ______________________________.

2. Almost all sociopaths are criminals or delinquents. T or F?

3. *Pedophilia* is the formal term for oral-genital sex. T or F?

4. What percentage of sex offenders inflict physical injury on their victims?

5% 10% 20% 40% 80%

Answers: **1.** conscience, anxiety, or guilt **2.** F **3.** F **4.** 5%

The Neuroses—When Anxiety Rules

Imagine for a moment the feeling of waiting to take an important test for which you are unprepared; or waiting to give a speech to a large audience of strangers; or waiting for a dentist to start work. You have almost certainly felt *anxiety* in one of these situations. Anxiety is similar to fear except that it is a response to a *nonspecific* threat or an *anticipation* of harm. When a person has "stage fright," we say he is anxious because it is not clear exactly what he fears.

Question: Is it abnormal to feel anxiety?

We all occasionally feel anxiety, and at times of great stress anxiety may be intense, but anxiety that is out of proportion to a given situation may reveal a problem:

> A college student appeared at the counseling center with a complaint that he was deathly afraid of examinations. . . . He had previously been involved in a confrontation with an instructor whom he accused of having administered an unfair test in that there was not enough time to answer all the questions. . . . He soon realized that the time limit had not been long enough because he had wasted most of his time in attempting to control his anxieties. He had already skipped two other examinations by remaining in bed petrified with his fears of failure (adapted from Suinn, 1975, p. 274).[2]

[2]From *Fundamentals of Behavior Pathology* by R. M. Suinn. Copyright © 1975. Reprinted by permission of John Wiley & Sons, Inc. Additional Suinn quotes in this chapter and the next are from the same source.

Fig. 21-3 Combat exhaustion resembles neurosis but is the result of prolonged exposure to stress. Most soldiers recover quickly when returned to a normal environment. (Photo by R. Ellison, Black Star.)

This brief excerpt demonstrates many of the characteristics of *neurotic* anxiety and neurotic behavior. Let us expand our previous definition of neurosis:

> A *neurosis* is an emotional disturbance in which high levels of anxiety, exaggerated fears, tension, extreme shyness, or other sources of discomfort cause a person to seek relief by adopting rigid defense mechanisms and unusual or self-defeating behavior patterns.

Some estimates of the frequency of neurosis run as high as 70 percent of the general population, but probably not more than 5 percent ever suffer a severe neurosis.

Question: Is a neurosis a nervous breakdown?

Neurotic behavior patterns may severely disrupt a person's life and almost always cause considerable misery, but neurosis rarely brings about a "breakdown." Actually, the term "nervous breakdown" has no formal meaning. What people usually have in mind when they use the term is best described as a *transient* (temporary) *situational disorder*. Transient situational disorders are the result of obvious environmental stresses that push a person beyond the ability to cope effectively. For example, a soldier may suffer *combat exhaustion* after an extended period of stress. Combat exhaustion is characterized by insomnia or repeated nightmares, loss of appetite, extreme sensitivity, unexplained crying, body tremors, hand wringing, and attacks of uncontrollable anxiety.

A similar emotional disturbance can result when a person is faced with sudden disaster like a flood, loss of a job, or a serious accident. The civilian equivalent of combat exhaustion is sometimes called a *traumatic neurosis* because of its clear connection to environmental stress. Transient situational disorders are usually successfully treated with rest, sedation, and a chance to "talk through" fears and anxieties.

Question: How is neurosis different from a transient situational disorder?

Transient situational disorders are sometimes called false neuroses because they disappear when stress is eased. In a true neurosis the person's anxiety is a lasting pattern that seems completely out of proportion to the situation. Consider, for example, the following description of Ethel B:

> . . . She was never completely relaxed, and complained of vague feelings of restlessness, and a fear that something was "just around the corner." Although she felt that she had to go to work to help pay the family bills, she could not bring herself to start anything new for fear that something terrible would happen on the job. She had experienced a few extreme anxiety attacks during which she felt "like I couldn't breathe, like I was sealed up in a transparent envelope. I thought I was going to have a heart attack. I couldn't stop shaking" (Suinn, 1975, p. 259).

Question: Do all neurotics feel like Ethel B?

Ethel B's problem would be described as an *anxiety neurosis*. Neurosis takes several forms. Each can be understood as an ineffective means of coping with anxiety or other personal discomfort. A description of several types of neurosis follows.

Anxiety Neurosis Anxiety neurosis is a relatively simple but very disturbing neurotic pattern characterized by continuous tension or anxiety that occasionally explodes into episodes of intense panic. An *anxiety attack*, which may last for a few minutes or for hours, causes sweating, apprehension, a pounding heart, and feelings of loss of control. The person often feels that he cannot breathe or that he is having a heart attack, going insane, or is about to die. It is sometimes said that the anxiety neurotic suffers from *free-floating anxiety* since an anxiety attack can be triggered by almost anything. Needless to say, the anxiety neurotic is unhappy and uncomfortable much of the time.

Phobic Neurosis *Phobias* are irrational fears that persist even when there is no real danger to a person. Some of the more common phobias have been given names:

Acrophobia—fear of heights
Agoraphobia—fear of open places
Claustrophobia—fear of closed spaces
Nyctophobia—fear of darkness
Pathophobia—fear of disease
Zoophobia—fear of animals

This list of possibilities is only partial: Phobias may be attached to almost any object or situation. Almost everyone has a few mild phobias: Fears of heights, closed spaces, or bugs and crawly things are common. A neurotic phobia differs from such garden-variety fears in that it produces overwhelming anxiety that may cause heart palpitations, vomiting, wild climbing and running, or fainting. The phobic person is so threatened that he will go to almost any length to avoid the feared object or situation. A person with a neurotic fear of water and drowning will not only avoid swimming and boats but, in addition, may be unable to visit a beach or take a bath. One individual treated by the author developed such a fear of public rest rooms that he would endure intense discomfort for hours or would travel across town to his home in order to urinate where he felt safe.

Hysterical (Conversion) Reaction *Conversion reactions* are said to occur when anxiety or severe emotional conflicts are "converted" into physical symptoms resembling disease or disability. Neurotic conversion reactions are usually quite dramatic. A soldier may go deaf or lame or may develop "glove anesthesia" just before a battle.

Question: What is "glove anesthesia"?

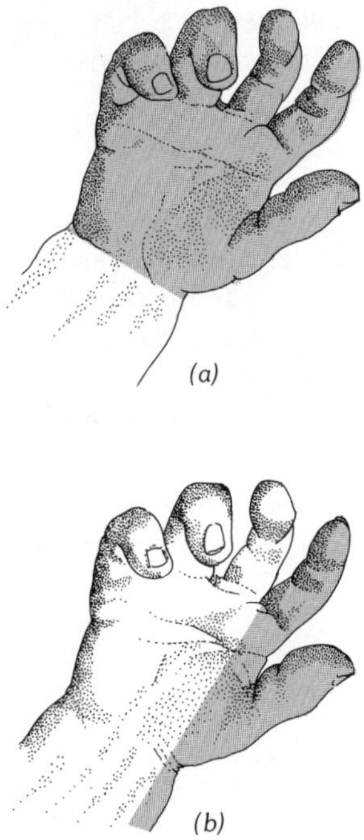

Fig. 21-4 "Glove" anesthesia is a conversion reaction in which the person loses feeling in areas of the hand that would be covered by a glove *(a)*. If anesthesia were physically caused, it would follow the pattern depicted in *(b)*.

"Glove anesthesia" is a loss of sensitivity in the areas of skin that would normally be covered by a glove. Glove anesthesia demonstrates that hysterical symptoms often contradict known medical facts. The system of nerves in the hands does not form a glovelike pattern and could not cause the observed symptoms. Conversion reactions are also revealed by a disappearance of symptoms when the "victim" is asleep, hypnotized, or anesthetized.

The physical symptoms of a conversion reaction usually serve to excuse the person from a threatening situation. In one case a college student who had a minor traffic accident awakened the following morning with a numbness in his legs and found himself unable to move them. A conversion reaction was suspected when it was noted that he did not seem at all disturbed by his inability to walk. Investigation revealed that his parents were pressuring him to stay in school although he wanted to quit and that he was not prepared for his final exams. If he failed his exams, he expected to be drafted (Suinn, 1975).

A final note of interest: Conversion reactions probably account for many of the so-called miracle cures attributed to faith healers or medical quacks. The hysterical neurotic who firmly believes he is being helped may undergo a miraculous cure but will usually develop a new symptom later.

Dissociative Reaction A *dissociative reaction* is a form of neurosis marked by striking episodes of *amnesia*, *fugue*, or *multiple personality*. *Amnesia* is the inability to recall one's name, address, or past. *Fugue* is physical flight to escape extreme threat or conflict. Fugue and amnesia are sometimes coupled. A person may wander away from work or school only to later find herself in a strange place without knowing how she got there. It can easily be seen that forgetting one's identity or fleeing unpleasant situations is a defense against anxiety that cannot be tolerated.

Multiple personality is a rare condition in which two or more separate personalities exist in an individual. The fictional story of *Dr. Jekyll and Mr. Hyde* is a well-known portrayal of *dual personality*. One of the most dramatic examples of multiple personality ever recorded is described in the book *Sybil* (Schreiber, 1973). Sybil is a woman who had sixteen complete and totally different personalities. Each personality had a distinct voice, vocabulary, and posture. One personality could play the piano (not Sybil), but the others could not. When a personality other than Sybil was in control, Sybil experienced a "time lapse" or memory blackout. For example, as a child she once "awoke" as a fifth grader and couldn't understand why she was not in her third-grade classroom. When she was asked to do a multiplication problem, she couldn't begin. Two years of her life were missing, and the personality that had inhabited her body had learned multiplication, but Sybil had not. Sybil's amnesia and alternate personalities developed during childhood when she was regularly beaten, locked in closets, perversely tortured, and almost killed. Sybil's first dissociations allowed her to escape by creating another person who would suffer torture in her place. In later years she developed additional personalities to defend against new stresses.

Obsessive-Compulsive Neurosis *Obsessions* are thoughts or images that intrude into consciousness against a person's will. You have probably experienced a mild obsessional thought in the form of some song or stupid commercial jingle that is repeated over and over in your mind. This may be irritating, but it is certainly not disturbing in any major sense. Neurotic obsessions are so disturbing that they cause anxiety or extreme discomfort. Obsessions may center on images of one's own violent death, feelings of being "dirty" or "unclean," feelings that one is about to lose control, or similar threatening preoccupations.

Obsessions usually give rise to *compulsions*. These are irrational acts a person feels driven to repeat. Typically the compulsive act helps control or block out anxiety caused by the obsession. A person who feels guilty or unclean because of a conflict about masturbation might be driven to wash his hands hundreds of times a day. A minister who finds profanities popping into his mind might take up compulsively counting his heartbeat to prevent their appearance. A young mother who repeatedly has an image of a knife plunging into her infant might count all the knives in the house several times a day and insist that they always be locked up. Of

Fig. 21-5 Is this compulsive behavior? A farmer collected millions of pieces of rope and twine to create this incredible ball. (Photo by Bernstein, International Press Service.)

course, not all obsessions and compulsions are this dramatic; many simply involve extreme orderliness and rigid routine. Compulsive rituals make a person feel more secure by keeping activities so structured that unexpected upsets are prevented.

Neurotic Depressive Reactions Depressive reactions are one of the most frequently occurring neuroses, accounting for approximately 25 percent of all treated cases. In a *depressive neurosis*, sadness and despondency are exaggerated and prolonged for unreasonable periods of time. The symptoms of neurotic depression are: lack of energy, unhappiness, limited movement, an extremely negative self-image, loss of sense of humor, and a loss of interest in other people.

Question: How is depressive neurosis different from normal depression?

Since its symptoms are similar to the feelings which accompany any depression, neurotic depression is identified by its maladaptive nature. If a loved one dies or a person suffers a major failure or setback, a period of mourning or depression is to be expected. Depression at these times represents an emotional readjustment and is soon resolved. When a person is in a continuous state of depression for months, we must look for causes that go beyond the incident that seemed to trigger the depression. Usually it is found that the person was unprepared to cope with a major loss because of a long series of former disappointments or because the person is emotionally dependent or immature. In any case, the triggering incident is merely the "last straw" that reveals an underlying maladjustment.

Theories of Neurosis—Three Ways to Construct a Neurosis

Question: What causes neurosis?

At least three major perspectives on the causes of neurosis can be identified. These are (1) the psychodynamic approach, (2) the humanistic approach, and (3) the behavioristic approach.

Psychodynamic Approach Freud was the first to propose a comprehensive explanation of neurosis. According to Freud, neurosis represents a raging conflict between the three subparts of the personality—the id, ego, and superego. Freud particularly emphasized anxiety caused by forbidden id impulses for sex or aggression which threaten to break through into behavior. Also important in the Freudian view is guilt generated by the superego in response to these impulses. Caught in the middle, the ego is overwhelmed by conflicting demands, and the person must adopt rigid defense mechanisms and inflexible behavior to prevent a disastrous loss of control.

Humanistic Approach Psychologist Carl Rogers interprets neurosis as the end product of a faulty *self-image* (Rogers, 1959). Rogers feels that the neurotic has built up an unrealistic picture of himself which leaves him vulnerable to contradictory information. Let's say, for example, that an essential part of a particular student's self-image is seeing himself as highly intelligent. If the student does poorly in his classes, he may deny or distort his perceptions of himself and of the situation. Rigid defense mechanisms, a conversion reaction, anxiety attacks, or other neurotic symptoms may result from the threat to his self-image. These symptoms in turn become new threats and require further distortions. We have, in other words, a classic example of a vicious cycle of maladjustment that feeds on itself once started.

Behavioristic Approach Behaviorists have generally rejected the two previous explanations of neurosis. The behavioristic position is that neurotic "symptoms" are learned just like any other behavior. A sample of behavioristic thinking follows.

One aspect of neurotic behavior all theorists agree upon is that it is ultimately self-defeating. This is largely summarized by the *neurotic paradox*. A paradox is a contradiction. The contradiction in neurotic behavior is that in the long run it makes the person more miserable, but its immediate effect is to make him feel temporarily less anxious.

Question: How does a pattern like this get started?

The behavioristic explanation is that the neurotic paradox is an example of *avoidance learning*. Avoidance learning is easily demonstrated in the laboratory:

> An animal is placed in a special cage. After a few minutes a light comes on, followed a moment later by a painful shock. After the shock begins, the animal escapes over a partition into a second chamber. After a few minutes, a light comes on in this chamber, and the shock is repeated there. At first, the animal only *escapes* shock, but soon it learns to *avoid* the shock by moving *before* the shock occurs. Once an animal learns to avoid the shock, it can be turned off altogether. A well-trained animal may then avoid the nonexistent shock indefinitely.

The same analysis can be applied to neurotic behavior. A behaviorist would say that anxiety has been conditioned to various situations and that the immediate reinforcement of *relief* from anxiety keeps the neurotic pattern alive. This is why neurotic behavior often looks very "stupid" to an outside observer.

There is probably a core of truth to each of the three explanations. Understanding a particular example of neurosis may be aided by combining parts of all three perspectives. Each perspective also suggests a different approach to treatment. Since the possibilities are numerous, discussion of therapy for neurosis and other problems is found later in two separate chapters (see Chapters 23 and 24).

A Final Note—You're O.K. . . . Really!

It is the author's hope that you will not fall prey to the psychological equivalent of "medical student's disease" after reading this chapter. Medical students, it seems, have a predictable tendency to notice in themselves the symptoms of each dreaded disease they learn about. As a psychology student you may have noticed what seems to be neurotic or other abnormal tendencies in your own behavior. If so, don't panic: this only shows that pathological behavior is an *exaggeration* of normal defenses and reactions, not that your behavior is pathological.

Learning Check

1. The most consistent symptom of neurosis is the presence of excessive

____________________.

2. Match the following:

______	Transient situational disorder	**A.**	Irrational fears
______	Anxiety neurosis	**B.**	Fugue
______	Phobic neurosis	**C.**	Extreme orderliness and rigid routine
______	Conversion reaction	**D.**	Exaggerated despondency
______	Dissociative reaction	**E.**	Combat exhaustion
______	Obsessive-compulsive neurosis	**F.**	Free-floating anxiety
______	Neurotic depression	**G.**	Mimics disease or disability

3. The humanistic explanation of neurosis emphasizes the importance of a faulty self-image. T or F?

4. The behavioristic explanation of neurosis is based on conflict between subparts of the personality. T or F?

Answers: **1.** anxiety **2.** E, F, A, G, B, C, D **3.** T **4.** F

Resources Summary

Mental or emotional disturbances are a major health problem. *Psychopathology* includes four major types of problems: *personality disorders*, *psychosomatic illness*, *neurosis*, and *psychosis*. The term "nervous breakdown" has no formal meaning, but nervous breakdowns do correspond somewhat to *transient situational disorders. Insanity* is a general term referring to legal responsibility, not to any of the above categories.

Formal definitions of normality usually take into account all or most of the following: *subjective discomfort*, deviation from *statistical norms*, *social nonconformity*, and the *cultural* or *situational context* of behavior. There are problems with each of these definitions of normality since all are *relative standards*. In practice a judgment of abnormality is a social act influenced by many factors.

Two frequently misunderstood personality disorders are *sociopathy* and *sexual deviance*. The sociopath lacks a *conscience* and has shallow emotional relationships with others. Few sociopaths are homicidal, and only a small proportion are criminals. Sexual deviance may be the most *relative* abnormality of all. Many "sexually deviant" behaviors are acceptable in other cultures. The sex offender is rarely dangerous and can best be characterized as inhibited and immature in his sexuality.

Neurosis is characterized by high levels of anxiety, rigid defense mechanisms, and self-defeating behavior patterns. Several patterns of neurotic behavior have been identified. Some of the major patterns and their principal symptoms are: *anxiety neuroses* (anxiety attacks), *phobic neuroses* (irrational fears), *conversion reactions* (symptoms resembling disease or disability), *dissociative reactions* (amnesia, fugue, or multiple personality), *obsessive-compulsive neurosis* (disturbing thoughts and rigid, driven behavior) and *depressive neurosis* (excessive depression unjustified by circumstances).

Three broad types of explanation for neurosis are: (1) a *psychodynamic* approach emphasizing unconscious conflicts within the personality, (2) a *humanistic* approach emphasizing the effects of a *faulty self-image*, and (3) a *behavioristic* approach which emphasizes the effects of previous learning, particularly *avoidance learning*.

Applications

Warning: Suicide May Be Hazardous to Your Health

"To be, or not to be? That is the question. . . ."

By the time you finish reading this page, someone in the United States will try to kill himself. Suicide is a very disturbing and widely misunderstood mental health problem. It ranks as the seventh cause of death in the United States, and approximately 1 person out of 100 has attempted suicide at some time in his or her life. Given these figures, it seems likely that you will sooner or later be affected by the suicide attempt of a friend, relative, neighbor, or co-worker. Check your knowledge of suicide against the following information.

Question: What factors affect suicide rates?

Season Suicide rates vary from city to city and time to time, but some general patterns emerge. Contrary to popular belief, there is little connection between major holidays like Christmas and the suicide rate. For reasons not clearly understood, the peak actually comes in May (Zung & Green, 1974).

Sex Men have the questionable honor of being better at suicide than women. Three times as many men as women *complete* suicide, but women make more attempts. More men than women succeed at suicide because they typically use a gun or an equally fatal technique. Women most often attempt a drug overdose, a method which leaves greater chance of help arriving before death occurs (Lester, 1972).

Age Age is also a factor in suicide. More than half of all suicides are committed by individuals over 45 years old. This may be changing—there has been a recent increase in suicide rates for adolescents and young adults.

Part of this increase comes from the ranks of college students where suicide is the leading cause of death. Contrary to popular belief, the most dangerous time for student suicide is the beginning (first six weeks) of a semester, not during final exams. School is a factor in some suicides, but only in the sense that suicidal students were not living up to their own extremely high standards. Many were good students. Other important factors in student suicide are chronic health problems (real or imagined) and interpersonal difficulties (some suicides are rejected lovers, but most are simply withdrawn and friendless) (Seiden, 1966).

Income Some professions, particularly medicine and psychiatry, show higher than average suicide rates. Overall, however, suicide is quite democratic. It is equally a problem of the rich and the poor (Labovity & Hagedorn, 1971).

Marital Status An additional factor in suicide is marital status. Marriage (when successful) may be the best natural deterrent to suicidal impulses. The highest suicide rates are found among the divorced; the next highest rates occur among the widowed; lower rates are recorded for single persons; and married individuals have the lowest rate of all.

Question: Why do people try to kill themselves?

One theory is that suicide is aggression directed inward. The suicidal person often feels that the world has treated him unfairly. His growing anger toward situations he cannot change may drive him to show others how badly they have treated him by taking his own life (Lester, 1968).

French sociologist Émile Durkheim attributed many suicides to what he called *anomie* (Durkheim, 1951). Anomie is a state of *alienation* brought about by rapidly changing social conditions that cause feelings of rootlessness, lack of identity, and unsatisfying personal relationships.

Immediate Causes The best explanation for suicide may simply come from a look at the conditions which precede it. Usually there is a history of interpersonal troubles with family, in-laws, or a lover or spouse. Often there is a drinking problem, sexual adjustment problems, or job difficulties (Humphrey, *et al.*, 1972). A combination of factors such as these lead to severe depression and a preoccupation with death as the "answer" to the person's suffering. There is usually a break in communication with others which causes the person to feel isolated and misunderstood. Self-image becomes very negative. The person feels "worthless" and wants to die (Lester, 1972).

A long history of such conditions is not always necessary to produce a desire for suicide. People who attempt suicide are not necessarily "mentally ill." Anyone may temporarily reach a state of depression severe enough to attempt suicide. Most dangerous for the average person are times of divorce, separation, failure, and bereavement. Each can create what seems like an intolerable situation and motivate an intense desire for escape.

Preventing Suicide—You Can Help

Question: Is it true that people who talk about or threaten suicide are rarely the ones who try it?

No, this is one of the major fallacies about suicide. Of every ten potential suicides, eight give warning beforehand (Shneidman *et al.*, 1965; Rudestam, 1971). A person who threatens suicide should be taken seriously. A potential suicide may say nothing more than, "I feel sometimes like I'd be better off dead." Warnings may also come indirectly. If a friend gives you a favorite ring and says, "Here, I won't be needing this any more," or if he comments, "I guess I won't get my watch fixed—it doesn't matter anyway," he may be *asking for help.*

Question: Is it true that suicide can't be prevented, that the person will find a way to do it anyway?

No. The decision to attempt suicide usually comes when a person is alone, depressed, and unable to view himself objectively. You *should* intervene if someone seems to be threatening suicide. It is estimated that about two-thirds of all suicide attempts fall in the "to be" category. That is, they are made by people who do not really want to die. Almost a third more are characterized by a "to be or not to be" attitude. These people are ambivalent or undecided about dying. Only about 3 to 5 percent of cases represent individuals who definitely want to die. Most people are, therefore, relieved when someone comes to their aid (Shneidman *et al.*, 1965). Remember that suicide is almost always a cry for help and that you *can* help.

Question: What is the best thing to do if someone threatens suicide or hints about it?

Suicide expert David Lester (1971b) believes that your most important task is to establish *rapport* with the person. You should offer support, acceptance, and legitimate caring. Lester gives some important suggestions about how to handle a potential suicide:

1. A suicidal person feels misunderstood. You should, therefore, try to accept the feelings the person is expressing. Telling the person

he really doesn't want to kill himself or listing reasons why he shouldn't, only adds to his feelings that no one understands him. This usually makes a bad situation worse. The person needs *acceptance* not reassurance.

2. Acceptance should extend to the idea of suicide itself. One of the worst things you can do is to say something like, "You're not thinking of doing something drastic, are you?" Hiding from suicide or trying to avoid talking about it makes the person feel wrong, unaccepted, and alone. Don't be afraid to talk about suicide directly. It is completely acceptable to ask, "Are you thinking of suicide?"

Establishing communication with a person may be enough to carry him through a difficult time. You may also find it helpful to get a day-by-day commitment from him to meet for lunch, to share a ride, and the like. Let the person know you *expect* him to be there. Such commitments, even though small, can be enough to tip the scales when a person is alone and thinking about suicide.

Don't end your efforts too soon. One of the most dangerous times for suicide is when a person suddenly seems to get better after a severe depression. Many experts agree that this often means the person has finally made the decision to end it all. The improvement in mood is deceptive because it comes from an anticipation that suffering is at an end (Lester & Lester, 1971).

There are over 200 centers for suicide prevention in the United States, and most sizable cities have mental health "crisis intervention" teams. Both services have staff trained to talk to potential suicides over the phone. Give a person who seems to be suicidal the number of one of these services and ask him to place it near his phone. Urge him to call you or the other numbers if he becomes frightened or impulsive. If a person seems on the verge of carrying out some action, don't worry about overreacting, call the police, crisis intervention, or a rescue unit. Needless to say, you should call immediately if a person is in the act of attempting suicide or if he or she has already taken a drug. The majority of suicide attempts come at temporary low points in a person's life and may never be repeated. Get involved—save a life!

Suicide—Summary of Misconceptions

The following is a list of misconceptions about suicide.

1. More women than men commit suicide.
2. College students are most likely to attempt suicide during final exam periods.
3. Anyone who would attempt suicide is mentally ill. Suicide is always the act of a psychotic person.
4. Suicide strikes more often among the poor.
5. Once a person becomes suicidal, he is suicidal forever (or will be repeatedly).
6. Suicides give no warning.
7. People who talk about suicide are rarely the ones who attempt it.
8. A person who attempts suicide really wants to die.
9. A sudden improvement in mood after a suicidal depression means that the danger has passed.
10. There is nothing that can be done to prevent suicide.

Remember: All these statements are *false*.

For Discussion

Is Normality in the Eye of the Beholder?

Question: How much do small differences in appearance affect perceptions of normality?

To answer this question, psychologists Ted Rosenthal and Glenn White (1971) arranged for a person they called "Bill" to visit two psychology classes. Bill was introduced to each class as a person who had "spent some time in a psychiatric ward." (Bill was actually a healthy undergraduate who had volunteered to take part in the experiment.) Following this introduction, Bill read "a few facts about himself" to the class. This description was quite neutral and gave no real hint of major psychological problems. Bill then left, and students were asked to rate his "severity of maladjustment" and also to rate the severity of "symptoms" he displayed. Bill's performance was repeated for a morning and an afternoon class. The only difference was that in the morning he had shoulder-length hair and wore jeans and a T-shirt, but in the afternoon he wore slacks and a sport coat (without tie) and had a fresh short haircut.

Overall, the college students who took part in this experiment judged Bill "sicker" in short hair and sport coat than with long hair and jeans. Students were then put into categories of "hip," "square," or "unclassified" on the basis of their own hair length and style of dress. It was found that "hip" students rated the short-haired Bill as "sickest" and "square" students rated him healthiest! Their judgments were, therefore, connected to their own personal appearance.

Question: These were untrained college students. Would a psychologist be influenced by hair length?

Certainly we would expect psychologists to be less affected by such superficial features as hair length and style of dress. But psychologists are still human and may at times be influenced by similar factors. In other experiments psycholosists were given psychological test results of nonexistent persons along with case histories suggesting "lower" or "middle-class" economic backgrounds. When the test results were attributed to persons with a "lower-class" background, such persons were judged to be more maladjusted, and predictions of chances for improvement were more negative (Haase, 1964; Levy & Kahn, 1970).

These studies demonstrate the subtle difficulties of making judgments about normality. They also make it clear that "mental health" must not be too narrowly defined lest it become a form of prejudice in which "abnormal" becomes "anyone not like me."

Questions for Discussion

1. How might perceptions of Bill differ if the students' parents had been the judges?
2. What effect might living in different parts of town, membership in an ethnic group, or growing up in a different culture have on perceptions of "normality"?

3. Can you think of a behavior that would be considered "abnormal" under any possible set of circumstances?
4. How would your perception of a person be likely to change if you knew he was an "ex-mental patient"?
5. To what extent does "maladjusted" or "sick" mean "different from me"?
6. Are standards of "normality" in our society broad enough to accommodate varying life-styles?
7. In what ways might our ultra-competitive society contribute to the development of a sociopathic personality?

Suggestions for Further Reading

Alvarez, A. *The Savage God: A Study of Suicide.* Bantam, 1973.

Dollard, J., and N. E. Miller. *Personality and Psychotherapy.* McGraw-Hill, 1950.

Goldstein, J. J., and J. O. Palmer. *The Experience of Anxiety: A Casebook.* Oxford, 1963.

Lester, G., and D. Lester. *Suicide: The Gamble with Death.* Prentice-Hall, 1971.

McMahon, F. B. *Abnormal Behavior, Psychology's View.* Prentice-Hall, 1976.

Parker, B. A. *Mingled Yarn: Chronicle of a Troubled Family.* Yale, 1972.

Schreiber, F. R. *Sybil.* Regency, 1973.

Psychosis

22

Chapter Preview

Psychosis—"Losing It"

> I'm a man 36 years of age, that in 1956-57 they changed the flag of the United States of America once by adding Alaska as a State to the Union and thus paving the way for Hawaii to become a state in 1959. That of course, gives me the "*capacity of the flag itself*" and therefore like any Congressional Medal of Honor winner, gives me the "*capacity of the President of the United States of America. . . .*
>
> . . . in 1955-56 civil authorities . . . some "small time" politicians got together on me and sand-bagged me brainwashed me and bugged me with a "*short-wave* Radio grid center, with an ultra-violet cross grid" called a "bug." Its sole purpose is to use a person's senses against himself so as to perjure and distort him to no end of humiliation . . . they vibrate your nerves physically with it and never ceases.
>
> . . . I'd been there several months before they gave me "ground privileges" and once on the grounds, they started frequencing my time all the more, vibrating the back of my neck, first flicking it to the front of my face, like a "whip" or a cat of 9 tails (Suinn, 1975, p. 432).

The excerpts above are taken from a letter written by a man experiencing a psychosis. They demonstrate some of the severe disturbances in thinking, behavior, speech, and emotions that accompany psychosis.

Psychosis also represents a loss of contact with reality. Novelist Joanne Greenberg (1964, p. 90) describes a split from reality this way:

> The walls dissolved and the world became a combination of shadows . . . all direction became a lie. The laws of physics and solid matter were repealed and the experience of a lifetime of tactile sensation, motion, form, gravity, and

light were invalidated. She did not know whether she was standing or sitting down, which way was upright, and from where the light, which was a stab as it touched her, was coming. She lost track of the parts of her body; where her arms were and how to move them. As light went spinning erratically away and back she tried to clutch at thoughts only to find that she had lost all memory of the English language.[1]

What is psychosis really like? What causes it? What can be done about it? For answers to these and related questions, read on.

Resources

Psychosis—When Things Really Go Wrong

Psychosis represents the most serious human reaction to stress. It can be considered comparable to a major physical illness in its capacity to disrupt a person's life.

Question: What is psychosis like?

A person experiencing a psychotic break undergoes a number of important changes. Following are descriptions of some of the major characteristics of psychosis.

Presence of Delusions *Delusions* are false beliefs that are held even when the facts contradict them. A person with the psychotic delusion that he is Jesus Christ will not be disturbed by an inability to walk on water or to perform miracles. Some common forms of delusion are: (1) *depressive* delusions—in which the person feels he has committed some horrible crime or sinful deed; (2) *somatic* delusions—such as belief that one's body is "rotting away" or that it is emitting foul odors; (3) delusions of *grandeur* —in which the individual thinks he is an extremely important person; (4) delusions of *influence*—in which the person feels that he is being controlled or influenced by other persons or unseen forces; and (5) delusions of *persecution*—in which the person feels others are "out to get him." (Reread the first quotation in the chapter preview, and you will find evidence of delusions of grandeur, influence, and persecution.)

Hallucinations and Sensory Changes *Hallucinations* are sensory experiences that occur in the absence of a stimulus. The most common psychotic hallucination is hearing voices, but the person may also feel insects "crawling under his skin," taste "poison" in his food, or smell "gas" his "enemies" are using to "get" him. Sensory changes may bring about extreme sensitivity to heat, cold, pain, or touch, or *anesthesia*, a loss of normal sensitivity.

[1]From *I Never Promised You a Rose Garden* by Hannah Green (Joanne Greenberg). Copyright © 1964 by Hannah Green. Reprinted by permission of Holt, Rinehart, & Winston, Publishers.

Disturbed Emotions Emotions may swing violently between extremes of elation or depression, or the person may be chronically hyperemotional, depressed, or emotionally "flat" or apathetic.

Major disturbances such as these, coupled with additional problems in thought, speech, memory, and attention bring about personality disintegration and a break with reality.

Question: How could a person function with all these problems?

Actually, the description above is somewhat exaggerated, since it is rare to find all these changes occurring at once. As a matter of fact, you would probably find a trip to a psychiatric institution disappointing if you expected to see flamboyant, dramatic, or bizarre behavior. Typically, psychotic behavior occurs in brief *episodes*. The symptoms of psychosis come and go and much of the time may be quite subtle.

Even a person who seems to be "out of it" is not necessarily totally unresponsive to his or her surroundings. In one interesting experiment, psychotics were interviewed in two ways. Some were told that the purpose of the interview was to determine if they were "ready for discharge." In this group, patients who were known to like the hospital acted very bizarre and disturbed during the interview. A second group was told that the interview was to determine if the patient should be allowed "open ward" privileges. In this case disturbed patients suddenly became amazingly free of symptoms (Braginsky & Braginsky, 1967).

This experiment shows that psychotic symptoms can be considered a primitive form of communication, the message being, "I need help," or "I can't handle it any more." This explanation becomes particularly evident when it is realized that one of the most universal symptoms of psychosis is difficulty in communicating verbally with others. Psychotic speech tends to be garbled and chaotic, sometimes sounding like no more than a "word salad."

Fig. 22-1 A typical scene in a state mental hospital. (Photo by Ray Zalesky, Black Star.)

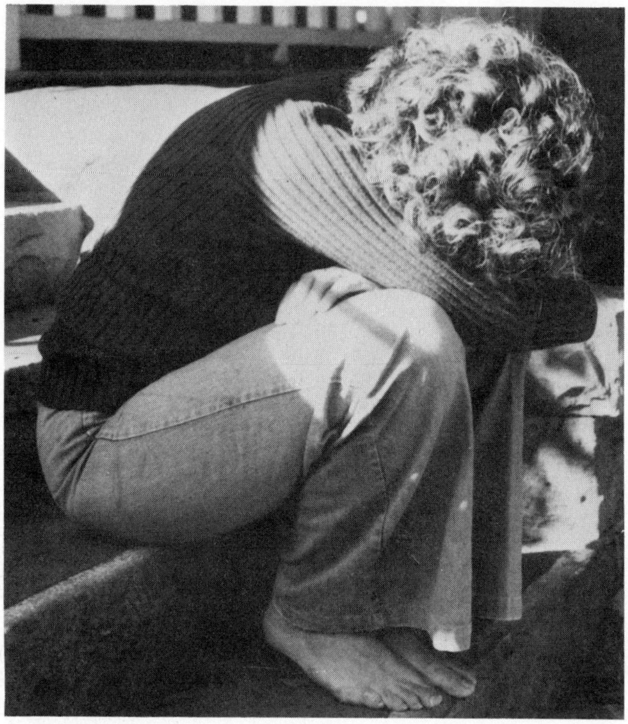

Fig. 22-2 In a depressive psychosis, suicidal impulses can be intense, and despair total.

Question: Are there different types of psychosis?

A psychosis based on known brain pathology related to disease, gunshot wound, accident, or other physical cause is termed an *organic psychosis*. A psychosis based on unknown or psychological factors is called a *functional psychosis*. The possible causes of functional psychosis are explored later in this chapter.

Organic Psychosis One example of organic psychosis is *general paresis*. General paresis occurs in a small number of cases of untreated syphilis. In advanced stages syphilis attacks brain cells and gradually brings about a deterioration in behavior. Most characteristic of general paresis is a loss of inhibition leading to shocking profanity and obscenity—the "dirty old man" syndrome.

A second source of organic psychosis that gives special cause for alarm is lead and mercury poisoning. Although relatively rare, such poisoning is entirely capable of damaging the brain and causing hallucinations, delusions, and a loss of emotional control. A particularly dangerous situation is found in many old houses and apartment buildings, since many are painted with old-style leaded paints. Children who eat this paint may become psychotic or retarded.

Senile psychosis is probably the most common of organic problems. Premature deterioriation of the brain caused by hardening of the arteries and other changes that accompany aging may bring about a loss of mental abilities. The individual suffering from a senile psychosis is usually confused, suspicious, and suffers a major loss of memory.

The three major types of functional psychosis are *paranoia*, *affective psychosis*, and *schizophrenia*. Information on each of these is provided on the following pages.

Paranoid Psychosis—An Enemy Behind Every Tree

Paranoia is an extremely rare form of psychosis. The true paranoid does not suffer from hallucinations, emotional excesses, or personality disintegration. The major characteristic of a paranoid is delusions of grandeur or persecution. Many self-styled reformers, absurdly jealous husbands or wives, crank letter writers, "Communist hunters," and the like, are paranoids.

The most frequent paranoid delusions center on feelings of persecution. The individual believes that someone or some group of people is plotting against him. The paranoid is usually intensely suspicious, believing that he must be on guard at all times against those who would mistreat him. The evidence a paranoid finds to support his beliefs is usually very unconvincing to others. Every detail of the paranoid's existence is woven into his version of "what's really going on." Buzzing during a telephone conversation may be interpreted as "someone listening," a stranger who comes to the door asking for directions may be seen as "really trying to get information," and so forth.

Paranoids are rarely treated or admitted to mental hospitals. This is because it is almost impossible to suggest to a paranoid that he needs help. A friend, relative, or psychologist who does so simply becomes part of the "conspiracy" to "persecute" him. Paranoids frequently lead lonely, isolated, and humorless lives marked by constant suspicion and hostility toward others. Paranoids are not necessarily dangerous to others, but they may be. A person who believes that "the Mafia" is slowly closing in on him may be moved to violence by his irrational fears. A person standing at the door with his hand in his coat pocket could become the target of a paranoid attempt at "self-defense."

Affective Psychosis—Peaks and Valleys

About 14 percent of patients admitted to mental hospitals suffer from affective reactions.

Question: How is an affective reaction different from other types of psychosis?

In addition to the usual disturbances of psychosis, affective reactions include persistent and excessive changes in mood or emotion. A person may be continuously loud, inappropriately elated, hyperactive, and energetic (*manic type*) or continuously sad and guilt-ridden (*depressive type*), or he may alternate between the two states (*manic-depressive* or *circular type*).

The manic individual throws himself into a whirlwind of activity characterized by extreme distractibility, rapid shifts in thoughts ("flight of ideas"), constant talking, and restless movement. In advanced stages, manic behavior becomes more and more incoherent, agitated, and out of control. Eating or sleeping may be ignored until the individual pushes himself into a state of total delirium. This brief excerpt from a case history illustrates manic behavior:

> Her husband had returned home to find her twirling around the living room bizarrely draped in her wedding gown tied with a bathtowel and wearing a lampshade. She gaily greeted him, laughed with an ear-piercing shrillness, and invited him to stay for the exciting "coming-out" party she was giving. Strewn on the table were a thousand handwritten invitations signed with a flourish and addressed to such dignitaries as the President of the United States, the justices of the Supreme Court, the Emperor of Japan. She made incessant noises: singing her own ballads, shouting mottoes, which she devised, reciting limericks, making rhyming sounds, and yelling obscenities (Suinn, 1970, p. 367).

Depressive reactions show a reverse pattern in which feelings of failure, sinfulness, worthlessness, and total despair predominate. The individual becomes extremely subdued and withdrawn and frequently becomes intensely suicidal. Depressive reactions pose one of the most serious threats to the survival of a disturbed individual since suicide attempted during a psychotic depression is rarely a "plea for help." The person intends to succeed and may give no prior warning. The excerpt below describes the condition of a woman admitted to a hospital in a psychotic depression.

> Her husband had brought her to the hospital because she had refused to eat for about three days, slept fitfully, and spent long hours staring off into space. She would speak to those around her, but only after more or less continuous coaxing. In very slow, monotonous speech she commented that she was talking to her dead sister who was wearing a white gown, but with a face eaten up by worms and with part of her eye socket missing. This hallucination was intermixed with some discussion between the patient and God that seemed to center around a mixture of pleading with Him to do something about the sister and reprimanding Him for letting her get into that condition (McMahon, 1976, p. 244).[2]

[2]From *Abnormal Behavior, Psychology's View*, F. B. McMahon. Copyright 1976. Reprinted by permission of Prentice-Hall, Inc., Englewood Cliffs, N.J.

Manic and depressive reactions are closely interrelated. When manic behavior occurs, it may still be considered a reaction to depression. The manic individual seeks to *escape* feelings of worthlessness and depression in an unending rush of activity.

Learning Check

1. A person who wrongly believes that his or her body is "rotting away" is suffering from:
   a. Depressive delusions
   b. Delusions of grandeur
   c. Somatic delusions
   d. Delusions of persecution
2. A person suffering from a psychosis is totally unresponsive to his or her surroundings. T or F?
3. A psychosis caused by lead poisoning would be termed a *functional* disorder. T or F?
4. Paranoia is the most common form of psychosis. T or F?
5. An affective psychosis is marked by a persistent lack of emotional response. T or F?

Answers: 1. c 2. F 3. F 4. F 5. F

Schizophrenia—Shattered Reality

Approximately half of all admissions to mental hospitals are diagnosed as *schizophrenic*. Schizophrenia is a major health problem: 1 person in 100 will become schizophrenic, and one-fourth of all hospital beds in the United States are occupied by schizophrenics. Most schizophrenics are young adults, but schizophrenia can occur at any age.

Question: Does a schizophrenic have two personalities?

"Schizophrenia" does not refer to having more than one personality. You will recall from the previous chapter that multiple personality is a dissociative reaction to neurosis. The word "schizophrenia" can be interpreted to mean "split-mind," but this refers to a split between thought and emotion. In schizophrenia, emotions may become blunted or "flat," or they may be very inappropriate. For example, a schizophrenic may smile or giggle when told his mother has died or may describe her death with no visible emotion. In addition, schizophrenia is characterized by: withdrawal from contact with others and a loss of interest in external activities; a breakdown of personal habits and ability to deal with daily events; and the delusions, hallucinations, and thought abnormalities that are found in other types of psychosis.

Question: Is there more than one type of schizophrenia?

Schizophrenia may ultimately turn out to be a whole series of related disturbances. For now, four major subtypes of schizophrenia can be identified.

Simple Schizophrenia Simple schizophrenia develops gradually, usually starting in adolescence. The individual becomes ever more withdrawn and isolated from his surroundings. He is usually seen as listless and apathetic by others and may be considered "odd," "shiftless," or "eccentric." Emotions are usually dulled, and the person seems to prefer to avoid contact and communication with others. Many simple schizophrenics go unnoticed and untreated and live out colorless and isolated lives on the fringes of society as vagrants, derelicts, or prostitutes.

Hebephrenic Schizophrenia Hebephrenic schizophrenia comes as close as any true psychiatric problem to matching the stereotyped portray-

Fig. 22-3 The hebephrenic schizophrenic's behavior is marked by silliness, laughter, bizarre, and often obscene behavior. (Photo by Benyas, Black Star.)

als of "insanity" found in movies and television. The hebephrenic's personality disintegration is almost complete. The result is silliness, laughter, and bizarre and often obscene behavior. The following excerpt is from the intake interview of a hebephrenic patient:

> *Dr.* I am Dr. ________. I would like to know something more about you.
> *Patient* You have a nasty mind. Lord!! Lord! Cat's in a cradle.
> *Dr.* Tell me, how do you feel?
> *Patient* London's bell is a long, long dock. Hee! Hee! (Giggles uncontrollably.)
> *Dr.* Do you know where you are now?
> *Patient* D______n! S______t on you all who rip into my internals! The grudgerometer will take care of you all! (Shouting) I am the Queen, see my magic, I shall turn you all into smidgelings forever!
> *Dr.* Your husband is concerned about you. Do you know his name?
> *Patient* (Stands, walks to and faces the wall) Who am I, who are we, who are you, who are they, (Turns) I . . . I . . . I . . .I!!! (Makes grotesque faces)
>
> Edna was placed in the women's ward where she proceeded to masturbate. She always sat in a chosen spot and in a chosen way, with her feet propped under her. Occasionally, she would scream or shout obscenities. At other times she giggled to herself. She was known to attack other patients. She began to complain that her uterus was attached to a "pipeline to the Kremlin" and that she was being "infernally invaded" by Communism (Suinn, 1975, pp. 449–450).

Catatonic Schizophrenia The catatonic seems to be in a state of total panic. This brings about a stuporous condition in which odd positions may be held for hours or even days. Sometimes a condition called "waxy flexibility" occurs. In this, the person can be arranged into any position like a mannequin. These periods of immobility may be similar to the tendency to "freeze" at times of great emergency or panic. There is evidence that the person is struggling desperately to control his inner turmoil because stupor may occasionally give way to outbursts of agitated and sometimes violent behavior. The following excerpt describes a catatonic episode:

> Manuel appeared to be physically healthy upon examination. Yet he did not regain his awareness of his surroundings. He remained motionless, speechless, and seemingly unconscious. One evening an aide turned him on his side to straighten out the sheet, was called away to tend another patient, and forgot to return. Manuel was found the next morning, still on his side, his arm tucked under his body, as he had been left the night before. His arm was turning blue from lack of circulation but he seemed to be experiencing no discomfort. Further examination confirmed that he was in a state of waxy flexibility (Suinn, 1975, p. 450).

Paranoid Schizophrenia Paranoid schizophrenia is the most common form of schizophrenic disorder. Paranoid schizophrenia, like paranoia, centers around delusions of grandeur and persecution, but in paranoid

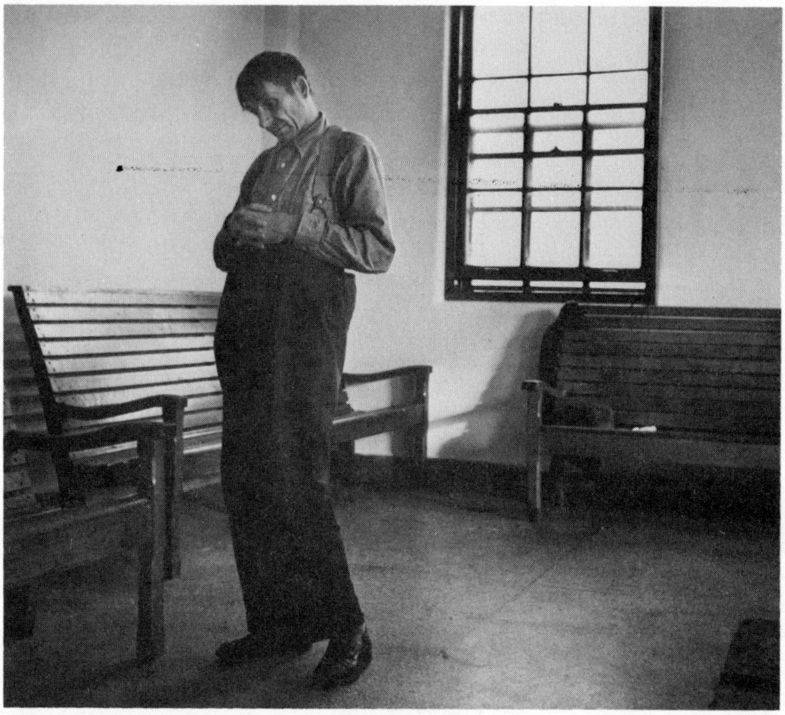

Fig. 22-4 Can the catatonic's rigid postures and stupor be understood in terms of abnormal body chemistry? (Photo by Jerry Cooke.)

schizophrenia there is a major personality disintegration not evident in paranoia. The paranoid schizophrenic also experiences hallucinations and has delusions that are more fragmented and unconvincing than those of the paranoid. Thinking that his mind is being controlled by the government or "cosmic rays from space" or that someone is trying to poison him, the paranoid schizophrenic may feel forced into violence to protect himself. Sirhan Sirhan, the assassin of Senator Robert F. Kennedy was a paranoid schizophrenic who was preoccupied with the delusion that he was the "savior of his people."

The four "types" of schizophrenia described occur most often in textbooks. In reality there is considerable overlap among the types, and a real patient may shift from one pattern of behavior to another at different times during the course of the psychosis.

The Causes of Schizophrenia—An Unsolved Riddle

Question: What causes schizophrenia?

Environment In the search for the causes of schizophrenia many psychologists have looked for unusual stresses in the schizophrenic's childhood. One intriguing theory is that the schizophrenic is *forced* to escape into psychosis by being placed in what British psychiatrist R. D. Laing calls a *position of checkmate* (1967, 1970). This idea can be illustrated by imagining that someone is standing over you with a large stick. This person gives you these instructions:

> In a moment I'm going to ask you if this stick is real. If you say "yes" I will hit you with it. If you say "no" then I will hit you with it. If you refuse to answer I will hit you with it.

Your reaction to this might very well be stammering, emotion, and a defensive crouch. To a person outside this situation your reactions might look "crazy." Similarly, Laing feels that the schizophrenic's strange thoughts and behavior are really an adaptation to an impossible environment. Laing and others also believe the families of schizophrenics constantly engage in *double-bind communication*. A double-bind message is one that places the listener in an unsolvable conflict like that posed above. For example, the mother of a schizophrenic might issue this typical double-bind message, "You don't really love me; you're only pretending you do." This statement asks for a show of love but makes showing love impossible. Anything the person does becomes "wrong."

Gregory Bateson provides another classic double-bind example.

> A young man who had fairly well recovered from an acute schizophrenic episode was visited in the hospital by his mother. He was glad to see her and impulsively put his arm around her shoulders whereupon she stiffened. He withdrew his arm and she asked, "Don't you love me anymore?" He then blushed and she said, "Dear, you must not be so easily embarrassed and afraid of your feelings." The patient was able to stay with her only a few minutes more and following her departure he assaulted an aide and was put in the tubs (Bateson *et al.*, 1956, pp. 258–259).

Although they are attractive, environmental explanations such as these are not enough to account for schizophrenia. This can be seen by comparing children raised in foster homes (with normal parents) to children raised by schizophrenic mothers. When the children of schizophrenic parents are raised away from their chaotic home environment, they are just as likely to become psychotic as before (Page, 1971).

Question: Does that mean that heredity is a factor in schizophrenia?

Heredity It is always difficult to separate the effects of heredity from the effects of environment. But studies with twins show that some individuals may inherit a *potential* for schizophrenia. For example, if one *identical* twin becomes schizophrenic (identical twins have identical heredity), then the other has a 50 percent chance of also becoming schizophrenic. When *fraternal* twins of the same sex are compared, the chances of mutual schizophrenia drop to about 12 percent (Gottesman & Shields, 1972). Other studies have shown that schizophrenia is more common among close relatives than distant relatives, and it tends to run in families (Reiss, 1974).

Question: How could someone inherit a susceptibility to schizophrenia?

Body Chemistry Drugs like LSD produce changes that partially mimic the symptoms of psychosis. Another connection between drugs and psychosis can be seen in the effects of large doses of amphetamines (speed), which produce a reaction that is almost identical to paranoid schizophrenia. Also, the same drugs (phenothiazines) that are effective in treating an amphetamine psychosis or an LSD overdose are effective in the treatment of schizophrenia (Mandell *et al.*, 1972). These similarities have suggested to many scientists that psychosis may be based on *biochemical abnormalities* which cause the body to produce some substance similar to a *psychedelic* (mind-altering) drug.

In the search for a biochemical basis for schizophrenia, almost every imaginable body fluid (blood, urine, saliva, etc.) of schizophrenic patients has been analyzed. A number of investigations have turned up promising leads. For example, some studies have focused on *adrenochrome*. Adrenochrome is a by-product of adrenaline. It is normally neutralized by the body but may accumulate in the body of a schizophrenic. Adrenochrome has a chemical structure similar to that of the drug *mescaline* (also a psychedelic). Volunteers who have taken adrenochrome experience sensory distortions like those of psychosis.

The implication of this research is that schizophrenics may be on a permanent drug trip caused by their own body chemistry (Hoffer, 1972). This line of thought has particular appeal since adrenaline is secreted by the body at times of stress. But it must be noted that this and related studies are still inconclusive since many chemical differences in schizophrenics can be traced to factors as simple as differences in diet or exercise.

In summary, the picture of psychosis that is emerging takes this general form: *Anyone* subjected to enough stress may be pushed to a psychosis, but some people inherit a difference in bodily chemistry that makes them more susceptible. The right combination of inherited potential and environmental stress then brings about important changes in basic brain chemicals or generates mind-altering substances in the body (McMahon, 1976).

Ultimately, distinctions between organic and functional psychosis may be dropped, and treatment for major disturbances may become more chemical than psychological, but, for now, psychosis remains an unsolved riddle and a tremendous challenge to scientific investigators.

Learning Check

Try to match the following:

____ **1.** Simple schizophrenia	**A.** Odd postures, immobility
____ **2.** Hebephrenic schizophrenia	**B.** Silliness, bizarre behavior

____	**3.**	Catatonic schizophrenia	**C.**	Conflicting message
____	**4.**	Paranoid schizophrenia	**D.**	Partially mimics psychosis
____	**5.**	Double bind	**E.**	Delusions of grandeur or persecution
____	**6.**	LSD	**F.**	Withdrawal, isolation

Answers: 1. F 2. B 3. A 4. E 5. C 6. D

Treatment—Medical Approaches to Psychiatric Disorders

Question: *Is mental illness incurable? If a person's symptoms temporarily disappear can an unexpected relapse occur?*

An organic psychosis cannot be "cured" in the usual sense, but it may be controlled with drugs and other techniques. Functional psychoses are often *permanently* cured. It is wrong to fear a "former mental patient" or to exclude him or her from work, friendships, or other social situations. A psychotic episode does not inevitably lead to a lifelong maladjustment, but it too often leads to unnecessary rejection based on the groundless fears of others.

Question: *What can be done about psychosis?*

Two basic forms of treatment can be distinguished. The first, called *psychotherapy*, can be described as two people talking about one person's problems. Psychotherapy is a special relationship between a counselor or psychologist and a person in trouble. Psychotherapy is applied to everything from a brief crisis to a neurosis or full-scale psychosis. Because approaches currently in use are so varied, a complete discussion of psychotherapy is found in the next two chapters.

A second major approach to treatment is *somatic* (bodily) *therapy*. The principal somatic treatments are *chemotherapy*, *electroshock therapy*, and *psychosurgery*. All these approaches have a distinct medical slant and are used primarily for the treatment of psychosis. Somatic therapy is usually carried out in the context of psychiatric *hospitalization*.

Drugs The atmosphere in mental hospitals changed radically in the mid-1950s with the widespread adoption of chemotherapy (key-moe-therapy). Chemotherapy is the use of drugs to control or alleviate the symptoms of emotional disturbance. Drugs are not very effective for treatment of neurosis. Most chemotherapy is used to combat psychosis. The three major classes of drugs used are *tranquilizers*, *antipsychotics*, and *energizers*. Tranquilizers calm agitated persons, energizers improve the mood of those who are depressed, and antipsychotics control hallucinations and other symptoms of psychosis.

Question: Are drugs a valid approach to treatment?

Drugs have greatly improved the chances for recovery from a psychiatric disorder. They have shortened the length of hospital stays and have made it possible for more individuals to be returned to the community where they may be treated on an "out-patient" basis.

Few experts would argue for a return to the conditions which existed before chemotherapy became available. But there are some drawbacks. First of all, drugs generally do not *cure* mental illness—they only temporarily relieve symptoms. Such relief may allow patients to benefit more fully from psychotherapy and other attempts to help them, but drugs alone do not remove underlying problems. As a matter of fact, patients may separate temporary improvement caused by a drug from improvement they consider genuine. As one patient told the author, "The drugs made me talk more and seem happy, but I knew I really wasn't."

The extensive use of drugs also raises the issue of balancing benefits against possible adverse side effects. Side effects can range from dry mouth, constipation, and confusion to a major deterioration of behavior or physical health.

Perhaps the most valid criticism of chemotherapy is the simple observation that it is overused. Apparently the temptation to reach for the prescription pad is great. Most observers agree that too many drugs are being given to too many people. Researcher David Rosenhan (see the applications section of this chapter) feels that drugs are no longer being given at therapeutic levels; rather, they are being used to keep patients docile and easy to manage. Many critics feel that the locks that came off the doors of old-style institutions have simply been replaced by "chemical locks." In the long run, concern over side effects and the overuse of drugs may temper the popularity of chemotherapy. But where psychosis is concerned, drugs are usually helpful and will remain a major mode of treatment for some time to come.

Shock Electroshock therapy (EST) is a rather drastic medical treatment for depression. In the usual EST session about 150 volts of electrical current is passed through the brain for slightly less than a second. This induces a convulsion and causes the patient to lose consciousness for a short time. Muscle relaxants and sedative drugs are given before EST to soften its impact. Treatments are administered in a series of 8 to 12 sessions spread over 3 to 4 weeks. There is some loss of memory for the period of the treatments, but memory usually returns within six months.

Question: How does shock help?

Actually, it is the convulsion brought on by the shock that is helpful. It is not known why EST works, but it does seem to help many depressed persons. Over 80 percent of cases of severe depression treated with EST show dramatic improvement (Thomas, 1954).

Since drugs can also be used to control depression, chemotherapy has partially replaced EST, but EST may be useful in treating a severely

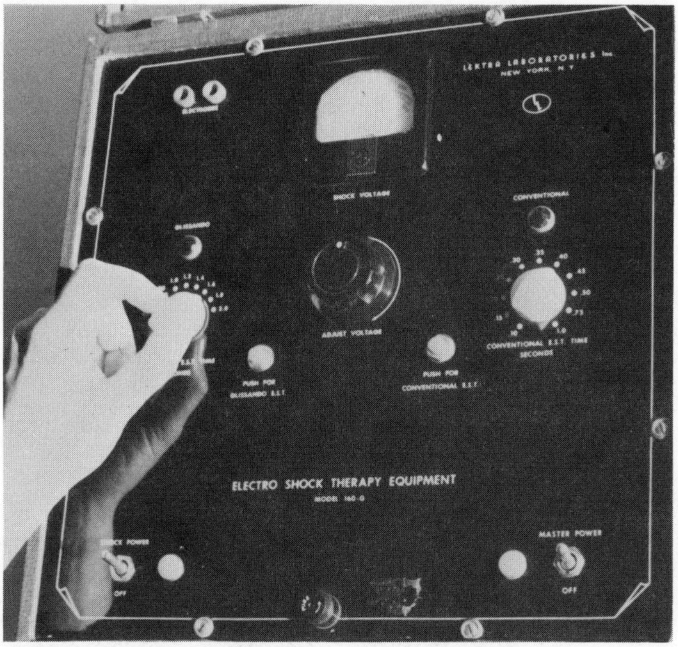

Fig. 22-5 A device used to administer EST as a means of treating severe depression.

suicidal patient or a person for whom drugs prove ineffective. Many people consider EST a distasteful procedure, and not all professionals support its use. As was the case with chemotherapy, the major problem with EST seems to be dangers of overuse and side effects. Some patients have had literally hundreds of shock treatments and have suffered ill effects in the process. In spite of these abuses, EST, when carefully used, may bring an end to wildly self-destructive behavior.

Surgery The most extreme biological treatment is *psychosurgery*, a general term applied to any surgical alteration of the brain. The best known psychosurgery is the *prefrontal lobotomy*. In the prefrontal lobotomy and related techniques, the frontal lobes are surgically disconnected from other areas of the brain. The original goal of this procedure was to calm a person who had not responded to any other type of treatment.

When the lobotomy was first introduced, there were enthusiastic claims for its success. But later studies suggest that the effects of psychosurgery are quite unpredictable. Some patients were calmed, some showed no noticeable change, and some became "vegetables." Psychosurgery also produces a high rate of undesirable side effects such as seizures, extreme lack of emotional response, and even stupor (Barahal, 1958). As if this were not enough, psychosurgery is also *irreversible*. Damage to the brain is permanent. This is one of the reasons that the use of chemotherapy has sharply limited use of psychosurgery. A drug can be given or taken away. You can't take back a lobotomy.

Hospitalization Somatic therapy, psychotherapy, and other techniques may require a special setting or special control for a period of time. Traditionally this has meant a trip to a psychiatric hospital or state institution. Hospitalization by itself may be considered a form of treatment since it removes a troubled individual from situations that may be provoking or maintaining the problem.

At its best, the hospital is a controlled environment in which diagnosis, support, refuge, and psychotherapy are provided. At worst, an institution can be a brutalizing experience that leaves a person less prepared to face the world than before.

New trends are rapidly improving the odds that hospitalization will be a positive experience. Hospital stays are now held to a minimum through use of "revolving-door" policies in which a patient is released as soon as possible and readmitted only if necessary. Also, provision in hospitals for

Fig. 22-6 Depending on the quality of the institution, hospitalization may be a refuge or a brutalizing experience. Many state "asylums" or mental hospitals are antiquated and in need of drastic improvement. (Photo by Jeff Albertson, Stock, Boston.)

recreation and rehabilitation is helping to end an old problem, that of the patient who becomes secure in the institution and fears a return to the community. Also useful are "halfway houses" and voluntary support groups which help the person make a successful return to the community.

Community Mental Health Programs—Hope and Help for Many

A bright spot in the area of mental health care has been the passage of federal legislation to encourage creation of community mental health centers. Community mental health centers attempt to shift emphasis away from institutionalization and hospitalization and seek new answers to mental health problems by providing short-term hospitalization, outpatient care, and special crisis or emergency services (Perlmutter & Silverman, 1972).

The most distinctive feature of community mental health centers is an emphasis on *prevention*. Consultation, education, and crisis intervention are used to end or prevent problems before they become serious. There have also been attempts to raise the general level of mental health in target areas by combating problems like unemployment, delinquency, and drug abuse.

Community mental health centers have made mental health services more accessible than ever before. Much of their work is made possible by *paraprofessionals*, individuals who work under the supervision of more highly trained staff. Some paraprofessionals are ex-addicts, ex-alcoholics, or ex-patients who have "been there." Many more are persons (paid or volunteer) who have skills in tutoring, crafts, counseling, or are simply warm, empathetic, and skilled at communication. There is a severe shortage of people working in mental health care. The contributions of paraprofessionals will undoubtedly continue to grow. A possible career as a paraprofessional should not be overlooked by the student planning to work in the field of mental health.

Learning Check

1. The use of chemotherapy has required longer hospital stays than before since drugs can only be given in a hospital. T or F?

2. Electroshock therapy is a modern form of psychotherapy. T or F?

3. EST is mainly used as a treatment for depression. T or F?

4. Psychosurgery can be reversed if it is unsuccessful. T or F?

5. The community mental health movement emphasizes prevention of mental health problems. T or F?

Answers: 1. F 2. F 3. T 4. F 5. T

Resources Summary

Psychosis is a break in contact with reality marked by *delusions*, *hallucinations*, *sensory changes*, and *emotional disturbances*. These changes, as well as other problems in thought, speech, memory, and attention, tend to be most prominent during short *episodes* of increased disturbance. An *organic* psychosis is based on known injuries or diseases of the brain. Other problems of unknown origin are termed *functional* psychosis. Three common causes of organic psychosis are untreated syphilis, poisoning, and senility.

Paranoia, *affective psychosis*, and *schizophrenia* are the three major functional disorders. A diagnosis of paranoia is almost totally based on delusions of grandeur or persecution and rarely involves personality disintegration. Affective psychosis involves extremes of mood, particularly elation (*manic type*), depression (*depressive type*), or an alternation between the two (*manic-depressive* or *circular type*).

Schizophrenia is the most frequently occurring psychosis. It is distinguished by a split between thought and emotion. Four major subtypes have been identified: *Simple schizophrenia* involves gradual withdrawal into almost total insulation from others; *hebephrenic schizophrenia* shows extreme personality disintegration and silly, bizarre, or obscene behavior; *catatonic schizophrenia* is marked by stupor and odd postures; and *paranoid schizophrenia* is characterized by outlandish delusions of grandeur and persecution coupled with personality breakdown. Explanations of schizophrenia emphasize a combination of *environmental stress*, *inherited susceptibility*, and *biochemical changes* in the body.

Three medical approaches to treatment of psychosis are *chemotherapy* (use of drugs), *electroconvulsive shock* (used mainly to treat depression), and *psychosurgery*. *Hospitalization* may also be considered a form of treatment. A new development in mental health care that seeks to avoid or minimize hospitalization is the creation of *community mental health centers*. Community mental health centers also have as their goal the *prevention* of mental health problems through education, consultation, and crisis intervention.

Applications

"On Being Sane in Insane Places"

Question: If people were committed to a psychiatric hospital by accident, would they be able to convince the staff to let them out?

David Rosenhan of Stanford University set out to answer this and the related question: "How accurately do psychiatric hospitals distinguish between people who are psychotic and those who are healthy?" To find out, Rosenhan and several colleagues had themselves committed (Rosenhan, 1973). Entrance to mental hospitals was gained by faking only one symptom. Rosenhan and the others complained of hearing voices which said "empty," "hollow," and "thud." In 11 out of 12 tries, they were admitted with a diagnosis of "schizophrenia."

After being admitted, these "pseudo-patients" dropped all pretense of mental illness. Yet, even though they acted completely normal, none of the researchers was ever recognized by hospital *staff* as a phony patient. Other patients were not so easily fooled. It was not unusual for a real patient to say to one of the researchers, "You're not crazy, you're checking up on the hospital!" or "You're a journalist."

Rosenhan and the others spent from one to seven weeks in hospitals before being discharged. The hospitals ranged from very modern and plush to ancient and shoddy. No matter how good the facilities or how good the hospital's reputation, Rosenhan found some very disturbing conditions.

Contact between staff and patients was very limited and sometimes marked by fear or hostility. It was found that attendants and staff only spent an average of 11.3 percent of their time out of the "cage," the glassed-in central compartment in the ward.

It was not unusual for the morning attendants to wake patients with a hostile call of: "Come on, you m _ _ _ _ _f _ _ _ _ _ _ s, out of bed!" When patients tried to talk with staff, they were often ignored or received strange replies. One pseudo-patient approached a psychiatrist and politely asked when he might get grounds privileges. The doctor's reply was, "Good morning, Dave. How are you today?"

Rosenhan found that therapy other than drugs was very limited. Daily contact of patients with psychiatrists, psychologists, or physicians averaged about *seven minutes*. On the other hand, the researchers were given a total of 2,100 pills to swallow. (Only two of these were actually taken, the rest being pocketed or flushed down the toilet.)

Patients tended to be treated as nonpersons. A nurse unbuttoned her uniform to adjust her bra in front of a room full of male patients. She was not being sexy; she just didn't consider the patients men. A patient would often be discussed by the staff while he was standing nearby. It was as if he were invisible.

A situation that sums up Rosenhan's findings better than any other is his note-taking. Rosenhan began taking notes by carefully jotting things on a small piece of paper hidden in his hand. He learned quickly that hiding was totally unnecessary. He was soon walking around with a clip-board and note pads, recording observations and collecting data. No one questioned this behavior. Note-taking was simply seen as a symptom of his "illness." As a matter of fact, Rosenhan found that anything he did was ignored. When a staff member manhandled a patient (as happened occasionally) Rosenhan would be right there—taking notes on the whole incident!

These observations clarify the failure of staff members to detect the fake patients. Because they were seen in the *context* of a mental ward and because they had been *labeled* schizophrenic, *anything* the pseudo-patients did was seen as a symptom of their "illness." To return to the original hypothetical question about talking your way out of an accidental commitment, it should be clear that it could be quite futile to say: "Look, this is all a mistake. I'm not crazy. You've got to let me out." The response might very well be: "Have you had these paranoid delusions for long?"

Many mental health professionals found Rosenhan's findings hard to believe. This led to a follow-up study in which the staff of another hospital was warned that one or more pseudo-patients were going to try to gain admission over the next three months. Thus alerted, the staff at this hospital tried to identify fake incoming patients. Among 193 candidates, 41 were labeled fakes by at least one staff member, and 19 more were labeled "suspicious." This only served to confirm Rosenhan's original findings since he never sent *any* patients—fake or otherwise—to this hospital!

It is an important final note that all of the normal people who served as pseudo-patients in the original studies were discharged as schizophrenics "in remission" (temporarily free of symptoms). In other words, the label that prevented hospital staff from seeing the normality of the researchers stayed with them when they left. Psychiatrist Karl Menninger (1964) has commented on a similar situation,

> A label can blight the life of a person even after his recovery from mental illness. A young doctor I knew suffered for a time from some anxiety and indecision. He consulted a psychiatrist and soon recovered. Unfortunately, a "tentative" diagnosis of schizophrenia got abroad—I don't know how—and the young doctor's professional career was seriously impaired. He was injured, not by mental illness but by a word.

Observations such as these are not a total condemnation of psychiatric hospitals. Many of the conditions Rosenhan encountered will be found in *any* hospital or other large institution. But Rosenhan's findings do carry an important message for professionals and nonprofessionals alike: *Labels can be dangerous*. As Stoller (1967, pp. 29–30) has said,

> When a person is labeled—neurotic, psychotic, executive, teacher, salesman, psychologist—either by himself or by others, he restricts his behavior to the role and even may rely upon the role for security. This diminishes the kind of experiences he is likely to have. Indeed, it is those groups whose members have shared labels—be it schizophrenic or executive—which are hardest to help move into intimate contact.

The terms reviewed in this and the previous chapter can, and do, aid communication about human problems. But if used carelessly, they may do great damage. Everyone has felt or acted "crazy" during brief periods of stress or high emotion. The person whose adjustment problems extend over a longer period of time is different from you or me only in the severity of his difficulty. It is therefore more productive to label problems than to label people. Think of the difference in impact between saying, "He is experiencing a serious emotional disturbance" and saying, "He is *a psychotic*." Which statement would you choose to have said about yourself?

It is also important to realize that a severely disturbed person will appreciate being treated normally. Rosenhan's research makes it clear that the person is not helped by being thrust into the role of a "patient." One former patient's comments clarify this last point:

> After I got back from the hospital, my friends tried to *act* like nothing had changed. But I could tell they weren't being honest. For instance, a friend invited me to dinner and everything went fine until I dropped my fork. Both my friend and his wife jumped up and stared at me like they thought I might explode. I was quite embarrassed.

For Discussion

Who Is "Crazy" and What Should Be Done about It?

Two well-known critics of traditional psychiatric treatment for "mental illness" are Thomas Szasz and Ronald D. Laing. Szasz (1966) believes that mental illness is a myth. Szasz charges that traditional medical concepts of disease have been wrongly applied to emotional problems. The "medical model," as this is called, treats such problems as "diseases" with "symptoms" that can be "cured." Szasz and a number of other experts prefer to view emotional disturbances as "problems in living." This view makes the goal of therapy "change" rather than "cure" and changes a "patient" to a "client."

Szasz has also questioned handling of the civil rights of psychiatric "patients." Szasz estimates there are 750,000 persons in mental hospitals, 90 percent of them involuntarily. He sees this as a serious mistake. To commit a person because he "might be dangerous to himself" is indefensible by Szasz's standards. The only legitimate reason for depriving a person of freedom is for being "dangerous to others," but then only if the person has broken the law by committing violence or by threatening to do so. Szasz considers the disturbed no more dangerous than a randomly selected group of citizens. He therefore rejects involuntary commitment as "punishment without trial, imprisonment without limit, and stigmatization without hope of redress" (1969, p. 57).

Szasz's position seems to be that a person has the right to be as "crazy" as he wants as long as he hurts no one else or doesn't break existing laws. Psychiatrist R. D. Laing takes a more extreme position. Laing believes that our world has become so "mad" that anyone adjusted to it is in serious trouble. He claims:

> The experience and behavior that are labeled schizophrenia are a special sort of strategy that a person invents in order to live in an unliveable world (1967, p. 56).[3]

Based on his respect for those who are unable or unwilling to "play the game" anymore, Laing set up an "anti-hospital" in London called Kingsley Hall. In Kingsley Hall no distinctions were made between patients and staff. Kingsley Hall was run as a self-governing communal arrangement without white coats and "chemical straitjackets." In Kingsley Hall "psychotics" were encouraged to explore the limits of their break from reality as a means of establishing a more honest relationship with the world. In this regard Laing has said:

> Madness need not be all breakdown. It may also be breakthrough. It is potentially liberation and renewal as well as enslavement and existential death.

It is undoubtedly a mistake to assume that the findings of David Rosenhan and the visions of people like Szasz and Laing justify abandon-

[3]From *The Politics of Experience*, R. D. Laing. Copyright © 1967 by R. D. Laing. Reprinted by permission of Penguin Books Ltd.

ing the tremendous advances in mental health care represented by current approaches. These people do, however, raise serious questions about the future. In an area as complex as treatment of major emotional disturbances, there is much room for improvement and innovation.

Questions for Discussion

1. What positive and negative roles do mental institutions play in society?
2. Is Szasz justified in his appraisal of mental institutions as simply prisons by another name?
3. Do you think Szasz and Laing are unrealistically romantic in their approach to mental illness, or are they the wave of the future?
4. Under what circumstances would you consider it reasonable for a stranger to be involuntarily committed? A friend? A close relative? Yourself?
5. In your opinion how could a person experiencing a severe "problem in living" be most effectively helped?
6. Should a mental patient have the right to:
   a. refuse medication
   b. demand legal counsel and alternative medical opinions
   c. refuse to work in a mental hospital or to choose the work that will be done
   d. communicate by phone, letter, or in person with anyone at any time
   e. keep personal property (including drugs, matches, pocketknives, and other potentially harmful materials)
   f. request an alternative to legal commitment to a mental hospital
7. In view of what you now know about the causes of psychosis, how valid do you consider the "medical model" of mental illness? What are the advantages and disadvantages of such a model? What are the advantages and disadvantages of a "psychological model"?

Suggestions for Further Reading

Braginsky, B. M., D. Braginsky, and K. Ring. *Methods of Madness: The Mental Hospital as a Last Resort.* Holt, 1969.

Coleman, J. C. *Abnormal Psychology and Modern Life.* Scott, Foresman, 1972.

Goffman, E. *Asylums.* Doubleday, 1961.

Grant, V. *This Is Mental Illness: How It Feels and What It Means.* Beacon, 1963.

Green, H. *I Never Promised You a Rose Garden.* New American Library, 1971.

Kesey, K. *One Flew Over the Cuckoo's Nest.* Viking, 1964.

Kleinmuntz, B. *Essentials of Abnormal Psychology.* Harper & Row, 1974.

Laing, R. D. *The Politics of Experience.* Ballantine, 1964.

Laing, R. D. *The Politics of the Family and Other Essays.* Pantheon, 1971.

Szasz, T. *The Myth of Mental Illness.* Delta, 1967.

Szasz, T. *The Manufacture of Madness.* Harper & Row, 1970.

23 Insight Therapy

Chapter Preview

Quiet Terror on a Spring Afternoon

The warm California sun shone brightly. A light breeze danced inland from the ocean. Outside my office window an assortment of small birds sang to a beautiful spring day. I could hear them between Susan's frightened sobs.

As a psychologist I see many students with personal problems. Still, I was somewhat surprised to see Susan standing at my office door. Her excellent work in class and her healthy casual appearance left me unprepared for her first words. "I feel like I'm losing my mind," she said. "Can I talk to you?"

In the next hour Susan sketched the features of her own personal hell. Her calm exterior hid a world of overwhelming fear, anxiety, and depression. She had lost several part-time jobs because at each one she began to fear her co-workers and the customers so much that she could barely bring herself to speak to them. Her absenteeism and embarrassing interchanges with customers would gradually lead to her dismissal. At school she felt "different" and was sure that other students could tell she was "weird." Several disastrous romances had left her terrified of men. Lately she had become so depressed that she had begun to think frequently of suicide. At times she became so terrified for no apparent reason that her heart pounded wildly and she felt that she was about to lose control of herself completely.

Susan's visit to my office was an important turning point. Emotional conflicts had made her existence a living nightmare. At a time when she was becoming her own worst enemy, Susan had realized that she needed the help and support of another person to overcome her problems. In Susan's case that person was a talented psychologist to whom I referred her. Combining various forms of psychotherapy, the psychologist was able to help Susan come to grips with her emotions and return a healthy balance to her personality.

This chapter emphasizes psychological *techniques currently used to alleviate problems like Susan's.* Insight *therapies, as these are called, can be distinguished from a special alternative approach called* behavior modification. *Behavior modification is discussed in the next chapter.*

Resources

Humpty-Dumpty sat on a wall.
Humpty-Dumpty had a great fall.
All the King's horses and all the King's men
Couldn't put Humpty together again.

Psychotherapy—Restoring Psychological Health

In our age of stress, conflict, and anxiety, who will put you together again, and how will they do it? Actually, the odds are that you will *not* experience a life-impairing emotional problem like Susan's, but if you did, what kind of help is available? In most cases, the answer is some form of *psychotherapy*.

Question: What is psychotherapy?

Psychotherapy is any psychological technique designed to facilitate positive changes in a person's personality, behavior, or adjustment. The psychotherapist has many approaches to choose from: psychoanalysis, desensitization, primal therapy, Gestalt therapy, logotherapy, Rogerian therapy, reality therapy, transactional analysis, behavior modification—to name but a few. Due to a recent explosive growth in the number of therapies, some confusion may exist concerning the differences among various approaches. It may be helpful to recognize that psychological problems are very complex and that the best approach for a particular person or problem will not always be the same. Also, psychotherapies vary considerably in emphasis. *Insight* therapies foster a deeper understanding of the assumptions, beliefs, emotions, and conflicts underlying a problem. *Action* therapies focus on directly changing troublesome habits and behavior. In *directive* therapies, the therapist guides the client strongly—giving instructions, offering interpretations, posing solutions, and sometimes even making important decisions for the client. *Nondirective* approaches place responsibility for the course of therapy on the client. In these, it is up to the client to discover his or her own solutions. *Individual* therapies proceed on a one-to-one basis between client and therapist. In *group* therapy, individual problems are resolved by making use of the special characteristics of the group setting. You should realize that psychotherapy need not be undertaken only as a means of solving a deep psychological problem or an immediate crisis. Some therapies are designed to encourage personal growth and enrichment for people who are already functioning effectively.

Psychotherapy—Humble Beginnings

The history of treatment for psychological problems gives ample reason for appreciating the humanity of modern therapies. Archaeological findings dating to the Stone Age suggest that most primitive approaches were marked by fear and superstitious belief in demons, witchcraft, and magic. One of the more dramatic "cures" practiced by primitive "psychotherapists" was a process called *trephinning.* A hole was bored, chipped, or bashed into the skull of the patient, presumably to relieve pressure or release evil spirits. Actually, trephining may have simply been an excuse to kill people who were unusual since few of the patients appear to have survived.

During the Middle Ages, treatment for the mentally ill in Europe focused on demonology. Abnormal behavior was attributed to supernatural forces like possession by the devil or the curses of witches and wizards. As treatment, *exorcism* was used to drive out the evil. For the fortunate, exorcism was a religious ritual. More often, it took the form of physical torture to make the body an inhospitable place for the devil to reside.

The idea that the emotionally disturbed are "mentally ill" and that they should be treated compassionately emerged after 1793. This was the year Philippe Pinel changed the Bicêtre Asylum in Paris from a squalid "madhouse" into a mental hospital by personally unchaining the inmates. Although almost 200 years have passed since Pinel began humane treatment for the emotionally disturbed, the process of improving conditions in psychiatric hospitals and of changing public attitudes toward psychotherapy continues today. Increased acceptance of the value of psychotherapy is a positive sign, but public attitudes toward the disturbed still tend to be colored by suspicion and fear. Perhaps as more people take part in psychotherapy as a growth experience, it will become more widely understood.

Question: When was psychotherapy developed?

The first true psychotherapy was developed around the turn of the century by Sigmund Freud. As a physician in Vienna, Freud was intrigued by the cases of *hysteria* (physical symptoms like paralysis or numbness without known physical cause) he encountered. Slowly Freud became convinced that the symptoms of hysteria were only the tip of the iceberg, that deeply hidden unconscious conflicts (frequently sexual in nature) were to blame. Based on this insight, Freud went on to develop his own comprehensive form of therapy. Since *psychoanalysis*, as Freud called his technique, is the "granddaddy" of most modern psychotherapies, let us examine it in some detail.

Psychoanalysis—Expedition into the Unconscious

Question: Isn't psychoanalysis the therapy where the patient lies on a couch?

Freud's patients usually reclined on a couch during therapy while Freud sat out of sight taking notes and offering interpretations. This arrangement was selected to encourage relaxation and a free flow of thoughts and images from the unconscious. It is the least important of several

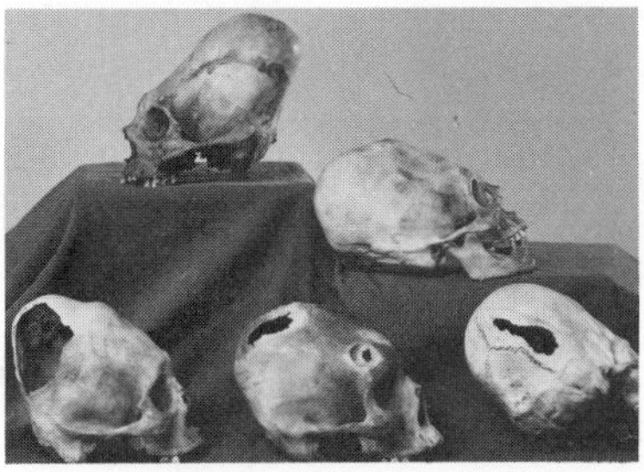

(a)

(b)

(c)

Fig. 23-1 Early approaches to the treatment of mental illness. *(a)* Primitive "treatment" for mental disorders sometimes took the form of boring a hole in the skull. *(b)* Many early asylums were no more than prisons with inmates held in chairs. *(c)* This late Nineteenth Century "treatment" was based on swinging the patient in a harness—presumably to calm the patient's nerves. (Photo *(a)* courtesy the University Museum, University of Pennsylvania; *(b)* courtesy the New York Public Library; *(c)* The Bettmann Archive.)

characteristics of psychoanalysis and has been abandoned by many modern analysts.

Question: How did Freud treat emotional problems?

Freud's theory stressed that repressed memories, motives, and conflicts—particularly those stemming from instinctual drives for sex and aggression—were the cause of neurosis. Although unconscious and repressed, these factors remain active in the personality, forcing the person to develop rigid ego-defense mechanisms and to devote excessive amounts of time and energy to compulsive and self-defeating behavior. Freud relied on four basic techniques to uncover the unconscious roots of neurosis (Freud, 1949).

1. *Free association.* During psychoanalysis, the patient must say whatever comes to mind without regard for whether it makes sense or is painful or embarrassing. Thoughts are allowed to move freely from one association to the next.
2. *Dream analysis.* The purpose of free association is to lower defenses so that unconscious material may emerge. Freud considered dreams an unusually good additional means of tapping the unconscious. Freud referred to dreams as "the royal road to the unconscious" because he felt that forbidden desires and unconscious feelings are more freely expressed in dreams. He distinguished between the *mani-*

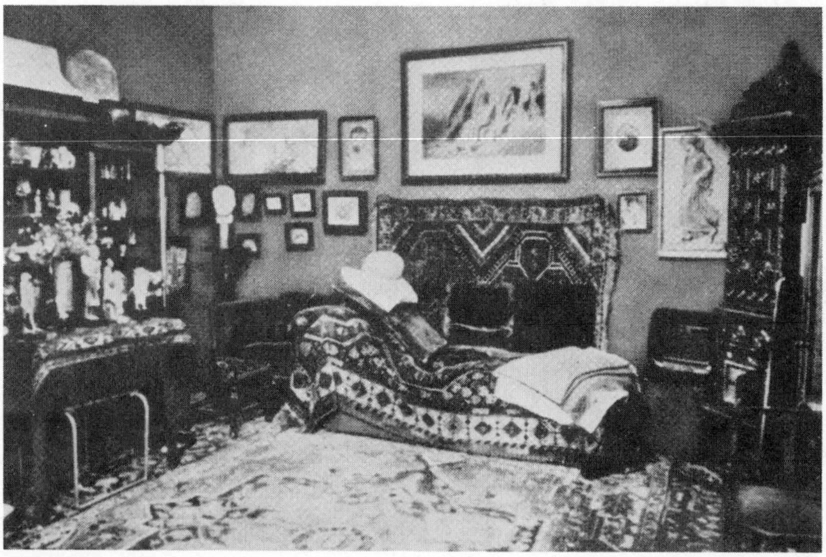

Fig. 23-2 The office of pioneering psychotherapist, Sigmund Freud. (Historical Picture Service.)

fest (obvious, visible) *content* and the *latent* (hidden) *content* of dreams. To appreciate fully the unconscious message of a dream, Freud sought to reveal its latent meaning by interpreting *dream symbols*. Let's say a young husband reports a dream in which he pulls a pistol from his waistband and aims at a target while his wife watches. The pistol repeatedly fails to discharge, and the man's wife laughs at him. Freud might see this as an indication of repressed feelings of sexual impotence, with the gun serving as a disguised image of the penis. (You may wish to refer back to Chapter 7 to review the discussion of Freudian dream interpretation there.)

3. *Analysis of resistance.* When free associating or describing dreams, the patient may *resist* talking or thinking about certain topics. Such resistances are said to reveal particularly important unconscious conflicts. As the analyst becomes aware of resistances, he brings them to the patient's awareness so they can be dealt with realistically.
4. *Analysis of transference.* The individual undergoing psychoanalysis may transfer feelings to the therapist that relate to important past relationships with others. At times the analyst may be reacted to as if he or she were a rejecting father, an unloving or overprotective mother, or a former lover. This is considered a prime opportunity to help the patient undergo an emotional reeducation. As the patient reexperiences repressed emotions, the therapist can help the patient recognize and understand them.

Question: Is psychoanalysis still used?

In its original form psychoanalysis requires three to five therapy sessions a week for up to seven years. Because of the huge amounts of time and money this requires, most psychodynamic therapists now substitute more direct interviewing for free association, and the length of therapy has been shortened considerably.

A more important question about psychoanalysis may be: "Does it work?" The development of newer more streamlined psychotherapies is in part due to questions about the effectiveness of psychoanalysis. One psychologist, H. J. Eysenck (1967), has gone so far as to suggest that psychoanalysis simply takes so long that there is a *spontaneous remission* of symptoms (improvement due to the mere passage of time). Eysenck's research indicates that the "cure rate" for psychoanalysis is no better than the rate of improvement without it. This viewpoint is fairly extreme. Undoubtedly many people have been helped by psychoanalysis. But to the modern therapist the questions remain: "When psychoanalysis works, why does it work? What procedures are essential and which are unnecessary?" Based on intuition, personal philosophy, clinical experience, and the personality theory they find most acceptable, modern psychotherapists have posed surprisingly varied answers to these questions. The sections which follow will help acquaint you with some of the therapies currently in use.

Learning Check

See if you can answer the following questions. If you miss any, review the previous sections.

Match

____**1.** Directive therapies	**A.** Change behavior
____**2.** Action therapies	**B.** Place responsibility on client
____**3.** Insight therapies	**C.** The client is guided strongly
____**4.** Nondirective therapies	**D.** Seek understanding

T or F?

____**5.** Pinel is famous for his use of exorcism.

____**6.** Freud developed trephining.

____**7.** A spontaneous remission of symptoms means that psychotherapy has succeeded.

Multiple choice

____**8.** In psychoanalysis, an emotional attachment to the therapist by the patient is called:

a. Free association
b. Resistance
c. Manifest association
d. Transference

Answers: **1.** C **2.** A **3.** D **4.** B **5.** F **6.** F **7.** F **8.** d

Humanistic Therapies—Restoring Human Potential

The goal of Freudian therapy is adjustment. The humanistic therapies outlined below are generally more optimistic. Most assume that it is possible for people to live rich and rewarding lives and to make full use of their potentials. Psychotherapy is seen as a means of giving natural tendencies toward mental health a chance to emerge.

Question: What is client-centered therapy? How is it different from psychoanalysis?

Client-centered Therapy The psychoanalyst delves into childhood, dreams, and the unconscious. Psychologist Carl Rogers has found it more

Fig. 23-3 Contemporary psychotherapist, Carl Rogers, originator of client-centered therapy. (Photo by Michael Rougier, Time-Life Picture Agency. © Time, Inc.)

productive to explore *conscious* thoughts and feelings. The psychoanalyst tends to take a position of authority from which he or she offers interpretations of what is "wrong" with the patient or of what dreams or childhood experiences "mean." Rogers believes that what is right or valuable for the therapist may not be right and valuable for the client. (Rogers prefers the term "client" to "patient.") Accordingly, client-centered therapy is *non-directive*. The client is the center of the process. He or she determines what will be discussed during each session.

Question: If the client runs things, what does the therapist do?

The therapist's job is to create an "atmosphere of growth" by maintaining four basic conditions. First, the therapist offers the client *unconditional positive regard*. In other words, the client is accepted *totally*. The therapist refuses to react with shock, dismay, or disapproval to anything the client says or feels. Total acceptance by the therapist is the first step to self-acceptance by the client. Second, the therapist attempts to achieve genuine *empathy* for the client by trying to see the world through the client's eyes and to feel some part of what he or she is feeling. As a third essential condition, the therapist strives to be *authentic* in his or her relationship with clients. The therapist must not hide behind his or her professional role. Rogers believes that phony fronts and facades destroy the growth atmosphere sought in client-centered therapy. Fourth, the therapist does not make interpretations, pose solutions, or offer advice. Instead, the therapist *reflects* the client's thoughts and feelings. By repeating or restating what the client has said or by telling the client what emotion he or she seems to be displaying, the therapist serves as a "psychological mirror" in which the patient learns to see himself more clearly and realistically. Rogers feels that a person armed with a realistic self-image and with a new level of self-acceptance will gradually discover solutions to life problems.

Rational Therapy According to Albert Ellis (1962, 1973), the basic idea of rational therapy is as easy as A-B-C. Ellis assumes that people become unhappy and develop self-defeating habits because of unrealistic or otherwise faulty beliefs.

Question: How are beliefs important?

Ellis analyzes the situation in this way: A stands for the *activating experience*, which the person assumes to be the cause of C, the emotional *consequence*. For instance, a person who is rejected (the activating experience) feels depressed, threatened, or hurt (the emotional consequence). Rational therapy shows the client that the true cause of difficulty is what comes between A and C. Between the activating experience and the emotional consequence stands B, the client's irrational and unrealistic *belief*. In this example, the unrealistic belief leading to unnecessary suffering is: "It is necessary that we be loved and approved by everyone at all times."

Question: Is rational therapy nondirective like client-centered therapy?

No. Rational therapists are very directive in their attempts to change a client's irrational beliefs and "self-talk." The therapist may directly attack clients' logic, challenge their thinking, confront them with evidence contrary to their beliefs, and may even assign "homework" for the clients.

Rational therapy has been criticized by some as superficial and argumentative, but Ellis' basic insight has considerable merit. Almost anyone can benefit from learning to recognize self-defeating beliefs. Here are three more *irrational assumptions* to look for in your own behavior: (1) One should be thoroughly competent, adequate, and achieving in all possible respects to be worthwhile; (2) it is awful and catastrophic when things are not the way one would like very much for them to be; and (3) one's past history has an all-important effect on present behavior; because something once strongly affected one's life, it will continue to do so indefinitely.

Existential Therapy Existential therapy focuses on problems of existence or "being in the world." Like client-centered therapy, its goals are self-knowledge and self-actualization.

Question: Then how are client-centered therapy and existential therapy different?

The major difference is one of emphasis. Client-centered therapy seeks discovery of the "true self" that has become hidden behind an artificial screen of defenses. By contrast, existential therapy emphasizes the idea of *free will*. That is, through *choices* one can *become* the person he or she wants to be. Existential therapist Rollo May has expressed deep concern about the loss of individual freedom, faith, and meaning in today's mass society. Existential therapy attempts to restore meaning and vitality to life so that the individual has the *courage* to accept the responsibility of making rewarding and socially constructive choices.

Question: What does an existential therapist do?

One example of existential therapy is Victor Frankl's *logotherapy* (Frankl, 1955). Frankl developed his approach on the basis of experiences in a Nazi concentration camp. In the camp Frankl observed the breakdown of countless prisoners as they were stripped of all hope and human dignity. Frankl felt that those who survived with their sanity did so because they had managed to hang on to a sense of *meaning* (logos). In some cases this was nothing more than the ultimate human freedom—the freedom to choose one's own attitude in any set of circumstances. Like most existential therapists, Frankl uses a very flexible approach centered around *confrontation*. The person is challenged to examine the quality of his or her existence and choices and to *encounter* the unique, intense here-and-now interaction of two human beings.

Learning Check See if you can answer the following questions.

Match

____**1.**	Client-centered therapy	**A.**	Meaning
____**2.**	Rational therapy	**B.**	Unconditional positive regard
____**3.**	Existential therapy	**C.**	Faulty beliefs
____**4.**	Logotherapy	**D.**	Choice and becoming

T or F?

____**5.** The rational therapist tries to *reflect* a client's thoughts and feelings.

____**6.** Client-centered therapy is *directive.*

____**7.** Confrontation and encounter are concepts of existential therapy.

Answers: 1. B 2. C 3. D 4. A 5. F 6. F 7. T

Group Therapy—Give Me Your Huddled Masses Yearning to Be Free

Question: Is group therapy just individual therapy with more than one person?

Most psychotherapies can be adapted for use in groups. Psychologists first tried working with groups as a practical response to the need for more therapists than were available. To their surprise, group therapy not only worked, it also offered some special advantages. In group therapy a person could *act out* or experience problems in addition to talking about them, and support was provided by other members who shared similar problems. Groups also helped form a bridge between therapy and real-life problems by providing a more realistic situation than the protected atmosphere of individual therapy. For reasons such as these, a number of specialized group techniques have emerged. Because they range from Alcoholics Anonymous to nude encounter, only a few representative approaches will be sampled here.

Psychodrama One of the first group approaches was developed by J. L. Moreno (1953) who called his technique psychodrama. In psychodrama an individual playacts roles and dramatic incidents resembling those that cause problems in real life. For example, a disturbed teenager might act out a typical family fight with the therapist playing his father, and other patients, his mother, brothers, and sisters. Moreno believes that insights and the emotional relearning from these enactments transfer to the real-life situations.

Gestalt Therapy The Gestalt therapy approach, which is most often associated with the late Frederick (Fritz) Perls (1969), is built around the idea that perception or awareness becomes disjointed and incomplete in the maladjusted individual.

Question: What does "Gestalt" mean?

The German word *Gestalt* means *whole* or complete. The Gestalt therapist seeks to help the individual rebuild thinking, feeling, and acting into connected wholes. Working in a group setting, the Gestalt therapist encourages the individual to become aware of his or her emotions by observing nonverbal cues like posture, voice, and eye or hand movements. To accomplish his goals, Fritz Perls used a collection of dramatic techniques with such flamboyant titles as "awareness training," "dream work," the "hot seat," and the "empty chair." In all these techniques and in his writings, Perls' one basic message comes through clearly: Emotional health comes from getting in touch with what you *want* to do, not what you *should* do, *ought* to do, or *should want* to do.

Encounter Groups and Sensitivity Training Abraham Maslow (1965) has observed that the humanistic movement in psychology has led people who are already effective in their behavior to display an interest in psychotherapy in the guise of sensitivity-training or encounter groups. Groups such as these were first developed in 1945 at the National Training Laboratories in Bethel, Maine. At first, they were called "T-groups" (training groups), but soon they took new forms and new names as they were adopted at Esalen and other "growth centers" around the country.

Question: What is the difference between sensitivity and encounter groups?

Sensitivity groups tend to be less confrontive than encounter groups. Participants take part in experiences that gently extend sensitivity to oneself and others. For example, the "trust walk," in which blindfolded participants are led about by "guides," is a typical exercise used to develop trust and confidence in others. Experiments in which group members try to communicate nonverbally with hands or eyes may be used to improve awareness of others. Body awareness may be explored through techniques like the "blind mill," in which participants close their eyes and walk about touching each other (in nonsexual ways). Techniques such as these foster personal growth without posing too great a threat to participants.

Fig. 23-4 A group therapy session. Sensitivity and encounter groups attempt to strip away superficialities and inhibitions. (Photo by Ken Heyman, Magnum.)

In encounter groups more intense emotion and communication may take place. An encounter group may meet only once or twice, many times, or in a *marathon* lasting eighteen hours or more (Stoller, 1972). In any case, the emphasis is on tearing down defenses and facades through discussion that can be brutally honest. Because of the danger of hostile confrontation or psychological damage, encounter-group members are carefully screened for freedom from severe emotional problems, and a trained leader or "facilitator" guides the group through difficult situations.

Question: Are sensitivity and encounter really psychotherapies?

Sensitivity and encounter groups can certainly be an exciting and valuable avenue for personal growth. They can also be a disaster if poorly run. Along with problems of poor leadership or group composition, there are additional dangers of disappointment and overreaction to group rejection. Also, the after-effects of rapid intimacy may pose a threat to existing relationships. Kurt Back (1972) may have summarized it best when he said: "Encounter groups may comfort, but they do not cure anything." A troubled individual should approach participation in an encounter group with some caution.

Transactional Analysis—Different Strokes for Different Folks

Transactional analysis (TA) is a rather unique approach to group therapy. In addition to helping a person change himself, TA seeks to change his transactions or interactions with others. Based on the assumption that

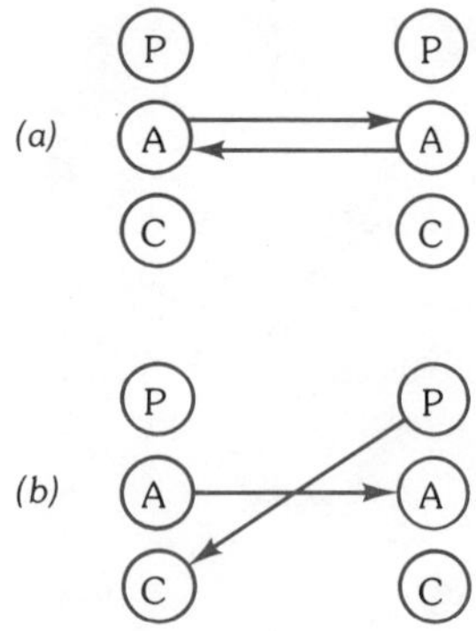

Fig. 23-5

one's problems reside in relationships with others, TA attempts to cure *relationships.*

Question: How can you cure relationships?

TA is based on a relatively simple personality scheme proposed by Eric Berne, (1961, 1964). Berne says the personality has three basic parts or *ego-states*. The *Child* is a carry-over from youth. The Child is primitive, impulsive, demanding, creative, and playful. The Child tends to say things like: "I want," "I need," "I won't," or, simply, "Wow." In addition to this perpetual child, Berne says we carry another product of our past in the form of the *Parent* ego-state. The Parent is an internal record of all the messages received from one's parents as personality developed. The Parent is very evaluative and restrictive. It is activated whenever you pass judgment on yourself or on another person. The Parent says: "You should," "You ought to," "Why didn't you," "That's good," "That's bad," and "Try harder." According to TA, people get into trouble when either the Parent or the Child controls the personality too much. People are therefore taught to place their *Adult* in command. The Adult is a mature and rational decision-making part of the personality. The Adult can bring about smooth personality functioning by nurturing and indulging the Child while resisting the excessive restrictions of the Parent.

Question: How does this analysis apply to interactions?

The P-A-C analysis can be extended to transactions between two people. A message can be sent from any of the ego-states in one person to any of the ego-states in the other. Trouble comes when *crossed* transactions occur (see Fig. 23-5). Diagram *(b)* represents a crossed transaction. For example, a man asks his wife, "Do you know where I left my glasses?" He has sent an Adult message to the wife's Adult ego-state. If she replies from the Adult [as in *(a)*] by saying: "No, I'm sorry, I don't" or "No, but let me help you look for them," then no crossing occurs. But if she replies: "Can't you take care of those things yourself?" or, even worse, "Who do you think I am, your mother?," then a crossed transaction has occurred. [She has replied Parent to Child as in (*b*).] Crossed transactions cause emotional flare-ups and misunderstandings, and they form the basis for a number of destructive psychological "games." As the individual in TA learns to recognize the Parent, Adult, and Child in himself and in others, destructive interactions can be avoided.

Learning Check

1. In psychodrama, people attempt to form meaningful wholes out of disjointed thoughts, feelings, and actions. T or F?
2. A T-group is a form of Gestalt therapy. T or F?
3. There are no dangers in participating in an encounter group. T or F?

4. The Adult is a mature and rational decision-making part of the personality. T or F?

5. Transactional analysis attempts to improve relationships by avoiding games and crossed transactions. T or F?

Answers: **1.** F. This is the goal of Gestalt therapy. **2.** F. "T-group" is another name for a sensitivity group. **3.** F **4.** T **5.** T

Psychotherapy—An Overview

Question: What do psychotherapies have in common?

The therapies we have sampled represent only a few of the approaches in use. One author, writing in 1959, counted at least 36 systems of psychotherapy (Harper, 1959). The examples cited were selected because they represent some of the basic variations in philosophy or technique and because they offer ideas that may be of immediate use to you. To understand more fully the basis for psychotherapy, let us briefly summarize what all techniques have in common.

All psychotherapies treated above include some combination of the following goals: insight, resolution of conflicts, an improved sense of self, a change in unacceptable patterns of behavior, better interpersonal relations, and an improved picture of oneself and the world. To accomplish these goals, psychotherapies offer:

1. *A caring relationship* between client and therapist. *Emotional rapport* based on warmth, friendship, understanding, acceptance, and empathy forms the basis for this relationship.
2. *A protected setting* in which emotional *catharsis* (release) can take place. Therapy provides a sanctuary in which the client is free to express fears, anxieties, and personal secrets without fear of rejection or loss of confidentiality.
3. All therapies to some extent offer a *explanation* or rationale for the suffering the client has experienced, and they propose a line of action that, if followed, will end this suffering.

These basic foundations of psychotherapy represent one of the more valuable lessons to be learned from this chapter. Together, they offer a useful perspective for meeting the challenge of helping a troubled friend or relative. More specific suggestions on this point will be found in the discussion which concludes the applications section of this chapter.

Resources Summary

Let us briefly summarize the psychotherapies discussed above. Freud's *psychoanalysis* was the first formal therapy. Psychoanalysis seeks a release of repressed thoughts and emotions from the unconscious. The psychoanalyst uses *free association*, *dream analysis*, and analysis of *resistance* and *transference* to reveal health-producing insights.

Client-centered therapy is nondirective and is dedicated to creation of an *atmosphere* of growth. *Unconditional positive regard*, *empathy*, *authenticity*, and *reflection* are combined to give the client a chance to solve his or her own problems.

In *rational* therapy clients learn to recognize and challenge *irrational beliefs* that cause undue suffering. Rational therapy is very directive.

Existential therapy focuses on the end result of the *choices* one makes in life. Clients are encouraged through *confrontation* and *encounter* to take responsibility for their choices and to create a meaningful existence.

Group therapy may be a simple extension of individual methods to more than one person or it may be based on techniques developed especially for groups. Two popular variations of group therapy are *psychodrama* and *Gestalt* therapy. Although not literally psychotherapy, *sensitivity* and *encounter* groups attempt to encourage positive personality change.

Transactional analysis is a special form of group therapy distinguished by its attempt to cure relationships as well as the individual.

Applications

Seeking Professional Help—When, Where, and How?

Question: How would I know if I should seek professional help at some point in my life?

Although there is no simple answer to this question, the following guidelines may be helpful.

1. If your level of psychological discomfort (unhappiness, anxiety, or depression, for example) becomes comparable to a level of physical discomfort that would cause you to see a dentist or physician, you should consider seeing a psychologist or a psychiatrist.
2. Another sign that should influence your decision is the occurrence of significant changes in observable behavior like the quality of your work (or school work), your rate of absenteeism, your use of drugs (including alcohol), or your relationships with others who are important to you.
3. Perhaps you have at some time urged a friend or relative to seek professional help and were then dismayed because they refused to recognize the extent of their problem. If *you* find friends or relatives making a similar suggestion, recognize that they may be seeing things more objectively than you.
4. If you have persistent or disturbing suicidal thoughts or impulses, you should seek help immediately.

Question: If I wanted to talk to a therapist, how would I find one?

Finding professional help can be somewhat bewildering, especially at a time when you are already under stress. Here are some tips on tracking down a therapist.

1. *The "yellow pages."* Psychologists are listed under "Psychologist" or in some cases under "Counseling Services." Psychiatrists are generally listed as a subheading under "Physicians." These listings will usually put you in touch with individuals in private practice.
2. *Community or county mental health centers.* Most counties and many cities in the United States now offer public mental health services. (These are listed in the phone book.) Public mental health centers usually provide counseling and therapy services directly and can make referrals to private therapists.
3. *Mental health associations.* Many cities have mental health associations organized by concerned citizens. Groups such as these usually keep listings of qualified therapists and of other services and programs in the community.
4. *Colleges and universities.* If you are a student, don't overlook counseling services offered by a student health center or special student counseling facilities.
5. *Newspaper advertisements.* Professional ethics prevent advertisements. Occasionally there are exceptions to this rule as when low-

cost "outreach" clinics try to make their presence known to the public, but in the case of an advertised service one should carefully inquire into the training and qualifications of its staff.

Question: How would I know what kind of a therapist to see? How would I pick one?

The choice between a psychiatrist and a psychologist is somewhat arbitrary. Both are trained to do psychotherapy, and while a psychiatrist can administer somatic therapy and prescribe drugs, a psychologist can work in conjunction with a physician if such services seem indicated. Fees for psychiatrists are usually higher, averaging around $45 an hour. Psychologists average from $25 to $35 an hour. With fees in mind, your decision may be influenced by whether or not you have health insurance that will cover the expense. If fees are a problem, keep in mind that many individual therapists charge on a sliding scale, or ability-to-pay basis and that community mental health centers almost always charge on a sliding scale. Some communities now have counseling services staffed by sympathetic paraprofessional counselors. Fees for these services are considerably lower. Group therapy is also much less expensive since the fee for the therapist's time is essentially divided among several people.

The training and professional qualifications of a therapist can usually be learned simply by asking. A reputable therapist will be glad to reveal his or her background. If you have any doubts, credentials may be checked and other helpful information can be obtained from local branches of any of the following organizations. You can also write to the addresses listed below.

The National Association for Mental Health
1800 N. Kent St.
Arlington, Va. 22209

The American Psychiatric Association
1700 18th St. N.W.
Washington, D.C. 20009

The American Psychological Association
1200 17th St. N.W.
Washington, D.C. 20036

The Association of Humanistic Psychology
146 Hoffman St.
San Francisco, Calif. 94114

The question of how to pick a particular therapist remains. The best means is to start with one short consultation with a respected psychiatrist or psychologist or with a counselor at a mental health center. This will allow the person you consult to evaluate the nature of your difficulty and recommend an appropriate type of therapy or a therapist who is likely to be helpful.

Question: How would I know whether or not to quit or ignore a therapist?

A balanced look at psychotherapies suggests that all *techniques* are about equally successful (Frank, 1973). However, all *therapists* are not equally successful. Far more important than the approach used are the therapist's personal qualities. The most consistently successful psychotherapists are those who are willing to use whatever method seems most helpful for a client. They are also distinguished by personal characteristics of warmth, integrity, sincerity, and empathy (Frank, 1973; Katz, 1972; Knight, 1949). It is perhaps most accurate to say that at this stage of development, psychotherapy is an art, not a science. Since the *relationship* between a client and therapist is the therapist's most basic tool, you must trust and easily relate to a therapist for therapy to be effective. There is always a temptation to avoid facing up to personal problems. With this in mind, you should give a therapist a fair chance and not give up too easily. But don't hesitate to change therapists or to terminate therapy if you lose confidence in the therapist or if you don't relate well to the therapist as a person.

Becoming a Community Mental Health Resource—How to Help

Question: What can be done to help a friend or relative who has a temporary personal problem or emotional crisis?

Everyone at one time or another will be faced with the task of comforting a troubled friend. For the majority of such upsets any caring, emotionally stable, empathic person can aid effectively. But how can you best give support? As was mentioned above, many observers consider the personal qualities of professional therapists more important than their specialized training. Jerome Frank (1973), Carl Rogers (1957), and others appear to be in agreement about two essential conditions for the person hoping to help in constructive personality change. These are:

1. An unconditional acceptance of the troubled person, an unshakable positive regard for him or her as a human.
2. A capacity to communicate to the person an understanding of the discomfort he or she is feeling.

We may call the second quality *empathy*, the ability to enter another person's private world, to understand feelings, and to share psychological pain. Because empathy and true caring cannot be faked, your support at times of crisis can be more valuable than anything the best-trained professional can offer. John O. Stevens (1971, pp. 129–130) has summarized:

> The way to really help someone is not to help him do anything but become more aware of his own experience—his feelings, his actions, his fantasies—and insist that he explore his own experience more deeply and take responsibility for it, no matter what that experience is.

Question: I'm still not sure exactly what is best to do when a friend wants to talk about a problem.

Several points may be kept in mind when "counseling" a friend.

Active Listening People frequently talk "at" each other without really listening. A person with problems needs to be heard. Make a sincere effort to listen to and understand the person. Let the person know you are listening through eye contact, posture, your tone of voice, and your replies.

Focus on Feelings Feelings are neither right nor wrong. By focusing on the person's feelings you can avoid making him or her defensive. Passing judgment on what is said prevents the free outpouring of emotion that is the basis for catharsis. For example, a friend confides that he has failed a test. Perhaps you know that he studies very little. If you say, "Maybe if you studied a little more you would do better," he will probably become defensive or hostile. Much more can be accomplished by saying, "You must feel very frustrated" or, simply, "How do you feel about it?"

Avoid Giving Advice It is not unreasonable to give advice when you are asked for it, but beware of the trap of the "Why don't you? Yes, but" game. According to Berne (1964), this "game" follows a pattern: Someone says, "I have this problem." You say, "Why don't you do thus and so?" The person replies, "Yes, but . . ." and then gives you several reasons why your suggestion won't work. If you make a new suggestion, the reply will once again be, "Yes, but . . ." because the person either knows more about his or her personal situation than you do or because he or she has reasons for avoiding your advice. The student described above knows he needs to study. His problem is to understand why he doesn't *want* to study.

Accept the Person's Frame of Reference W. I. Thomas said, "Things perceived as real are real in their effect." Try to resist the temptation to contradict the person with your point of view. Since we all live in different psychological worlds, there is no "correct" view of a life situation. If a person feels that his point of view is understood, he will feel freer to examine it objectively and to question his perspective.

Reflect Thoughts and Feelings One of the most productive things you can do when "counseling" a friend is to give feedback by simply restating what is said. This is also a good way to encourage a person to talk. If he or she seems to be at a loss for words, restate his or her last sentence. For example:

Friend: I'm really bummed out about school. I can't get interested in any of my classes. I flunked my Spanish test, and somebody stole my notebook for psychology.

You: You're really down about school, aren't you?
Friend: Yeah, and my parents are hassling me about my grades again.
You: You're feeling pressured by your parents?
Friend: Yeah, damn.
You: It must make you angry to be pressured by them.

As simple as this sounds, it is extremely helpful to someone trying to sort out his feelings. Try it. If nothing else, you'll develop a reputation as a fantastic conversationalist!

Maintain Confidentiality Your efforts to help will be wasted if you fail to respect the privacy of someone who has confided in you. Put yourself in the person's place. Don't gossip.

These guidelines are not an invitation to play "junior therapist." A professional therapist is prepared to attack a serious problem from a position of experience and expertise, and formal therapy provides a protected and confidential arena in which problems can be solved. We simply urge you to recognize the role each of us plays in providing two of the greatest mental health resources available at any cost: friendship and honest communication.

Questions for Discussion

1. What preconceptions did you have about psychotherapy? Has your understanding of therapy changed? Has your attitude changed?
2. Which of Ellis' irrational assumptions do you consider most self-defeating? Can you think of other irrational assumptions that seem to cause problems?
3. Do you agree with Rollo May that there has been a loss of individual freedom, faith, and meaning in today's society? Why or why not?
4. Which form of psychotherapy do you find the most attractive? Why?
5. What psychological services are available in your area? Would you know how to find or make use of them? What factors would affect your decision to seek help?
6. Describe a time when you helped someone resolve a personal problem. Describe a time when you were unsuccessful in helping. What factors seemed to make the difference?

Suggestions for Further Reading

Axline, V. *Dibs: In Search of Self.* Houghton Mifflin, 1964.

Berne, E. *Games People Play.* Grove, 1964.

Burton, A. (ed.). *Twelve Therapists.* Jossey-Bass, 1972.

Frankl, V. *Man's Search for Meaning.* Simon and Schuster, 1970.

Freud, S. *General Introduction to Psychoanalysis.* Simon and Schuster, 1969.

Perls, F. *Gestalt Therapy Verbatim.* Real People Press, 1969.

Rogers, C. *Client-centered Therapy.* Houghton Mifflin, 1951.

Rotter, J. B. *Clinical Psychology.* 2nd ed. Prentice-Hall, 1971.

Ruitenbeck, H. M. *The New Group Therapies.* Avon, 1970.

24 Behavior Modification

Chapter Preview

News Item June Clark, age 17, of Miami, Florida, started sneezing January 4, 1966, while recovering from a kidney ailment in the James M. Jackson Memorial Hospital. Her sneezing was stopped after 155 days on June 8, 1966, by the use of electric aversion therapy.

Behavior Modification and the Twilight Zone

In the previous chapter we discussed psychotherapy based upon insight. *The concern of this chapter is an entirely different approach to therapy, called* behavior modification.

Behavior modification is an exciting and controversial form of therapy. Psychologists who use behavior modification (behavior therapists) *feel that insight, or understanding of one's problems, is unnecessary. Instead, behavior therapists try to change directly or remove troublesome* behavior. *June Clark, the girl described above, didn't need to delve into her past emotions and conflicts. She needed to quit sneezing! Similarly, behavior modification has helped people to stop drinking, smoking, hiccoughing, stuttering, and molesting children. Behavior modification can be used to lose weight or to increase eating in the pathologically underweight. It has improved study habits, work output in factories, and speech in retarded and disturbed children, and it has increased the amount of time a psychotic patient will go without hallucinating. Also, through behavior modification, people have conquered fears of heights, snakes, public speaking, sexual intimacy, and automobiles. The list of possible applications is practically endless. It is almost certain that you will discover a useful technique for self-improve-*

ment while reading this chapter. But before we begin with some new terms, here is something to think about.

The Twilight Zone? *Pretend for a moment that you work for the telephone company and that you have been sent to repair a phone. Picture a pleasant professional building, one similar to the buildings in which your own doctor and dentist are found. Inside the front door is an office bustling with quiet activity. Through the windows of side offices you see discussions taking place between clients and well-dressed therapists. You ask where the defective phone is. A secretary tells you it is in the opposite end of the building and asks you to follow her. She opens a door on your left. As you step through it, your mind reels.*

In confusion you rapidly scan your surroundings. You are in a tavern! In the dim light you see a bar and heavily padded stools. Behind the bar, a bartender polishes glasses in front of a large mirror and a row of bottles. Lighted displays advertising beer glow softly from the wall, and music flows from an unseen speaker.

Catching sight of the secretary again, you wind your way through the tables and hurry to a door on the opposite side of the room. Once again you are in an ordinary office. But over your shoulder you see the bartender close the door behind you, and the strains of an old Sinatra tune die abruptly with a click of the latch.

What's happening here? Was it a hallucination? A movie set? A modern version of Alice in Wonderland? *A hideout for the CIA? For an answer, read further.*

Resources

Behavior Modification—Animal, Vegetable, or Mineral?

Question: In general, how does behavior modification work?

Behavior modification is based on one principal assumption: People have *learned* to be the way they are. Consequently, if they have learned habits that cause problems, then they can *unlearn* them or *relearn* more appropriate habits. Broadly speaking, "behavior modification" is a term referring to any attempt to use the learning principles of *classical* or *operant conditioning* to change human behavior.

Question: I'm not sure I remember how classical conditioning works.

Classical conditioning was described in Chapter 8. It is the process of learning originally studied by the Russian physiologist Ivan Pavlov. Here is a brief review of Pavlov's principles:

> A previously neutral stimulus (the *conditioned stimulus*) is followed by a stimulus (the *unconditioned stimulus*) which always produces a response (the *unconditioned response*). Eventually the conditioning stimulus begins to pro-

> duce the response directly. The response is then called a *conditioned response*. Thus, for a child the sight of a hypodermic needle (CS) is followed by pain (UCS), which causes anxiety or emotional discomfort (UCR). Eventually the sight of a hypodermic (the conditioned stimulus) may produce anxiety (a conditioned response) *before* the child feels any pain.

Question: What does classical conditioning have to do with behavior modification?

Classical conditioning may be used to associate discomfort with a bad habit. Psychologists call discomfort used this way an *aversion*. An aversion may be used to combat an undesirable habit as it was in the case of the girl who sneezed for 155 days. Use of the technique is called *aversion therapy*, and it is one form of behavior modification.

The Behavior Therapist's Toolbox—Aversion Therapy, or a Little Pain Goes a Long Way

Imagine that you are eating an apple. Suddenly you discover that you have just bitten a large green worm in half. You vomit. Months pass before you can eat an apple again without feeling ill. You have experienced a *conditioned aversion* to apples.

Question: "Conditioning an aversion" was mentioned as an application of classical conditioning in behavior modification. How is a conditioned aversion used in therapy? Can you give an example of the actual procedures?

In aversion therapy an individual learns to associate a strong aversion (or negative emotional response) to an undesirable habit like smoking, drinking, or gambling. Aversion therapy has also been used to cure hiccoughs, sneezing, stuttering (Goldiamond, 1965), vomiting (Lang & Melamed, 1969), bed-wetting (Wickes, 1958), and to help homosexuals who want to change their sexual orientation (Feldman & MacCulloch, 1964).

An excellent example of aversion therapy is provided by the work of Roger Vogler. Dr. Vogler works with alcoholics who have been unable to stop drinking. For many patients aversion therapy is a last chance. They have often been threatened with desertion by relatives and friends, have lost their jobs, and have tried Alcoholics Anonymous, psychotherapy, detoxification, vitamin therapy, and even Antabuse therapy. (Antabuse is a drug that causes an alcoholic to become violently nauseated after he drinks.) Here is a typical aversion procedure:

> While drinking an alcoholic beverage, painful (although noninjurious) electric shocks are delivered to the patient's hand. From the patient's point of view the shocks are unpredictable; he never knows for sure when one is due. Most of the time, however, the shocks come as the patient is beginning to take a drink of alcohol.

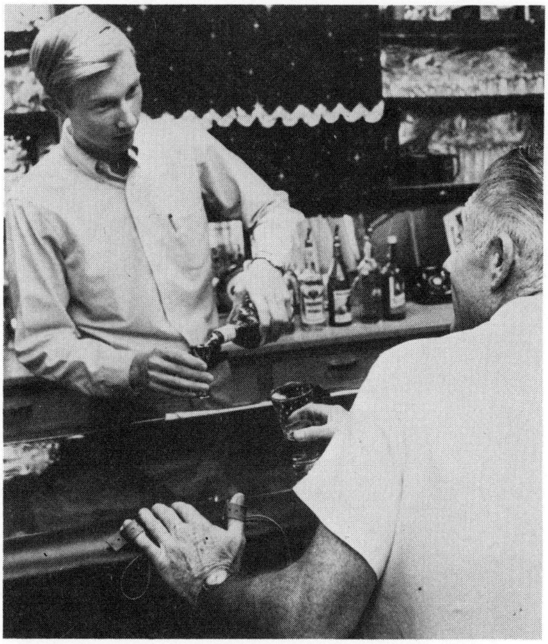

Fig. 24-1 · Aversion therapy for drinking. The sights, smells, and tastes of drinking are associated with unpleasant electrical shocks applied to the hand. (Photo by Kurt Gunther, *Camera 5.*)

This *response-contingent* (or response-connected) shock obviously takes the immediate pleasure out of drinking. It also causes the patient to develop a conditioned aversion to drinking. The sight and smell of alcohol and the motions of drinking begin to have a capacity to make the individual very uncomfortable.

Question: But can't the person tell when it is "safe" to drink and when it is not?

Transfer, or *generalization*, of aversion conditioning to the "real world" is a problem. Dr. Vogler has constructed in his office a vivid recreation of a "friendly neighborhood tavern," complete with a bar, tables, soft lights, music, and a bartender. Also provided are a "living room," a "bedroom," and a "kitchen." Patients undergo aversion therapy in a setting as much like the normal site of their drinking as possible, and carry-over of the aversion training is improved.

Recently Dr. Vogler has added a more subtle dimension to his conditioning procedures. His bartender is trained to provoke patients into becoming argumentative and obnoxious after they get drunk. This presumably is not too hard to do with a drunk who is being shocked! Videotapes of the patient are made and replayed for him or her later. Most people are apparently not aware of how unattractive they are while they are drunk. Seeing themselves as obnoxious drunks adds to the aversion patients come to feel for drinking.

Question: I'm not sure I'm comfortable with the idea of treating humans this way.

People are often disturbed (shocked?) by such methods. It must be emphasized that patients usually volunteer for aversion therapy because it helps them overcome a destructive habit. Also, aversion therapy is often backed up with supportive counseling and psychotherapy. But, most importantly, as behaviorist Donald Baer puts it: "A small number of brief, painful experiences is a reasonable exchange for the interminable pain of a lifelong maladjustment" (Baer, 1971).

Learning Check

Before continuing, see if you can answer these questions. If not, review the preceding section.

1. What two types of conditioning are used in behavior modification?

______________________ and ______________________________________

2. Aversion therapy is used to combat what?

____

3. Shock, pain, or discomfort play what role in conditioning an aversion? (circle one) conditioned stimulus, unconditioned stimulus, unconditioned response, conditioned response

4. If shock is used to control drinking, it must be what?

______________________-contingent

5. A major problem with aversion therapy is what?

____

Answers:

1. classical and operant **2.** undesirable habits **3.** unconditioned stimulus **4.** response **5.** transfer, or generalization

The Behavior Therapist's Toolbox—Desensitization

Assume you are a swimming instructor who wants to help a child overcome fear of the high diving board. How might you proceed? Directly forcing a terrified child off the high board could be psychologically disastrous.

Obviously, a better approach would be to begin by teaching the child to dive off the edge of the pool. Then the child could be taught to dive off the low board, followed by a platform 6 feet above the water, and then an 8-foot platform. As a last step the child could try the high board.

This *ordered set of steps* is called a *hierarchy*. The hierarchy allows the child to undergo *adaptation*. Gradually the child adapts to the high dive and overcomes fear, much as one adapts to the cool water of a swimming pool on a hot day. When the child has overcome the fear, a psychologist would say that *desensitization* has occurred. Desensitization is also based on the principle of *reciprocal inhibition*, developed by Joseph Wolpe (1958). Reciprocal inhibition means that one emotional state can prevent the occurrence of another. For instance, it is impossible to be anxious and relaxed at the same time. If we have managed to get our subject on to the high board in a relaxed state, anxiety and fear responses will be inhibited. Repeated times on the high board should cause fear in the situation to disappear. Again we would say that the person has been *desensitized*. In general, desensitization (that is, a reduction in fear) is usually brought about by gradually approaching a feared stimulus while maintaining complete relaxation.

Question: What is desensitization used for?

Desensitization is primarily used to help people unlearn or countercondition phobias or strong anxieties. Almost everyone has a phobia or two. Many people fear heights, snakes, public speaking, spiders, and so forth. Usually these cause little difficulty because the individual carefully avoids fear-producing situations. However, consider the following: a teacher with stage fright, a student with test anxiety, a salesperson who fears people, an aspiring pole-vaulter who fears heights, or a newlywed with a fear of sexual intimacy. Each may be hampered enough by fears or anxieties to seek aid.

Question: I understand how some of these fears could be desensitized by gradual approach—like the child on the high dive. But how would a therapist use desensitization to combat fear of sexual intimacy?

Desensitization usually involves three steps. First, the patient and the therapist *construct a hierarchy*. This is a list of fear-provoking situations involving the phobia and ranging from the least disturbing situation to the most disturbing one. Second, the patient is taught *exercises that produce total relaxation*. Once the patient is relaxed, he proceeds to the third step by trying to *perform the least disturbing item* on his list. For a fear of heights (acrophobia) this might be: "(1) standing on a chair." The first item is repeated until no anxiety is felt. Any change from complete relaxation is a signal to the patient that she must repeat the relaxation process before continuing. Slowly patients move up the hierarchy: "(2) climb to the top of a small foot ladder"; "(3) look down a flight of stairs"; and so on, until the last item is performed without fear: "(20) fly in an airplane."

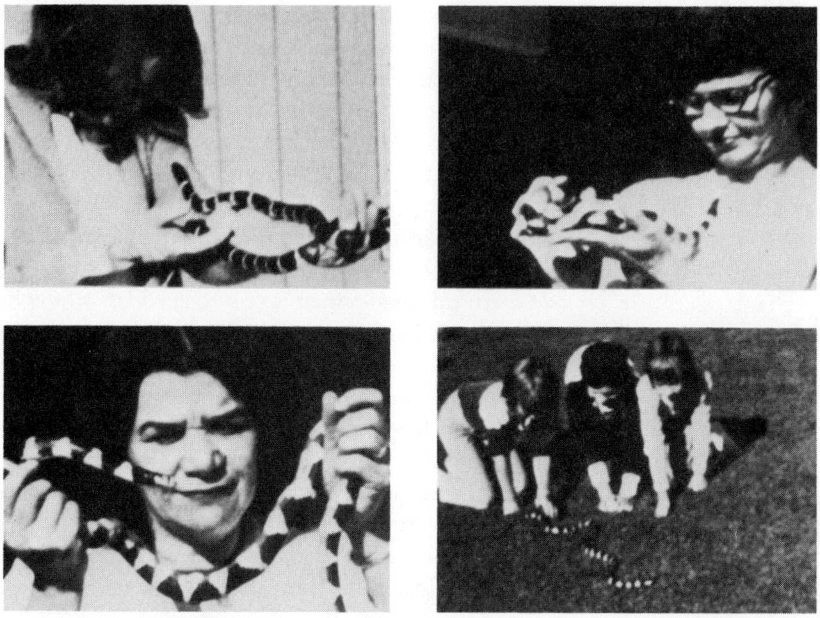

Fig. 24-2 Treatment of a snake phobia by desensitization. The photographs show models interacting with snakes. To overcome their own fears, phobic subjects observed the models. (Bandura *et al.*, 1969; photos courtesy of Albert Bandura.)

For a person with a fear of heights, the steps of the hierarchy might be acted-out. Often, however, acting-out is totally impractical. Fortunately, desensitization works almost as well when a patient *vividly imagines* each of the steps of the hierarchy. If the steps can be visualized without anxiety, fear in the actual situation is reduced. Here is a sample of the hierarchy imagined by a twenty-four-year-old married woman to overcome the fear and disgust she felt for sexual intercourse. (Some steps are left out to shorten the list.)

1. Dancing with and embracing husband while both fully clothed.
2. Being kissed on cheeks and forehead.
3. Being kissed on lips.
4. Sitting on husband's lap, both fully dressed.
5. Husband kisses neck and ears.
6. Husband caresses hair and face.
•
•
•
17. Having intercourse in bed in the dark.
18. Having intercourse in the nude in a dining room or living room.
19. Changing positions during intercourse.
20. Having intercourse in the nude while sitting on husband's lap.
(Adapted from Lazarus, 1964.)

Mrs. A was able to imagine the last steps in this hierarchy without experiencing anxiety after a three-month period of desensitization. Accordingly, she and her husband reported that their sexual and marital adjustments were greatly improved.

Learning Check

Answer these questions before going on.

1. An ordered set of steps is called a what? ______________

2. Desensitization is based on what two principles? ______________

and ______________ ______________

3. What are the three steps in desensitization?

____

____

Answers: **1.** hierarchy **2.** adaptation and reciprocal inhibition **3.** construct a hierarchy, learn relaxation, imagine the steps of the hierarchy

All The World Is a . . . Skinner Box?

Question: Aversion therapy and desensitization are forms of behavior modification based on classical conditioning. Where does operant conditioning fit in?

The principles of *operant conditioning* have been developed by B. F. Skinner and his associates mostly through laboratory research with animals. The operant principles most frequently used by behavior therapists to deal with *human* behavior are:

1. *Positive reinforcement.* An action that is followed by reward will occur more frequently. If a child whines and gets attention, he will whine more frequently. If you get A's in your psychology class, you may become a psychology major.
2. *Nonreinforcement.* An action that is not followed by reward will occur less frequently.
3. *Extinction.* If a response is not followed by reward after it has been repeated many times, it will go away. After winning 3 times, you pull the handle on a slot machine 30 times more without a payoff. What do you do? You go away. So does the response of handle pulling (for that particular machine, at any rate).
4. *Punishment.* If a response is followed by discomfort or an undesirable effect, the response will be suppressed (but not necessarily extinguished).

5. *Shaping.* Shaping means rewarding actions that are closer and closer approximations to a desired response. If a response is complicated, it may never occur to be rewarded. If I want to reward a retarded child for saying "ball," I may begin by rewarding him for saying anything that starts with a *b* sound.
6. *Stimulus control.* Responses tend to come under the control of the situation in which they occur. If I set my clock 10 minutes fast I can get to work on time in the morning. My departure is under the stimulus control of the clock even though I know it is fast.
7. *Time out.* A time-out procedure usually involves removing the individual from a situation in which reinforcement occurs. Time out prevents reward from following an undesirable response; it is a variation of nonreinforcement.

(For a more thorough review of operant principles return to Chapter 8.)

As simple as these principles may seem, they have been used very effectively by behavior modification specialists to overcome difficulties in work, home, school, and industrial settings.

The Behavior Therapist's Toolbox—Nonreinforcement and Extinction

An extremely overweight mental patient had a persistent and disturbing habit: She stole food from other patients. No one could persuade her to stop stealing or to diet. For the sake of her health, a behavior therapist assigned her a special table in the ward dining room. If she approached any other table, she was immediately removed from the dining room. Since her attempts to steal food went unrewarded, they rapidly disappeared. Additionally, any attempt to steal from others usually resulted in the patient's missing her own meal (Ayllon, 1963).

Question: What operant principles did the therapist in this example use?

He used *nonreward* to produce *extinction*. Most frequently occurring human behaviors lead to some form of reward. An undesirable response can be eliminated by *identifying* and *removing* the rewards which maintain it. But people don't always do things for food, money, or other obvious rewards. Most of the rewards which maintain human behavior are more subtle. *Attention*, *approval*, and *concern* are common yet powerful reinforcers for humans. For instance, in a classroom one often finds that misbehaving children are surrounded by others who giggle and pay attention to them. If seating is rearranged so that the disruptive children are surrounded by less responsive students, misbehavior decreases. Attention from a teacher (even scolding) can also be a reinforcer. An experiment showed that when teachers paid extra attention to classroom misbehavior, it increased. It increased even when attention took the form of saying things like "Sit down!" When misbehaving children were *ignored* and

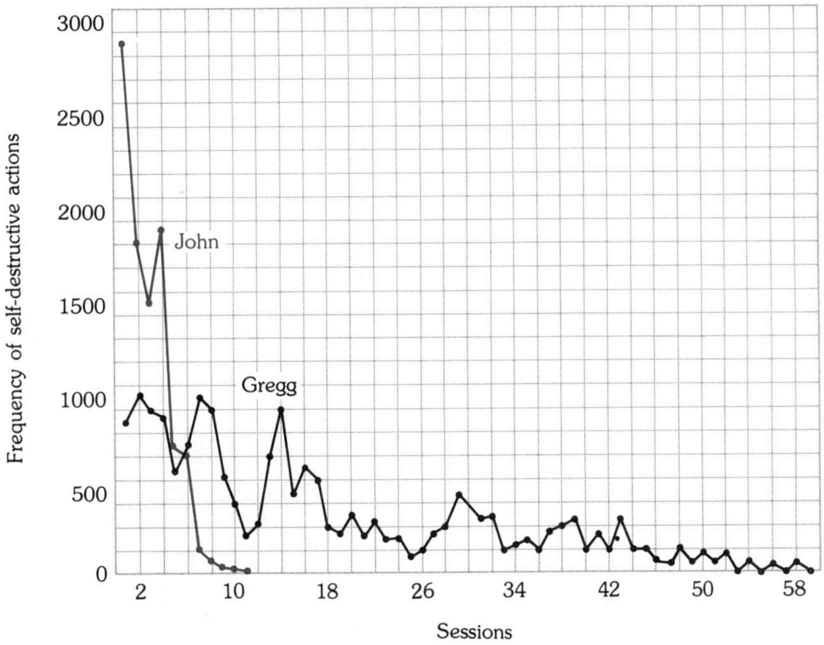

Fig. 24-3 This graph shows extinction of self-destructive behavior in two autistic boys. Before extinction began, the boys received attention and concern from adults for injuring themselves. During extinction, self-damaging behavior was ignored. (Adapted from Lovaas and Simmons, 1969.)

attention was given to children who were *not* misbehaving, misbehavior decreased (Madsen *et al.*, 1968).

Question: How are nonreward and extinction applied in therapy?

Nonreward and extinction can eliminate many problem behaviors. Frequently, difficulties center around a limited number of particularly disturbing responses. A typical strategy used in institutions is called *time out*. Time out means refusing to reward maladaptive responses, usually by refusing to play the *attention* game. Another form of time out is to remove an individual immediately from the setting in which an undesirable response occurs so that the response will not be rewarded. For example:

> Fourteen-year-old Josh periodically appeared in the nude in the activity room of a training center for disturbed juveniles. This always generated a great deal of attention from staff and other patients. Usually Josh was returned to his room and confined there. During this "confinement" he often missed doing his usual chores. As an experiment he was placed on time out. The next time he appeared nude, counselors and other staff members greeted him normally and then ignored him. Attention from other patients rapidly subsided. Sheepishly he returned to his room and dressed.

Learning Check

1. If an undesirable response is not rewarded, it will? ____________

2. Attention is a powerful ____________________ for humans.

3. Nonreward is sometimes called? ____________________

4. The process of gradually rewarding closer approximations to a final desired response is called? ____________________

Answers: 1. extinguish 2. reinforcer 3. time out 4. shaping

The Behavior Therapist's Toolbox—Reinforcement and Token Economies

This section might be called "Throwing a Lifeline to the 'Unreachable' " or "What Do You Say to a Schizophrenic?" A distressing problem faced when dealing with severe mental illness is how to "break through" to a patient who cannot, or will not, communicate. Mental patients sometimes spend years in hospitals without noticeable improvement. Even the patient who is willing to talk about his or her problem may make little visible progress toward mental health.

Question: *What can be done in such circumstances?*

An approach to therapy rapidly growing in popularity is based on the use of *tokens*. Tokens are *symbolic* rewards that can be exchanged for real rewards. Tokens may be printed slips of paper, plastic "poker" chips, check marks, points, or "gold stars." Whatever form they take, tokens serve as rewards because they may be exchanged for candy, food, cigarettes, recreation, or other privileges. Tokens are being used in mental hospitals, halfway houses for drug addicts, schools for the retarded, programs for delinquents, and in ordinary classrooms. Their use is usually associated with dramatic improvements in behavior and overall adjustment.

Learning research and everyday experience point out the power of positive reinforcement to change behavior. If a response is followed by reward, it will occur more frequently. Using tokens, a therapist can *immediately* reward a positive response. This feature of tokens allows a therapist to use operant shaping to influence behavior directly instead of vaguely urging patients to "get themselves together."

So that incentives will have maximum impact, the therapist selects specific *target behaviors* that could or should be improved, then reinforces them with tokens. For example, an uncommunicative mental patient might initially be given a token each time he says a word. Next, he might only be given tokens for speaking a complete sentence. Later, he could gradually

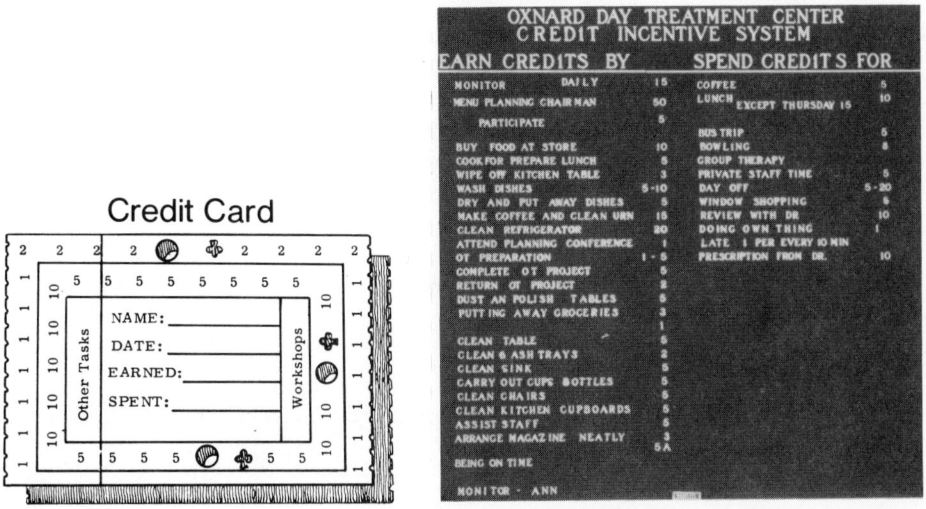

Credit Card
NAME:
DATE:
EARNED:
SPENT:
Other Tasks
Workshops
OXNARD DAY TREATMENT CENTER
CREDIT INCENTIVE SYSTEM
EARN CREDITS BY
SPEND CREDITS FOR
MONITOR DAILY 15
MENU PLANNING CHAIRMAN 50
PARTICIPATE 5
BUY FOOD AT STORE 10
COOK FOR PREPARE LUNCH 5
WIPE OFF KITCHEN TABLE 3
WASH DISHES 5-10
DRY AND PUT AWAY DISHES 5
MAKE COFFEE AND CLEAN URN 15
CLEAN REFRIGERATOR 20
ATTEND PLANNING CONFERENCE 1
OT PREPARATION 1-5
COMPLETE OT PROJECT 5
RETURN OT PROJECT 2
DUST AN POLISH TABLES 5
PUTTING AWAY GROCERIES 3
CLEAN TABLE 5
CLEAN 6 ASH TRAYS 2
CLEAN SINK 5
CARRY OUT CUPS BOTTLES 5
CLEAN CHAIRS 5
CLEAN KITCHEN CUPBOARDS 5
ASSIST STAFF 5
ARRANGE MAGAZINE NEATLY 3
BEING ON TIME
MONITOR - ANN
COFFEE 5
LUNCH EXCEPT THURSDAY 15 10
BUS TRIP 5
BOWLING
GROUP THERAPY
PRIVATE STAFF TIME 5
DAY OFF 5-20
WINDOW SHOPPING
REVIEW WITH DR 10
DOING OWN THING 1
LATE 1 PER EVERY 10 MIN
PRESCRIPTION FROM DR. 10

Fig. 24-4 Pictured above are the tokens used in one token economy system; also pictured are credit values for various activities. Tokens may be exchanged for items or for privileges listed on the board. (Photographs courtesy of Dr. Robert P. Liberman.)

be required to speak more frequently, then to answer questions, and eventually to carry on a short conversation in order to receive tokens. In this way, patients who have not spoken more than a few words for months or years have been returned to the world of normal communication.

Full-scale use of tokens in an institutional setting leads to the development of a *token economy*. In a token economy, patients are rewarded with tokens for a wide range of socially desirable or productive activities. They must *pay* tokens for privileges or for engaging in problem behavior. For example, tokens are given to patients who get out of bed, dress themselves, take required medication, arrive for meals on time, and the like. Work at constructive activity like gardening, cooking, or custodial duties may also earn tokens. Patients *must exchange* tokens for meals and for privileges like private rooms, movies, and passes for off-ward activities. Sometimes tokens can be exchanged for items at a commissary or ward "store." Patients are *charged* tokens for behavior like staying in bed, disrobing in public, talking to themselves, fighting, crying, and similar target behaviors.

In a token economy program, staff members ensure that patients earn tokens easily for constructive behavior, but fine them heavily for destructive responses. This provides the therapists with leverage. Patients are both pushed and enticed toward normality. The result can be a radical change in a patient's overall adjustment and morale. Patients have an incentive to change and are held responsible for their maladaptive habits and actions. Many "hopelessly" retarded, mentally ill, and delinquent people have been returned to a productive life by means of a token economy.

Learning Check

1. When symbolic rewards are used in a behavior modification program, they are called? ________________

2. An advantage of tokens is that they can be used to ________ ________________________ a desired response.

3. Tokens are used to change specific actions. These actions are called? ________________ ________________

4. When an entire treatment program is centered on the use of tokens, it is called what? ________________ ________________

Answers: **1.** tokens **2.** reward immediately **3.** target behaviors **4.** token economy

Resources Summary

Before discussing some applications of behavior modification, let us review some of the more important terms used so far. Behavior modification is a form of psychotherapy that uses the learning principles of *classical* and *operant conditioning* to change directly or improve human functioning. Classical conditioning is the basis for *aversion therapy*—a technique used to combat destructive habits. Classical conditioning is also used to overcome fears and anxieties in a process called *desensitization*. Through the control of rewards and punishments, operant conditioning is used to *extinguish* undesirable habits or to promote constructive behavior. The most frequently used operant principles are: positive reinforcement, nonreinforcement, extinction, punishment, shaping, stimulus control, and time out. A special form of operant conditioning therapy called a *token economy* makes use of *symbolic rewards* to improve behavior.

Applications

Applying Behavioral Principles to Yourself

"Last week I didn't even know what a 'behavior mortifier' was and now I are one!"

"Throw out the snake oil, ladies and gentlemen, and throw away your troubles. Doctor B. Havior Modification is here to put an end to all human suffering."

True? Well, not quite. Behavior modification is not a cure-all. Its effective use is often very complicated and requires a great deal of experience and expertise. Also, for many problems behavior modification is a poor choice by comparison to insight therapy. Still, it does offer a straightforward solution to many of the problems that bedevil us.

It would be a serious mistake to presume that you could effectively apply the principles of behavior modification to major personal problems. As we have mentioned elsewhere in this book, professional help is available and should be sought when a significant problem exists. For lesser difficulties there is a good chance that you might succeed in modest attempts to apply the principles of behavior modification to yourself. Let us see how this might be done.

Applying Aversion Therapy—Boosting Your "Will Power"

"Have you ever decided to quit smoking cigarettes, watching television too much, eating too much, drinking too much, or driving too fast?"

"Well, one of those applies. I have decided several times to quit smoking."

"When have you decided?"

"Usually after I am reminded of how dangerous smoking is—like when I heard that my uncle had died of lung cancer. He smoked constantly."

"If you have decided to quit 'several times' I assume you haven't succeeded?"

"No, the usual pattern is for me to become upset about smoking and then to cut down for a day or two."

"You forget the disturbing image of your uncle's death, or whatever, and start smoking again."

"Yes, I suppose if I had an uncle die every day or two, I might actually quit!"

The use of electric shock to condition an aversion seems remote from everyday problems. However, some activities are naturally aversive if engaged in to excess. For example, a common method of using aversion therapy to reduce smoking is to have the smoker sit in a small unventilated booth and smoke three or four *cartons* of cigarettes nonstop. Even a heavy smoker comes away from such an experience with a new distaste for cigarettes and smoking. Repeating this procedure periodically can create an aversion strong enough to reduce smoking.

Question: I don't think I could actually do that myself. Besides, I don't think it would work for overeating.

Since the oversmoking procedure involves considerable discomfort, it is unlikely that one would complete it without the guidance of a therapist. However, there is an alternative that can be used to help cut down on smoking as well as eating and other less naturally aversive habits.

Procedure Obtain six 3 x 5 cards and on each write a brief description of a scene related to the habit you wish to control. The scene should be so *disturbing* or *disgusting* that thinking about it would temporarily make you very uncomfortable about indulging in the habit. For smoking the cards might read:

1. I am in a doctor's office. The doctor looks at some reports and tells me I have lung cancer. He says a lung will have to be removed and sets a date for the operation.
2. I am in bed under an oxygen tent. My chest feels caved in. There is a tube in my throat. I can barely breathe.
3. I wake up in the morning and smoke a cigarette. I begin coughing up blood.
4. Other cards would continue along the same line.

For overeating the cards might read:

1. I am at the beach. I get up to go for a swim and I overhear people whispering to each other: "Isn't that fat disgusting?"
2. I am at a store buying clothes. I try on several things that are too small. The only things that fit look like rumpled sacks. Salespeople are staring at me.
3. And so forth.

The trick, of course, is to get yourself to imagine or picture vividly each of these disturbing scenes *several times a day*. Imagining the scenes can be accomplished by placing them under *stimulus control*. Simply choose something you do *very frequently* each day (like getting a cup of coffee or getting up from your chair). Next make a rule: Before you can get a cup of coffee, or get up from your chair, or whatever you have selected as a cue, you must take out your stack of cards and *vividly picture* the scene described on the top card. Imagine the scene for 30 seconds. After visualizing the top card, move it to the bottom so the cards are rotated. Make up new cards each week. This technique may sound like "playing games with yourself," but it can be a great help if you want to cut down on a bad habit (based on the technique developed by Lloyd Homme). Try it!

Applying Desensitization Therapy—Overcoming Common Fears

You have prepared for two weeks to give a speech in a large class. As your turn approaches, your hands begin to tremble and perspire. Your heart pounds, and you find it difficult to breathe. You say to your body, "Relax!" What happens? Nothing!

The key to desensitization is relaxation. To inhibit fear, one must *learn* to relax. Here is a method for achieving complete deep-muscle relaxation.

> Tense the muscles in your right arm until they tremble. Hold them tight for about 5 seconds and then let go. Allow your hand and arm to go limp and to relax completely. Repeat the procedure. Releasing tension two or three times will allow you to feel whether or not your arm muscles have relaxed. Repeat the tension-release procedure with your left arm. Compare it to your right arm. Repeat until the left arm is equally relaxed. Apply the tension-release technique to your right leg; to your left leg; to your abdomen; to your chest and shoulders. Clinch and release your chin, neck, and throat. Wrinkle and release your forehead and scalp. Tighten and release your mouth and face muscles. As a last step, curl your toes and tense your feet. Then release. Practice relaxation with the tension-release method until you can achieve complete relaxation quickly (5 to 10 minutes).

After you have practiced relaxation once a day for a week or two, you will begin to be able to tell when your body (or a group of muscles) is tense. Also you will begin to be able to relax on command. Once you have learned to relax, the next step is to identify the fear you would like to control and construct a *hierarchy*.

Procedure for Constructing a Hierarchy Make a list of situations (related to the fear) that make you anxious. Try to list at least 10 situations. Some should be very frightening and others only mildly frightening. Write a short description of each situation on a separate 3 x 5 card. Place the cards in order from the least disturbing situation to the most disturbing. Here is a sample hierarchy constructed by a student with a fear of public speaking:

1. Given an assignment to speak in class.
2. Thinking about the topic and the date the speech must be given.
3. Writing the speech; thinking about delivering the speech.
4. Watching other students speak in class the week before speech date.
5. Rehearsing the speech alone; pretending to give it to the class.
6. Delivering the speech to a roommate; pretending he is the teacher.
7. Reviewing the speech on the day it is to be presented.
8. Entering the classroom; waiting and thinking about the speech.
9. Being called; standing up; facing the audience.
10. Delivering the speech.

When the relaxation exercises have been mastered and the hierarchy constructed, set aside time each day to work on reducing your fear. Begin by performing the relaxation exercises. When you are completely relaxed, visualize the scene on the first card (the least frightening scene). If you can *vividly picture* and imagine yourself in the first situation twice *without a noticeable increase in muscular tension*, proceed to the next card. Also, as you progress through the cards, relax yourself between each card. Each day stop when you reach a card that you cannot visualize without tension after three attempts. On each successive day begin one or two cards before the one on which you stopped the previous day. Continue to work with the cards until you can visualize the last (most anxiety-provoking) situation without experiencing tension (techniques are based on Wolpe, 1969).

Using this approach one should be able to reduce significantly the fear or anxiety often associated with things like public speaking, entering darkened rooms, asking questions in large classes, heights, talking to members of the opposite sex, taking tests, and so forth. Even if you are unable to reduce a fear successfully, you will have learned to place relaxation under voluntary control. This can be a valuable skill in and of itself. You will become aware of how often during the day you add a burden of unnecessary tension to your workload. Controlling unnecessary tension can increase energy and efficiency.

Applying Operant Conditioning—Improving Habits

Would you like to increase the number of hours you spend studying each week? Would you like to exercise more, attend more classes, concentrate longer, or read more books? All these activities and many others can be improved by following these simple rules:

1. *Choose a target behavior.* Identify the activity you want to change.
2. *Record a baseline.* Record how much time you currently spend performing the target activity.
3. *Establish goals.* Remember the principle of shaping and set realistic goals for gradual improvement on each successive week. Also, set daily goals that add up to the weekly goal.
4. *Choose reinforcers.* If you meet your daily goal what reward will you allow yourself? Daily rewards might be watching TV, eating a candy bar, socializing with friends, playing a musical instrument, or whatever *you* enjoy. Also establish a weekly reward. If you reach your weekly goal, what reward will you allow yourself? A movie? A dinner out? A weekend hike?
5. *Record your progress.* Keep accurate records of the amount of time spent each day on the desired activity.
6. *Reward successes.* If you meet your daily goal, collect your reward. If you fall short, be honest with yourself and skip the reward. Do the same for your weekly goal.

If you have trouble finding rewards or if you don't want to use the entire system, simply remember this: Anything *done often* can serve as reinforcement for another activity. For example, if you watch television every night and want to study more, make it a rule that you cannot turn on the TV until you have studied for an hour (or whatever length of time you choose). Then lengthen the study requirement each week.

Here is a sample of one student's plan to improve study habits.

1. Target behavior: number of hours spent studying for school
2. Recorded baseline: an average of 15 minutes per day for a weekly total of 1¼ hours
3. Goal for the first week: an increase in study time to 20 minutes per day; weekly goal of 2 hours total study time
   Goal for second week: 25 minutes per day and 2½ hours per week
   Goal for third week: 30 minutes per day and 3 hours per week
   Ultimate goal: to reach and maintain 8 hours per week study time
4. Daily reward for reaching goal: 1 hour of guitar playing in the evening; no playing if the goal is not met
   Weekly reward for reaching goal: go to a movie or buy a record album

For Discussion

Behavior Modification—To Control or Not to Control? That Is the Question

Obviously, if one *voluntarily* uses behavior modification to lose weight, to increase study time, to unlearn a phobia, or to face a public speaking engagement, problems of control and personal freedom are avoided. But should behavior modification be used by some people to change or control others? B. F. Skinner argues in his book *Beyond Freedom and Dignity* that everyone is already controlled by the environment and the consequences of actions. Skinner's premise is that such control might just as well be rational and orderly instead of haphazard.

Question: I have some misgivings about controlling people. Is behavior modification widely accepted by psychologists?

Behavior modification is exciting to those who have used it because it often works. It is frightening to many others for the same reason. They fear that the widespread use of behavior modification is capable of thrusting us into a world like that in George Orwell's book *1984* or in Stanley Kubric's movie *A Clockwork Orange*. Both depict a world in which people are controlled and molded against their will. Traditional psychotherapists and other opponents of behavior modification also claim that it is dehumanizing and that it removes the symptoms of psychological problems without dealing with their causes. Behavior modifiers counter by saying the symptom *is* the problem, and *learning* is the cause. They also argue that humanistic or insight therapists like Carl Rogers are really controlling their clients through the subtle rewarding effects of approval and attention (Truax, 1966).

Behavior Modification: Are You for or against It? Let us say that an autistic child is mutilating himself. He bites his fingertips off or repeatedly pounds his head against his knee, chews his shoulder until the bone shows, or bangs his head on the corner of a steel cabinet. Using behavior modification, psychologist Ivar Lovaas has successfully ended such actions even when other approaches have failed (see Chapter 17). The benefits of using behavior modification seem clear in this situation. But elsewhere the use of behavior modification might be superficial or undesirable.

The use of behavior modification in public schools, prisons, mental institutions (students sometimes argue that there is no difference among these three), and other "captive" groups is more open to question. For example, prisoners at Atascadero State Hospital for the Criminally Insane and at the California Medical Facility in Vacaville have been given a drug called Anectine as part of an aversion therapy program to deal with homosexuality, chronic violence, and similar problems. Anectine paralyzes the respiratory system for up to two minutes, causing an intense feeling of suffocation. Prisoners have little choice about participation in this treatment. In many cases the "therapy" is effective, but at what cost in human terms? In the confines of a total institution, can participating in such a program really be considered free choice?

The proper place for behavioral control in a free society is a complex issue. Where do you stand on the use of behavior modification?

Questions for Discussion

1. Under what conditions would you condone the use of behavior modification? When would you oppose it?
2. Based on the techniques described, would you cooperate with a therapist who wanted to make use of behavior modification? Are there some techniques you find acceptable and others not?
3. Select a bad habit you would like to break or a positive behavior you would like to encourage and tell how you might use behavior modification to alter your behavior. Be explicit.
4. Some critics have charged that the use of tokens in the classroom encourages students to expect artificial rewards. Behavior theorists reply that explicit rewards are better than inconsistent rewards like praise and attention. What are the advantages and drawbacks represented by each position?
5. How do you feel about the use of behavior modification in prisons and psychiatric hospitals? Is behavior modification any different from the involuntary administration of tranquilizers or other drugs? Why or why not?

Suggestions for Further Reading

London, P. *Behavior Control.* Perennial Library, 1971.

Tharp, R., and R. Wetzel. *Behavior Modification in the Natural Environment.* Academic, 1969.

Ullman, L. P., and L. Krasner. *Case Studies in Behavior Modification.* Holt, 1965.

Watson, D., and R. Tharp. *Self-Directed Behavior: Self-Modification for Personal Adjustment.* Brooks/Cole, 1972.

Wolpe, J. *Practice of Behavior Therapy.* Pergamon, 1967.

Wolpe, J., and A. A. Lazarus. *Behavior Therapy Techniques.* Pergamon, 1966.

Contents

Self and Others

Unit Seven

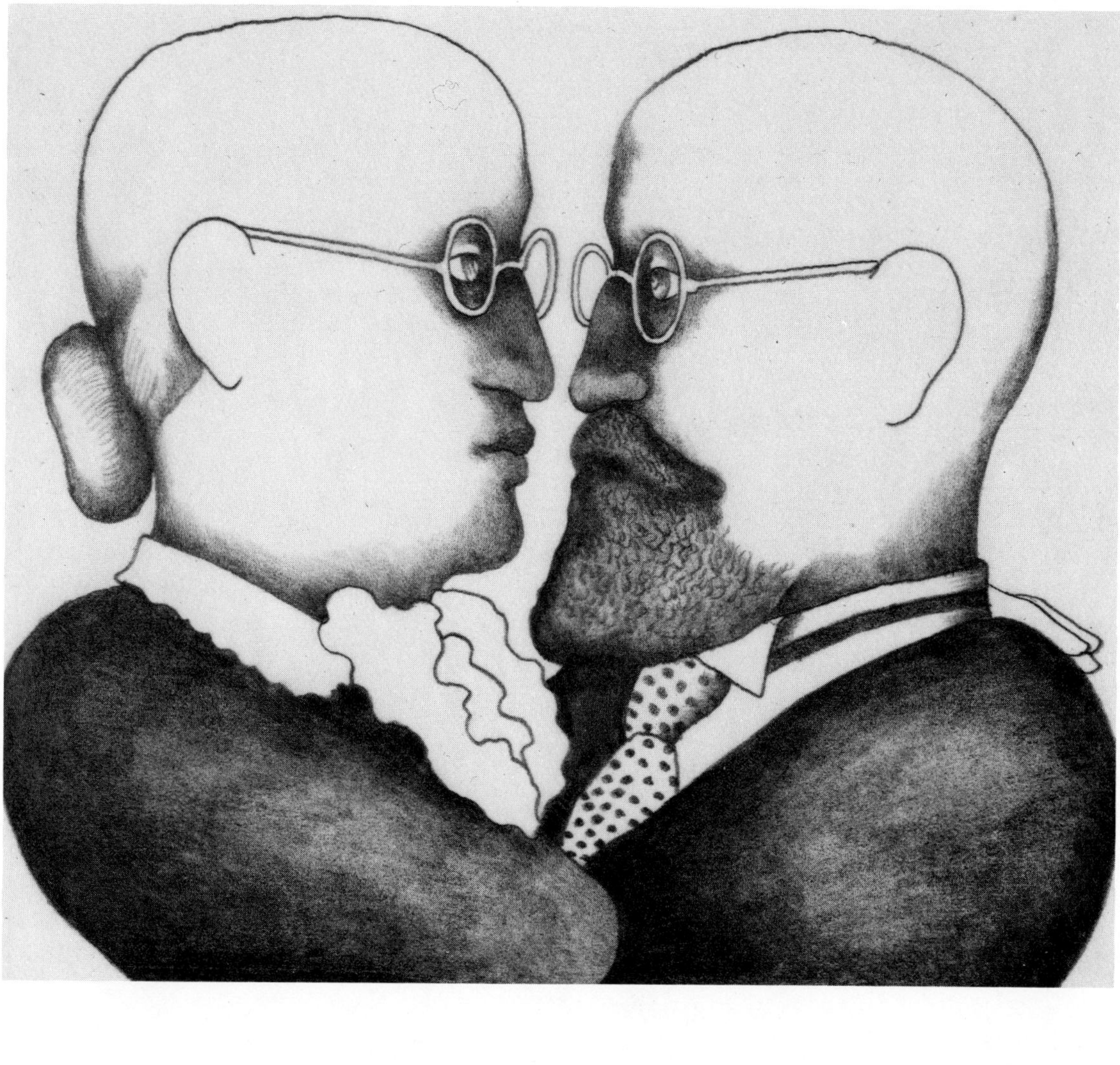

Human Sexuality

25

Chapter Preview

That Magic Word

Sex /seks/, *n* **1:** one of the two divisions of organisms formed on the distinction of male and female

You are by nature a sexual creature. This inescapable reality springs from the basic biology of reproduction and the division of people into male and female gender. So far-reaching are the effects of this division that personal identity and personal adjustment cannot be adequately understood without some reference to sexuality. With this in mind, a discussion of some of the more important psychological aspects of human sexuality follows.

Before reading further, you may find it interesting to see if you can correctly answer the following questions. The answers are listed below the quiz. The reasons for the answers can be found in this chapter.

Human Sexuality Quiz *Indicate which of the following statements are true and which are false.*

1. *Female pleasure in intercourse is greatly affected by penis size. T or F?*
2. *Male sexual potency is closely related to penis size. T or F?*
3. *Excessive masturbation causes mental or physical harm. T or F?*
4. *Nocturnal emissions ("wet dreams") are an indication of sexual disorders. T or F?*

5. *Women do not experience nocturnal orgasms. T or F?*

6. *Women ejaculate when sexual climax occurs. T or F?*

7. *Simultaneous orgasm is essential for complete sexual satisfaction and compatibility. T or F?*

8. *Women are incapable of multiple orgasms. T or F?*

9. *Women have two kinds of orgasm—vaginal and clitoral. T or F?*

10. *Alcohol is a sexual stimulant. T or F?*

11. *Castration or sterilization destroys the sex drive. T or F?*

12. *A person's sex life comes to an end after age forty to fifty. T or F?*

Answers: All the above statements are false.

Resources

The Development of Sex Differences

It has been said that the one thing you will never forget about a person is that person's sex. Considering the number of activities, relationships, conflicts, pressures, and choices that are influenced by one's sex, it is little wonder that considerable attention is directed toward it. Before considering sexuality more directly, let us take a brief look at some general male/female differences which underlie sexual behavior.

The basic physical differences between males and females can be divided into *primary* and *secondary* sexual characteristics. Primary sexual characteristics refer to the sexual and reproductive organs themselves: the penis, testes, and scrotum in males; and the ovaries, uterus, and vagina in females. Secondary characteristics appear at puberty. In females, secondary characteristics involve development of the breasts, broadening of the hips, and other changes in body shape. Males develop facial and body hair, and the voice deepens. These changes signal physical readiness for reproduction. Readiness for reproduction is especially evident in the female *menarche* (onset of menstruation). From then until *menopause* (the end of regular monthly fertility cycles), a woman can bear children.

Question: What causes the development of sexual differences?

Both primary and secondary sexual characteristics are closely related to the action of *sex hormones* in the body (hormones are chemical substances secreted by glands of the endocrine system). The *gonads* (or sex glands) affect sexual development and behavior by secreting *estrogens* (the feminine hormones) and *androgens* (male hormones). The gonads in the male are the *testes*, and in the female, the *ovaries*. The *adrenal* glands (located on top of the kidneys) are a secondary source of sex hormones in both males and females. At puberty, the adrenals add to the development of secondary sexual characteristics.

Interestingly, all individuals normally produce both estrogens and androgens. It is the balance of these substances that influences sexual differences. In fact, the development of male or female genitals before birth is largely due to the presence or absence of *testosterone* (one of the androgens).

Genetic sex is determined at the instant of conception. Two X chromosomes cause development of a female. An X chromosome plus a Y chromosome produces a male. If the Y chromosome is present, testes de-

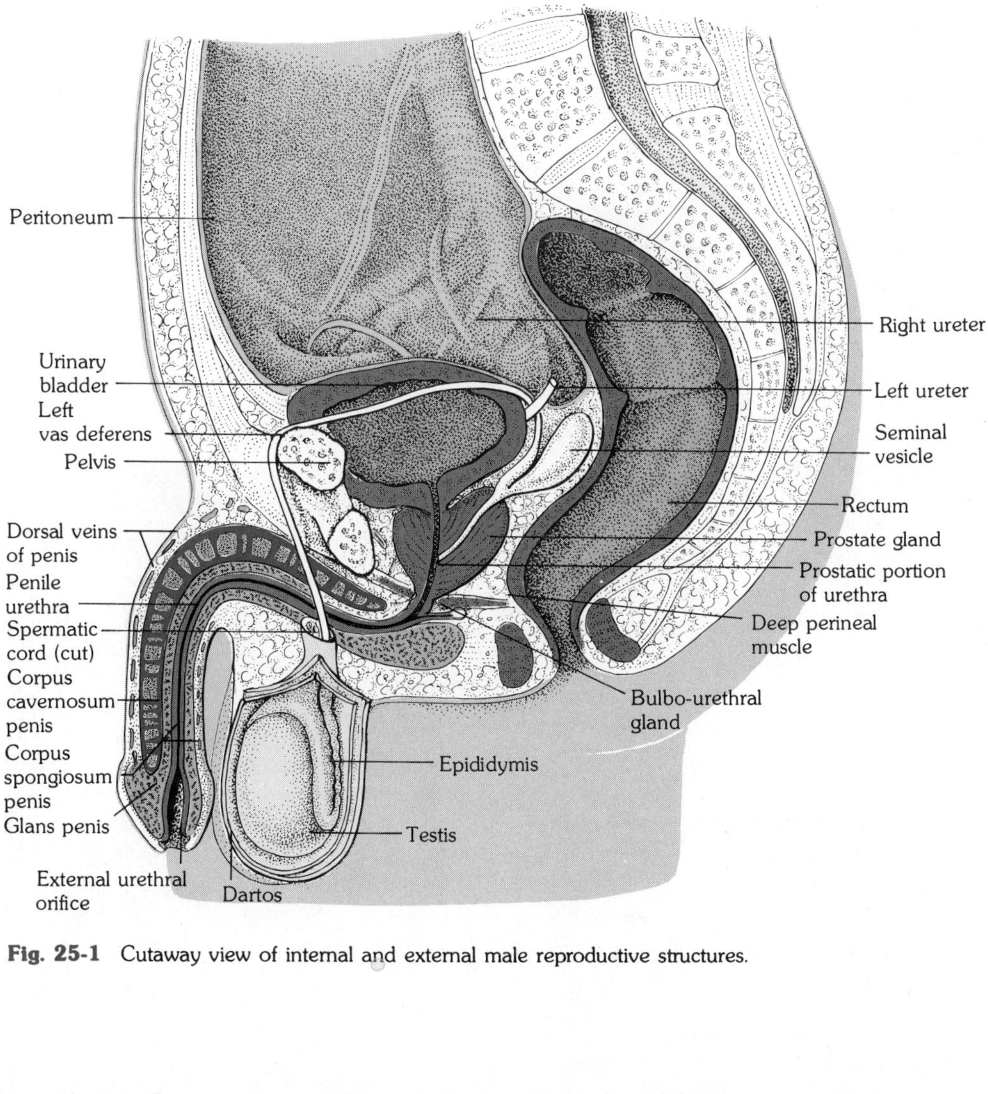

Fig. 25-1 Cutaway view of internal and external male reproductive structures.

velop in the embryo and supply testosterone. Testosterone stimulates growth of the penis and other male reproductive structures. In the absence of this supply of androgens, the embryo will develop feminine reproductive organs, regardless of its genetic sex. Nature's primary impulse, then, is to make a female (Money, 1965) (see Fig. 25-3).

Hormonal problems at the crucial time before birth may result in *hermaphroditism* (defects in sexual development, particularly those resulting in dual or ambiguous sexual anatomy). For instance, a developing female may be exposed to excessive androgen due to genetic defects or the effects of drugs administered to her mother. As a result, the child is born with a combination of male and female genitals. In addition to determining genital development, some researchers believe that the balance of sex hormones before birth may also permanently "sex-type" the brain (Levine, 1966). Changes in the brain are then thought to explain later differences between males and females in aggressiveness, dominance, and sexuality.

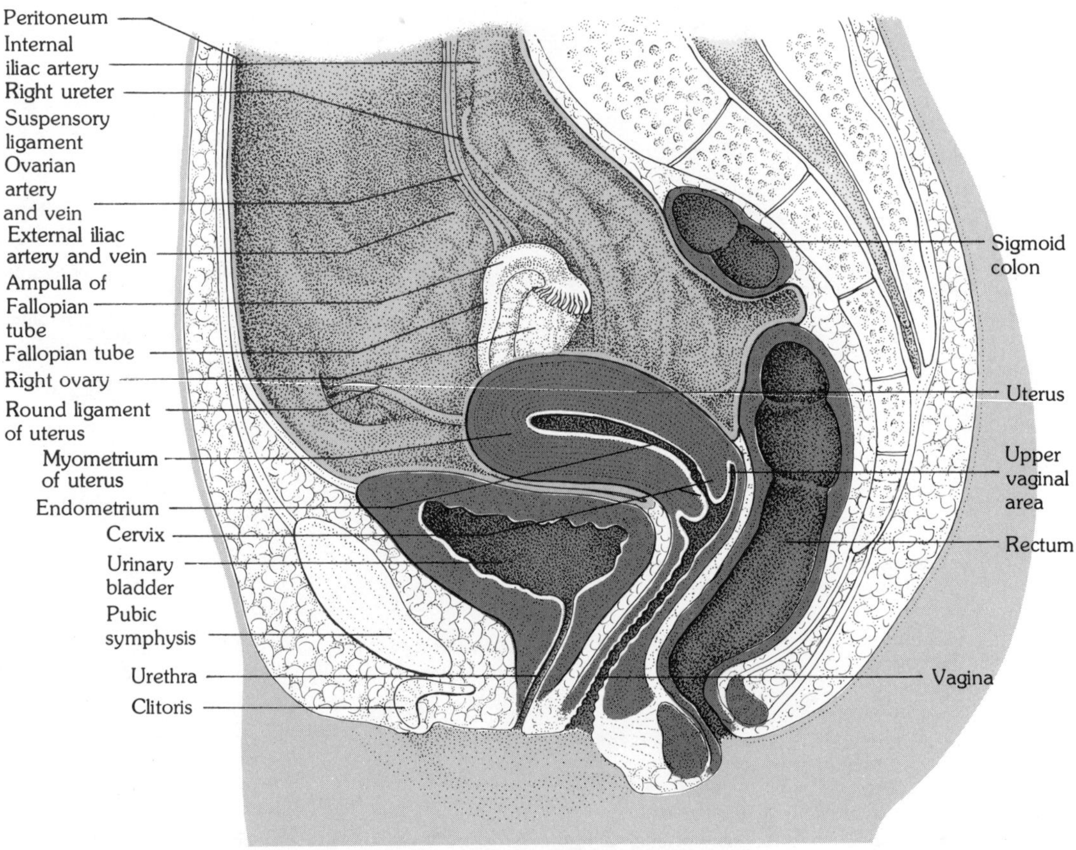

Fig. 25-2 Cutaway view of internal and external female reproductive structures.

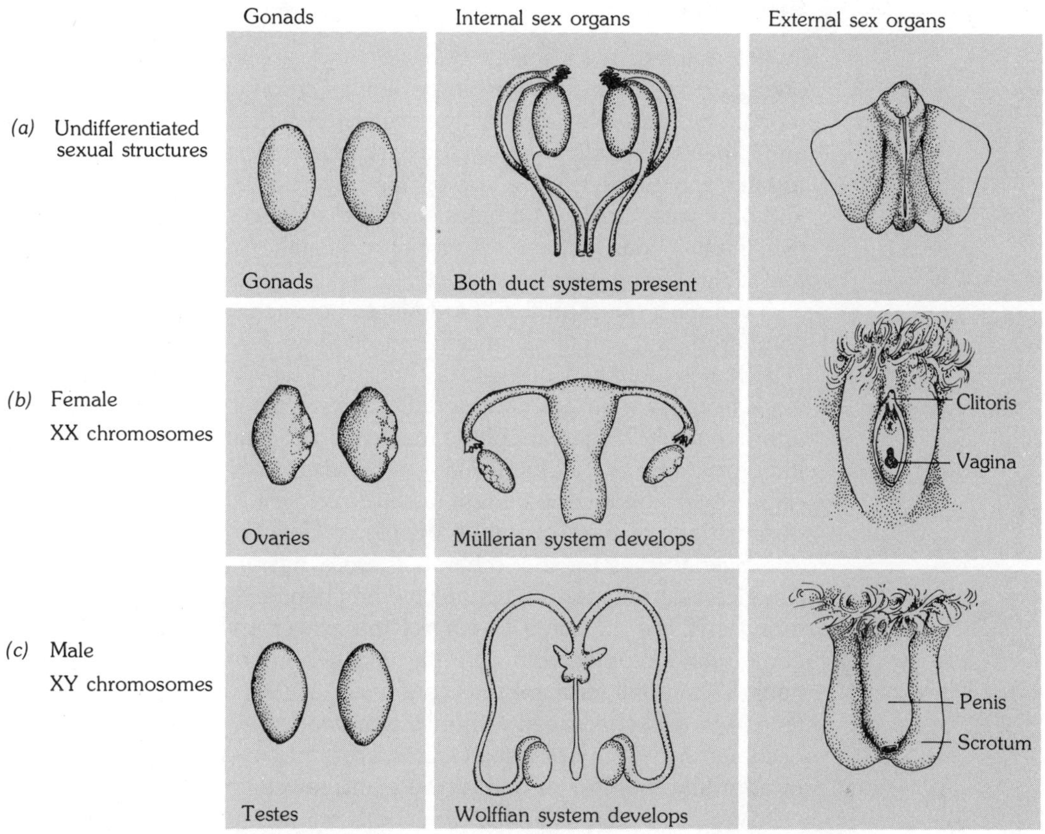

Fig. 25-3 Development of the reproductive organs. Row *a* shows that the sex organs are initially the same in the human male and female. Row *b* shows the differentiation that occurs in females (i.e., when androgen is absent). Row *c* shows the differentiation that occurs in males (i.e., when androgen is present). (From Schneider, A. M. and Tarshis, B., *An Introduction to Physiological Psychology.* Copyright © 1975 by Random House. Reprinted by permission of Random House.)

Question: Does that mean there is a physical basis for male and female traits?

Not necessarily. Levine's research is very controversial, and where humans are concerned, there is much evidence to suggest that most important sex-linked behavior is learned. Cases of hermaphroditism emphasize this point. If we compare two individuals having the same degree of hermaphroditism—one raised as a boy and the other as a girl—we will find that the person raised as a girl will act like and consider herself a girl, and the individual raised as a boy will act like and identify himself as a boy (Money, 1970; Hampson & Hampson, 1961). Based on a survey of a wide range of evidence, Weisstein (1975) concluded that there is no "natural" male or female behavior.

Sex Roles

In determining adult sexual behavior and sex-linked personality traits, one's *sex role* is probably as important as chromosomal, genital, or hormonal sex. Sex role refers to the pattern of behavior that is encouraged and expected of individuals on the basis of gender. In our culture, boys are usually encouraged to be strong, fast, aggressive, dominant, achieving, and otherwise "male." Females have typically been expected to be sensitive, intuitive, passive, and emotional and to take "naturally" to household and child-rearing chores.

We must question the "naturalness" of such sex roles when they are compared with variations in different cultures. For example, Ethel Albert (1963) has identified numerous cultures in which women do the heavy work because men are considered too weak for it. In the Soviet Union, approximately 75 percent of the medical doctors and a large proportion of the work force are women. Many more examples can be cited, but perhaps one of the most pertinent is anthropologist Margaret Mead's (1935) observations of the Tchambuli people of New Guinea.

Sexual roles for the Tchambuli are a nearly perfect reversal of the American stereotypes. Tchambuli women handle the fishing and manufacturing and are expected to control the power and economic life of the community. Women also take the initiative in courting and sexual relations. Tchambuli men, on the other hand, are expected to be dependent, flirtatious, and concerned with their appearance. Art, games, and theatrics occupy most of the Tchambuli males' time, and males are particularly fond of adorning themselves with flowers and jewelry.

We have tried to briefly show both the reality, and the frequent artificiality, of male and female differences. Where human sexual behavior is concerned, we will again find differences that are both real and arbitrary.

Learning Check

To check your progress, answer the following questions:

1. The basic physical differences between males and females can be divided into ____________________ and ____________________ sexual characteristics.

2. The development of both types of sexual characteristics is closely related to the action of sex hormones in the body: the female hormones, called ____________________, and the male hormones, called ____________________.

3. When or at what point in development is genetic sex determined? ______________________________

4. Most important sex-linked behavior is inborn, that is, "natural" male or female behavior. T or F?

Answers: **1.** primary and secondary **2.** estrogens, androgens **3.** at conception **4.** F

Sexual Behavior

Question: When does sexual behavior first appear in humans?

A capacity for sexual arousal is apparent at birth or soon after. Sexual researcher Alfred Kinsey verified instances of *orgasm* (sexual climax) in boys as young as five months old and girls as young as four months (Kinsey *et al.*, 1948, 1953). Kinsey also found that children aged two to five spontaneously engage in manipulation and exhibition of their genitals. Various forms of sexual behavior continue through childhood and adolescence, but as a child matures, cultural norms place greater restrictions on sexual activities. Still, 50 percent of males and 25 percent of females report having engaged in preadolescent sex play. In adulthood, norms continue to shape sexual activity along approved lines. In our culture, sex between children, incest (sex between close relatives), prostitution, homosexuality, and extramarital sex all tend to be discouraged. As was the case with sex-role behavior, it can be seen that such restrictions are somewhat arbitrary. A comparison of many cultures shows that less restriction is usually accompanied by more sexual activity of all kinds. If cultural restrictions are disregarded, it can be said that any sexual act engaged in by consenting adults is "normal" if it does not hurt anyone.

Sexual Arousal

Question: Is it true that men are more easily sexually aroused than women?

On the basis of their questionnaire studies of sexuality, Kinsey and his colleagues (1948, 1953) concluded that men are more easily aroused than women. Men also reported more frequent arousal to visual stimuli of an explicit nature (such as pornographic movies) than did women. Women were more likely to be aroused by movies, fiction, or poetry that emphasized romance more than sex.

Question: But haven't women's attitudes toward sex changed since 1953 when Kinsey did this study?

A more recent study (Mosher, 1973) suggests that current attitudes may not be as liberalized as one might expect. Women are still more inclined to respond negatively to explicit pictures of sex than are men. Unmarried university females, who were shown fairly graphic films of intercourse, rated their reactions more negatively than did a comparable group of male students.

However, these differences seem to be largely psychological. This can be seen in a study that compared the *physical* arousal of men and women to erotic stimuli. When shown pictures of various sexual activities, women again rated the material less stimulating than did men. But when ratings of physical reactions in the genital area were compared, there were *no* significant differences between men and women (Sigusch *et al.*, 1970). This finding suggests that women are no less sexually aroused by erotic stimuli than men, although they are more likely to reject such arousal.

Question: When does the sex drive reach its peak?

If capacity for arousal is measured by the frequency of orgasm (as a result of masturbation or intercourse), the peak of male sexual activity occurs at age eighteen. Married women show maximum arousal (again measured by frequency of orgasm) at approximately thirty years of age (Kinsey *et. al.*, 1953). Maximum responsiveness, therefore, appears to occur significantly later in females than it does in males.

Question: What causes differences in sex drive?

Attitudes toward sex, past experience, and recency of sexual release are all obviously important, but physical factors also play a role. In males the strength of the sex drive is related to the amount of *androgen* secreted by the testes. When the supply of androgens dramatically increases at puberty, sex drive does likewise. Surprisingly, androgen, which is the male hormone, is also important to the female sex drive. In addition to estrogen, the ovaries produce small amounts of androgen. Evidence from clinical studies suggests that this androgen is as essential to a normal sex drive in women as it is in men. When women are given androgen for medical reasons, they often report increased sexual drive. Some women also report a relationship between arousal and various times during their monthly period. If such a relationship does exist it is probably not too important since sexual activity in the human female may occur at any time during the monthly cycle (including during menstruation).

Question: Are nocturnal emissions ("wet dreams") an indication of an unusually strong sex drive? Do they ever indicate sexual disorders? Do both men and women experience nocturnal orgasms?

According to Kinsey's studies, about 85 percent of males and 35 percent of females have had sexual dreams that resulted in orgasm. These experiences typically begin during adolescence and may continue to be a form of sexual outlet throughout adulthood. Kinsey found some reduction in the number of men experiencing nocturnal orgasms after marriage, but no change among women. Any connection between other sexual activities and the frequency of nocturnal orgasm remains essentially unproved. Nocturnal orgasm may best be considered a completely normal (if relatively unimportant) form of sexual release.

Question: Does alcohol stimulate the sex drive?

No. Alcohol is a *depressant*. As such, it may lower *inhibitions* that would normally keep *any* prohibited behavior in check. This probably accounts for alcohol's reputation as an aid to seduction since it may lower sexual inhibitions.* However, as a depressant, alcohol just as often has a negative effect on sexual response.

Question: Does removal of the testes or ovaries abolish the sex drive? Also, what happens to the sex drive in old age?

In lower animals, castration (surgical removal of the testicles) or removal of the ovaries usually completely abolishes sexual activity in *inexperienced* animals. Sexually experienced animals (particularly higher animals like monkeys) may show little immediate change in sexual behavior. In humans, the effects of male or female castration vary. Because of the reduction in androgens, some individuals show a decline in sex drive, but many others experience no change in sexual desire.

There is typically a natural decline in sex drive that accompanies aging and reduction in sex hormone output. However, sexual activity does not come to an unavoidable end. In some cases men and women in their ninety's have continued active sex lives. The crucial factor for an extended sex life appears to be regularity. Individuals who fairly regularly engage in intercourse after ages forty to fifty have little difficulty in later years (Masters & Johnson, 1970).

Masturbation

Masturbation may be defined as deliberate self-stimulation which causes sexual arousal or orgasm. Masturbation is one of the most basic forms of human sexual behavior. Rhythmic self-stimulation has been observed in infants under one year of age. With increased maturity, masturbation in the male usually takes the form of stroking or other manipulation of the penis. Female masturbation most often centers on stimulation of the clitoris or the tissues immediately surrounding it.

The following are some questions commonly asked about masturbation.

Question: In adulthood, do more men masturbate than women?

Yes. Of the women who took part in Kinsey's survey (1953), 60 percent reported that they had masturbated at some time. Of the males, 95 percent reported that they have masturbated (Kinsey *et al.*, 1948).†

Question: Do more men masturbate to orgasm than do women?

Yes. Of the women interviewed by Kinsey, 58 percent reported masturbating to orgasm. By their middle teens, all but a few males have experi-

*Humorist Ogden Nash once summarized this bit of folklore by saying, "Candy is dandy, but liquor is quicker."

†Some cynics add ". . . and the other 5 percent lied!"

enced orgasm through masturbation (Simon & Gagnon, 1973). The lower frequency reported by females probably more represents sexual inhibition among women in our culture than a physical difference in responsiveness.

Question: Is it wrong for masturbation to continue after marriage?

In some instances masturbation after marriage may represent hostility toward a mate. Generally speaking, however, masturbation is a valid sexual activity at any age and may continue after marriage without posing any threat to the relationship.

There is nothing "immature" or infantile about masturbation. As a matter of fact, masturbation may be related to sexual response in other activities. For example, 85 percent of a group of women who had masturbated before marriage reported achieving orgasm during the first year of marriage. By comparison only about 65 percent of a group of women who did not masturbate achieved orgasm during the first year of marriage (Kinsey *et al.*, 1953).

Question: Is it true that more educated and refined people avoid masturbation?

No. Kinsey and his associates found that masturbation is most frequent among men and women with higher education.

Question: Is there any way in which masturbation can cause mental harm?

In the past, frightening stories about potential physical and mental ill effects abounded in the folklore surrounding masturbation. Thirty years ago a child might be told that masturbation would cause insanity, acne, sterility, or other such nonsense. "Self-abuse," as it was often called, has enjoyed a long and unfortunate history of religious and medical condemnation.

The contemporary view is that masturbation is a normal and acceptable sexual outlet. No knowledgeable authority on human sexuality would deny this, and enlightened parents are well aware of it. Still, many a child has been punished or made to feel guilty for touching his or her genitals. In a survey of adult women, Kinsey (1953) found that more than 50 percent of those who had masturbated reported some disturbance over it.

Reports such as Kinsey's are disturbing since there is absolutely no harm caused by masturbation itself. The only possible negative effects of masturbation are the fear, guilt, or anxiety that occur when an individual has learned negative attitudes toward it.

Question: Is there any physical harm that can be caused by masturbation?

No. As psychologist Eleanor Hamilton (1969) comments:

> The truth is that autoeroticism is self-determining, like eating, indulging in a sport, or any other natural functions. . . . If you overmasturbate you feel uncomfortable in your genital area. Nothing more, nothing less—as simple as that.

James McCary (1973) states the opinion of the vast majority of authorities when he summarizes that masturbation:

> is normal and beneficial, part of growing up, part of self-discovery, a stepping-stone toward the youth's eventual role as an adult sexual being. . . . It cannot be called abnormal in any case, since the practice is so widespread (p. 110).

Learning Check

1. A capacity for sexual arousal is apparent at birth or soon after. T or F?
2. If cultural restrictions are disregarded, it can be said that any sexual act engaged in by consenting adults is "normal" if it does not hurt anyone. T or F?
3. According to the Kinsey reports, men reported more frequent sexual arousal to explicit visual stimuli (such as pornographic movies or pictures), while women were more likely to be aroused by stimuli that emphasized romance more than sex. T or F?
4. It is possible and normal for sexual activity to continue to ages eighty or ninety. T or F?
5. Masturbation can cause physical harm, according to the latest research reports. T or F?

Answers: 1. T 2. T 3. T 4. T 5. F

Human Sexual Response

Objective information about human sexual response has recently been expanded by the work of gynecologist William Masters and psychologist Virginia Johnson (1966, 1970). In a controversial series of experiments, interviews, and controlled observations, Masters and Johnson directly studied sexual intercourse and masturbation in nearly 700 males and females. The information they obtained has significantly improved our understanding of human sexuality.

Sexual response in both males and females can be divided into four phases: (1) *excitement*, (2) *plateau*, (3) *orgasm*, and (4) *resolution* (see Fig. 25-4).

Male Response Sexual arousal in the male is signaled by erection of the penis during the excitement phase. There is also a significant change in heart rate, an increase in blood flow to the genitals, enlargement of the testicles, erection of the nipples, and numerous other bodily changes. If sexual stimulation ends, the excitement phase will gradually subside. Continued stimulation moves the individual into the plateau phase in which physical changes and subjective feelings of arousal become more intense. An end to stimulation during this phase will be resolved more slowly and

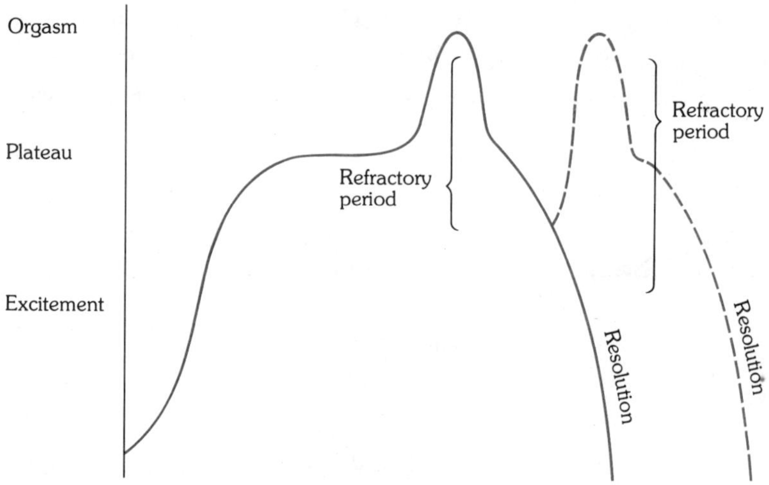

Fig. 25-4 Male sexual response cycle. (Reproduced by permission from Frank A. Beach (ed.), *Sex and Behavior*, N.Y., John Wiley & Sons, Inc., 1965.)

may produce considerable frustration. Further stimulation during the plateau phase brings about a reflex release of accumulated tension resulting in sexual climax, or orgasm. In the mature male, orgasm is accompanied by ejaculation (release of seminal fluid) and is followed by a short *refractory period* during which no amount of continued stimulation will produce a second orgasm. (Many men cannot even be stimulated to erection until the refractory phase has passed.) Only rarely is the male refractory period followed by a second orgasm. Orgasm is usually followed by *resolution*, a return to lower levels of sexual tension and arousal.

Female Response Although the timing and intensity of the phases vary considerably from individual to individual, the basic pattern of response for women is the same as that for men. During the excitement phase of arousal, a complex pattern of changes takes place to prepare the vagina for intercourse. These changes correspond to erection in the male. Also (as in the male) the nipples become erect, pulse rate changes, and the skin may become flushed. Most women go through a plateau stage comparable to that in the male, although a few follow a pattern of response that essentially skips the plateau. During orgasm, from three to ten muscular contractions of the vagina, uterus, and related structures serve to discharge accumulated sexual tension. Contrary to the belief of some women, no form of ejaculation accompanies female orgasm. Vaginal lubrication produced during the earlier stages of arousal probably accounts for the misconception of those women who believe they have ejaculated. Both orgasm and resolution in the female usually last longer than they do in the male. After orgasm, many females return to the plateau phase and may be stimulated to orgasm again before resolution.

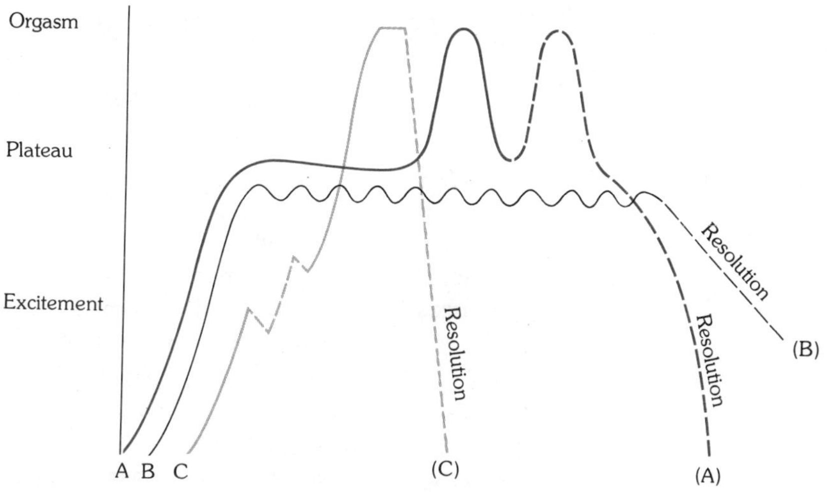

Fig. 25-5 Female sexual response cycle. (Reproduced by permission from Frank A. Beach (ed.), *Sex and Behavior*, N.Y.: John Wiley & Sons, Inc. 1965.)

Before the work of Masters and Johnson, there was considerable debate about whether a difference exists between female orgasm associated with the vagina and orgasm derived from stimulation of the clitoris. Sigmund Freud had contended in his writings that a clitoral orgasm was an immature form of female response. Since the clitoris is the female structure most comparable to the penis, Freud felt that women whose orgasmic experiences centered on the clitoris had not fully accepted their femininity. Masters and Johnson exploded this myth by showing that there is absolutely no difference in physical response no matter what form of stimulation produces orgasm. As a matter of fact, the vagina is quite lacking in nerve endings for touch. Most sensations during intercourse, therefore, come from stimulation of the clitoris and other external tissues. It now seems apparent that sensations from many sources are fused together into the total experience of orgasm and that for the female one of the most important sources of these sensations is the clitoris (Fisher, 1973). To downgrade the "clitoral orgasm" ignores the basic physiology of female sexual response.

Male and Female Responses Compared

The research of Masters and Johnson indicates that the similarities between male and female sexual responses outweigh the differences. However, the differences which do exist may have a significant effect on sexual adjustment. For example, it was found that women typically go through the sexual phases more slowly than do men. During lovemaking, from 10 to 20 minutes is usually required for a woman to go from excitement to orgasm. Males may experience all four stages in as little as 4 minutes.

These differences should be kept in mind by couples seeking sexual compatibility.

Question: Does this mean that a couple should try to time lovemaking to promote simultaneous orgasm?

At one time the concept of simultaneous orgasm (both partners reaching sexual climax at the same time) was considered the ideal goal of lovemaking. More recently, it has been rejected as an artificial concern that may reduce satisfaction instead of enhance it. It is one thing to be aware of differences in male and female responses, and it is quite another to become preoccupied with such differences. To paraphrase one expert (Lowen, 1965):

> To govern the timing of orgasm by the response of either partner destroys the natural flow of feeling that alone guarantees mutual satisfaction. This point cannot be stressed too strongly. Inhibiting the buildup of the excitation for the sake of one partner limits the possibility of mutual satisfaction, whereas the opposite enhances that possibility.

It is more advisable to aim for the satisfaction of both partners through some combination of intercourse and manual stimulation than it is to self-consciously inhibit spontaneity.

Question: Does slower response mean that women are less sexual than men?

Definitely not. During masturbation, 70 percent of females reach orgasm in 4 minutes or less. This finding casts serious doubts on the idea that female response is actually slower. Slower female response during intercourse probably occurs because stimulation to the clitoris is less direct. It might be said that the male simply provides too little stimulation for more rapid female response, not that the female is in any way inferior.

Question: Does penis size affect female response?

Masters and Johnson found that the vagina adjusts to the size of the penis and that subjective feelings of pleasure and intensity of orgasm are not related to penis size. They also found that while individual differences exist in flaccid penis size, there tends to be much less variation in size during erection. Contrary to popular belief, there is no relationship between penis size and male sexual potency.

Question: Men almost always reach orgasm during intercourse, but many women do not. Does this indicate that women are less sexually responsive?

Again, the evidence argues against any lack of female sexual responsiveness. It is true that about one woman in three does not experience orgasm during the first year of marriage. However, this does not imply lack of physical responsiveness since most of these women have reached orgasm through masturbation. Also, the peak of female responsiveness does not occur until about age thirty.

In another regard, the female is clearly more responsive. Only about 5 percent of males are capable of multiple orgasm (and then only after an unavoidable refractory period). Masters and Johnson's findings suggest that most women who regularly experience orgasm are capable of multiple orgasm. Whereas the male is almost always limited to a second orgasm at most, some women report having several orgasms in rapid succession.

Attitudes toward Sexual Behavior

There is considerable debate among psychologists about whether more liberal attitudes toward sexuality have actually been translated into new sexual freedoms. At one extreme it has been predicted that:

> Sexual experience will tend to begin earlier—in fact as soon as the body becomes capable of sexual satisfaction, at the age of twelve or thirteen. Teenagers will take it for granted that sexual intercourse is as natural as kissing, provided there are no unfortunate consequences (Wilson, 1966, p. 187).

Others believe that sexual behavior has remained essentially unchanged for the past 20 years. From this point of view, the "sexual revolution" has been mostly verbal—people are simply talking about sex more now than they were in the past (Miller & Siegal, 1972).

An accurate description of the effects of liberalized attitudes toward sex seems to lie somewhere between these two views. There *have* been changes in sexual behavior. However, these are generally quite moderate. For example, in the early 1950s, Kinsey found that among college-educated subjects, 27 percent of twenty-one-year-old females and 51 percent of twenty-one-year-old males had engaged in sexual intercourse. In 1968, Packard reported that 43 percent of a comparable sample of females and 57 percent of males had engaged in intercourse at least once.

More importantly, this limited change in sexual behavior (confined mostly to females) does not appear to represent a move toward loose or promiscuous sexuality. Although it is true that sexual intercourse by unmarried couples is more freely accepted, most couples emphasize mutual commitment and a loving relationship as a requirement for sexual involvement. In this regard, premarital sex today often parallels the behavior of engaged couples 20 years ago (Simon & Gagnon, 1973).

Another recent study of sexual attitudes and behavior revealed a pattern of liberal attitudes but personal conservatism. In a poll of its readers, *Psychology Today* magazine found that 80 percent accepted extramarital sex under some circumstances. But in practice only 40 percent of married men and 36 percent of married women had actually had extramarital sexual experience (Athenasiou, Shaver, & Travis, 1970). Another survey of more conservative couples found that only 28 percent reported extramarital sexual experience (Johnson, 1970).

Fig. 25-5 Liberalized sexual attitudes have added new conflicts to many relationships. (Photo by Susan Miller.)

Another issue related to liberalized sexual attitudes concerns the plight of the individual who is not ready for, or interested in, greater sexual freedom. One writer notes:

> After several years of propaganda about sexual liberation on campus, many college psychiatrists and counselors are beginning to pay attention to the problems of the students who don't particularly want to be liberated (Adams, 1973).

Apparently some individuals feel pressured into sexual behavior because it is "expected." However, pressures such as these probably come more from the individual than from peers. After a survey of the sexual adjustment of college students, Andrew Barclay (1971) concluded that for many students:

> pleasure in life comes from waiting for the appropriate person to come along; hence sexual behavior will take place in the context of marriage. These individuals will be able to relate to others in an open and honest way, which includes communicating their desires to remain celibate for the time being.[1]

[1]From *Sexuality: A Search for Perspective* by Grummer and Barclay. Copyright © 1971 by Litton Educational Publishing, Inc. Reprinted by permission of D. Van Nostrand Company.

Learning Check

1. The research of Masters and Johnson indicates that the similarities between male and female sexual responses outweigh the differences. T or F?
2. During lovemaking, from 10 to 20 minutes is usually required for a woman to go from excitement to orgasm, while the male may experience all four stages of sexual response in as little as 4 minutes. T or F?
3. Simultaneous orgasm of the male and female is the ultimate goal in lovemaking. T or F?
4. Recent research shows there is considerable evidence that open discussion and more liberal views regarding sexual behavior is causing loose or promiscuous sexuality. T or F?

Answers: 1. T 2. T 3. F 4. F

Resources Summary

Physical differences between males and females can be divided into *primary* (genital) and *secondary* (bodily characteristics). The development of both is greatly influenced by the balance of *androgens* (male hormones) and *estrogens* (female hormones) in the body. In humans *sex roles* (expected behavior based on gender) generally override other sex-based differences in determining adult personality characteristics.

Sexual behavior is quite "natural," being apparent soon after birth and expressed in various ways throughout life. There appears to be little difference in sexual responsiveness between males and females, although females may be more likely to reject some forms of arousal than males. The sex drive for males appears to peak at age eighteen and for females at age thirty. Sex drive in both males and females is related to bodily levels of androgen.

Nocturnal emissions are a normal if unimportant form of sexual release. *Castration* may or may not influence sex drive in humans.

Masturbation is a normal and completely acceptable sexual outlet. It can cause no physical harm and only causes psychological distress when a person fears it or feels guilty because of negative attitudes.

Human sexual response can be divided into four phases: (1) *excitement*, (2) *plateau*, (3) *orgasm*, and (4) *resolution*. Both males and females may go through all four stages in 4 or 5 minutes. But during intercourse females typically take longer than this—from 10 to 20 minutes. There do not appear to be any differences between "vaginal orgasms" and "clitoral orgasms" in the female. Mutual orgasm has been abandoned by most sex counselors as the ideal in lovemaking.

Attitudes towards sex have become more liberalized, but actual changes in sexual behavior have been rather gradual. Generally speaking, the greatest change has been in the number of people willing to talk openly about sex.

Applications

Sexual Problems

The origin of many sexual problems may be summarized in this way:

> Our competitive culture provides a constant pressure for performance. In the sexual area, this pressure concerns potency, responsiveness, and more and better orgasms as standards against which one must measure oneself. Sexual performance thus becomes a major source of personal stress. It is little wonder that counselors are finding their clients in anxiety and desperation about sexuality (Jacobs & Whiteley, 1975).

Question: What are the most common sexual problems? How are they treated?

The two main problems encountered by men are *primary impotence* and *secondary impotence*. The most frequent female complaints are *frigidity* and *orgasmic dysfunction*.

Primary Impotence Primary impotence is the inability to maintain an erection for sexual intercourse. Primary impotence may be an occasional or continuous problem. If it is a repeated pattern, it is usually very disturbing to the man and his sexual partner. Repeated primary impotence should be distinguished from an *occasional* inability to achieve or maintain an erection. Fatigue, excessive consumption of alcohol, anger, and anxiety can all cause temporary impotence in healthy males.

It is important to recognize that occasional impotence is normal, since overreaction to it may generate fears and doubts that will contribute to further impotence. It is particularly important at such times for the female partner to avoid expressing anger, disappointment, or embarrassment. The woman who offers patient reassurance helps prevent the establishment of a vicious cycle.

Primary impotence as a continuing problem is rarely caused by physical illness, disease, or damage. Most cases are caused by psychological factors. Anxiety about sex in general, guilt because of an extramarital affair, resentment or hostility toward one's sexual partner, fear of ability to perform, and similar conflicts and emotions are common sources of chronic impotence.

Treatment for primary impotence usually begins with discussion of the fears and psychological blocks behind the problem. The man learns that he cannot consciously will an erection and that his disability is not a reflection on his manhood. To further free him of his fears (particularly that of failure), the man and his partner are usually assigned a series of exercises to perform. This technique, called *sensate focus*, directs attention to natural sensations of pleasure and builds communication skills.

In sensate focus, the couple is initially told to take turns stroking various parts of each other's bodies. They are instructed to carefully avoid any genital contact at first. Instead, they are to concentrate on giving pleasure and on signaling what is most gratifying to them. This takes the pressure to perform off the male and allows him to learn to give pleasure as a means of receiving it. Over a period of days or weeks, the couple proceeds to more intense physical contact involving the breasts and genitals. As inhibitions are reduced and natural arousal begins to replace fear, the successful couple moves on to normal intercourse.

Secondary Impotence Secondary impotence is the term applied to *premature ejaculation*. Ejaculation may be considered premature if a man cannot delay sexual climax long enough to satisfy his partner in at least one half of their lovemaking attempts (Masters & Johnson, 1970). Premature ejaculation is a very common problem in male sexual adjustment. Theories advanced to explain it have ranged from the idea that it may represent hostility toward the female partner (since it deprives her of satisfaction) to the suggestion that most early male sexual experiences tend to encourage rapid climax (such as those taking place in the back seat of a car and masturbation). Whatever the cause, secondary impotence can cause serious difficulty, especially in the context of long-term relationships.

Treatment of secondary impotence is usually quite successful. The procedures are relatively simple. The most common is the "squeeze technique" used by Masters and Johnson. The woman stimulates her partner manually until he signals that ejaculation is about to occur. She then firmly squeezes the tip of the penis to inhibit orgasm. When the man feels he has control, stimulation is repeated. Gradually the man acquires the ability to delay orgasm sufficiently for satisfactory intercourse.

Frigidity Female frigidity is usually defined as a persistent lack of interest in sex or an inability to derive pleasure from sexual intercourse. A definition such as this implies that the male partner is sexually adequate in terms of freedom from secondary impotence and that he has a commitment to ensuring gratification of the female. Many cases of "frigidity" can be most accurately understood as a problem the couple shares, not just as the woman's problem.

Beyond this, frigidity can often be traced to frightening childhood experiences like molestations (often by older relatives), incestuous relations that produce lasting guilt, a harshly religious background in which sex is considered evil, or cold, unloving childhood relationships. Also common is the need to maintain control over emotions, deep-seated conflicts over being female, and extreme distrust of others, especially males (Masters & Johnson, 1970).

Orgasmic dysfunction is the inability to achieve orgasm during intercourse. It may or may not involve complete inhibition of sexual response. Often it is clear that the woman is not *sexually* unresponsive; she is, instead, *heterosexually* unresponsive. This can be seen in that she may achieve orgasm easily by masturbation. Treatment for frigidity and orgasmic dysfunction takes the same basic form as it does for primary impotence in the male. Counseling and emotional support are coupled with use of the sensate focus method to help the woman and her partner achieve sexual compatibility.

Solving sexual problems can be very difficult. The problems described above are rarely solved without professional help. If a serious sexual difficulty is not resolved in a reasonable amount of time, the aid of an appropriately trained psychologist, physician, or counselor should be sought. The longer the problem is ignored, the more difficult it is to solve, but professional help is available.

Sexual Adjustment

Question: What can be done to improve sexual adjustment?

It is often useless to separate sexual adjustment from the broader context of a relationship. Conflict and unresolved anger in other areas frequently take their toll in sexual adjustment, and mutually satisfying relationships tend to carry over into sexual relations. Sex is not just a performance or a skill to be mastered like playing tennis. It is a form of communication and an extension of a relationship. Couples with strong and open relationships can probably survive most sexual problems. A couple with a satisfactory sex life but a poor relationship rarely lasts.

Sex researchers and therapists Masters and Johnson (1970) have discussed how sexual partners can best approach disagreements about each other's sexual needs and wishes. When disagreements arise over issues like frequency of intercourse, who initiates lovemaking, or what behavior is appropriate, Masters and Johnson believe that the rules should be "each partner must accept the other as the final authority on his or her own feelings." Partners are urged to be *responsive* to each other's needs at an *emotional* level and to recognize that all sexual problems are *mutual*. Failures should always be shared without placing blame. Masters and Johnson feel that it is particularly important to avoid the "numbers game." That is, couples should avoid being influenced by statistics on the "average" frequency of intercourse, by stereotypes about sexual potency, and by the superhuman sexual exploits portrayed in movies and magazines.

Question: Are there any other guidelines for maintaining a healthy emotional relationship?

In a study that compared happily married couples with unhappily married couples, Navran (1967) found that in almost every regard the happily married couples showed superior *communication* skills. Many theorists agree that communication is facilitated by observing the following guidelines (after Bach & Wyden, 1969).

Avoid "Gunnysacking" Persistent feelings, whether positive or negative, need to be expressed. Gunnysacking refers to saving up feelings and complaints. These are then "dumped" during an argument or used as ammunition in a fight. Gunnysacking is very destructive to a relationship.

Be Open about Feelings Happy couples not only talk more, they convey more personal feelings and show greater sensitivity to their partners' feelings.

> . . . in a healthy relationship, each partner feels free to express his likes, dislikes, wants, wishes, feelings, impulses, and the other person feels free to react with like honesty to these. In such a relationship, there will be tears, laughter, sensuality, irritation, anger, fear, baby-like behavior, and so on (Jourard, 1963, p. 343).

Don't Attack the Other Person's Character Whenever possible, expressions of negative feelings should be given as statements of one's own feelings, not as statements of blame. It is far more constructive to say: "It makes me angry when you leave things around the house" than it is to say: "You're a slob!"

Don't Try to "Win" a Fight Constructive fights are aimed at resolving shared differences, not at establishing who is right or wrong, superior or inferior.

Recognize that Anger Is Appropriate Constructive and destructive fights are not distinguished by whether or not anger is expressed. A fight is a fight, and anger is appropriate. As is the case with any other emotion in a relationship, anger should be expressed. However, constructive expression of anger requires that couples fight fair by sticking to the real issues and not "hitting below the belt."

For Discussion

Touching—Does It Always Have Sexual Implications?

The whole thing began because Sidney Jourard is a people-watcher. One day, sitting in a coffeehouse in San Juan, Puerto Rico, where he was a Peace Corps consultant, he wondered how many times the couple at the next table would touch each other in one hour. During the next two years, he did the same thing in London and Paris while studying at London's Tavistock Clinic. When he went to Gainesville, Florida, to teach in the psychology department of the University of Florida, he checked out an American couple for the one hour. The two people at the Gainesville table touched each other twice in one hour. In Paris the touch total for one hour was one hundred ten. In San Juan, one hundred eighty. And in London? In London, the two people touched each other not at all.

From this information you must draw your own conclusions. The professor, back at Gainesville, Florida, teaching, being a therapist and practicing Hatha Yoga, refuses to. But his interest led him to make further surveys.

He issued booklets to his Gainesville students, fifty-four male and eighty-four female. Each booklet contained four diagrams of the body divided into twenty-four zones, the idea lifted (he says with a straight face) from a butcher's meat-chart. He then asked his students to report, anonymously of course, which area of their bodies had been touched by mother, father, best-friend-same-sex, and best-friend-opposite-sex. Furthermore, each student was asked to show which zones of these four chums the student had touched. Time range: within the last year. The charts on this show the result.

Here Jourard *will* draw conclusions about "body accessibility."

"If you're out of love," says the professor, "you're out of touch."

"There isn't a great deal of body contact going on outside the strictly sexual context. It's almost as if all possible meanings of a touch are eliminated except the caress with the sexually arousing intent. . . . Most regions of a young adult's body remain untouched unless one has a close friend of the opposite sex, and that depends on the relationship going on between them."

One of our touch taboos, then, is that we equate touch with sexuality. Unless the relationship is sexual therefore, *mustn't touch*.

Jourard goes on to say that in family physical contact the daughters are "the favored ones." Her parents touch her more than they would if she were a boy. Right up into her twenties. Parents stop touching boys about the time they reach what used to be called The Age of Reason—when one can commit sin. Furthermore, a girl's mother is allowed, or allows herself (having herself once been a favored one), to give frequent touches to a girl's hair. One half the parents get to touch her on her lips, and half manage a literal pat on the back. But—taboo, taboo—only 13 percent of the girls received a paternal pat on the bottom, and none of the girls touched or were touched by their fathers in the genital area. (Not quite the case with regard to male students and Mamma.)

Outside the Best-Friend-Opposite-Sex category very little touching goes on, but when it does happen between lovers, the professor says, "There is a virtual deluge of physical contact all over the body. . . . I suspect that the transformation from virginity or even preorgasmic existence to the experience of having a sexual climax is so radical as to be equivalent to a kind of rebirth."

For Jourard, in our maddeningly crowded world, touch may be our salvation. "I think that body contact has the function of confirming one's bodily being," he says. . . . Yet how can one learn to touch lovingly if one is not permitted to touch and be touched when young? To touch and be touched at times *other* than when making love?

"It's a blunted way of life," Jourard says. "People need physical contact to increase awareness and sensitivity to the body. But, instead, we use our relationship with others as a means to increase our status and social position. We are afraid to let others get close because then we are trapped. . . . The price we pay for this estrangement is loneliness" (H. E. F. Donohue, 1968).

Questions for Discussion

1. Do your patterns of touching and being touched correspond to those found by Jourard?
2. In what ways does sexual contact differ from nonsexual touching?
3. Do you feel as Jourard does that people should touch more? Why or why not?
4. Would you be jealous if your spouse or lover were touched (in a nonsexual way) by a person of the same sex? Opposite sex?
5. Do you think the "sexual revolution" will increase touching by encouraging openness or decrease it by defining more casual touching as potentially sexual?

Suggestions for Further Reading

Bach, G., and P. Wyden. *The Intimate Enemy.* Morrow, 1969.

Cherniak, D., and A. Feingold (eds.). *Birth Control Handbook.* Journal offset (Montreal), 1971.

Fisher, S. *Body Consciousness.* Prentice-Hall, 1973.

Katachadourian, H. A., and D. T. Lunde. *Fundamentals of Human Sexuality.* Holt, 1972.

Masters, W., and V. Johnson. *Human Sexual Response.* Little, Brown, 1966.

——— *Human Sexual Inadequacy.* Little. Brown, 1970.

O'Neill, N., and R. O'Neill. *Open Marriage.* Avon, 1972.

Pomeroy, W. B. *Dr. Kinsey and the Institute for Sex Research.* New American Library, 1973.

Social Psychology I

26

Chapter Preview

Preedy at the Seashore

The following account by author William Sansom describes an incident in which Preedy, a vacationing Englishman, makes his first visit to the beach at his summer hotel in Spain:

> . . . it was time to institute a little parade, the parade of the Ideal Preedy. By devious handlings he gave any who wanted to see the title of his book—a Spanish translation of Homer, classic thus, but not daring, cosmopolitan too—and then gathered together his beach-wrap and bag into a neat sand-resistant pile (Methodical and Sensible Preedy), rose slowly to stretch at ease his huge frame (Big-Cat Preedy), and tossed aside his sandals (Carefree Preedy, after all).[1]

Does this sound familiar? Like Preedy, you may become intensely aware of your actions when making an "entrance" at a party, dance, meeting, or sporting event. We all tend to talk, act, and even think differently when we know others are watching.

Humans are born in the presence of at least one other person and are surrounded by people until death. The journey through life can be lonely at times, but, undeniably, humans are social animals. Any doubt about our social nature can be dispelled by imagining what it would be like to be completely alone: visualize the impact of putting this book down, walking outside, and finding the streets silent and deserted, forever. Contrast this imagined solitude with the real-world clamor of groups, crowds, clubs, clans, families, gangs, audiences, organizations, communities, tribes, societies and nations.

[1]From "A Contest of Ladies." In *The Stories of William Sansom* by William Sansom. Copyright © 1963 Hogarth Press. Reprinted by permission.

Social psychology *is the study of how people behave in the presence (real or implied) of others. Some of the groups just mentioned are formal and organized; others are* unorganized. *All influence the behavior of their members. The fascinating interplay of individual and group behavior has been the target of an immense amount of psychological study, too much, in fact, for us to cover in any detail. Therefore, this chapter and the next are "social psychology samplers." We hope you will agree that the topics selected are interesting and thought-provoking. Some of the questions investigated in this chapter are: If someone asked you to electrocute a stranger, would you do it? Who are you attracted to, and why? Must people conform?*

Resources

Humans in a Social Context—People, People, Everywhere

We are born into an organized society. Established values, expectations, and behavior patterns are present when we arrive. So too is *culture*, an ongoing pattern of life that is passed from one generation to the next. Some representations of culture that are readily visible are language, marriage customs, concepts of ownership, and sex roles.

Groups On a day-to-day level, the groups to which a person belongs form his or her most immediate social environment. Each person is a member of many groups: the family, teams, church groups, work groups, and so on. In each group the individual occupies a *position* in the structure of the group. *Roles* are different behavior patterns displayed in connection with a particular social position. There are expectations associated with playing each of the following roles: mother, teacher, employer, student. Some roles are *ascribed*, meaning they are not under the individual's control: male or female, adolescent, inmate. *Achieved* roles are those which are attained voluntarily: wife, teacher, scientist, bandleader.

Question: What effect does role playing have on behavior?

Roles allow us to anticipate the behavior of others. When a person is acting as a physician, mother, clerk, or police officer, certain behaviors are expected. In general, roles are quite useful because they streamline many of our daily interactions with others. However, roles have a negative side too. It is not unusual for a person to occupy two or more conflicting roles. Getting caught in a *role conflict* can be quite uncomfortable or frustrating. Consider, for example, the traffic court judge whose son is brought before him with a violation.

Position in a group also determines one's *status*. In most groups higher status is associated with special privileges and respect. Status can operate very subtly to influence behavior in many situations. For example, in one interesting experiment an old Rambler and a new Chrysler Imperial were repeatedly driven through an intersection in downtown Palo Alto,

California. The cars were maneuvered so that they were at the front of the line of waiting cars at the traffic signal. When the signal turned green, the test cars failed to move, until someone honked. Eighty-four percent of the following cars honked at the Rambler, but only 50 percent honked at the Imperial (Doob & Gross, 1968). Perhaps this explains some of the American preoccupation with status symbols.

Question: Are there other dimensions of group membership?

Groups are made up of people who are in some way interrelated. Two very important dimensions of any group are its *structure* and *cohesiveness.* Group structure is the organization of roles, communication pathways, and power in the group. Organized groups like the Army or an athletic team have a high degree of structure. Informal friendship groups may or may not be highly structured. Group cohesiveness is basically an indication of the degree of attraction among group members. Cohesiveness is the basis for much of the power that groups exert over their members.

A very important aspect of the functioning of any group is its norms. *Norms* are standards of conduct which prescribe appropriate behavior in a given situation.

Question: How are norms formed?

One early investigation of pressures toward uniformity and the formation of group norms made use of a striking illusion called the *autokinetic effect.* In a completely darkened room a stationary pinpoint of light will appear to drift or move about (it is therefore "autokinetic" or "self-moving"). Muzafer Sherif (1935) found that estimates of how far the light moves vary widely from person to person. However, when two or more people give estimates at the same time, their judgments rapidly converge. There is a similar convergence of attitudes, beliefs, and behavior among members of most groups.

Now that you are armed with this brief introduction to group functioning, let us turn to a look at a basic human need.

Learning Check

1. "Male," "female" and "adolescent" are examples of ____________ ____________ roles.

2. Status refers to a set of expected behaviors associated with a social position. T or F?

3. Social psychology is the study of how people behave ____________ ______________________________.

Answers: **1.** ascribed **2.** F **3.** in the presence of others.

The Need for Affiliation—Come Together

Question: Why do people choose to associate with others?

We have already observed that the *need to affiliate* appears to be a basic human characteristic. Why? Probably because affiliation helps meet needs for approval, support, friendship, and information. We also seek company to alleviate fear or anxiety. An experiment in which college women were threatened with painful electric shock serves as an illustration:

Zilstein's Shock Shop

A man introduced as Dr. Gregor Zilstein ominiously explained to arriving subjects, "We would like to give each of you a series of electric shocks. Now I feel I must be completely honest with you and tell you these shocks will hurt, they will be painful." In the room was a frightening electrical device that seemed to verify Zilstein's intentions. While waiting to be shocked, each subject was given a choice of waiting alone or with other subjects. Women frightened in this way more often chose to wait with others than did subjects told that the shock would be a mild tickle or tingle (Schachter, 1959).

Apparently the frightened women found it comforting or reassuring to be with others. The tempting conclusion is: "Misery loves company." But this is not completely accurate. In a later experiment, women expecting to be shocked were given the option of waiting with other shock subjects, with women waiting to see their advisors, or alone. Most subjects chose to wait with other future "victims." In short, misery seems to love miserable company! In general we tend to seek the company of people in circumstances similar to our own.

Question: Is there a reason for this?

Yes, other people provide information for evaluating one's own reactions. When a situation is threatening or unfamiliar, or when a person is in doubt, *social comparisons* serve as a guide for behavior.

Social Comparison Theory In some cases objective standards for self-evaluation exist. If I want to know how tall I am, I simply get out a yardstick. But how do I know if I am a good athlete, guitarist, worker, parent, or friend? How do I know if my views on politics, religion, or the latest rock album are correct? The only yardstick available for such evaluations is provided by comparing myself to others. Eminent social psychologist Leon Festinger (1954) was among the first to point out that group membership fills needs for *social comparison*. When there are no objective standards, we must turn to others to evaluate our actions, feelings, opinions, or abilities. When students congregate to "compare notes" after a classroom exam, they satisfy needs for social comparison.

Festinger emphasizes that social comparisons are not made randomly, or on some ultimate scale. To illustrate, let's say we ask a student if he is a good tennis player. If he were to compare himself to a professional, the answer would be "no." But this tells little about his relative ability. In his group of tennis partners, he might be considered an excellent player. Useful personal evaluation requires comparison with people of similar backgrounds, abilities, and circumstances. On a fair scale of comparison, our tennis player knows he is good and takes pride in his skills.

In the same way, thinking of yourself as successful, talented, responsible, or fairly paid, depends entirely on whom you compare yourself to. Social comparison theory holds that a desire for self-evaluation determines what groups are joined and provides a general motive for associating with others.

Question: Don't people also affiliate out of attraction for each other?

They do, of course. The next section tells why.

Interpersonal Attraction—Social Magnetism?

"Birds of a feather flock together." "Familiarity breeds contempt." "Opposites attract." "Absence makes the heart grow fonder." Interest in what attracts people to one another has spawned an extensive folklore about what factors are important. This is understandable, since *interpersonal attraction* is the basis for most voluntary social relationships.

Question: What attracts people to each other?

Social psychologist Elliot Aronson (1969) lists several things that determine who you are likely to become friends with.

Physical Proximity It may be difficult to admit, but our friends (or even lovers) are selected more on the basis of opportunity than we might like to believe. Nearness plays a powerful role in determining friendships. In a study of friendship patterns in a campus married-student housing complex, it was found that the closer people lived to each other, the more likely they were to be friends (Festinger et al., 1950). People in love like to think they have found the "one and only" person in the universe for them. In reality they have probably found the one and only person in a 5 mile radius!

Of course, nearness alone is not enough to create a relationship, and familiarity may "breed contempt" when there is a mismatch of personalities. Also, some relationships are successfully maintained over large distances. Let's consider some other factors in attraction.

Physical Attractiveness As might be expected, beautiful people are consistently rated more attractive than those of average appearance. This is another example of the "halo effect" (see Chapter 19) in which it is assumed that attractive people are also intelligent, witty, honest, and so on. To the majority of us it may be reassuring to know that beauty seems mainly to be a factor in initial acquaintance. Later, more substantial personal qualities become important (Berscheid & Walster, 1974).

Competence We are also attracted to those who are talented or competent, but there is an interesting twist to this:

Clever but Clumsy

In an experiment on attraction, college students listened to one of four tapes of a supposed candidate for the "College Quiz Bowl." On two of the tapes the person was represented as highly intelligent; on the other two he was depicted as average in ability. One of the "intelligent" and one of the "average" tapes included an incident in which the candidate clumsily spilled coffee on himself. Those listening to the tapes rated as most attractive the superior candidate who blundered, and as least attractive the student who was average and clumsy. The superior but clumsy student was more attractive than the student who was only superior (Aronson, 1969).

The upshot of this experiment seems to be that we like people who are competent, but human.

Similarity One of the most consistent findings about interpersonal attraction is that people with similar backgrounds, interests, attitudes, or beliefs are attracted to each other (Byrne, 1971). This is probably at least partially due to the reinforcing value of seeing our beliefs and attitudes affirmed by others. It shows we are "right" and reveals that they are clever people as well!

Question: Then is it fair to say that, "Birds of a feather flock together"?

Generally yes, but this is only half of the story. To an extent it is also true that "opposites attract."

Complementary Need Systems Relationships may be formed on the basis of complementary needs, as well as on similarities. For example, an extremely domineering person and a very submissive person may make a better couple than two domineering persons. Complementary needs are humorously illustrated by this fabled conversation between a sadist and masochist: "Beat me!" said the masochist. "No!" replied the sadist! More seriously, research suggests that similarity and complementarity are not conflicting principles of attraction. It appears that similarity is important in the initial stages of building a relationship; whereas complementary needs may be necessary to sustain it (Kerckhoff & Davis, 1962).

Social Exchange Theory Many of the factors we have listed can be understood in terms of maximizing rewards while minimizing "costs" in any social exchange. When a relationship ceases to be attractive, people often say, "I'm not getting anything out of it any more." Actually they probably are, but their costs—in terms of effort, aggravation, or lowered self-esteem—have exceeded their rewards. According to social exchange theory, a relationship must be *profitable* to endure.

The idea that people seek comfortable or mutually beneficial relationships does not completely explain some aspects of interpersonal attraction. To complete the picture, we must also consider Aronson's gain-loss theory.

Question: I'll bite! What's gain-loss theory?

Gain-Loss Theory This approach holds that gains in liking or approval are more rewarding than constant liking. The person who plays "hard to get" makes use of this principle by staging an apparent increase in liking. Aronson also holds that a loss of liking or affection is more punishing than consistent dislike. That is, a falling-out with a friend is more painful than the constant dislike of an enemy. These ideas have been tested in an intriguing experiment:

Does She Like Me?

After each of seven staged "conversations," female college students were allowed to overhear another "student" (actually an actress) give her "honest opinion" of the real subject. Over the course of the experiment some subjects heard the other "student" say consistently flattering things about them *(positive* condition). Others heard repeatedly unfavorable comments about themselves *(negative* condition). A third group heard negative evaluations at first, but these became positive by the last session *(gain* condition). The fourth group heard initially positive comments that later became more negative *(loss* condition). After the seven conversations, subjects were interviewed to determine their liking for the other "student" (Aronson & Linder, 1965).

Question: What were the results?

Aronson's theory predicts that the gain condition should cause more liking than the positive condition, and that the loss condition should cause more dislike than the negative condition. A look at Figure 26-1 will show this was the case. "Winning" acceptance from another person or "losing" it has a powerful effect on attraction. Perhaps we are most attracted to those who slowly learn to like us because they show themselves to be discriminating in their choice of friends!

An added implication of gain-loss theory is that "You always hurt the one you love." Aronson contends that a compliment from a stranger is more flattering (because it is a gain) than one from a friend or spouse (because it is expected). But the reverse is also true: An insult from a stranger represents little or no loss, but a slight by a friend or spouse is costly. It is therefore difficult to compliment, but easy to hurt, the one you love.

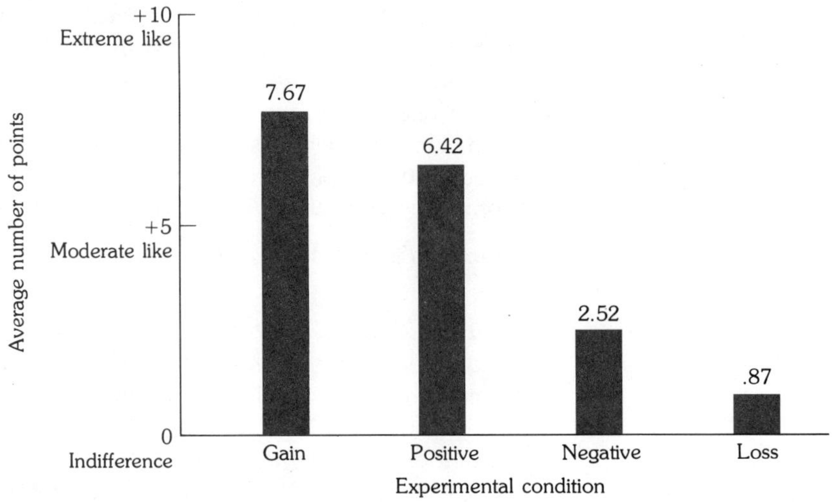

Fig. 26-1 Reported liking for the confederate in the Aronson-Linder study. (After Aronson and Linder, 1965.)

Question: You mention love, how does it differ from liking?

Romantic Love One well-known newspaper columnist likes to ask of teenage romance, "Is it love or sex?" For those involved this may be an academic question, since mutual attraction is strong either way. Just the same, it may be more accurate on occasion to say, "I'm in lust," than it is to say, "I'm in love." All of which raises the question, what is love? Can it be measured? Is love distinct from intense liking? An innovative research program carried out by Zick Rubin (1973) provides some answers.

Until recently, love has been a taboo subject for psychological research. Moreover, love is difficult to study because it is unclear if it should be treated as an emotion, a need, or an attitude. Rubin chose to think of love as an attitude held by one person toward another. This allowed him to develop "liking" and "love" scales (see Box 26-1) for the measurement of each "attitude." Next, he contracted dating couples through a poster that read in part:

ONLY *DATING* COUPLES CAN DO IT!
GAIN INSIGHT INTO YOUR RELATIONSHIP
BY PARTICIPATING IN A UNIQUE SOCIAL-PSYCHOLOGICAL STUDY
. . . AND GET PAID FOR IT TOO!

Couples who agreed to participate were asked to complete each scale twice: once with their date in mind and once for a close friend of the same sex.

Box 26-1 Sample Love-scale and Liking-scale Items Each scale consists of 13 items similar to those shown. Scores on these scales correspond to other indications of love and liking. (Reprinted by permission of Zick Rubin.)

Love Scale

1. If __________ were feeling bad, my first duty would be to cheer him (her) up.
2. I feel that I can confide in __________ about virtually everything.
3. I find it easy to ignore __________'s faults.

Liking Scale

1. When I am with __________, we almost always are in the same mood.
2. I think that __________ is unusually well-adjusted.
3. I would highly recommend __________ for a responsible job.

Question: What were the results?

Scores for love of partner and love of friend differed more than those for liking (see Table 26-1). In other words, dating couples liked *and* loved

Fig. 26-2 What attracts people to each other? (Photo by Philip Jon Bailey, Stock, Boston.)

Table 26-1 Love and Liking for Date and Same-Sex Close Friend

	Mean Scores	
Condition	*Women*	*Men*
Love for partner	89.46	89.37
Liking for partner	88.48	84.65
Love for friend	65.27	55.07
Liking for friend	80.47	79.10

(Rubin, 1970, p. 268.)

their partners, but mostly liked their friends. Women, however, were a little more "loving" of their friends than were men. Does this reflect real differences in the strength of male friendships and female friendships? Probably not, since it is more acceptable in our culture for women to express love for one another than it is for men.

In a later test of the accuracy of the love scale, Rubin recorded the amount of time subjects spent gazing into each other's eyes. He found that couples spent much more time looking into each other's eyes than did strangers, and that couples who had scored high on the love scale (strong love) did more mutual gazing than those who scored low (weak love). These findings provide some insight into the absorbtion of romantic love. As the song says, "Millions of people go by, but they all disappear from view—'cause I only have eyes for you." (Rubin, 1970).

At this point we have primarily considered forces that draw people together. In the next section we will consider forces that keep people apart.

Learning Check

Before reading more, check your comprehension with the following questions.

1. Women threatened with electric shock in an experiment generally chose to wait alone or with other women not taking part in the experiment. T or F?
2. The need to affiliate is related to interest in social comparison. T or F?
3. Social comparisons are made pretty much at random. T or F?
4. Interpersonal attraction is increased by all but one of the following. (Which does not fit?) physical proximity, competence, similarity, social costs
5. According to Aronson, the strongest interpersonal attraction is created by
   a. gains in liking
   b. a loss in liking
   c. constant liking

6. Women rate their friends higher on the love scale than do men. T or F?

Answers: 1. F 2. T 3. F 4. social costs 5. a 6. T

Personal Space—Invisible Boundaries

An interesting aspect of social behavior is the effort people expend to regulate the space around their bodies. Each person has an invisible "spatial envelope" that defines his or her *personal space* and extends "I" or "me" boundaries past the skin.

Question: *What effect does personal space have on behavior?*

Maintaining and regulating personal space directly affects many social interactions. There are unspoken rules covering the interpersonal distance considered appropriate for formal business, casual conversation, waiting in line with strangers, and other situations. The study of rules for the personal use of space is called *proxemics* (Hall, 1966).

The existence of personal space and the nature of proxemics can be demonstrated by "invading" the space of another person. The next time you are talking with an acquaintance, move closer and watch the reaction. Most people show immediate signs of discomfort and step back to re-establish their original distance. Those who hold their ground turn to the side, look away, or position an arm in front of themselves as a kind of psychological barrier to intrusion. If you persistently edge toward your subject, you should find it easy to move him several feet from his original position.

Question: *Would this work with a good friend?*

Possibly not. Conventions governing comfortable or acceptable distances vary according to relationships as well as activities. Hall (1966) identifies four basic zones.

Intimate Distance For most American adults, the most private personal space extends about 18 inches out from the skin. Entry within this space is reserved for special people or circumstances. Lovemaking, comforting others, cuddling children, and massage all take place within this space. So does wrestling!

Personal Distance This is the distance maintained in comfortable interaction with friends. It extends from about 1½ to 4 feet from the body. Personal distance basically keeps people within "arms' reach" of each other.

Social Distance Impersonal business and casual social gatherings take place in a range of about 4 to 12 feet. This distance eliminates most possibilities of touching, and formalizes conversation by requiring greater voice projection. "Important people" in many offices use the width of their imposing desks to maintain social distance while conducting business.

Public Distance When people are separated by more than 12 feet, interactions take on a decidedly formal quality. People look "flat" and the voice must be raised. Formal speeches, lectures, business meetings, and the like, are conducted at public distance.

Spatial Behavior Violations of personal space at each distance tend to cause the "invaded" person to move away or become defensive (Dabbs, 1972). In one study, experimental assistants sat down a foot or less from other students studying in a library. In most cases other seats were available. As the "invader" busied himself, the other student typically stopped, put an arm up, and in most cases left a few minutes later (Sommer, 1969). When it is impossible to maintain distance (for example, in a crowded elevator or a dentist's chair) privacy is most often maintained by avoiding eye contact.

Territoriality Personal space also extends to areas that become our "territory." For example, in the library, readers protect their territory by marking it with coats, handbags, books, or other personal belongings (Sommer, 1969). "Saving a place" at a theater or library also demonstrates the tendency to identify a space as "ours." Respect for the temporary ownership of space is widespread. It is not unusual for a person to "take over" an entire table or study room by looking sufficiently annoyed when others intrude. Your own personal territory may include your room, specific seats in many of your classes, or a particular table in the cafeteria or library that "belongs" to you and your friends.

Social Influence—Follow the Leader

Question: What is social influence?

Imagine a traffic signal brightly flashing the word: WAIT. As you and a number of other pedestrians wait for it to change, a well-dressed man in a suit crosses against the light. How many people follow him? Do you think the answer would be different if the man were dressed in a denim shirt, patched pants, and scuffed shoes? One of the most heavily researched topics in social psychology concerns the effects of *social influence.* When people interact they almost always affect one another's behavior. The street-corner setting was used in a well-known experiment on social influence. As you might have guessed, more people followed the well-dressed man than the one dressed in shabby clothes (Lefkowitz *et al.*, 1955).

In another sidewalk experiment, various numbers of people were assembled on a busy New York City street. On cue they all looked at a sixth-floor window across the street. A camera recorded the number of passersby who also stopped to stare. The larger the initial group, the more people were influenced to join in staring at the window (Milgram *et al.*, 1969).

Question: Are there different kinds of social influence?

These are only two of countless possible examples of social influence. To help organize thinking about social influence, McGuire (1969) has identified five situations in which it occurs:

1. *Suggestion situations*—where repeated communication is presented, often without explanation.
2. *Conformity situations*—where communication of differences between individual and group actions, norms, or values is made.
3. *Group discussion*—where, through group dynamics and social interaction, tailored arguments and counter-arguments occur.
4. *Persuasive messages*—where carefully considered and polished arguments are presented in one-way communication.
5. *Intensive indoctrination* (brainwashing)—where all of the above are used simultaneously.

Everyday behavior is highly influenced by all of the above except number 5. Perhaps the most pervasive in their effects are conformity situations.

Conformity—Odd Man Out

When John first started working at the Fleegle Flange Factory he found it easy to process 300 flanges an hour, while those around him averaged only 200. Other workers told him to slow down and take it easy. "I get bored," he said and continued to do 300 flanges an hour. At first John had been welcomed, but now conversations broke up when he approached and other workers laughed or ignored him when he spoke. Although he never made a conscious decision to conform, in another week John's output had slowed to 200 flanges an hour.

As mentioned earlier, all groups have shared rules of conduct called *norms.* The broadest norms, defined by society as a whole, establish "normal" or acceptable behavior in most situations. Comparing hair styles, habits of speech, dress, eating habits, and social customs in two or more cultures makes it clear that we all conform to social norms. In fact, a degree of uniformity is necessary if we are to interact comfortably. Imagine being totally unable to anticipate the actions of others. In stores, schools, and homes this would be frustrating and disturbing. On the highways it would be lethal.

Perhaps the most basic of all group norms is (as John discovered), "Thou shalt conform!" (Suedfeld, 1966). This is equally true for the Hell's Angels, the Daughters of the American Revolution, a street-corner gang, or the board of directors of a large corporation. Groups of all kinds exert considerable pressures toward uniformity on their members. Like it or not, everyday life is filled with instances of conformity.

Fig. 26-3 All groups expect a degree of conformity from their members. (Photo by Andy Mercado, Jeroboam.)

Question: How strong are group pressures for conformity?

The Asch Experiment One of the better known experiments on conformity was staged by Solomon Asch in the early 1950s. Asch's experiment is best appreciated by placing yourself in the position of a subject. Assume that you have volunteered to take part in a psychological study of perception. You are seated at a table with six other students. Your task is actually quite simple. On each trial you are shown two large cards. On one card is a single "standard" line. On the second card are three "comparison" lines of varying length (see Fig. 26-4). You are asked to select the comparison line on each card that is closest in length to the standard.

As the testing begins, each subject announces an answer for the first card. When your turn comes, you find yourself in complete agreement with the others. "This isn't hard at all," you say to yourself. For several more trials your answers correspond to those of the other group members. Then comes a shock. All six people announce that line number 1 matches the standard, and you were about to say line number 3 matches. Suddenly you feel alone and upset. You nervously look at the cards again as the room falls silent. Everyone seems to be staring at you as the experimenter awaits your answer. Do you yield to the group?

In this experiment the other "students" were all accomplices coached to give the wrong answer on about a third of the trials. Few real subjects suspected trickery; hence, the group pressure created was very realistic (Asch, 1956).

Question: *How many people yielded to group pressure?*

Subjects conformed to the group on about one-third of the critical trials. Seventy-five percent of those tested yielded at least once. The significance of these results is underscored by the fact that other people tested alone errored in less than 1 percent of their judgments. Those who yielded to group pressures were clearly denying what their eyes told them.

Question: *Do you mean they actually saw things differently?*

Individual Factors in Conformity Interviews with Asch's subjects showed that conformity occurred at three levels. A few subjects yielded at the *perceptual* level, having convinced themselves that they actually saw the line as reported by others. More often, yielding was *judgmental*, in that subjects felt they did not understand the task, or did not want to spoil the experiment. Subjects who wore glasses were particularly likely to yield at the judgmental level. The largest number of subjects were aware they were yielding, and were upset about it, but conformed in fear of being ridiculed or excluded by the group. This represents yielding at the *action* level.

Question: *Are some people more susceptible to group pressures than others?*

A variety of experiments have shown that people with high needs for structure or certainty are more likely to be influenced. People who are anxious, low in self-confidence, or who are concerned with the opinions or approval of others are also more susceptible.

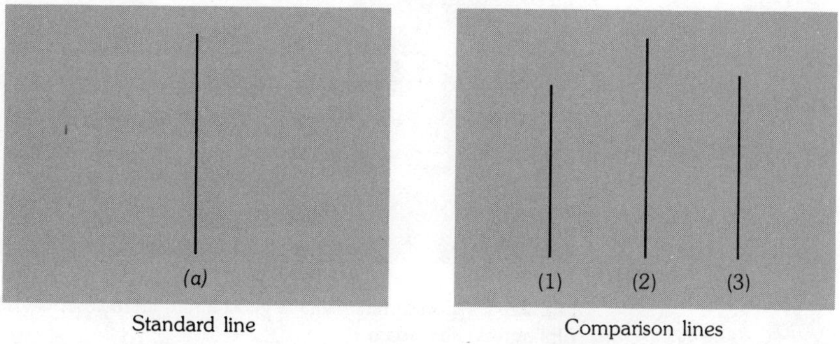

Fig. 26-4 Stimuli used in Solomon Asch's conformity experiments.

Question: How do groups enforce norms?

Group Factors in Conformity In most of our experiences with groups we have been rewarded with acceptance and approval for conformity, and threatened with rejection or ridicule for nonconformity. These reactions are called *group sanctions.* Negative sanctions (or punishments) for non-conformity range from laughter, staring, or social disapproval to complete rejection or formal ostracism. This is illustrated by later experiments in which Asch made up groups of six real subjects and one trained dissenter. When "Mr. Odd" announced his wrong answers, he was greeted with derisive laughter and sidelong glances.

Question: Wouldn't the effectiveness of group sanctions depend on the importance of the group?

Yes, and this is why the Asch experiments are impressive. Since these were only temporary groups, sanctions were informal and rejection had no lasting importance.

Question: What factors, besides importance of the group, affect the degree of conformity?

Fig. 26-5 Conformity: What's good about it? In what ways is it undesirable? (Photo by Alphapress, Jeroboam.)

Earlier we described an experiment in which passersby were influenced by a group of people staring at a building. We noted that the larger the group, the greater the number of people influenced. In Asch's face-to-face groups the *size* of the majority also made a difference, but a surprisingly small one. The number of conforming subjects increased dramatically as the majority was increased from two to three people. However, a majority of three produced about as much yielding as a majority of eight. Next time you want to talk someone into (or out of) something, take two friends along and see what a difference it makes!*

Even more important than the size of the majority is its *unanimity*. Having at least one person in your corner can greatly reduce pressures to conform. When Asch provided subjects with an ally (who also opposed the majority by giving the correct answer), conformity was lessened. In terms of numbers, a unanimous majority of three is more powerful than eight with one dissenting. Perhaps this accounts for the rich diversity of human attitudes, beliefs, opinions, and life-styles. If you can find at least one other person who sees things as you do (no matter how weird), you can be relatively secure in your opposition to other viewpoints.

Social Power

In trying to understand the ways in which people are able to influence each other it is helpful to distinguish among five types of *social power* (French & Raven, 1959). *Reward power* lies in the ability to reward a person for complying with desired behavior. Teachers try to exert reward power over their students through the use of grades. Employers command reward power by their control of wages and bonuses. *Coercive power* is based on the ability to punish a person for failure to comply. Coercive power is the basis for most statute law, in that fines or imprisonment are used to control behavior. *Legitimate power* comes from acceptance of a person as an agent of an established social order. For example, elected leaders and supervisors have legitimate power. So does a teacher in the classroom, but outside the classroom that power would have to come from another source. *Referent power* is based on respect for or identification with a person or a group. The person "refers to" the source of referent power for direction. *Expert power* is based upon recognition that another person has knowledge or expertise necessary for achieving a goal. Allowing teachers or experts to guide behavior because you believe in their ability to produce desirable results is an example. Physicians, lawyers, psychologists, and plumbers have expert power.

A person who has power in one situation may have very little in another. In those situations where a person has power, he or she is described as an *authority*. In the next section we will investigate *obedience*. Obedience is a special type of conformity to the demands of an authority.

*Sometimes it helps if the two are large and mean-looking.

Learning Check

1. The study of the interpersonal use of space is called proxemics. T or F?

2. The effect one person's behavior has on another is called ________________.

3. In conformity, repeated communication is presented—often without explanation. T or F?

4. Conformity is a normal aspect of social life. T or F?

5. Nonconformity is punished by negative group ________________.

Answers:

1. T **2.** Social influence **3.** F, this describes suggestion **4.** T **5.** sanctions

Obedience—Would You Electrocute a Stranger?

The question is this: If ordered to do so, would you shock a man with a known heart condition who is screaming and asking to be released? Certainly we can assume that few people would do so. Or can we? In Nazi Germany obedient soldiers (once average citizens) helped slaughter over nine million people. A more recent example of the same phenomenon is Lt. William Calley's massacre of helpless Vietnamese civilians at My Lai. Do such inhumane acts reflect deep character flaws? Are they the acts of heartless psychopaths or crazed killers? Or are they simply the result of obedience to authority? What are the limits of such obedience? These are questions which puzzled social psychologist Stanley Milgram (1965) when he began a provocative series of studies on obedience.

Question: How did Milgram study obedience?

Like the Asch experiments, Milgram's research is best appreciated by imagining yourself as a subject. Place yourself in this situation.

Milgram's Study Imagine answering a newspaper ad to take part in a "learning" experiment at Yale University. When you arrive you are immediately paid $4.50. A coin is flipped and a second subject, a pleasant-looking man in his fifties, is designated the "learner." By chance you have become the "teacher."

Your task is to read a list of word pairs to be memorized by the learner. You are to punish him with an electrical shock each time he makes a mistake. The learner is taken to an adjacent room and you watch as he is seated in an "electric chair" apparatus and electrodes are attached to his wrists. You are then escorted to your position in front of a "shock generator." On this device is a row of 30 switches labeled from 15 to 450 volts and accompanied by descriptions ranging from "Slight Shock" to "Extreme Intensity Shock" and finally "Danger Severe Shock." Your instructions are to administer a shock each time the learner makes a mistake. You are to begin with 15 volts and then move one switch (15 volts) higher for each additional mistake.

The experiment begins, and the learner soon makes his first error. You flip a switch. More mistakes. Rapidly you reach the 75-volt level. The learner moans after each shock. At 100 volts he complains he has a heart condition. At 150 volts he says he no longer wants to continue and demands release. At 290 volts he screams and says he can no longer give answers.

At some point during the experiment you begin to protest to the experimenter. "That man has a heart condition," you say; "I'm not going to kill that man." The experimenter says, "Please continue." Another shock and another scream from the learner and you say, "You mean I've got to keep going up the scale? No, sir. I'm not going to give him 450 volts!" The experimenter says, "The experiment requires that you continue." For the remainder of the experiment the learner refuses to answer any more questions and screams with each shock (Milgram, 1965).

Question: I can't believe many people would do this. What happened?

Milgram also doubted that many people would obey his orders, and when he polled a group of psychiatrists before the experiment they predicted that less than 1 percent of those tested would obey. The astounding fact is that 65 percent of those tested obeyed completely by going all the way to the 450-volt level. No one stopped short of 300 volts ("Severe Shock").

Question: Was the "learner" injured?

The time has come to reveal that the "learner" was actually an actor who turned a tape-recorder on and off in the "shock room." No shocks were ever administered, but the dilemma for the "teachers" was quite real. Subjects protested, sweated, trembled, stuttered, bit their lips, and laughed nervously. Clearly they were disturbed by what they were doing, but most obeyed the experimenter's orders.

Question: Why did so many people obey?

Milgram's Follow Up Some have suggested that the prestige of Yale University contributed to subjects' willingness to obey. Could subjects have assumed that the professor running the experiment would not really allow anyone to be hurt? To investigate this possibility, the experiment was rerun in a shabby office building in nearby Bridgeport, Connecticut. There was nothing in either the location or the experimenter's appearance to inspire confidence. Under these conditions fewer people obeyed (48 percent), but the reduction was minor.

Milgram was quite disturbed by the willingness of people to knuckle under to authority and to senselessly shock someone. In later experiments, he tried in various ways to reduce obedience. He found that distance between the "teacher" and the "learner" was of importance. When subjects were in the same room as the learner, only 40 percent were fully obedient. When they were face-to-face with the learner and required to force his hand down on a "shock plate," only 30 percent obeyed. Distance from the authority also had an effect. When the experimenter delivered his orders over the phone, only 22 percent obeyed.

Milgram's research raises nagging questions about our willingness to commit antisocial or inhumane acts commanded by a "legitimate authority." The excuse so often given by war criminals: "I was only following orders," takes on new meaning in this light. Milgram suggests that when directions come from an authority, people rationalize that they are not personally responsible for their actions.

Question: Aren't you taking an overly dim view of obedience?

Obedience to authority is obviously necessary and desirable in many circumstances. Just the same, it is probably true, as C. P. Snow (1961) has observed, "When you think of the long and gloomy history of man, you will find more hideous crimes have been committed in the name of obedience than in the name of rebellion." With this in mind, let us end this discussion on a more positive note. In one of his experiments, Milgram found that group support can greatly reduce destructive obedience. When

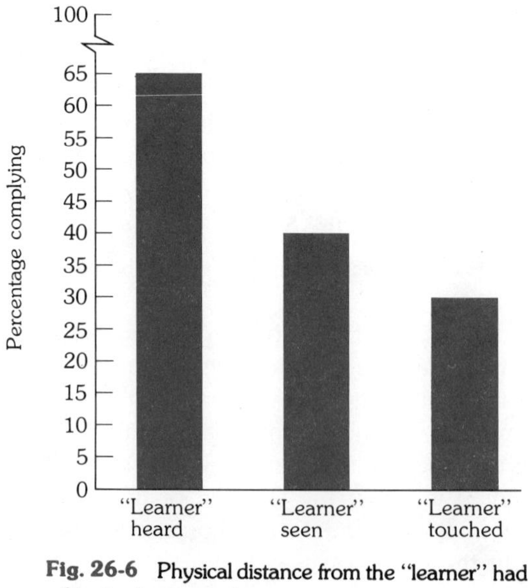

Fig. 26-6 Physical distance from the "learner" had a significant effect on the percentage of subjects obeying orders.

real subjects saw two other "teachers" (both actors) resist orders and walk out of the experiment, only 10 percent continued to obey. Thus, a personal act of courage or moral fortitude by one or two members of a group may free others to disobey misguided or unjust authority.

Learning Check

1. Would you electrocute a stranger? ______________________

2. Obedience in Milgram's experiments was related to:
a. distance between learner and teacher
b. distance between experimenter and teacher
c. obedience of other teachers
d. all of the above

3. Obedience is conformity to ______________________.

Answers: **1.** answer will vary **2.** d **3.** authority

Resources Summary

Social psychology studies humans as members of groups. *Group roles, status* and *norms* exert considerable influence on people. *Affiliation* is based on various factors including alleviation of anxiety and desires for *social comparison. Interpersonal attraction* is related to nearness, physical attractiveness, competency, similarity, and complementary needs. *Romantic love* has been studied as a special kind of attitude. It seems to differ from liking. The study of *personal space* is called *proxemics. Social influence* refers to the effect one person's behavior has on another. *Conformity*, demonstrated in the Asch experiments is a very important form of social influence. *Obedience*, as investigated by Milgram, is a form of conformity particularly susceptible to misuse.

Applications

Assertive Training—Standing Up for Your Rights

Have you ever:

> Hesitated to question an error on a restaurant bill because you were afraid of making a scene?
>
> Backed out of asking for a raise or a change in working conditions?
>
> Said "yes" when you wanted to say "no"?
>
> Been afraid to question a grade that seemed unfair?

Most of us have been rewarded, first as children, and later as adults, for compliant, obedient, or "good" behavior. Perhaps this is why so many people find it difficult to assert themselves. Or perhaps non-assertion is related to the anxiety that accompanies "making a scene" or feeling disliked by others. Whatever the causes, some people are so seriously inhibited that they suffer tremendous anguish in any situation requiring poise, self-confidence, or self-assertion. Fortunately for these people, behavior therapist Joseph Wolpe (and others) have pioneered a therapeutic technique called *assertive training*.

Question: What is done in assertive training?

Assertive training is a very direct procedure. By using group exercises, videotapes, mirrors, and staged conflicts, the behavior therapist teaches assertive behavior. People learn to practice honesty, disagreeing, questioning authority, and assertive postures and gestures. As their self-confidence improves, non-assertive clients are taken on "field trips" to shops and restaurants where they practice what they have learned.

Non-assertion requiring therapy is unusual. Nevertheless, many people become tense or upset in at least some situations in which they must stand up for their rights. For this reason, many people have found the techniques and exercises of assertive training helpful. If you have ever eaten a carbonized steak when you ordered it rare, or stood in silent rage as a clerk ignored you, the following discussion will be of interest.

Self-Assertion The first step in assertive training is to convince yourself of three basic rights: You have the right to refuse, to request, and to right a wrong. Self-assertion involves standing up for these rights by speaking out in your own behalf.

Question: Is self-assertion just getting things your own way?

Not at all. A basic distinction can be made between self-assertive and aggressive behavior. Assertion is a direct, honest expression of feelings and desires. It is not exclusively self-serving, since pent up anger can be very destructive to relationships. People who are non-assertive are usually patient to a fault. In contrast, aggression does not take into account the feelings or rights of others. Aggression is an attempt to get one's own way no matter what. Assertion techniques emphasize firmness, not attack.

The basic idea in assertive training is that each assertive action is practiced until it can be repeated even under stress. For example, let's say it really angers you when a store clerk waits on several people who arrived after you did. To improve your assertiveness in this situation you would begin by *rehearsing* the dialogue, posture, and gestures you would use to confront the clerk or the other customer. Working in front of a mirror can be very helpful. If possible, you should *role play* the scene with a friend. Be sure to have your friend take the part of a really aggressive or irresponsible clerk, as well as a cooperative one. Rehearsal and role playing should also be used when you expect a possible confrontation with someone: For example, if you were going to ask for a raise, challenge a grade, or confront a landlord.

Question: Is that all there is to it?

No, another important principle is *overlearning* When you rehearse or role play assertive behavior, it is essential to continue practice until your responses become almost automatic. This helps prevent becoming flustered in the actual situation.

One more technique you may find useful is the *broken record.* A good way to prevent assertion from becoming aggression is to simply restate your request as many times and as many ways as necessary. As an illustration, let's say you are returning a pair of shoes to a store. After two wearings the shoes fell apart but you bought them two months ago and no longer have a receipt. The broken record sounds something like this:

Customer: I would like to have these shoes replaced.

Clerk: Do you have a receipt?

Customer: No, but I bought them here and since they are defective I would like to have you replace them.

Clerk: I can't do that without a receipt.

Customer: I understand that, but I want them replaced.

Clerk: Well, if you'll come back this afternoon and talk to the manager . . .

Customer: I've brought these shoes in because they are defective.

Clerk: Well, I'm not authorized to replace them.

Customer: Yes, well, if you'll replace these, I'll be on my way.

Notice that the customer has not attacked the clerk or created an angry confrontation. Simple persistence is often all that is necessary for successful self-assertion.

To summarize, self-assertion is not instant poise, confidence, or self-assurance. It is a way of combating anxieties associated with life in an impersonal and sometimes intimidating society. If you are interested in more information, you can consult a book entitled *Your Perfect Right* by Robert Alberti and Michael Emmons.

For Discussion

Passive Compliance and "Little Murders"

Social scientists used to worry about our becoming a nation of sheep. As we have seen, social pressures for uniformity can be powerful. The regimentation of modern life is still cause for concern, but recently the emphasis has shifted to *passivity* rather than simple conformity. Milgram's experiment is not the only example of excessive or unquestioning obedience. In one study conducted by Martin Orne (1962), subjects were presented with a thoroughly boring task. They were given sheets of numbers and asked to add up each pair of adjacent numbers. After finishing a sheet, subjects were directed to pick up a card upon which were instructions to tear the completed sheet into a minimum of 32 pieces, to go on to the next sheet, and then to pick up another card. The experimenter departed, commenting that he would return eventually. Quite incredibly, many subjects worked on this meaningless task for several hours, with few outward signs of anger.

Question: Could it be that people cooperated because they didn't want to ruin the experiment?

Yes, it's possible this degree of passive compliance is limited to artificial experiments. However, researcher Thomas Moriarty (1975) has recently demonstrated passivity under more realistic conditions. Moriarty became interested in the "little murders" of daily life: the personal insults, rebuffs, and sacrifices of dignity that have become so common. Moriarty observed that many people will put up with almost anything to avoid a confrontation. He decided to put this passive, "no-hassle" attitude to experimental test.

In one experiment two subjects (one actually an accomplice) were given a difficult test in a very small room. The two subjects were seated back-to-back and left alone to work. As soon as the experimenter left, the phoney subject turned on a portable cassette tape-player at full volume. Subjects who failed to complain were treated to 17 minutes of nerve-wracking rock music. The accomplice was instructed to turn the music off only after a third request. In this particular experiment, 80 percent of the subjects said nothing, although they glared, cupped their ears, stopped work, and so forth. An interview later showed that most were angry or annoyed, but were afraid to tell the other "subject" to be quiet.

Again there is a possibility that the passivity observed in this study is unique to the experimental setting. However, when Moriarty and his students staged loud conversations behind theater patrons or people studying in a library, very few protested. In other naturalistic experiments, people were accosted in phone booths. The experimenter explained that he had left a ring in the booth and asked if the subject had found it. When the subject said "no," the experimenter demanded that the subject empty his pockets. Most did.

In these and similar situations, people passively accepted having their personal rights trampled, even when objecting presented no threat to the person's safety. Have we become, as Moriarty puts it, "a nation of willing victims"?

Questions for Discussion

1. What would have been an assertive response to the situations described above? An aggressive response?
2. Would it be possible to be completely nonconforming (that is, to not conform to *some* group norm)?
3. How serious, in your estimation, are problems of conformity, obedience, and passivity?
4. How has physical proximity influenced your choice of friends?
5. Modern warfare allows killing to take place impersonally and at a distance. How does this relate to Milgram's experiments?
6. If a waiter or waitress wanted to use gain-loss theory to earn larger tips, how should he or she act in contact with customers?
7. People of different nationalities often have different norms for personal space. What would you expect to happen in a conversation between two people with very different proxemic habits?
8. Can you think of a personal experience in which you were subjected to group pressures like those in the Asch experiment? How did you feel? Did you yield?
9. In view of the Milgram obedience experiment, do you think the civil disobedience of the civil-rights and anti-war movements was justified? Why or why not?

Suggestions for Further Reading

Aronson, E. *The Social Animal.* Viking, 1972.

Brown, R. *Social Psychology.* Free Press, 1965.

Goffman, E. *The Presentation of Self in Everyday Life.* Doubleday, 1959.

Hall, E. T. *The Hidden Dimension.* Doubleday, 1966.

Homans, G. C. *Social Behavior: Its Elementary Forms.* Harcourt Brace Jovanovich, 1961.

27 Social Psychology II

Chapter Preview

Doomsday for the Seekers

Mrs. Keech was receiving messages from superior beings on a planet called Clarion. On their journeys to Earth they had detected a fault in the earth's crust that would submerge the North American continent in a natural disaster of unimaginable proportions. The date of this event was to be December 21. However, Mrs. Keech and her band of followers, who called themselves the Seekers, had no fear of the impending disaster. Their plans were to assemble on December 20 when they expected to be met at midnight by a flying saucer and taken to safety in outer space.

The night of December 20 arrived, and the Seekers assembled at Mrs. Keech's house. Many had given up jobs and possessions in preparation for their departure. Expectations were high and commitment was total, but as the night wore on, midnight passed and the world continued to exist. It was a bitter and embarrassing disappointment to all concerned.

Question: Did the group break up then?

The amazing twist to this story, and the aspect that intrigued social psychologists, was that the Seekers became more convinced than ever before that they and Mrs. Keech had been right. At about 5 A.M. Mrs. Keech announced that she had received a message explaining that the Seekers had saved the world. Before the night of December 20, the group had been uninterested in convincing other people that the world was coming to an end. Now they called newspapers, magazines, and radios to explain what had happened and to convince others of their accomplishment.

How do we explain this strange turn in the behavior of Mrs. Keech's doomsday group? The answer seems to lie in the concept of cognitive dissonance. *Cognitive dissonance also helps to explain many aspects of attitude change. Watch for a discussion of cognitive dissonance in the following material.*

Resources

Attitudes—Belief + Emotion + Action

What is your attitude toward: birth control, marijuana, Republicans, higher education, Chevrolets, psychology? The answers have far-reaching effects on your behavior. The effects of attitudes are intimately woven into the way a person views the world and acts toward it. Our tastes, friendships, votes, preferences, and goals are all touched by attitudes.

Question: What specifically is an attitude?

An *attitude* is a learned predisposition to respond to people, objects, or institutions in a positive or negative way. Attitudes are one of the more heavily studied aspects of social functioning. This is because attitudes summarize past experience and predict or direct future actions. A person's personality and social relationships are deeply interconnected with attitudes.

"Your attitude is showing," is sometimes said. This seems like a simple statement, but actually there are three ways in which attitudes are expressed. Most attitudes have a *belief component*, an *emotional component*, and an *action component.* Consider, as an example, your attitude toward gun control. You will have beliefs about whether or not gun control would affect rates of crime or violence; you will have emotional responses to guns, find them either attractive and desirable or threatening and destructive. And you will have a tendency to seek out or to avoid gun ownership. The action component of your attitude will probably also include support of organizations that urge or oppose gun control.

Question: How do people acquire attitudes?

Attitude Formation Attitudes are acquired in three basic ways. Sometimes through *direct contact* with the object of the attitude—like opposing pollution when a nearby factory ruins your favorite river. Attitudes are also learned through *interaction* with others holding the attitude—if you live in a vegetarian household, chances are you will become a vegetarian. Attitudes are also acquired through the effects of *child rearing.* For example, if both parents belong to the same political party, chances are two out of three that the child will belong to the same party as an adult (Campbell *et al.*, 1954.

In the previous chapter we discussed group forces which operate to bring about conformity: there is little doubt that many of the attitudes we hold are influenced by group *membership.* For example, in one classic study, discussion groups were formed to discuss the case of a juvenile delinquent. Most group members took the position that what the boy needed was love, kindness, and friendship. As a test of group pressures on attitudes, a person was introduced into the group who advocated extreme punishment.

Question: How did group members react to the "deviant"?

At first they directed almost all of their comments to him. In effect, they seemed to be trying to change his attitudes toward greater agreement with the group. However, if the deviate stuck to his position, an interesting thing happened. The deviate was almost completely excluded from further conversation. After the discussion was complete, group members were asked to anonymously rank members in terms of their desirability for continued group membership. The deviate was strongly rejected in these ratings. Both the strength of group pressures for conformity and the difficulty of holding deviant attitudes are clearly visible in this experiment (Schachter, 1951).

A number of other factors may contribute to the formation of attitudes. Schools and peer groups undoubtedly influence the formation of attitudes in childhood. *Peer group influences* can be particularly strong. Parents often lament many of the ideas and attitudes their children "pick up" from their friends. Attitudes are also influenced by the *mass media.* As Marshal McLuhan puts it, we are "massaged" by the media, meaning:

Fig. 27-1 Attitudes are an important dimension of social behavior. (Photo by Hap Stewart, Jeroboam.)

threatened, urged, cajoled, persuaded, and otherwise influenced. Ninety-eight percent of American homes have a television set, which is on an average of 6 hours a day. The accumulative effect of the values thus channeled into homes clearly has an effect on the attitudes of many people. As mentioned elsewhere in this book, some psychologists are particularly concerned with the casual attitudes toward violence portrayed on TV. Also of concern are the stereotyped images of male and female roles and racial or ethnic identities found on "the tube."

Some attitudes are formed quite inadvertently through *chance conditioning*. Let's say, for instance, that you have had three encounters in your lifetime with psychologists. If by chance all three were negative, you might take an unduly dim view of psychology and psychologists. In the same way, people often develop strong attitudes toward cities, restaurants, or parts of the country on the basis of one or two unusually good or bad experiences with each.

Question: Why are some attitudes acted upon while others are not?

To understand why some attitudes seem to have more influence than others it must be recognized that attitudes in general can be quite irrational. Some attitudes rest almost entirely on the emotional component and represent a strong feeling of like or dislike that may not be backed up by facts or actions. At other times, our attitudes are based on sound factual arguments but carry little emotional impact. Even when an attitude is based on strong emotion and clear-cut beliefs, it may not be acted upon. For example, a person has concluded that automobiles contribute significantly to pollution and strongly objects to pollution, but for convenience continues to drive to work every day.

Question: How are such discrepancies explained?

The answer lies in the fact that attitudes are only one of many determinants of action in a particular situation. The *immediate consequences* of one's actions weigh heavily on the choices that are made. The person who objects to pollution but continues to drive is responding to the immediate convenience of driving. A person with strongly negative attitudes toward the police may act with decorum in their presence. In short, there are often large differences between privately expressed attitudes and public behavior. We typically do not act fully to express even our most strongly held attitudes.

Question: Can attitudes be measured?

Attitude Measurement There are a number of approaches to the measurement of attitudes. In some cases, individuals are simply asked in a straightforward manner to express attitudes toward a particular issue. For example, a person might be asked in an *open-ended interview*: "How do you feel about strip mining?" The second approach, which has been particularly useful as a measure of attitudes toward various national or ethnic groups, is a *social distance scale.* Social distance indicates the degree to which a person would be willing to have contact with another person. The person is asked to indicate his or her willingness to admit members of a particular group to various levels of social closeness ranging from "would exclude from my country" to "would admit to marriage in my family."

Use of *attitude scales* is one of the most common approaches to attitude measurement. Attitude scales consist of statements expressing various possible attitudes on a particular issue. For example, "socialized medicine would destroy the quality of health care in this country" or "this country desperately needs a national health care program." Subjects are asked to express agreement or disagreement with each item on a five-point scale ranging from "strongly agree" to "strongly disagree." By computing scores on all items, a person can be rated in terms of overall acceptance or rejection of a particular issue.

Attitude measures, particularly as they have been used in public polls, have provided much useful information about the feelings of large segments of the population. However, it is again important to remember that expressed attitudes and behavior may differ. Publicly expressed attitudes favoring racial or sexual equality often crumble in situations involving a conflict of interest. A "racially enlightened" individual, for instance, may act quite bigoted when equal employment opportunity laws threaten a chance for employment.

Attitude Change—Or Why the "Seekers" Went Public

Although attitudes are relatively stable, they are subject to change. Some attitude change can be understood in terms of the concept of *reference groups.* A reference group is one whose values and attitudes are seen by the individual as being relevant to his or her own. Reference group membership need not be physical. It depends instead on who an individual identifies with or cares about. In the 1930s Theodore Newcomb studied real life attitude change among students at Bennington College. Most students came from conservative homes, but Bennington was a very liberal school. Newcomb found that most students shifted significantly toward more liberal attitudes during their 4 years at Bennington. Those who did not change maintained parents and hometown friends as their primary reference group (typified by one student's statement, "I decided I'd rather stick to my father's ideas"). Those who did change primarily identified with the campus community. Notice that all students could count the college and their families as membership groups, but one or the other tended to become their reference group.

We all know from personal experience that profound experiences may dramatically alter attitudes. A man who gives up drinking after nearly dying in an accident while drunk serves as an example. To bring about attitude change, psychologists have experimented with creating such experiences through *role playing.* Janis and Mann (1965) asked women who

Fig. 27-2 Attitudes are rooted in reference groups. (Photo by Alphapress, Jeroboam.)

were known smokers to play the role of a cancer patient. A physician told each of the women that he had some "bad news": she had lung cancer and would have to undergo immediate surgery. The women played out the part by asking questions about the surgery, if it might fail, and so on. Women in the role-playing group drastically reduced their smoking. Those who listened to a tape recording of similar information showed little change.

Question: Why should role playing have more effect than hearing the same information?

Cognitive Dissonance Theory Certainly emotional impact and realism have some effect, but part of the explanation also lies in the concept of *cognitive dissonance.*

Question: What is cognitive dissonance?

Cognitions are thoughts. Dissonance means clashing. The influencial theory of cognitive dissonance (Festinger, 1957) states that contradicting or clashing thoughts cause discomfort. We have a need for *consistency* in our thoughts and actions. If people can be made to act in a way that is inconsistent with their attitudes, they may change one or both to bring them into agreement. For example, a smoker is told on every pack that cigarettes may endanger his life. He lights up and smokes. How does he resolve the tension between this information and his actions? He could quit smoking, but it may be easier to convince himself that smoking is not really so dangerous. To do this he will seek examples of people who have lived long lives as heavy smokers, and he will associate with other smokers who support his attitude. He will also avoid information concerning the link between smoking and cancer. Cognitive dissonance theory also suggests that people tend to reject new information that contradicts ideas they already hold, in a sort of "don't-bother-me-with-the-facts-my-mind-is-made-up" strategy.

Recall now the account of Mrs. Keech and her doomsday group. Why did their belief in Mrs. Keech's messages increase after the world failed to end? Why did they suddenly become interested in convincing others of the correctness of their beliefs? Cognitive dissonance explains that after publicly committing themselves to their beliefs, they had a strong need to maintain their stand. No matter what the evidence, convincing others was a way of adding additional proof that they were right.

Question: Acting contrary to one's attitudes does not always bring about change. How does cognitive dissonance account for this?

The amount of *reward* or *justification* for acting contrary to one's real beliefs determines the amount of dissonance created. In a now classic study, college students performed an extremely boring task consisting of turning wooden pegs in a board for an extended time. Afterward they were asked to help lure others into the experiment by pretending it was interesting and enjoyable. Students paid $20 for lying to others did not change their own negative opinion of the task. Those who were paid only $1 later rated the experience as actually being pleasant and interesting. In other words, those paid $20 experienced no dissonance (anybody would lie for $20). Those paid $1 were faced with the conflicting thought, "I lied, but I had no good reason to." Rather than admit to themselves that they had lied, these students changed their attitude toward what they had done (Festinger & Carlsmith, 1959).

Brainwashing—Can Attitude Change Be Forced?

Most people associate the term "brainwashing" with techniques used by the Chinese on American prisoners during the Korean War. Through various types of "thought reform," the Chinese were able to coerce approximately 16 percent of these prisoners to sign false confessions (Schein *et al.*, 1957). More recently, the celebrated Patricia Hearst case rekindled public interest in the possibility of inducing involuntary changes in attitudes, beliefs, or personal loyalties.

Question: What is brainwashing? How does it differ from other persuasive techniques?

Instances of attempted persuasion are extremely numerous in our society. Advertisers, politicians, educators, religious organizations, and others actively seek to alter attitudes and opinions. To an extent their efforts resemble brainwashing, but there is an important difference: brainwashing requires a *captive* audience. If you are offended by a television commercial, you can tune it out. Prisoners in the POW camps in Korea (and later in Vietnam) were completely at the mercy of their captors. James McConnell has noted that complete control over the environment allows a degree of psychological manipulation that would be impossible in a normal setting.

Question: How does captivity facilitate persuasion?

McConnell identifies three techniques used for brainwashing: (1) The "target" person is isolated from other people who would support his original attitudes. (2) The "target" is made completely dependent on his captors for satisfaction of his needs. (3) The indoctrinating agent is in a position to reward the "target" for changes in attitudes or behavior.

Brainwashing typically begins with an attempt to make the "target" feel completely helpless. Physical and psychological abuse, lack of sleep, humiliation, and isolation serve to *unfreeze* former values and beliefs. *Change* comes about when exhaustion, pressure, and fear become unbearable. The prisoner reaches the breaking point and signs a false confession or cooperates to gain relief. When he does, he is suddenly rewarded with praise, privileges, food, or rest. The continued coupling of hope and fear with additional pressures for conformity then serves to *refreeze* new attitudes (Schein *et al.*, 1961).

Question: How permanent are changes caused by brainwashing?

In most cases the dramatic alteration in attitudes brought about by brainwashing is temporary. Most "converted" prisoners who returned to the United States after the Korean War eventually reverted to their original beliefs and repudiated their indoctrinators.

Although we tend to think of coercive persuasion as unacceptable and immoral, its use may not be restricted to brainwashing. In the United States more than 80 percent of all criminal cases are solved by confession. Most confessions come while a suspect is being interrogated by a police officer. Police interrogations are obviously quite successful. Yet everyone knows of cases in which innocent people have confessed to crimes they did not commit, and frequently we read of persons retracting confessions made during an interrogation.

Question: Why do innocent people confess to crimes they did not commit?

After studying police manuals and procedures, Philip Zimbardo (1967a) states, "I am now convinced that the secret inquisitorial techniques of our police force are sometimes more highly developed, more psychologically sophisticated, and more effective than were those of the Chinese Communists." Although many would disagree with this opinion, it is, indeed, thought provoking.

Prejudice—Attitudes that Injure

Prejudice is a negative attitude or a *prejudgment* tinged with unreasonable suspicion, fear, or hatred. Prejudice that is institutionalized and backed by social power structures is referred to as *racism*. Recent changes in law and social customs have supposedly opened the doors for racial equality. But unfortunately, it is too often the case that these theoretical opportunities are never converted into real changes. In many cases they create higher expectations that cause frustration when they go unfulfilled. In other words, prejudice cannot be legislated out of existence.

Question: How do prejudices develop?

One theory suggests that prejudice represents a form of *scapegoating*. Scapegoating, you may recall, is a form of displaced aggression in which hostilities generated by frustration are redirected to other targets. One interesting test of this hypothesis was conducted at a summer camp for young men. Subjects were given a difficult test they were sure to fail. Additionally, completing the test caused them to miss a trip to the theater (normally the high point of their weekly entertainment). Attitudes toward Mexicans and Japanese were measured before the test and after they had failed it and missed the entertainment. Subjects in this study consistently rated members of these two groups lower after they had been frustrated (Miller & Bugelski, 1970).

At times the development of prejudice (like other attitudes) can be traced to direct experiences with members of the rejected group. A child who is repeatedly bullied by members of a particular racial or ethnic group may develop resentment that forms the core of a lifelong dislike for other members of the group. The tragedy in such cases is that once such an antipathy is established, it prevents accepting additional, more positive experiences which could reverse the damage.

Gordon Allport (1958) concluded that there are two important sources of prejudice. *Personal prejudice* occurs when members of another racial or ethnic group represent a threat to the individual's security or comfort. For example, members of another group may be viewed as competitors for jobs. Another type of prejudice occurs simply through the individual's adherence to *group norms*. In other words, you may have no personal reason for disliking out-group members but you do so because you are expected to.

The Prejudiced Personality Other research suggests that prejudice at times is a general personality characteristic.

Question: Do you mean some people are more prone to prejudice than others?

Apparently some are. Theodore Adorno and his associates (1950) have conducted extensive research on what they call the *authoritarian personality*. These researchers started out by studying anti-Semitism, as a means of understanding the social climate that existed in Germany during World War II. In the process they found that people who are prejudiced against one group tend to be prejudiced against all *out-groups*.

Question: What are the characteristics of the prejudice-prone personality?

The authoritarian personality can be described as a collection of personal attitudes and values marked by rigidity, inhibition, and oversimplification. The authoritarian tends to be very *egocentric*—he considers only members of his own national, ethnic, or religious group acceptable. He is also overwhelmingly concerned with power, authority, and obedience. To measure these qualities, the "F" scale was created. (The "F" stands for "fascism.") This is an attitude scale made up of statements such as the following—to which the authoritarian readily agrees (Adorno *et al.*, 1950):

> Obedience and respect for authority are the most important virtues children should learn.
>
> People can be divided into two distinct classes: the weak and the strong.
>
> If people would talk less and work more, everybody would be better off.
>
> What this country needs most, more than laws and political programs, is a few courageous, tireless, devoted leaders, in whom the people can put their faith.
>
> Nobody ever learns anything really important except through suffering.

As children, authoritarians were usually severely punished and learned to fear authority (and to covet it) at an early age. Authoritarians are not happy people.

Intergroup Conflict—The Roots of Prejudice

An unfortunate by-product of the human proclivity for forming groups is that group membership often limits contact with people in other groups. Additionally, groups themselves may come into conflict. Both events tend to foster unpleasant feelings and prejudices toward the out-group. The bloody clash of opposing forces in Ireland, in South Africa, and in hometown U.S.A. are reminders that intergroup conflict is a widespread problem of modern life. Daily we read of jarring clashes between nations, communities, races, and political, religious, or ethnic groups. In many cases intergroup conflict is accompanied by *stereotyped* images of out-group members and by bitter prejudice.

Question: What exactly do you mean by a stereotype?

A stereotype is an oversimplified image of people who fall into a particular category. As psychologist Gordon Allport (1958) puts it: "Given a thimbleful of facts . . . [we] rush to make generalizations as large as a

Fig. 27-3 Intergroup conflict. (Photo by Eileen Christelow, Jeroboam.)

tub." Stereotypes tend to simplify people into "us" and "them" categories. Actually, aside from the fact that they always oversimplify, stereotypes may be either positive or negative. Table 27-1 shows stereotyped images of various national and ethnic groups and their changes over the years. Notice that many of the qualities listed are desirable.

Stereotypes held by the prejudiced tend to be unusually irrational. When given a list of negative statements about other groups, prejudiced individuals agree with most of them. Particularly revealing is the fact that they often agree with conflicting statements. Thus, Jews are both "pushy" and "standoffish" or blacks are "ignorant" and "sly" to the prejudiced person. In one study, prejudiced subjects even expressed negative attitudes toward two non-existent groups, the "Piraneans" and the "Danirians." As further testimony to the irrationality of stereotypes, we may note that when a prejudiced person meets a pleasant or likable member of a rejected group, the out-group member tends to be perceived as "an exception to the rule," not as a disconfirmation of the stereotype.

Question: How do stereotypes and intergroup tensions develop?

Two experiments, both in unlikely settings and both using children as subjects, offer some insight into these problems.

Table 27-1 University Students' Characterization of Ethnic Groups, 1933 and 1967

Trait	Percent Checking Trait 1933	1967	Trait	Percent Checking Trait 1933	1967
	Americans			*Irish*	
Industrious	48	23	Pugnacious	45	13
Intelligent	47	20	Witty	38	7
Materialistic	33	67	Honest	32	17
Progressive	27	17	Nationalistic	21	41
	Germans			*Jews*	
Scientific	78	47	Shrewd	79	30
Stolid	44	9	Mercenary	49	15
Methodical	31	21	Grasping	34	17
Efficient	16	46	Intelligent	29	37
	Italians			*Blacks*	
Artistic	53	30	Superstitious	84	13
Impulsive	44	28	Lazy	75	26
Musical	32	9	Ignorant	38	11
Imaginative	30	7	Religious	24	8
Revengeful	17	0			

Source: M. Karlins, T. L. Coffman, & G. Walters. "On the Fading of Social Stereotypes: Studies in Three Generations of College Students." *Journal of Personality and Social Psychology*, 1969, 13: 1, 1–16.

An Experiment in Prejudice What is it like to be discriminated against? Those who have never experienced discrimination probably can't imagine it. In a unique experiment, elementary school teacher Jane Elliot sought to give her pupils a direct experience with prejudice. On the first day of the experiment Elliot announced that brown-eyed children were to sit in the back of the room and that they could not use the drinking fountain. Blue-eyed children were given extra recess time and got to leave first for lunch. At lunch brown-eyed children were prevented from taking second helpings, because they would "just waste it." Mixing of brown-eyed and blue-eyed children was prevented, and the blue-eyed children were told they were cleaner and smarter.

At first Elliot had to maintain these imposed conditions of prejudice. She also made an effort to constantly criticize and belittle the brown-eyed children. To her surprise the blue-eyed children rapidly joined in and soon were outdoing her in the viciousness of their attacks. The blue-eyed children began to feel superior, and the brown-eyed children felt just plain awful. Fights broke out. Test scores of the brown-eyed children fell.

Question: How lasting were the effects of this experiment?

The effects were short-lived, because two days later the roles of the children were reversed. Before long the same destructive effects occurred again, but this time in reverse. The implications of this experiment are unmistakable. In less than one day it was possible to get children to hate each other because of their eye color and *status inequalities.* Certainly the effects of a lifetime of real racial or ethnic prejudice are infinitely more powerful and destructive.

Question: What can be done to combat prejudice?

Equal-Status Contact Progress has been made through attempts to educate the general public about the lack of justification for prejudicial attitudes. Changing the belief component of an attitude has long been known to be one of the most direct means of changing the entire attitude. Thus, when people are made aware that minority group members share the same goals, ambitions, feelings, and frustrations as they do, intergroup relations may be improved.

However, this is not the whole answer. As we noted earlier, there is often a wide difference between attitudes and actual behavior. Until non-prejudicial behavior is engineered, changes can be quite superficial. Sev-

Fig. 27-4 Racial and ethnic pride are gradually replacing stereotypes and discrimination. (Photo by Hank Lebo, Jeroboam.)

eral lines of thought (including cognitive dissonance theory) suggest that more frequent *equal-status* interaction between groups in conflict should reduce prejudice and stereotypes.

Question: But does it?

One study suggests it does. Women who lived in integrated and segregated housing projects were compared for changes in attitude toward their black neighbors. In the integrated project, black and white families lived next door to one another. In the segregated project, they lived on separate floors. Those in the integrated project showed favorable shifts in attitude toward members of the other racial group. Those in the segregated project showed no change or actually became more prejudiced than before (Deutsch & Collins, 1951). The conclusion of this particular study was that contact must be on an equal footing if it is to reduce prejudice between whites and blacks (or other segregated groups). Certainly this must be viewed as a worthwhile goal. As Kenneth Clark (1965) has said, "Racial segregation, like other forms of cruelty and tyranny, debases all human beings—those who are its victims, those who victimize, and in quite subtle ways, those who are merely accessories."

Superordinate Goals Let us now consider one more revealing study of intergroup conflict and its reduction. Muzafer Sherif and his associates conducted an ingenious experiment with 11-year-old boys at a summer camp. When they arrived at camp, the boys were separated into two groups and housed in cabins that were physically separated. At first the groups were kept apart to build up in-group friendships. Development of pride and identification with the in-group was encouraged by participation in cooperative games and activities. Soon each group had a flag, a name (the "Rattlers" and the "Eagles"), and had staked out its own territory. At this point the two groups were placed in competition with each other. After a number of clashes, disliking between the two groups bordered on hatred. Outright hostility erupted as the boys baited each other, started fights, and raided each other's cabins (Sherif *et al.*, 1961).

Question: Were they allowed to go home hating each other?

As an experiment in the reduction of intergroup conflict, and to prevent the boys from remaining enemies, various strategies were tried to reduce tensions. Having leaders from each group meet did nothing. Just getting the groups together also did little. When the groups were invited to eat together, the event became a free-for-all. Finally, emergencies were staged at the camp which required cooperation among members of the groups. For example, the water supply was damaged in a way that required all the boys to work together to repair it. Creation of this and other *superordinate* goals served to restore relations between the two groups. As members were forced to cooperate, hostilities subsided.

The concept of superordinate goals is one that needs greater emphasis in group conflict. Even feuding groups will often unite to meet a common threat. Perhaps some of the pressing problems facing the human race will prove a blessing in disguise. When a threat becomes worldwide, perhaps people everywhere will be better able to see that their well-being is deeply intertwined with that of others.

There can be little question that we need more people who are willing to help other people. In the applications section of this chapter we will examine some of the forces that operate to prevent people from helping. Also discussed are a few glimmerings about how to enhance *prosocial* (as opposed to antisocial) behavior.

Resources Summary

Attitudes are learned dispositions made up of a *belief* component, an *emotional* component, and an *action* component. Attitudes may be formed by direct contact, interaction with others, and *child rearing* practices. Groups also exert pressures on attitudes held by their members. Peer group influences, the mass media, and chance conditioning also appear to be important. Attitudes are measured using such approaches as *open-ended interviews*, *social distance scales*, and *attitude scales.* Attitude change is related to *reference group* membership and to significant personal experiences (which may be engineered through *role playing*). The maintenance and change of attitudes is also accounted for by needs for consistency. Cognitive dissonance theory explains the dynamics of such needs.

Brainwashing is a form of forced attitude change that depends on control of a person's total environment. Three steps in brainwashing are *unfreezing*, *changing*, and *refreezing* attitudes and beliefs.

Prejudice is a negative attitude held toward members of various *out-groups.* One theory attributes prejudice to *scapegoating.* A second account says that prejudice can be *personal* or *group* inspired. The prejudiced person tends to have an *authoritarian personality.*

Intergroup conflict gives rise to hostility and the formation of *stereotypes. Status inequalities* tend to build prejudice. *Equal-status* contact tends to reduce it. Muzafer Sherif and others have emphasized the concept of *superordinate goals* as a key to the redirection of intergroup conflict: racial, religious, ethnic, and national.

Applications

Helping—Prosocial Behavior

Late one night in March, 1964, tenants of a Queens, New York, apartment building watched and listened in horror as a young secretary named Kitty Genovese was murdered on the sidewalk outside. From the safety of their rooms, no fewer than 38 people heard the agonized screams as her assailant stabbed her, was frightened off, and returned to stab her again. Kitty Genovese's murder took over 30 minutes, but none of her neighbors tried to help. None even so much as called the police. Perhaps it is understandable that no one wanted to "get involved." After all, it could have been a violent lovers' quarrel; or helping might have meant risking personal injury. But what prevented these people from at least calling the police?

Question: Isn't this an example of the alienation of city life?

News reports treated this incident as evidence of a breakdown in social ties caused by the impersonality of the city. While it is true that urban living can be dehumanizing, this does not fully explain the *bystander apathy* observed in this and similar emergencies. According to social psychologists Bibb Latané and John Darley (1968), failure to help is related to the *number* of people present. The more potential helpers present, the lower the chances that help will be given.

Question: Why would people be less willing to help when others are present?

In Kitty Genovese's case the answer is that everyone thought *someone else* would help. The dynamics of this effect can be illustrated with a hypothetical example: Two motorists have stalled at roadside, one on a sparsely travelled country road and the other on a busy freeway. Who gets help first? On the freeway, where hundreds of cars pass every minute, each driver assumes someone else will help. Personal responsibility for helping is spread so thin no one takes action. On the country road, the first person to arrive will probably stop, since the responsibility is clearly his. In general, Latané and Darley assume that bystanders are not apathetic or uncaring; they are inhibited by the presence of others.

Bystander Intervention There are four "decision points" a person must pass through before giving help. First he must *notice* that something is happening. Next he must *define* the event as an emergency. Then he must *take responsibility.* Finally, he must *select* a course of action. Laboratory experiments have shown that each step can be influenced by the presence of other people.

Noticing What would happen if you fainted and collapsed on the sidewalk? Would someone stop to help? Would people think you were drunk? Would they even *notice* you? Latané and Darley suggest that if the sidewalk is crowded, few people will even see you. This has nothing to do with people blocking each other's vision. Instead, it is related to widely accepted norms against staring at others in public. People in crowds carefully "keep their eyes to themselves."

Question: Is there any way to prove this is a factor in bystander apathy?

As a test of this idea, students were asked to fill out a questionnaire either alone or in a room full of people. While the students worked, a thick cloud of smoke was blown into the room through a ventilator. Most subjects alone in the room noticed the smoke immediately. Few of the people in groups noticed the smoke, even when it became difficult to see through it. Subjects working in groups politely kept their eyes on their papers and avoided looking at others (or the smoke). In contrast, those who were alone scanned the room from time to time.

Defining an Emergency The smoke-filled room also shows the influence others have on defining a situation as an emergency. After subjects in groups noticed the smoke, they cast sidelong glances at others in the room. Apparently they were searching for clues to help interpret what was happening. No one wanted to overreact or to make a fool of himself if there was no emergency. However, each subject, coolly surveying the reactions of others, was herself also being surveyed. In real emergencies, people sometimes underestimate the need for action because each is attempting to appear calm. In short, until someone acts, no one acts.

Taking Responsibility Perhaps the most crucial step in the helping sequence is assuming responsibility. In this case, groups limit helping by causing a *diffusion of responsibility.*

Question: Is that like the unwillingness of drivers to offer help on a crowded freeway?

Exactly. It is the feeling that no one is personally responsible for helping. This was demonstrated in an experiment in which students took part in a group discussion over an intercom system. Actually there was only one real subject in each group; the others were tape-recorded confederates of the experimenter. Each subject was placed in a separate room (supposedly to maintain confidentiality), and discussions of college life were begun. During the discussion, one of the "students" simulated an epileptic-like seizure and called out for help. In some cases, subjects thought they were alone with the seizure victim. Others believed they were members of three- or six-person groups. Subjects who thought they were alone with the "victim" of this staged emergency reported it immediately or tried to help. Some subjects in the three-person groups failed to respond and those who did were slower. In the six-person groups, over a third of the subjects took no action at all. People in this experiment were obviously faced with a conflict like that in many real emergencies: Should they be helpful and responsible, or should they "mind their own business"? Many were influenced toward inaction by the presence of others.

Question: People do help in some emergencies. How are these different?

It is not always clear what makes the difference. Helping behavior is a complex event, influenced by many variables. One naturalistic experiment staged in a New York City subway gives a hint of the kind of things that may be important. When a "victim" (actor) "passed out" in a subway car, he received more help when carrying a cane than when carrying a liquor bottle. More importantly, however, was the fact that most people were willing to help in either case. In addition, there was little evidence of a diffusion of responsibility: the number of people didn't seem to matter much (Piliavin *et al.*, 1969). These observations are encouraging, but they tell little about how to increase the incidence of helping behavior.

Question: Is there really anything that can be done?

There is evidence that people who see others helping are more likely to offer help themselves. For example, motorists were much more likely to stop to help a woman fix a tire when they had just passed another woman being helped by someone (Bryan & Test, 1967). By offering help, you make a double contribution. You will have assisted directly, and you will have encouraged others to help.

For Discussion

Psychology and Urban Stress—Life in the Big City

Everyone has his or her own list of complaints about living in, or visiting, a large city. Traffic congestion, pollution, crime, and impersonality are urban problems that immediately come to mind. To this list psychologists have added crowding, noise, and overstimulation as significant sources of urban stress. Recent psychological research has begun to clarify the impact of each of these conditions on human functioning.

Crowding Overpopulation ranks as one of the most serious problems facing the world today. Nowhere are the effects of overpopulation more evident than in the crowded buses, subways, and living quarters of our big cities. The subjective discomforts of overcrowding are familiar to most people, but is there any way to assess the effect crowding has on people? One approach is to investigate the effects of overcrowding among animals. Although the results of animal experiments cannot be considered conclusive for humans, they point to some disturbing effects.

Question: For example?

In an interesting experiment John Calhoun (1962) let a group of laboratory rats reproduce without restriction in a confined space. Calhoun provided plenty of food, water, and nesting materials for the rats. All the rats lacked was space. At its peak the colony numbered 80 rats yet was housed in a cage designed to comfortably hold about 50. Overcrowding in the cage was further exaggerated by actions of the two most dominant males, who staked out private territory at opposite ends of the cage, gathered harems of eight to ten females, and prospered. This forced the remaining rats into a small middle area where severe crowding resulted.

Question: What effect did crowding have on the animals?

A high incidence of pathological behavior developed in both males and females. Females abandoned nest-building and caring for their young. Pregnancies decreased and infant mortality ran extremely high. Many of the animals became indiscriminately aggressive and went on rampaging attacks at others. Abnormal sexual behavior was rampant, with some animals displaying hypersexuality, bisexuality, homosexuality, or complete sexual passivity. Many of the animals died, apparently from stress-caused diseases. The connection between these problems and overcrowding is unmistakable.

Question: But does this apply to humans?

Many of the same pathological behaviors can be observed in crowded inner-city ghettos. It is therefore tempting to assume that violence, social disorganization, and declining birth rates as seen in these areas are directly related to crowding. The connection remains unproven, however, because nutritional, educational, income, and health care disadvantages suffered by those living in the inner city may also be to blame. Because of such uncertainties, research efforts in psychology are beginning to focus on urgent social problems.

While overcrowding ranks high among the crises which face us, it is only one of the "superordinate" problems that press for world attention. What other problems can you identify that have community-wide, nationwide, or worldwide effects? Can these problems be used to draw humanity together? Or do they bode a threatening and uncertain future? What role will psychology and psychologists play in the alleviation of such problems? What role will psychology play in your life?

Suggestions for Further Reading

Allport, Gordon. *The Nature of Prejudice.* Doubleday, 1958.

Cohen, Arthur. *Attitude Change and Social Influence.* Basic Books, 1964.

Festinger, L., H. W. Riecken, and S. Schachter. *When Psychology Fails.* University of Minnesota Press, 1956.

Festinger, Leon. *A Theory of Cognitive Dissonance.* Stanford University Press, 1957.

Insko, C. A. *Theories of Attitude Change.* Appleton-Century-Crofts, 1967.

Zimbardo, P. G., and E. B. Ebbesen. *Influencing Attitudes and Changing Behavior.* Addison-Wesley, 1969.

Statistics*

The Use of Statistics in Psychology

From the multitude of observations they make daily, psychologists try to extract meaningful information by precisely describing and summarizing what they have seen. This is greatly aided by assigning numbers to observed events. To illustrate, let's say you are describing a child's behavior for a one-day period. You report that the child played for long periods during the day, fought with playmates occasionally, and cried frequently when he failed to get his own way. Notice how ambiguous this description is: What are "long" periods? How often is "occasionally," or "frequently"? A more *quantitative* report might read like this:

> The child engaged in three major behaviors—playing, fighting, and crying. He played 3 times for 1 hour or more, twice for 30–60 minutes, and 12 times for 0–30 minutes. In 12 waking hours, the child fought with a playmate 4 times and cried 27 times for a total of 1.6 hours.

By applying numerical measurements to the child's behavior, precision is increased, and the clarity of our observations is vastly improved.

Quantifying Data There are several ways in which *measurement* (assigning numbers to observations) can be done. The least effective type of measurement is made on a *nominal* (naming) *scale* in which numbers are simply used to classify objects or events into categories. An excellent example of this is found on computerized application forms which classify

*This appendix was contributed by Daniel Downey, Ph.D.

people "male or female," "single or married," etc., and then assign a number (1 or 2) to indicate the category.

Another type of measurement rank-orders objects or events on an *ordinal scale.* Position on an ordinal scale indicates only more or less of some characteristic (height, intelligence, age, etc.) For example, it is common in the United States to assign numbers to graduating college students on the basis of grade point average (GPA). Thus, in a class of 150 students, the rank of 1 goes to the highest GPA score, the rank of 2 to the next highest, and so on. Notice that on an ordinal scale, intervals between rankings need not be equal. The difference in GPA between students ranked 1 and 2 may not be the same as that between those ranked 19 and 20.

The most satisfactory scales of measurement are *interval* and *ratio scales.* In ratio scales, the intervals along the scale are equal. Thus, precise statements can be made about how much greater or smaller measurements are from one another. Running speed is a good example of a ratio scale because a runner traveling at 10 feet/second can be said to be running four times as fast as one running 2.5 feet/second. An additional property of ratio scales is that they possess a true zero point at which no quantity of the behavior being measured exists. Running speed satisfies this requirement (since inactivity represents zero running speed) as does a scale measuring units of length (for example, a yardstick), where zero indicates the absence of any length.

In an interval scale, units on the scale are equal, but the zero point is arbitrarily chosen. On a Farenheit thermometer, for example, intervals are equal (they are marked off in multiples of 10 degrees) and it takes just as much added heat to move from 25 to 26° as it does to move from 99 to 100°. However, one cannot say that 100° is twice as hot as 50° or that at 0° temperature ceases to exist.

Descriptive Statistics

The first of two major divisions of statistical methods is *descriptive statistics.* Descriptive statistics are used to summarize large amounts of data. For example, if we were to list the test scores for athletic aptitude of 100 students, we could get an idea of the capabilities of each. But to describe this data to someone else, we would have to read the whole list. Descriptive statistics provide a number of useful ways of "boiling down" a mass of numbers so that they become more meaningful and more readily communicated to others. In the following sections, we will consider three descriptive techniques: *graphical statistics*, measures of *central tendency*, and measures of *variability*.

Graphical Statistics Large amounts of information can be neatly summarized by use of a *frequency distribution.* To form a frequency distribution the entire range of possible scores is broken down into *classes* of equal size. Next the number of scores falling in each class is recorded. Table A-1 shows hypothetical "raw" scores on an athletic aptitude test taken by 100 students. In Table A-2 the raw data have been condensed into a frequency distribution. Notice now much clearer the scores of the entire group become.

Frequency distributions are often expressed *graphically* to make them more "visual." *Histograms*, as these are called, are constructed by labeling frequencies on the ordinate (vertical axis) and class intervals on the abscissa (horizontal axis); next, bars are drawn for each class interval; the height of each bar is determined by the number of scores in each class (see Fig. A-1). An alternative way of graphing a distribution of scores is the more familiar *frequency polygon* seen in the lower panel of Fig. A-1. Here, points are placed at the center of each class interval to indicate the number of cases. Then, the dots are connected by straight lines.

Measures of Central Tendency A measure of central tendency is simply a number describing a "middle score" around which other scores fall. Two commonly used measures of central tendency are the mean and the median. Table A-3 shows the raw data for a hypothetical experiment in which two groups of subjects were tested for running speed in a foot race. One group was given the drug amphetamine (a stimulant); the other received nothing. Is there a difference between scores for the two groups? It's difficult to tell without computing an average.

One type of average is the *mean*, computed by adding all the scores for each group and dividing by the number of scores. Notice in Table A-3 that the means show a difference for the two groups.

The mean is sensitive to extremely high or low scores in a distribution and, consequently, does not always give the best measure of central tendency. In such cases, the middle score in a group of scores, called the *median*, is used instead. The median is found by ranking scores from the highest to the lowest and selecting the score that falls in the middle. If there is an even number of scores, there will be no "middle score." This problem is handled by taking the two scores which "share" the middle spot, and averaging them to get a median (see bottom panel of Table A-3).

Table A-1 Raw Scores of Athletic Aptitude

55	86	52	17	61	57	84	51	16	64
22	56	25	38	35	24	54	26	37	38
52	42	59	26	21	55	40	59	25	57
91	27	38	53	19	93	25	39	52	56
66	14	18	63	59	68	12	19	62	45
47	98	88	72	50	49	96	89	71	66
50	44	71	57	90	53	41	72	56	93
57	38	55	49	87	59	36	56	48	70
33	69	50	50	60	35	67	51	50	52
11	73	46	16	67	13	71	47	25	77

Table A-2 Frequency Distribution of Athletic Aptitude Scores

Class Interval	*Number of Persons in Class*
0–19	10
20–39	20
40–59	40
60–79	20
80–99	10

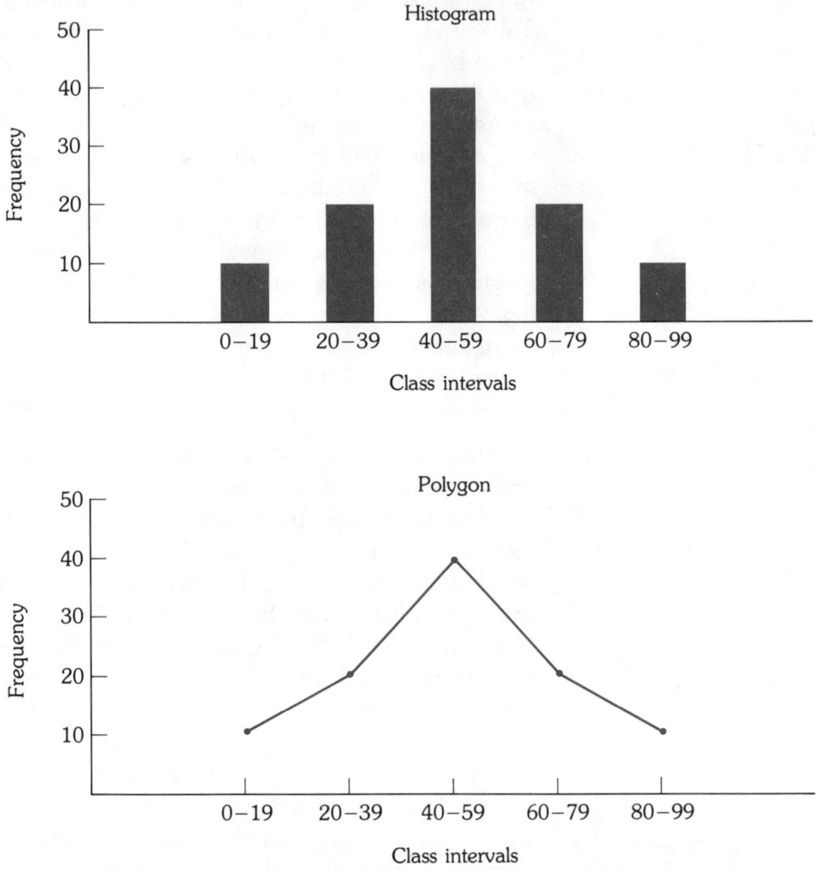

Fig. A-1 Frequency histogram and frequency polygon of raw scores of athletic aptitude contained in Table A-1.

A final measure of central tendency is the *mode*, which simply represents the most frequently occurring score in a distribution. In psychology the mode is rarely used. In practice the mean is the most commonly used measure.

Measures of Variability It is not enough to simply know the average score in a distribution; usually, we would also like to know if scores are clustered closely about the mean or scattered widely. Measures of *variability* attach a numerical value to the "spread" of scores. If you look again at Table A-3, you will notice that the scores within each group vary so widely that no more than two or three people share the same score. How can we convey this fact?

The simplest way would be to use the *range*, which is the spread between the highest and lowest scores. In group 1 of our experiment, the

Table A-3 Raw Scores for Running Speed in a 1000 meter Foot Race with and without Amphetamine

Subject	Group 1 0 mg. amphetamine	Group 2 10 mg. amphetamine
1	6.5 min.	5.4 min.
2	6.7 min.	6.0 min.
3	7.3 min.	6.3 min.
4	6.5 min.	3.3 min.
5	5.8 min.	5.6 min.
6	5.5 min.	6.0 min.
7	7.0 min.	6.0 min.
8	6.9 min.	3.1 min.
9	6.0 min.	6.2 min.
10	6.8 min.	6.1 min.
Sum	65	54
Mean	6.5 min.	5.4 min.
Median	6.6 min.	6.0 min.

Mean $= \frac{\Sigma X}{N}$ or $\frac{\text{sum of all scores, } X}{\text{number of scores}}$

$$\text{Mean}_{Gp.1} = \frac{\Sigma 6.5+6.7+7.3+6.5+5.8+5.5+7.0+6.9+6.0+6.8}{10} = \frac{65}{10} = 6.5$$

$$\text{Mean}_{Gp.2} = \frac{\Sigma 5.4+6.0+6.3+3.3+5.6+6.0+6.0+3.1+6.2+6.1}{10} = \frac{54}{10} = 5.4$$

$\text{Median}_{Gp.1}$ = 5.5;5.8;6.0;6.5;6.5;6.7;6.8;6.9;7.0;7.3

$$= \frac{6.5 + 6.7}{2} = 6.6$$

$\text{Median}_{Gp.2}$ = 3.1;3.3;5.4;5.6;6.0;6.0;6.0;6.1;6.2;6.3

$$= \frac{6.0 + 6.0}{2} = 6.0$$

[shaded box] = middle score(s)

highest score is 7.3 and the lowest is 5.5; thus, the range is 1.8 (7.3 minus 5.5 equals 1.8). In group 2, the highest score is 6.3, and the lowest is 3.1; this makes the range 3.2. Scores in group 2 are more spread than those in group 1.

A better measure of variability is the *standard deviation.* To obtain the standard deviation, the deviation (or difference) of each score from the mean is found and then squared (multiplied by itself). These squared deviations are then added and averaged (the total is divided by the number of deviations). Taking the square root of this average yields the standard deviation (see Table A-4). Notice again that the variability for group 1 (0.54) is smaller than that for group 2 (where the standard deviation is 1.13).

A particular advantage of the standard deviation is that it can be used to "standardize" scores in a way that gives them greater meaning. For example, John and Susan have both taken psychology midterms, but in different classes. John received a score of 118, and Susan scored 110. Who did better? It is impossible to tell without knowing what an average score was on each test, and whether John and Susan scored at the top, middle, or bottom of their classes. We would like to have one number that gives all this information. A number that does this is the *z-score.*

To convert original scores to z-scores, the mean is subtracted from the score and the resulting number is divided by the standard deviation for the group of scores from which the original came. To illustrate, Susan had a

Table A-4 Computation of the Standard Deviation

	Group 1—Mean = 6.5	
	Deviation (d)	*Deviation Squared* (d^2)
6.5−6.5=	0	0
6.7−6.5=	.2	.04
7.3−6.5=	.8	.64
6.5−6.5=	0	0
5.8−6.5=	−.7	.49
5.5−6.5=	−1.0	1.00
7.0−6.5=	.5	.25
6.9−6.5=	.4	.16
6.0−6.5=	−.5	.25
6.8−6.5=	.3	.09
		2.91

$$SD = \sqrt{\frac{\text{sum of } d^2}{N}} = \sqrt{\frac{2.91}{10}} = \sqrt{.291} = 0.54$$

	Group 2—Mean = 5.4	
	Deviation (d)	*Deviation Squared* (d^2)
5.4−5.4=	0	0
6.0−5.4=	.6	.36
6.3−5.4=	.9	.81
3.3−5.4=	−2.1	4.41
5.6−5.4=	.2	.04
6.0−5.4=	.6	.36
6.0−5.4=	.6	.36
3.1−5.4=	−2.3	5.29
6.2−5.4=	.8	.64
6.1−5.4=	.7	.49
		12.76

$$SD = \sqrt{\frac{\text{sum of } d^2}{N}} = \sqrt{\frac{12.76}{10}} = \sqrt{1.276} = 1.13$$

score of 110 in a class with a mean of 100 and a standard deviation of 10; her z-score is +1.0 (see Table A-5). John's score of 118 came from a class having a mean of 100 and a standard deviation of 18; thus his z-score is also +1.0 (see Table A-5). Originally it looked like John did better on his midterm than did Susan, but we now see that, relatively speaking, their scores were equivalent. Compared to other students, each was an equal distance above average.

The Normal Curve

When chance events are recorded, we find that some outcomes have a high probability and occur very often; others have a lesser probability and occur infrequently; still others have little probability and occur rarely. As a result, the distribution (or tally) of chance events resembles a *normal curve* (see Fig. A-2). Most psychological traits or events are determined by the action of a large number of factors. Therefore, like chance events, measures of psychological variables tend to approximate a normal curve. For example, direct measurement has shown such characteristics as height, digit memory-span, and intelligence to be distributed normally. In other words, many people have average height, memory ability, and intelligence; but as we move above or below average, fewer and fewer people are found.

It is very fortunate that many psychological variables are distributed "normally," because a great deal is known about the mathematical properties of the normal curve. One relevant to the preceding discussion is the fixed relationship between the standard deviation and the normal curve; specifically, the standard deviation measures off constant proportions of the curve above and below the mean. For example, in Fig. A-3, notice that 68 percent of all cases (IQ scores, memory scores, heights, or whatever) fall between one standard deviation above and below the mean (± 1 SD); 95 percent of all cases fall between ± 2 SD; and 99 percent of the cases can be found between ± 3 SD from the mean.

Table A-6 gives a more complete account of the relationship between z score and the percentage of cases found in a particular portion of the normal curve. Notice for example, that 93.3 percent of all cases fall below

Table A-5 Computation of a z-Score

$$z = \frac{X - \overline{X}}{SD} \quad \text{or} \quad \frac{\text{score} - \text{mean}}{\text{standard deviation}}$$

Susan: $z = \dfrac{110 - 100}{10} = \dfrac{+10}{10} = +1.0$

John: $z = \dfrac{118 - 100}{18} = \dfrac{+18}{18} = +1.0$

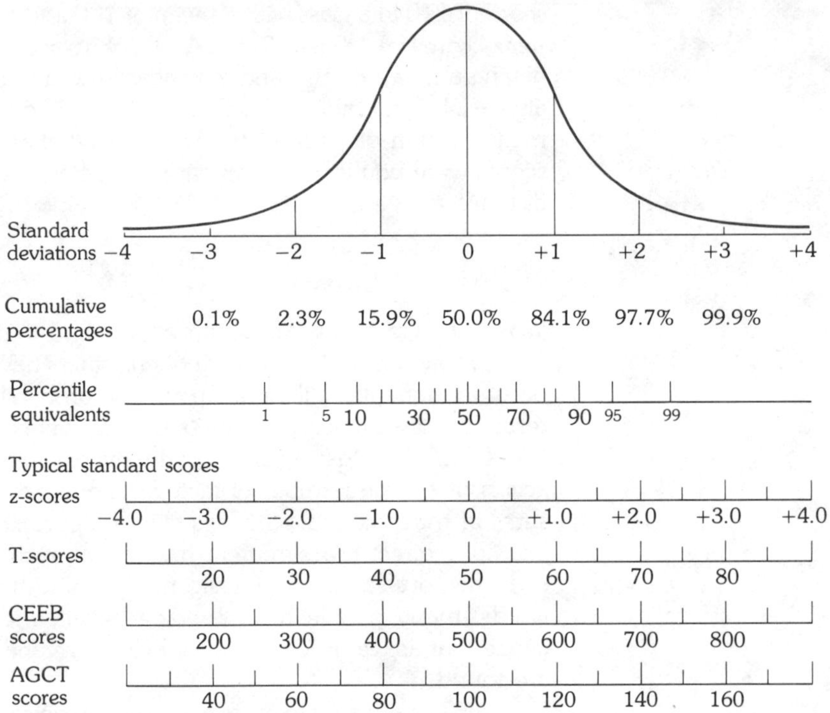

20
40
60
80

Fig. A-2 The normal curve. Scales show the relationship of standard deviation, z-scores, and other measures to the curve.

a *z* score of +1.5. A *z* score of 1.5 on a test (no matter what the original or "raw" score was) would be a good performance, since approximately 93 percent of all scores fall below this mark. Relationships between the standard deviation (or *z* scores) and the normal curve are invariant, making possible useful comparisons between various tests or groups of scores.

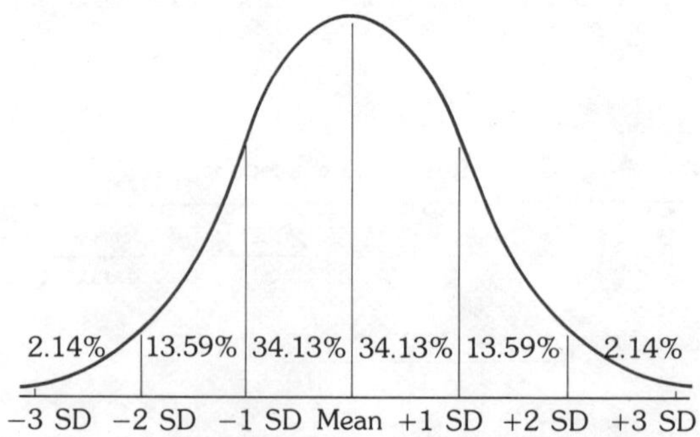

Fig. A-3 Relationship between standard deviation and the normal curve.

Table A-6 Area Under the Normal Curve as a Percentage of Total Area for a Variety of z-Scores

z score	*Percentage of Area to the Left of this Value*	*Percentage of Area to the Right of this Value*
−3.0 SD	00.1	99.9
−2.5 SD	00.6	99.4
−2.0 SD	02.3	97.7
−1.5 SD	06.7	93.3
−1.0 SD	15.9	84.1
−0.5 SD	30.9	69.1
0.0 SD	50.0	50.0
+0.5 SD	69.1	30.9
+1.0 SD	84.1	15.9
+1.5 SD	93.3	06.7
+2.0 SD	97.7	02.3
+2.5 SD	99.4	00.6
+3.0 SD	99.9	00.1

Inferential Statistics

Let's say a psychologist studies the effects of isolation and loneliness on a group of monkeys. Is he or she interested only in this particular group? Usually not, since, except in rare instances, psychologists seek to discover general laws of behavior which apply widely to human and animal species. *Inferential statistics* are techniques that allow us to make inferences. That is, they allow us to generalize from the behavior of small groups of subjects to that of the larger groups they represent.

Samples and Populations In any scientific investigation, we would like to observe the entire set or *population* of subjects, objects, or events being studied. However, this is usually impossible or impractical. Observing all Catholics, all cancer patients, or all mothers-in-law could be both impractical (since all are large populations) and impossible (since people change denominations, may be unaware of having cancer, and change their status as relatives). In such cases, *samples* or smaller cross sections of a population are selected, and observations of the sample are used to draw conclusions about the entire population.

The major requirement for any sample is that it be *representative.* That is, the sample group must truly reflect the composition and characteristics of the larger population. Referring to our hypothetical study of the effects of amphetamine on running speed, it would be essential that the sample of 20 college students from whom data is collected be representative of the general population of college students. Even then, we could only generalize our conclusions to all college students (or perhaps to all college-age persons). Our sample would not be representative of "people in general." A very important aspect of representative samples is that their members are chosen at *random*; that is, each member of the population must have an equal chance of being included in the sample.

Significance of Differences between Groups in an Experiment

In our hypothetical experiment we observed that the average running speed for subjects who were given the drug amphetamine was faster than that of control subjects who received no drug. Certainly this is an interesting result. But could it have occurred by chance? If two groups were repeatedly tested (with neither receiving any drug), their averages would sometimes differ. How much must the two averages differ before we can consider them real (not due to chance)? Tests of *statistical significance* provide an estimate of how often experimental results could have occurred by chance alone. The results of a test of statistical significance are stated as a probability giving the odds that the observed difference was due to chance. In psychology, any experimental outcome attributable to chance 5 times or less out of 100 (in other words, a probability of .05 or less) is considered significant. In the amphetamine experiment we have used as an example, the probability is .025 ($p \leq .025$). This allows us to conclude that the drug actually did affect running speed.

Correlation

Many of the statements that psychologists make about behavior do not result from the use of experimental methods. Rather, they come from keen observations and measurement of existing phenomena. A psychologist might note, for example, that the higher one's socioeconomic and educational status, the greater the variety of sexual behavior engaged in. Or that grades in high school are excellent predictors of how well an individual will do in college. Or even that as rainfall levels increase within a given metropolitan area, crime rates are drastically reduced. In these instances, we are dealing with the fact that two variables are co-relating (varying together in some orderly fashion).

Correlational methods are descriptive statistics which give a number, called the *coefficient of correlation*, indicating the degree of relationship between two measures. The simplest way of visualizing a correlation is to construct a *scatter diagram*. In a scatter diagram, two measures (grades in high school and grades in college, for instance) are obtained. One measure is indicated by the X axis and the second by the Y axis. The scatter diagram plots the intersection of each pair of measurements as a single point. Many such measurement pairs give pictures like those in Fig. A-4.

Fig. A-4 also shows scatter diagrams of three basic kinds of relationships between variables (or measures). The left panel shows a *positive* relationship, one in which increases in scores on one variable are associated with increases in the others; for example, higher high school grades (X) are

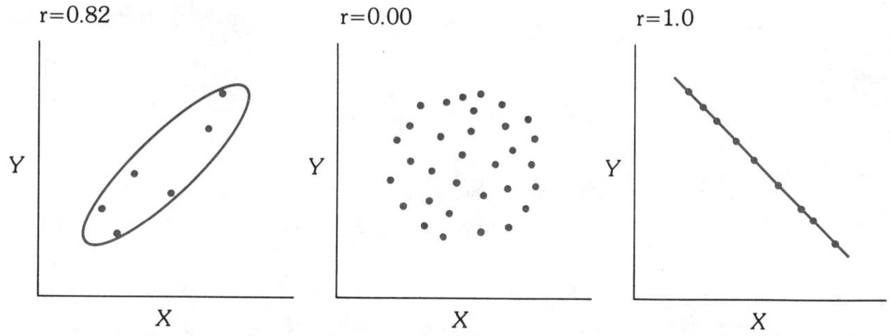

Fig. A-4 Scatter diagrams showing various degrees of relationship for a positive, zero, and negative correlation.

associated with higher college grades (Y). A *zero* correlation (no relationship) is pictured in the middle panel of Fig. A-4. This might be the result of comparing subjects' hat sizes (X) to their college grades (Y). In the right panel is a scatter diagram showing a *negative* relationship (or correlation). Notice that as values on one measure increase, those on the second become smaller. An example might be the relationship between level of anxiety and classroom test scores: higher anxiety is correlated with lower scores.

In summary, remember that each point in a scatter diagram represents a subject's scores on two variables and that the shape of the resulting distribution of scores indicates whether a relationship is positive, negative, or non-existent.

The numerical value of a correlation coefficient may range from +1.0 for a perfect positive correlation to −1.0 for a perfect negative relationship. Lack of any relationship is indicated by a correlation coefficient of 0. The most popular method for calculating the correlation coefficient (called *r*) is summarized by this formula:

$$r = \frac{\Sigma \text{ (deviations } x) \cdot \text{(deviations } y)}{\sqrt{\text{(deviations } x)^2 \cdot \text{(deviations } y)^2}}$$

Here, one of each paired measures is called the *x* variable and the other the *y* variable. Deviations refer to the difference between each score and its respective mean. The mathematical symbol Σ refers to the summation of the paired products of *x* and *y* deviations of each individual subject.

Interpreting Correlations When two variables are correlated, the occurrence of one is associated with the occurrence of the other, and the value of *r* tells to what extent measurements of one variable coincide with those of the second. Of what value is this? Suppose we construct a new test of musical aptitude by assembling tasks that a musically gifted individual would be expected to possess: ability to follow rhythm, to label notes played on a musical scale, to detect harmonies, and so forth. We prepare to put our test in use. But how do we know it measures musical ability and not some other quality like intelligence, motivation, or simple hearing acuity?

To find out we could compare scores on our test to established criteria for musical aptitude. These criteria might include relative success in a musical program, scores on other tests of musical aptitude, and teachers' ratings of how rapidly beginning students learn musical skills. By showing a high positive correlation between scores on these criteria and on our test, we would be saying that they are associated or, in effect, that they measure the same thing: musical aptitude. By using this procedure we have established the *validity* of our test.

Correlation coefficients can also be used to measure the *reliability* of a test (the ability of a test to give the same score on repeated administrations). In this case, we would select a group of individuals, give them a test once and then retest them some time in the future. If a test is reliable, the correlation between the two sets of scores will be large and positive.

Correlations are particularly valuable for making *predictions.* If we know two measures are correlated, and we know a person's score on one measure, we can predict his or her score on the other. For example, most colleges have formulas which make use of multiple correlations to decide which prospective students have the best chances for success. Usually the formula includes such "predictors" as high school GPA, teacher ratings, and scores on the Scholastic Aptitude Test (SAT) or some equivalent. Although none of the predictors is perfectly correlated with success in college, together they correlate highly and provide a useful technique for screening applicants.

Correlation and Causation It is very important to recognize that the existence of a correlation between two measures does not mean that one causes the other: *Correlation does not prove causation.* When a correlation exists, the best we can say is that two variables are related. Of course, this does not mean that it is impossible that two correlated variables are causally related. Rather, it means that we cannot *conclude* that a causal relationship exists on the basis of a correlation. To establish causality, an experiment must be performed (see Chapter 2).

Often two correlated variables are related through the influence of a third variable. For example, we might observe that the more hours students devote to studying the better their grades. Although it is tempting to conclude that more studying produces (causes) better grades, it is possible (indeed, it is probable) that grades and the amount of study time are both related to the amount of motivation or interest a student has.

The distinction between having data that indicate causality versus that which indicates relationship of unknown origin is one that should not be forgotten. Since we rarely run experiments in daily life, the information on which we act is largely correlational. This should make us more humble and more tentative in the confidence with which we make pronouncements about human behavior.

Glossary

Absolute Threshold A point indicating the minimum amount of physical energy necessary to produce a sensation.

Accommodation Changes in the shape of the lens of the eye which serve to focus objects at varying distances. Also, the adaptation of old concepts and thinking habits to new information (Piaget).

Achievement Motivation A need for success or the attainment of excellence.

Adaptation In general, adjustment to environmental demands. In connection with the senses, refers to a gradual decline in response to a constant stimulus.

Addiction Physical dependency on a drug.

Adrenal Glands Source of adrenaline, a hormone secreted during emotional arousal. Also, a source of other important hormones.

Affect Pertaining to emotion or feelings.

Afferent or Sensory Nerves Incoming sensory fibers.

Affiliation Motive The desire to associate with other people.

Age Regression Return of a hypnotized subject to a younger age.

Alpha Wave A relatively large, slow brain-wave pattern indicating the individual is in a passive state of relaxed awareness.

Altered State of Consciousness Any nonordinary mental state including meditation, hypnosis, and drug induced states.

Ambivalance Holding opposite emotions such as love and hate toward some person or object.

Amnesia Loss of memory (partial or complete) for past events.

Amphetamines Class of drugs acting as central nervous system stimulants. Not known to be physically addictive but may cause strong psychological dependency.

Anesthesia Loss of bodily sensation.

Anthropomorphic Fallacy The temptation to attribute human thoughts, feelings, and motives to animals.

Antidepressants Drugs which counteract depression or despondency by elevating the individual's mood.

Antipsychotics Drugs which alleviate psychotic symptoms, making it easier to treat psychiatric problems.

Anxiety A feeling of painful or apprehensive uneasiness closely related to fear. Especially characterized by dread or anticipation of some unclear threat.

Aphasias Speech disturbances resulting from damage to certain areas in the temporal lobe of the brain.

Approach-Avoidance Conflict Unpleasant condition in which a person is simultaneously attracted to and repelled by the same goal.

Assessment Evaluation or measurement.

Attention Orienting toward or focusing on some stimulus.

Attitude A predisposition having emotional, belief, and behavioral components that determines a person's reaction toward a particular social stimulus.

Autokinetic Effect The apparent movement of a stationary pinpoint of light displayed in a dark room. Often occurs as a result of suggestion.

Autonomic Nervous System (ANS) Division of the peripheral nervous system concerned with involuntary functions of the body.

Aversive Conditioning Use of an unpleasant or painful stimulus to reinforce learning.

Avoidance Learning Learning procedure in which the occurrence of a particular response results in postponement or prevention of an unpleasant stimulus.

Babinski Reflex Curling and spreading of the toes that occurs when the sole of an infant's foot is stroked.

Barbiturates Addictive drugs that depress activity of the central nervous system. Barbiturate intoxication resembles intoxication caused by alcohol.

Behaviorism School of psychology holding that overt observable behavior is the only worthwhile subject for psychological study.

Behavior Modification Application of principles of learning to change or eliminate maladaptive or abnormal behavior.

Biased Sampling Selection of subjects for an experiment or public opinion poll that gives some subjects a greater chance of being included than others.

Binocular Cues Any cue for depth perception requiring two eyes.

Biofeedback A technique allowing a subject to monitor and control his or her own internal bodily functions.

Blind Spot A portion of the retina where the optic nerve leaves the eye. No visual receptors are found at the blind spot.

Brain Lesion Destruction of brain tissue experimentally, accidentally, or through disease.

Brainstorming A group problem-solving technique in which ideas are offered freely, imaginatively, and initially without evaluation as to their practicality.

Brainwashing Engineered or forced change in attitudes and beliefs.

Central Nervous System (CNS) The brain and spinal cord.

Chemotherapy Use of psychoactive drugs for the treatment of mental disturbances.

Chromosomes Rodlike structures within the nucleus of each cell that carry the genes. Normal human cells carry 23 pairs of chromosomes.

Circadian Rhythms A rhythmic pattern of bodily changes following an approximate 24-hour cycle.

Clairvoyance Form of extrasensory perception (ESP) in which objects or events are perceived without the aid of normal sensory systems.

Classical Conditioning A basic form of learning discovered by Pavlov in which existing (reflex) responses are attached to new stimuli by pairing of the stimuli with those which naturally elicit the response.

Client-centered Therapy A form of therapy designed by Rogers in which the client assumes responsibility for solving his or her own problems. The therapist's role is to clarify and assist, not to give advice.

Closure Gestalt term for the perceptual tendency to complete figures by "closing" or ignoring small gaps.

Coding Organizing information for efficient memory storage and retrieval.

Cognition The process of thinking, knowing, or processing information.

Cognitive Dissonance An imbalance between one's thoughts, beliefs, attitudes, or behavior. According to the theory, cognitive dissonance is a tension state people are motivated to reduce.

Compulsion An act the individual feels driven to repeat, often against his or her will.

Conditioned Response A learned response that becomes attached to the conditioned stimulus in classical conditioning.

Conditioned Stimulus In Pavlovian conditioning, a previously neutral stimulus which acquires the capacity to evoke a response as the result of association with an unconditioned stimulus.

Conditioning The process of learning by association discovered by Pavlov. Also sometimes used to refer to operant learning.

Cones Visual receptors in the eye responsible for color vision and daylight visual acuity.

Conscience Internalized sense of right and wrong. In Freudian theory, the superego.

Consolidation Theoretical process by which material is solidified as a permanent memory in the brain after being learned.

Constructs Explanatory concepts inferred from observable events but not directly observable themselves.

Contact Comfort A pleasant and reassuring feeling human and animal infants derive from touching or clinging to something soft and warm, usually the mother.

Control Eliminating, identifying, or equalizing all factors in an experiment that could affect the outcome.

Control Group A group in a psychological experiment exposed to all experimental conditions except the independent variable.

Convergence The simultaneous turning inward of the two eyes as they focus on nearby objects.

Convergent Thought Thinking directed toward discovery of a single established correct answer. Conventional thinking.

Conversion Reaction Type of neurosis characterized by physical symptoms resulting from anxiety or stress. Anxiety which is hysterically converted into physical symptoms.

Cornea Clear outer membrane covering the eyeball.

Corpus Callosum A large nerve unit in the middle of the brain connecting the two hemispheres. Serves to transfer information from one hemisphere to the other.

Correlation A statistical index indicating the degree to which two measures are related.

Cretinism A form of mental retardation resulting from a malfunction of the thyroid gland.

Critical Period A time during which a certain event must occur in an organism's life if development is to occur normally.

Dark Adaptation The process by which the eye adapts to conditions of low illumination. Principally, by a shift to rod vision.

Defense Mechanisms Habitual and unconscious psychological devices used to reduce or avoid anxiety.

Delusions False beliefs held against all evidence to the contrary. Symptomatic of some psychotic disorders.

Denial A defense mechanism in which we merely deny the existence of a problem or an unpleasant reality.

Denotative The objective dictionary meaning of a word or concept.

Dependent Variable The variable (usually a behavior) which reflects changes in the independent variable.

Depressive Neurosis Prolonged and severe depression triggered by a stressful event but representing an overreaction to it.

Depressive Psychosis A form of psychosis characterized by the deepest possible despondency.

Depth Perception The ability to see three-dimensional space and to accurately estimate distances.

Difference Threshold The smallest change in a physical stimulus that can be detected by an observer.

Discrimination (learning) The ability to detect differences between two or more objects or events. Often brought about by reinforcement of responses to one stimulus but not the other.

Disjunctive Concepts Concepts defined by the presence of at least one of a number of features.

Displacement In Freudian theory, the rechanneling of energy from one target or activity to another. Often used as a defense mechanism as when aggression is displaced on someone or something other than the actual source of frustration.

Dissociative Reaction An unusual form of neurosis including amnesia, fugue, and multiple personality which allows the indivdual to completely separate himself from thoughts and actions he finds unacceptable.

Divergent Thinking Thinking which produces many ideas or alternatives. Creative or unconventional thinking.

DNA (Deoxyribonucleic Acid) Large and complex chemical molecules found in chromosomes and believed to be the substance of which genes are composed.

Drive The psychological representation of internal need states, for example, hunger, thirst, etc.

EEG (Electroencephalogram) Record of the electrical activity of the brain made by attaching electrodes to the scalp.

Ego In Freudian terminology, the portion of personality in conscious control of behavior. The ego reconciles the demands of the id, superego, and external reality.

Egocentric Being unable to take a viewpoint other than one's own.

Eidetic Imagery The ability to retain an image long enough to use it as a source of information. Basically, a photographic memory.

Fantasy A product of the imagination determined mainly by one's motives or feelings. Fantasy may be used as an escape mechanism.

Feedback Knowledge of results relaying the effect of some action.

Figure-Ground Gestaltist's observation that some aspects of a stimulus pattern appear to stand out as an object (figure) while others appear to stand in the background (ground).

Fixation The tendency to repeat wrong solutions or faulty responses as a consequence of frustration. In Freudian theory, lasting conflicts developed during a particular stage of development as a result of frustration or overindulgence during that stage.

Fixed-interval Schedule A schedule of reinforcement in which reinforcement is administered following a fixed period of time after the previous reinforcement. For example, every 3 minutes.

Fixed-ratio Schedule A schedule of reinforcement in which a predetermined number of responses must be made before reinforcement is delivered. For example, one reinforcement may be delivered for every five responses.

Fovea A small depression in the center of the retina containing the greatest concentration of cones and providing the sharpest vision.

Fraternal Twins Twins conceived from two separate eggs. Fraternal twins are no more alike genetically than other siblings.

Free Association A technique of psychoanalysis in which the person says anything that comes into his mind regardless of how embarrassing or unimportant it may seem.

Free-floating Anxiety Feelings of dread or apprehension that cannot be traced to any particular source.

Frigidity An abnormal lack of sexual desire.

Frontal Lobotomy Destruction of the frontal lobes of the brain, or separation of the frontal lobes from the remainder of the brain.

Frustration An internal emotional state resulting from interference with satisfaction of a motive or blocking of goal-directed behavior.

Fugue A neurotic dissociative reaction characterized by taking flight and by a loss of memory for events prior to or during the act of fleeing.

Functional Fixedness Rigidity in problem solving caused by an inability to see novel uses for familiar objects.

Functional Psychosis A psychosis with no apparent biological basis.

Galvanic Skin Response (GSR) A change in the electrical resistance of the skin associated with arousal or anxiety.

General Adaptation Syndrome (GAS) Selye's description of a consistent pattern of reactions to prolonged stress occurring in three states: alarm, resistance, and, finally, exhaustion.

General Paresis An organic psychosis that results when syphilis attacks the brain.

Generalization The transfer of a learned response from one stimulus or set of circumstances to others that are in some way like the original stimulus.

Genes The carriers of hereditary characteristics found in the nucleus of every cell.

Gerontologist One who studies the effects of aging.

Gestalt A German word meaning form or pattern. Also, the school of psychology emphasizing the study of perception, learning, and thinking in whole units not by analysis into parts.

Gestalt Therapy A psychotherapy developed by Perls and others which emphasizes immediate experience and participation of the whole person in any activity.

Gonads The sex glands—testes in males and ovaries in females.

Group Therapy Any form of psychotherapy taking advantage of the special characteristics of group interaction. Patients work out personal problems with the help of other group members and the guidance of a trained therapist.

Habituation A decrease in the strength of a reflex caused by repeated elicitation.

Hallucinations Experiencing imaginary sensations such as seeing, hearing or smelling things which don't exist in the real world.

Halo Effect The tendency to generalize a favorable or unfavorable impression to unrelated details of personality.

Hebephrenic Schizophrenia A form of psychosis characterized by giddy, obscene, or silly behavior and including a severe disintegration of personality.

Heredity A transmission of physical and psychological characteristics from parents to offspring through genes.

Hippocampus A structure in the brain associated with the regulation of emotion and the transfer of information from short-term memory to long-term memory.

Homeostasis Steady state of physiological equilibrium maintained by various bodily mechanisms.

Hormone A bodily chemical transported by body fluids that has an effect on physiological functioning or psychological behavior.

Hospitalism A pattern of deep depression observed in institutionalized infants; marked by weeping and sadness and a lack of normal response to other humans.

Hue The psychological aspect of vision related to the wavelength of light; the color of a stimulus.

Hydrocephaly A type of mental retardation caused by accumulation of cerebrospinal fluid within the brain.

Hyperopia A visual defect causing farsightedness.

Hypnosis An altered state of consciousness characterized by relaxation, focused attention, and increased susceptibility to suggestion.

Hypochondria An excessive preoccupation with minor bodily problems or a neurosis characterized by complaints about illnesses which seem to be imaginary.

Hypothalamus A small area at the base of the brain which regulates many aspects of motivation and emotion particularly hunger, thirst, and sexual behavior.

Hypothesis The predicted outcome of an experiment or an educated guess about the relationship between variables.

Hysterical Neurosis An abnormal reaction in which psychological problems are given expression as physical symptoms or disabilities. Usually expressed as paralysis or insensitivity in the absence of any actual organic disorder.

Id According to Freud, the id is the most primitive part of the personality which supplies energy and which demands immediate gratification of needs, drives, and desires.

Identical Twins Twins who develop from the same egg and who, therefore, have an identical hereditary makeup.

Identification A process in personality development in which a person becomes like an admired adult by incorporating the adult's goals and values into his or her own behavior. Also used as a defense mechanism in adulthood.

Imprinting A rapid and relatively permanent type of learning occurring within a limited period of time early in life.

Incentive A goal object valued by an individual that can be employed to motivate behavior.

Independent Variable In an experiment, the variable manipulated by the experimenter in order to study its effect on the dependent variable.

Innate Inborn or hereditary traits.

Insight A sudden reorganization of the elements of a problem causing the solution to become self-evident. Also refers to one's understanding of one's own behavior or motives.

Instinct Complex unlearned behaviors that are species-specific and relatively uniform.

Instrumental Conditioning Also called operant conditioning. Learning brought about when voluntary responses are affected by their consequences; specifically, the effects of positive and negative reinforcement, nonreinforcement, and punishment.

Intellectualization A psychological defense mechanism in which anxiety or emotion is removed from a situation by thinking or speaking of it in very formal or abstract terms.

Intelligence Quotient (IQ) An index of intelligence defined as a person's mental age divided by his or her chronological age and multiplied by 100.

Interference Theory The theory of forgetting which holds that previously learned material interferes with the storage of new material or that recalling previous learning is prevented by recent learning.

Intermittent Reinforcement Reinforcement occurring irregularly or unexpectedly (partial reinforcement).

Intrauterine Environment The chemical and physical environment existing in the womb before birth.

Introspection A psychological technique used to examine one's own conscious experience. Self-observation of one's thoughts, feelings, and sensations.

Introvert An individual who prefers being alone, who withdraws from social contact, or who is self-centered.

Iris Colored circular muscle of the eye that opens and closes to admit more or less light into the eye.

Isolation A psychological defense involving the separation of contradictory feelings or ideas into "logic-tight" compartments.

Kinesics The study of expression or communication through movement and gestures.

Kinesthesis The sense of bodily position, muscle movement, or equilibrium.

Latency In Freudian theory, the period from age six until puberty characterized as a quiet interruption of psychosexual development.

Latent Learning Learning which occurs without obvious reinforcement and which is not apparent until reinforcement is provided.

Learned Helplessness A learned inability to overcome environmental obstacles or to avoid punishment.

Learning In general, any relatively permanent change in behavior that can be attributed to experience but not to such factors as fatigue, maturation, injury, etc.

Lens A transparent structure at the front of the eye which focuses images on the retina.

Libido In Freudian terminology, the sexual energy involved in the functioning of personality, primarily sexual in nature.

Limbic System A collection of interconnected brain structures whose functions include smell and emotional reactions.

Linguistic Determinism Hypothesis proposed by Whorf that the language one speaks shapes perceptions of reality and influences thought.

Localization of Function The theory that particular psychological functions are represented by particular parts of the brain.

Logotherapy Therapy which emphasizes the need to find meaning in life.

Long-term Memory Memory of events for relatively long periods, usually presumed to be based on permanent storage of information transferred from short-term memory.

Manic Extremely excited, hyperactive, or irritable.

Manic-Depressive Psychosis A psychosis in which a person swings in mood from elation or excitement to deep depression.

Masochism Deriving sexual gratification from pain inflicted on the self by others.

Massed Practice Continuous practice without rest periods or interruption as distinct from distributed practice.

Maturation The emergence and development of personal characteristics in an orderly sequence as a result of underlying physical growth.

Meditation A contemplative exercise for the production of relaxation, heightened awareness, or spiritual revelation.

Menopause The female "change of life" signaled by the end of regular monthly menstrual periods.

Mescaline A psychoactive drug derived from the peyote cactus which has properties similar to LSD.

Metabolism The rate of energy production and expenditure in the body.

Microcephaly A type of mental retardation characterized by a very small scull which prevents normal brain development.

Microsleep A momentary shift in brain-wave patterns to those of sleep.

MMPI (Minnesota Multiphasic Personality Inventory) The most widely used self-rating personality test.

Mnemonic Device Any technique or strategy to assist remembering.

Modeling A type of imitation in which an individual mimics behavior performed by another person (the model).

Mongolism (Down's Syndrome) A hereditary abnormality associated with the presence of 47 chromosomes rather than the usual 46. Characterized by a shortened life expectancy, mental retardation, and unusual physical features.

Monocular Pertaining to the function of one eye. For example, monocular cues for depth perception are those involving the use of only one eye.

Morphemes The smallest meaningful units in a language.

Motive A drive or force within the organism that activates behavior or directs it toward a goal.

Motor Skills Learned skills having an element of physical dexterity or requiring the coordination of muscular movements.

Multiple Personality A rare form of neurosis in which an individual maintains two or more distinct personalities; classified as a dissociative reaction.

Myopia A visual defect making it difficult to focus distant objects (nearsightedness).

Naturalistic Observation Observation and recording of naturally occurring behavior that is not manipulated experimentally.

Negative Reinforcement Increasing the probability of a response by terminating or withdrawing an unpleasant stimulus upon completion of the response.

Nervous System A network of neurons that interconnects sensory receptors and effector organs to produce behavior and conscious experience.

Neurons Individual nerve cells that form the basic structure of the nervous system.

Neurosis A behavior disturbance primarily characterized by excessive anxiety, minor distortions of reality, and subjective discomfort. Neuroses appear to be psychological in origin. Typically, they do not completely prevent a person from attending school, holding a job, or maintaining relationships.

Night Blindness A condition in which vision becomes impaired in low levels of illumination.

Nondirective Therapy See *Client-centered Therapy*.

Nonsense Syllable A meaningless syllable usually consisting of a consonant, a vowel, and a consonant; used in experiments on retention and memory.

Normal Curve A bell-shaped curve having known mathematical properties. Characterized by a large number of scores in the middle tapering toward each end.

Norms Accepted social rules for behavior to which the individual members of a group tend to conform.

NREM Sleep Sleep periods during which there is a minimum of eye movements and little or no dreaming.

Object Constancy Tendency to perceive objects in the same way even when our view of them changes.

Object Permanence Recognition that objects continue to exist when they cannot be seen. Very young children appear to believe that objects cease to exist when they are out of sight.

Obsessions Recurring irrational or disturbing thoughts a person cannot prevent.

Obsessive-Compulsive Neurosis Extreme preoccupation with certain thoughts and compulsive performance of certain behaviors both of which occur in ritualistic or unavoidable fashion.

Oedipus Conflict A Freudian concept referring to a boy's sexual attachment to his mother.

Olfaction The sense of smell.

Operant Conditioning Type of learning which occurs when an organism "operates" on the environment. The consequences of a response affect its probability of reoccurrence.

Optic Nerve The large nerve carrying visual impulses from each eye to the brain.

Oral Stage The Freudian stage of psychosexual development in which the individual is preoccupied with his mouth.

Organic Psychosis A psychotic disorder caused by clearly identifiable physiological or genetic factors.

Orgasm A climax and release of sexual excitement.

Ovaries Female sex organs that produce hormones and ova (eggs).

Overlearning Practice that is continued beyond the point of mere mastery of memorized material or of a skill.

Paranoia A psychotic state characterized by delusions of persecution.

Paranoid Schizophrenia A psychosis characterized by delusions of persecution or grandeur and accompanied by severe disturbances of thought and emotion.

Parapsychology The scientific study of extra-normal psychological events, e.g., extrasensory perception.

Partial Reinforcement Reinforcement administered only after a portion of the total responses in a particular situation (also called intermittent reinforcement).

Peer Group A group of people of one's own age and of equal or similar background.

Perception The process of meaningfully organizing sensation.

Phallic Stage The Freudian developmental stage in which the individual is preoccupied with pleasure derived from the genital organs.

Phenylketonuria (PKU) A metabolic disorder causing the accumulation of phenylaline in the body and leading to mental retardation.

Phobia An intense and unrealistic fear of some specific object or situation.

Phonemes The basic sounds of a language that can be distinguished from one another.

Pitch Psychological experience of high or low tones corresponding to the physical dimension of frequency.

Placebo An inactive substance given in the place of a drug in psychological research or by physicians who wish to treat chronic aches and pains by suggestion.

Positive Reinforcement Rewards or stimuli that increase the probability of a response they have followed.

Prenatal Events occurring before the birth of a child.

Presbyopia Farsightedness caused by aging.

Primary Impotency In the male, total inability to perform sexually.

Primary Reinforcers Unlearned reinforcers. Usually those that satisfy physiological needs.

Primate A member of the family of mammals including humans, apes, and monkeys.

Proactive Inhibition Forgetting that occurs when previous learning interferes with more recent learning.

Projection Attributing to others unacceptable impulses or feelings as a means of defending against anxiety.

Projective Tests Psychological tests making use of unstructured stimuli. The subject is presumed to project his or her own thoughts and impulses onto the stimulus.

Psychiatrist A medical doctor with additional training in the diagnosis and treatment of mental illness.

Psychoanalysis A Freudian approach to therapy emphasizing free association, dream interpretation, and transference.

Psychoanalyst A mental health professional (usually a medical doctor) trained to practice psychoanalysis.

Psychodrama A technique of psychotherapy in which people act out personal conflicts in the presence of other people who play supporting parts.

Psycholinguist A psychologist who specializes in the study of language.

Psychology The scientific study of behavior and conscious experience.

Psychopath An individual who appears to make no distinctions between right and wrong and who feels no guilt about destructive or antisocial behavior.

Psychopathology Abnormal or maladaptive behavior. Literally, mental sickness.

Psychophysics The study of the relationship between physical stimuli and the sensations evoked by them in a human observer.

Psychosexual Stages In Freud's theory of personality development, the following stages: oral, anal, phallic, and genital.

Psychosis A severe psychological disturbance characterized by loss of contact with reality, by hallucinations and delusions, and by withdrawal, and usually requiring hospitalization.

Psychosomatic Illnesses Disorders in which actual physical damage results from psychological stress.

Psychotherapy General term referring to any form of psychological treatment for behavioral disorders. Most often used to refer to verbal interaction between the client and a trained mental health professional.

Punishment The delivery after a response of an event or stimulus that tends to reduce the probability of that response.

Pupil The dark spot at the front of the eye through which light moves in reaching the retina.

Rationalization Explaining away one's shortcomings in such a way as to avoid responsibility.

Rational Therapy A direct and forceful therapy in which clients learn to abandon irrational and self-defeating behavior and beliefs.

Reaction Formation A psychological defense mechanism in which unconscious anxiety-producing impulses are controlled by behaving in exactly the opposite way.

Recall Detailed remembering in the absence of memory cues.

Recognition Memory in which previously learned material is correctly identified as that which has been seen before.

Reference Group Any group with which the individual identifies psychologically and uses as a standard for social comparison.

Regression Return to earlier behavior patterns appropriate to a child or younger person particularly as a response to stress.

Reinforcement Any stimulus that brings about learning or increases the frequency of the response. Often simply a reward.

Relearning Learning again something previously learned. Used as a measure of memory for prior learning.

Reliability An important characteristic of any test. A test that is reliable gives the same score on each administration.

Remission Disappearance of symptoms of a psychological disorder.

REM Sleep Rapid eye movement sleep corresponding to periods of dreaming.

Repression Pushing out or barring from consciousness unwanted memories, impulses, or feelings.

Resistance Blocks that occur in psychoanalysis during free association.

Respondent Conditioning Another term for classical conditioning.

Retention Storage or memorization of information.

Retina The photosensitive lining at the back of the eye containing rods and cones.

Retrieval Extracting stored information from memory.

Retroactive Inhibition The interference of new learning with the memory of previously learned material.

Retrograde Amnesia Loss of memory for events preceding a head injury or other amnesia-producing event.

RNA (Ribonucleic Acid) A chemical substance similar to DNA and believed to be involved in learning and memory.

Rods Visual receptors in the retina which are responsive to low levels of illumination but which produce only black-white vision.

Role Particular type of behavior one is expected to exhibit when occupying a particular position within a group.

Schedule of Reinforcement A rule for determining which response will be reinforced.

Schizophrenia A functional psychosis characterized by withdrawal from reality, apathy, and in some cases, delusions and hallucinations.

Secondary Impotence In the male, unsatisfactory sexual performance caused by premature ejaculation.

Secondary Reinforcement A previously neutral stimulus that acquires reinforcement through association with primary reinforcers.

Sensation A subjective response to a physical stimulus.

Sensory Adaptation A reduction in sensory response to any unchanging form of stimulation.

Set A predisposition to respond in a certain way.

Sex Roles Learned behavior which fits societal expectations concerning proper behavior for males and females.

Shaping Gradual molding of responses to a final desired pattern by reinforcing successive approximations of it.

Short-term Memory (STM) The retention of information for brief periods without rehearsal. The first step in the creation of permanent memories.

Social Comparison Making judgments about ourselves through comparison with others.

Socialization The process of learning to live in a particular culture by adopting socially acceptable behavior.

Sociopath Another name for the psychopath.

Spaced Practice Learning trials or practice sessions spread over an extended period of time and including a number of rest periods.

Species A classification comprising closely related plants or animals potentially able to breed with one another.

Species-specific Behavior Patterned behavior that is exhibited by all normal members of a particular species.

Spontaneous Recovery The sudden reappearance of a learned response after apparent extinction.

Status An individual's position in a group or social system.

Stereotype An inaccurate and rigid concept used to refer to members of an outgroup.

Stimulus Any physical energy which has some effect on an organism and which evokes a response.

Sublimation A psychological defense mechanism involving the expression of socially unacceptable impulses in a socially acceptable way. For example, converting greed into a successful business career.

Subliminal Perception of a stimulus presented below the threshold for conscious recognition.

Superego In Freud's theory of personality, the superego represents parental values and the rules of society; basically, the unit which acts as the conscience.

Syllogism A logical format for reasoning consisting of a major and a minor premise and a conclusion.

Synapse The microscopic space over which nerve impulses travel in the junction of two neurons.

Synesthesia Experiencing one sensory modality in terms of another. For example, "seeing" sounds as colors.

Tachistoscope A mechanical device capable of flashing words or pictures on a screen for very short periods of time. Used in perceptual testing, especially in studies of subliminal perception.

Telepathy A form of ESP in which thoughts are transferred from a sender to a receiver without direct contact.

Temperament The physical foundation of personality including such things as prevailing mood, sensitivity, energy levels, etc.

Testes The male sex organs located in the scrotum. The source of sperm and male sex hormones.

Testosterone Male sex hormone responsible for the development of secondary sexual characteristics.

Timbre The psychological aspect of sound that corresponds to the complexity of a tone.

Tolerance Refers to a condition in drug addiction brought about by the body's ability to withstand increased amounts of the drug. As tolerance develops, the dosage must be increased to produce the same reaction a smaller dosage once produced.

Traits (Personality) Enduring attitudes and personal qualities that an individual tends to display in most life situations.

Transactional Analysis (TA) A therapeutic technique designed to improve awareness of one's transactions (interchanges) with others.

Transduction Changing one form of energy into another.

Transference Refers to the tendency of a patient to transfer feelings to the therapist which correspond to feelings held toward important figures in the patient's past.

Transient Situational Disorder A psychological disturbance resembling neurosis but directly related to intense environmental stress; usually a temporary reaction.

Unconditioned Response In classical conditioning this is the unlearned response that is innately elicited by the unconditioned stimulus. Usually a reflex response.

Unconditioned Stimulus A stimulus innately capable of eliciting a response.

Unconscious That part of a person's mind or personality which contains impulses and desires not directly known to the person.

Validity The ability of a test to measure what it purports to measure.

Variable Interval Schedule A schedule of reinforcement that varies the time period between reinforcements.

Variable Ratio Schedule A schedule in which the number of responses required to produce reinforcement varies.

Vestibular Senses Concerned with balance or equilibrium, the vestibular senses are produced by the semicircular canals located close to the inner ear.

Visual Acuity The clarity of visual perception.

White Noise An auditory stimulus made up of all audible frequencies of sound. White noise sounds like a hiss or a waterfall.

References

Adams, J. A. *Human Memory*. New York: McGraw-Hill, 1967.

Adams, James Ring. "Sex Revolution Casualties." *The Wall Street Journal*, Oct. 1, 1973, p. 10.

Adorno, T. W., E. Frenkel-Brunswik, D. J. Levinson, and R. N. Sanford. *The Authoritarian Personality*. New York: Harper, 1950.

Albert, E. M. "The Roles of Women: Question of Values." In *The Potential of Women* edited by Farber and Wilson. New York: McGraw-Hill, 1963.

Allport, G. W. *The Nature of Prejudice*. Garden City, N.Y.: Anchor Books, Doubleday & Company, 1958.

——— *Pattern and Growth in Personality*. New York: Holt, Rinehart, & Winston, 1961.

Allport, G. W. and H. S. Odbert. "Trait-Names: A Psycholexical Study," *Psychological Monographs*, 1936, No. 211.

American Medical Association, Department of Mental Health. "The Crutch that Cripples: Drug Dependence, Part I." *Today's Health*, 1968, 46 (9), pp. 11-12, 70-72.

Anastasi, A. and J. P. Foley, Jr. *Differential Psychology* (3rd ed.). New York: Macmillan, 1958.

Anastasi, A. and J. P. Foley Jr. *Differential Psychology* (3rd ed.). New York: Macmillan, 1958.

Aronson, E. "Some Antecedents of Interpersonal Attraction." In *Nebraska Symposium on Motivation*, edited by W. J. Arnold and D. Levine. Lincoln: University of Nebraska Press, 1969.

Aronson, E. and D. Linder. "Gain and Loss of Esteem as Determinants of Interpersonal Attractiveness." *Journal of Experimental and Social Psychology*, 1965, 1, pp. 156-171.

Asch, S. E. "Studies of Independence and Conformity: A Minority of One against a Unanimous Majority." *Psychological Monographs*, 1956, 70, No. 416.

Asimov, I. *Is Anyone There?* Garden City, N.Y.: Doubleday, 1967.

——— *The New Intelligent Man's Guide to Science*. New York: Basic Books, 1965.

Athenasiou, R., P. Shaver, and C. Tavris. "Sex." *Psychology Today*, 1970, 4 (2), pp. 37-52.

Avard, B. K. and J. R. Brobeck. "Hypothalamic Control of Food Intake in Rats and Cats." *Yale Journal of Biological Medicine*, 1951, 24, pp. 123-140.

Averill, J. R. "Grief: Its Nature and Significance." *Psychological Bulletin*, 1968, 70, pp. 721-748.

Ayllon, T. "Intensive Treatment of Psychotic Behavior by Stimulus Satiation and Food Reinforcement." *Behavior Research and Therapy*, 1963, 1, pp. 53-61.

Ayllon, T., E. Haughton, and H. B. Hughes. "Interpretation of Symptoms: Fact or Fiction?" *Behavior and Therapy*, 1965, 3, pp. 1-7.

Azrin, N. H., R. R. Hutchinson, and R. McLaughlin. "The Opportunity for Aggression as an Operant Reinforcer during Aversive Stimulation." *Journal of Experimental Analysis of Behavior*, 1965, 8, pp. 171-180.

Bach, G. and P. Wyden. *The Intimate Enemy*. New York: Morrow, 1969.

Back, K. W. "The Group Can Comfort but It Can't Cure." *Psychology Today*, 1972, 6 (7), pp. 28-35.

Baer, D. M. "Let's Take Another Look at Punishment." *Psychology Today*, Oct. 1971.

Baltes, P. B. and K. W. Schaie. "Aging and I.Q.: The Myth of the Twilight Years." *Psychology Today*, 1974, 7 (10), pp. 35-40.

Bandura, A. *Aggression: A Social Learning Analysis.* Englewood Cliffs, N.J.: Prentice-Hall, 1973.

———"Vicarious Processes: A Case of No-Trial Learning." In *Advances in Experimental Social Psychology*, Vol. 2, edited by L. Berkowitz. New York: Academic Press, 1965, pp. 1-55.

Bandura, A. and T. L. Rosenthal. "Vicarious Classical Conditioning as a Function of Arousal Level." *Journal of Personality and Social Psychology*, 1966, 3, pp. 54-62.

Bandura, A., D. Ross, and S. A. Ross. "Vicarious Reinforcement and Imitative Learning." *Journal of Abnormal and Social Psychology*, 1963, 67, pp. 601-607.

Bandura, A. and R. Walters. *Adolescent Aggression.* New York: Ronald, 1959.

Bandura, A. and R. Walters. *Social Learning and Personality Development.* New York: Holt, 1963.

Barahal, H. S. "1000 Prefrontal Lobotomies: Five to Ten Year Follow-up Study." *Psychiatric Quarterly*, 1958, 32, pp. 653-678.

Barber, T. X. "Suggested ('Hypnotic') Behavior: The Trance Paradigm Versus an Alternative Paradigm." Harding, Mass. Medfield Foundation, Report No. 103, 1970.

———"Toward a Theory of Pain: Relief of Chronic Pain by Prefrontal Leucotomy, Opiates, Placebos, and Hypnosis." *Psychological Bulletin*, 1959, 56 (6), pp. 430-460.

Barclay, A. M. "Sex and Personal Development in the College Years." In *Sexuality: A Search for Perspective*, edited by D. Grummer and A. Barclay. Princeton, N.J.: D. Van Nostrand, 1971, pp. 311-332.

Barron, F. "The Psychology of Imagination." *Scientific American*, 1958, 199 (3), pp. 150-170.

Basedow, R. H. *The Australian Aborigine.* Adelaide, Australia: F. W. Peerce and Sons, 1925.

Bateson, G., D. D. Jackson, J. Haley, and J. Weakland. "Toward a Theory of Schizophrenia." *Behavioral Science*, 1956, 1, pp. 251-264.

Beecher, H. K. *Measurement of Subjective Responses: Quantitative Effects of Drugs.* New York: Oxford University Press, 1959.

Bengelsdorf, I. S. "Alcohol, Morphine Addictions Believed Chemically Similar." *Los Angeles Times*, March 5, 1970, Part II, p. 7.

Benson, H. *The Relaxation Response.* New York: Morrow, 1975.

Berlyne, D. "Curiosity and Exploration." *Science*, 1966, 153, pp. 25-33.

Berne, E. *Games People Play.* New York: Grove Press, 1964.

———*Transactional Analysis in Psychotherapy.* New York: Grove Press, 1961.

Berscheid, E. and E. Walster. "Physical Attractiveness." In *Advances in Experimental and Social Psychology*, Vol. VII, edited by L. Berkowitz. New York: Academic Press, 1974.

Bettelheim, B. *The Informed Heart.* New York: Free Press, 1960.

Bloom, B. *Stability and Change in Human Characteristics.* New York: Wiley, 1964.

Bluestone, H. and C. L. McGahee. "Reactions to Extreme Stress: Impending Death by Execution." *American Journal of Psychiatry*, 1962, 119, pp. 393-396.

Bourne, L. E., Jr. and E. J. Archer. "Time Continuously on Target as a Function of Distribution of Practice." *Journal of Experimental Psychology*, 1956, 51, pp. 25-33.

Bower, G. H. "How to . . . uh . . . Remember." *Psychology Today*, Oct. 1973, pp. 63-70.

Bower, G. H. and M. C. Clark. "Narrative Stories as Mediators for Serial Learning." *Psychonomic Science*, 1969, 14, pp. 181-182.

Bowlby, J. *Attachment and Loss, Volume I: Attachment.* New York: Basic Books, 1969.

———*Attachment and Loss, Volume II: Separation and Anxiety.* New York: Basic Books, 1973.

Brady, J. V. "Ulcers in Executive Monkeys." *Scientific American*, 1958, 199, pp. 95-100.

Braginsky, B. M. and D. D. Braginsky. "Schizophrenic Patients in the Psychiatric Interview: An Experimental Study of Their Effectiveness at Manipulation." *Journal of Consulting Psychology*, 1967, 31, pp. 543-547.

Bridges, K. M. B. "Emotional Development in Early Infancy." *Child Development*, 1932, 3, pp. 324-334, 340.

Brown, R. and D. McNeill. "The 'Tip of the Tongue' Phenomenon." *Journal of Verbal Learning and Verbal Behavior*, 1966, 5, pp. 325-337.

Bruch, H. "Transformation of Oral Impulses in Eating Disorders: A Conceptual Approach." *Psychiatry Quarterly*, 1961, 35, pp. 458-481.

Bruner, J. S., et al. *Studies in Cognitive Growth.* New York: Wiley, 1966.

Bruner, J. S. and C. C. Goodman. "Value and Need as Organizing Factors in Perception." *Journal of Abnormal and Social Psychology*, 1947, 42, pp. 33-44.

Bruner, J. S. and L. Postman. "On the Perception of Incongruity: A Paradigm." *Journal of Personalty*, 1949, 18, pp. 206-223.

Bryan, J. H., and M. A. Test. "Models and Helping: Naturalistic Studies in Aiding Behavior." *Journal of Personality and Social Psychology*, 1967, 6, pp. 400-407.

Buchwald, A. "Psyching Out." *The Washington Post*, June 20, 1965.

Burtt, H. E. "An Experimental Study of Early Childhood Memory: Final Report." *Journal of General Psychology*, 1941, 58, pp. 435-439.

Butler, R. "Curiosity in Monkeys." *Scientific American*, 1954, 190 (18), pp. 70-75.

Butler, R. and H. F. Harlow. "Persistence of Visual Exploration in Monkeys." *Journal of Comparative Physiological Psychology*, 1954, 47, pp. 258-263.

Byrne, D. *The Attraction Paradigm.* New York: Academic Press, 1971.

Cabanac, M. and P. Duclaux. "Obesity: Absence of Satiety Aversion to Sucrose." *Science*, 1970, 168, pp. 496-497.

Calhoun, J. B. "A 'Behavioral Sink.' " In *Roots of Behavior*, edited by E. L. Bliss. New York; Harper & Row, 1962.

Cameron, P., R. Frank, M. Lifter, and P. Morrissey. "Cognitive Functionings of College Students in a General Psychology Class." Paper presented at the meeting of the A.P.A., San Francisco, Sept. 1968.

Campbell, A., G. Gurin, and W. E. Miller. *The Voter Decides.* New York: Harper & Row, 1954.

Campbell, C. "Transcendence Is as American as Ralph Waldo Emerson." *Psychology Today*, 1974, 7 (11), pp. 37-38.

Canadian Government's Commission of Inquiry. *The Non-Medical Use of Drugs.* Baltimore: Penguin, 1971.

Cannon, W. B. "Hunger and Thirst." In *A Handbook of General Experimental Psychology*, edited by C. Murchinson. Worcester, Mass.: Clark University Press, 1934.

———" 'Voodoo' Death." *American Anthropologist*, 1942, 44, pp. 169-181.

———*The Wisdom of the Body.* New York: Norton, 1932.

Cannon, W. B. and A. L. Washburn. "An Exploration of Hunger." *American Journal of Physiology*, 1912, 29, pp. 441-454.

Carmen, R. and W. R. Adams. *Study Skills: A Student's Guide for Survival.* New York: Wiley, 1972.

Carmichael, L., H. P. Hogan, and A. A. Walter. "An Experimental Study of the Effect of Language on the Reproduction of Visually Perceived Form." *Journal of Experimental Psychology*, 1932, 15, pp. 73-86.

Carroll, J. B. *Language and Thought.* Englewood Cliffs, N.J.: Prentice-Hall, 1964.

Cartwright, R. In *Dream Psychology and the New Biology of Dreaming*, edited by M. Kramer. Springfield, Ill.: Charles C Thomas, 1969.

Casler, L. "The Effects of Extra Tactile Stimulation on a Group of Institutionalized Infants." *Genetic Psychology Monographs*, 1965, 71, pp. 137-175.

Cattell, R. B. "Personality Pinned Down." *Psychology Today*, 1973, 7, pp. 40-46.

———*The Scientific Analysis of Personality.* Baltimore: Penguin, 1965.

Ceraso, J. "The Interference Theory of Forgetting." *Scientific American*, April 1967.

Chess, S., A. Thomas, and H. G. Birch. *Your Child Is a Person: A Psychological Approach to Parenthood without Guilt.* New York: Viking, 1965.

Chomsky, N. *Language and Mind.* New York: Harcourt Brace Jovanovich, 1968.

Chown, S. M. and H. Heron. "Psychological Aspects of Aging in Man." *Annual Review of Psychology*, 1965, Vol. 16.

Clark, K. B. *Dark Ghetto.* New York: Harper & Row, 1965.

Cleckley, H. *The Mask of Sanity* (4th ed.). St. Louis: Mosby, 1964.

Cofer, C. N. and M. H. Appley. *Motivation: Theory and Research.* New York: Wiley, 1964.

Cohen, J. *Secondary Motivation.* Chicago: Rand McNally, 1970.

Cohen, S. *The Drug Dilemma.* New York: McGraw-Hill, 1969.

Coleman, J. *Abnormal Psychology and Modern Life* (4th ed.). Glenview, Ill.: Scott, Foresman, 1972.

Coleman, J. C. "Facial Expression of Emotion." *Psychology Monthly*, 1949, No. 296.

———*Psychology and Effective Behavior.* Glenview, Ill.: Scott, Foresman, 1969.

Coleman, J. C. and C. L. Hammen. *Contemporary Psychology and Effective Behavior.* Glenview, Ill.: Scott, Foresman, 1974.

Comfort, A. *A Good Age.* New York: Crown, 1976.

Coopersmith, S. "Studies in Self-Esteem." *Scientific American*, 1968, 218, pp. 96-106.

Cornsweet, T. N. *Visual Perception.* New York: Academic Press, 1970.

Cortes, J. B. and F. M. Gatti. *Delinquency and Crime: A Biopsychological Approach.* New York: Seminar, Press, 1972.

Cowles, J. T. "Food Tokens as Incentives for Learning by Chimpanzees." *Comparative Psychology*, Monograph 14, No. 5, Whole No. 71.

Cox, C. M. *Genetic Studies of Genius.* Vol. II. Stanford, Calif.: Stanford, University Press, 1926.

Crancer, A., Jr., J. M. Dille, J. C. Delay, J. E. Wallace, and M. D. Haykin. "Comparison of the Effects of Marijuana and Alcohol on Simulated Driving Performance." *Science*, 1969, 164, pp. 851-854.

Cronbach, L. *Essentials of Psychological Testing* (3rd ed.). New York: Harper & Row, 1970.

Dabbs, J. M. "Sex, Setting and Reactions to Crowding on Sidewalks." *Proceedings of the 80th Annual Convention of the American Psychological Association*, 1972, 7, pp. 205-206.

Darley, J. M. and B. Latane. "Bystander Intervention in Emergencies: Diffusion of Responsibility." *Journal of Personality and Social Psychology.* 1968, 8, pp. 377-383.

Darwin, C. *The Expression of Emotion in Man and Animals.* Chicago: The University of Chicago Press, 1965. (First published, 1872.)

Davis, D. M. "Self-Selection of Diet by Newly Weaned Infants." *American Journal of Diseases of Children*, 1928, 36, pp. 651-679.

Deese, J. and S. H. Hulse. *The Psychology of Learning* (3rd ed.). New York: McGraw-Hill, 1967.

Dement, W. "The Effect of Dream Deprivation." *Science*, 1960, 131, pp. 1705-1707.

Dement, W. and E. Wolpert. "The Relation of Eye Movements, Body Mobility and External Stimuli to Dream Content." *Journal of Experimental Psychology*, 1958, 55, pp. 543-553.

Dennenberg, V. H. "Stimulation in Infancy, Emotional Reactivity, and Exploratory Behavior." In *Neurophysiology and Emotion*, edited by D. C. Glass. New York: Russell Sage Foundation and Rockefeller University Press, 1967.

Dennis, W. amd M. Dennis. "The Effects of Cradling Practices upon the Onset of Walking in Hopi Children." *Journal of Genetic Psychology*, 1940, 56, pp. 77-86.

Deutsch, H. *Neurosis and Character Types*. New York: International Universities Press, 1965.

Deutsch, M. and M. E. Collins. *Interracial Housing*. Minneapolis: University of Minnesota Press, 1951.

Dinello, F. A. "Stages of Treatment in the Case of a Diaper Wearing Seventeen-Year-Old Male." *American Journal of Psychiatry*, 1967, 124, pp. 94-96.

Dixon, J. "Jeanne Dixon Strikes Back at Scientists Who Knock Astrology." *National Star*, Sept. 30, 1975, p. 5.

Dollard, J., et al. *Frustration and Aggression*. New Haven: Yale University Press, 1939.

Dollard, J. and N. E. Miller. *Personality and Psychotherapy: An Analysis in Terms of Learning, Thinking and Culture*. New York: McGraw-Hill, 1950.

Donohue, H. E. F. *Where Should You Touch?* The Hearst Corporation, 1968.

Doob, A. N. and A. E. Gross. "Status of Frustrator as an Inhibitor of Horn-Honking Responses." *Journal of Social Psychology*, 1968, 76, pp. 213-218.

Dostoevsky, F. *Crime and Punishment*. Translated by C. Garnett. New York: Collier & Son, 1917.

Downey, D. *Personal Communication*. Tempe, Ariz.: Casales Press, 1976.

Duncker, K. "On Problem Solving." *Psychological Monographs*, 1945, 58, No. 270.

Durkheim, E. *Suicide: A Study in Sociology*. Translated by J. A. Spaulding and G. Simpson. New York: Free Press, 1951.

Ebbinghaus, H. *Memory: A Contribution to Experimental Psychology*. Translated by H. A. Ruger and C. E. Bussenius. New York: New York Teacher's College, Columbia University, 1913. (Originally published, Leipzig: Altenberg, 1885.)

Ehrenberg, P. "A Last Memoir." In *What I Have Learned*, edited by N. Cousins. New York: Simon & Schuster, 1968.

Elkind, D. "Giant in the Nursery—Jean Piaget." *The New York Times Magazine*, May 26, 1968.

Ellis, A. "The No Cop-Out Therapy." *Psychology Today*, 1973, 7 (2), pp. 56-60, 62.

———*Reason and Emotion in Psychotherapy*. New York: Lyle Stuart, 1962.

Erikson, E. H. *Insight and Responsibility*. New York: Norton, 1964.

———*Childhood and Society* (2nd ed.). New York: Norton, 1963.

Eysenck, H. J. "New Ways in Psychotherapy." *Psychology Today*, June 1967, p. 40.

———*Sense and Nonsense in Psychology*. Harmondsworth, Middlesex, England: Penguin Books Ltd., 1957, 1958.

Fantz, R. L. "Pattern Vision in Newborn Infants." *Science*, 1963, 140, pp. 296-297.

Faraday, A. *Dream Power*. New York: Coward, 1972.

Farber, L. H. "Ours Is the Addicted Society." *The New York Times Magazine*, Dec. 11, 1966.

Farnum G., P. S. Graubard, and H. Rosenberg. "Little Brother Is Changing You." *Psychology Today*, March 1974.

Fast, J. *Body Language*. New York: M. Evans, 1970.

Feldman, M. P. and M. J. MacCulloch. "A Systematic Approach to the Treatment of Homosexuality by Conditioned Aversion: Preliminary Report." *American Journal of Psychiatry*, 1964, 121, pp. 167-171.

Ferster, C. B. "The Autistic Child." *Psychology Today*, 1968, 2, pp. 35-37, 61.

———"Positive Reinforcement and Behavioral Deficits of Autistic Children." *Child Development*, 1961, 32, pp. 437-456.

Festinger, L. *A Theory of Cognitive Dissonance*. Stanford, Calif.: Stanford University Press, 1957.

———"A Theory of Social Comparison Processes." *Human Relations*, 1954, 7, pp. 117-140.

Festinger, L. and J. M. Carlsmith. "Cognitive Consequences of Forced Compliance." *Journal of Abnormal and Social Psychology*, 1959, 58, pp. 203-210.

Festinger, L., S. Schachter, and K. Back. *Social Pressures in Informal Groups: A Study of a Housing Project*. New York: Harper, 1950.

Fisher, S. *The Female Orgasm*. New York: Basic Books, 1973.

Fleming, J. "Field Report: The State of the Apes." *Psychology Today*, Jan. 1974, 46.

Frank, J. D. "The Demoralized Mind." *Psychology Today*, 1973, 6 (11), pp. 22-31, 100-101.

Frankenburg, W. K. and J. B. Dodds. "The Denver Developmental Screening Test." *The Journal of Pediatrics*, 1967, 71 (2), pp. 181-191.

Frankl, V. *The Doctor and the Soul*. New York: Knopf, 1955.

———*Man's Search for Meaning*. New York: Washington Square Press, 1963.

French, J. R. P., Jr. and B. H. Raven. "The Bases of Social Power." In *Studies in Social Power*, edited by D. Cartwright. Ann Arbor: The University of Michigan Press, 1959.

Freud, S. *The Interpretation of Dreams*. London: Hogarth, 1900.

———*An Outline of Psychoanalysis*. New York: Norton, 1949.

———"Psychopathology of Everyday Life." In *The Basic Writings of Sigmund Freud*. New York: Random House, 1938.

———*Leonardo da Vinci and A Memory of His Childhood*. (1910a). Standard edition, Vol. 11. London: Hogarth, 1957, pp. 59-137.

Friedman, M. and R. Rosenman. *Type A*. New York: Knopf, 1974.

Gagné, R. M. and E. A. Fleishman. *Psychology and Human Performance*. New York: Holt, Rinehart & Winston, 1959.

Galanter, E. "Contemporary Psychophysics." In *New Directions in Psychology*, Vol. 1. New York: Holt, Rinehart & Winston, 1962, pp. 87-156.

Gandhi, M. Speech delivered March 23, 1922.

Gardner, M. "Dermo-Optical Perception: A Peek Down the Nose." *Science*, 1966, 151, pp. 654-657.

Gardner, R. A. and B. T. Gardner. "Teaching Sign Language to a Chimpanzee." *Science*, 1969, 165, pp. 664-672.

Gates, A. I. "Recitation as a Factor in Memorizing." In *The Psychology of Learning* (2nd ed.), edited by J. Deese. New York: McGraw-Hill, 1958.

Gesell, A., et al. *The First Five Years of Life*. New York: Harper Bros., 1940.

Gibran, K. *The Prophet*. New York: Knopf, 1951.

Gibson, E. J. and R. D. Walk. "The 'Visual Cliff.' " *Scientific American*, 1960, 202 (4), pp. 67-71.

Ginott, H. G. *Between Parent and Child: New Solutions to Old Problems*. New York: Macmillan, 1965.

Gitter, A. G., H. Black, and D. Mostofsky. "Race and Sex in the Perception of Emotion." *Journal of Social Issues*, 1972, 28, pp. 63-78, 170.

Goldenson, R. M. *The Encyclopedia of Human Behavior*, Vol. 2. Garden City, N.Y.: Doubleday, 1970b.

Goldiamond, I. "Fluent and Non-Fluent Speech (Stuttering): Analysis and Operant Techniques for Control." In *Research in Behavior Modification*, edited by L. Krasner and L. P. Ullman. New York: Holt, Rinehart & Winston, 1965.

Gordon T. *P.E.T. Parent Effectiveness Training: A Tested New Way to Raise Children*. New York: Peter H. Wyden, 1970.

Gottesman, I. I. and J. Shields. *Schizophrenia and Genetics*. New York: Academic Press, 1972.

Gould, R. "Growth Toward Self-Tolerance." *Psychology Today*, Feb. 1975.

Green, H. (Joanne Greenberg). *I Never Promised You a Rose Garden*. New York: Holt, Rinehart & Winston, 1964.

Greenspoon, J. "The Reinforcing Effect of Two Spoken Sounds on the Frequency of Two Responses." *American Journal of Psychology*, 1955, 50, pp. 409-416.

Greenwald. H. (Ed.). *Active Psychotherapy*. Chicago: Aldine, 1967, quoted in *Psychosources*, edited by E. Shapiro. New York: Bantam, 1973, p. 147.

Gregory, R. L. *The Intelligent Eye*. New York: McGraw-Hill, 1970.

Gresham, S., W. Webb, and R. Williams. "Alcohol and Caffeine: Effects on Inferred Visual Dreaming." *Science*, 1963, 140, pp. 1226-1227.

Grinspoon, L. "Marijuana." In *Altered States of Awareness: Readings from* Scientific American. San Francisco: Freeman, 1972.

Grinspoon, L. and P. Hedblom. "Amphetamines Reconsidered." *Saturday Review*, July 8, 1972. (Special Issue.)

Guilford, J. P. "Creativity." *American Psychologist*, 1950, 5, pp. 444-454.

———*Personality*. New York: McGraw-Hill, 1959.

Haase, W. "The Role of Socio-Economic Class in Examiner Bias." In *Mental Health of the Poor*, edited by F. Reissman, J. Cohen, and A. Pearl. New York: Free Press, 1964, pp. 241-247.

Haefele, J. W. *Creativity and Innovation*. New York: Reinhold, 1962.

Hall, C. *The Meaning of Dreams*. New York: McGraw-Hill, 1966.

Hall, E. T. *The Hidden Dimension*. Garden City, N.Y.: Doubleday, 1966.

Hall, G. S. *Senescence, The Last Half of Life*. New York: Appleton-Century-Crofts, 1922.

Hamburg, P. A. and D. T. Lunde. "Sex Hormones in the Development of Sex Differences in Human Behavior." In *The Development of Sex Differences*, edited by E. Maccoby. Stanford, Calif.: Stanford University Press, 1966, pp. 1-24.

Hamilton, E. *Sex Before Marriage*. New York: Meredith Press, 1969.

Hampson, J. L. and J. C. Hampson. "The Ontogenesis of Sexual Behavior in Man." In *Sex and Internal Secretions*, Vol. 2, edited by W. C. Young. Baltimore: Williams & Wilkins, 1961, pp. 1401-1432.

Harlow, H. F. and M. K. Harlow. "Learning to Love." *American Scientist*, 1966, 54, pp. 244-272.

Harlow, H. F. and M. K. Harlow. "Social Deprivation in Monkeys." *Scientific American*, 1962, 207, pp. 136-146.

Harlow, H. F. and M. K. Harlow. "The Young Monkeys." *Psychology Today*, 1967, 1 (5), pp. 40-47.

Harlow, H. F. and R. R. Zimmerman. "The Development of Affectional Responses in Infant Monkeys." *Pro-*

ceedings of The American Philosophical Society, 1958 (102), pp. 501-509.

Harlow, J. M. "Recovery from the Passage of an Iron Bar Through the Head." *Massachusetts Medical Society*, 1868, 2, pp. 327ff.

Harper. *Psychoanalysis and Psychotherapy*. Englewood Cliffs, N.J.: Prentice-Hall, 1959.

Harris, I. D. *The Promised Seed: A Complete Study of Eminent First and Later Sons*. New York: Free Press, 1964.

Hartmann, E. L. *The Functions of Sleep*. New Haven: Yale University Press, 1973.

Hartmann, E. L., P. Verdone, and F. Snyder. "Longitudinal Studies of Sleep and Dreaming Patterns in Psychiatric Patients." *Journal of Nervous Mental Disorders*, 1966, 142, pp. 117-126.

Hartshorne, H. and M. A. May. *Studies in the Nature of Character. Volume I: Studies in Deceit*. New York: Macmillan, 1928.

Hastorf, A. and H. Cantril. "They Saw a Game: A Case Study." *Journal of Abnormal and Social Psychology*, 1954, 49, pp. 129-134.

Hayakawa, S. I. "The Use and Misuse of Language." In *Science and Human Affairs*, edited by R. E. Farson. Palo Alto, Calif.: Science and Behavior Books, 1965, pp. 95-113.

Hayes, C. *The Ape in Our House*. New York: Harper & Row, 1951.

Hearst, E. "Psychology Across the Chess Board." In *Readings in Psychology Today*. Del Mar, Calif.: CRM, 1969, pp. 16-23.

Heath, R. G. "Electrical Self-Stimulation of the Brain in Man." *The American Journal of Psychiatry*, 1963, 120 (6), pp. 571-577.

Hebb, D. O. *Organization of Behavior*. New York: Wiley, 1949.

———*A Textbook of Psychology* (2nd ed.). Philadelphia: Saunders, 1966.

———"What Psychology Is About." *American Psychologist*, 1974, 29, pp. 71-79.

Heinstein, M. I. "Behavioral Correlates to Breast-Bottle Regimes Under Varying Parent-Infant Relationships." *Monographs of the Society for Research in Child Development*, 1963, 28 (4), pp. 1-61.

Heller, J. *Catch 22*. New York: Simon & Schuster, 1961.

Hellman, H. *Biology in the World of the Future*. New York: Hayden, 1971.

Helson, H. *Adaptation—Level Theory*. New York: Harper, & Row, 1964.

Hernandez-Peon, R., H. Scherrer, and M. Jouvet. "Modification of Electric Activity in Cochlear Nucleus during 'Attention' in Unanesthetized Cats." *Science*, 1956, 123, pp. 331-332.

Hess, E. H. "Imprinting." *Science*, 1959, 130, pp. 133-141.

Hess, E. H. and J. M. Polt. "Pupil Size as Related to Interest Values of Visual Stimuli." *Science*, 1960, 132, pp. 349-350.

Hilgard, J. "Learning and Maturation in Preschool Children." *Journal of Genetic Psychology*, 1932, 41, pp. 36-56.

Hilton, I. "Differences in the Behavior of Mothers Toward First and Later Born Children." *Journal of Personality and Social Psychology*, 1967, 7, pp. 282-290.

Hoffer, A. *Description, Diagnosis, Theory and Treatment of Schizophrenia*. Karpat, 1972.

Hoffman, M. L. "Conscience, Personality, and Socialization Techniques." *Human Development*, 1970, 13 (2), pp. 90-126.

Hohmann, G. W. "Some Effects of Spinal Cord Lesions on Experienced Emotional Feelings." *Psychophysiology*, 1966, 3, pp. 143-156.

Holland, M. K. *Using Psychology: Principles of Behavior and Your Life*. Boston: Little, Brown, 1975.

Holmes, T. and M. Masuda. "Psychosomatic Syndrome." *Psychology Today*, April 1972, p. 71.

Holmes, T. H. and R. H. Rahe. *Journal of Psychosomatic Research*, 1957.

Horner, M. S. "Fail: Bright Women." *Psychology Today*, 1969, 3 (6), pp. 36-38.

Horwitz, W. A., C. Kestenbaum, E. Person, and L. Jarvik. "Identical Twin—'Idiot Savants' Calendar Calculators." *The American Journal of Psychiatry*, 1965, 121, pp. 1075-1079.

Hsia, Y. and C. H. Graham. "Color Blindness." In *Vision and Visual Perception*, edited by C. H. Graham. New York: Wiley, 1965, pp. 395-413.

Humphrey, J. A., D. Puccio, G. D. Niswander, and T. M. Casey. "An Analysis of the Sequence of Selected Events in the Lives of a Suicidal Population: A Preliminary Report." *Journal of Nervous Mental Disorders*, 1972, 154, pp. 137-140.

Hunt, J. McV. *Intelligence and Experience*. New York: Ronald Press, 1961.

Hunter, W. S. "The Delayed Reaction in Animals and Children." *Behavior Monographs*, 1913 (2).

Hutman, S. "Marijuana Issue Lives." *ACLU Open Forum*, July/Aug. 1975, 50 (7).

Huxley, A. *The Doors of Perception*. Baltimore: Penguin, 1971.

———"Human Potentialities." In *Science and Human Affairs*, edited by R. E. Farson. Palo Alto, Calif.: Science and Behavior Books, 1965.

Jacobs, M. and J. M. Whiteley. "Approaches to Sexual Counseling." *Counseling Psychologist*, 1975, 5, pp. 3-8.

Jacobson, A., A. Kales, D. Lehmann, and J. R. Zweizia. "Somnambulism: All Night EEG Studies." *Science*, 1965, 148, pp. 975-977.

Jacobson, L. E. "The Electrophysiology of Mental Activities." *American Journal of Psychology*, 1932, 44, pp. 677-694.

James, W. *The Varieties of Religious Experience.* New York: New American Library, 1958.

Janis, I. L. *Psychological Stress.* New York: Wiley, 1958.

Janis, I. L. and L. Mann. "Effectiveness of Emotional Role-playing in Modifying Smoking Habits and Attitudes." *Journal of Experimental Research in Personality*, 1965, 1, pp. 84-90.

Jarvik, L. F., C. Eisdorfer, and J. E. Blum (Eds.). *Intellectual Functioning in Adults.* New York: Springer, 1973.

Jarvik, M. E. "Ciba Found." *Symposium of Animal Pharmacology Drug Action*, edited by H. Steinberg et. al., 1964.

Jellinik, E. M. *The Disease Concept of Acoholism.* New Haven: Hill House Press, 1960.

Jenkins, J. G. and K. M. Dallenbach. "Oblivescence During Sleep and Waking." *American Journal of Psychology*, 1924, 35, pp. 605-612.

John, E. R. *Mechanisms of Memory.* New York: Academic Press, 1967.

Johnson, J. J. "Sticking with First Responses on Multiple-Choice Exams: For Better or for Worse?" *Teaching of Psychology*, 1975, 2 (4).

Johnson, R. E. "Some Correlates of Extramarital Coitus." *Journal of Marriage and Family*, 1970, 32, pp. 449-456.

Joint Commission on Mental Illness and Health. *Action for Mental Health.* New York: Basic Books, 1961.

Jones, E. *The Life and Work of Sigmund Freud.* New York: Basic Books, 1953.

Jourard, S. M. "Healthy Personality and Self-Disclosure." *Mental Hygiene*, 1959, 32, pp. 449-507.

———*Personal Adjustment* (2nd ed.). New York: Macmillan, 1963.

Kagan, J. *Change and Continuity in Infancy.* New York: Wiley, 1971.

———*Personality Development.* New York: Harcourt Brace Jovanovich, 1969.

———"What Is Intelligence?" *Social Policy*, 1973, 4, pp. 88-94.

Kagan, J. and R. E. Klein. "Cross-Cultural Perspectives on Early Development." *American Psychologist*, 1973, 28, pp. 947-961.

Kamiya, J. "Conscious Control of Brain Waves." *Psychology Today*, 1968, 1, pp. 57-66.

Kanfer and Goldfoot. 1966, cited in Sternbach. *Pain.* New York: Academic Press, 1968.

Kanner, L. *Child Psychiatry.* Springfield, Ill.: Charles C Thomas, 1957.

Kapleau, P. *The Three Pillars of Zen.* New York: Harper & Row, 1966.

Kastenbaum, R. and R. Aisenberg. *The Psychology of Death.* New York: Springer, 1972.

Katz, B. J. "Finding Psychiatric Help Can Be Traumatic Itself." *The National Observer*, 1972.

Kelley, H. H. "The Warm-Cold Variable in First Impressions of Persons." *Journal of Personality*, 1950, 18, pp. 431-439.

Kellogg, L. A. and W. N. Kellogg. *The Ape and the Child.* New York: McGraw-Hill, 1933.

Kerckhoff, A. C. and K. E. Davis. "Value Consensus and Need Complementarity in Mate Selection." *American Sociological Review*, 1962, 27, pp. 295-303.

Kessler, J. *Psychopathology of Childhood.* Englewood Cliffs, N.J.: Prentice-Hall, 1966.

Keys, A., J. Brôzek, A. Henschel, O. Mickelson, and H. L. Taylor. *The Biology of Human Starvation.* Minneapolis: University of Minnesota Press, 1950.

Kiell, N. (Ed.). *The Psychology of Obesity: Dynamics and Treatment.* Springfield, Ill.: Charles C Thomas, 1973.

Kinsbourne, M. "Eye and Head Turning Indicates Cerebral Lateralization." *Science*, 1972, 176, pp. 539-541.

Kinsey, A., W. Pomeroy, and C. Martin. *Sexual Behavior in the Human Female.* Philadelphia: Saunders, 1953.

Kinsey, A., W. Pomeroy, and C. Martin. *Sexual Behavior in the Human Male.* Philadelphia: Saunders, 1948.

Kleitman, N. "Physiological Cycling." In *Psychophysiological Aspects of Space Flight*, edited by B. E. Flaherty. New York: Columbia University Press, 1961, pp. 158-165.

Kleitman, N. and E. Kleitman. "Effect of Non-24-Hour Routines of Living on Oral Temperature and Heart Rate." *Journal of Applied Physiology*, 1953, 6, pp. 283-291.

Klineberg, O. *The Human Dimension in International Relations.* New York: Holt, Rinehart & Winston, 1964.

Knight, R. P. "A Critique of the Present Status of the Psychotherapies." *Bulletin of the New York Academy of Medicine*, 1949, 25, pp. 100-114.

Koestler, A. *The Act of Creation.* New York: Macmillan, 1964.

———*The Ghost in the Machine.* New York: Macmillan, 1968.

Kohlberg, L. "The Cognitive-Developmental Approach to Socialization." In *Handbook of Socialization Theory and Research*, edited by A. Goslin. Chicago: Rand McNally, 1969.

———"The Development of Children's Orientation Toward a Moral Order: 1. Sequence in the Development of Moral Thought." *Vita Humana*, 1963, 6, pp. 11-33.

Köhler, I. "Experiments with Goggles." *Scientific American*, 1962, Offprint No. 465, pp. 62-72.

Köhler, W. *The Mentality of Apes.* New York: Harcourt Brace Jovanovich, 1925.

Krech, D., M. R. Rosenzweig, and E. L. Bennett. "Relations between Brain Chemistry and Problem Solving among Rats Raised in Enriched and Impoverished

Environments." *Journal of Comparative and Physiological Psychology*, 1962, 55, pp. 801-807.
Kübler-Ross, E. *On Death and Dying.* New York: Macmillan, 1969.

Labovitz, S. and R. Hagedorn. "An Analysis of Suicide Rates among Occupational Categories." *Social Inquiry*, 1971, 41, pp. 67-72.
Laing, R. D. *The Divided Self.* New York: Pantheon, 1970.
———*The Politics of Experience.* New York: Pantheon, 1967.
———*The Politics of the Family and Other Essays.* New York: Pantheon, 1971.
Lake, A. "Get Thin, Stay Thin." *McCalls*, 1973, 100 (4).
Landuet, T. K. and M. W. M. Whiting. "Infantile Stimulation and Adult Stature of Human Males." *American Anthropolgist*, 1964, 66, pp. 1007-1028.
Lang, P. J. and B G. Milamed. "Avoidance Conditioning Therapy of an Infant with Chronic Ruminative Vomiting." *Journal of Abnormal Psychology*, 1969, 74, pp. 1-8.
Lappé, F. M. *Diet for a Small Planet.* New York: Ballantine, 1971.
Laurendeau, M. and A. Pinard. *Causal Thinking in the Child.* New York: International Universities Press, 1962.
Lazarus, A. H. "The Treatment of Chronic Frigidity by Systematic Desensitization." In *Experiments in Behavior Therapy*, edited by H. J. Eysenck, New York: Pergamon, 1964.
Lazarus, R. S. "Emotions and Adaptation: Conceptual and Empirical Relations." In *Nebraska Symposium on Motivation*, edited by W. J. Arnold. Lincoln: University of Nebraska Press, 1968.
Leavitt, H. J. and H. Scholsberg. "The Retention of Verbal and Motor Skills." *Journal of Experimental Psychology*, 1944, 34, pp. 404-417.
Leboyer, Frederick. *Birth without Violence.* New York: Knopf, 1975.
Lee, E. S. "Negro Intelligence and Selective Migration: A Philadelphia Test of the Klineberg Hypothesis." *American Review*, 1951, 16, pp. 227-232.
Leeper, R. W. "A Study of a Neglected Portion of the Field of Learning: The Development of Sensory Organization." *Pedagogical Seminary and Journal of Genetic Psychology*, 1935, 46, pp. 41-75.
Lefkowitz, M., R. R. Blake, and J. S. Mouton. "Status Factors in Pedestrian Violation of Traffic Signals." *Journal of Abnormal and Social Psychology*, 1955, 51, pp. 704-706.
Lennenberg, E. "On Explaining Language." *Science*, 1969, 164, pp. 635-643.
Lester, D. "Attempted Suicide as a Hostile Act." *Journal of Psychology*, 1968, 68, pp. 243-248.
———"Relationship of Mental Disorder to Suicidal Behavior." *New York State Journal of Medicine*, 1971b, 71, pp. 1503-1505.
———*Why People Kill Themselves: A Summary of Research on Suicidal Behavior.* Springfield, Ill.: Charles C Thomas, 1972.
Lester, G. and D. Lester, *Suicide: The Gamble with Death.* Englewood Cliffs, N.J.: Prentice-Hall, 1971.
Levine, S. "Infantile Stimulation: A Perspective." In *Stimulation in Early Infancy*, edited by A. Ambrose. New York: Academic Press, 1969.
———"Sex Differences in the Brain." *Scientific American*, 1966, 214, 4, pp. 84-90.
Levy, M. R. and M. W. Kahn. "Interpreter Bias on the Rorschach Test as a Function of Patients' Socioeconomic Status." *Journal of Projective Techniques and Personality Assessment*, 1970, 34, pp. 106-112.
Lewin, K. *A Dynamic Theory of Personality.* New York: McGraw-Hill, 1935.
Liebett, R. E. "Taste Deprivation and Weight Determinants of Eating Behavior." *Journal of Personality and Social Behavior*, 1968, 10, pp. 107-116.
Lifton, R. J. "Psychological Effects of the Atomic Bomb in Hiroshima: The Theme of Death." *Daedalus*, Summer 1963, pp. 462-497.
Lilly, J. C. "Mental Effects of Reduction of Ordinary Levels of Physical Stimuli on Intact, Healthy Persons." *Psychiatric Research*, 1956, 5, pp. 1-9.
Lindesmith, A., A. Strauss, and N. Denzin. *Social Psychology* (4th ed.). Hinsdale, Ill.: Dryden Press, 1975.
Lindsley, D. B., J. Bowden, and H. W. Magoun. "Effect upon the EEG of Acute Injury to the Brain Stem Activating System." *EEG and Clinical Neurophysiology*, 1949, 1, pp. 475-486.
Lipinski, E. and B. G. Lipinski. "Motivational Factors in Psychedelic Drug Use by Male College Students." In *Drug Awareness*, edited by R. E. Hormon and A. M. Fox. New York: Discus Books, published by Avon, 1970.
Lorenz, K. Z. "Imprinting." *The Auk*, 1937, 54, pp. 245-273.
Lovaas, O., G. Freitag, V. Gold, and I. Kassorla. "Experimental Studies in Childhood Schizophrenia: Analysis of Self-Destructive Behavior." *Journal of Experimental Child Psychology*, 1965, 2, pp. 67-84.
Lovaas, O., G. Freitag, M. Kinder, B. Rubenstein, B. Schaeffer, and J. Simmons. "Establishment of Social Reinforcers in Two Schizophrenic Children on the Basis of Food." *Journal of Experimental Child Psychology*, 1966, 4, pp. 109-125.
Lowen, A. *Love and Orgasm.* New York: Macmillan, 1965.
Luby, E., J. Grissell, C. Frohman, H. Lees, B. Cohen, and J. Gottlieb. "Biochemical, Psychological and Behavioral Responses to Sleep Deprivation." *Academic Science*, 1962, 96, p. 71.

Luce, G. G. *Body Time: Physiological Rhythms and Social Stress.* New York: Pantheon, 1971.

———"Current Research on Sleep and Dreams." *Health Service Publication* No. 1389. U.S. Department of Health, Education, and Welfare. 1965.

Luce, G. G. and E. Peper. "Mind Over Body, Mind Over Mind." *The New York Times Magazine*, Sept. 12, 1971.

Ludwig, A. M. "Altered States of Consciousness." *Archives of General Psychiatry*, 1966, 15, pp. 225-233.

Lugo, J. O.and G. L. Hershey. *Human Development.* New York: Macmillan, 1974.

Luh, C. W. "The Conditions of Retention." *Psychological Monographs*, 1922, 31, No. 22.

Luria, A. R. *The Mind of a Mnemonist.* New York: Basic Books, 1968.

Lykken, D. T. "Psychology and the Lie Detector Industry." *American Psychologist*, 1974, 29, pp. 725-739.

———"A Study of Anxiety in the Sociopathic Personality." *Journal of Abnormal and Social Psychology*, 1957, 55, pp. 6-10.

MacFarlane, J. W., W. L. Allen, and M. P. Honzik. "A Developmental Study of the Behavioral Problems of Normal Children between 21 Months and 14 Years." *University of California Publication of Child Development*, 1954, 2 (169), p. 334.

MacKinnon, D. W. "The Nature and Nurture of Creative Talent." *American Psychologist*, 1962. 17 (7), pp. 484-495.

Madsen, C. H., Jr., W. C. Becher, D. R. Thomas, L. Koser, and E. Plager. "An Analysis of the Reinforcing Function of 'Sit Down' Commands." In *Readings in Educational Psychology*, edited by R. K. Parker. Boston: Allyn & Bacon, 1968.

Maier, N. R. F. *Frustration.* New York: McGraw-Hill, 1949.

Mandell, A. J., D. S. Segal, R. T. Kuczenski, and S. Knapp. "The Search for the Schizococcus." *Psychology Today*, Oct. 1972, pp. 68-72.

Marañon, I. "Contribution a l'etude de l'action emotive de l'adrenaline." *Franc. D'endocrinol*, 1924, 2, pp. 301-305.

Martin, J. H. "An Experiment with the 'Talking Typewriter.' " In *Panorama of Psychology*, edited by N. H. Pronko. Belmont, Calif.: Brooks/Cole, 1969, pp. 219-224.

Maslow, A. H. *The Farther Reaches of Human Nature.* New York: Viking, 1971.

———*Motivation and Personality.* New York: Harper, 1954.

———*Motivation and Personality* (2nd ed.). New York: Harper & Row, 1970.

———"A Philosophy of Psychology: The Need for a Mature Science of Human Nature." In *Humanistic Viewpoint in Psychology*, edited by F. T. Severin. New York: McGraw-Hill, 1965, pp. 17-33.

———*The Psychology of Science.* Chicago: Henry Regnery, 1969.

———"Self-Actualization and Beyond." In *Challenges of Humanistic Psychology*, edited by J. F. T. Bugental. New York: McGraw-Hill, 1967.

———*Toward a Psychology of Being* (2nd ed.). New York: Van Nostrand, 1968.

Masters, W. H. and V. E. Johnson. *Human Sexual Response.* Boston: Little, Brown, 1966.

Masters, W. H. and V. E. Johnson. *The Pleasure Bond: A New Look at Sexuality and Commitment.* Boston: Little, Brown, 1970.

Maugh, T. H., II. "Marihuana: The Grass May No Longer Be Greener." *Science*, 1974a, 185, pp. 683-685.

———"Marihuana (II): Does It Damage the Brain?" *Science*, 1974b, 185, pp. 775-776.

Maupin, E. W. "Individual Differences in Response to a Zen Meditation Exercise." *Journal of Consulting Psychology*, 1965, 29, pp. 139-145.

Max, L. W. "Experimental Study of the Motor Theory of Consciousness: IV. Action-Current Responses in the Deaf during Awakening, Kinesthetic Imagery, and Abstract Thinking." *Journal of Comparative Psychology*, 1937, 24, pp. 301-344.

Mayer, J. *Overweight: Causes, Cost, and Control.* Englewood Cliffs, N.J.: Prentice-Hall, 1968.

McCary, J. L. *Sexual Myths and Fallacies.* New York: Schocken Books, 1973.

McClelland, D. C. *Studies in Motivation.* New York: Appleton-Century-Crofts, 1955.

———"Risk Taking in Children with High and Low Need for Achievement." In *Motives in Fantasy Action and Society*, edited by J. W. Atkinson. New York: Van Nostrand, 1958.

———"Achievement and Entrepreneurship." *Journal of Personality and Social Psychology*, 1965, 1, pp. 389-393.

———*The Achieving Society.* New York: Van Nostrand, 1961.

———"Testing for Competence Rather than 'Intelligence.' " *American Psychologist*, 1973, 28, pp. 1-14.

McConnell, J. V. "Memory Transfer through Cannibalism in Planarians." *Journal of Neuropsychiatry*, 1962, 3 (suppl. 1), pp. 542-548.

McConnell, J. V., A. L. Jacobson, and D. P. Kimble. "The Effects of Regeneration upon Retention of a Conditioned Response in the Planarian." *Journal of Comparative and Physiological Psychology*, 1959, 52, pp. 1-5.

McGaugh, J. L. "Time-Dependent Processes in Memory Storage." In *Controversial Issues in Consolidation of the Memory Trace*, edited by J. L. McGaugh and M. J. Herz. New York: Atherton, 1970.

McGinnies, E. "Emotionality and Perceptual Defense." *Psychological Review*, 1949, 56, pp. 244-251.

McGuire, W. J. "The Nature of Attitudes and Attitude Change." In *The Handbook of Social Psychology*, Vol. 3, edited by G. Lindzey and E. Aronson. Reading, Mass.: Addison-Wesley, 1969.

McMahon, F. B. *Abnormal Behavior, Psychology's View.* Englewood Cliffs, N.J.: Prentice-Hall, 1976.

———"A Contingent-Item Method for Constructing a Short Personality Questionnaire." *Journal of Applied Psychology*, 1964, pp. 197-200.

McMurrary, G. A. "Experimental Study of a Case of Insensitivity to Pain." *Archives of Neurological Psychiatry*, 1950, 64, pp. 650-667.

McNeil, D. "Developmental Psycholinguistics." In *The Genesis of Language: A Psycholinguistic Approach*, edited by F. Smith and G. A. Miller. Cambridge, Mass.: MIT Press, 1966.

Mead, M. *Sex and Temperament in Three Primitive Societies.* New York: Morrow, 1935.

Mehrabian, A. "Significance of Posture and Position in the Communication of Attitude and Status Relationships." *Psychological Bulletin*, 1969, 71, pp. 359-372.

Melzack, R. "Shutting the Gate on Pain." *Science Year: The World Book Science Annual.* Palo Alto, Calif.: Field, 1974.

Melzack, R. and T. H. Scott. "The Effects of Early Experience on the Response to Pain." *Journal of Comparative and Physiological Psychology*, 1957, 50, pp. 155-161.

Melzack, R. and D. Wall. "Pain Mechanisms: A New Theory," *Science*, 1965, 150, pp. 971-979.

Menninger, K. "Psychiatrists Use Dangerous Words." *Saturday Evening Post*, April 25, 1964.

Milgram, S. "Some Conditions of Obedience and Disobedience to Authority." *Human Relations*, 1965, 18, pp. 57-76.

Milgram, S., L. Bickman, and L. Berkowitz. "Note on the Drawing Power of Crowds of Different Size." *Journal of Personality and Social Psychology*, 1969, 13, pp. 79-82.

Miller, G. A. "Language and Psychology." In *New Directions in the Study of Language*, edited by E. H. Lennenberg. Cambridge, Mass.: MIT Press, 1964, pp. 89-107.

Miller, G. "The Magical Number Seven, Plus or Minus Two: Some Limits on Our Capacity for Processing Information." *Psychological Review*, 1956, 63, pp. 81-87.

———"On Turning Psychology Over to the Unwashed." APA Paper, 1969.

Miller, H. L. and P. S. Siegal. *Loving: A Psychological Approach.* New York: Wiley, 1972.

Miller, N. E. "Experimental Studies of Conflict." In *Personality and the Behavior Disorders*, Vol. I, edited by J. McV. Hunt. New York: Ronald Press, 1944, pp. 431-465.

———"The Frustration-Aggression Hypothesis." *Psycological Review*, 1941, 48, pp. 337-342.

———"Learning of Visceral and Glandular Responses." *Science*, 1969, 163, pp. 434-445.

Miller, N. E. and R. Bugelski. "The Influence of Frustration Imposed by the In-group on Attitudes Expressed Toward Out-groups." In *Social Psychology in Life*, edited by R. I. Evans and R. M. Rozelle. Boston: Allyn & Bacon, 1970.

Miller, N. E. and L. V. Di Cara. "Instrumental Learning of Heart Rate Changes in Curarized Rats; Shaping and Specificity to Discriminative Stimulus." *Journal of Comparative and Physiological Psychology*, 1967, 63, pp. 12-19.

Millinson, J. R. *Principles of Behavior Analysis.* New York: Macmillan, 1967.

Milner, B. "Memory Disturbance After Bilateral Hyppocampal Lesions." In *Cognitive Processes and the Brain*, edited by P. Milner and S. Glickman. Princeton, N.J.: Van Nostrand, 1965, pp. 97-111.

Minami, H. and K. M. Dallenbash. "The Effect of Activity upon Learning and Retention in the Cockroach." *American Journal of Psychology*, 1946, 59, pp. 1-58.

Mischel, W. *Personality and Assessment.* New York: Wiley, 1968.

Money, J. "Psychosexual Differentiation." In *Sex Research: New Developments*, edited by J. Money. New York: Holt, Rinehart & Winston, 1965, pp. 3-23.

———"Sex Hormones and Other Variables in Human Eroticism." In *Sex and Internal Secretions*, Vol. VIII, edited by W. C. Young. Baltimore: Williams & Wilkens, 1961.

———"Sexual Dimorphision and Homosexual Gender Identity." *Psychological Bulletin*, 1970, 6, pp. 425-440.

Moreno, J. L. *Who Shall Survive?* New York: Beacon House, 1953.

Moriarty, T. "A Nation of Willing Victims." *Psychology Today*, April 1975, pp. 43-50.

Moritz, A. P. and N. Zamchech. "Sudden and Unexpected Deaths of Young Soldiers." *American Medical Association Archives of Pathology*, 1946, 42, pp. 459-494.

Moruzzi, G. and H. W. Magoun. "Brain Stem Reticular Formation and Activation of the EEG." *EEG and Clinical Neurophysiology*, 1949, 1, pp. 455-473.

Moser, D. "The Nightmare of Life with Billy." *Life*, May 7, 1965.

Mosher, D. L. "Sex Differences, Sex Experience, Sex Guilt, and Explicitly Sexual Films." *Journal of Social Issues*, 1973, 29 (3).

Munn, N. L., L. D. Fernald, Jr., and P. S. Fernald. *Introduction to Psychology* (2nd ed.). Boston: Houghton Mifflin, 1969.

Murray, E. J. *Sleep, Dreams, and Arousal.* New York: Appleton-Century-Crofts, 1965.

Mussen, P. H., J. J. Conger, and J. Kagun. *Child Development and Personality* (3rd ed.). New York: Harper & Row, 1969.

Nachman, M. "Learned Taste and Temperature Aversions Due to Lithium Chloide Sickness After Temporal Delays." *Journal of Comparative and Physiological Psychology*, 1970, 73, pp. 22-30.

National Institute of Mental Health. "First Annual Report on the Health Consequences of Marijuana Use." 1971.

Navran, L. "Communication and Adjustment in Marriage." *Family Process*, 1967, 6 (2), pp. 173-184.

Neufeld, R. W. "The Effect of Experimentally Altered Cognitive Appraisal on Pain Tolerance." *Psychonomic Science*, 1970, 20 (2), pp. 106-107.

Neugarten, B. "Grow Old Along with Me! The Best Is Yet to Be." *Psychology Today*, Dec. 1971, p. 45.

Neuringer, A. J. "Superstitious Key Pecking After Three Peck-Produced Reinforcements." *Journal of the Experimental Analysis of Behavior*, 1970, 13, pp. 127-134.

Newsweek, March 4, 1974.

Olds, J. and P. Milner. "Positive Reinforcement Produced by Electrical Stimulation of Septal Area and Other Regions of Rat Brain." *Journal of Comparative and Physiological Psychology*, 1954, 47, pp. 419-427.

Olds, J. and M. E. Olds. "Drives, Rewards, and the Brain." In *New Directions in Psychology II,* edited by F. Barron et al. New York: Holt, Rinehart & Winston, 1965, pp. 329-410.

Orne, M. T. "On the Social Psychology of the Psychological Experiment: With Particular Reference to Demand Characteristics and Their Implications." *American Psychologist*, 1962, 17, pp. 776-783.

Ornstein, R. E. *The Psychology of Consciousness.* San Francisco: Freeman, 1972.

Osgood, C. E. "The Nature and Measurement of Meaning." *Psychological Bulletin*, 1952, 49, pp. 197-237.

Oswald, I. *Sleeping and Waking: Physiology and Psychology.* New York: American Elsevier, 1962.

Overmier, J. B. and M. E. P. Seligman. "Effects of Inescapable Shock upon Subsequent Escape and Avoidance Learning." *Journal of Comparative and Physiological Psychology*, 1967, 63, pp. 23-33.

Owens, W. A., Jr. "Age and Mental Abilities: A Longitudinal Study." *Genetic Psychology Monograph*, 1953, 48, pp. 3-54.

Owens, W. A., Jr. "Age and Mental Abilities: A Second Adult Follow Up." *Journal of Educational Psychology*, 1966, 57, pp. 311-325.

Packard, V. *The Sexual Wilderness.* New York: David McKay, 1968.

Page, J. D. *Psychopathology.* Chicago: Aldine, 1971.

Paivio, A. "Mental Imagery in Associative Learning and Memory." *Psychological Review*, 1969, 76, pp. 241-263.

Parnes, S. J. *Creative Behavior Workbook.* New York: Scribners, 1967.

Paul, G. L. *Insight vs. Desensitization in Psychotherapy.* Stanford, California: Stanford University Press, 1966.

Pavlov, I. P. *Conditioned Reflexes*, translated by G. V. Anrep. New York: Dover, 1927.

Penfield, W. "Brain's Record of Past a Continuous Movie Film." *Science News Letter*, April 27, 1957, p. 265.

———*The Excitable Cortex in Conscious Man.* Springfield, Ill.: Charles C Thomas, 1958.

———*The Mystery of the Mind: A Critical Study of Consciousness and the Human Brain.* Princeton, N.J.: Princeton University Press, 1975.

Penfield, W. and L. Roberts. *Speech and Brain Mechanisms.* Princeton, N.J.: Princeton University Press, 1959.

Perin, C. T. "A Quantitative Investigation of the Delay of Reinforcement Gradient." *Journal of Experimental Psychology*, 1943, 32, pp. 37-51.

Perlmutter, F. and H. A. Silverman. "CMHC: A Structural Anachronism." *Social Work*, 1972, 17, pp. 78-84.

Perls, F. *Gestalt Therapy Verbatim.* Lafayette, Calif.: Real People Press, 1969.

Peterson, L. R. and M. J. Peterson. "Short-Term Retention of Individual Verbal Items." *Journal of Experimental Psychology*, 1959, 58, pp. 193-198.

Phillips, J. L. *Origins of Intellect: Piaget's Theory.* San Francisco: Freeman, 1969.

Piaget, J. *The Origins of Intelligence in Children.* New York: International Universities Press, 1952.

———*The Psychology of Intelligence.* New York: Norton, 1951 (original French, 1945).

Piliavin, I. M., J. Rodin, and J. A. Piliavin. "Good Samaritanism: An Underground Phenomenon?" *Journal of Personality and Social Psychology*, 1969, 13, pp. 289-299.

Pines, M. "How Three-Year-Olds Teach Themselves to Read—and Love It." *Harper's Magazine*, May 1963, pp. 58-64. Harper & Row.

———"Infants Are Smarter than Anybody Thinks." *The New York Times Magazine*, Nov. 29, 1970, pp. 32-33; 110; 114-120.

———"Why Some Three-Year-Olds Get A's and Some Get C's." *The New York Times Magazine*, July 6, 1969, pp. 4-5, 10-17.

Playboy, 1969, 16 (2), p. 46.

Premack, A. J. and D. Premack. "Teaching Language to an Ape." *Scientific American*, October 1972, pp. 92-99.

Premack, D. "The Education of S*A*R*A*H." *Psychology Today*, September 1970, pp. 54-58.

Pritchard, R. M. "A Collimator Stabilizing System." *Quarterly Journal of Experimental Psychology*, 1961, 13, pp. 181-183.

Pronko, N. H. "Are Geniuses Born or Made?" In *Panorama of Psychology.* Belmont, Calif.: Brooks/Cole, 1969, pp. 215-219.

Rahula, W. *What the Buddha Taught.* New York: Grove Press, 1959.

Reiss, D. "Competing Hypothesis and Waring Factions: Applying Knowledge of Schizophrenia." *Schizophrenia Bulletin*, Spring 1974, No. 8.

Rethlingshafer, D. and E. D. Hinckley. "Influence of Judge's Characteristics upon the Adaptation Level." *American Journal of Psychology*, 1963, 76, pp. 116-123.

Rhine, J. *New World of the Mind.* New York: Sloane, 1953.

Riesen, A. H. "Effects of Early Deprivation of Phobic Stimulation." In *The Biosocial Basis of Mental Retardation*, edited by S. Osler and R. Cooke. Baltimore, Md.: Johns Hopkins Press, 1965.

Robinson, F. P. *Effective Behavior.* New York: Harper & Row, 1941.

Rock, I. and L. Kaufman. "The Moon Illusion II." *Science*, 1962, 136, pp. 1023-1031.

Rogers, C. "Learning to Be Free." A paper given at a session on "Conformity and Diversity" in the conference on "Man and Civilization," sponsored by the University of California School of Medicine, San Francisco, Calif.: Jan. 28, 1962.

———"The Necessary and Sufficient Conditions of Therapeutic Personality Change." *Journal of Consulting Psychology*, 1957, 21, pp. 95-103.

Rogers, C. R. *On Becoming a Person: A Therapist's View of Psychotherapy.* Boston: Houghton, Mifflin, 1961.

———"A Theory of Therapy, Personality, and Interpersonal Relationships, as Developed in the Client-Centered Framework." In *Psychology: A Study of a Science*, Vol. 3, edited by S. Koch. New York: McGraw-Hill, 1959.

Rogers, J. M. "Drug Abuse—Just What the Doctor Ordered." *Psychology Today*, Sept. 1971, pp. 16-24.

Romanes, G. J. *Animal Intelligence.* New York: Appleton-Century-Crofts, 1912.

Rosenhan, D. L. "On Being Sane in Insane Places." *Science*, 1973, 179, pp. 250-258.

Rosenthal, R. "Clever Hans: A Case Study of Scientific Method." Introduction to *Clever Hans: (The Horse of Mr. Von Osten)*, O. Pfungst. New York: Holt, Rinehart & Winston, 1965.

———*Experimenter Effects in Behavioral Research.* New York: Appleton-Century-Crofts, 1966.

———"Interpersonal Expectations: Effects of the Experimenter's Hypothesis." In *Artifact in Behavioral Research*, edited by R. Rosenthal and R. L. Rosnow. New York: Academic Press, 1969, pp. 182-277.

Rosenthal, R. and K. L. Fode. "The Effect of Experimenter Bias on the Performance of the Albino Rat." *Behavioral Science*, 1963a, 8, pp. 183-189.

Rosenthal, R. and L. Jacobson. *Pygmalian in the Classroom: Teacher Expectation and Pupil's Intellectual Development.* New York: Holt, Rinehart & Winston, 1968.

Rosenthal, T. L. and G. M. White. "On the Importance of Hair in Student's Clinical Inferences." *Journal of Clinical Psychology*, 1972, 28 (1), pp. 43-47.

Rubin, Z. "Measurement of Romantic Love." *Journal of Personality and Social Psychology*, 1970, 16, pp. 265-273.

———*Liking and Loving: An Invitation to Social Psychology.* New York: Holt, Rinehart & Winston, 1973.

Ruch, F. L. and W. W. Ruch. "The K Factor as a (Validity) Suppressor Variable in Predicting Success in Selling." *Journal of Applied Psychology*, 1967, 51, pp. 201-204.

Ruch, F. L. and P. G. Zimbardo. *Psychology and Life* (8th ed.). Glenview, Ill.: Scott, Foresman, 1971.

Rudestam, K. E. "Stockholm and Los Angeles: A Cross-Cultural Study of the Communication of Suicidal Intent." *Journal of Consulting and Clinical Psychology*, 1971, 36 (1), pp. 82-90.

Russell, W. and P. Nathan. "Traumatic Amnesia." *Brain*, 1964, 69, p. 280.

Sage, W. "ESP and the Psychology Establishment." *Human Behavior*, Sept.-Oct. 1972.

Sansom, W. "A Contest of Ladies." In *The Stories of William Sansom.* London: Hogarth, 1963.

Scarr-Salapatch, S. and R. A. Weinberg. "When Black Children Grow Up in White Homes. . . ." *Psychology Today*, Dec. 1975.

Schachter, S. "Communication, Deviation, and Rejection." *Journal of Abnormal and Social Psychology*, 1951, 46, pp. 190-207.

———*Emotion, Obesity and Crime.* New York: Academic Press, 1971.

———*Psychology of Affiliation.* Stanford, Calif.: Stanford University Press, 1959.

Schachter, S. and L. P. Grose. "Manipulated Time and Eating Behavior." *Journal of Personality and Social Psychology*, 1968, 10, pp. 98-106.

Schachter, S. and B. Latané. "Crime, Cognition, and Autonomic Nervous System." In *Nebraska Symposium on Motivation*, edited by D. Levine. Lincoln: University of Nebraska Press, 1969.

Schachter, S. and J. Singer. "Cognitive, Social and Physiological Determinants of Emotional State." *Psychological Review*, 1962, 69, pp. 379-399.

Schein, E. H., W. F. Hill, A. Lubin, and H. L. Williams. "Distinguishing Characteristics of Collaborators and Resistors among American Prisoners of War." *Journal of Abnormal and Social Psychology*, 1957, 55, pp. 197-201.

Schein, E. H., I. Schneier, and C. H. Barker. *Coercive Persuasion.* New York: Norton, 1961.

Schlosberg, H. "Three Dimensions of Emotion." *Psychological Review*, 1954, 61, pp. 81-88.

Schneider, A. M. and B. Tarshis. *Physiological Psychology*. New York: Random House, 1975.

Schneidman, E. S. "You and Death." *Psychology Today*, 1971, 5 (1), pp. 43-45, 74-80.

Schneidman, E. S., N. L. Farherow, and L. Cabista. *Some Facts about Suicide Causes and Prevention*. Washington, D.C.: U.S. Government Printing Office, 1965.

Schreiber, F. R. *Sybil*. Chicago: Regency, 1973.

Scott, E. M. and E. L. Verney. "Self-Selection and Diet. VI: The Nature of Appetites for B Vitamines." *Journal of Nutrition*, 1947, 34, pp. 471-480.

Scott, J. P. "The Development of Social Motivation." In *Nebraska Symposium on Motivation*, edited by D. Levine. Lincoln: University of Nebraska Press, 1967, pp. 111-132.

Sears, R. R., E. E. Maccoby, and H. Levin. *Patterns of Child Rearing*. Evanston, Ill.: Row, Peterson, 1957.

Seiden, R. H. "Campus Tragedy: A Study of Student Suicide." *Journal of Abnormal Psychology*, 1966, 71, pp. 389-399.

Seligman, M. E. P. "For Helplessness: Can We Immunize the Weak?." In *Readings in Psychology Today* (2nd ed.). Del Mar, Calif.: CRM, 1972.

———"Submissive Death: Giving Up on Life." *Psychology Today*, 1974, 7, pp. 80-85.

Selye, H. *The Stress of Life*. New York: Knopf, 1953.

Senden, M. V. *Space and Sight*. Translated by P. Heath. Glencoe, Ill.: Free Press, 1960.

Shaffer, L. F. "Fear and Courage in Aerial Combat." *Journal of Consulting Psychology*, 1947, 11, pp. 137-143.

Shaffer, L. F. and E. J. Shoben, Jr. *The Psychology of Adjustment* (2nd ed.). Boston: Houghton Mifflin, 1956.

Shapiro, D., B. Tursky, E. Gershon, and M. Stein. "Effects of Feedback and Reinforcement on the Control of Human Systolic Blood Pressure." *Science*, 1969, 163, pp. 588-590.

Shattock, E. H. *An Experiment in Mindfulness*. London: Rider, Hutchinson Publishing Group, 1958.

Sheffield, F. D., J. J. Wulff, and R. Backer. "Reward Value of Copulation without Sex Drive Reduction." *Journal of Comparative and Physiological Psychology*, 1951, 44, pp. 3-8.

Sheils, M. and S. Monroe. "A Ban on I.Q. Tests?" *Newsweek*, March 22, 1976, p. 49.

Sheldon, W. H. *Atlas of Men: A Guide for Somatotyping the Adult Male at All Ages*. New York: Harper, 1954.

Sherif, M. "A Study of Some Social Factors in Perception." *Archives of Psychology*, 1935, 27, No. 187.

Sherif, M., O. J. Harvey, B. J. White, W. R. Hood, and C. W. Sherif. *Intergroup Conflict and Cooperation: The Robbers Cave Experiment*. Institute of Group Relations, University of Oklahoma, 1961.

Shiffrin, R. M. "Forgetting: Trace Erosion or Retrieval Failure?." *Science*, 1970, 168, pp. 1601-1603.

Shirley, M. M. *The First Two Years*. Institute of Child Welfare, Monograph No. 7. Minneapolis: University of Minnesota Press, 1933.

Siffre, M. "Six Months Alone in a Cave." *National Geographic*, 1975, 147 (3), pp. 426-435.

Sigusch, V., G. Schmidt, A. Reinfeld, and I. Wiedmann-Sutor. "Psychological Stimulation: Sex Differences." *Journal of Sex Research*, 1970, 6 (1).

Simon, W. and J. Gagnon. "Psychosexual Development." In *Human Sexuality: Contemporary Perspectives*, edited by E. S. Morrison and V. Borosage. Palo Alto, Calif.: Mayfield, 1973.

Skeels, H. M. "Adult Status of Children with Contrasting Early Life Experiences." *Monograph of the Society for Research in Child Development*, 1966, 31 (3).

Skinner, B. F. *Beyond Freedom and Dignity*. New York: Bantam, 1971.

———"Pigeons in a Pelican." *American Psychologist*, 1960, 15, pp. 28-37.

Smith, B. M. *The Polygraph in Contemporary Psychology*. San Francisco: Freeman, 1971.

Smith, E. M., H. O. Brown, J. E. P. Toman, and L. S. Goodman. "The Lack of Cerebral Effects of D-Tubo-Curarine." *Anesthesiology*, 1947, 8, pp. 1-14.

Snow, C. P. "Either-Or." *Progressive*, February 1961. p. 24.

Snyder, S. H. "The True Speed Trip: Schizophrenia." *Psychology Today*, Jan. 1972.

Soal, S. G. and F. Bateman. *Modern Experiments in Telepathy*. New Haven: Yale University Press, 1964.

Sommer, R. *Personal Space: The Behavioral Basis of Design*. Englewood Cliffs, N.J.: Prentice-Hall, 1969.

Sorokin, P. A. *The American Sex Revolution*. Boston: Porter Sargent, 1956.

Sperling, G. "Successive Approximations to a Model for Short Term Memory." *Acta Psychologica* (Amsterdam), 1967, 27, pp. 285-292.

Sperry, R. W. "The Eye and the Brain." *Scientific American*, 1956, Offprint No. 465, pp. 48-52.

———"The Great Cerebral Commissure." *Scientific American*, 1964, 210, pp. 42-52.

———"Hemisphere Deconnection and Unity in Conscious Awareness." *American Psychologist*, 1968, 23, pp. 723-733.

Spiesman, J. C., R. S. Lazarus, A. M. Mordkoff, and L. A. Davidson. "The Experimental Reduction of Stress Based on Ego-Defense Theory." *Journal of Abnormal and Social Psychology*, 1964, 68, pp. 367-380.

Spitz, R. A. "Hospitalism: An Inquiry into the Genesis of Psychiatric Conditions in Early Childhood." In *The Psychoanalytic Study of the Child*, Vol. I. New York: International Universities Press, 1945, pp. 53-74.

Spitzer, H. F. "Studies in Retention." *Journal of Educational Psychology*, 1939, 30, pp. 641-656.

Staub, E., B. Turskey, and G. E. Schwartz. "Self-Control and Predictability: Their Effects on Reactions to Aversive Stimulation." *Journal of Personality and Social Psychology*, 1971, 18 (2), pp. 157-162.

Stern, C. "Hereditary Factors Affecting Adoption: A Study of Adoption Practices." *Child Welfare League of America*, 1956, 2, p. 53.

Stevens, J. O. *Awareness: Exploring, Experimenting, Experiencing.* Lafayette, Calif.: Real People Press, 1971.

Stoller, F. H. "The Long Weekend." *Psychology Today*, 1967, 1 (7), pp. 28-33.

———"Marathon Groups: Toward a Conceptual Model." In *New Perspectives on Encounter Groups*, edited by L. N. Solomon and B. Berzon. San Francisco: Jossey-Bass, 1972, pp. 171-194.

Strange, J. R. *Abnormal Psychology.* New York: McGraw-Hill, 1965.

Stratton, G. M. "Vision without Inversion of the Retinal Image." *Psychological Review*, 1897, 4, pp. 341-360, 463-481.

Suedfeld, P. *Social Processes.* Dubuque, Iowa: Wm. C. Brown, 1966.

Suinn, R. M. *Fundamentals of Behavior Pathology.* New York: Wiley, 1970.

———*Fundamentals of Behavior Pathology* (2nd ed.). New York: Wiley, 1975.

Swensen, C. H. *Introduction to Interpersonal Relations.* Glenview, Ill.: Scott, Foresman, 1973.

Szasz, T. S. "The Crime of Commitment." *Psychology Today*, 1969, 2 (10), pp. 55-57.

———"The Ethics of Addiction." *Harpers*, April 1972.

———"Mental Illness Is a Myth." *The New York Times Magazine*, June 12, 1966.

Tanner, J. M. "Growing Up." *Scientific American*, September 1973, pp. 34-43.

Tart, C. T. "The 'High' Dream: A New State of Consciousness." In *Altered States of Consciousness*, edited by C. Tart. Garden City, N.Y.: Anchor Books, Doubleday & Company, 1969.

Ten Danger Signals of Depression. The National Association for Mental Health, Virginia.

Terman, L. M. and M. Oden. *The Gifted Group in Mid-Life.* Vol. 5, *Genetic Studies of Genius.* Stanford, Calif.: Stanford University Press, 1959.

Terman, L. M. and M. A. Merrill. *Stanford-Binet Intelligence Scale.* Boston: Houghton Mifflin, 1937 (revised ed., 1960).

Thigpen, C. H. and H. M. Cleckley. *The Three Faces of Eve.* New York: McGraw-Hill, 1957.

Thomas, A., S. Chess, and H. G. Birch. *Temperament and Behavior Disorders in Children.* New York: New York University Press, 1968.

Thomas, D. "Prognosis of Depression with Electrical Treatment." *British Medical Journal*, 1954, 2, p. 950.

Thompson, R. I. *Foundations of Physiological Psychology.* New York: Harper & Row, 1967.

Thoreau, H. D. *Walden or Life in the Woods.* New York: Houghton Mifflin, 1893.

Time, August 1968, p. 15.

Time, January 8, 1973.

Time, March 4, 1974.

Tobin, R. L. "Murder on Television and the Fourteen-Year-Old." *Saturday Review*, 1972, 55, pp. 39-40.

Tolman, E. C. and C. H. Honzik. "Introduction and Removal of Reward and Maze Performance in Rats." *University of California Publications in Psychology*, 1930, 4, pp. 257-275.

Tolman, E. C., B. F. Ritchie, and D. Kalish. "Studies in Spatial Learning: II. Place Learning Versus Response Learning." *Journal of Experimental Psychology*, 1946, 36, pp. 221-229.

Toman, W. "Birth Order Rules All." *Psychology Today*, December 1970.

Trotter, R. J. "Obesity and Behavior." *Science News*, August 3, 1974.

Truax, C. B. "Reinforcement and Non-Reinforcement in Rogerian Psychotherapy." *Journal of Abnormal Psychology*, 1966, 71, pp. 1-9.

Tryon, R. C. "The Genetics of Learning Ability in Rats." *University of California Publications in Psychology*, 1929, 4, pp. 71-89.

Turnbull, C. M. "Some Observations Regarding the Experiences and Behavior of the Bambuti Pygmies." *American Journal of Psychology*, 1961, 74, pp. 304-308.

Ulrich, R. E., T. J. Stachnik, and N. R. Stainton. "Student Acceptance of Generalized Personality Interpretations." *Psychological Reports*, 1963, 131, pp. 831-834.

U.S. National Commission on the Causes and Prevention of Violence. *To Establish Justice to Insure Domestic Tranquility; The Final Report.* New York: Praeger, 1970.

Valins, S. "Cognitive Effects of False Heart-Rate Feedback." *Journal of Personality and Social Psychology*, 1966, 4, pp. 400-408.

———"Emotionality and Information Concerning Internal Reactions." *Journal of Personality and Social Psychology*, 1967, 6, pp. 458-463.

Van Eeden, F. "A Study of Dreams." *Proceedings of the Society for Psychical Research*, 1913, 26, pp. 431-461.

Van Lawick-Goodall, J. *In the Shadow of Man.* New York: Houghton Mifflin, 1971.

Verhave, T. "The Pigeon as a Quality Control Inspector." *American Psychologist*, 1966, 21, pp. 109-115.

Von Frisch, K. *Bees: Their Vision, Chemical Senses and Language.* Ithaca, N.Y.: Cornell University Press, 1950.

Wallace, R. and H. Benson. "The Physiology of Meditation." *Scientific American*, 1972, 226, pp. 84-90.

Wallach, M. A. and N. Kogan. *Modes of Thinking in Young Children*. New York: Holt, Rinehart & Winston, 1965.

Waller, J. A. "Drugs and Highway Crashes." *Journal of the American Medical Association*, 1971, 215, pp. 1477-1482.

Watson, J. B. *Behaviorism* (revised ed.). Chicago: The University of Chicago Press, 1930.

———"Psychology as the Behaviorist Views It." *Psychological Review*, 1913, 20, pp. 158-177.

Watson, J. B. and R. Rayner. "Conditioned Emotional Reaction." *Journal of Experimental Psychology*, 1920, 3, pp. 1-14.

Wechsler, D. *The Measurement and Appraisal of Adult Intelligence* (4th ed.). Baltimore: Williams & Wilkins, 1958.

Weil, A. T., N. E. Zinberg, and J. M. Nelson. "Clinical and Psychological Effects of Marijuana in Man." *Science*, 1968, 162, pp. 1234-1242.

Weinland, J. D. *How to Improve Your Memory*. New York: Barnes & Noble, 1957.

Weisstein, N. "Psychology Constructs the Female." In *Perspectives on Psychology*, edited by I. S. Cohen. New York: Praeger, 1975, pp. 318-331.

Weitzenhoffer, A. M. and E. R. Hilgard. *Stanford Hypnotic Susceptibility Scales Forms A and B*. Palo Alto, Calif.: Consulting Psychologists Press, 1959.

Wells, W. D. and B. Siegel. "Stereotyped Somatotypes." *Psychological Reports*, 1961, 8, pp. 77-78.

Wenger, M. A., F. N. Jones, and M. H. Jones. *Physiological Psychology*. New York: Holt, Rinehart & Winston, 1956.

West, J., H. Janszen, B. Lester, and F. Cornelison, Jr. "Psychosis of Sleep Deprivation." *Annals of the New York Academy of Science*, 1962, 96, p. 66.

Whimbey, A. "Something Better than Binet?" *Saturday Review*, June 1, 1974.

White, B. L. and R. Held. "Plasticity of Sensorimotor Development in the Human Infant." In *The Causes of Behavior*, Vol. I (2nd ed.), edited by J. F. Rosenblith and W. Allinsmith. Boston: Allyn & Bacon, 1966.

White, B. L. and J. C. Watts. *Experience and Environment*, Vol. I. Englewood Cliffs, N.J.: Prentice-Hall, 1973.

Whorf, B. L. "Science and Linguisitcs." *Technology Review*, 1940, 34, pp. 229-231, 247-248.

Whyte, W. H. *The Organization Man*. New York: Simon & Schuster, 1956.

Wickes, I. G. "Treatment of Persistent Enuresis with the Electric Buzzer." *Archives of Diseases in Childhood*, 1958, 33, pp. 160-164.

Williams, R. L., et al. "Sleep Patterns in Young Adults: An EEG Study." *Electroencephalography and Clinical Neurophysiology*, 1964, pp. 376-381.

Wilson, C. *Sex and the Intelligent Teenager*. Essex, England: Anchor Press, 1966.

Winterbottom, M. R. "The Relationship of Childhood Training in Independence to Achievement Motivation." Unpublished Doctoral Dissertation, Ann Arbor, Mich.: University of Michigan, 1953.

———"The Relationship of Need for Achievement to Learning Experiences in Independence and Mastery." In *Motives in Fantasy, Action, and Society*, edited by J. W. Atkinson. Princeton, N.J.: Van Nostrand, 1958.

Wolfe, J. B. "Effectiveness of Token Rewards for Chimpanzees." *Comparative Psychological Monographs*, 1936, 12 (5), Whole No. 60.

Wolpe, J. *The Practice of Behavior Therapy*. New York: Pergamon, 1969.

———*Psychotherapy by Reciprocal Inhibition*. Stanford, Calif.: Stanford University Press, 1958.

Wordsworth, W. "Intimations of Immortality from Recollections of Early Childhood." In *Complete Poetical Works of William Wordsworth*. New York: Houghton Mifflin, 1904, p. 353.

Zarcone, V. et al. "REM Deprivation and Schizophrenia." In *Recent Advances in Biological Psychiatry*, edited by J. Wortis. New York: Plenum Press, 1971.

Zigler, E. "On Growing Up, Learning and Loving." *Human Behavior*, March 1973.

Zimbardo, P. G. *Psychology and Life* (9th ed.). Glenview, Ill.: Scott, Foresman, 1975.

———"Toward a More Perfect Justice." *Psychology Today*, 1967, 1 (3), pp. 44-46.

Zung, W. W. K. and R. H. Green, Jr. "Seasonal Variation of Suicide and Depression." *Archives of General Psychiatry*, 1974, 30, pp. 89-91.

Index

†

T

U